T0202651

Lecture Notes in Computer Science   11587

Commenced Publication in 1973
Founding and Former Series Editors:
Gerhard Goos, Juris Hartmanis, and Jan van Leeuwen

More information about this series at http://www.springer.com/series/7409

Norbert Streitz · Shin'ichi Konomi (Eds.)

Distributed, Ambient and Pervasive Interactions

7th International Conference, DAPI 2019
Held as Part of the 21st HCI International Conference, HCII 2019
Orlando, FL, USA, July 26–31, 2019
Proceedings

 Springer

Editors
Norbert Streitz 🆔
Smart Future Initiative
Frankfurt am Main, Germany

Shin'ichi Konomi
Learning Analytics Center
Kyushu University
Fukuoka, Japan

ISSN 0302-9743   ISSN 1611-3349   (electronic)
Lecture Notes in Computer Science
ISBN 978-3-030-21934-5   ISBN 978-3-030-21935-2   (eBook)
https://doi.org/10.1007/978-3-030-21935-2

LNCS Sublibrary: SL3 – Information Systems and Applications, incl. Internet/Web, and HCI

This Springer imprint is published by the registered company Springer Nature Switzerland AG
The registered company address is: Gewerbestrasse 11, 6330 Cham, Switzerland

Foreword

The 21st International Conference on Human-Computer Interaction, HCI International 2019, was held in Orlando, FL, USA, during July 26–31, 2019. The event incorporated the 18 thematic areas and affiliated conferences listed on the following page.

A total of 5,029 individuals from academia, research institutes, industry, and governmental agencies from 73 countries submitted contributions, and 1,274 papers and 209 posters were included in the pre-conference proceedings. These contributions address the latest research and development efforts and highlight the human aspects of design and use of computing systems. The contributions thoroughly cover the entire field of human-computer interaction, addressing major advances in knowledge and effective use of computers in a variety of application areas. The volumes constituting the full set of the pre-conference proceedings are listed in the following pages.

This year the HCI International (HCII) conference introduced the new option of "late-breaking work." This applies both for papers and posters and the corresponding volume(s) of the proceedings will be published just after the conference. Full papers will be included in the *HCII 2019 Late-Breaking Work Papers Proceedings* volume of the proceedings to be published in the Springer LNCS series, while poster extended abstracts will be included as short papers in the HCII 2019 *Late-Breaking Work Poster Extended Abstracts* volume to be published in the Springer CCIS series.

I would like to thank the program board chairs and the members of the program boards of all thematic areas and affiliated conferences for their contribution to the highest scientific quality and the overall success of the HCI International 2019 conference.

This conference would not have been possible without the continuous and unwavering support and advice of the founder, Conference General Chair Emeritus and Conference Scientific Advisor Prof. Gavriel Salvendy. For his outstanding efforts, I would like to express my appreciation to the communications chair and editor of *HCI International News,* Dr. Abbas Moallem.

July 2019   Constantine Stephanidis

HCI International 2019 Thematic Areas and Affiliated Conferences

Thematic areas:

- HCI 2019: Human-Computer Interaction
- HIMI 2019: Human Interface and the Management of Information

Affiliated conferences:

- EPCE 2019: 16th International Conference on Engineering Psychology and Cognitive Ergonomics
- UAHCI 2019: 13th International Conference on Universal Access in Human-Computer Interaction
- VAMR 2019: 11th International Conference on Virtual, Augmented and Mixed Reality
- CCD 2019: 11th International Conference on Cross-Cultural Design
- SCSM 2019: 11th International Conference on Social Computing and Social Media
- AC 2019: 13th International Conference on Augmented Cognition
- DHM 2019: 10th International Conference on Digital Human Modeling and Applications in Health, Safety, Ergonomics and Risk Management
- DUXU 2019: 8th International Conference on Design, User Experience, and Usability
- DAPI 2019: 7th International Conference on Distributed, Ambient and Pervasive Interactions
- HCIBGO 2019: 6th International Conference on HCI in Business, Government and Organizations
- LCT 2019: 6th International Conference on Learning and Collaboration Technologies
- ITAP 2019: 5th International Conference on Human Aspects of IT for the Aged Population
- HCI-CPT 2019: First International Conference on HCI for Cybersecurity, Privacy and Trust
- HCI-Games 2019: First International Conference on HCI in Games
- MobiTAS 2019: First International Conference on HCI in Mobility, Transport, and Automotive Systems
- AIS 2019: First International Conference on Adaptive Instructional Systems

Pre-conference Proceedings Volumes Full List

1. LNCS 11566, Human-Computer Interaction: Perspectives on Design (Part I), edited by Masaaki Kurosu
2. LNCS 11567, Human-Computer Interaction: Recognition and Interaction Technologies (Part II), edited by Masaaki Kurosu
3. LNCS 11568, Human-Computer Interaction: Design Practice in Contemporary Societies (Part III), edited by Masaaki Kurosu
4. LNCS 11569, Human Interface and the Management of Information: Visual Information and Knowledge Management (Part I), edited by Sakae Yamamoto and Hirohiko Mori
5. LNCS 11570, Human Interface and the Management of Information: Information in Intelligent Systems (Part II), edited by Sakae Yamamoto and Hirohiko Mori
6. LNAI 11571, Engineering Psychology and Cognitive Ergonomics, edited by Don Harris
7. LNCS 11572, Universal Access in Human-Computer Interaction: Theory, Methods and Tools (Part I), edited by Margherita Antona and Constantine Stephanidis
8. LNCS 11573, Universal Access in Human-Computer Interaction: Multimodality and Assistive Environments (Part II), edited by Margherita Antona and Constantine Stephanidis
9. LNCS 11574, Virtual, Augmented and Mixed Reality: Multimodal Interaction (Part I), edited by Jessie Y. C. Chen and Gino Fragomeni
10. LNCS 11575, Virtual, Augmented and Mixed Reality: Applications and Case Studies (Part II), edited by Jessie Y. C. Chen and Gino Fragomeni
11. LNCS 11576, Cross-Cultural Design: Methods, Tools and User Experience (Part I), edited by P. L. Patrick Rau
12. LNCS 11577, Cross-Cultural Design: Culture and Society (Part II), edited by P. L. Patrick Rau
13. LNCS 11578, Social Computing and Social Media: Design, Human Behavior and Analytics (Part I), edited by Gabriele Meiselwitz
14. LNCS 11579, Social Computing and Social Media: Communication and Social Communities (Part II), edited by Gabriele Meiselwitz
15. LNAI 11580, Augmented Cognition, edited by Dylan D. Schmorrow and Cali M. Fidopiastis
16. LNCS 11581, Digital Human Modeling and Applications in Health, Safety, Ergonomics and Risk Management: Human Body and Motion (Part I), edited by Vincent G. Duffy

http://2019.hci.international/proceedings

7th International Conference on Distributed, Ambient and Pervasive Interactions (DAPI 2019)

Program Board Chair(s): **Norbert Streitz,** *Germany,* **and Shin'ichi Konomi,** *Japan*

- Yasmine Abbas, USA
- Ashir Ahmed, Bangladesh
- Andreas Braun, Germany
- Maria Antonietta Grasso, France
- Nuno Guimaraes, Portugal
- Jun Hu, The Netherlands
- Pedro Isaias, Australia
- Kristian Kloeckl, USA
- Nicos Komninos, Greece
- Seongil Lee, South Korea
- Antonio Maña, Spain

- Takuya Maekawa, Japan
- Irene Mavrommati, Greece
- Tatsuo Nakajima, Japan
- Anton Nijholt, The Netherlands
- Guochao (Alex) Peng, P.R. China
- Carsten Roecker, Germany
- Atsushi Shimada, Japan
- Reiner Wichert, Germany
- Chui Yin Wong, Malaysia
- Woontack Woo, South Korea

The full list with the Program Board Chairs and the members of the Program Boards of all thematic areas and affiliated conferences is available online at:

http://www.hci.international/board-members-2019.php

HCI International 2020

The 22nd International Conference on Human-Computer Interaction, HCI International 2020, will be held jointly with the affiliated conferences in Copenhagen, Denmark, at the Bella Center Copenhagen, July 19–24, 2020. It will cover a broad spectrum of themes related to HCI, including theoretical issues, methods, tools, processes, and case studies in HCI design, as well as novel interaction techniques, interfaces, and applications. The proceedings will be published by Springer. More information will be available on the conference website: http://2020.hci.international/.

General Chair
Prof. Constantine Stephanidis
University of Crete and ICS-FORTH
Heraklion, Crete, Greece
E-mail: general_chair@hcii2020.org

http://2020.hci.international/

Contents

Perception and Emotion in DAPI

IoT and Big Data

Movement Awareness

An Analysis of the *GESTURES* Installation Game

Andrew Hieronymi[✉]

Pennsylvania State University, University Park, PA 16802, USA
athl3@psu.edu

Abstract. This paper is about an installation game currently in development titled *GESTURES*. The *GESTURES* project is a study of movement in the context of the arts. It aims to create an interactive experience requiring sequences of gestures, choreographed movements learned through repetition and optimization. Custom input devices provide the participant with an experience of hand-eye coordination inspired by the strategies of post-modern dance phrasing, thus placing *GESTURES* at the intersection of performance, game design, interactive art and biomechanics.

The paper asks the following question: How can digital interactive systems inform us about our human movements on an experiential level? More specifically, how can an installation with custom hardware and software help bring awareness to a participant of the sequential steps between thought movement, physical movement and computational movement?

Keywords: Human-computer interaction · Interactive art · Video games · Embodiment

1 Introduction

"[…] the pleasure comes from the gesture, from acting oneself out." (Flusser 2014)

This paper is about an installation game currently in development titled *GESTURES*. The *GESTURES* project is a study of movement in the context of the arts. It aims to create an interactive experience requiring sequences of gestures, choreographed movements learned through repetition and optimization. Custom input devices provide the participant with an experience of hand-eye coordination inspired by the strategies of post-modern dance phrasing, thus placing *GESTURES* at the intersection of performance, game design, interactive art, and biomechanics. While changes may still be made to the design described here, this analysis offers an opportunity to reflect on the installation's approach to movement in relation to these various fields.

The paper asks the following question: How can digital interactive systems inform us about our human movements on an experiential level? More specifically, how can an installation with custom hardware and software help bring awareness to a participant of the sequential steps between thought movement, physical movement and computational movement? (Sutil 2015) These sequential steps can be seen as the digitally

© Springer Nature Switzerland AG 2019
N. Streitz and S. Konomi (Eds.): HCII 2019, LNCS 11587, pp. 3–15, 2019.
https://doi.org/10.1007/978-3-030-21935-2_1

augmented equivalent of Heidegger's "ready-to-hand" and "present-at-hand" states, which he describes when one engages with technology. Media theorist James Ash describes Heidegger's states as follows:

> "When swinging a hammer without thinking about it, time is experienced corporeally as the movement of particular muscles and joints in the body and the relation between these movements [*ready-to-hand*]. As a detached *present-at-hand* object, the hammer is experienced cognitively as a series of elements or traits that might be measured quantitatively through the weight of the hammer or its length." (Ash 2015)

The installation attempts to give participants movement awareness when engaging with a digital interface as their attention shifts between these two distinct states.

The type of movements encountered in *GESTURES* is controlled movements that are carried out in a certain order with a certain timing. This is the type of movements encountered when driving a car, playing an instrument, or dancing. These are also the type of movements executed when playing video games. These prescribed movements need to be learned (present-at-hand) in order to be carried out successfully. In dance for instance, during the learning process dancers are actively thinking about how to execute the steps until the movements are internalized and dancers can perform them without thinking consciously (ready-to-hand). The same process happens in video games, in which players learn to engage with the game world through the various sensors of their input devices until they can manipulate them without conscious thought.

Today, a user interacting with a digital interface is involved in a specific type of cybernetic circuit comparable to a conversation between a user and a computer with the following steps: user input, process thinking, interface output, user thinking, user input and so on. We have become cyborgs, our movements augmented and reacting in sync with the computer system. This ubiquitous contemporary technology, the user interface, finds its most sophisticated and complex expression in the choreographed movements of video games.

As our bodies interact with computer systems, analog movements are transformed into digital signals. Those signals are then translated into information, which is sent back to us. How can the computer, as a machine that strictly manipulates symbols, communicate something back to the participant about their movements beyond quantitative data? Does affect come into play? According to new media artist Nathaniel Stern, the limitations of digital media to translate accurately the richness of our human gestures into digital information is a potential source of exploration for interactive artists, which can reveal a better awareness of the complexities of our bodies' coordinated gestures:

> "Interaction is a limitation - but also an amplification. At its limits, interactive art disrupts our relational embodiment, and thus attunes us to its potential." (Stern 2013)

GESTURES invites non-gamers to engage in physical movement and play with the installation. Participants use custom controllers, long human-height flexible sticks anchored to the ground with springs at their bases and accelerometer sensors at their extremities. These flexible custom controllers are stiff and robust enough to resist human-scale forces without breaking. They require whole-body physical movement to activate. Participants control with the sticks the orientation, rotation, speed and pressure of a circular shape or *puck* they see projected in front of them leaving trails as the shape moves about a two-dimensional field. Collision of the shape with previous trails leads to their gradual erasure. In the process of making marks and engaging with the interface participants generate a history of their gestural decisions visible in the shape, angle, pressure level and direction of the marks created.

The paper is divided into six sections, each providing a framework for understanding the type of movement awareness participants experience while using GESTURES. The sections are *GESTURES* as: lab experiment; interface; video game; dance; mirror; mark making.

2   *GESTURES* as Lab Experiment

The *GESTURES* project is a single-participant installation game. Its physical setup is the following: in a darkened room, two custom controllers stand in front of a wall-sized projection at a distance of about 10 ft. The two custom controllers are identical and resemble ski poles in that they are meant to be handheld by their top extremities while the participant is standing. The controllers are gripless, smooth wooden sticks anchored to the ground with springs at their bases allowing the participant to bend them in all directions. A small sensor (Bosch's BNO055 absolute orientation sensor) is affixed to the top of the controllers registering the orientation, rotation and acceleration of how the sticks bend as the participant manipulates them. The sensor's data is captured by an Arduino microcontroller. It is then sent to a computer with custom software that uses the data in real time to update the graphics displayed on the projector.

This type of setup, in which a participant's gestures are captured by sensors and gathered as data is reminiscent of the process found in scientific lab experiments. *GESTURES* started as a collaborative research project between the author, faculty Joseph Cusumano (Engineering Science and Mechanics), and Jonas Rubenson (Kinesiology) at Penn State. Both Rubenson and Cusumano conduct research on gait optimization using such lab experiments. They set up experiments using motion control sensors to test hypotheses and gather data based on the physical responses from their test subjects. Data is collected and analyzed using conventional quantitative measures and the results are presented in peer-reviewed papers and published in scientific journals.

Prior to *GESTURES*, all three collaborated on a multi-user interactive installation titled *Walking in Patterns* (2017). At the time, Rubenson and Cusumano were interested in collaborating on an installation game using similar technologies as their experiments but used in a different context.

Walking in patterns is a gallery-based installation game in which two participants attempt to optimize their walking on treadmills by watching their silhouetted movement projected on a wall. They duck to avoid their silhouette colliding with a virtual waving ceiling generated by the other participant's height fluctuation while at the same time weaving colored lines and triggering sonic patterns.

Instead of an investigator telling testers what to do, the installation allows participants to discover gradually the rules of the system as well as the way their movement affected the behavior of the other participant and vice-versa. The thinking behind the design was that an intervention used to study gait optimization provides better quality data if the conditions placed the test subjects in a setting in which they have agency over their movements independently of the investigator. Playing a game relying on walking was seen as a way to think differently about how to design future data-collecting approaches about gait optimization.

The philosopher Hubert Dreyfus reached a similar conclusion regarding testers in controlled lab experiments in his 1980 paper about skill acquisition:

> "[...] when the same task can be described as a sequence of formal operations, and alternatively as a familiar concrete problem, the subject's behavior dramatically improves when he is presented the task in a concrete everyday form." (Dreyfus 1980)

A later single player iteration of the installation allowed Rubenson's PhD candidate Kirsty McDonald to make significant discoveries about human locomotion in constrained environments. (McDonald et al. 2019)

The *GESTURES* installation is the next attempt by the collaborators to merge artistic and scientific concerns in a single interactive installation. As Cusumano summarizes:

> "The dynamical complexity of the device, together with its structural simplicity, lends itself to human interactions in a way that promotes gestural explorations. How the human neuromotor system organizes itself when complex and communicative movements are involved is a challenging problem at the cutting edge of movement neuroscience. By coupling the whole body with the device's action, we will open up avenues to interesting fundamental research (for example on the energetics of such movements) that could also have significant implications in clinical, therapeutic contexts." (pers. comm.)

Physical installations using motion sensors allow for the design of interfaces where the interaction of the participants requires real-world movements (running, ducking, gesturing). It is in the gap between where that physical behavior would happen in a real-world context versus a staged scenario - what Rubenson calls a "closed-loop feedback" (pers. comm.) - that the participants' subjective experience of the installation can unfold. In the context of *GESTURES*, this subjective experience is centered on a heightened awareness of the role of the body when interacting with digital interfaces.

3   *GESTURES* as Interface

When a participant stands in front of the *GESTURES* installation projection, they see a small two-dimensional puck-like shaped circle. Inside the circle is an arrow pointing to the right. Both the circle and the arrow have jagged edges. They appear pixelated as if drawn on a low-resolution display. The background of the application is a grid of squares of a resolution of 195×195. The circle has a diameter of 15 squares. The two stick-shaped controllers allow for the manipulation of this puck.

The left stick controls the simulated acceleration, direction and orientation of the puck on the 2D surface. As it is pushed forward or backward, the puck accelerates or decelerates. As it is bent left or right, it rotates left or right. If the puck reaches the limits of the screen it wraps around to the opposite side and continues its forward motion.

The right input device controls the trails the puck makes as it moves. If the stick is pushed forward or backward, a trail will be drawn on the screen, the trail's width corresponding to the diameter of the puck. The angle of the stick will determine the brightness value of the trail. The more the stick is bent the lighter the trail. As it is bent left or right, the brightness value will increase only left or right. If the stick is bent backwards, the motion of the puck will leave no trail.

To summarize, the stick-shaped custom input devices allow real-time control of a circular shape on a projection with the possibility of leaving trails as it moves about the surface. The sticks resemble joysticks found inside plane cockpits. The dual sticks also reference analog thumb sticks found on most contemporary gamepads.

The pixelation effect is not trying to emulate an older system for a "retro" effect. Instead it is there to remind the participants of the basic building block of a visual display: graphical user interfaces made of grids of pixels whose color or brightness value is arranged to look like images and are updated in real time to create the illusion of motion and by extension, interaction.

Enlarging the dual sticks so that not only the thumbs are engaged but also the whole upper body allows for an emphasis on the role of the body during real-time interaction with a digital interface. The game artist and scholar Mary Flanagan explored this emphasis in her 2006 installation game *Giant Joystick* in which she created "a large, functioning game controller [serving] as an interface to a shift in embodied experience." (Flanagan 2006) Flanagan enlarged an original Atari 2600 joystick to a height of about eight feet with which participants could play emulated versions of Atari 2600 games. Because of the size of the input device, at least two players were needed to play what used to be single-player games, leading to a more embodied as well as collaborative experience, in contrast with the more common multi-player competitive gameplay prevalent in commercial videogames.

As new media artist and theorist Simon Penny writes, interfaces originally created by the military to help humans interact with computers were seen as a temporary fix until machines could run unassisted (Penny 2017). As human computer interfaces proliferated, issues concerning their usability grew and interfaces became increasingly user-friendly. Today's interaction with our devices integrates natural gestures such as real-time audiovisual responses to finger taps and swipes. This interaction seems so seamless and "natural" that the interface becomes transparent unless technical glitches occur. The installation setup of *GESTURES* with human-size input devices encourages participants to consider the various building blocks of the interface they engage with, from the custom hardware to the pixelated grid that constitutes its visual display.

4   *GESTURES* as Video Game

The *GESTURES* application allows participants to control a puck moving on the screen in front of them. When pushing the right stick forward, trails appear following the moving puck. The trails are as wide as the puck and their brightness corresponds to the speed of the puck (lighter when going faster). Additional rules apply: as the puck generates a trail and encounters in its path an existing trail drawn previously, it will keep drawing its current trail over the older trail. The older trail will gradually fade as its brightness value diminishes. The amount of fading of the older trails when colliding with the puck will depend on its speed and pressure level. The slower the puck and the more pressure applied, the faster the fade. As participants engage with the interface and develop an understanding of its logic, they might be compelled to control the appearance and pattern of the trails they create by manipulating the puck. The erasure of the trails might not be desirable; therefore they will attempt to master the responsiveness of the sticks in order to control the path and speed of the puck.

Thus, participants need to learn the coordination skills required to move the puck at the right speed and time its rotation to avoid collision with older trails. If it goes too fast or does not rotate fast enough it might collide with other trails. Alternatively, if it goes too slow, it might fade the older trails faster. This process of kinesthetic learning is what makes video game interaction such a rich source of study when investigating skill acquisition. As sociologist David Sudnow writes in his landmark study *Pilgrim in the Microworld*:

"If you engage a human body through eyes and fingers in a precisely scripted interaction with various sorts of computer-generated events, what seem like quite complex skills are rapidly acquired by regular repetition. Sequences of events can be scheduled into readily mastered routines of progressive difficulty, and a program of timed transitions can be organized, programming you, in turn, at an economically desirable rate." (Sudnow 1983)

Learning to manipulate the sticks accurately allows participants to get intimate with the resistance and give the sticks provide to control the acceleration and deceleration of the pucks' various properties, i.e., motion, orientation and pressure. In order to acquire those skills they need to practice and gradually internalize the hand/arm/body-eye coordination corresponding to each device since the controls of the circle (motion, orientation, pressure) are not mapped intuitively to the two sticks. In other words, because the sticks look and behave identically participants are required to internalize the role of each stick and its impact on the puck's behavior.

Because the sticks' input corresponds to typical gamepad's thumb sticks they feel familiar but at the same time because of their size they engage the participants' hand/arm/body and keeps them aware of the role their bodies play. It is the amplification of the interactions (Stern) through these oversized input devices that emphasize what game theorist Brendan Keogh defines as "distributed presence":

"A key aspect of understanding videogames as an embodied experience is identifying how the player feels a sense of presence "in" the virtual world of the videogame while remaining aware that they are situated in the actual world. It is a liminal, distributed presence across worlds and across bodies that is never resolved and that is fundamental to how videogames are experienced." (Keogh 2018)

If we use game theorists Salen and Zimmerman's definitions of *play*, "play is free movement within a more rigid structure" (Salen and Zimmerman 2004) and *game*, "a game is a system in which players engage in an artificial conflict, defined by rules, that results in a quantifiable outcome" (Salen and Zimmerman 2004) we can see that *GESTURES* most certainly provides a playful experience. It can also provide a video game experience if participants decide to engage with it in pursuit of a "quantifiable outcome". In the case of *GESTURES*, this outcome would be the mastery of the puck's motion and pressure level in order to avoid the accidental erasure of trails. It is ultimately up to the participants to decide their level of commitment and their desire to pursue a goal-oriented versus an open-ended interaction with the system.

5   *GESTURES* as Dance

Similarities can be found between the sequence of moves video game players and dancers need to learn in order to perform in their respective mediums. Those similarities exist even though video game players' actions are goal-oriented and use fingers on a controller and eyes on a screen, whereas dancers use their bodies to produce aesthetic stimulus on their audience. Game theorist Graeme Kirkpatrick points out the resemblance between the trial-and-error processes of both practices:

> "Since it is difficult, we have to persist until we get it right. In so doing, we gradually master the move, much as a dancer learns a new sequence or position, so that when we encounter the right kind of situation later in the game we may get through on the first or second attempt." (Kirkpatrick 2011)

Beginner and expert practitioners alike generally experience this learning process as long as the choreography or game matches their skill level. If there is a mismatch, the dancer or gamer might experience frustration or boredom depending on the situation. Post-modern choreographers have questioned this road to mastery required by dancers by creating pieces in which the learning process is less linear.

Yvonne Rainer, for example, is a dancer and choreographer whose work in the 1960's challenged some of the conventions of classical dance most notably notions of spectacle and virtuosity. During that period, Rainer often collaborated with visual artists associated with the minimal art movement. In her famous dance piece *Trio A* (1966), her choreography was inspired by everyday tasks-oriented activities such as for instance walking, eating and carrying bricks. In the years following its introduction, Rainer used *Trio A* as a framework to teach workshops in which participants could perform the piece without the rigorous requirements of classical training. *Trio A* is physically demanding and has a learning curve but is accessible to the everyday participant. As Reiner's choreography challenges her art form's conventions, it provides both dancer and spectator with a new awareness of the everyday movements enacted in the performance. She writes that:

> "The display of technical virtuosity and the display of the dancer's specialized body no longer make any sense. Dancers have been driven to search for an alternative context that allows for a more matter-of-fact, more concrete, more banal quality of physical being in performance, a context wherein people are engaged in actions and movements making a less spectacular demand on the body and in which skill is hard to locate." (Rainer 1965)

If we associate the difficulty of learning sequenced moves in video games to the technical abilities of the dancer, *GESTURES* is closer to the no-spectacle no-virtuosity of *Trio A*. It proposes to the participant the option to learn and develop skills in order to experience the piece but does not penalize or prevent them from enjoying the experience because of a lack of skill. Because *GESTURES* is an interactive art installation exhibited in an art-gallery setting participants are expected to interact with it for a relatively short period of time (less then 10 min on average). The duration presents similarities with *Trio A*'s time stamp (four-and-a-half minutes).

Also, comparable to *Trio A*, moment-to-moment interaction with *GESTURES* presents a certain evenness in emotional engagement without the typical catharsis players experience in commercial videogames. For Rainer, in *Trio A*

> "[…] no one part of the series is made any more important than any other. […] A great variety of movement shapes occur, but they are of equal weight and are equally emphasized". (Rainer 1965)

Ultimately *GESTURES* is not attempting to mimic dance choreographies, but instead is borrowing some of the post-modern dance phrasing strategies exemplified by *Trio A* in order to question and reflect on the complex gestures video game players execute. Inspired by Rainer's choreography, *GESTURES* attempts to provide a smoother, more mindful learning process for participants engaging with a playful interactive experience without the tension resulting from reward/punishment systems, competitiveness and audio visual immersion that commercial game interfaces usually offer.

6 *GESTURES* as Mirror

Since the very beginning of its brief history, interactive art has been concerned with making participants aware of the closed loop in which they are taking part: user input, process thinking, interface output, user thinking, user input, and so on. This cybernetic circuit common to all human-computer interactive systems transforms us into cyborgs, our movements augmented and reacting in sync with the digital interface. Interactive artists have attempted to encourage participants to observe critical distance from their experience in order to reflect on it. Early pioneer Myron Krueger created his interactive installation *Videoplace* (1972–1990s) using a camera as a sensor. The silhouettes of the participants were captured and projected on a screen facing them. A series of mini-game-like interactions allowed participants to experience real-time interactivity. This setup became ubiquitous in new media art during the 1990s and was also coopted by the videogame industry in the following decades Sony's Eyetoy (2003), Microsoft's Kinect (2010): custom camera sensors using a mirror-like setup putting the focus of gameplay on the participant's bodily movements. New media artist Daniel Rozin uses a similar setup to create mirror-like physical interfaces with a great range of materials, notably wood:

> "Wooden Mirror is a comment on digital artifacts and interfaces - a comment on how computer applications reveal information and reflect their users and the process of production. The textured surface of Wooden Mirror, which responds so playfully to our movements, help us to understand the conventional computer screen as both a window and a mirror." (Bolter and Gromala 2003)

New media artist David Rokeby in his installation *Very Nervous System* (1986–1990) uses computer vision as a motion sensor but instead of a visual display MIDI sounds provide feedback to the various movements of the participant. Rokeby also references a self-reflective setup in his essay *Transforming Mirrors*:

> "The self-image is the known reference against which the phenomena of transformation are registered. [...] These impressions are immediately translated into sounds or music, reflecting and accompanying the gestures, thereby transforming the interactor's awareness of his or her body. In both cases, the character of the experienced phenomenon is discovered as a change in a representation of the self." (Rokeby 1995)

Through the trails that it creates, *GESTURES* also aims to provide a mirror-like setup. As the participant bends the sticks, the puck moves and reacts in real time. The trails it leaves give the participant a constant visual trace of the speed, pressure and orientation of the physical input applied with the custom sticks.

The visuals are intentionally limited in mirroring the gestures of the participant. After all, the simulated puck is moving in a 2D space and is not reflecting realistically the 3D movements of the sticks and by extension the participant. This discrepancy between a rich, analog input and a restricted, pixelated, digital output emphasizes this gap instead of attempting to hide it.

Digital systems today have become very effective at creating highly immersive experiences. The popularity of Virtual Reality in digital entertainment is a telling example. In Virtual Reality systems, the emphasis and technological innovation focuses on the visual experience, often recycling existing input devices from traditional gaming interfaces. This approach demonstrates a desire by the entertainment industry to continue a long tradition of gaze-centric media production neglecting the role of the body and it's crucial role in experiencing the world around us. As immersive, gaze-centric technologies such as virtual reality are gaining ground with computer users worldwide, it seems all the more urgent to remind ourselves about the body we inhabit:

> "VR is an illusion of control over reality, nature, and especially over the unruly, gender-and-race-marked, essential mortal body... With virtual reality we are offered the vision of a body-free universe." (Balsamo 1995 cited in Monteiro 2017)

An installation like *GESTURES* attempts to reveal instead of conceal the shortcomings of computation in translating human gestures into digital information. Those shortcomings hopefully break temporarily the cybernetic circuit participants are engaged in and bring their attention to the gestures they perform.

7 *GESTURES* as Mark Making

As a participant engages with *GESTURES*, applying pressure with the right stick creates trails. A trail is a thick line the width corresponding to the diameter of the puck. The brightness and pixelation of the trail corresponds to the amount of pressure and speed of the puck. The faster the puck the brighter the trail, the more pressure applied the least amount of pixelation on the trail. Older trails fade gradually as the puck collides with them. The result of a play session with *GESTURES* can vary between a jumble of interweaving lanes of various opacities to a very controlled all-over pattern of trails reflecting the intention, skill and dedication of the participant. What do these trails represent? Can they be seen as original digital drawings or a history of the participant's gestures?

Robert Ryman, a New York painter contemporary of Yvonne Rainer, (they were born four years apart) has also been classified as an artist belonging to the minimal art movement of the sixties. His stark approach to painting focuses on the materiality of the support (canvas, frame, pigment) and the mark making of the brush. His palette is most often restricted to the color white not because he is interested in that color in particular but because he does not want other colors to distract from the focus of the mark and how it is applied on the surface. In a recent exhibition catalog, artist Charles Gaines notes that:

> "He [Ryman]e laid them out [the brushstrokes] across the picture plane usually in an allover and evenly dispersed pattern exploiting their nuanced, gestural quality not as design but as material fact. Their organization reads more like a taxonomic display, functional and utilitarian; as Vittorio Colaizzi has said, "each stroke is a record of its application." (Gaines 2017)

It could be said that minimal artists like Ryman (and Rainer) are attempting a more "objective" approach to their art practice, an approach in which instead of infusing the movement or the mark with expressive meaning, they let the medium speak for itself. Both the choreography and the painting are what they are and it is up to the audience to experience and appreciate the medium in its essence.

In the late nineteenth century, French scientist and chronophotographer Étienne-Jules Marey was conducting early experiments with photography attempting to capture movement. Contrary to his contemporary Eadweard Muybridge, he was less interested in decomposing movement in its consecutive postures but in representing the duration of movement between postures. (Manning 2009) Media theorist Erin Manning describes Marey's work as a line that "does not simply represent movement: it creates the feeling of movement. We are moved by what we do not actually see. The elasticity of the image feels like a drawing vision drawing." (Manning 2009)

This idea of creating a "feeling of movement" is central to *GESTURES*. The installation was not designed to operate strictly as a drawing tool. The marks left while creating trails will hardly allow the participant to draw anything specific. Instead, the trails provide a visual history of the way the controllers were manipulated. At the moment of writing the installation was not tested sufficiently to be able to assert that visual history can provide enough information to get a significant understanding of the types of gestures that were accomplished during a session. Ultimately, provided there are enough screenshots of the finished traces it will be possible to generate a taxonomy of gestures that could not only be informative about the participant's interaction history but also have an affective (aesthetic) effect. It would provide a visual feeling of movement. "Movement is no longer asked to express something outside it: movement becomes its own artwork." (Manning 2009)

8 Conclusion

To conclude with some final thoughts, we will reflect first on why movement awareness in interaction design can have value for participants, and second how the *GESTURES* installation game attempts to achieve movement awareness.

As we have seen, movement awareness is the state in which someone is conscious of their gestures (Heidegger's present-at-hand). In general it can be said that unless something perturbs the gesture (tool malfunction or accident for example) or someone makes a conscious decision to be present and alert about one's gestures (mindfulness), gestures are performed unconsciously (Heidegger's ready-to-hand).

In order for a gesture to be performed unconsciously it first has to be learned. As we learn a gesture, our awareness declines until we perform it unconsciously, without actively thinking about it. The philosopher Hubert Dreyfus breaks down the skill acquisition process into "five developmental stages […] novice, competence, proficiency, expertise and mastery." (Dreyfus 1980) In this process, students go from "analytic thought to intuitive response". Pilots for instance, go from the awareness of flying to the experience of flying. If they suddenly reflect upon what they are doing, they will be degrading their flying performance.

Both Heidegger and Dreyfus, as they formulate their understanding of movement awareness, focus on a person's interaction with a given technology (handling a hammer, flying a plane). When interacting with digital media, a cybernetic circuit develops between the user and the computer creating a loop mediated by the interface through input/output devices. This closed loop can have various effects on the awareness of the user as they experience various mental states such as immersion, relaxation and escapism, or oscillation between reflection and action.

Immersion can occur for instance when videogame players get caught in a heightened sense of present, what game theorist James Ash describes as *envelope power*. Commercial videogame designers actively work in developing interfaces that encourage this particular state because it

> "draws upon players' habitual capacities to sense difference to alter the relationship between their temporal anticipation and recollection in order to encourage continued engagement and consumption of the products they are using." (Ash 2015)

Relaxation and escapism from and through digital media can happen as in the case of cultural writer Shaad D'Souza who describes his need to escape the constant lure of mobile device notifications by engaging in videogame play. D'Souza chooses games requiring minimal skill such as navigating aimlessly a character in an open world while avoiding goals or direct challenges. D'Souza notes:

> "Gaming, a tactile activity that requires my full focus, is one of the few activities I've found that doesn't encourage me to check my phone every five minutes. […] It seems counterintuitive, but gaming provides for me the kind of peace and relaxation that's becoming harder and harder to find." (D'Souza 2019)

As for oscillation between reflection (analytic thought) and action (intuitive response), it is a mental state encountered most typically when engaging with interactive artworks. According to media theorist Katja Kwastek:

"The epistemic potential of interactive art is based on an oscillation between flow and distancing and between action and reflection that originates in the processes of interaction." (Kwastek 2013)

The *GESTURES* installation game does not encourage learning mastery from the participants, or immersion, escapism or relaxation through the use of audiovisual representations of virtual worlds. It also does not aim to generate a back and forth movement between action and reflection. Instead, the installation aims to make the participants aware of their bodies' movements and gestures during interaction with the interface.

According to new media artist Simon Penny, the history of computing that lead to the current information age was based on a clear mind/body split inherited from a Cartesian mindset. This mindset emphasizes abstraction and "logical manipulation of abstract symbols" over "embodied practices". (Penny 2017) The denigration of the body in cultural computing is exemplified today by the current enthusiasm for technologies such as Virtual Reality that emphasize a gaze-centric disembodied immersive experience.

GESTURES attempts to provide an interactive experience in which movement awareness is encouraged by letting participants make decisions on the type of interaction they are interested in pursuing. Participants can attempt to fill the screen with marks (game), focus on the rhythm of their bodily gestures (dance), and/or be attentive to the relationship between gesture and mark (mirror and mark-making). As they gradually learn to manipulate the custom input devices to control the screen-based puck, participants can observe how their body is engaged and how skills are acquired. The interface does not encourage immersion and does not provide easy visual gratification. The emphasis is on the constant movement between user input and display output with visual marks providing a history of moment-to-moment decision-making.

The type of movement awareness that GESTURES is aiming to bring about in participants can be compared to the description artist Ken Koren gives of the Zen tea ceremony:

"Nonthinking repetition of mechanical forms allows one to concentrate simply on being without the distraction of having to make decisions, artistic or otherwise. (Another aspect of this practice is the belief, from Zen, that the body, not language, is the repository of knowledge and technique." (Koren 2008)

Can GESTURES pretend to encourage mindfulness in participants? It remains to be seen as the installation is still in development. Nonetheless creating installations with this goal in mind seems for this author to be a worthy attempt at reacting to the unprecedented levels of anxiety, distraction and addiction for which contemporary digital media is responsible.

References

Ash, J.: The Interface Envelope: Gaming, Technology, Power. Bloomsbury Academic an Imprint of Bloomsbury Publishing, Inc., New York (2015)

Balsamo, A.: Technologies of the Gendered Body: Reading Cyborg Women. Duke University Press, Durham (1995)

Dreyfus, S.E., Dreyfus, H.L.: A Five-Stage Model of the Mental Activities Involved in Directed Skill Acquisition. University of California, Berkeley (1980)

Flanagan, M.: Giant Joystick (2006). https://maryflanagan.com/work/giant-joystick/. Accessed 01 Jan 2019

Flusser, V.: Gestures. University of Minnesota Press, Minneapolis (2014)

Gaines, C.: Robert ryman's reality: between literalism and expression. In: Hoban, S., Courtney, J. M. (eds.) Robert Ryman. Yale University Press, New Haven (2017)

Gromala, D., Bolter, J.D.: Windows and Mirrors: Interaction Design, Digital Art and the Myth of Transparency. MIT Press, Cambridge (2003)

Keogh, B.: A Play of Bodies: How We Perceive Videogames. MIT Press, Cambridge (2018)

Kirkpatrick, G.: Aesthetic Theory and the Video Game. Manchester University Press, New York (2011)

Koren, L.: Wabi-Sabi for Artists, Designers Poets & Philosophers. Imperfect Publishing, Point Reyes (2008)

Kwastek, K.: Aesthetics of Interaction in Digital Art. MIT Press, Cambridge (2013)

Manning, E.: Relationscapes: Movement, Art Philosophy. MIT Press, Cambridge (2009)

McDonald, K., Hieronymi, A., Cusumano, J., Rubenson, J.: Optimization in Human Walking: Decoupling Whole-Body Energetics and Local Muscle Effort (2019, Unpublished)

Monteiro, S.: The Fabric of Interface, Mobile Media, Design, and Gender. MIT Press, Cambridge (2017)

Penny, S.: Making Sense: Cognition, Computing, Art, and Embodiment. MIT Press, Cambridge (2017)

Rainer, Y.: A quasi survey of some "minimalist" tendencies in the quantitatively minimal dance activity midst the plethora, or an analysis of Trio A. In: Battcock, G. (ed.) Minimal Art. University of California Press, Berkeley (1965)

Rokeby, D.: Transforming mirrors: subjectivity and control in interactive media. In: Penny, S. (ed.) Critical Issues in Interactive Media. SUNY Press, Albany (1995)

Salen, K., Zimmerman, E.: Rules of Play: Game Design Fundamentals. MIT Press, Cambridge (2004)

D'Souza, S.: https://www.theguardian.com/games/2019/mar/22/its-ironic-but-gaming-can-be-an-escape-from-our-hyper-connected-screen-filled-life. Accessed 28 Mar 2019

Stern, N.: Interactive Art and Embodiment: The Implicit Body as Performance. Gylphi Limited, Canterbury (2013)

Sudnow, D.: Pilgrim in the Microworld. Warner Books, New York (1983)

Sutil, N.S.: Motion and Representation: The Language of Human Movement. MIT Press, Cambridge (2015)

AquaBot: An Interactive System for Digital Water Play

Lijuan Liu[1], Cheng Yao[1(✉)], Yuyu Lin[1], Yang Chen[1], Ziyu Liu[2], and Fangtian Ying[3]

[1] College of Computer Science and Technology, Zhejiang University,
Hangzhou, China
{liulijuan,Yaoch}@zju.edu.cn
[2] College of Computer Software Technology, Zhejiang University,
Hangzhou, China
miclzy@126.com
[3] Hubei University of Technology, Wuhan, China
yingft@gmail.com

Abstract. Water is a ubiquitous substance in everyday life and has been found in many cultures as a game medium. With advances in digital technology and computer-aided design, there is a great potential for water games which can create new interactive experiences for players. In this paper, we take an interest in digital games with physical water and propose AquaBot an interactive water game system. It includes an underwater robot and a wearable wristband. The robot can change existing state such as light, color, and movement, based on its interaction with player and environment. The wearable device is used to control and interact with the robot. We test AquaBot system through two interactive scenarios, the results show that users' feedback is positive and many of them are willing to experience in future water play. In addition, we discuss design factors of interaction with underwater robot from water environment, human and device. The intent of this paper is to inspire other researchers to explore and study digital water play and interaction with underwater robot.

Keywords: Digital water play · Interaction with underwater robot · Water environment · Design factor

1 Introduction

Water is one of the most abundant compounds on earth, and about three-quarters of the world's area is covered with water. Popular aquatic activities like water sport, water theme park, water game provide players with special experience. Recently, Human-Computer Interaction related research has received significant attention in game experience design. Games research field is advancing from playing with digital content using a keyboard, to using bodies to play with digital content, towards a future where we experience our bodies as digital play [3]. While most previous work has focused on ground-based exercise activities, there has been an immense interest in various water activities [1]. Besides, an underwater robot is designed mostly for industrial, educational

N. Streitz and S. Konomi (Eds.): HCII 2019, LNCS 11587, pp. 16–27, 2019.
https://doi.org/10.1007/978-3-030-21935-2_2

and scientific research. In this paper, we are concerned with underwater entertainment applications. Advances in computing, digital and robot technology have inspired the creation of novel water game design. Those advancements let to improved sensing and interacting technologies that support new forms of digital water play.

In this paper, we present AquaBot system towards digital game with physical water. The system supports interaction between human, robot and environment. It includes two parts: underwater robot and wearable wristband. The underwater robot can perceive the environmental information to give corresponding feedback, it can also complete the interactive task according to the commands issued by the player. Now, it can support color, light, vibration and movement changes. Players can send the command to adjust the robot's state through wristband. We also explore the design factors of interaction with underwater robot from human, device and water environment. Those factors are beneficial to consider when design water-related interaction. Our main contributions are as follows:

- Proposing a digital water play system supporting multiple interactions and experiences.
- Using the body to control underwater robot which makes interaction more natural.
- Exploring the design factors of interaction with underwater robot.

2 Related Work

Water environment is unconventional and sometimes is risky for players to attend, there is less amount of existing HCI work in such an underwater environment than in land domain. Technological advancements such as game console accessories allowing for bodily play, wearable technologies and sensors in mobile phones enabling digital games [3]. In this paper we focus on interactions beyond the screen and land situation, we explore the digital water play and water-related interaction experience.

With the advances in technologies, studies on water games have been made. Water Ball Z is a novel interactive two-player water game that allows kids and young adults to "fight" in a virtual world with actual physical feedback [15]. It engages people in a real and fun experience where a hit is physically manifested via a water spray. The paper by Choi et al. [1] proposed MobyDick, a smartphone-based multi-player game in which a group of swimmers coordinates themselves in order to achieve the common goal of hunting an AR monster in the water. AquaCAVE [5] is a computer-augmented swimming pool with rear-projection acrylic walls that surround a swimmer, providing a CAVE-like immersive stereoscopic projection environment. Bellarbi [7] explored augmented and mixed reality technologies in aquatic leisure activities, he proposed an underwater AR game using the DOLPHYN device which can be used at water surface as well as underwater using a tuba. Jain [6] presents Amphibian VR system that provides an immersive SCUBA diving experience through a convenient terrestrial simulator. Users lie on their torso on a motion platform with their outstretched arms and legs placed in a suspended harness. It could simulate buoyancy, drag and temperature changes through various sensors. In underwater game, wireless data exchange among users and devices need to be supported and it also needs to overcome several key technical challenges as well as human factor constraints.

Recently, the demand for advances in underwater robot technologies is growing and will eventually lead to fully autonomous, specialized, reliable underwater robotic vehicles [9]. Some researchers have successfully applied underwater robots to digital water games. In the experience process, we have to consider the interaction between human, underwater robot, and the environment. Swimoid is a swim support system using an underwater buddy robot [4] to recognize, follow, and present information to the swimmer. While there are some problems in this system, it's difficult to control the robot with increasing water resistance. Users can't interact with the display for a long time because of the limitation of breathing capacity. Pell [8] presents Gravity Well an interactive shallow-water system that supports bodily play through water-movement interactions. The robot can provide a real-time visual response to the player's human-aquatic movement interactions and change color with touch.

Within the context of the underwater environment, there are many factors that may influence the quality of interactions. The existing studies on underwater interaction design strategies may be classified into two categories: giving instructions to robots from human; tracking human using some sensors mounted on robots [4]. Wu [10] proposed a preliminary human factors model to study interactions between human and semi-autonomous underwater vehicles. Raffe [11] proposed a taxonomy of six degrees of water contact and four categories of player and computer design features to be considered during the design and development of digital water play experience.

Inspired by previous researches and technologies, we propose AquaBot an interactive digital game with physical water which can give different color, light, movement feedback according to the interaction with human and environment. We also explore the design factors of interaction with underwater robot with the AquaBot system.

3   System Description

AquaBot system contains two parts, an underwater robot and a wearable wristband. The wristband is a waterproof part worn by the player to response for the interaction with the robot. The underwater robot is the main interactive device and plays a critical role in the whole system because of its interactive property like color, light, movement. Compared to the studies about HCI and HRI in land domains, the biggest challenge of underwater interaction is that some communication channels available in land become unavailable underwater. We need to test and find a suitable communication channel that can be used in our system. Besides, all of our devices need to be waterproof and can be immersed in water.

3.1   Interaction Framework

Figure 1 illustrates the interaction framework of AquaBot system, it includes three essential factors: AquaBot, human and water environment. AquaBot amplifies the interactions between underwater robot, wristband, player, water environment through visual perception, haptic perception and behavior interaction. The system has two data input ways: the monitoring data from the wristband and the data collected from the underwater robot. The wearable wristband is used for detecting hand gesture and send commands to the robot. The underwater robot consists of LED, vibration motor, propeller, temperature sensitive material for interaction output. The interaction between the AquaBot system and the environment is mainly through sound and temperature information. Human interacts with the system is through body gesture and active operation. The interaction between human and water environment is reflected in the contact degree between hand and water: above the water surface, on the water surface, and under the water. Arduino for computational processing, and Bluetooth for data communication.

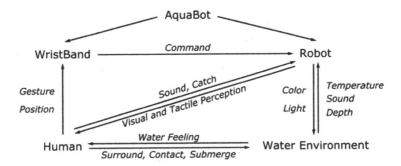

Fig. 1. Interaction framework of AquaBot

3.2 Underwater Robot

The appearance of the underwater robot is a bionic design based on jellyfish and is made by 3D printing (Fig. 2). At the outermost layer of the robot, we applied a temperature sensitive paint. When the temperature is below 31 °C, the paint will show blue, and when the temperature is above 31 °C, the blue paint will become transparent. So that it can interact with the environment to change its color according to temperature.

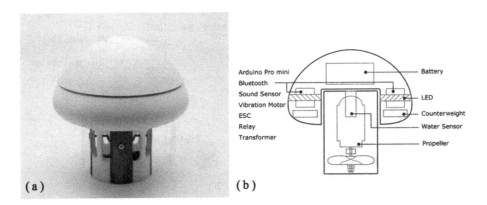

Fig. 2. (a) Underwater robot of AquaBot; (b) Internal structure of underwater robot.

The robot is powered by a 12 V lithium battery and can continue to work underwater for 20 min. We use Bluetooth as the communication method for several reasons. Firstly, our water environment is set in a glass jar with the size of 80 × 45 × 45 cm. Bluetooth module can work in this underwater environment; Another Bluetooth module is installed on the wristband, it's convenient for data transmission; The connection of Bluetooth is easier than other methods while meeting system function. But Bluetooth can only achieve short-distance data transmission, it needs the player and robot to stay within 5 m.

Under the action of the propeller, the robot can perform floating and dive movement under water. The propeller provides 11 N thrust at 12 V. We use a duct to help it generate more force. We also add counterweights inside the robot to keep it balanced under water. The Arduino Pro Mini is used to control the robot. The water sensor can detect whether the robot is in a water environment. When leaving the water environment, the propeller will stop working. The sound sensor can detect ambient sound with a volume threshold of 50 dB and the robot will be activated when the sound is above 50 dB for more than 1 s. The vibration motor provides a vibrating touch. The LED strip is available in a variety of colors. If no interaction occurs for more than 5 min, the robot will start to "sleep". The connection part of the robot is waterproofed by a silicone ring.

3.3   Wristband

The wristband needs to be worn by the player to participate in the game (Fig. 3). It acts as an operation tool between the human and the robot. It converts the human action commands into data and sends them to the robot. The wristband is powered by a 9 V dry battery. The Arduino Pro Mini is used as the control system. Data communication is done with the Bluetooth module. We use the MPU-6050 module to detect gestures. The water sensor on the side is used to detect the contact degree between the hand and the water. It can be detected that the hand is not in contact with water, is located on the water surface, and is completely immersed in water. The other electronic components of the wristband are placed in the waterproofed box.

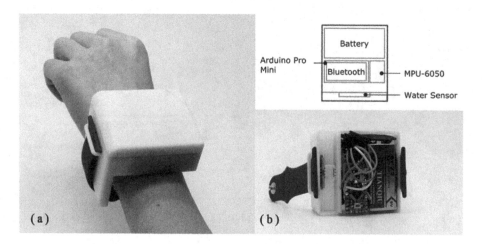

Fig. 3. (a) Wristband of AquaBot; (b) Internal structure of Wristband.

3.4   Interaction and Control

AquaBot supports interaction with human and the environment. When the ambient temperature is lower than 31 °C, the robot remains blue, and when the temperature is higher than 31 °C, the robot will change color from blue to transparent (Fig. 4). When the ambient sound is above 55 dB, the robot will wake up and flash the blue light (Fig. 5).

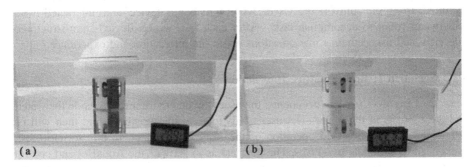

Fig. 4. Robot changes color with temperature: (a) The water temperature is 28.9 °C and the robot remains blue color. (b) The water temperature is 56.3 °C, the blue paint gradually fades and becomes transparent. (Color figure online)

Players need to wear the wristband when interacting with the robot. AquaBot will give feedback based on human gestures. The player claps, the robot is activated when the sound exceeds 50 dB and the light flashes. When the hand is not in contact with the water, the arm raises upwards, the robot will float up; when the arm moves down, the robot will dive; when the user swings the arm to the left or right, the color of the robot can be switched; when the hand puts over the robot and touches the water surface, the robot will float up to touch the player's palm and the light becomes red; when the hand is completely immersed in the water and close to the robot, the robot will dive down. Catch the robot and take it out of the water, the propeller will stop working. At the same time, the robot will flash the light and the vibration module is triggered to provide the hand with a vibrating touch.

Fig. 5. Robot is awakened by the sound and flash light. (Color figure online)

4   Interactive Application Scenarios

In order to improve and evaluate the performance of AquaBot and understand how users would use our system, we organized 2 scenario tests for different interaction: body gesture interaction and underwater interaction. The tests were implemented indoors, the robot was placed in a 90 × 45 × 45 cm glass jar. Added water to the glass jar, the depth of the water was 30 cm. All participants are aged from 20 to 32 and were recruited from our university. Users wore wristband device and interacted with underwater robot to accomplish tasks. After each test, we conducted semi-structured interview and asked them some questions about the interaction and experience.

4.1   Scenario 1: Body Gesture Interaction

Scenario 1 involves two environments: the user is in an environment outside the water, and the robot is in the water. The user needs to wear the wristband and then will be introduced the function and operation of the AqucaBot system. In this scenario test, users need to complete two tasks. The first task is to activate the AquaBot and control its floating and dive movements by gestures (Fig. 6a). The second task is to change the color of the robot's light through gesture control and set it to the color they like (Fig. 6b).

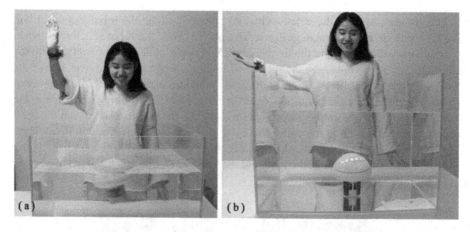

Fig. 6. Body gesture interaction: (a) Raising arm to control the robot float up; (b) Swing arm to change the color of robot. (Color figure online)

All users showed great interest in the interaction process. Some users said that when they experienced the AquaBot, they were surprised that they could control the underwater robot without touching the water. P3 said the system was very interactive and provides a new water game experience. P6 said that this system gave her a new understanding of underwater robots. During the test, we found that the task of controlling the robot's movement was the most popular, and some participants experienced this task many times.

4.2   Scenario 2: Underwater Interaction

In scenario 2, users need to touch the water surface and immerse in the water. The water sensor in the wristband would perceive the situation when hand contacts with the water. In this scenario, users are told to complete 2 tasks. The first task is to put the hand on the top of the robot and let the palm touch the water (Fig. 7a). The second task is to immerse the hand underwater, catch the robot and take it out of the water (Fig. 7b, c).

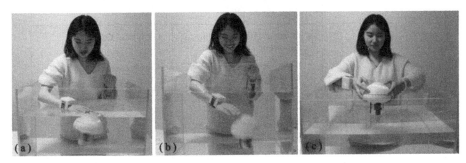

Fig. 7. Underwater interaction: (a) Putting hand on the water surface, the robot would float up, touch the palm and bright red light; (b) Immersing hand in the water and closing to the robot, the robot would dive down to try to escape; (c) Catching the robot and taking it out of the water, the robot would flash red color and vibrate. (Color figure online)

The test results reflect the user's surprise for the AquaBot, especially when the hand puts on the water surface, the robot floats up to touch the user's palm, and lights up red. One of the users said: "This experience made me feel like a pet is approaching me, then gently kissing my palm and shy blushing." This interaction makes the underwater robot emotional.

Another user said that he likes to catch robots underwater. In this process, the robot would dive down when the hand closes to it, and when taking it out of the water, it would vibrate and try to get rid of the arrest. But some users said that the robot's up and down movement is too singular, and if it can support multiple directions of movement in the water, it will make this interaction more interesting.

In this scenario, we just let the user immerse the hand in the water to interact and not all of the body immerse in the water. This setup is sufficient to reflect the existing functions of the AquaBot, but there are some limitations because we have not fully observed the interaction of the entire body when it is submerged under water.

Interaction Factors	Properties	AquaBot
Water Environment	• Depth • Temperature • Pressure • Visibility • Light • Sound • Water Flow • None-open Water Environment • Open Water Environment	• None-open Water Environment • Depth • Temperature • Light • Sound
Human	• Physical and Psychological Condition • Water Skill • Education • Technique Level • Operation Ability • Experience • Movement • Body Gesture • Perception (visual, auditory, olfactory, taste, touch)	• Physical Condition • Body Gesture • Movement • Visual Perception • Tactile Perception
Device	• Water Proof • Hardware • Software • Material • Interaction Mode • Communication • Power • Appearance • Operation • Function	• Underwater Robot and Wristband • Bluetooth • Temperature Sensitive Material • Battery:12V DC • Body Gesture • Temperature Interaction • Sound Interaction • Light Interaction • Arduino

Fig. 8. Design factors of interaction with underwater robot.

5   Design Factors

Human-Computer Interaction Design is accepted and rapidly spread over the world, at the preliminary stage, it applies to visual interface design, such as multimedia game and immersive circumstance design, later interaction concern becomes one of the product entities [12]. Through the process of designing AquaBot system, we learned that some designers are unfamiliar with digital water play and interaction with underwater robot. And many land-based digital design principles and methods are not suitable for underwater environment. These issues inspired us to summarize and propose a series of design strategies of digital game with physical water. Digital water play design needs to consider multiple factors, and these factors may influence the quality or even the success of the interaction. In this paper, we discuss three factors: water environment, human, device (Fig. 8) on the interaction of underwater robot.

5.1 Water Environment

We discuss two environments: the real open water environment such as the ocean and lake, the non-open water environment such as swimming pool and water tank. The temperature, depth, stability, visibility, and light of water are all factors that can influence the outcome of the interaction. These factors can also be used as triggers for interaction under certain conditions. In addition, the complex terrain of the underwater environment and other disturbances around the water environment can also affect the interactive experience.

5.2 Human

Human play an important role in digital water play. For human, the primary consideration is physical condition and water skill in the underwater environment, which is important for some interactions that require full body immersion into the water. Moreover, the educational background, technical level, and operational ability of people are also factors that can affect the system. The ways in which users participate in interaction include body gesture, movement, voice control, sight interaction, brain wave control, facial expression, perception (visual, auditory, olfactory, taste, touch), pulse, body surface temperature, galvanic skin response, etc. If the interaction scenario requires multiple people to complete, then the person also needs to have the ability to work in teams.

5.3 Device

Due to the special environment under water, the device needs to be waterproof, and underwater communication is also a challenge. The four means of communication through underwater are using acoustic waves, EM waves, optical signals, optical fiber cables [13]. In these ways that acoustic waves generally carry information inside the water because of various drawbacks of other signals. In addition to the limitations of the technology itself, noise near the water can also affect the transmission, such as waves, ships, weather, etc. Besides, the multipath channel and Doppler Effect will also affect underwater transmission [13].

The size, appearance, operation interface, operation mode of the device are all factors that need to be considered in underwater interaction design. And they are the most relevant factors to human. The power of the device underwater is mainly from the battery. Generally, we need an operator to control underwater device like a remote controller, a mobile phone, etc. But this is a traditional way of controlling, the interaction is unnatural and lacks some interests.

6   Discussion and Future Work

AquaBot is a digital underwater play system that includes an underwater robot and a wristband. This system can support the natural interaction of people in three different water environments. But there are still some limitations in the current system. First, our systems are currently only used in the shallow and stable water environment, it is not tested in open water environments such as lake and ocean. Then we use Bluetooth as the communication method, which only supports transmission within a few meters of water. There are some problems in the design of the underwater robot that needs to be improved, and the movement of the robot under water is not very stable. During the movement, the robot has some inclination in the water. Moreover, the robot is still unable to support long-term work and needs to be charged in time.

In the future work, we will continue to study the research of digital water play. We will improve the underwater movement of AquaBot, adjust the structural design, and ensure that the robot can maintain stable floating and dive underwater. We will also explore the underwater multidimensional motion of robots to provide more forms of interaction. For underwater communication, we will adopt more mature and stable methods, such as acoustic waves. We will also try to increase the depth of water and study the interaction of complex underwater environments. Study other parts of the body when contact the water and participate in the interaction. We will also enrich the interaction between the environment, human and device, and provide more interesting experiences.

7 Conclusion

This paper introduces AquaBot, a novel digital water play system that provides water play experience with digital technologies. The system includes two parts underwater robot and wristband which support interaction with human and environment. Through the exploration of different scenarios, it can be seen that bringing digital and intelligent elements into water play provides new interactions and experiences. In this paper, we also discuss the design factors of interaction with underwater robot, we hope this will inspire more researchers to study digital water play.

References

1. Choi, W., Oh, J., Park, T., et al.: MobyDick: an interactive multi-swimmer exergame. In: Proceedings of the 12th ACM Conference on Embedded Network Sensor Systems, Memphis, TN, USA, pp. 76–90. ACM (2014)
2. Bachlin, M., Forster, K., Troster, G.: SwimMaster: a wearable assistant for swimmer. In: Proceedings of the 11th International Conference on Ubiquitous Computing, Orlando, Florida, pp. 215–224. ACM (2009)
3. Mueller, F.F., Byrne, R., Andres, J., Patibanda, R.: Experiencing the body as play. In: Proceedings of the 2018 CHI Conference on Human Factors in Computing Systems, April, Montreal, QC, Canada. ACM, April 2018
4. Ukai, Y., Rekimoto, J.: Swimoid: a swim support system using an underwater buddy robot. In: Proceedings of the 4th Augmented Human International Conference, Stuttgart, Germany, pp. 170–177. ACM (2013)
5. Yamashita, S., Zhang, X., Rekimoto, J.: AquaCAVE: augmented swimming environment with immersive surround-screen virtual reality. In: Proceedings of the 29th Annual Symposium on User Interface Software and Technology, Tokyo, Japan, pp. 183–184. ACM (2016)

6. Jain, D., Sra, M., Guo, J., Marques, R., et al.: Immersive terrestrial Scuba diving using virtual reality. In: Proceedings of the 2016 CHI Conference Extended Abstracts on Human Factors in Computing Systems, San Jose, CA, USA, pp. 1563–1569. ACM (2016)
7. Bellarbi, A., Domingues, C., Otmane, S., Benbelkacem, S., Dinis, A.: Augmented reality for underwater activities with the use of the DOLPHYN. In: 2013 10th IEEE International Conference on Networking, Sensing and Control, Evry, France, pp. 409–412. IEEE (2013)
8. Pell, S.J., Mueller, F.F.: Gravity well: underwater play. In: CHI 2013 Extended Abstracts on Human Factors in Computing Systems, Paris, France, pp. 3115–3118. ACM (2013)
9. Chutia, S., Kakoty, N.M., Deka, D.: A review of underwater robotics, navigation, sensing techniques and applications. In: Proceedings of the Advances in Robotics, New Delhi, India. ACM (2017)
10. Wu, X., Stuck, R.E., Rekleitis, I., Beer, J.M.: Towards a human factors model for underwater robotics. In: Proceedings of the Tenth Annual ACM/IEEE International Conference on Human-Robot Interaction Extended Abstracts, Portland, OR, USA, pp. 159–160. ACM (2015)
11. Raffe, W.L., Tamassia, M., Zambetta, F., Li, X., Pell, S.J., et al.: Player-computer interaction feature for designing digital play experiences across six degrees of water contact. In: CHI PLAY 2015 Annual Symposium on Computer-Human Interaction in Play, October, London, United Kingdom, pp. 295–305. ACM (2015)
12. Qu, Y., Chong, D., Liu, W.: Bringing interaction design methods and experimental technologies together into designing and developing interactive products. In: Proceeding of the 11th Asia Pacific Conference on Computer Human Interaction, Bangalore, India, pp. 102–107. ACM (2013)
13. Pranitha, B., Anjaneyulu, L.: Review of research trends in underwater communications-a technical survey. In: 2016 International Conference on Communication and Signal Processing, April, Warangal, India, pp. 1443–1447. IEEE (2016)
14. Muminov, S., Yun, N.-Y., Shin, S.-W., Park, S.-H., et al.: Biomimetic fish robot controlling system by using underwater acoustic signal. In: 2012 9th Annual IEEE Communications Society Conference on Sensor, Mesh and Ad Hoc Communications and Networks, pp. 106–108. IEEE (2012)
15. Hoste, L., Signer, B.: Water Ball Z: An augmented fighting game using water as tactile feedback. In: 8th International Conference on Tangible, Embedded and Embodied Interaction, Munich, Germany, pp. 173–176. ACM (2014)

Security in Smart Toys: A Systematic Review of Literature

Lara Pontes[1]([✉]), Gustavo Coutinho[1], Patrick C. K. Hung[2],
and Benjamin Yankson[2]

[1] Federal Institute of Education Science, and Technology of Ceará, Jaguaribe, Brazil
larajdspontes@gmail.com, gustavo.coutinho@ifce.edu.br
[2] University of Ontario Institute of Technology, Oshawa, Canada
patrick.hung@uoit.ca, benyyank@gmail.com

Abstract. Smart toys are traditional toys embedded with technological intelligence that enhances the toys functionalities to match the need of children in an ever-advancing technological savvy generation. Due to some weaknesses present in their embedded features, the sale and the use of this type of product have been driving some great concernments related to cyber-security. Therefore, this systematic review mapped the current research areas in smart toy security, collect data and show the available works on the subject in question. For conducting this survey, we used electronic resources such as ACM Digital Library, Science Direct (Elsevier) and Scopus in the period between 2014 to 2018. This research protocol was developed by the research question, data sources and search strategies, data extraction and synthesis. After completing all these processes, we selected and analyzed a range of 26 studies from an initial set of 731. We considered the suggestions presented in the analyzed studies about keeping children's data secured while using smart toys and we came to the conclusion that there is a significant growth in the studies about it, although there is not any study implementing a security model in these toys or a guideline of how to use it safely.

Keywords: Smart toys · Security information · Child-toy interaction

1 Introduction

Toys have always been present in people's lives, either as an educational and playful element in school or as a form of entertainment for children in their daily lives. In general, toys play an important role in children cognitive and motor development [24]. With toys, children can learn new things and develop fundamental elements in their personality and socialization behavior [6,39]. As the society began witnessing technological advancement, most parents began buying new and available mobile or computational devices for their children [27]. As a consequence of it, the toy industry implemented technology in traditional toys, leading the smart toys emersion [22].

N. Streitz and S. Konomi (Eds.): HCII 2019, LNCS 11587, pp. 28–38, 2019.
https://doi.org/10.1007/978-3-030-21935-2_3

Smart toys are traditional toys embedded with technological intelligence that enhances the toys functionalities to match the need of children in an ever-advancing technological savvy generation [29]. A smart toy can be considered as an Internet of Things (IoT) device with Artificial Intelligence (AI) designed for providing a unique child-toy interaction by responding to users actions [11,13]. Some smart toys can have face and voice recognition capabilities performed through their embedded features and tools such as microphone, camera, and recording and speech devices, making themselves look more attractive and fun [2]. Even though smart toys represent a significant technological breakthrough, some studies have shown that criminals can target such toys since they store sensitive information, their vulnerable user base, and some cybersecurity violations related to their privacy policies [31].

Recently, some smart toys companies have recognized that they can collect and store children's data and share it with trusted third parties; however, few of these companies fully encrypt user data or clearly state how they can use it [5]. Smart toys can track the location of children using GPS features, store pictures, videos, and audios, connect to the internet and cloud, and allow personal information exchanges through smartphone applications [7]. The information smart toys can gather, if accessed by the wrong person, can have severe consequences for users, mainly because most parents have no prior knowledge about the smart toys security policies, and children are considered as vulnerable and defenseless online users [19]. As a result of the security breaches present in smart toys, some federal governments all over the world have enacted cybersecurity laws aiming to ensure the confidentiality, integrity, and availability protection of young children data, and the technology information research community in this field has shown a relevant growth as well [4,20].

A systematic review stands out as constituting a series of relevant studies on a specific subject, which may be related, presenting criticism and praise and making general comments on the subject. A systematic review is considered as secondary research, because it is made with the union of primary studies elaborated by other authors, is characterized by being both qualitative and quantitative research and presenting the "state of the art" about a certain subject [15,25]. This type of review helps to gather knowledge about a specific area of study, to identify recommendations for future research, to establish the context of a research topic or problem, and to identify the main methodologies and research techniques used in a particular topic or field of research [17].

This systematic review brings an approach to the threats that children may be exposed by using smart toys and which safety practices should be used to avoid such problems. The protocols used for the selection of studies were: research questions, search strategies, selection criteria, and results synthesis. A total of 26 primary studies published from 2014 to 2018 were selected in electronic resources as ACM Digital Library, Science Direct (Elsevier) and Scopus, which addressed topics related to safety gaps in smart toys and the mechanisms that could protect children from the use of smart toys. Finally, we evaluate if these studies present concepts and security practices related to the reliability, availability, and integrity of infant information, and at the last moment, we describe the methods and type of validation adopted.

2   Developing the Protocol

This systematic review of the literature presents an overview of the security of smart toys. To plan this review, we divided it into three phases (Fig. 1). In the first phase, we searched manually for studies about smart toys, and we used snowballing strategies in the relevant articles for this work. During the development of the protocol, we evaluate the state-of-art of some chosen studies, and we checked if there was a considerable quantity of primary studies available in the literature. After the studies selection, we looked into their content and analyzed which information related to security in smart toys needed to be established, and which requirements should be adopted while conducting this review.

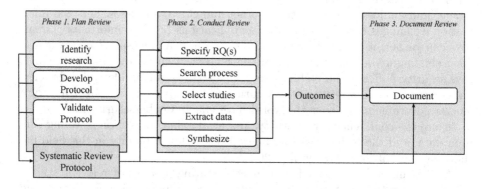

Fig. 1. Diagram representing an overview of the systematic review process. Adapted from [17].

In the second phase, we delimit the information that we needed to extract from the primary studies through one research question. During the searching process, we chose the electronic resources, and we set the string search we used in this stage. For selecting the studies, we delimit inclusion and exclusion criteria to filter the initial set of retrieved studies. After having the final list of selected studies, we extracted and separated their content based in categories. The Sects. 2.1–2.5 provide more details about this stage.

2.1   Research Question

To formulate the research question, we considered the topic of this approach and the principle of the acronym PICO. According to [16], this acronym outlines the critical elements of a well-elaborated research question, based in its word letters, which is stood for: Population, Intervention, Comparison, and Outcome.

The search question composition according to the acronym PICO is shown in Table 1. The research question *"How to ensure that smart toys are secure enough for children?"* was defined considering the requirements mentioned above.

Table 1. Search question composition according to the acronym PICO.

Denomination	Abbreviation	Search question componentes
Population	P	Children (aged from 0–9 years old)
Intervention	I	Smart toys
Comparison	C	Information security
Outcome	O	Security assurance

2.2 Data Sources and Search Strategy

In order to perform an automated search process, we used electronic resources such as digital libraries and indexing systems to find relevant papers. The digital libraries that we used in this work were ACM Digital Library[1] and Science Direct (Elsevier)[2], and as an indexing system, we included the Scopus[3].

Table 2. List of eletronic resources and number of retrieved studies.

Eletronic resource	Studies retrieved	Studies selected
ACM Digital Library	303	7
Science Direct	228	6
Scopus	190	17
Total of remaining studies without duplicates		26

We set a search string (Fig. 2) to narrow the scope of our search and collect accurate studies. To build it we considered the research question main terms and its synonyms, and we used Boolean operators, wildcards, quotations marks, and parentheses as well. We applied the search string in titles, abstracts and keywords of the retrieved studies, and we adapted it according to the electronic resources formats.

This stage took place in December 2018, and it retrieved an initial set of 721 primary studies.

---

[1] www.acm.org.

[2] www.sciencedirect.com.

[3] www.scopus.com.

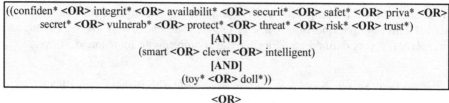

Fig. 2. Search string used to automate the search process.

2.3 Study Selection

We summarized a range of inclusion and exclusion criteria to filter the initial set of studies. The inclusion criteria (IC) used were: studies published from 2014 to 2018 (IC1); studies written in English (IC2) and studies peer-reviewed (IC3). For the exclusion criteria (EC) were delimited: studies not included in the information technology field (EC1); duplicated or same authorship studies (EC2); studies that do not address technology designed for the infant user (EC3), and studies that do not address smart toys (EC4) (Table 3).

Table 3. Inclusion and exclusion criterias and the number of studies filtered.

ID	Description	Number of studies
IC1	Published from 2014 to 2018	313
IC2	Written in English	308
IC3	Peer-reviewed	239
EC1	Not included in the information technology field	131
EC2	Duplicated	124
EC3	Do not address technology designed for the infant user	81
EC4	Do not address smart toys	30

To filter the initial set of primary studies based on the criteria mentioned above we count with the electronic resources delimiters and mechanisms for exporting the bibliographic details in formats for EndNote[4].

After applying the inclusion and exclusion criteria in the initial set of studies, we selected 30 studies. In these 30 studies, we found four studies repeated among the electronic resources, remaining a total of 26 primary studies included in this study.

---

[4] www.endnote.com.

2.4   Data Extraction and Synthesis

During the data extraction, we separated the selected studies into categories to evaluate their relevance for this approach. To synthesize the studies content, some requirements in an excel sheet delimit the details that articles would have regarding their approach, validation methods, contribution type, and approach. Moreover, this procedure helped to compare and summarize the findings of the primary studies included in this work, along with the information we need to answer the research questions.

2.5   Threats to Validate the Protocol

Some threats found throughout this systematic review are presented below, as well as how to mitigate them:

Selection of Relevant Studies: Search strings were used to perform an automatic search in the databases. The terms of the search string were extracted from the formulated search query. To make sure that relevant works were not missed in the automatic search, keyword synonyms were included in the search string.

Missing Relevant Studies: Although the search string shown in Fig. 2 was used on the indexing systems presented in Table 2, some relevant articles may not have been returned. This threat was avoided by presenting the list of articles found to experts in the area to indicate whether any relevant articles were missing.

3   Systematic Review Reports

In this section, we address some security gaps in smart toys and procedures that can contribute to the improvement of smart toys mentioned in the studies selected for this review. From an initial sample of 731 papers, we identified 26 primary studies (3.55%) that match the selection criteria of this systematic review. The primary studies selected for the analysis were categorized according to their approach and type, as mentioned in the data extraction step.

3.1   How to Ensure that Children Are Secure Enough?

Data Confidentiality. The studies [8, 10, 12, 14, 21, 23, 30, 32, 33, 35] are categorized as case studies that address data confidentiality tests with intelligent toys, such as Hello Barbie, Dinno, Hello Kitty, My Friend Cayla, Smart Toy Bear, and HereO Watch, among others. According to these studies, smart toys easily store and/or collect images of the physical activity status of their users (walking, running, sitting, etc.), location history information through a camera, microphone, GPS and several others. And as a solution to this issue, these studies suggest the synchronization of apps that allow to check and keep track on the child usage; the avoidance of default passwords in differing products and passwords that cannot be changed by users; and control over GPS activation. And still, according to them, the toy company should adopt privacy policies that aim to protect the data collected by the smart toys and aware parents to read their guidelines.

The studies categorized as surveys works such as [8,9,35,36] consider that each intelligent toy should have its privacy policy, describing the information and including the collection, management, sharing and retention of personal data of a user. The studies also point to the need for further research into the underlying mechanisms regarding the compliance of children with connected toys, as one of the studies noted the ability of a (third) agent to influence children's moral judgments through interaction.

The only primary study selected and categorized as a systematic review is [1]. According to this study, the information technology research community has had many discussions about confidentiality issues in smart toys that store personal information. Hence, this study showed that a toy connected to the internet should guarantee user privacy by encrypting their data when sending information to a third party.

The works categorized as bibliographic studies as [3,10,12,18,26,28,30,34, 38] show that smart toys must comply with the traditional safety standards of common toys and, as online services, must also comply with digital privacy laws. Most of these articles highlight that to protect children data it is necessary to implement a transparent and workable method that allows parents to have control over the information of their children that are being shared. According to these works, the end-user requirements in smart toys need to be created specifically for their base of users, considering their needs and vulnerability.

In general, most of the studies that mention data confidentiality practices have shown that smart toys should ask their user before collecting their personal information, such as voice recordings, photographs, videos, location history, or any personal information that identifies users, specifically children. In addition, the literature has suggested that such toys should provide a clearer meaning for identifying personal data in case of the end of use, loss, theft or transition of owners. It is necessary to restrict the total amount of personal data stored locally in the toy and require some form of authentication to access all the recorded data.

Data Integrity. In the work [10], categorized as a case study that approaches data integrity, the authors mention that while using a remote server to have access to the information kept in a smart toy, the information security would be guaranteed by enforcing a physical and administrative restriction that does not allow unauthenticated software updates.

In the bibliography work [37], is proposed an intelligent model of data exchange oriented to toy edge computing that can support isolated IoT systems to perform secure interconnection with a distributed P2P way. Moreover, there is the implementation of the intelligent toy data exchange platform with distributed accounting technology, which guarantees the integrity and consistency of the data, while providing accountability, transparency, and efficiency to the network.

In the bibliography study [28], the author suggests creating a model that allows parents to create privacy rules and receive acknowledgments about their children's confidential location data. [26, 34], mentioned in their work that would be necessary create a version control so that it is possible to return the data to the previous version (if they have been accidentally changed or deleted).

Data Availability. The works categorized as study of cases as [10, 21, 30, 32] suggest the implantation of maintenance in the physical structure of toys, the establishment of compatible programs and the realization of all the necessary updates to the system. Also, they mention that the toys should allow parents to review or delete data collected from their children, such as recordings or voice images, and track what data a company is using and for what purpose the company is transmitting that data.

The bibliography studies that approaches the guarantee of data availability such as [3, 26, 28, 30, 38, 40] mention that a backup system (remote or in the cloud) should be implanted in the smart toy to be used in case there is an event that was not caused by human interaction, such as equipment failures, that can erase user data.

4   Conclusions

An exploratory study on the security of smart toys is relevant because they are a reality for some children, and its related possible negative information privacy impacts are clear according to studies reviewed. Shortly, with the diffusion of IoT, smart toys will become popular and will be used not only as an educational tool or a form of entertainment; but integrated as part of the child day to day activities and as their companions. It is necessary, as new technologies emerge, the development and adoption of security practices that follow the evolution of these connected devices. Hence, this systematic review contributes to the identification of works that deal with security gaps in toys that can help to mitigate the risks to children information privacy and safety.

After analyzing the suggestions about information security practices in smart toys presented in the 26 primary studies selected for this review, we came to the conclusion that the studies about security in smart toys have grown significantly in the last few years mainly due to the expansion of the market of smart toys. Although several studies available in the literature already address security gaps in smart toys, the majority of them only mention superficially some steps that should be taken to reduce this security breaches, and there is not any study that substantially implements a security model that can enhance security practices in smart toys yet. Also, many types of research have shown that parents can help to mitigate the risks exposed by smart toys features, but it is still necessary to conduct an investigation that presents a guideline that parents should follow to avoid data breaches in smart toys.

References

1. de Albuquerque, A.P., Kelner, J.: Toy user interfaces: systematic and industrial mapping. J. Syst. Archit. (2018)
2. Brito, R., Dias, P., Oliveira, G.: Young children, digital media and smart toys: how perceptions shape adoption and domestication. Br. J. Educ. Technol. **49**(5), 807–820 (2018)
3. de Carvalho, L.G., Eler, M.M.: Security tests for smart toys. In: ICEIS, no. 2, pp. 111–120 (2018)
4. Chaudhuri, A.: Internet of things data protection and privacy in the era of the general data protection regulation. J. Data Prot. Priv. **1**(1), 64–75 (2016)
5. Chowdhury, W.: Toys that talk to strangers: a look at the privacy policies of connected toys. In: Arai, K., Bhatia, R., Kapoor, S. (eds.) FTC 2018. AISC, vol. 880, pp. 152–158. Springer, Cham (2019). https://doi.org/10.1007/978-3-030-02686-8_12
6. Delprino, F., Piva, C., Tommasi, G., Gelsomini, M., Izzo, N., Matera, M., et al.: ABBOT. In: Advanced User Interfaces (AVI), pp. 1–9. ACM (2018)
7. D'Hooge, H., Dalton, L., Shwe, H., Lieberman, D., O'Malley, C.: Smart toys: brave new world? In: CHI 2000 Extended Abstracts on Human Factors in Computing Systems. pp. 247–248. ACM (2000)
8. Druga, S., Williams, R., Park, H.W., Breazeal, C.: How smart are the smart toys? Children and parents' agent interaction and intelligence attribution. In: Proceedings of the 17th ACM Conference on Interaction Design and Children, pp. 231–240. ACM (2018)
9. Fantinato, M., et al.: A preliminary study of hello Barbie in Brazil and Argentina. Sustain. Cities Soc. **40**, 83–90 (2018)
10. Haynes, J., Ramirez, M., Hayajneh, T., Bhuiyan, M.Z.A.: A framework for preventing the exploitation of IoT smart toys for reconnaissance and exfiltration. In: Wang, G., Atiquzzaman, M., Yan, Z., Choo, K.-K.R. (eds.) SpaCCS 2017. LNCS, vol. 10658, pp. 581–592. Springer, Cham (2017). https://doi.org/10.1007/978-3-319-72395-2_53
11. Holloway, D., Green, L.: The internet of toys. Commun. Res. Pract. **2**(4), 506–519 (2016)
12. Hung, P.C.K., Iqbal, F., Huang, S.-C., Melaisi, M., Pang, K.: A glance of child's play privacy in smart toys. In: Sun, X., Liu, A., Chao, H.-C., Bertino, E. (eds.) ICCCS 2016. LNCS, vol. 10040, pp. 217–231. Springer, Cham (2016). https://doi.org/10.1007/978-3-319-48674-1_20
13. Ihamäki, P., Heljakka, K.: The internet of toys, connectedness and character-based play in early education. In: Arai, K., Bhatia, R., Kapoor, S. (eds.) FTC 2018. AISC, vol. 880, pp. 1079–1096. Springer, Cham (2019). https://doi.org/10.1007/978-3-030-02686-8_80
14. Jones, M.L., Meurer, K.: Can (and should) hello Barbie keep a secret? In: 2016 IEEE International Symposium on Ethics in Engineering, Science and Technology (ETHICS), pp. 1–6. IEEE (2016)
15. Kitchenham, B., Brereton, O.P., Budgen, D., Turner, M., Bailey, J., Linkman, S.: Systematic literature reviews in software engineering-a systematic literature review. Inf. Softw. Technol. **51**(1), 7–15 (2009)
16. Kitchenham, B., Mendes, E., Travassos, G.H.: A systematic review of cross-vs. within-company cost estimation studies. In: Proceedings of the 10th International Conference on Evaluation and Assessment in Software Engineering, pp. 81–90. BCS Learning & Development Ltd. (2006)

17. Kitchenham, B.A., Budgen, D., Brereton, P.: Evidence-Based Software Engineering and Systematic Reviews, vol. 4. CRC Press, Boca Raton (2015)
18. Kshetri, N., Voas, J.: Cyberthreats under the bed. Computer **51**(5), 92–95 (2018)
19. Kucirkova, N., Ng, I., Holtby, J.: From mirrors to selfies: protecting children's data for personalised learning and future growth (2017)
20. de Lima Salgado, A., do Amaral, L.A., Castro, P.C., de Mattos Fortes, R.P.: Designing for parental control: enriching usability and accessibility in the context of smart toys. In: Tang, J.K.T., Hung, P.C.K. (eds.) Computing in Smart Toys. ISCEMT, pp. 103–125. Springer, Cham (2017). https://doi.org/10.1007/978-3-319-62072-5_7
21. Mahmoud, M., Hossen, M.Z., Barakat, H., Mannan, M., Youssef, A.: Towards a comprehensive analytical framework for smart toy privacy practices. In: Proceedings of the 7th Workshop on Socio-Technical Aspects in Security and Trust, pp. 64–75. ACM (2018)
22. Mazur, I., Rakauskas, F., Rosa, A.: Use of information and communication technology in logistics operations of storage: a case study of application in industry of toys. Indep. J. Manag. Prod. **9**(5), 623–639 (2018)
23. McReynolds, E., Hubbard, S., Lau, T., Saraf, A., Cakmak, M., Roesner, F.: Toys that listen: a study of parents, children, and internet-connected toys. In: Proceedings of the 2017 CHI Conference on Human Factors in Computing Systems, pp. 5197–5207. ACM (2017)
24. Mironcika, S., de Schipper, A., Brons, A., Toussaint, H., Kröse, B., Schouten, B.: Smart toys design opportunities for measuring children's fine motor skills development. In: Proceedings of the Twelfth International Conference on Tangible, Embedded, and Embodied Interaction, pp. 349–356. ACM (2018)
25. Moher, D., et al.: Preferred reporting items for systematic review and meta-analysis protocols (PRISMA-P) 2015 statement. Syst. Rev. **4**(1), 1 (2015)
26. Ng, G., Chow, M., Salgado, A.L.: Toys and mobile applications: current trends and related privacy issues. In: Hung, P.C.K. (ed.) Mobile Services for Toy Computing. ISCEMT, pp. 51–76. Springer, Cham (2015). https://doi.org/10.1007/978-3-319-21323-1_4
27. Plowman, L.: Researching young children's everyday uses of technology in the family home. Interact. Comput. **27**(1), 36–46 (2015)
28. Rafferty, L., et al.: Towards a privacy rule conceptual model for smart toys. In: Tang, J.K.T., Hung, P.C.K. (eds.) Computing in Smart Toys. ISCEMT, pp. 85–102. Springer, Cham (2017). https://doi.org/10.1007/978-3-319-62072-5_6
29. Rivera, D., García, A., Martín-Ruíz, M.L., Alarcos, B., Velasco, J.R., Oliva, A.G.: Secure communications and protected data for a internet of things smart toy platform. IEEE Internet Things J. **6**(2), 3785–3795 (2019)
30. Shasha, S., Mahmoud, M., Mannan, M., Youssef, A.: Playing with danger: a taxonomy and evaluation of threats to smart toys. IEEE Internet Things J. **6**(2), 2986–3002 (2018)
31. Shasha, S., Mahmoud, M., Mannan, M., Youssef, A.: Smart but unsafe: experimental evaluation of security and privacy practices in smart toys. ArXiv Pre-Print (2018)
32. Streiff, J., Kenny, O., Das, S., Leeth, A., Camp, L.J.: Who's watching your child? Exploring home security risks with smart toy bears. In: 2018 IEEE/ACM Third International Conference on Internet-of-Things Design and Implementation (IoTDI), pp. 285–286. IEEE (2018)

33. Valente, J., Cardenas, A.A.: Security & privacy in smart toys. In: Proceedings of the 2017 Workshop on Internet of Things Security and Privacy, pp. 19–24. ACM (2017)
34. Verdoodt, V., Clifford, D., Lievens, E.: Toying with children's emotions, the new game in town? The legality of advergames in the EU. Comput. Law Secur. Rev. **32**(4), 599–614 (2016)
35. Williams, R., Machado, C.V., Druga, S., Breazeal, C., Maes, P.: My doll says it's ok: a study of children's conformity to a talking doll. In: Proceedings of the 17th ACM Conference on Interaction Design and Children, pp. 625–631. ACM (2018)
36. Xia, L., Bisong, L., Qian, W., Ya, L.: Analysis on quality and safety of toys for children—based on the survey data of Beijing. In: Xhafa, F., Patnaik, S., Zomaya, A.Y. (eds.) IISA 2017. AISC, vol. 686, pp. 880–889. Springer, Cham (2018). https://doi.org/10.1007/978-3-319-69096-4_125
37. Yang, J., Lu, Z., Wu, J.: Smart-toy-edge-computing-oriented data exchange based on blockchain. J. Syst. Archit. **87**, 36–48 (2018)
38. Yankson, B., Iqbal, F., Hung, P.C.K.: Privacy preservation framework for smart connected toys. In: Tang, J.K.T., Hung, P.C.K. (eds.) Computing in Smart Toys. ISCEMT, pp. 149–164. Springer, Cham (2017). https://doi.org/10.1007/978-3-319-62072-5_9
39. Yilmaz, R.M.: Educational magic toys developed with augmented reality technology for early childhood education. Comput. Hum. Behav. **54**, 240–248 (2016)
40. Zhang, W., Lu, Z., Wu, Z., Wu, J., Zou, H., Huang, S.: Toy-IoT-oriented data-driven CDN performance evaluation model with deep learning. J. Syst. Archit. **88**, 13–22 (2018)

Presentation of Information Uncertainty from IoBT for Military Decision Making

Adrienne Raglin[(⊠)]

Army Research Laboratory, Adelphi, MD 20783, USA
adrienne.j.raglin.civ@mail.mil

Abstract. The goal of this paper is to investigate uncertainty of information introduced at the final decision point and ways this information can be presented to potentially improve decision making. Uncertainty expressions and representations from different fields of study will be explored in this paper. While uncertainty is important to all types of decision making there is a focus on a simple task that is representative of a military relevant task in this paper. Supporting this effort will be the results from a recent experimental study where information from simulated Internet of Battlefield Thing (IoBT) devices were presented to Soldiers for a simplified decision making task with and without an uncertainty of information value given at preset decision making points. The presentation of this information was done in the Android Tactical Assault Kit (ATAK) which is a mapping engine that allows precision targeting, intelligence on surrounding land formations, navigation, and situational awareness. For this experimental study the software was modified to add a decision making component within the ATAK interface. Analysis of the data will help influence additional directions for future research and experimentation.

Keywords: Decision making · Uncertainty · Visualization

1 Introduction

The Internet of Things (IoT) is defined as "a variety of objects or things that are able to interact with each other through unique addressing schemes [1]." IoT was listed as one of six "Disruptive Civil Technologies" by the US National Intelligence Council. The strength of IoT has been its impact to everyday life and how individuals use this new capability. IoT systems are expanding from commercial application the government or DoD, in the form of Internet of Military Things or Internet of Battlefield Things (IoBT) [2]. But the use of IoBT systems to solve defense problems is not trivial or straightforward. The challenges to the realization of IoBT include the organization and management of the large and heterogeneous set of devices, as well as how individuals will make sense of the diverse data that comes from these devices. If IoBT devices provide new sources of data, then they will have a significant impact on decision making. Like all technology, the benefits come with possible uncertainty from the operation of the devices to the information that the devices generate. This leads to the question like what and how uncertainty of information will be represented and presented to decision makers, particularly in military operations.

N. Streitz and S. Konomi (Eds.): HCII 2019, LNCS 11587, pp. 39–47, 2019.
https://doi.org/10.1007/978-3-030-21935-2_4

A decision is defined as a conclusion or a resolution reached after consideration or the action or process of deciding something. While, decision making is the thought process of selecting a logical choice from the available options. When trying to make a good decision, a person must weigh the pros and cons of each option and consider all the alternatives. Ideally, a person must also be able to predict the possible outcomes of multiple options and determine which option is the best for the particular situation [3]. This includes making the decision with uncertainties in mind. Multiple theories for decision making exist, however common threads like uncertainty may be seen across the various concepts.

Whether it is Herbert Simon's three step theory, Colonel John Boyd's "Observe, Orient, Decide and Act" (OODA) loop, or the military decision making process (MDMP), the ability to grasp uncertainty is a key element of decision making. From a military standpoint the requirements of decision making across the echelons drives the effect of uncertainty as the time available to make a decision is compressed from months to seconds as one approaches the tactical edge. The inclusion of IoBT devices in decision making will increase the volume of data available to base decisions on, but may also cause new sources of uncertainties.

Equally important is the expression and presentation of this data along with any associated uncertainty. The uncertainty may be related to the ambiguity, limitations, and constraints linked with the devices and the device data. Critical to decision making is any uncertainty related to possible risks that shape the final decision. While uncertainty measures of information can be interjected into multiple steps prior to and after the final decision in this paper the focus is on uncertainty presented prior to the final decision or act.

2 Decisions and Decision Making

2.1 Models for Decision Making

There are several models for decision making. Three have been selected to highlight in this paper. The first was developed by Herbert Simon the Nobel Prize winner known for his decision making theory categorized in three steps: intelligence activity, design activity, and choice activity [4]. In his paper, Herbert Simon discussed those things that affected a rational decision: lack of knowledge, cognitive limitations, and time constraints which can cause uncertainty. Lack of knowledge is due to the problem that all the information that will generate the optimal decision is not always known or available to the decision maker.

The second is the OODA loop decision cycle developed by Colonel John Boyd from the United States Air Force [5]. As a military strategist, COL Boyd's creation was primarily applied to combat operations and included five steps: observe, orient, decide, and act. In Boyd's 1987 talk "Organic Design for Command and Control" he stated that uncertainty places the biggest part in the observe and orient steps. In these steps, uncertainty is in the managing of information including the evolution, the inconsistencies, the incompleteness, and the dependencies from the sources of the observations [5].

The third, is the military decision making process (MDMP) [6]. The MDMP is iterative, linking the commander, the staff, subordinate headquarters, and the partners' activities to make decisions for successful missions. There are seven basic steps in the MDMP. In the MDMP, Receipt of Mission and Production of Orders are critical anchors serving as the start and end steps of the process. Between these anchor points five steps are identified: mission analysis, course of action (COA) development, course of action analysis, course of action comparison, and course of action approval. Having an idea of the uncertainty that impacts the decision is needed ideally at each step in the process.

3 Uncertainty

3.1 Presentation of Uncertainty

In the book "The Design of Everyday Things" [7] the author stated "Great precision is not required." If this is true, then how do we represent uncertainty information? How do we present uncertainty information that positively impacts decision making, making decisions that are robust and adaptive?

Although not a new problem, presentation of uncertainty is a continual challenge. The seemingly never-ending struggle to display information from sources that may not be intuitive and that may grow exponentially from the devices and the data supports the need to continue investigating the presentation of uncertainty. The questions how much information is needed to aid decision makers and how to aid decision makers with the ability to understand the uncertainties associated with the information are always relevant in this space. Moreover, continuing the investigation of how uncertainty can be presented can be useful as new technology such as IoT and IoBT are integrated into sources of data for decision making.

Graphical representations can be extremely useful for presenting uncertainty. Quantitative analysis uses techniques such as analysis of variance, point estimates, confidence intervals, and least squares regression to determine relationships with the data's independent and dependent variables. These techniques can use a variety of graphs such as scatter plots, histograms, probability plots, box plots, and spectrum plots. For example, in regression analysis the estimated relationship between variables can be shown between the conditional expectation of the dependent variables and fixed independent variables. If there is a linear relationship between the variable, y_i and dependent variable, x_i, parameters, α and β with error, ε_i their relationship can be described with the following equation:

$$y_i = \alpha x_i + \beta + \varepsilon_i, i = 1, \ldots, n$$

Applying a confidence band can represent the uncertainty of the function based on limited or noisy data. Figure 1 shows an example of a scatter plot with confidence bands with probability of 0.95 and a collection of confidence intervals constructed with coverage probability of 0.95.

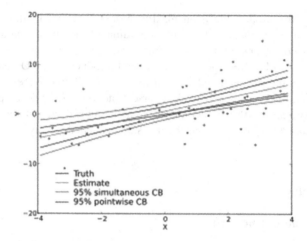

Fig. 1. Example graph of confidence bands for an example of a linear regression analysis. (wiki: https://en.wikipedia.org/wiki/Confidence_and_prediction_bands)

Uncertainty in this case can be calculated using equations of the distribution to reflect uncertainty in the estimation, probability of a poor fit, or sample noise across the data. In the case of a scatter plot, as in example in Fig. 1 where a trend line is shown that represents the function used to estimate the actual data. Seeing how the sample data varies in reference to the model or estimated function can provide a visual representation of the uncertainty, particularly if your model is being used for the prediction of future data points. Ideally, there would be no divergence between the output generated by the model and the future data but this is not always the case. A simple graph as in Fig. 2 can be used to show this divergence of data to imply that there is an increased uncertainty.

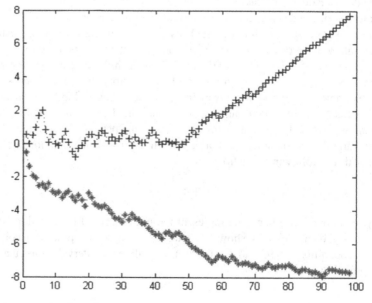

Fig. 2. An example of data that diverges from expected values. (https://www.mathworks.com/matlabcentral/answers/249350-find-diverging-point-of-two-arrays)

Graphs that show error bars to represent variability can visually indicate error of uncertainty in measurement. Figure 3 is an example [8]. One caution is to ensure that the true value is not lost in presenting the uncertainty. Yau's paper discusses the challenge from a data statistics point of view where standard errors, confidence intervals, and likelihoods are hard to capture graphically. In traditional approaches usually a range or confidence interval is shown where the middle is the mean or median and a line shows other possible values. In this approach there can be a loss of details in the data and explanations are sometimes needed for the confidence intervals [8].

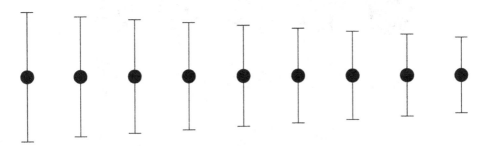

Fig. 3. An example graph with error bars.

Other traditional graphical representations include boxplots, histograms, and scatter plots. The boxplot presents the minimum and maximum range of data values, the upper and lower quartiles, and the median. Confidence levels are shown by changing the width of the plots. The width of the box is related to the size of the data, if notches are present they are related to the significant differences of the medians.

Another visualization option is where a distribution shows variation in a sample or spread of possible values or decisions. In this option multiple outcomes are presented as lines that represent all the different paths indicating that there is not just one outcome, but the use of too many lines or paths can overwhelm the information itself. Also, additional description is need to understand what the variations mean and the uncertainty connection to the individual options. An example graph is in Fig. 4 [8].

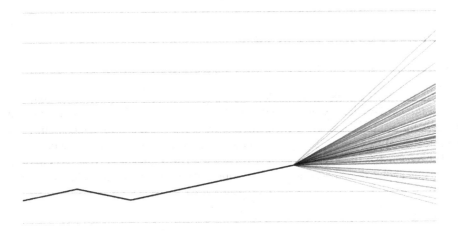

Fig. 4. An example showing spread in values or decisions.

Animation, gitter gauges are also ways to show uncertainty. Even simulations where different results are shown one at a time to create an overall picture can be used but losing the thread of uncertainty across results can occur. Adding obscurity to indicate uncertainty by using transparency, color scale, or blur as the outcomes increase or as the outcomes have different uncertainties is possible. Figure 5 shows an example; this approach requires interpretation of the fuzziness or opaqueness [8].

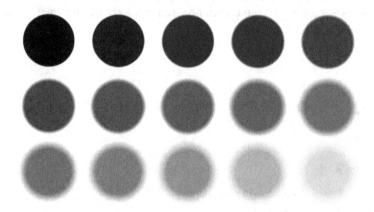

Fig. 5. An example visual using transparency to represent uncertainty.

Using a descriptive statement such as better than, about, we doubt, unlikely, etc. is another way to represent uncertainty. This technique requires interpretation and consensus of the meanings associated with each term [8].

Also, a numerical value for uncertainty can be calculated and presented at the time of decision making. This value can inform the decision makers on the state of information they are using, for example information from a set of IoBT devices. This number could use a scale from 0 to N to represent the level of uncertainty, where 0 is the lowest level of uncertainty. This approach was selected for the pre-pilot study discussed in the following section.

4   Uncertainty Measure in IoBT

4.1   Motivation

For the military "discovery, characterization, and tracking of relevant, available and useful things, dynamically in time and space" [2] are part of the information gathering process for making decisions. IoBT can be used to provide this information which can be categorized as sources from people, buildings, and the environment. The behaviors and characteristics of the devices and the network are definitely needed prior to making a decision and as decision changes throughout a task or a mission. In addition, the vast amounts of IoBT data, the information sharing criteria, and the mission relevance for this data needs to be considered for decision making. Along with this is the need for any uncertainty associated with this data to be provided to the decision maker. How this data is presented can influence the usefulness of the data and how it impacts the decision. As a first step towards looking at the usefulness of presenting uncertainty of this information as a numerical value a pre-pilot study was conducted and discussed in the following section.

5 Pre-pilot User Study Using the Uncertainty of Information Value

5.1 Description

The pre-pilot user study was the first attempt for us to investigate how the presentation of uncertainty can support decision making, which may be applicable to military situations. In this study, at each decision point information based on a notional IoBT device informs to the participant on which direction to take along a route. The information is a simulated notice from the IoBT device of the state of the route for a given direction. For example, if a right turn along the route is clear then the report says that this direction should be taken. Part of the study is to also present this report with an uncertainty value that indicates any uncertainty related to the information from the IoBT device. The primary research question was to determine if including information from the IoBT data to soldiers along with a number that represented the uncertainty of the data would affect the decision to take action in a helpful way. The number was presented as a value but was not identified as a probability. The higher the number, the more uncertain the information. This uncertainty value was incorporated into the interface of the software for the task.

The experiment followed a within-subjects design consisting of two blocks. Each block consisted of four trials, two with the uncertainty of information value and two without. Participants were asked to complete the simple task. All participants were shown a series of routes with multiple decision points.

A random number was assigned to the participants and no additional demographic information was collected from the participants for this pre-pilot user study. Upon arrival, participants were given an introduction describing the study. If they chose to participate, participants who volunteered to do the study were provided with consent forms and were divided into two groups. They were all seated at tables and given a tablet with the ATAK software installed. Participants were then given instructions on how to use the tablet and software (including the interface).

ATAK is a mapping engine that allows for precision targeting, intelligence on land, navigations, and situational awareness. This system is under development by a variety of government laboratories. Navigation using GPS maps can be overlaid with symbols and Cursor on Target data to show situational awareness of events. The fictional route was displayed in the ATAK software on the tablet. At selected points along the route a window displayed information describing whether the path was blocked (with and without a number that represents the uncertainty of the information). At the end of the trials the participants were debriefed and dismissed.

The modified ATAK interface consisted of three components: (I) The ATAK Map display, in which the route was shown (Fig. 6); (II) The Information Dialog Box, which presented the information from the device with and without the uncertainty values (Fig. 7); and (III) a timer indicating remaining time to complete objective.

Fig. 6. A figure caption is always placed below the illustration. Short captions are centered, while long ones are justified. The macro button chooses the correct format automatically.

5.2   Results and Discussion

Data from two participants were taken to first determine if there was a difference in the decisions made with and without the uncertainty of information as a numerical value. For each participant there are four decision points per trail with a total of four trails. This selected sample data shows two of the decisions were the same for one of the participants but none of the decisions were the same for the other participant. From all the samples analyzed only 10% of the decisions were the same. This implies the uncertainty of information value presented numerically possibly changed the decisions. Of course, there are many influences to the decisions the participants made, from the vigilance during the study to biases when making this type of simple decision.

After completion of the task in ATAK, a questionnaire was given and one of the questions was what additional information was needed to make a better decision. Most

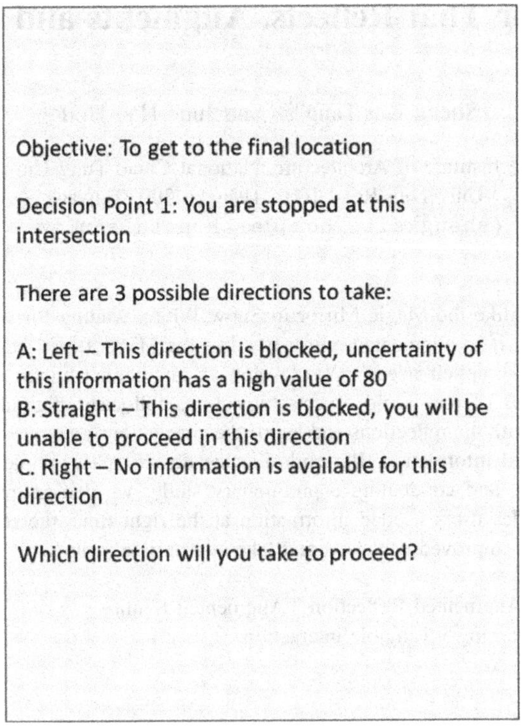

Objective: To get to the final location

Decision Point 1: You are stopped at this
intersection

There are 3 possible directions to take:

A: Left – This direction is blocked, uncertainty of
this information has a high value of 80
B: Straight – This direction is blocked, you will be
unable to proceed in this direction
C. Right – No information is available for this
direction

Which direction will you take to proceed?

Fig. 7. Figure showing presentation of information for the decision points in the study.

of the participants wanted additional insights to the value in terms of what was behind
the value that made it either high, medium, or low. In future user studies this information will be incorporated and presented with the value.

References

1. Atzori, L., Iera, A., Morabito, G.: The internet of things: a survey. Comput. Netw. **54**(15), 2787–2805 (2010)
2. Kott, A., Swami, A., West, B.: The internet of battle things. Computer **49**, 70–75 (2016). https://doi.org/10.1109/MC.2016.355
3. http://www.businessdictionary.com/definition/decision-making.html
4. Simon, H.A.: Theories of decision-making in economics and behavioral science. Am. Econ. Rev. **49**(3), 253–283 (1959)
5. Boyd, J.: OODA loop. Technical report, Center for Defense Information (1995)
6. US Marine Corps: Marine Corps Planning Process (2010)
7. Norman, D.: The Design of Everyday Things: Revised and Expanded Edition. Constellation (2013)
8. Yau, N.: Visualizing uncertainty in data. FlowingData (2017)

A Mirror That Reflects, Augments and Learns

Sheng Kai Tang[✉] and June Hao Hou

Graduate Institute of Architecture, National Chiao Tung University,
University Road 1001, Hsinchu 300, Taiwan
{shengkait, jhou}@arch.nctu.edu.tw

Abstract. Unlike the Magic Mirror in Snow White, waiting for users' active requests, what if an augmented mirror was like the Mirror of Erised, capable of serving users' implicit needs? We develop an augmented mirror system that reflects images of real-world objects by nature, collocates digitally rendered information with the reflections and learns the correlations among users, objects and augmented information. By exploring the design space, implementing an actual system, and conducting a preliminary study, we demonstrate that our system provides users needed information at the right time, thereby allowing them to make improved decisions and take appropriate actions.

Keywords: Augmented Reflection · Augmented Reality ·
Correlation learning · Tangible interaction

1 Introduction

Mirrors by nature reconstruct a duplicated world optically through reflecting photons of light from the real world to human's eyes. Standing in front of a mirror, a user can perceive not only his/her own figure but also surroundings, including objects, other figures and spaces. This made mirrors essential household necessities, fulfilling different functionalities at various locations. For example, a full-length mirror not only assists users for dressing when placed in the bedroom but also creates illusion of more space when hanging on the wall of the living room.

Researchers tried to extend the functionalities of mirrors by augmenting digital properties on top of the reflective reality. These technical discoveries, in general, were categorized as the study of Augmented Reflection. In contrast to Augmented Reality, Augmented Reflection overlays 3D digital information on the reflection of the real world instead of the real world itself. This technique has the potential to realize many household use cases and scenarios, requiring 3D floating information, wearable-device-free interaction and two-handed direct manipulation [1, 3, 4, 6, 10, 12].

Most of the related works have mainly focused on developing technological advances, aiming at reflective optics and computational geometry, to combine natural and rendered optical information. Related systems have successfully aligned the reflections of real-world objects with their 3D corresponding information to create high fidelity illusion of coexistence. However, such augmented mirrors, being similar to the Magic Mirror in the story of Snow White (Fig. 1), still follows the conventional

© Springer Nature Switzerland AG 2019
N. Streitz and S. Konomi (Eds.): HCII 2019, LNCS 11587, pp. 48–58, 2019.
https://doi.org/10.1007/978-3-030-21935-2_5

interaction model, where information retrievals are triggered by users' determined inquiries according to their explicit demands.

Fig. 1. Magic Mirror in the story of Snow White answers Evil Queen's requests [13].

What if an augmented mirror was like the Mirror of Erised (Fig. 2), capable of serving users' implicit needs instead of waiting for their explicit requests? Could this proactive capability provide even more intuitive interaction than what the current model does? Our vision is that augmented mirrors are not only a passive portal for users to access augmented information of everyday objects, but also an active server to dynamically fulfill users' instant needs, elicited from their day-to-day interactions with physical objects and associated information.

Fig. 2. Mirror of Erised in Harry Potter shows the most desperate desire of a person's heart [11].

To explore this vision, we propose an advanced augmented mirror system that reflects images of real-world objects by nature, collocates digitally rendered information with the reflections and further learn the correlations among users, objects and augmented information.

2   Related Works

There are two kinds of augmented mirror systems, one uses the video see through technique, the other implements the optical combinator concept.

In video see through systems, the mirrors are large format displays, showing digital information overlaying on top of the 2D video streams, captured by high resolution cameras. This approach is easier technically and popular in commercial applications, such as i-Mirror [15], Toshiba's Virtual 3D Dressing Room [14] and Adidas virtual mirror [2]. The limitation is that they have fixed and slightly tilted perspectives, caused by the positions of camera.

The optical combinator systems, which realize the true Augmented Reflection idea, combine a half-silvered mirror with a 2D display to collocate digital rendered 3D information with the reflection of real world. This implementation creates magical illusion, making users to believe the 3D digital rendered information truly exist, such as The Mixed Reality Mirror Display [4], Air Drum [3], and Holoflector [6]. These systems rely on tracking the user's head position to generate dynamic perspectives, hence limiting to single user scenarios. Furthermore, the lack of depth and stereo affects the comfort of visual perception.

3   Design Space

According to the vision, we divide the design space into three parts to explore, including augmentation, interaction and correlation.

3.1   Augmentation

Most published research results addressing the issue of augmenting reflections with virtual elements have primarily dealt with the technical aspects of it, creating the illusion of coexistence by developing view dependent 3D rendering algorithms. However, less work has been done on exploring design possibilities, arranging virtual and reflected elements in numerous ways to generate diverse design solutions. We hence identified a framework suggesting various information placements for different use cases.

Around. Augmentations can be placed around the reflection of an object, making the best use of the surrounded 3D virtual space instead of being limited by the real estate of a 2D screen. Virtual elements, such as texts, lines and graphics, can be placed close to a mirrored object as an annotation, be put between mirrored objects to illustrate their relations, and be located near where users are gazing at to draw attention. The tabletop surface nearby an object can provide physical affordances for users to interact with the touchable Graphical User Interface (GUI) elements on the mirrored tabletop (Fig. 3A).

On. Augmentations can be attached on the surface of the reflection of an object, enhancing the object's surface properties. Virtual elements, such as underlines, frames, symbols, and backgrounds, can be attached to highlight or modify existing information. 2D GUI elements, such as icons, buttons, and hyperlinks can be added as interactive properties, triggering additional functionalities, and linking them to external information on websites or clouds (Fig. 3B).

Inside. Augmentations can be embedded inside the reflection of an object, becoming a hidden layer of information to be revealed when needed. Virtual elements, such as volumes, structures and contents, can simulate internal properties, which users physically have difficulty perceiving and inspecting. This internal information can be predefined contents providing corresponding information on demand, synchronized real world inputs updating states of contents in real time, and even simulated volumetric data according to users' direct inputs (Fig. 3C).

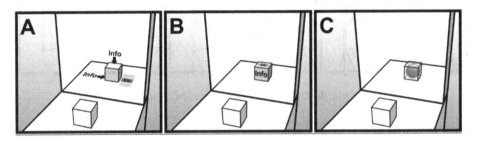

Fig. 3. Design space for augmentation design.

3.2   Interaction

The current interaction techniques for augmented reflection enable users to use physical tools, two hands, and the body to interact with virtual contents in the mirror. These techniques highly rely on hand-eye coordination skills, performing physical actions to align with visual feedback in the mirror. However, we believe tangible mediated interaction can provide physical affordances, and hence can be more intuitive. Therefore, we developed three tangible mediated interactions to assist, which are object-mediated, surface-mediated and face-mediated interactions.

Object-Mediated. The significant advantage of an augmented mirror is that it allows users to have two-handed direct manipulation of physical objects. Since having the full control of physical objects via hands, users can use one hand to slightly move an object to call out the information, pick up/put down the object to switch functionalities, and rotate it to adjust properties. Users can also use two hands to manipulate the proximity of two physical objects to specify their relationships or transfer properties from one to another (Fig. 4A).

Surface-Mediated. 2D GUI elements are augmented on the mirrored tabletop to leverage the affordance of the physical tabletop surface for users to interact with. Popular touch actions, such as tap to select, swipe to browse, and drag to move, are supported. The same touch actions can be applied on the GUI elements attached on the surface of a mirrored object, enabling users to trigger the associated functionalities described in the augmentation session (Fig. 4B).

Face-Mediated. In addition to using hands to manipulate tangible user interfaces and fingers to operate graphical user interfaces of our mirror system, a user's face can become an input channel by deploying a facial recognition technique. A user's presence in front of the mirror extracts augmented information and functionalities belonging to him/her. Using a finger to point at distinct parts of a face, such as eyes, nose, mouth, etc., can also retrieve augmented information accordingly (Fig. 4C).

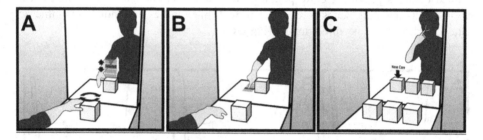

Fig. 4. Design space for interaction design.

3.3   Correlation

Current augmented mirror systems, like other augmented reality systems, manually bind physical objects with their augmented information, ensuring that users always receive the right information regarding the target objects. However, there are hidden correlations among objects, information, and users, which only emerge during the actual and frequent interactions on a daily basis and have not been addressed yet. These correlations might reflect users' behavior patterns and even implicit needs, and hence are valuable to advancing our augmented mirror system.

Dependency. Our system not only can recognize users' presences but also can identify objects the users are using. When objects are frequently manipulated by the users, the system learns and builds dependencies between the objects and the users. In addition to one object mapping to one user, an object can belong to multiple users, while a user can also own many objects (Fig. 5A).

Group. The objects belonging to a user can be further categorized into different groups according to the ways that the user interact with them. A user might collect different objects before using them, revealing the user's intention of forming these objects into group. A user might use one object after another within a short period of time, also showing that these objects have a higher chance of becoming a group (Fig. 5B).

Sequence. Objects in a group might contain hidden orders, providing rules for the system to predict users' possible next steps. Users always use objects with various functions in diverse orders to fit different purposes, forming unique sequences. Our system recognizes and learns these sequences, and later reminds a user of his/her belongings, keeps a user in the right procedure, and recommends to other users how to achieve similar goals (Fig. 5C).

Fig. 5. Design space for correlation design.

4 Use cases

After exploring and defining the general design principles for developing the augmented mirror, we further extended these generic principles to three demonstration scenarios, to provide a better understanding and envision real benefits.

4.1 Hallway

A user always leaves a car key on the table in front of the mirror when arriving home. The mirror is gradually aware of the fact that the user owns the key. When the user checks his or her appearance in front of the mirror before going out, the mirror augments a graphical reminder around the key to draw the user's attention. The mirror also displays a UI with two icons, which represent ignition and garage door, on the mirrored table top nearby the key. The user touches one button to start the car for warming up and the other to open the gate of the garage remotely (Fig. 6).

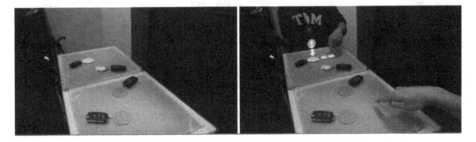

Fig. 6. Interacting with Erised in the hallway setting.

4.2 Kitchen

A wife puts a food material on the countertop with a mirror attached vertically. She seasons the material with seasoning A, seasoning B, and seasoning C in turn. When her hand moves the seasoning cans, the volumetric renderings are displayed on the mirrored cans showing the remain amounts. When noticing that the can of seasoning B has a few servings of seasoning left, she lifts up then puts down the can to call out an augmented menu. She rotates the can to highlight the 'buy' function in the menu and lifts up then puts down the can again to select. The selection triggers the connection to the supermarket and orders a new can of seasoning B (Fig. 7B, C). She then uses a knife to cut the material into four pieces, and the mirror learns the locations where she has cut the material.

Some days later, the husband must cook himself, while the wife is on a business trip. When he puts the material that his wife prepared for him on the counter (Fig. 7A), the way in which his wife previously cooked the material is augmented on the mirrored image of the material step by step, including what seasonings to use, what sequence to follow, and where to cut the material (Fig. 7D).

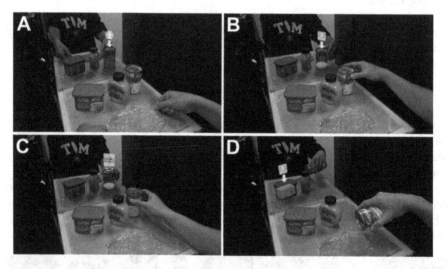

Fig. 7. Interacting with Erised in the kitchen setting.

4.3   Bathroom

One day, a female buys four facial care products for her forehead, eyes, nose, and mouth, and puts them on the wash stand in front of a mirror. She always consciously takes a little cream with her finger from a specific care product, then puts it on the related part of the face. Or she always unconsciously uses her fingers and hands to check the parts of her face, before using the care products. These conscious and unconscious actions are learned by the mirror.

Another day, a male living with the female uses his finger to check the nose in front of the mirror. As soon as he feels that he might need some care products for his nose, he notices that there is an augmented indicator on a bottle (Fig. 8A). When he uses his finger to point to different parts of the face, there are augmented indicators showing up on other bottles in turn accordingly. He picks and opens the can for nose and touches a button nearby the can to link to a website showing the product details and instructions (Fig. 8C, D).

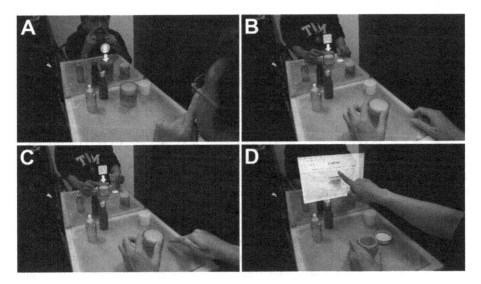

Fig. 8. Interacting with Erised in the bathroom setting.

5 System Implementation

To achieve the above-mentioned use cases, we built customized hardware and developed software by integrating several popular toolkits and algorithms.

5.1 Hardware

The developed system has two hardware modules, a mirror module, and a tabletop module. The mirror module has a 39 cm × 56 cm half-silvered mirror overlaying on a 24-in. LCD display to merge virtual and real images. The mirror module also has a Microsoft Kinect 2 attached on top of it to capture depth image for facial recognition and tracking.

The mirror module is placed on the tabletop module, which consists of a 39 cm 39 cm translucent table top, a 1920 px × 768 px camera with an IR lens covered facing upwards 40 cm from the bottom of the tabletop, and two 30 × 30 IR led panels illuminating the tabletop from below as well. This setting limits the camera to only see IR-reflective tabletop activities (Fig. 9).

5.2 Software

To realize the high-fidelity illusion of the coexistence of mirrored and digitally rendered images, we implemented the popular Eye Dependent 3D Rendering Algorithm. The Microsoft Kinect 2 on the mirror module captures the depth image of the user and recognizes and tracks the user's head position [7]. In the 3D digital scene, the moving head position is further bound with a perspective camera looking into the viewport on the LCD screen behind the half-silvered mirror.

We adopted the reacTIVision framework to make the tabletop module an interactive surface capable of recognizing and tracking fiducial markers and finger touches [5]. The recognized marker identifications (IDs) are pointers to the associated augmented information and GUI elements. The continuous actions of lifting up then putting down a marker are interpreted as a click event, while rotating the marker is used for rotary control. A finger touch can be recognized to trigger, swipe, and drag-and-drop GUI elements.

To identify different users in front of the mirror, we implemented a facial identification module based on NodeJS Support Vector Machine (SVM) API [9]. The Kinect HD Face API recognizes users' faces and identifies the position of each facial element, including forehead, eyes, nose, and mouth. The relative positions between these elements are then calculated to define five unique features of a face. These features are ultimately fed into an SVM to train.

We also used the NodeJS Hidden Markov Model (HMM) API [8] to implement the correlation module building the relationships between users, objects and information. The computed results of the facial recognition module and the recognized marker IDs of the reaTIVsion toolkit and the GUI elements triggered by the finger touch are defined as attributes to train the HMM, predicting the augmented information for the users and physical objects (Fig. 9).

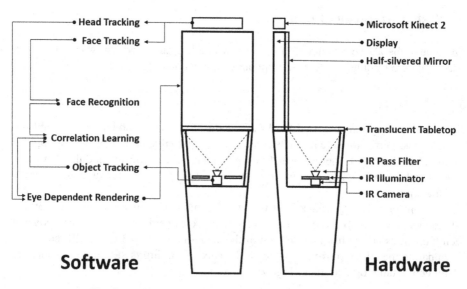

Fig. 9. Software and hardware design and implementation.

6 Preliminary Evaluation and Results

To collect feedbacks, we invited eight users to experience our augmented mirror and conducted a preliminary study.

Since the correlation module requires a relatively large dataset and takes time to train, it was difficult to demonstrate during the user tests. Therefore, we pre-trained the models for the three demonstration scenarios and let the users to experience the training results. The users directly manipulated the physical objects to interact with the mirror and answered a questionnaire containing seven Likert Scale questions. After the questionnaire, we interviewed the users to acquire explanations for their answers.

The results of our survey indicated some benefits the system provides, including:

- The users feel that the effect of augmenting virtual elements with the mirrored objects is magical.
- They would love to have such a smart mirror at home to assist them with their daily activities.
- The augmented indicators serve to remind them with a relatively "calm" way compared to conventional pop-up notifications of mobile phones.
- Manipulating the physical objects to call out related digital information and GUI elements is intuitive.
- They feel the next-step instructions help them to continue their tasks without searching online or asking family members.
  Some problems were also identified, including:
- There was difficulty in focusing on the merged images in the mirror, (using one eye is better than two eyes).
- The rendered images were a little bit dark.
- Some latencies occurred while users were moving their heads too fast, causing the rendered and mirror images to be unmatched.
- The touch sensitivity and precision were not high enough and caused some operational issues.

7   Conclusion, Limitations and Future Works

According to the collected data, we concluded that augmented reflection offered an intuitive and convenient way for users to retrieve digital information of everyday objects with the freedom to use both their hands, and without wearing and carrying any additional device. The study also revealed that the augmented information of predicted correlations provides users needed information at the right time, allowing them to make better decisions and take the appropriate actions. Most of the cons found in this study, such as poor rendering performance, insufficient brightness, occlusion problems and lack of visual depth, were technical issues and noted for future improvements and further study.

References

1. Riviere, J.B.D.L., Dittlo, N., Emmanuel, O., Kervegant, C., Courtois, M.: Holocubtile: 3D multitouch brings the virtual world into the user's hands. In: Proceedings of ITS 2010, p. 311 (2010)
2. Eisert, P., Rurainsky, J., Fechteler, P.: Virtual mirror: real-time tracking of shoes in augmented reality environments. In: Proceedings of ICIP 2007 (2007)

3. Ho, W., Li, A., Fu, H.: Augmented reflection of reality. In: Proceedings of SIGGRAPH 2012 Emerging Technologies, p. 3:1 (2012)
4. Hara, T., Oda, M.: Mixed reality mirror display. In: Proceedings of SIGGRAPH Asia 2012 Emerging Technologies, pp. 16:1–16:3 (2012)
5. Kaltenbrunner, M.: reacTIVision and TUIO: a tangible tabletop toolkit. In: Proceeding of ITS 2009, pp. 9–16 (2009)
6. Holoflector. http://research.microsoft.com/apps/video/default.aspx?id=159487 Accessed 24 Sept 2015
7. Kinect for Windows SDK 2. https://msdn.microsoft.com/en-us/library/dn782034.aspx Accessed 08 Jan 2018
8. NPM Hidden Markov Model. https://www.npmjs.com/package/hidden-markov-model Accessed 08 Jan 2015
9. NPM Support Vector Machine. https://www.npmjs.com/package/node-svm Accessed 08 Jan 2018
10. Plasencia, D.M., Berthaut, F., Karnik, A., Subramanian, S.: Through the combining glass. In: Proceedings of UIST 2014, pp. 341–350 (2014)
11. Mirror of Erised. http://harrypotter.wikia.com/wiki/Mirror_of_Erised Accessed 08 Jan 2018
12. Sato, H., Kitahara, I.,Ohta, Y.: MR-mirror: a complex of real and virtual mirrors, In: Proceedings of VMR 2009, pp. 482–491 (2009)
13. Mirror, Mirror On The Wall. https://www.theodysseyonline.com/mirror-the-wall Accessed 08 Jan 2018
14. Virtual 3D Dressing Room. https://www.youtube.com/watch?v=YAPmC6priqY Accessed 11 Jan 2018
15. Ushida, K., Tanaka, Y., Naemura, T., Harahima, H.: i-mirror: an interaction/information environment based on a mirror metaphor aiming to install into our life space. In: Proceeding of ICAT 2002 (2002)

Towards an Understanding of College Students' Perceptions of Smart Home Devices

Christine E. Wania[✉]

The College at Brockport, State University of New York, Brockport, NY, USA
cwania@brockport.edu

Abstract. The concept of a smart home has evolved over several decades. There are many advantages and potential advantages of smart homes, smart home devices and smart living. There are also disadvantages, risks and concerns with smart home devices. There has been significant work examining adults' perceptions of smart home technologies and devices, particularly in adults over the age of 40 in the areas of energy policy and assistive technologies. There has not been as much work examining perceptions of adults under the age of 40. The goal of this research is to further understand college students' familiarity with smart home devices, use of smart home devices, willingness to use such devices, and the perceived advantages and disadvantages of smart home devices. This study extends previous research by gathering college students' perceptions of smart home devices. The results of this study suggest that most of the college students surveyed perceived some usefulness and potential benefits of smart home devices, but they also had many concerns. Less than half of the college students surveyed indicated a desire to use smart home devices. A deeper understanding of younger adults' perceptions, expectations, and concerns may assist device manufacturers, researchers, and potential users of smart home devices. Further work is needed in this area.

Keywords: Consumer perceptions · Internet of Things (IoT) · Smart home · Smart home devices · Smart home technology · Smart living · Ubiquitous computing · User perceptions

1 Introduction

The concept of a smart home has evolved over time [28, 30, 36, 37]. Smart homes and smart home devices have been discussed in literature and researched in many disciplines for several decades. There are many advantages [36, 42] and also disadvantages [9, 18, 42] of smart homes and smart home devices. Research has been conducted in an attempt to understand perceptions of smart home devices and use of such devices. Many research methods have been utilized. Researchers have conducted focus groups [13, 15], interviews [6, 17], surveys [5, 17, 22], observational studies and home visits [7]. Several smart homes have also been built and studied at universities including Drexel University, Georgia Institute of Technology, and University of Colorado, Boulder. Much of the empirical work in this area has focused on adults over the age of 40. There has been significant work examining adults' perceptions of smart home technologies

© Springer Nature Switzerland AG 2019
N. Streitz and S. Konomi (Eds.): HCII 2019, LNCS 11587, pp. 59–74, 2019.
https://doi.org/10.1007/978-3-030-21935-2_6

and devices, particularly in adults over the age of 40, in the areas of energy policy [6, 17, 26], and assistive medical and healthcare technologies [13, 15, 31]. There has been some work examining younger adults' perceptions of smart home technology and devices [18, 22], but not to the same extent as other populations. However, younger adults are certainty a target population for such devices in a market that has rapidly grown and is predicted to continue to rapidly grow [4].

One goal of this research is to further understand college students' familiarity with smart home devices, use of smart home devices, willingness to use such devices, and perceptions of advantages and disadvantages of smart home devices. The other goal of this research is to further refine the survey instrument used in this study prior to distributing the survey to a wider population. This study extends previous research by gathering perceptions from a population that has not been studied as extensively as other populations. A brief review of related work is included in the following section.

2 Background and Related Work

Smart homes and smart home devices have been discussed in literature for decades and researched in many disciplines for decades. During this time the concept of a smart home has evolved. This evolution began with the smart home and is now referred to by some as smart living [36]. The first use of the term smart house has been attributed to the American Association of House Builders, in 1984 [25]. Although similar concepts had been described prior to the 1980s. Smart homes in the 1980s contained many large (r) devices and lots, and lots of wires [23]. The smart homes of today are closely related to ubiquitous computing [40] and the Internet of Things (IoT). The concept of smart living extends the conveniences and functionality of smart home devices to everyday life, not limited to the confines of a home.

2.1 From Smart Homes to Smart Living

There is currently no agreed upon definition of a smart home, a smart home device or smart living, and different disciplines and industries have varying definitions. Aldrich defines a smart home as "as a residence equipped with computing and information technology which anticipates and responds to the needs of the occupants, working to promote their comfort, convenience, security and entertainment through the management of technology within the home and connections to the world beyond." [2, p. 17]. Aldrich [2] proposed five classifications of smart homes: homes which contain intelligent objects, homes which contain intelligent communicating objects, connected homes, learning homes, and attentive homes. Not only are smart homes intelligent, connected, and able to communicate, but, according to Aldrich they learn and are aware and attentive to the needs and desires of the occupants [2]. Solaimani, Keijzer-Broers, Bouwman [36] extend Aldrich's definition by adding communication, education and healthcare to the list of things that a smart home promotes.

The concept of smart living extends the concept of a smart home outside of the home, to focus on intelligent living, and not just focus on devices in the home [36]. As Weiser stated "The most profound technologies are those that disappear" [40, p. 94].

The smart home devices and technologies of today seem to have disappeared and be the invisible computers described by Norman [33]. These invisible computers exist in many everyday devices we are already accustomed to having in our homes.

Smart home devices have been studied in many disciplines including: Architecture and Construction, Computer Science, Cybersecurity, Energy Policy, Healthcare, Human Computer Interaction, and Networking, among others. Smart home devices have been studied in these disciplines for varying reasons such as reducing energy consumption, providing independence and healthcare to older adults, and for comfort, convenience and security. There have been many large-scale smart home projects including the Aware Home at Georgia Institute of Technology [27, 28], and the Drexel Smart House [19]. Academic and industry researchers have examined smart home advantages, disadvantages, challenges and accomplishments. Reviews of the literature are provided in various disciplines [1, 16, 36].

Smart home devices have been developed in many areas including, but not limited to: energy, entertainment, healthcare, and security. Advances in technology have allowed for new developments. As the technology has advanced and prices have decreased, it seems as though there is more interest in smart home devices and smart living. Interest in smart home devices can be seen in new product development, product sales, and the Consumer Electronics Show [11, 12]. In 2019 smart home technologies were named one of the 5 technology trends to watch by the Consumer Technology Association [4].

Another way to examine interest in this area is by inspecting Google Trends. Google Trends examined in January 2019 for the time period of 2004–2018 indicate an increase in searches that include terms such as smart home and several similar variants beginning in and around 2013. Note: the Amazon Echo was introduced in 2014 and Google purchased Nest Labs in 2014.

In the literature, potential advantages and disadvantages of smart home devices vary based on the industry, application and the specific smart home device. Some of the advantages or benefits of various smart home devices discussed in the literature include: convenience, comfort, safety, security, cost savings, energy savings, and time savings. Research suggests that consumers have adopted these devices for convenience, safety, security, to save money [6, 15, 31, 43], and in some cases simply as a desire to be identified as an early adopter [29].

There are also many concerns, risks and disadvantages of smart home devices described in the literature including: control, cost, interoperability, privacy, reliability, security and usability [6–9, 29]. In some cases consumers simply do not see a need for smart home devices. Edwards and Grinter [20] identified seven challenges of smart homes, including the need for a systems administrator or someone to manage the smart home. Some of the barriers and challenges with adoption described by Gann et al. [21] and Edwards and Grinter [20] appear to still be barriers and challenges today.

According to the Consumer Technology Association, smart home product revenues were more than $3.3 billion in 2017 [4]. The Consumer Technology Association's 2018 *U.S. Consumer Technology Sales & Forecasts* report predicts that sales of smart home products will double between 2018 and 2022, with revenues surpassing $6.9 billion in 2022 [4]. Clearly there is currently interest in smart home devices. However, we still do not understand enough about peoples' perceptions of these devices.

2.2   Technology Adoption, Acceptance and Use: Theoretical Frameworks

There are many theoretical models or frameworks for understanding adoption, acceptance and use of emerging technologies. A brief review of several such frameworks is provided here. The diffusion process described by Rogers in Diffusion of Innovations suggests that innovation is communicated over time through particular channels [35]. Rogers describes the innovation decision making process that includes five steps: knowledge, persuasion, decision, implementation and confirmation [35]. The decision phase includes a decision to adopt or reject a technology. In this diffusion process as described by Rogers, the first adopters are categorized as innovators, followed by early adopters, early majority, late majority and laggards [35]. This framework also addresses communication networks, diffusion networks, personal networks and reaching critical mass [35].

The Technology Acceptance Model (TAM) [14] focuses on organizational systems and the acceptance of such systems by end users in an organization. TAM suggests that perceived usefulness and perceived ease of use are of particular importance in the acceptance of technology by end users. TAM suggests that perceived usefulness and perceived ease of use determine behavioral intent to use a technology [14]. The Unified Theory of Acceptance and Use of Technology (UTAUT) by Venkatesh, Morris, Davis, Davis [38] built on previous frameworks, including TAM, and considered individual acceptance and use of technology, primarily in organizations. UTAUT contains four constructs that provide a richer understanding of individual acceptance and use of technology in organizations: performance expectancy, effort expectancy, social influence and facilitating conditions [38].

Unified Theory of Acceptance and Use of Technology II (UTAUT2) by Venkatesh, Thong, Xu [39] extends UTAUT [38] and addresses consumer acceptance and use of technology. In addition to the four constructs in UTAUT that are adapted for the consumer context, UTAUT2 contains three additional constructs: hedonic motivation, price value and habit [39]. These constructs deserve a bit of explanation. In this context, performance expectancy refers to the benefits to consumers from the use of a particular technology [39]. Effort expectancy refers to the amount of effort/ease associated with the use of a particular technology [39]. Social influence refers to one's perception of others' beliefs about one's use of a particular technology. Facilitating conditions refer to one's perceptions about the availability of resources and support [39]. Hedonic motivation is the fun or pleasure one perceives from using a particular technology [39]. Price value refers to the cost/benefit tradeoffs [39]. The last construct, habit, according to Venkatesh et al. is a "perceptual construct that reflects the results of prior experiences" [39, p. 161]. For further information refer to [39]. These theoretical frameworks and models provide some context within which we can further examine and explore the adoption and use of new technologies.

2.3   Smart Home and Smart Living Literature

Much has been written about smart homes and smart living. In this literature, perceptions of smart home devices vary. Several literature reviews have been conducted including those by Alaa, Zaidan, Zaidan, Taal, Kiah [1], Chan, Esteve,

Escribe, Campo [10], Demiris and Hensel [16], and Solaimani, Keijzer-Broers and Bouwman [36]. Alaa et al. [1] provide a review of 229 publications. Demiris and Hensel [16] provide a review of 114 publications. Chan et al. [10] provide a review of smart home projects along with the systems used in the smart homes. Solaimani et al. [36] provide a review of 154 publications. Solaimani et al. [36] identify four domains within smart living literature: organization, finance, service, and technology. Alaa et al. provide a taxonomy of smart home literature and divide the literature into four classes and several subclasses [1].

Several methods have been used to investigate perceptions of smart home technology. Bernheim Brush, Lee, Mahajan, Agarwal, Saroiu, Dixon [7] conducted home visits "in the wild" at 14 homes with at least one smart home device, or home automation device, as they referred to in their work. Bernheim Brush et al. spoke with 31 people in the 14 households. Bernheim Brush et al. found that many households were happy with their experiences with smart home devices. Although these users were happy with their experiences, they encountered challenges including: inflexibility, manageability, security, and high cost of ownership [7].

Balta-Ozkan, Davidson, Bicket, Whitmarsh [6] conducted workshops and expert interviews to understand barriers to the adoption of smart home technologies, specifically related to energy efficiency. Balta-Ozkanet et al. found that experts perceive barriers related to complexity, interoperability, privacy, reliability and security. However, Balta-Ozkan et al. found that consumers concerns are related to: cost, loss of control, privacy, reliability, security, trust and utility (or lack thereof) [6].

Rainie and Duggan [34] at the PEW Research Center conducted a survey and online focus groups. Raine and Duggan state "the phrase that best captures Americans' views on the choice between privacy vs. disclosure of personal information is, "It depends."" [34]. Rainie and Duggan [34] surveyed a nationally representative sample of 461 Americans, using parameters from the March 2013 Census Bureau's Current Population Survey (CPS). This survey included 235 men and 226 women. Two-hundred thirty participants were between ages 18–49 and 231 participants were age 50 and above. Participants were asked to indicate whether or not you would be willing to share information about themselves in exchange for getting something they might need or enjoy [34]. Raine and Duggan report that 27% of the adults surveyed found a smart thermostat acceptable. Fifty-five percent found a smart thermostat not acceptable, and 17% felt as though it depends [34].

Apthorpe, Shvartzshnaider, Mathur, Reisman, Feamster [3], using a survey based on the Contextual Integrity privacy framework, gathered data from 1731 adults in the United States. Based on the results of their survey Apthorpe et al. [3] concluded that user privacy perceptions are context dependent and diverse in this area. Zheng, Shvartzshnaider, Mathur, Reisman, Feamster conducted 11 semi-structured interviews with smart home device owners [43]. Their work suggests that user opinions depend on perceived benefits [43]. The findings in [43] suggest that users trust manufacturers, but do not take action to verify that they are being protected and that users are unaware of some privacy risks. The findings in Zheng et al. suggest that desires for convenience dictate privacy related behaviors [43].

Lau, Zimmerman, Schaub [29] conducted a diary study and interviews with 17 smart speaker users and 17 non-users. Lau et al. investigated perceptions of benefits, risks and concerns with smart speakers, such as Amazon Echo. In this study, non-users did not see the purpose or value of the devices and non-users did not trust the device companies [29]. Their findings suggest that users of the smart speakers did not fully understand privacy risks, expressed few privacy concerns and were mixed on their level of trust in the companies [29]. Lau et al. suggest "people are choosing to trade privacy for convenience" [29]. Lau et al. provide recommendations to device manufacturers, regulators and policy makers to address privacy protections and data practices [29]. Nikou [32] conducted a survey of 156 individuals in an attempt to understand what influences intentions. Their findings suggests that perceived usefulness, attitudes towards technology and social influence impact adoption decisions [32].

In an attempt to further understand perceptions and use of smart home technologies, research groups have designed, constructed and studied smart homes [27, 28]. Many including Nikou [32] have investigated adoption of smart home technologies using some of the frameworks discussed above. Others have conducted focus groups [13, 15], interviews [3, 17, 43], surveys [5, 17, 22], observational studies and home visits [7] and mined publically available information from consumers [8]. Some have utilized multiple research methods [6, 29, 41]. The methods used in this study are described in the following section.

3   Method

A survey instrument was used to gather data. The survey was developed after a review of the literature and consideration of the theoretical frameworks described in the previous section. The survey contains questions and statements similar to those used elsewhere, such as [17]. There was a tradeoff between the length of the survey instrument and the number of items that could be addressed.

The survey gathered demographic information, familiarity with smart home devices, ownership of smart home devices and perceptions of a few specific smart home devices. The survey included a summary of three smart home devices: Amazon Echo, Nest thermostat, and Ring doorbell. The summary included information about functionality and price. This information was gathered from the product pages on the manufacturer websites. The survey asked for an indication of the extent of disagreement or agreement with 14 statements for each device with the following Likert-type responses: strongly disagree, disagree, neither disagree nor agree, agree and strongly agree. The survey contained statements such as: I feel that the Ring doorbell (or a similar video doorbell) would be useful. Each time that a device was listed in the survey it was listed with (or a similar <fill in the blank> device) where fill in the blank contained a brief description of the device. The survey also included open-ended questions.

The survey was distributed on paper. The survey was administered in multiple sections of an introductory computer science course at a liberal arts college in the fall of 2017. The survey was distributed in one class session. Participation was voluntary and students received no remuneration. Students took approximately 25 min to complete the survey.

Data from the completed surveys was entered into an excel spreadsheet. The data was checked twice for accuracy. Prior to analyzing the pilot data the data was examined for missing responses. Seventy-six participants completed the survey. Of those 76 participants, 18 of them did not complete the entire survey. Sixty-eight of the 76 participants responded to all questions. Instead of selecting a method such as replacing missing values with the mean, incomplete survey data was not used in this analysis. Therefore this analysis includes data only from the 68 participants who answered all the questions. To simplify reporting in this paper, strongly disagree and disagree have been combined into disagree and similarly strongly agree and agree have been combined. For simplification and readability in the reporting of the results, percentages have been rounded at two decimal places. The results of this research are discussed in the next section.

4   Results

Sixty-eight college students responded to all the survey questions. The data from the 68 participants is included in this analysis. The majority of the college students, 80.9%, were between the ages of 18 and 21. Most students, 64.7%, identified as male and 73.5% Caucasian. All of the 68 participants owned a smartphone and most reported using their smartphone extensively: 42.65% for more than 5 h a day; 45.69% for 3–4 h a day and 11.76% for 1–2 h a day. All but one of the participants owned a laptop or desktop computer. Many participants, 70.59%, also owned a gaming console.

Most of the participants, 95.59%, used social media or were a member of more than one social network, with Facebook, 77.94%; Instagram, 73.53%; and Snapchat, 80.88%; being the mostly frequently used. Many participants, 57.35%, reported using the Internet 5 or more hours a day; followed by 36.76%, reported using the Internet 3–4 h; and 5.89%, for 1–2 h a day. Approximately two-thirds, 66.18%, of participants reported mostly using their smartphone to access the Internet, followed by laptop, 17.65%; desktop, 11.75%; and gaming console, 4.41%.

Almost all the participants were familiar, to some extent, with smart home devices: 7.35% extremely familiar; 20.59% familiar; 35.29% somewhat familiar; and 26.47% slightly familiar. While some participants, 10.29%, indicated they were not at all familiar with smart home devices. Most of the participants, 76.47%, did not own a smart home device or live in a residence with a smart home device. Of the 16 participants, 23.53%, who owned or lived in a residence with smart home devices, most (11 participants) only had one smart home device. The most commonly reported device was the Amazon Echo, followed by the Nest thermostat. One participant lived in a residence with more than 5 smart home devices. This participant reported that a family member who worked in a technology related field. Four participants had 2 smart home devices in their residences, which included WeMo outlets, Philips Hue lightbulbs, and Bluetooth deadbolts.

The survey included several questions about perceptions of smart home devices. Participants were asked if they thought three smart home devices would be useful. More than half of the participants agreed that the three smart home devices included in the survey would be useful, as seen in Fig. 1. However, many were unsure about the usefulness of the devices and more than 10% of the participants did not feel that the devices would be useful.

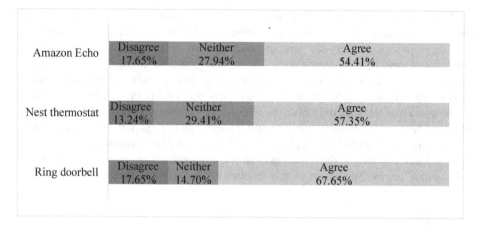

Fig. 1. Responses to: I feel <device> would be useful

Participants were asked about possible advantages of each smart home device including: convenience, comfort, security, and saving time and money. More than half of the participants agreed that the three devices would provide convenience as seen in Table 1. More participants agreed that the Nest thermostat would provide convenience, as compared to the Amazon Echo and the Ring doorbell.

Table 1. Responses to: I feel <device> would provide convenience

	Disagree	Neither	Agree
Amazon Echo	7.35%	25.00%	67.65%
Nest thermostat	10.29%	14.70%	75.00%
Ring doorbell	8.82%	19.12%	72.06%

Participants had varying levels of agreement about smart home devices providing comfort and security. In terms of comfort, 61.76% of participants agreed the Ring doorbell would provide comfort, compared to 47.06% for the Nest thermostat and 26.47% for the Amazon Echo. Participants had varying perceptions about smart home devices providing security. Many of participants, 73.53%, agreed that the Ring doorbell would provide security, 16.18% were unsure and 10.29% disagreed. Very few participants felt as though the Amazon Echo and Nest thermostat would provide security, only 5.88% and 2.94% respectively agreed that these devices would provide security.

Participants were also asked about their perceptions of the smart home devices saving them time and money. Participants had varying levels of agreement as seen in Tables 2 and 3. More than half of the participants agreed that the Amazon Echo and

Nest Thermostat would save them time. Many did not feel as though the devices would save them time and many were unsure.

Table 2. Responses to: I feel <device> would save me time

	Disagree	Neither	Agree
Amazon Echo	23.53%	22.06%	54.41%
Nest thermostat	26.47%	22.06%	51.47%
Ring doorbell	39.71%	23.53%	36.76%

Many participants did not feel as though the smart home devices would save them money and many participants were unsure. Of the three devices, more participants agreed that the Nest thermostat would save them money, compared to the Amazon Echo and the Ring doorbell as seen in Table 2.

Table 3. Responses to: I feel <device> would save me money

	Disagree	Neither	Agree
Amazon Echo	64.70%	20.59%	14.71%
Nest thermostat	22.06%	44.12%	33.82%
Ring doorbell	76.47%	16.18%	7.35%

Participants were asked about potential concerns of each smart home device including: cost, ease of use, interoperability, level of control, privacy, reliability, and trust. Cost was a concern for many participants as seen in Table 4. More participants agreed that they were concerned about the cost of the Nest thermostat and the Ring doorbell when compared to the Amazon Echo. For some participants cost was not seen as a concern in making a decision to use a particular device.

Table 4. Responses to: I feel cost would be a concern in deciding to use <device>

	Disagree	Neither	Agree
Amazon Echo	47.06%	13.24%	39.71%
Nest thermostat	22.06%	26.47%	51.47%
Ring doorbell	20.59%	22.06%	57.35%

More than half of the participants agreed that privacy would be a concern in deciding to use a smart home device as seen in Table 5. Almost 80% of participants agreed that privacy would be a concern in deciding to use the Amazon Echo. Over 60% of participants agreed that privacy would be a concern in deciding to use the Nest thermostat and the Ring doorbell. Some participants were not sure if privacy would be a concern and some did not feel as though privacy would be a concern.

Table 5. Responses to: I feel privacy would be a concern in deciding to use <device>

	Disagree	Neither	Agree
Amazon Echo	11.76%	8.82%	79.41%
Nest thermostat	20.59%	16.18%	63.24%
Ring doorbell	14.71%	20.59%	64.71%

More than 60% of participants agreed that trusting an organization with their usage information would be a concern in deciding to use a particular smart home device as seen in Table 6. Less than 15% of participants did not feel as though trusting organizations with their usage data was a concern and some participants were unsure.

Table 6. Responses to: I feel trusting an organization with my usage information would be a concern in deciding to use <device>

	Disagree	Neither	Agree
Amazon Echo	11.76%	16.18%	72.06%
Nest thermostat	13.24%	25.00%	61.76%
Ring doorbell	14.71%	13.24%	72.06%

More than 60% of participants agreed that not having full control of a smart home device was a concern in deciding to use a particular smart home device as seen in Table 7. Some participants were unsure and less than 20% of participants did not see this as a concern.

Table 7. Responses to: I feel not having full control of <device> would be a concern

	Disagree	Neither	Agree
Amazon Echo	17.65%	13.24%	69.12%
Nest thermostat	13.24%	11.76%	75.00%
Ring doorbell	14.71%	20.59%	64.71%

Some participants agreed that ease of use would be a concern in deciding to use a smart home device as seen in Table 8. Some participants were unsure and many participants did not perceive ease of use to be concern in deciding to use a particular device. Participants were also asked about interoperability and reliability. Less than half of the participants expressed that interoperability with other devices would be a concern in deciding to use a particular device. Approximately half of the participants agreed that reliability would be a concern in deciding to use a particular smart home device.

Table 8. Responses to: I feel ease of use would be a concern in deciding to use <device>

	Disagree	Neither	Agree
Amazon Echo	41.18%	23.53%	35.29%
Nest thermostat	42.65%	35.29%	22.06%
Ring doorbell	35.29%	32.35%	32.35%

Participants were also asked if they would use the devices, responding to statements such as: I would use the Nest thermostat (or a similar thermostat). Less than 40% of the participants indicated that they would use each of the devices as seen in Fig. 2. Most of the participants indicated that they would not use the devices or they were unsure.

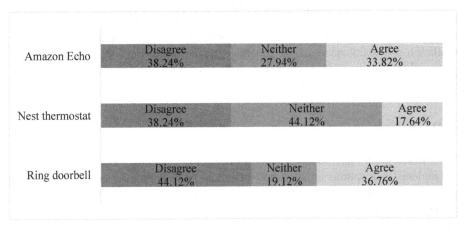

Fig. 2. Responses to: I would use <device>

The survey also included open-ended questions. For each of the three smart home devices included in the survey, participants were asked: What information, if any, would you need before deciding to use this technology? Participants had more questions and comments about the Nest thermostat, followed by the Ring doorbell and then the Amazon Echo. Many participants indicated that they did not need any further information. The most common responses for all three devices included questions of comments about where and how their data would be stored, used and shared. There were 37 responses related to data storage, access, and usage. Examples of comments include: What does Nest do with my location data? What information, if any, Nest will keep a record of? Where is the information stored and who can access it? If they record my voice without me knowing and who can access my data that the company receives… Do they save my voice recordings!? and What information it is taking from me personally and does it save pictures of people at my door?

Following questions and comments regarding how data is stored, used and shared, the next largest category included questions about the functionality of the devices. Examples include: Does it need to be always plugged in in order to be used? What happens if a leaf blows by? Do I get a pop-up message from the motion sensors every time? and How do people ringing the doorbell know if they are being filmed?

The next most frequently occurring responses were indications that they would not use the smart home device. There were 18 responses that specifically mentioned that they would not use a device. Three participants wrote comments indicating that they would not use each of the smart home devices. There were nine other participants who indicated that they would not use one of the devices. Examples of these comments include: I would not use it, Not going to use it, so none, and I'd never use it. Some responses indicated that they would use a particular technology, but would not buy it, for example: I would use it but I wouldn't buy one for privacy reasons. Responses also indicated a need for further explanation of the benefits of smart home devices and/or a lack of understanding about the utility of the smart home devices. Examples of comments include: What would be the benefit? Using the internet yourself takes 5 s, I feel like it is useless; Don't be lazy, walk to your door; and Seems pointless. Responses also included cost concerns, privacy concerns, security concerns, reliability concerns, installation and maintenance concerns/questions and a desire to read reviews or talk with people who have used a particular device, among other things. A discussion of the results is included in the following section.

5   Discussion

This research contributes to smart home research by providing some insight into college students' perceptions of smart home devices. Considering the expectations about the rate at which sales of smart home devices are predicted to continue to grow [4], this population will likely be a target population in the sales of smart home devices. This research suggests that there are many potential issues to be addressed. It is possible that some people are not ready for this paradigmatic shift inside their homes. A brief discussion of the results is included here.

Approximately half of the college students surveyed expressed that they believe the smart home devices are useful. However, most of the college students did not express a willingness or desire to use the devices. The results of this study suggest that the perceived benefits of the three smart home devices varied. This is not surprising considering the differences among the smart home devices. Many of the students surveyed agreed that there were potential benefits, but also had concerns about using the devices.

Convenience was one of the benefits that the college students recognized with each of the smart home devices. Previous research with other populations also found a desire for such convenience [29, 34, 43]. TAM [14] suggests that perceived usefulness and perceived ease of use determine behavioral intent to use a technology [14]. The findings in Nikou [32] also suggest that perceived usefulness is one factor that influences smart home technology adoption decisions. In this research more than half of the surveyed college students perceived some usefulness for each the smart home devices. It appears as though this is one area that might require further attention from smart home device manufacturers and researchers.

In this research, the college students surveyed were more concerned with trusting organizations with their data and potentially not having full control of the devices, compared to the other concerns. Most participants were also concerned about privacy, reliability and cost. Ease of use and interoperability were not as concerning to as many participants. Privacy and trust were concerns among the college students surveyed in this research, as well as concerns with a lack of perceived utility and/or lack of understanding about the smart home devices. Some researchers have examined smart home devices with a particular focus on privacy. Apthorpe et al. [3] based their work on the Contextual Integrity privacy framework. It appears as though examining smart home device acceptance, adoption and use with a focus on privacy might provide further insights.

Approximately a third of the college students surveyed were concerned with ease of use. Seeing as how the college students surveyed are digital natives, it is not surprising that many of them are not as concerned with ease of use. However, this requires further investigation. Considering that most of the participants did not own any smart home devices it is not surprising that they are not (yet) concerned with interoperability of devices. Cost was a concern for many of college students surveyed. Venkatesh et al. [39] suggest there is a complex relationship between price value, hedonic motivation and habit. The sentiment of "it depends" seen in previous research [34] seems to be the case in this study also.

Although there are many frameworks that focus on understanding technology acceptance, adoption and use, and frameworks that focus on privacy, it is possible that we currently do not have a framework that is most appropriate for understanding the acceptance, adoption and use of smart home technologies. Further work is needed in this area to understand these complex relationships.

6 Conclusion

There are many advantages and potential advantages of smart homes devices. There are also disadvantages and concerns with the use of such devices. This study extends previous research by gathering college students' perceptions of smart home devices. This group has not been studied as extensively as other populations. Approximately 90% of the college students surveyed were familiar, to some extent, with smart home devices. Approximately 75% of the college students surveyed did not own a smart home device or live in a residence with a smart home device. The results of this study suggest that many of the college students surveyed perceived some usefulness and potential benefits of smart home devices, but they also had many concerns. Less than half of the college students surveyed indicated a desire to use the three smart home devices mentioned in this research. Further understanding younger adult perceptions, expectations, and concerns may assist device manufacturers, researchers, and potential users of such devices. In an industry that is predicted to continue to rapidly grow, it appears as though we still have many questions to answer and many issues to address. Further work is needed.

7 Limitations and Future Work

A survey is only one of many ways to gather perceptions. The sample population in this research is limited to college students in a particular course. This gathered perceptions about a few specific smart home devices and did not encompass all types of smart home devices. All of these limitations are acknowledged. The goal of this research was to work towards an understanding of college students' perceptions of smart home devices and to further refine the survey instrument for future use with a larger population.

Based on the results of this survey, modifications were made to this survey. After further refinement we intent to gather feedback from a larger group of college students. We are also expanding the list of smart home devices included in the survey. As this work continues we may begin to understand more about the complexities in the acceptance, adoption and use of smart home technologies, and the frameworks through which we can further understand these complex relationships.

References

1. Alaa, M., Zaidan, A.A., Zaidan, B.B., Talal, M., Kiah, M.L.M.: A review of smart home applications based on Internet of Things. J. Netw. Comput. Appl. **97**, 48–65 (2017). https://doi.org/10.1016/j.jnca.2017.08.017
2. Aldrich, F.K.: Smart homes: past, present and future. In: Harper, R. (ed.) Inside the Smart Home, pp. 17–39. Springer, London (2003). https://doi.org/10.1007/1-85233-854-7_2
3. Apthorpe, N., Shvartzshnaider, Y., Mathur, A., Reisman, D., Feamster, N.: Discovering smart home internet of things privacy norms using contextual integrity. In: Proceedings of the ACM on Interactive, Mobile, Wearable and Ubiquitous Technologies, vol. 2, no. 2, pp. 1–23 (2018). https://doi.org/10.1145/3214262
4. Arnold, B.: Consumer technology association. In: 5 Technology Trends to Watch (2019). https://www.cta.tech/News/Annual-Publications.aspx
5. Balta-Ozkan, N., Amerighi, O., Boteler, B.: A comparison of consumer perceptions towards smart homes in the UK, Germany and Italy: reflections for policy and future research. Technol. Anal. Strateg. Manag. **26**(10), 1176–1195 (2014). https://doi.org/10.1080/09537325.2014.975788
6. Balta-Ozkan, N., Davidson, R., Bicket, M., Whitmarsh, L.: Social barriers to the adoption of smart homes. Energy Policy **63**, 363–374 (2013). https://doi.org/10.1016/j.enpol.2013.08.043
7. Bernheim Brush, A.J., Lee, B., Mahajan, R., Agarwal, S., Saroiu, S., Dixon, C.: Home automation in the wild: challenges and opportunities. In: Proceedings of the SIGCHI Conference on Human Factors in Computing Systems, pp. 2115–2124. ACM (2011). https://doi.org/10.1145/1978942.1979249
8. Bian, J., et al.: Mining Twitter to assess the public perception of the "Internet of Things". PLoS One **11**(7), e0158450 (2016). https://doi.org/10.1371/journal.pone.0158450
9. Blue, L., Vargas, L., Traynor, P.: Hello, is it me you're looking for?: differentiating between human and electronic speakers for voice interface security. In: Proceedings of the 11th ACM Conference on Security & Privacy in Wireless and Mobile Networks, pp. 123–133. ACM (2018). https://doi.org/10.1145/3212480.3212505
10. Chan, M., Estève, D., Escriba, C., Campo, E.: A review of smart homes—present state and future challenges. Comput. Methods Programs Biomed. **91**(1), 55–81 (2008). https://doi.org/10.1016/j.cmpb.2008.02.001
11. Consumer Technology Association. Consumer Electronics Show (2019)
12. Consumer Technology Association. Consumer Resource Guides: Smart Homes. https://www.cta.tech/Consumer-Resources/Guides/Smart-Home.aspx
13. Coughlin, J.F., D'Ambrosio, L.A., Reimer, B., Pratt, M.R.: Older adult perceptions of smart home technologies: implications for research, policy & market innovations in healthcare. In: 29th Annual International Conference of the IEEE Engineering in Medicine and Biology Society, EMBS 2007, pp. 1810–1815. IEEE (2007). https://doi.org/10.1109/iembs.2007.4352665

14. Davis, F.D., Bagozzi, R.P., Warshaw, P.R.: User acceptance of computer technology: a comparison of two theoretical models. Manag. Sci. **35**(8), 982–1003 (1989). https://doi.org/10.1287/mnsc.35.8.982
15. Demiris, G., et al.: Older adults' attitudes towards and perceptions of 'smart home' technologies: a pilot study. Med. Inform. Internet Med. **29**(2), 87–94 (2004). https://doi.org/10.1080/14639230410001684387
16. Demiris, G., Hensel, B.K.: Technologies for an aging society: a systematic review of "smart home" applications. Yearb. Med. Inform. **17**(01), 33–40 (2008). https://doi.org/10.1055/s-0038-1638580
17. Dimitrokali, E., Mackrill, J., Jennings, P., Khanna, S., Harris, V., Cain, R.: Exploring homeowners' perception and experiences in using a domestic smart home heating controller. Indoor Built Environ. **24**(7), 1010–1032 (2015). https://doi.org/10.1177/1420326x15606186
18. Dorai, G., Houshmand, S., Baggili, I.: I know what you did last summer: your smart home internet of things and your iphone forensically ratting you out. In: Proceedings of the 13th International Conference on Availability, Reliability and Security, p. 49. ACM (2018). https://doi.org/10.1145/3230833.3232814
19. Drexel Smart House. Drexel University. http://www.drexelsmarthouse.com/
20. Edwards, W.K., Grinter, R.E.: At home with ubiquitous computing: seven challenges. In: Abowd, G.D., Brumitt, B., Shafer, S. (eds.) UbiComp 2001. LNCS, vol. 2201, pp. 256–272. Springer, Heidelberg (2001). https://doi.org/10.1007/3-540-45427-6_22
21. Gann, D., Barlow, J., Venables, T.: Digital Futures: Making Homes Smarter. Chartered Institute of Housing, Coventry (1999)
22. Gaul, S., Ziefle, M.: Smart home technologies: insights into generation-specific acceptance motives. In: Holzinger, A., Miesenberger, K. (eds.) USAB 2009. LNCS, vol. 5889, pp. 312–332. Springer, Heidelberg (2009). https://doi.org/10.1007/978-3-642-10308-7_22
23. Gibbs, W.W.: As we may live. Sci. Am. **283**(5), 36–40 (2000). https://doi.org/10.1038/scientificamerican1100-36
24. Google Trends. https://trends.google.com/trends/
25. Harper, R.: Inside the Smart Home. Springer, Heidelberg (2003). https://doi.org/10.1007/b97527
26. Jensen, R.H., Strengers, Y., Kjeldskov, J., Nicholls, L., Skov, M.B.: Designing the desirable smart home: a study of household experiences and energy consumption impacts. In: Proceedings of the 2018 CHI Conference on Human Factors in Computing Systems, p. 4. ACM (2018). https://doi.org/10.1145/3173574.3173578
27. Kidd, C.D., et al.: The aware home: a living laboratory for ubiquitous computing research. In: Streitz, N.A., Siegel, J., Hartkopf, V., Konomi, S. (eds.) CoBuild 1999. LNCS, vol. 1670, pp. 191–198. Springer, Heidelberg (1999). https://doi.org/10.1007/10705432_17
28. Kientz, J.A., Patel, S.N., Jones, B., Price, E.D., Mynatt, E.D., Abowd, G.D.: The Georgia tech aware home. In: In CHI 2008 Extended Abstracts on Human Factors In Computing Systems, pp. 3675–3680. ACM (2008). https://doi.org/10.1145/1358628.1358911
29. Lau, J., Zimmerman, B., Schaub, F.: Alexa, are you listening?: privacy perceptions, concerns and privacy-seeking behaviors with smart speakers. In: Proceedings of the ACM on Human-Computer Interaction, vol. 2, no. CSCW, p. 102 (2018). https://doi.org/10.1145/3274371
30. Marr, B.: The Best Must-Have Smart Home Gadgets Available Today. Forbes (2018). https://www.forbes.com/sites/bernardmarr/2018/09/10/the-best-must-have-smart-home-gadgets-available-today/#486d5fdf18c8
31. Mihailidis, A., Cockburn, A., Longley, C., Boger, J.: The acceptability of home monitoring technology among community-dwelling older adults and baby boomers. Assist. Technol. **20**(1), 1–12 (2008). https://doi.org/10.1080/10400435.2008.10131927

32. Nikou, S.: Consumers' perceptions on smart home and smart living. In: Twenty-sixth European Conference on Information Systems (ECIS 2018), Portsmouth, UK (2018)
33. Norman, D.A.: The Invisible Computer: Why Good Products Can Fail, the Personal Computer Is so Complex, and Information Appliances Are the Solution. MIT Press, Cambridge (1998)
34. Rainie, L., Duggan, M.: Privacy and Information Sharing. Pew Research Center, December 2015. http://www.pewinternet.org/2016/01/14/2016/Privacy-and-Information-Sharing/
35. Rogers, E.M.: Diffusion of Innovations, 4th edn. Free Press, New York (1995)
36. Solaimani, S., Keijzer-Broers, W., Bouwman, H.: What we do–and don't–know about the smart home: an analysis of the smart home literature. Indoor Built Environ. **24**(3), 370–383 (2015). https://doi.org/10.1177/1420326x13516350
37. Venkatesh, A.: Computers and other interactive technologies for the home. Commun. ACM **39**(12), 47–54 (1996). https://doi.org/10.1145/240483.240491
38. Venkatesh, V., Morris, M.G., Davis, G.B., Davis, F.D.: User acceptance of information technology: toward a unified view. MIS Q. 425–478 (2003). https://doi.org/10.2307/30036540
39. Venkatesh, V., Thong, J.Y., Xu, X.: Consumer acceptance and use of information technology: extending the unified theory of acceptance and use of technology. MIS Q. **36**, 157–178 (2012). https://doi.org/10.2307/41410412
40. Weiser, M.: The computer for the 21st century. Sci. Am. **265**(3), 94–104 (1991). https://doi.org/10.1038/scientificamerican0991-94
41. Wilkowska, W., Ziefle, M., Himmel, S.: Perceptions of personal privacy in smart home technologies: do user assessments vary depending on the research method? In: Tryfonas, T., Askoxylakis, I. (eds.) HAS 2015. LNCS, vol. 9190, pp. 592–603. Springer, Cham (2015). https://doi.org/10.1007/978-3-319-20376-8_53
42. Wilson, C., Hargreaves, T., Hauxwell-Baldwin, R.: Benefits and risks of smart home technologies. Energy Policy **103**, 72–83 (2017). https://doi.org/10.1016/j.enpol.2016.12.047
43. Zheng, S., Apthorpe, N., Chetty, M., Feamster, N.: User perceptions of smart home IoT privacy. In: Proceedings of the ACM on Human-Computer Interaction, vol. 2, no. CSCW, p. 200 (2018). https://doi.org/10.1145/3274469

Managing Changes Initiated by Industrial Big Data Technologies: A Technochange Management Model

Fei Xing[1(✉)], Guochao Peng[1], Tian Liang[1], Simin Zuo[1], and Shuyang Li[2]

[1] Sun Yat-sen University, Panyu District, Guangzhou 510000, China
xingf5@mail2.sysu.edu.cn
[2] The University of Sheffield, Sheffield S10 2TN, UK

Abstract. With the adoption of Internet of Things and advanced data analytical technologies in manufacturing firms, the industrial sector has launched an evolutionary journey toward the 4th industrial revolution, or so called Industry 4.0. Industrial big data is a core component to realize the vision of Industry 4.0. However, the implementation and usage of industrial big data tools in manufacturing firms will not merely be a technical endeavor, but can also lead to a thorough management reform. By means of a comprehensive review of literature related to Industry 4.0, smart manufacturing, industrial big data, information systems (IS) and technochange management, this paper aims to analyze potential changes triggered by the application of industrial big data in manufacturing firms, from technological, individual and organizational perspectives. Furthermore, in order to drive these changes more effectively and eliminate potential resistance, a conceptual technochange management model was developed and proposed. Drawn upon theories reported in literature of IS technochange management, this model proposed four types of interventions that can be used to copy with changes initiated by industrial big data technologies, including human process intervention, techno-structural intervention, human resources management intervention and strategic intervention. This model will be of interests and value to practitioners and researchers concerned with business reforms triggered by Industry 4.0 in general and by industrial big data technologies in particular.

Keywords: Industry 4.0 · Industrial big data · Technochange management · Interventions · Conceptual model

1 Introduction

Since 2010s, a wide range of innovative and advanced information and communication technologies (ICTs) have emerged in our society, such as internet of things (IoT), cyber-physical-systems (CPS), advanced sensor technology, cloud computing, big data, and artificial intelligence (AI). These technologies are increasingly integrated into the manufacturing industry, and so are shifting the traditional mode of production toward smart manufacturing [1, 2].

© Springer Nature Switzerland AG 2019
N. Streitz and S. Konomi (Eds.): HCII 2019, LNCS 11587, pp. 75–87, 2019.
https://doi.org/10.1007/978-3-030-21935-2_7

The basic concept of smart manufacturing is an intelligent production pattern, in which original physical manufacturing devices are enriched with embedded items (e.g. sensors, actuators, electronic tags, etc.) that are connected to the network wirelessly [3]. In this context, a wide variety of data with respect to production process can be acquired and collected continuously in real time, and then be cleaned, correlated, stored, mined and analyzed. Moreover, the analytical results are fed back to different production devices to realize precision manufacturing and machine self-monitoring/control/maintenance. As a result, this smart manufacturing paradigm can shorten product lead-time, enable personalized, flexible and decentralized production, facilitate decision making, and maximize the utilization of resources [4].

In order to guide the national manufacturing industry to realize these benefits, the German government initially proposed a strategic plan named "Industry 4.0" at Hannover Messe in 2013. This strategy has since then been widely appreciated and adopted by other nations in Europe, and even countries across other continents (e.g. USA, China, Japan) [5]. In light of this, researchers highlighted that industrial big data plays a crucial role in any Industry 4.0 initiatives [6–9].

It is important to stress that, the implementation and usage of industrial big data will not only bring in new technological upgrades, but more importantly can also lead to essential changes and organizational reforms in manufacturing companies. Historically, changes caused by the usage of new information systems are often subjected to various internal resistance and hindrance, which can lead to major technical and business failure [10]. For the implementation of Enterprise Resource Planning (ERP) systems for example, anecdotal evidence showed that ERP project failure could result in hundreds of thousands of US dollars in economic loss, and more seriously could even trigger business bankruptcy [10]. Consequently, researchers from the information systems (IS) field highlighted that successful implementation of IT/IS projects in enterprises should be supported by adequate change management theories and methods, particularly technochange management theories, which refers to theoretical concepts and methods used to handle technology-driven organizational changes [11–13]. It can therefore be argued that these technochange management theories will also be important and applicable to the implementation and usage of industrial big data applications.

However, an extensive review of the current literature showed that most studies in the field of industrial big data focus mainly on technical and engineering aspects, like algorithm optimization [14, 15], data modeling development [16, 17], data and cyber security [18, 19], or basic conceptual introduction such as concept interpretation and generalization, benefits and challenges of the usage of industrial big data [20, 21]. In fact, success of industrial big data or Industry 4.0 strategy depends on the maturity of related technologies mentioned above, however, technochange management theory and approaches from an IS perspective are arguably important in the process of technical implementation and business transformation. In light of this discussion, there is currently very limited understanding and research related to changes derived from the implementation and usage of industrial big data in a manufacturing context and suitable methods to handle these changes. Therefore, this paper aims to fill this research gap through identifying potential changes caused by industrial big data implementation and investigating effective interventions that can help manufacturing organizations to cope with these emerging changes.

The results derived from this study will be important to researchers and business managers who are interested in not just the development of industrial big data and realization of Industry 4.0, but more crucially to the successful transformation for the whole manufacturing enterprise owing to the application of industrial big data. The rest of the paper is structured as follows: the next section presents the nature of industrial big data. Subsequently, an explanation of IS technochange management is given, followed by a discussion of changes triggered by industrial big data and effective interventions to cope with these changes. Finally, a theoretical technochange management model is presented with conclusions drawn.

2   Nature of Industrial Big Data

Ever since the beginning of industrial revolution, advances in technology has resulted in severe changes and improvements in social development, particularly in the manufacturing industry. In the past, the first industrial revolution was the manufacturing of goods with machines, that is well-known as mechanization. The second industrial revolution was the realization of mass production with the assistance of electric power, followed by the digital or 3rd industrial revolution, in which electronics and IT were adopted in production [22]. At present, due to rapid development and wide application

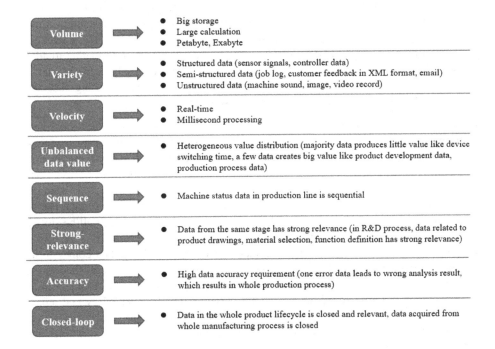

Fig. 1. Characteristics of industrial big data

of cyber physical system (CPS), internet of things (IoT), advanced sensor technology, communication technology, computer and science technology, these technologies are increasingly adopted and deployed in manufacturing field. Therefore, manufacturing industry is experiencing a major leap forward, which can be considered as the 4th industrial revolution or Industry 4.0 [23].

To be specific, for instance, under the help of advanced sensor technology and communication technology, various types of sensors and actuators are installed in different devices and production lines, tremendous amounts of industrial data particularly real-time machine data (e.g. switching time, machine logs, real-time alarm, temperature) and product data (e.g. quality assurance, raw material codes) is collected, transferred and stored in cloud server [24]. Moreover, those collected industrial data are scrubbed, screened and analyzed by the aid of cloud computing and relative data process technology like machine learning, deep learning approaches (e.g. navie bayes, convolution neural network, k-means clustering algorithm) [25]. Furthermore, data analysis results will be fed back to the production process in order to realize intelligent control, smart deployment, predictive diagnosis and precise management over raw materials, production device, detection device and even the whole manufacturing process, which is considered as the vision of Industry 4.0. Under this circumstance, there is no doubt that industrial big data plays and will continue to play an increasingly important role toward realizing Industry 4.0.

When many authors (e.g. [24, 25]) emphasized on the production sets of industrial big data, other researchers indicated that industrial big data actually contains a much wider coverage that goes beyond the boundary of production units. In particular, Yan et al. argued that industrial big data refers to all types of data generated from the whole product life cycle, covering sales, product design and development, production, procurement, supply chain, stock control, delivery, and after-sales services [26]. Lee et al. pointed out that industrial big data also includes Internet data related to market trends, customer behavior, and competitor performance [20]. A further analysis of the literature [14, 16, 24, 27] suggested that, these various categories of industrial big data can be generated and collected from three types of sources, including:

- Management information systems. A large amount of industrial big data is derived from internal management information systems like ERPs, supply chain management (SCM) systems, customer relationship management (CRM) systems, manufacturing execution systems (MES), product lifecycle management (PLM) systems, etc. For example, there are lots of product design data in PLM, such as product drawings, CAD, CAE, and bill of materials (BOM) of product. Besides, data related to operation and customer like staff behavior, KPIs, stock records can all be stored in management information systems.
- Shop-floor machines. The complex component of industrial big data comes from shop-floor machines. The machine data is mainly acquired and collected from various sensors that are integrated in production lines, such as data of machine temperature, rotating speed, fault detection, product quality, availability and repair rate. In reality, shop-floor machine data is regarded having three characteristics, that is, real-time, dynamism and uncertainty. At present, large amounts of machines are

working in factory synchronously. Under this circumstance, shop-floor machine data has the fastest growth and vital significance in maintaining the machine health.

- External environment. External data is the third category of industrial big data from the perspective of data source, and refers to data that is not included in the enterprise in-house systems. According to the study conducted by McKinsey, nearly 90% external data is generated from internet, including internet market data (e.g. news, blog, etc.), raw material data, data related to competitor's product, etc. [28].

Interestingly, compared with the popular word 'big data' that discussed widely by both academic and the media, industrial big data possesses partial overlapped characteristics (e.g. volume, variety and velocity) as big data, but it still has its unique features, for instance, sequence, strong-relevance, accuracy and closed-loop [26], as detailed in Fig. 1.

3 IS Technochange Management

The concept of technochange was firstly coined by Markus, who defined that "*Using IT in ways that can trigger major organizational changes creates high-risk, potentially high-reward situations, that called technochange*" [12]. A technochange management initiative is not merely an IT-based project or an organizational change program, but the combination of both (Table 1 summarizes their differences in detail). Generally, a pure IT project usually has a strong technological focus on improving technical performance (e.g. processing speed, reliability, functionality) of the system, but may pay less attention to organizational, management and human-related problems. Meanwhile, a pure organizational change program pays close attention to people and business issues, but may have nothing to do with the adoption of new technologies [12, 29]. In contrast, a technochange management program is characterized by completeness, effectiveness and feasibility, and combines technical solutions with considerations regarding organizational structure, processes, business culture, and human needs [30]. In short, a technochange management program is an integrated initiative that manages organizational changes in conjunction with the adoption and usage of information technologies.

Table 1. Technochange vs IT project and organizational change program [12]

	IT project	Organizational change program	Technochange management
Solutions	New information technology adopted	Changes of people, structure, culture, policy	Changes due to information technology implementation
Approaches	Normally led by IT manager	Normally led by CEO and HR manager	All departments of enterprise cooperate comprehensively, typically led by CEO and other branch managers collaborate together

(*continued*)

Table 1. (*continued*)

	IT project	Organizational change program	Technochange management
IT expert	Very important, manage the quality of new information technology	Insignificant	Balanced, IT expert should work with other department's managers to redesign work processes and related organizational components
Target	Technology performance (e.g. response speed, security)	Organizational performance (e.g. flat structure, a good corporate culture)	Reasonable organizational changes in conjunction with implementation of information technology (e.g. organizational structure change, job redesign, new reward system)

Under the concept of technochange management, the term "intervention" should be highlighted. An intervention can be defined as a set of sequenced and planned activities that can systematically improve organization deficiencies and members' attitudes, values, skills and interpersonal relationships, and so make the organization and its people adapt to new changes more effectively [29]. With this definition in mind, many research studies (e.g. [30, 31]) demonstrated that changes initiated by new information technologies are complicated, and so the corresponding interventions used to cope with these changes will vary according to the actual project contexts and organizational needs. For example, the adoption of ERP system emphasizes integrity and consistency of the enterprise as a whole rather than independent work among different departments [32]. In this case, past routine work and jobs will be adjusted and replaced, which needs more communication and information sharing among a variety of units within an organization and co-ordination of personnel to make sure successful application of ERP. The intervention of business process reengineering is thus often applied in ERP projects to facilitate changes related to process redesign [33]. On the other hand, employees need to use the new ERP system on a daily basis to improve their work performance. A comprehensive training program should thus be designed and used as an intervention to equip different types of users with the needed technical skills [31].

When there is a rich number of literature discussing technochange management and related interventions in an IS context, this discussion has currently not been much extended to the application of industrial big data technologies. As an important component to realize Industry 4.0, industrial big data will undoubtedly trigger essential changes and even reforms in organizations. The relevance of existing interventions to deal with these changes will also need to be further explored and considered. The next section attempts to provide further insights, derived from the literature review as well as our previous research work and practical experiences, to address these knowledge gaps.

4   Technochange Management for Industrial Big Data Applications

4.1   Potential Changes Initiated by Industrial Big Data

The application of industrial big data will inevitably trigger technological upgrades and changes in user companies. These technical changes will have substantial influences on individual's daily work, and eventually lead to profound transformation across the whole organization. This section provides a detailed profile of potential changes caused by industrial big data, respectively in technological, individual and organizational levels.

Technological Changes. As discussed in Sect. 2, industrial big data is huge in terms of volume and it has different attributes, sources and structures, which thus raise new challenges to traditional data processing and analyzing infrastructures. In order to cope, manufacturing firms need to use more updated and efficient data storage and analytical technologies to maximize the utilization of industrial big data, as outlined in Fig. 2. In particular, cloud computing technologies (such as Google File System or GFS, MapReduce) and big data processing platforms (like Hadoop) are widely perceived as driving forces to boost technological reforms, as well as to enable smart automation and predictive management, in the Industry 4.0 environment [16].

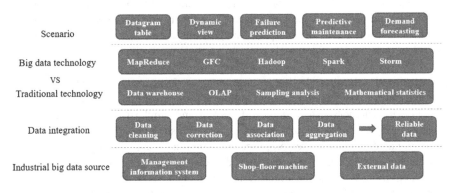

Fig. 2. Basic components of industrial big data process

Individual Changes. Hackman and Oldham proposed a job characteristics model that has impacts on employees' work satisfaction and motivation [34]. This model comprises of five core elements, namely:

- Skill variety: jobs involving a variety of skills and activities can better motivate and attract employees;
- Task identity: jobs with clearly-defined tasks and goals are more likely to lead to positive feelings of achievement;
- Task significance: jobs with clear meaning, significance and impact can make employees feel more satisfied;

- Autonomy: employees generally enjoy the level of freedom given to them to accomplish their tasks;
- Job feedback: employees want to be told when they are doing well and when they are not.

It can be argued that the intensive application of industry big data will result in changes of individual employee in all of these five elements:

- **Changes in skill variety:** many traditional jobs (e.g. product quality assurance, stock control) will be replaced by intelligent machines with support of analytical results derived from industrial big data. Employees are also required to develop and learn new skill sets, e.g. certain degree of data modelling and data analysis capabilities that can help them make better decision in work.
- **Changes in task identity & significance:** Industrial big data runs through the whole product lifecycle and connect all units together, and so making the enterprise more integrative. Individual tasks and roles will need to be refined and precisely defined. In this context, people and machines' work will coordinate and interrelate with each other. Tasks done by individuals will also have greater importance and impact organization-wide.
- **Changes in autonomy:** Analytical results and predictions derived from industrial big data tools can empower employees and allow them to have more autonomy in making work plans and decisions.
- **Changes in job feedback:** Industrial big data enables managers and front-line staff to understand better their job performance in a timely and clear manner. Meanwhile, according to the needs of enterprise, suggestions are provided based on industrial big data analysis for individuals to improve their work efficiency.

Organizational Changes. In the environment of Industry 4.0, technological and individual change will lead to profound organizational reform throughout the enterprise eventually. Researchers (e.g. [30, 31]) disclosed and emphasized that organizational change is a long-term process and cannot be accomplished in one go. According to the organizational diagnosis model proposed by Cummings and Worley [35], organizational changes can occur in four essential aspects, including organizational structure, management process, human resource systems and business strategy. The application of industrial big data can have far-reaching impacts on all of these organizational aspects:

- **Changes in organizational structure:** The application of industrial big data tools and intelligent automatic systems will reduce the demand of team leaders in shop floor and even middle managers in the tactical level. This will enable a flatter, more decentralized, and networked nature of organizational structure. In addition, new functional units and job positions (e.g. big data center, data analyst, data scientist, etc.) will also be set up to support the organization in the new technological environment.
- **Management process:** In traditional management process, managers can only adopt a reactive approach to deal with business issues when they occur. With support of predictive analysis done by industrial big data applications, managers can now become more proactive and take early actions to deal with production and business problems before they even happen.

- **Human resource systems:** Human resource systems consist of mechanisms for employing, appraising and rewarding members in the organization. Organizations should hire more staffs who has the ability to perform well in the environment of industry 4.0. Moreover, organization should provide some training course for staffs to develop data-driven awareness and data analysis skills.
- **Strategy:** Business strategy will be formulated driven by data analytical results rather than top managers' experience and intuition. As a result, resources (human, finance, technology) can be assigned and used more scientifically and efficiently.

4.2 Interventions Applied in the Usage of Industrial Big Data

It was clearly demonstrated from the above discussion that, in order to realize the full potential of industrial big data applications, individuals need to change not only their original ways of working but also their roles, behaviors and attitudes. Moreover, the organization as a whole will need to undergo severe reform in order to suit the new technological environment. Successful advancement of these individual and organizational changes can accelerate technological changes, on the contrary, it can create strong internal resistance and even lead to technical failure during the adoption of industrial big data technologies [35].

In order to copy with the changes triggered by the application of industrial big data, four types of interventions commonly adopted in IS projects can be considered and used during the adoption of industrial big data tools, namely human process interventions, technostructural interventions, human resource management interventions, and strategic interventions.

Human Process Interventions. Human process interventions derive mainly from the disciplines of psychology and it refers to actions and programs taken to improve interpersonal relations [36]. In an organization, the major aim of human process interventions is to strengthen the relationships and cooperation among employees in different departments and across all levels [36]. The basic approaches of human process interventions include team building, process consultation, organization confrontation meeting and interpersonal communication training [37]. When an organization implements an industrial big data application, it requires all units to work together along the entire product life cycle. Human process interventions can thus help to break down departmental boundaries and barriers and so facilitate effective usage of industrial big data tools organization-wide.

Technostructural Interventions. Technostructural interventions are concerned with both new technologies and structure of the organization [38]. The main purpose of technostructural intervention is to change and improve the organizational structure according to the needs of the changing technology environment. Typical technostructural interventions include structural redesign, downsizing, business process reengineering, high-involvement, job enrichment, etc. [38]. In particular, structural redesign and business process reengineering are two typical and important interventions applied in IS projects in general and industrial big data projects in particular.

84   F. Xing et al.

Human Resource Management Interventions. Human resource management interventions are associated with issues like hiring, appraising, rewarding, developing and supporting employees in organizations [35]. With the implementation of industrial big data tools, traditional labor-intensive production mode will be replaced by smart manufacturing mode gradually. This will put forward a demand for new personal skills and new knowledge of employees. Human resource management interventions, such as goal re-setting, reward system redesign, coaching and mentoring can encourage employees to develop new skills, enable people with the right quality to be selected, and ensure staff with good performance to be rewarded in the new technological environment.

Strategic Interventions. Strategic interventions are associated with the changing of business goals and transforming the organization to keep pace with internal and external changing environments [39]. Specifically, strategic interventions include organization redesign, integrated strategic change, culture redesign, dynamic strategy making, etc. [40]. As discussed earlier, industrial big data applications will have long-term and profound impacts on enterprise strategy making. Therefore, organization needs to have a long-term plan based on their business strategy rather than concerning about short-term needs. Strategic interventions (especially culture redesign and dynamic strategy making) can be applied by manufacturing companies to ensure they have a healthy organizational culture and strategic decision making environment to deploy and use industrial big data applications effectively in the long-term plan.

4.3 Technochange Management Model

Based on analysis and discussions made above, a technochange management model for industrial big data is proposed and developed, as shown in Fig. 3.

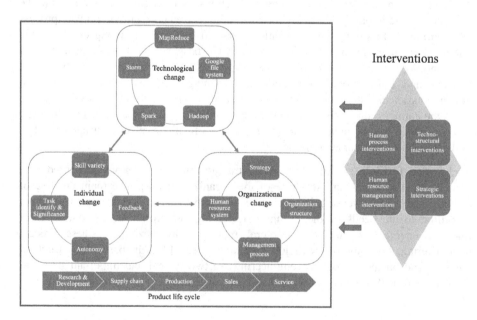

Fig. 3. Conceptual technochange management model for industrial big data

As shown in the model, for any manufacturing firms, technology, individual and organization are closely interrelated with each other. As such, technological changes can always lead to essential changes in individual and organizational levels. Moreover, individual and organizational changes can in turn either facilitate or hinder technological changes in enterprises. In order to cope with potential resistance to these changes, the four types of technochange management techniques and interventions will need to be selected and used as relevant in industrial big data projects.

5 Conclusion

For nearly two decades, the concept of technochange management has attracted the attention of both IS researchers and practitioners. It is arguable that effective management of individual and organizational changes can substantially increase the possibility of IS success. It is deemed that this argument can be highly applicable and suitable to the context of industry 4.0 in general and the usage of industrial big data tools in particular, but it is hard to retrieve current literature to support and explore this phenomenon. We therefore try to explore in this paper different types of potential changes initiated by the adoption of industrial big data technologies, as well as to demonstrate how a variety of technochange techniques and interventions can be useful in this context. A conceptual technochange management model is then developed and proposed to sum up these insights. More importantly, this conceptual model can serve as a theoretical foundation to guide future research on this topic, and can also be used as the basis for high-level change management planning in practice. We admit that technochange management in the context of industrial big data projects is a very complicated topic, and that the proposed model is relatively simple. However, we attempt to use this paper to bridge the concepts of technochange management, industry 4.0 and industrial big data, and hope more in-depth research can be done on this increasingly important topic in the near future.

References

1. Wan, J., Cai, H., Zhou, K.: Industrie 4.0: enabling technologies. In: 2014 International Conference on Intelligent Computing and Internet of Things (ICIT), pp. 135−140. IEEE (2015)
2. Zheng, P., et al.: Smart manufacturing systems for Industry 4.0: conceptual framework, scenarios, and future perspectives. Front. Mech. Eng. 1−14 (2018)
3. Lucke, D., Constantinescu, C., Westkämper, E.: Smart factory-a step towards the next generation of manufacturing. In: Mitsuishi, M., Ueda, K., Kimura, F. (eds.) Manufacturing Systems and Technologies for the New Frontier, pp. 115–118. Springer, London (2008). https://doi.org/10.1007/978-1-84800-267-8
4. Kang, H.S., et al.: Smart manufacturing: Past research, present findings, and future directions. Int. J. Precis. Eng. Manuf. Green Technol. 3(1), 111–128 (2016)
5. Gilchrist, A.: Introducing industry 4.0. In: Industry 4.0, pp. 195–215. Apress, Berkeley (2016)

6. Li, J., Tao, F., Cheng, Y., et al.: Big data in product lifecycle management. Int. J. Adv. Manuf. Technol. **81**(1–4), 667–684 (2015)

7. Kang, H.S., Lee, J.Y., Choi, S.S., et al.: Smart manufacturing: past research, present findings, and future directions. Int. J. Precis. Eng. Manuf. Green Technol. **3**(1), 111–128 (2016)

8. Santos, M.Y., Sa, J.O., Andrade, C., et al.: A big data system supporting bosch braga industry 4.0 strategy. Int. J. Inf. Manag. **37**(6), 750–760 (2017)

9. Raguseo, E.: Big data technologies: an empirical investigation on their adoption, benefits and risks for companies. Int. J. Inf. Manag. **38**(1), 187–195 (2018)

10. Peng, G., Baptista Nunes, M.: Identification and assessment of risks associated with ERP post-implementation in China. J. Enterp. Inf. Manag. **22**(5), 587–614 (2009)

11. Aladwani, A.M.: Change management strategies for successful ERP implementation. Bus. Process Manag. J. **7**(3), 266–275 (2001)

12. Markus, M.L.: Technochange management: using it to drive organizational change. J. Inf. Technol. **19**(1), 4–20 (2004)

13. Harison, E., Boonstra, A.: Essential competencies for technochange management: towards an assessment model. Int. Inf. Manag. **29**(4), 283–294 (2009)

14. Ding, X., Tian, Y., Yu, Y.: A real-time big data gathering algorithm based on indoor wireless sensor networks for risk analysis of industrial operations. IEEE Trans. Industr. Inf. **12**(3), 1232–1242 (2016)

15. Minor, B.D., Doppa, J.R., Cook, D.J.: Learning activity predictors from sensor data: algorithms, evaluation, and applications. IEEE Trans. Knowl. Data Eng. **29**(12), 2744–2757 (2017)

16. O'Donovan, P., Leahy, K., Bruton, K., O'Sullivan, D.T.: An industrial big data pipeline for data-driven analytics maintenance applications in large-scale smart manufacturing facilities. J. Big Data **2**(1), 25 (2015)

17. Liu, Q., Qin, S.J., Chai, T.: Unevenly sampled dynamic data modeling and monitoring with an industrial application. IEEE Trans. Ind. Inform. **PP**(99), 1 (2017)

18. Esposito, C., Castiglione, A., Martini, B., Choo, K.K.R.: Cloud manufacturing: security, privacy, and forensic concerns. IEEE Cloud Comput. **3**(4), 16–22 (2016)

19. Flatt, H., Schriegel, S., Jasperneite, J., Trsek, H., Adamczyk, H.: Analysis of the cyber-security of industry 4.0 technologies based on RAMI 4.0 and identification of requirements. In: 2016 IEEE 21st International Conference on Emerging Technologies and Factory Automation (ETFA), pp. 1–4. IEEE, September 2016

20. Lee, J., Ardakani, H.D., Yang, S., Bagheri, B.: Industrial big data analytics and cyber-physical systems for future maintenance & service innovation. Procedia CIRP **38**, 3–7 (2015)

21. Wan, J., et al.: A manufacturing big data solution for active preventive maintenance. IEEE Trans. Industr. Inf. **13**(4), 2039–2047 (2017)

22. Lasi, H., Fettke, P., Kemper, H.G., Feld, T., Hoffmann, M.: Industry 4.0. Bus. Inf. Syst. Eng. **6**(4), 239–242 (2014)

23. Shrouf, F., Ordieres, J., Miragliotta, G.: Smart factories in Industry 4.0: a review of the concept and of energy management approached in production based on the Internet of Things paradigm. In: 2014 IEEE International Conference on Industrial Engineering and Engineering Management (IEEM), pp. 697–701. IEEE, December 2014

24. Xu, X., Hua, Q.: Industrial big data analysis in smart factory: current status and research strategies. IEEE Access **5**, 17543–17551 (2017)

25. Najafabadi, M.M., Villanustre, F., Khoshgoftaar, T.M., Seliya, N., Wald, R., Muharemagic, E.: Deep learning applications and challenges in big data analytics. J. Big Data **2**(1), 1 (2015)

26. Yan, J., Meng, Y., Lu, L., Li, L.: Industrial big data in an industry 4.0 environment: challenges, schemes, and applications for predictive maintenance. IEEE Access **5**, 23484–23491 (2017)
27. Mourtzis, D., Vlachou, E., Milas, N.: Industrial big data as a result of IoT adoption in manufacturing. Procedia CIRP **55**, 290–295 (2016)
28. Manyika, J., et al.: Unlocking the Potential of the Internet of Things. McKinsey Global Institute (2015)
29. Markus, L., Bashein, R.: Interorganizational Technochange: How to Make Successful Choices in Electronic Partner Integration. Society for Information Management, Advanced practices council (2006)
30. Mattia, A.: A multi-dimensional view of socio-technical information systems research and technochange. Rev. Bus. Inf. Syst. **15**(4), 11–18 (2011)
31. Jackson, S., Philip, G.: A techno-cultural emergence perspective on the management of techno-change. Int. J. Inf. Manage. **30**(5), 445–456 (2010)
32. Staehr, L., Shanks, G., Seddon, P.B.: An explanatory framework for achieving business benefits from ERP systems. J. Assoc. Inf. Syst. **13**(6), 424 (2012)
33. Chen, I.J.: Planning for ERP systems: analysis and future trend. Bus. Process Manag. J. **7**(5), 374–386 (2001)
34. Hackman, J.R., Oldham, G.R.: Motivation through the design of work: test of a theory. Organ. Behav. Hum. Perform. **16**(2), 250–279 (1976)
35. Cummings, T.G., Worley, C.G.: Organization development and change. Cengage learning (2014)
36. Sturman, M.C.: Implications of utility analysis adjustments for estimates of human resource intervention value. J. Manag. **26**(2), 281–299 (2000)
37. Jackson, S.E., Schuler, R.S.: Understanding human resource management in the context of organizations and their environments. Annu. Rev. Psychol. **46**(1), 237–264 (1995)
38. Bunce, D., West, M.A.: Stress management and innovation interventions at work. Hum. Relat. **49**(2), 209–232 (1996)
39. Rajagopalan, N., Spreitzer, G.M.: Toward a theory of strategic change: a multi-lens perspective and integrative framework. Acad. Manag. Rev. **22**(1), 48–79 (1997)
40. Herrmann, P., Nadkarni, S.: Managing strategic change: the duality of CEO personality. Strateg. Manag. J. **35**(9), 1318–1342 (2014)

Designing a Cyber Physical System Prototype for the Leaching Process in Producing High-Purity Materials

Simin Zuo[1(✉)], Guochao Peng[1], Yuanshan Zhang[1], Fei Xing[1], Le Qin[1], and Jiangfeng Tang[2]

[1] Sun Yat-sen University, Panyu District, Guangzhou, China
zuosm@mail2.sysu.edu.cn
[2] Guangdong Huanuo Qingeng Material Science Co. Ltd., Guangzhou, China

Abstract. Accompanied with the emerging concept of Industry 4.0, manufacturing companies in any sectors are attempting to transform their hitherto production equipment into cyber physical systems (CPSs), with the aims of improving efficiency across the whole production line and enhancing core business competitiveness. Focusing on the material manufacturing sector, this paper presents and discusses the design of a CPS prototype used in the leaching process for producing high-purity materials. This prototype contains three components/layers, namely sensor installation for data collection, wireless data transmission using ZigBee, and finally data storage and visualization. This CPS prototype design is particularly useful and practically transferrable to material manufacturing companies, especially those involving high purity material production, during their journey towards realizing Industry 4.0.

Keywords: Prototype · Cyber physical system · High purity materials · Smart factory · Data visualization

1 Introduction

The term Industry 4.0 was firstly corned and proposed at the 2012 Hannover Fair [1]. This concept has then brought the world into the trend of the new generation of industrial reform. The architecture of Industry 4.0, including sensors, Internet of Things (IoT), cyber physical systems (CPS), cloud-based data integration, standardized intelligent control, and visualized monitoring, allows human beings to communicate with physical items (both production machines and even end products) more effectively [2–4].

On the other hand, throughout the world, high-purity materials, which plays a crucial role in various fields and supports the development of a large number of high-tech industries, have penetrated into each part of social life, national economy and national defense construction. More specifically, high-purity materials have a variety of uses, from daily necessities (e.g. solar cells, non-toxic iron pots, decorative materials, etc.) to modern high-tech fields such as high-purity metals, alloys, graphite, semiconductors and insulators [5]. The largest application field for high-purity materials is the microelectronics industry [5]. With the accelerated development of science and

© Springer Nature Switzerland AG 2019
N. Streitz and S. Konomi (Eds.): HCII 2019, LNCS 11587, pp. 88–98, 2019.
https://doi.org/10.1007/978-3-030-21935-2_8

technology and economic construction, the global demand for high-purity materials has been increasing substantially. And the requirements for the performance and quality of high-purity materials will also become higher and higher.

Based on the importance of high purity materials, the manufacturing industry of high purity materials should develop towards intelligent manufacturing under the impetus of industry 4.0 environment. CPS is the core of industry 4.0 and intelligent manufacturing. The main roles of CPS are to fulfill the agile and dynamic requirements of production, and to improve the effectiveness and efficiency of the entire industry [6].

Even today, there are many fields of applications for CPS, such as medical equipment, driving safety and driver assistance systems for automobiles, industrial process control and automation systems, assistance systems for controlling the power supply in terms of optimized use of renewable energies [1]. These are all applications of CPS in manufacturing: Ford Motor Company's service-oriented architecture [7]; Cloud manufacturing jointly researched between KTH and Sandvik, Sweden [8]; FESTO preindustrial system, MiniProd [9, 10]; Model-driven manufacturing systems [11]. In recent years, research and applications of CPS have been active in such areas like transportation, smart home, robotic surgery, aviation, defence, critical infrastructure, etc. [7]. However, smart manufacturing technology, especially CPS, is not widely used and discussed in the production of high-purity materials.

Therefore, this paper proposes a CPS prototype system to realize data measurement, storage and real-time monitoring of sensors installed on high-purity material mechanical equipment. All the data generated by the high-purity material production process hides huge unpredictable value. The establishment of CPS will be beneficial to optimize the production process and promote the development of high purity material industry. This paper presents and discusses the technical features and functions of this prototype, which can serve as a model to be followed by researchers and practitioners in the field.

2 CPS and High-Purity Material Production

2.1 The Importance of CPS in the Production of High-Purity Materials

In the production of most high-purity materials without intelligent transformation, although the production process in conventional laboratories and factories is controlled by mechanical equipment, it is difficult to monitor changes of all process parameters in real time. If all the data cannot be monitored synchronously, then real-time changes in the production process cannot be mastered efficiently, and the quality of high purity materials cannot be well controlled, thus resulting in the decline of output value and quality. When a problem occurs, information related to the problem is collected and an analysis will be conducted subsequently to find out the cause of the problem [12].

Because CPSs combine information and materials, decentralization and autonomy play an important role in improving the overall industrial performance [13]. CPSs are capable of increasing productivity, fostering growth, modifying the workforce performance, and producing higher-quality goods with lower costs via the collection and analysis of malicious data [14]. Therefore, it is urgent for factories to establish an innovative, reliable and easy-to-use CPS prototype system to control material leaching and other production processes. In this way, the output and quality of high purity materials can be guaranteed, and the competitiveness of enterprises can be enhanced, thus supporting the development of high technology.

According to the current literature, studies on material purification (e.g. [15–17]) and CPS development (e.g. [18–20]) are two separated fields of research. As such, there is a lack of study to bridge the gap and consider CPS development and usage in the production of high purity materials.

2.2   Using CPS in the Leaching Process of High-Purity Material Production

The production of high purity materials is the core of the development of high purity materials industry, which realizes the deep integration between information system and manufacturing process, one information system and another information system, and results an intelligent manufacturing system through CPS and intelligent manufacturing technology. The system can control the whole process of manufacturing with timely feedback information improving the competitiveness of the industry, and promote the development of high purity materials industry.

In the process of making high-purity materials, material purification is an indispensable and crucial step, which controls the purity and precision of the final high-purity materials. During the process of material purification, it not only controls the amount of material input and output, but also the time of reaction, reaction temperature etc. Those can affect the final quality of high-purity materials. And it can be said that the leaching process is the most important milestone in material purification, and the success of the leaching process also means the success of high-purity material production.

In that case, it's extremely important for us to design a CPS prototype of the leaching process to realize the control of the most important part of the high purity material manufacturing, due to the important role of leaching process. In our research, based on the requirements of material purification of high-purity material enterprises, the existing mechanical equipment is modified, and sensors needed in the process of material purification are added to collect and analyze data. Finally, the prototype system design of real-time display and monitoring of temperature, speed, environment and other changes is realized.

3   Design of the Prototype

3.1   Prototype Architecture

In order to transform the original high-purity material leaching equipment into CPS, our designed prototype contains three components/layers, namely sensor installation for data collection, wireless data transmission using ZigBee, and finally data storage and visualization.

The specific hardware frame and the flow of information transition are directly shown in Fig. 1. The collected data is obtained from two types of sensors, including temperature sensors and PH sensors, which are added into the original high-purity equipment. Subsequently, the data of each equipment will be sent to the corresponding processing terminal. Then all the processing terminals transfer the processed date to the ZigBee gateway through ZigBee communication. Finally, the whole data is obtained in PC via USB interface from the ZigBee gateway for further data processing and analysis.

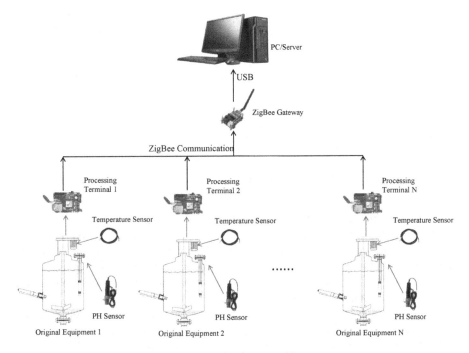

Fig. 1. Prototype hardware architecture

3.2   Sensor Deployment

To maximize the utilization of spaces of the container, all the used sensors (e.g. temperature and PH sensors) are assembled as an integral unit. The modified device is shown in Fig. 2. As the composite sensor unit is fixed inside the container, the tightness can be pursued by the less intervention during the production process. Furthermore, the data processing terminal will read the digital data automatically and send it to data base timely, instead of relying on manual measurement in traditional manner.

Temperature and PH values are two very important objects for our leaching monitoring, so we must choose suitable sensors for obtaining them. Moreover, the ADC (analog-to-digital conversion) module is needed, since the terminal or PC only process and store the digital information rather than analog information.

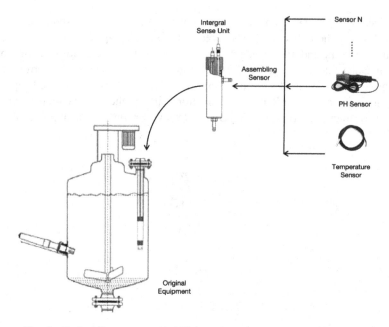

Fig. 2. Embedding sensors into high-purity material leaching equipment

For temperature measurement, DS18B20 (a contact temperature sensor with digital signal output) was selected and used. This DS18B20 sensor is not just small in size but is also very convenient to use. All sensing components and conversion circuits are integrated in a circuit which looks like a triode. The probe is directly contacted with the solution in the vessel of which temperature values can be obtained and transferred to the MCU through the DuPont line.

For the PH sensor, its working principle is closely related to the primary battery system, that is, the PH value is calculated by the voltage. Since the voltage generated by the PH sensor is small, it needs to be amplified before sending to the MCU. Here we design the ADC module on the MCU to obtain the ultimate digital PH value.

These sensors are very important direct data source for the system, just like sensing organs for people. However, these sensors as electronic measuring instruments themselves, have measurement errors caused by thermal noise, which naturally have a great influence on the accuracy of the measurement results, thereby causing trouble for analysis after data collection. Therefore, we need to make robust correction to the collected data, so that the random error can be smaller, that is to say, a filter is added after these measuring instruments.

3.3   Wireless Transmission

In order not to miss any critical data of the leaching process, we need to measure the data of the solutions in multiple chemical reaction vessels at each step. It means that each container needs to be fitted with a temperature and PH sensor accordingly. After the leaching equipment is embedded with sensors, we need to distinguish the data collected by these sensors in different containers and integrate the data for subsequent processing and analysis. To this end, we use a star network (Fig. 3) to solve the above problems. Since wired communication requires a large number of interfaces and is likely to cause wiring chaos, we choose wireless communication as the communication method between network nodes in combination with the actual production environment. This also makes it easy to add network nodes during subsequent device transitions.

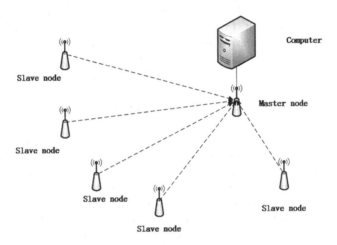

Fig. 3. Star network

ZigBee [21] is a low-power wireless communication technology based on the IEEE802.15.4 [22] standard. The development environment under Windows is IAR Embedded Workbench. There is a lot of open source code here, which greatly reduces our workload, so we can easily achieve wireless data transmission under various conditions. This is convenient for the expansion of the prototype.

Although the CC2530 [23] chip on the ZigBee development board is only a microprocessor with the weak computing power, it is enough to support the ZigBee technology. In addition, it communicate with the temperature sensor to read the temperature data, and communicate with the ADC module to obtain the converted value and convert it to PH value through the corresponding function relationship. Also it can do some mathematical calculations as the filter processing. Combined with the terminal, the raw data collected by the sensor is first transferred to the CC2530 chip for filtering. Then the filtered data is ready for wireless transmission. Finally the data collected at each slave nodes in the star network is aggregated into the master node of the star network by wireless transmission.

3.4   PC-End Software

After the data collected at each slave nodes is aggregated into the master node of the star network by wireless transmission, the next question is how to transfer the overall data to the computer. Here we took the serial communication technology for use, using the CH340G chip on the development board to connect to the USB port of the PC. The key is that the computer should know how to read the data form the MCU, so that the computer is possible to carry out storage and realize real-time data visualization.

Golang is an open source programming language that makes it easy to build simple, reliable, and efficient software [24]. So we choose Golang to achieve data transmission. Next, we use the serial tool written in Golang to read the incoming data from the device received by the computer port for further data analysis. Goserial is a simple-go package to allow users to read and write from the serial port as a stream of bytes. This allows the data in the MCU to be transferred to the computer for later processing.

After completing the data transfer from the device to the local computer, in order to facilitate the future data analysis process, we choose to transfer the data read in the computer software to the database for storage via the TCP connection. The TCP protocol is a connection-oriented, reliable, byte stream based transport layer communication protocol running on the fourth layer of the TCP/IP network model, so reliability can be guaranteed during data transmission. The data will be stored in the database of the remote computer, so that a centralized node allows departments of different functions to connect and complete their tasks, and achieve data sharing.

The above steps complete the collection, reading and storage of the data. The next step is to implement data visualization. Because the front-end interface is written by the Java language, the open source JFreeChart package is used to achieve data visualization, and the WebService interface is used to obtain the data in the database. Finally, the data is parsed into the data types available for JFreeChart through Google's gson parsing package.

To realize real-time visualization of data, we use JFreeChart's sequence diagram correlation function to create a special function to generate images based on data. When the front-end calls, an empty image instance can be generated by passing in the corresponding image name and image ordinate name. Then the data in JSON format in the database can be obtained through the WebService interface, and the JSON data can be parsed into the required data type through the gson package. Then the data can be transferred into the required time series set by calling the relevant function of the image instance, so that, the data will appear on empty images. The front-end can display the data in real time by setting the process in a thread that refreshes once a second (Fig. 4).

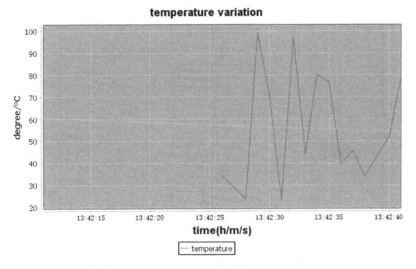

Fig. 4. Visualization interface

3.5   Summing up the Overall Design of the Prototype

Figure 5 shows the design of a complete CPS prototype. As shown in the figure, according to the direction of the data flow, the following steps are required to implement CPS. First we need to add sensors to the high purity material leaching equipment. According to the requirements of the company, we add sensors related to the data types (temperature, PH, etc.) to be measured in the actual material leaching process. After installing sensors, it is necessary to collect data of multiple sensors on the MCU, and then transmit them to another MCU through wireless, and finally transmit them to the computer through the serial port. The data transmitted to the computer is stored in the database and displayed in real time on computer and mobile phone. Finally, the leaching equipment is automatically regulated and controlled to form a cycle.

Now the prototype design of the high purity material leaching process has realized the collection, transmission, analysis and monitoring of the key data. In the future, we will continue to implement the following functions: automatic control, self-diagnosis and early warning analysis. In addition to the leaching process, the prototype of this CPS can be extended to other production processes of high purity materials, and finally realize the intelligent manufacturing of high purity materials manufacturing industry.

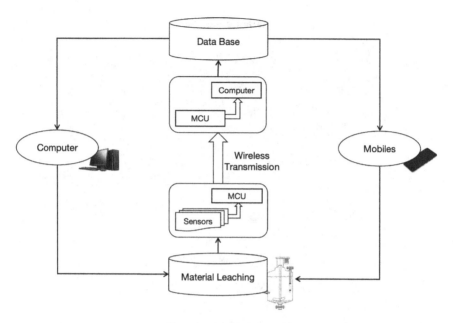

Fig. 5. Prototype design

4 Conclusions

This paper proposed a designed prototype system for the high purity material leaching process, which helped establish a complete visualization system for the high purity material leaching process, enabling the plant to observe and analyze the required data in real time. In the future project, the research will continue to realize data screening, real-time monitoring, self-diagnosis, early warning analysis and automatic regulation, and finally complete the construction of the entire CPS. The establishment of the CPS prototype based on the leaching process of high-purity materials can gradually make all the equipment in the manufacturing process become intelligent, forming a comprehensive upgrade of the high-purity material industry. It is also expected to provide ideas for the intelligent equipment transformation of other enterprises.

High purity material plays an important role in the development of national economy and is also an important indicator of national science and technology development level. In the context of industry 4.0, the only way for industry to make steady progress and finally push forward industrial reform is to master and develop core technologies like CPS.

References

1. Jazdi, N.: Cyber physical systems in the context of Industry 4.0. In: 2014 IEEE International Conference on Automation, Quality and Testing, Robotics, May 2014, pp. 1–4. IEEE (2014)
2. Schlechtendahl, J., Keinert, M., Kretschmer, F., Lechler, A., Verl, A.: Making existing production systems Industry 4.0-ready. Prod. Eng. 9(1), 143–148 (2015)

3. Schmidt, R., Möhring, M., Härting, R.C., Reichstein, C., Neumaier, P., Jozinović, P.: Industry 4.0-potentials for creating smart products: empirical research results. In: Abramowicz, W. (ed.) BIS 2015. LNBIP, pp. 16–27. Springer, Cham (2015). https://doi.org/10.1007/978-3-319-19027-3_2

4. Thoben, K.D., Busse, M., Denkena, B., Gausemeier, J.: System-integrated Intelligence–New Challenges for Product and Production Engineering in the Context of Industry 4.0 (2014)

5. Becker, J.S., Dietze, H.J.: State-of-the-art in inorganic mass spectrometry for analysis of high-purity materials. Int. J. Mass Spectrom. **228**(2–3), 127–150 (2003)

6. Lu, Y: Industry 4.0: a survey on technologies, applications and open research issues. J. Ind. Inf. Integr. **6**, 1–10 (2017)

7. Wang, L., Törngren, M., Onori, M.: Current status and advancement of cyber-physical systems in manufacturing. J. Manuf. Syst. **37**, 517–527 (2015)

8. Wang, L.: An overview of function block enabled adaptive process planning for machining. J. Manuf. Syst. **35**, 10–25 (2015)

9. Ribeiro, L., Barata, J., Ferreira, J.: An agent-based interaction-oriented shop floor to support emergent diagnosis. In: 2010 8th IEEE International Conference on Industrial Informatics (INDIN), July 2010, pp. 189–194. IEEE (2010)

10. Ferreira, P., Lohse, N., Ratchev, S.: Multi-agent architecture for reconfiguration of precision modular assembly systems. In: Ratchev, S. (ed.) IPAS 2010. IFIPAICT, pp. 247–254. Springer, Heidelberg (2010). https://doi.org/10.1007/978-3-642-11598-1_29

11. Wang, L., Wang, X.V., Gao, L., Váncza, J.: A cloud-based approach for WEEE remanufacturing. CIRP Ann. Manuf. Technol. **63**(1), 409–412 (2014)

12. Lee, C.K.M., Yeung, C.L., Cheng, M.N.: Research on IoT based cyber physical system for industrial big data analytics. In: IEEE International Conference on Industrial Engineering and Engineering Management (IEEM), pp. 1855–1859. IEEE (2015)

13. Ivanov, D., Sokolov, B., Ivanova, M.: Schedule coordination in cyber-physical supply networks Industry 4.0. IFAC-PapersOnLine **49**(12), 839–844 (2016)

14. Rüßmann, M., et al.: Industry 4.0: the future of productivity and growth in manufacturing industries. Boston Consulting Group **9**(1), 54–89 (2015)

15. Brown, E., Kumi-Barimah, E., Hömmerich, U., Bluiett, A.G., Trivedi, S.B.: Material purification, crystal growth, and spectroscopy of Tm-doped KPb2Cl5 and KPb2Br 5 for 2 μm photonic applications. J. Cryst. Growth **393**, 159–162 (2014)

16. Mateker, W.R., et al.: Improving the long-term stability of PBDTTPD polymer solar cells through material purification aimed at removing organic impurities. Energy Environ. Sci. **6**(8), 2529–2537 (2013)

17. Huisman, J.L., Schouten, G., Schultz, C.: Biologically produced sulphide for purification of process streams, effluent treatment and recovery of metals in the metal and mining industry. Hydrometallurgy **83**(1–4), 106–113 (2006)

18. Monostori, L.: Cyber-physical production systems: roots, expectations and R&D challenges. Procedia Cirp **17**, 9–13 (2014)

19. Leitão, P., Colombo, A.W., Karnouskos, S.: Industrial automation based on cyber-physical systems technologies: prototype implementations and challenges. Comput. Ind. **81**, 11–25 (2016)

20. Lee, J., Bagheri, B., Kao, H.A.: A cyber-physical systems architecture for industry 4.0-based manufacturing systems. Manuf. Lett. **3**, 18–23 (2015)

21. Lee, J. S., Su, Y.W., Shen, C.C.: A comparative study of wireless protocols: Bluetooth, UWB, ZigBee, and Wi-Fi. In: 33rd Annual Conference of the IEEE on Industrial Electronics Society, IECON 2007, November 2007, pp. 46–51. IEEE (2007)

22. Baronti, P., Pillai, P., Chook, V.W., Chessa, S., Gotta, A., Hu, Y.F.: Wireless sensor networks: a survey on the state of the art and the 802.15. 4 and ZigBee standards. Comput. Commun. **30**(7), 1655–1695 (2007)
23. Xin, Z., et al.: Research on the ZigBee network and equipment design based on the cc2530. Sens. Transducers **158**(11), 89 (2013)
24. The Go Programming Language. https://golang.org/

Smart Cities and Built Environments

On the Relationship Between Accuracy of Bus Position Estimated by Crowdsourcing and Participation Density

Kenro Aihara[1,2,3(✉)], Piao Bin[1], and Hajime Imura[4]

[1] National Institute of Informatics,
2-1-2 Hitotsubashi, Chiyoda-ku, Tokyo 101-8430, Japan
`kenro.aihara@nii.ac.jp`
[2] The Graduate University for Advanced Studies, Hayama, Japan
[3] Joint Support-Center for Data Science Research,
Research Organization of Information and Systems, Tokyo, Japan
[4] Hokkaido University, N-13, W-8, Sapporo, Hokkaido 060-8628, Japan

Abstract. The authors proposed a methodology of bus location service by crowdsource. In the conventional bus location service, a GPS receiver or the like for positioning the bus vehicle and a communication line for transmitting the position information are necessary for each bus and it causes expensive cost, whereas in this methodology, the BLE beacon and the application of the service installed in users' smartphone transmits the beacon signal and the position information of the smartphone using the communication line of users' smartphone so as to reduce the cost of bus operators.

In order to grasp the position of each bus at any time on the server, one of the following is required: (1) At least one service user always exists for each bus, and (2) It is possible to estimate the position with high accuracy where there is no service user in a section.

If contributing to the realization of smart city by grasping the situation in the town by crowdsourcing, it is extremely important to clarify the precision with respect to density that may be given as a relation between the number of users who participate in the program for grasping this situation and the size of the town.

In this paper, the authors examine and show the relationship between the density of data collection and the accuracy of interpolation for the section where data is missing, using the position information actually obtained using the proposed application.

Keywords: Internet of Things · Smart and hybrid cities · Crowdsensing · Crowdsourcing

© Springer Nature Switzerland AG 2019
N. Streitz and S. Konomi (Eds.): HCII 2019, LNCS 11587, pp. 101–112, 2019.
https://doi.org/10.1007/978-3-030-21935-2_9

1   Introduction

We have researched and proposed crowdsourcing which can collect and share the location information of mobile phones cheaply in a public place like a bus. Citizen participation is an indispensable factor in the realization of smart city, but crowdsourcing, which enables this technically, is an important issue. In order to grasp the situation of the city by crowdsourcing, the density of data collection is necessary. For example, if you want to grasp the traffic volume of a certain area at any time, you need to collect the traffic conditions of various places in the area by crowdsourcing, but for some partial areas only once in several days It is not always said that it is insufficient to grasp traffic conditions of partial areas. The required density depends on the quality of the service, but if you know the amount of traffic per hour for the entire area, for example when it is defined in the service, it is simply at least one question per hour. It is necessary to provide information.

Here, as an approach to realize a service with a lower density, it is conceivable to accurately interpolate or estimate a portion where data is missing. In the case of the traffic volume on the road, since the constraints such as the network topology can be used, the density in a planar sense is not necessary, and the state of the unknown section may be estimated from the information of the surrounding road sections to be connected. Therefore, to maintain the service quality, it neccessary to obtain the balance between the estimation accuracy and what degree of density of collected data can be obtained.

In this paper, we will examine the estimation accuracy of the density of the user and its surrounding "data collector" and the bus position by simulation based on actually acquired data by taking the location information service of the bus by crowdsourcing as an example.

2   Background

2.1   Crowdsourcing for Civil Problems

The term "crowdsourcing" was described by Howe in 2006 [6] and defined that crowdsourcing is the act of taking a task traditionally performed by a designated agent and outsourcing it by making an open call to an undefined but large group of people [7]. This can take the form of peer-production, but is also often undertaken by sole individuals [5].

The concept of smart cities can be viewed as a recognition of the growing importance of digital technologies for a competitive position and a sustainable future [10]. Although the smart city-agenda, which grants ICTs with the task to achieve strategic urban development goals such as improving the life quality of its citizens and creating sustainable growth, has gained a lot of momentum in recent years.

Tools such as smartphones offer the opportunity to facilitate co-creation between citizens and authority. Such tools have the potential to organize and stimulate communication between citizens and authority, and allow citizens to participate in the public domain [4,12]. One example is FixMyStreet[1] that enables citizens to report broken streetlights and potholes [9]. It is important that these approaches will not succeed automatically and social standards like trust, openness, and consideration of mutual interests have to be guaranteed to make citizen engaging in the public domain challenging.

Waze[2] is another crowdsourcing service to collect data of traffic. Even though Waze provides users to traffic information collected from users and route navigation function, it seems not enough to motivate users to get involved in, because recommended routes are not as adequate as car navigation appliances, especially in Japan where such appliances are well-developed.

2.2 Bus Location Services

Route bus system is a fundamental transit service. However, due to a progress of motorization, the number of bus passengers has been gradually decreasing especially in suburban areas. As a result, the decline in passengers has led to a decline in unprofitable routes and it is in a vicious circle that accelerates the decline of passengers. To attract more choice passengers to route buses, the transit service must not only have a high level of service in terms of frequency and travel time but also must be reliable [13]. Although such efforts often come at a substantial cost, one inexpensive way to improve unreliability from the user perspective is providing real-time transit information.

A bus location service, or realtime bus tracking service, provides up-to-date bus location and estimated times of arrival at bus stops. Most existing bus location systems (e.g., [8,11]) use onboard location sensors, such as GPS receivers, to perceive the current location and then send it to a server. In these systems, it is necessary to prepare a communication line, such as cellular phone network, and GPS receiver in advance.

Another model is a bus detector installed on the environment side along the route detects the ID of the nearby bus and sends it to the server. Typically, these detectors are installed at the bus stop and detect the passing bus. Detectors installed at the bus stop need a communication line for transmitting data to the server.

Both models have high initial cost of equipment and operational cost of communication, and there is a problem in introducing services.

3 Target Service: Ride Around-the-Corner

Here we describe the target service of crowdsourced bus location service "Ride around-the-corner. (Ride ATC)" in blief [2]. The key idea of the service model is that collecting bus locations is not by bus operators but by onboard passengers. To collect them, a smartphone application of bus tracker is provided to public.

---

[1] https://www.fixmystreet.com/.

[2] https://www.waze.com/.

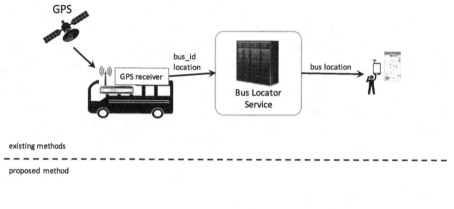

existing methods

- -

proposed method

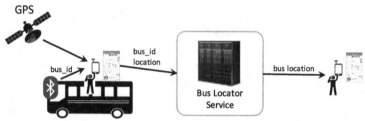

Fig. 1. Comparison of methods

Figure 1 shows the proposed method, compared with existing ones. Typical existing methods are equipped with onboard location sensors, such as a GPS receivers, and transmitters. Every perceived latest location will be sent to the server frequently through a wireless communication line, such as cellular phone. That is, bus operators must prepare such devices and a communication line for each bus vehicle.

On the other hand, in this model, bus operators only install Bluetooth beacons on each bus vehicle. Instead of installing a location sensor on the bus, the proposed method uses a passenger's smartphone and our application. An onboard beacon broadcasts its own identification number nearby. In the case of Bluetooth, its range is usually several tens of meters. When the application on passenger's smartphone detects specific Bluetooth information including UUID and vehicle identification number, it perceives its location and transmit it with the vehicle information to the server.

The application shows current locations of buses in operation on bus transit services, while it detects nearby buses around users and transmits bus IDs with time and location of detection to the service platform. That is, locations of buses are collected by users.

3.1   Onboard Beacon

For enabling mobile applications detect IDs of buses, Bluetooth beacons are deployed on buses. In our preliminary experiment, we set one beacon for each bus vehicle, because the range of Bluetooth signal is usually several tens of meters and that can cover the whole vehicle.

Each beacon broadcasts the common service UUID and its own identification number. For IDs, we use the same major number for bus vehicles and an unique minor number. Ids of buses and relations to the fleet are stored in a database in the server. In addition to IDs of buses, some static information, such as bus routes and timetables, are given to the server database. The system can identify which bus on which route the beacon is on by the correspondence table of major and minor number, vehicle and route in the database.

3.2   Mobile Applications

We are preparing two as a mobile application related to this Ride ATC. One, of course, is the Ride ATC application itself. It is an application that can check the bus position used by the user wishing to know the bus position. The other is "Drive around-the-corner. (DriveATC)" application which is a related service.

These two applications differ in target users, but both have the function of notifying the bus position information when detecting the bus beacon signal. Therefore, the location information of the bus will be collected from various mobiles who act in the streets. The idea of around-the-corner, crowdsourcing service is to promote understanding of the situation of the city as a whole by sharing necessary information mutually between services in this manner.

Ride ATC Application. The Ride ATC application provides users with current locations of buses in operation. It indicates the position of the buses on the map. The user can check it and estimate arrival time of their possible target bus on map beforehand so that it is possible to minimize the waiting time at the bus stop without missing it.

While the user is using the application in both the foreground and the background, the Ride ATC application scans a specific range of Bluetooth IDs. Once it detects an ID nearby, the application obtains location from onboard sensors. The location data with bus IDs and time are collected and pooled in the local data store and then transmitted to the service platform.

On the platform, current positions are updated and estimated by using collected bus IDs with spatiotemporal information and static information in database.

Drive ATC Application. The authors have developed and provides a driving recorder service called "Drive around-the-corner." since February 2015 [1,3]. Drive ATC has the function of collecting behavior logs and posts of events and delivering information around current position.

Before driving, users mount their own smartphone and connect a cable for power supply if neccessary (Fig. 2), and then start recording in the application (Fig. 3).

Drive ATC users naturally use this application as a drive recorder, but when the application simultaneously detects a beacon signal of the neighboring ATC service, such as onboard beacons on the bus, it has the function of sending it to the server together with the position information like the Ride ATC application.

Fig. 2. Mounting smartphones on car.

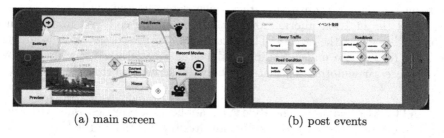

(a) main screen   (b) post events

Fig. 3. "Drive: around-the-corner." application. Traffic information, events posted from users, events extracted from sensor data, and footprints are shown in map of main screen.

3.3   Grasping Bus Location and Estimating Arrival Time

If at least one passenger who enables the Ride ATC is onboard, the service grasps the current location of the bus. Therefore, at least one user of the Ride ATC gets on a bus, this service gets effective. Conversely, it is not possible to acquire the location information of the bus where there is no user onboard. In other words, the more users want to know the location of the bus, the more practical this service will be.

The signal of the beacon on the bus can be received not only within the bus but also in the vicinity of the outside of the bus (Fig. 4). For example, in the case where the bus passes by the side of the user walking on the sidewalk, the user can provide the location information of the bus to the service.

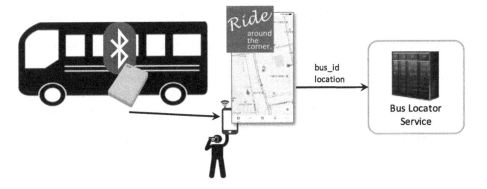

Fig. 4. Detecting onboard beacons from outside the bus

Table 1. Collected data of Ride ATC

Detector	Number of records
By onboard passengers	12,346
From outside of the bus	1,920

4   Density and Accuracy

4.1   Accuracy

The accuracy of position information is discussed from two viewpoints.

On the other hand, regarding the density of data, it is considered that positioning and communication are carried out generally once per minute in the conventional method of installing a GPS receiver on the bus. In the method of installing the detector at the bus stop, since the position of the bus is detected only when the bus approaches the bus stop, its density is smaller and it is impossible to grasp the behavior between bus stops. In the proposed method, the user can continuously measure and transmit the position information while detecting the beacon, and in the current implementation of the Ride ATC, these are performed every second.

4.2   Acquired Data

We conducted experiments on data acquisition in cooperation with the Hokkaido Chuo Bus in March 2018. We prepared passengers who are eight users of the application, and acquired data over specific routes over two days. We set up a beacon on 38 buses used for six routes and set up a beacon at 150 bus stops on that route. Table 1 shows number of data collected at the experiments. This table shows the number of beacons detected by passengers over two days of use.

When getting on the bus where the beacon was installed, the beacon is detected without problems and sent to the server. Although detailed verification was not completed, beacon detection was able to be performed in the range of roughly 50 m.

What the authors want to pay attention to here is that it can detect the bus beacon even from outside the bus. Here, 1920 out of all 14,266 detections was other than the bus that passengers themselves take. These include the case of detecting a beacon of another bus passed by both while getting on another bus and while on the roadside. This indicates that this service can detect the location of the bus even if it is not necessarily on the target bus. The authors suppose that users of Drive ATC can also detect the bus beacon and provide information.

4.3   Settings

Service Quality. As a service quality, here we define an interval to update the bus location is 15 s as a baseline. One reason is that the traditional bus location services in the urban bus route where the bus stops are short and then the information is too coarse at intervals longer than 1 min. And also in the major bus location service operated in Japan, such as Business Navitime Bus Location Service, which collects the location information by installing the device onboard, the update frequency is about 15 s.

Evaluation Index. In the method of crowdsourcing targeted here, since it depends on whether or not the user is on the bus, this paper regards each section (between bus stops) as a unit. In normal operation, in addition to business related factors, such as existence of passengers who get on or off at the bus stop, it is impossible to move in the scheduled travel time due to external factors such as traffic signals, road congestion and obstacles on the road. Here, the influence on these estimation accuracy for each section s at i^{th} run is defined as an error rate as follows.

$$r_{si} = \frac{(observed\ travel\ time)_i}{(expected\ travel\ time)_i} \tag{1}$$

This error rate indicates how deviated per 1 min travel time.

Data Blank. As a result of the experiment, it seems that location is detected almost every second inside the range of beacon signal, although the beacon detection timing depends on the OS of the smartphone. Therefore, if at least one user is aboard, this Ride ATC notifies the location of the bus which changes moment every second, and it can be said that it realizes real time positioning superior to the baseline service notified every 15 s. Figure 5 shows an example of collected data. The red triangle marker indicates the position and movement direction. The size of the marker depends on the speed. Naturally, the moving speed is changing every moment.

Fig. 5. An example of collected data on map

Target Route. In this paper, the authors focus on the bus route passing through the area around Sapporo terminal station where traffic congestion occurs burstingly in Sapporo city and the travel time of the bus is greatly affected because the necessity of bus location service is low in the case of routes whose schedule is not much disturbed.

Using the actual movement record of this route gathered using Ride ATC, the error rate was calculated from the running condition of each route section.

We selected a bus route of Hokkaido Chuo Bus between Sapporo terminal station and Asabu bus terminal. The route consists of twelve bus stops and the total journey is about 4.3 km. Usually it takes 18 min. However, if there is snowfall in the winter season, it may take twice this time in severe cases.

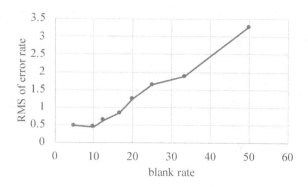

Fig. 6. Error rate

Table 2. Relationship between error rate and data blank rate

Blank rate (%)	RMS of error rate
5.0	0.487
10.0	0.443
12.5	0.635
20.0	1.237
25.0	1.641
50.0	3.269

4.4 Results

The root mean square of the error rate calculated from the actual data acquired in this route was 0.866. Among the actually acquired data, there was a delay of three minutes for the scheduled route of 18 min. Also, there was one that took four minutes in the section where the travel time was one minute on the timetable.

Figure 6 and Table 2 show a result of the relationship between error rate and data blank rate. The data blank section is randomly extracted at a given ratio, the value of root mean square of the error rate is calculated, and the average value of five tests is shown.

As a result, if the blank rate is less than this, it can not be said that it can be used as a service, but it can be said that it can maintain a certain level of service even for intermittent data collection on an congested route. It is suggestive that the blank rate at the same level as actual RMS, 0.866, was just below 20%.

5   Conclusion

In this paper, the authors examine and show the relationship between the density of data collection and the accuracy of interpolation for the section where data is missing, using the position information actually obtained using the proposed application.

The authors have been doing preliminary experiments. Under the cooperation of Sapporo city and the Hokkaido Chuo Bus, we are proceeding with the operation verification using the developed Ride ATC application. We will proceed with verification of methodology and social implementation by carrying out larger-scale demonstration.

Acknowledgment. The authors would like to thank City of Sapporo, Hokkaido Government, Hokkaido Chuo Bus Co., Ltd. for their cooperation with this research. Part of this research was supported by "Research and Development on Fundamental and Utilization Technologies for Social Big Data" of the Commissioned Research of National Institute of Information and Communications Technology (NICT), Japan.

References

1. Aihara, K., Bin, P., Imura, H., Takasu, A., Tanaka, Y.: On feasibility of crowd-sourced mobile sensing for smarter city life. In: Streitz, N., Markopoulos, P. (eds.) DAPI 2016. LNCS, vol. 9749, pp. 395–404. Springer, Cham (2016). https://doi.org/10.1007/978-3-319-39862-4_36
2. Aihara, K., Bin, P., Imura, H., Takasu, A., Tanaka, Y.: Collecting bus locations by users: a crowdsourcing model to estimate operation status of bus transit service. In: Streitz, N., Konomi, S. (eds.) DAPI 2018. LNCS, vol. 10921, pp. 171–180. Springer, Cham (2018). https://doi.org/10.1007/978-3-319-91125-0_14
3. Aihara, K., Imura, H., Piao, B., Takasu, A., Tanaka, Y.: Mobile crowdsensing to collect road conditions and events. In: Yasuura, H., Kyung, C.-M., Liu, Y., Lin, Y.-L. (eds.) Smart Sensors at the IoT Frontier, pp. 271–297. Springer, Cham (2017). https://doi.org/10.1007/978-3-319-55345-0_11
4. Amichai-Hamburger, Y.: Potential and promise of online volunteering. Comput. Hum. Behav. **24**(2), 544–562 (2008)
5. Howe, J.: Crowdsourcing: a definition. Crowdsourcing tracking the rise of the amateur (2006)
6. Howe, J.: The rise of crowdsourcing. Wired Mag. **14**(6), 1–4 (2006)
7. Howe, J.: Crowdsourcing: How the Power of the Crowd is Driving the Future of Business. Random House, New York (2008)
8. Kanatani, N., Sasama, T., Kawamura, T., Sugahara, K.: Development of bus location system using smart phones. In: Proceedings of SICE Annual Conference, vol. 2010, pp. 2432–2433 (2010)
9. King, S.F., Brown, P.: Fix my street or else: Using the internet to voice local public service concerns. In: Proceedings of the 1st International Conference on Theory and Practice of Electronic Governance, pp. 72–80 (2007)
10. Schuurman, D., Baccarne, B., De Marez, L., Mechant, P.: Smart ideas for smart cities: investigating crowdsourcing for generating and selecting ideas for ict innovation in a city context. J. Theoret. Appl. Electron. Commer. Res. **7**(3), 49–62 (2012)

11. Shigihara, I., Arai, A., Saitou, O., Kuwahara, Y., Kamada M.: A dynamic bus guide based on real-time bus locations - a demonstration plan. In: 2013 16th International Conference on Network-Based Information Systems (NBIS), pp. 436–438 (2013)
12. Stembert, N., Mulder, I.J.: Love your city! an interactive platform empowering citizens to turn the public domain into a participatory domain. In: International Conference Using ICT, Social Media and Mobile Technologies to Foster Self-Organisation in Urban and Neighbourhood Governance (2013)
13. Watkins, K.E., Ferris, B., Borning, A., Rutherford, G.S., Layton, D.: Where is my bus? Impact of mobile real-time information on the perceived and actual wait time of transit riders. Transp. Res. Part A: Policy Pract. **45**(8), 839–848 (2011)

reTessellate: Modular Dynamic Surfaces Reactive to Socio-Environmental Conditions

Mostafa Alani[1,2(✉)] and Arash Soleimani[3]

[1] Tuskegee University, Tuskegee, AL 36088, USA
malani@tuskegee.edu
[2] Al-Iraqia University, Baghdad, Iraq
[3] Kennesaw State University, Marietta, GA 30060, USA
asoleiml@kennesaw.edu

Abstract. This paper presents the design, fabrication, and programming of a reconfigurable structure. The structure is comprised of modular, programable units, which can be stacked together, and collectively construct surfaces that shape-shifts in response to the surrounding physical and social conditions aiming at enhancing the link between occupants and the built environment.

Keywords: Reconfigurable structures · Embedded computation · Interaction design · Algorithmic thinking · Form transformation · Tessellations · Built environment · Architectural robotics

1 Background

Reconfigurable structures are well established within our built environments and exist all around us. For instance, doors and windows are some of the earliest examples of reconfigurable structures that provide a dynamic manipulation of the building layout to satisfy various conditions. Examples across different building typologies exist from tiny houses (in which reconfigurable structures play a key role in space planning) to public spaces. In airports, for instance, passenger boarding bridge changes shape and position to facilitate a convenient and safe connection between the building and the aircraft (Fig. 1).

Fig. 1. Passenger boarding bridges (image credits: Wikimedia).

© Springer Nature Switzerland AG 2019
N. Streitz and S. Konomi (Eds.): HCII 2019, LNCS 11587, pp. 113–123, 2019.
https://doi.org/10.1007/978-3-030-21935-2_10

With the technology being increasingly embedded in various aspects of our lives, reconfigurable structures have become more responsive and intelligent in our everyday life. For instance, doors can sense an incoming motion and react accordingly. Building envelopes can dynamically control the amount of light that enters the building. Additionally, mechanical systems can be added to such list since they allow for adaptation of interior quality in response to climatic conditions and human behavior. Building components such as windows, walls and movable partitions, doors, screen systems, louver and shading devices, and operable vents can allow for adaptation of the building in response to human needs.

The integration of responsive features in Architecture, offers the opportunity to experience buildings as living, changeable organs versus buildings being static entities. Buildings with reconfigurable structures can be designed in a way that their appearance, permeability, and affordances can (un)predictably change in response to environmental changes and their occupants. Le Corbusier, famous Swiss-French architect and the pioneer of modernist architecture (1887–1965), used the term "household equipment" and referred to the house as a "machine for living in" to define an architecture that involves operable and reconfigurable elements. In the 1970s, avantgarde thinkers like Nicholas Negroponte suggested that advancements in computation and artificial intelligence would soon make buildings smarter while being capable of intelligently recognizing users' activities and environmental changes for a more customizable and adaptive living condition [1]. "Negroponte proposes that responsive architecture is the natural product of the integration of computing power into built spaces and structures. He also extends this belief to include the concepts of recognition, intention, contextual variation, and meaning into computed responses and their successful and ubiquitous integration into architecture" [1]. Today, automated reconfigurable structures have become more commonplace and are frequently integrated in building envelopes as a tool for enhancing human comfort and energy efficiency.

In this paper, what we refer to as reconfigurable and responsive structures encompasses all building elements that are able to change and adapt in real-time in response to socio-environmental conditions in order for accommodating the contingencies of everyday life. We argue that computation and reconfigurable structures can converge and be embedded at different scales of the built environment, in particular, architectural surfaces, which can produce more flexible, responsive, and intelligent spaces aiming to optimize our social and physical experience of architectural spaces that we live in.

2   Research Through Design Approach

The field of Human Computer Interaction (HCI) is experiencing an increasing interest in Research through Design (RtD) as a research method which can offer distinct advantages to the HCI community. RtD's contribution to the HCI field has been characterized in different ways and many of them view RtD as a canonical type of design-research activity. For instance, Frayling [2] referred to *developmental work* which involves "a customization of a piece of technology to do something no one had considered before, and communicating the results." In *action research*, "a research diary tells, in a step-by-step way, of a practical experiment in the studios, and the resulting report aims to contextualize it to communicate the results" [2]. In general, RtD offers researchers the opportunity to cope with messy design-research problems that are unclear or not well situated in other methods of research. RtD also enforces designers and researchers to focus on the work of future, instead of the present or the past. Additionally, RtD makes designers think about the logics and ethics of the design process rather than solely focusing on the final outcome [3].

This paper presents an exemplar case of research through design as a result of an iterative design process. The proposed, fully functioning prototype was designed and tested during different phases as we improved the usability and efficiency of the system.

3 The Backstory

The design-research work presented in this paper started as a response to social conditions in public spaces aiming at answering the question of "how can the environment adapt to the human needs within public spaces?" The theoretical stance builds upon Christopher Alexander's concept of positive and negative spaces. In his discussion of positive and negative spaces, Alexander argues that "people feel comfortable in spaces which are *positive*; and people feel relatively uncomfortable in spaces which are *negative*". He later established a link between the positive-negative concept and the shape of the indoor walls in which he explains that straight walls "make no sense in human or structural terms" and to create a social, inviting space the shape of the wall needs to be concave when possible (especially in thick walls) [4]. The Reconfigurable Wall System (RWS) came as a response in order to provide various configurations offering both feelings interchangeably (Fig. 2). The configurations are (1) embrace, (2) repellent, and (3) delineate [5].

This paper revisits the RWS and further elaborates the opportunities to design a flexible, intelligent structure, which can be integrated in various parts of the built environment while responding to various socio-environmental conditions.

4 Tessellations in Nature as a Source of Inspiration

Nature provides a fascinating source of inspiration for pattern development, surface subdivisions, and close-packing, i.e., tessellations. The existence of tessellations in nature relates, in many cases, to optimization purposes by producing "economical structural solutions to some given set of conditions" [6]. Various examples exist in nature which have been shaped, evolved, and refined over time through evolutionary processes. Some tessellations can be seen directly with the naked eye such as the honeycomb structures, patterns in animals' skins, and cracked mud; whereas, some are invisible to the naked eye, such as the living cell structures [6] (Fig. 3).

This paper employs tessellations to subdivide surfaces and focuses on three types of tessellations: regular tessellations, semi-regular tessellations, and tessellations with regular polygons. Mathematically, tessellation is defined as the repetition of polygonal shapes infinitely to fill a surface area while leaving no gaps between the polygons [6].

Fig. 2. The Reconfigurable Wall System (RWS). Top right: conceptual design; top left: programing and sensing experimentation; bottom: fully-functioning prototype.

For regular tessellations the surface is subdivided into smaller sections using identical, congruent regular polygons. There are only three possible scenarios in the case of regular tessellations: triangular-, square-, and hexagonal-based subdivisions. In semi-regular tessellations, more than one congruent regular polygon is employed. However, the collection of geometries within the subdivided surface should be identical from any point in the surface, otherwise the type of tessellation will fall under the category of tessellation with regular polygons [6]. Both semi-regular tessellations and tessellation with regular polygons provide a good opportunity for morphing different tessellations within a surface area (Fig. 4).

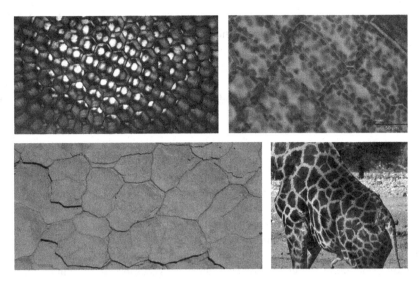

Fig. 3. Tessellations in nature. Top left: hexagonal pattern in a honeycomb; top right: microscopical leaf structure; bottom left: cracked mud; and bottom right: Voronoi structure on giraffe's skin (image credits: Wikimedia)

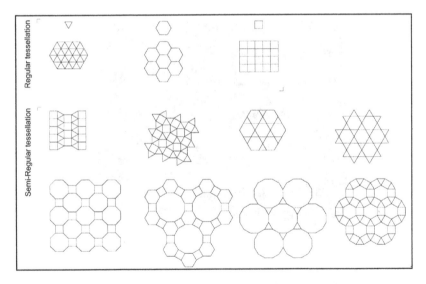

Fig. 4. Regular tessellations and semi-regular tessellations.

5 Design Process

Our team investigated the possibility of extending applications of reconfigurable structures in different building components. Through investigating various tessellating systems, this paper presents a Dynamic Modular Tessellation (DMT) system–reTessellate—in the form of units that can be stacked to form a structure, which can be used in various architectural surfaces e.g. celling, building façade, and walls.

Significant hardware and software modifications were conducted on the RWS. The following sections discuss detailed modifications.

5.1   Hardware Design

In order to create a flexible surface structure which fits in a variety of situations, the design of the new system hardware has to be flexible enough to cover various type of tessellation systems while prioritizing "minimum inventory/maximum diversity" design strategies.

The current system hardware consists of three main components: a repetitive unit, a repetitive structure, and the core units. The repetitive unit is the basic building block of the system that hosts the core unit (Fig. 5). The repetitive unit can be disassembled into two pieces—male and female—when necessary. A consideration was given to how this geometry can be repeated to construct various novel tessellations.

The repetitive structure is the product of continuously stacking the repetitive unit to fill the required area. The system can be assembled to form all the possible regular tessellation structures (triangular-, square-, and hexagonal-based tessellations), semi-regular tessellations, and tessellations with regular polygons. This feature significantly increases structural flexibility and provide an opportunity to seamlessly morph between various types of regular tessellation systems (Fig. 6).

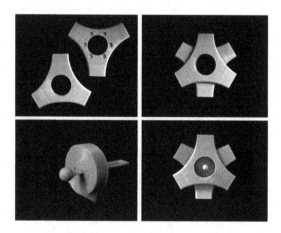

Fig. 5. Top: the repeated unit; and bottom: the core and its installation.

The core, on the other hand, is also modular, and different modules can be attached to the repetitive units to offer a variety of reconfigurable and transfigurable environmental settings. For instance, the module presented in Fig. 7 (Left) is a linear actuator module. This module function in a similar way that the RWS works (a push and pull mechanism). The study also examined the design of other modules that can control origami folding star units as a responsive shading device (Fig. 7).

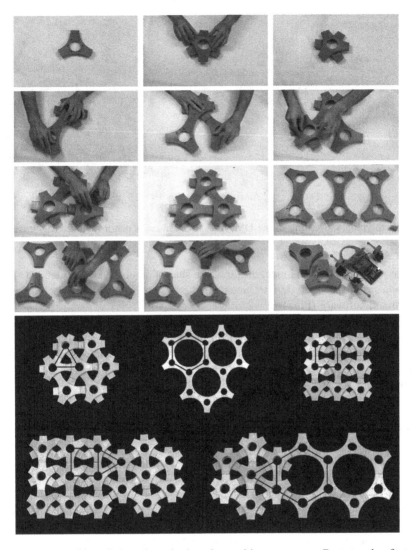

Fig. 6. Top: assembly of the triangular-based repetitive structure. Bottom: the first row, employing the DMT units to assemble triangular-, hexagonal-, and square-based tessellations; the second row, morphing the structural system.

5.2 Software Development

The Dynamic Modular tessellation system was programmed using Rhinoceros' Grasshopper and Firefly. The latter acted as the primary communication tool between Grasshopper and the Arduino microcontroller. Two algorithms were developed to provide two primary dialogue modes:

(1) the preset interaction; and (2) the responsive interaction (sensing the environment).

Fig. 7. Prototyping and testing of the DMT unit. Left: linear actuator module. Right: origami-star as a shading device.

In the preset interaction mode, the structure shapeshifts based on hardcoded values. This mode provides testing environment of the system functionality including both hardware and software (Fig. 8).

In the responsive interaction mode, the system reconfigures in response to the data collected from the surrounding environment through embedded sensors. The structure integrates a Microsoft Kinect motion sensor, which is utilized with "skeletal mapping" and depth information within the Grasshopper plugin to understand nearby occupants (Fig. 9).

6   Discussion of the System's Current State

The DMT system offers two types of configurations: per-configuration and post-configuration. Both configuration modes depend on expected activities within the space. The pre-configuration mode is the initial setup of the system. In the pre-configuration mode, the designer gets to choose the type of tessellations and the installation modules. The post-configuration mode is the capability of the system to shapeshift to accommodate post-occupancy needs.

Tessellations offered many advantages to the design of the DMT system. A surface that is constructed from the DMT units provides an excellent opportunity to be reconfigured and customized during the design and fabrication phase using "minimum inventory" of the modular units. The DMT surfaces is capable of morphing the internal structural subdivisions of the surface between various stacking systems. Such a feature makes it possible to have a single responsive surface which offers different configurations at different points while being controlled by a single control center. For instance, consider the corridor presented in Fig. 10 which reimagines passengers' corridors public spaces. The DMT system is forming a surface that is being morphed from square-based tessellation to a hexagonal based tessellation (i.e., aperture system). The wall structure aims to better accommodate passengers' activities in crowded corridors while the aperture system controls light intensity in the interior spaces.). The aperture is also capable of morphing into a triangular-based tessellation.

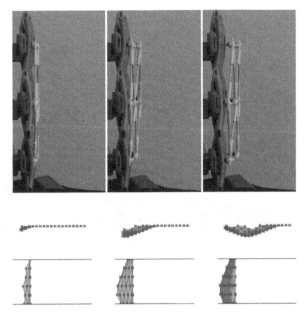

Fig. 8. Preset interaction mode (preprogrammed wave).

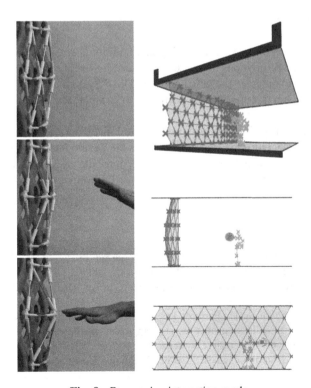

Fig. 9. Responsive interaction mode

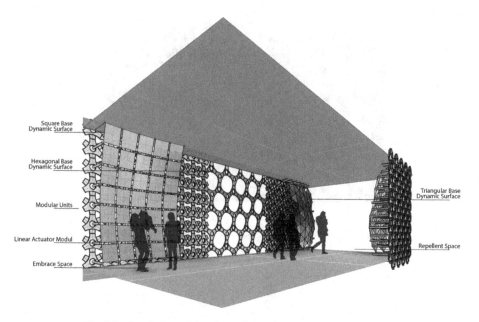

Fig. 10. Rendering of the dynamic modular tessellation (DMT).

7   Future Works

The next step is to conduct usability testing and additional software adjustments. The current modular design provides a great environment for testing the system in different scenarios. We aim to enhance the efficacy of the DMT System by conducting different usability studies. User groups will be recruited to evaluate the system usability and functionality.

Additionally, the DMT system is envisioned to be able to teach itself and improve its behavior over time. Our next step also includes the development of "algorithms that improve through experience," which ultimately contribute to a more intelligent dialogue between the occupants, the structure, and the built environment [7].

References

1. Sterk, T.D.E.: Building upon negroponte: a hybridized model of control suitable for responsive architecture. Autom.Constr. **14**(2), 225–232 (2005)
2. Frayling, C.: Research in art and design. Royal College of Art Research Papers, vol. 1, no. 1, April 1993 (1994)
3. Zimmerman, J., Stolterman, E., Forlizzi, J.:. An analysis and critique of Research through Design: towards a formalization of a research approach. In: Proceedings of the 8th ACM Conference on Designing Interactive Systems, August, pp. 310–319. ACM (2010)
4. Alexander, C.: A Pattern Language: Towns, Buildings. Construction. Oxford University Press, Oxford (1977)

5. Alani, M., Soleimani, A., Murray, E., Bah, A., Leicht, A., Sajwani, S.: The reconfigurable wall system: designing a responsive structure reactive to socio-environmental conditions. In: Streitz, N., Konomi, S. (eds.) DAPI 2018. LNCS, vol. 10922, pp. 167–177. Springer, Cham (2018). https://doi.org/10.1007/978-3-319-91131-1_13

6. Pearce, P.: Structure in Nature is a Strategy for Design. MIT Press, Cambridge (1990)

7. Tegmark, M.: Life 3.0: Being Human in the Age of Artificial Intelligence. Knopf (2017)

A User-Centric Design Framework for Smart Built Environments
A Mixed Reality Perspective

Archi Dasgupta, Mohamed Handosa, Mark Manuel, and Denis Gračanin(⊠)

Department of Computer Science, Virginia Tech,
2202 Kraft Drive, Blacksburg, VA 24060, USA
gracanin@vt.edu

Abstract. Smart Built Environments (SBEs) empowered by the Internet of Things (IoT) dramatically augment the capabilities of traditional built environments by imbuing everyday objects with computational and communication capabilities. SBEs primarily consist of three types of components: architectural elements, embedded technology (smart objects) and enhanced interaction modalities. As smart objects hold the ability to change the state of the environment, inefficient design of smart configurations can lead to potentially harmful conditions affecting the safety and security of the inhabitants. The interaction scenarios and space use pattern of SBEs are also notably different from traditional built environments. But, to the best of our knowledge, there has been limited work on developing a consolidated design framework addressing the three interdependent SBE elements and evaluating the safety and security of the IoT application environment. We propose an SBE design framework based on the traditional architectural design process. The framework combines the technological aspects of SBEs with the traditional architectural design process while leveraging Building Information Modeling (BIM) and participatory design. We describe a Mixed Reality(MR)-based reference framework implementation that is particularly helpful for representing, visualizing and modeling the vast amount of data, digital components and novel SBE interaction scenarios.

Keywords: Internet of Things · Smart Built Environment ·
Mixed Reality · Human computer interaction ·
Human-centered computing

1 Introduction

Imagine a built space that is empathetic to your needs; a physical environment that goes beyond obvious user-interaction and has the ability to derive your cognitive state and activity pattern and respond accordingly. The idea of such smart environments is not new, but the emergence of IoT has dramatically broadened the scope of SBEs and given rise to revolutionary ideas like a smart, connected

© Springer Nature Switzerland AG 2019
N. Streitz and S. Konomi (Eds.): HCII 2019, LNCS 11587, pp. 124–143, 2019.
https://doi.org/10.1007/978-3-030-21935-2_11

world. This emerging idea of the SBE is set to be the future of all built environments and it needs a trans-disciplinary design approach as it encompasses fields like computer science, electrical engineering, architecture, industrial design etc.

IoT-based SBEs include fundamentally different and enhanced capabilities compared to the traditional built environments. Traditional built environments consist of basic building elements and plain physical objects offering primitive interactions, basic use cases and direct affordances. SBEs on the other hand, consist of three major components– basic building elements, embedded technologies and enhanced interaction modalities. The computational and communication capabilities embedded with everyday physical objects enable augmented affordances and multi-modal interactions, thus affecting users' spatial usage pattern and interaction scenarios [17]. As a result the spatial design is dependent on smart functionality.

In-spite of these inherent differences, SBE designers still follow the traditional architectural design processes and implement the architectural design, technology design and interaction design as three separate processes. The segregation of processes result in the three components being merely layered on top of each other rather than being completely merged towards a unified goal. Consequently, the potential of an SBE to enhance its users' overall spatial experience or positively impact their spatial use pattern is not fully utilized.

Therefore, it is imperative for SBE designers to adopt a trans-disciplinary approach and adopt a unified design framework that considers the interdependency of the three key elements from the very beginning of the SBE design process. But to the best of our knowledge, there has not been much work on developing such a comprehensive framework for SBE design, previous efforts being focused mostly on addressing technological issues associated with SBE.

We describe a unified SBE design framework by integrating embedded technology perspectives and user-centered interaction design principles with the traditional architectural design process. The proposed framework leverages Building Information Modeling (BIM) and enables participatory design by having users as active participants in the design process. It also helps ensure a safe, secure and user-centric design approach for SBEs.

We also describe a mixed reality (MR)-based reference implementation of the proposed framework. The use of MR is particularly helpful for representing and modeling the vast amount of data, digital components and novel interaction scenarios associated with SBEs.

2   Related Work

Architecture is increasingly becoming a major concern for smart environment design and interaction with SBE because when embedded interactive technologies work as architectural elements, it influences the activity flow of the occupants and functional layout of the built environment. Wiberg et al. [30] for example, describe a restaurant in Umea, Sweden, where the inclusion of an RFID-device-based ordering service changed the layout of the restaurant to become significantly different from those of traditional restaurants. Hence architectural design process needs to be an integral part of SBE design. In this section, we first discuss the traditional architectural design process.

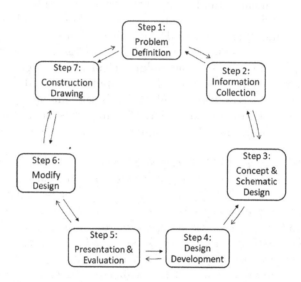

Fig. 1. Traditional architectural design process [6].

The traditional built environments (TBE) consist of basic building blocks (i.e., wall, column, floor, window) and plain physical objects (i.e., furniture, fixture) [6]. For TBEs, the defining elements are– places (points of activities with a sense of boundary), paths (space characterized by a tendency towards mobility), domains (well defined areas consisting of places and paths), thresholds (functional and physical boundaries between spaces) and objects (elements that define a space) [20,23,25,28]. So, the TBE design process primarily focuses on the design issues of the physical environment and we briefly describe a comprehensive outline of the TBE design process based on the related literature [5,9,10,18,22].

As illustrated in Fig. 1, the first step consists of problem definition and program analysis for understanding the functional requirements, usage pattern, budget, client's perspective, etc. Step 2 is information collection to understand the topography, climate, regulations, etc. Step 3 consists of concept development and schematic design analyzing client's lifestyle, spatial use pattern and cultural preferences. Step 4 is mass design, structural design, etc. by drawing a flow diagram and finally developing an architectural design. Step 5 consists of presenting the proposed design to the stakeholders using models, 2D drawings, rendered images, etc. Step 6 is detail design and construction documents. Finally, the construction phase begins.

As for SBE, the related research and current practices do not yet offer a comprehensive framework for SBE design. We briefly discuss the related works that addresses different SBE design issues and proposes novel approaches for addressing those issues. Zhang et al. [31] integrate BIM with the smart functionality design and management of SBEs by including smart object profiling and information exchange data. They also implement a framework to identify possible defects in the design. Lertlakkhanakul et al. [19] worked on a data model for a building and a virtual platform simulating smart home services. The integration of context-aware data model, digital representation of place and user and web services enable a user-oriented approach to visualize invisible services and configuration of smart capabilities. Inada et al. [15] emphasize on the ECA (event, condition, action) rules for designing sensor-driven services where possible conflicts need to be addressed. Guinard et al. [14] describe the importance of a detailed description of the building environment for designing an efficient indoor wireless sensor network. Jeng et al. [17] propose a 3D smart space design concept where space (furniture, fixture, etc.) is viewed as one dimension. The other two dimensions are ubiquitous computing technology and living (safety, security, etc.). Different devices influencing a common set of environmental factors need to be considered based on their spatial context as architectural features effect the efficiency of a built form [31].

In a framework for human computer interaction (HCI) and sustainable home technology, Makonin et al. [21] proposed an ecosystem consisting of the occupants, components of the home, context and dependencies between these. They mentioned the case study of North House to show how to achieve net-zero performance using customized energy systems, smart facade and automated optimization. But the house was not successful in balancing occupancy comfort with optimal energy efficiency, ultimately leading the house occupants to disable the system in favor of their own personalized settings for the house. Rowland et al. [26] emphasize on understanding the primary users, stakeholders and the consequences of networked technologies for designers of connected products. Dourish et al. [11] discuss studying tangible interfaces and interactive behavior together with ubiquitous computing. Weiser's idea of UbiComp [29] proposes that the most successful technologies are those that are invisible and yet pervasive. This theory exploits our natural skills and activities and tries to make technology blend into our environment. SBE designers would benefit from keeping this in mind while designing smart environments.

We also explore novel assistive technology for supporting the design process. Lertlakkhanakul et al. [19] note there is limited research into introducing virtual reality or web services to the SBE design process to simulate complex, invisible smart services to end users or even designers. They introduce a web-based virtual platform to engage end users in the design process by allowing them to configure smart services.

There has been previous research into the use of immersive technologies for traditional architectural design as they enable visualization and exploration of the designed space before it is constructed [4,32]. It also has the potential to aid in surveying a model of the site, topography, etc. without having to be there physically [2]. An omni-directional treadmill allows users to move in the virtual environment. Campbell et al. [5] studied and compared designs of a built form designed with virtual reality (VR) and more traditional methods and reported the advantages and shortcomings of VR systems.

MR technologies can overcome some shortcomings of VR. MR devices allow for the projection of the designed space onto the real world in real scale and allow for 3-dimensional interaction with them [2]. MR based social interactions testbed can be used to study users' situated interaction in an SBE [8]. Virtual twins of the smart objects can also be used to interact with the physical objects in an SBE [13].

3   Problem Definition

In an SBE, the use pattern of a physical space maps to the underlying computing infrastructure. So the pattern of situated interaction is inherently different from a traditional architectural space. But, to the best of our knowledge, there is no existing defined framework for SBE design. As a result, the traditional architectural design approach is still being used for the physical design of an SBE. The technological aspects of the SBE are designed as an entirely separate process.

Additionally, the literature review shows that the related works on SBE design mostly address only the technological aspects of SBE design. As a result SBEs often do not cater to a smart living pattern and human-human/human-object relationship aspects [16,17].

So, the research problems addressed in this paper are as follows:

– Develop a framework for assisting the SBE design process by modifying the traditional architectural design process leveraging BIM and user-centred design approach. We use a trans-disciplinary approach including architectural design, smart functionality design and interaction design.
– Describe an immersive technology based reference implementation of the framework. We emphasize on overcoming the shortcomings of traditional 2D representations for represent the enhanced capabilities and abstract components of SBEs.

4   Proposed Approach

We developed a unified, trans-disciplinary framework addressing the interdependency of architectural elements, embedded technology and interaction-modalities by modifying the traditional architectural design process. Our aim is to assist in the holistic SBE design process by combining architectural design and smart functionality design within the same process.

Smart functionality design means the design of the smart capabilities of the space. A smart space is able to perceive user's presence and activity and change the configuration of the environment accordingly. For example, we consider a flexible smart living room in home office context that enables maximum use of space in a small house. The living room transforms into a home office by day and to an expanded living room by evening using an automated movable wall in the design.

The design process of such flexible, smart space needs to consider architectural aspects as well as the design of automatic configuration. Our framework provides a step by step process describing necessary aspects ranging from user requirement collection to an overview of system architecture for an SBE.

An SBE has the following three dimensions [17]:

1. Built Environment: Physical components like wall, floor, furniture, appliances, etc.
2. Embedded Technology: Sensing technology, networking technology, display, etc.
3. Living Requirements: Safety, efficiency, etc.

Our described framework (Fig. 2) modifies the traditional architectural design process (Fig. 1) for meeting the needs of SBE design. This framework consists of four phases- schematic design phase, design development phase, presentation/evaluation phase and construction phase. Each phase consists of multiple steps including detailed guidelines described below:

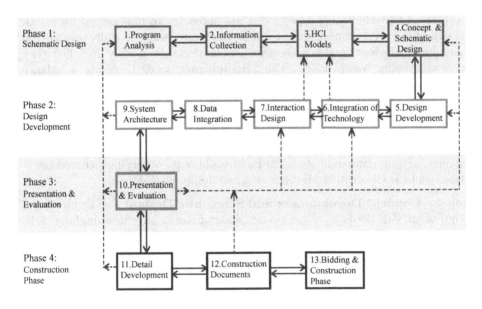

Fig. 2. SBE design framework.

PHASE 1—Schematic Design (Fig. 3 Left):

Step 1—Program Analysis: Understanding the client's requirements for the SBE along with the usage pattern, context, ecological factors, socio-cultural factors, etc. Ecological factors are the components of the operational network of an SBE (e.g., third party application developers).

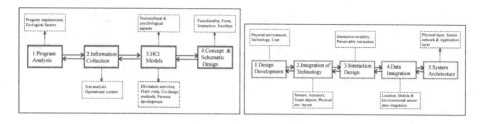

Fig. 3. Left: Phase 1—Schematic design. Right: Phase 2—Design development.

Step 2—Site Analysis, Contextual Information: Operational context is important because SBE designs for urban areas, rural areas or the wilderness would need to address different sets of constraints (e.g., unhindered Internet access and power supply). As the spatial arrangement and architectural design support the functionality of the device [26], standard architectural dimensions need to be considered for installing IoT devices.

Step 3—HCI Models: Users' time-based routines, user-user/user-device relationships and psychological aspects etc. are necessary to understand for avoiding superficial and unnecessary technological intervention. Fully automated smart home devices might make users uncomfortable if they feel like they are always being watched [26]. The SBE designer needs to create a balance between learned automation, programmed automation and fully automatic or user-initiated actions, based on user's preference, e.g., North house did not balance optimal energy efficiency with occupancy comfort resulting in the users option to disable automation [21]. Hence, we introduce HCI models [26] within the SBE design framework. These models include—(1) Elicitation activities (e.g., personas, activity time-line etc.). (2) Field visits (e.g., observing situated interaction) and (3) Generative Methods (e.g., co-design workshops).

Step 4—Concept Development and Schematic Design: The architectural design of an SBE needs to accommodate smart functionality meaningfully. SBE components that influence the space design are smart objects (walls, floors, etc.), smart devices and furniture/fixtures enabled with smart functionality (smart fridge, smart meter, etc.). Schematic design of the space needs to follow the mapping of situated interaction with these smart objects to ensure adaptability [4].

PHASE 2—Design Development: Designing the components of an SBE based on the context study and client's requirements (Fig. 3 Right):

Step 1—Architectural Design: The architectural layout needs to be responsive to the novel interaction and activity diagram of the smart space. For example, flexible space or movable wall scenarios accommodated by architectural design. In SBEs, architectural components work as interaction modalities and smart objects function as architectural components. Hence, planning and layout of sensors and actuators need to be integrated into the architectural design process of SBE.

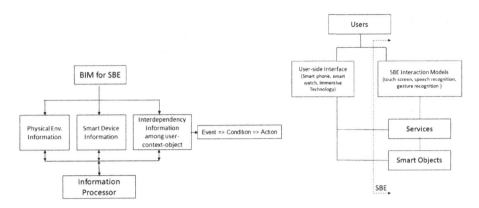

Fig. 4. Left: BIM model for SBE design. Right: Interaction modalities.

Step 2—Leveraging BIM For Integration of technology with physical environments: Traditional BIM consists of information about the physical infrastructure. We propose that the BIM model (Fig. 4 Left) needs to include smart device data and inter-dependency of smart functionality, context, user and devices. Also the constraining factors of sensors to address issues that affect performance of a smart object. For example, placing a temperature sensor too close to a furnace/cooler causes interference with its functionality. Also, trigger/affect information needs to be included for generating warnings to detect conflicting services. For example, occupancy sensor instructing curtain to open and turn on light simultaneously. The designer needs to program specific instructions to handle these scenarios. We promote participatory design by introducing users' preference data in the BIM by including their preferences on event–condition–action. For example, each resident of the house gives input on their preferred automated setting of light, temperature, etc. for different tasks.

Step 3—Interaction and Interface Design: The boundary between physical and digital space is slowly disappearing with dynamic interfaces being integrated into everyday objects. As the nature of HCI dramatically changes, a major challenge in SBE design is developing an well defined interaction model which does not pose cognitive burden to the user or confuse them. A clear boundary needs to be defined for starting and end points and multi modal interaction needs to be supported by the model. A natural mapping between action and perception helps users understand and feel comfortable in a space.

There are two types of interaction modalities—direct interaction (switches, input devices, etc.) and indirect interaction (gesture, voice command, automation etc.). We suggest a balanced, hybrid user-side (direct) and SBE side (indirect) interaction (Fig. 4 Right). For example, the lighting and HVAC system can be semi-automated with options for the users to override the system using voice command or manual switch.

Step 4—Acquiring Data from the Environment: Smart objects gather data about the state of the objects and respond to changing conditions and user-interaction. Typically three types of sensors are used in SBEs:

1. Location sensors: Detect human presence using web cameras, optical and magnetic sensors, etc.
2. Mobile sensors: Detect gestures, motion, etc.
3. Environmental sensors: Measure humidity, temperature, etc.

The major challenge in system design lies in successfully combining the heterogeneous sensors and actuators with a software platform to develop a responsive environment and smooth user experience. The steps in our proposed system are collecting the sensor data, integrating them in a central system and programming the cause and effect (Fig. 5). The proposed framework uses a singular protocol for sending data from smart objects and dynamically creating digital representations for them. The framework supports both cloud and local installation enabling the system to be completely autonomous and independent.

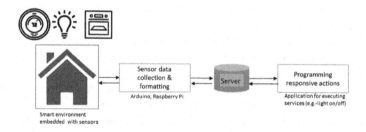

Fig. 5. Acquiring data from SBE.

Step 5—System Architecture: An integrated platform controls the whole system making the SBE responsive to a changing environment. Sensors and actuators send data to a server, an application accesses the data and determines the role and behavior of smart devices. Data analysis tools help in improving the building performance (Fig. 5).

There are three layers in the system architecture:

1. Spatial system: Spatial planning of the environment.
2. Sensor networks: Collecting environmental parameters like temperature, humidity, etc.
3. Services and Application layer: Using collected data for controlling and monitoring building's conditions.

There are some other necessary aspects that need to be considered in the SBE design process. They are stated below:

Energy Efficiency: Additional objectives of an SBE includes improving comfort, operational cost reduction, energy consumption reduction, etc. [24]. So, efficient use of building systems, improving life cycle of building utilities, etc. are necessary criteria for SBE design.

Laws and Regulations: It is very important to know about the relevant laws and regulations before embarking on the design process because SBEs collect a lot of personal data from the users [26]. As it is a comparatively new field the regulations are still not very concrete.

Privacy and Security Aspect: The unique characteristics of SBE enabled by IoT, i.e., use of distributed control, heterogeneous attack surfaces and scale make it hard to provide security and privacy. Eavesdropping is easier as majority of the communication is Wireless. IoT devices have low computing capability and limited energy resource, so complex schemes cannot be implemented for enabling security [3]. End devices belong to various organizations making the management of passwords a challenging task. So there needs to be unified human centered approach for solving this issue. A major concern regarding privacy is the uneasiness among users at being constantly watched or listened to by smart devices. The increasingly pervasive collection of data is a serious privacy concern as it gives away a virtual biography revealing behavioral and lifestyle patterns.

User Safety: In an SBE, it is common to have multiple actuated devices that are capable of acting independently, without user supervision. In such a space with several independently-acting smart objects there is a possibility that the interaction of these smart objects might produce safety hazards for the SBE inhabitants. For example a collision between the SBE user and a moving wall could take place while changing the spatial configuration of the SBE. To prevent hazards like this, the SBE needs to have a system in place that is capable of supporting real-time hazard detection [12]. Such a system would have to constantly monitor the state of the SBE and its inhabitants in order to warn the inhabitants and to take mitigative action against these safety hazards.

PHASE 3—Presentation and Evaluation: The steps in this phase are discussed below:

Step 1—Presenting the Ideas for Feedback and Evaluation: Computer drafting, drawing and 3D models are predominantly used for development and presentation of architectural ideas [4]. But these tools have limitations in case of SBE design. Novel immersive simulation techniques can assist in evaluating the enhanced SBE capabilities and also as input-output modality. Re-configurable spaces, automated configurations etc. can be simulated to understand capability and spatial impact.

An immersive platform has potentials for remote and in-situ collaboration with other consultants. Figure 6 shows an immersive walk through a home interior. Incorporating editing capabilities within the immersive platform allows the designer to make necessary changes and test different iterations of the design at different scales [1,27]. This technology can in fact reinvent the architectural/SBE design process [2].

Step 2—Improve the Design and go back to Phase 1: Based on the feedback from stakeholders, the designer needs to return to the first step and reconsider design decisions for a proper balance between events and actions.

PHASE 4—Construction Phase:

Step 1—Detail development and construction documents: Construction documents include detail working drawings and specifications for guiding construction.

Fig. 6. Visualizing the designed space on top of user's physical environment.

Step 2—Bidding and Construction: After selecting a contractor the designer oversees the construction.

5   MR-Based Reference Implementation of the Framework

We describe a MR-based implementation of the SBE design framework in a smart home context. Since SBE prototype building is expensive and challenging, using immersive MR technology helps simulating the abstract affordances of a smart space to benefit both the user and designer. It also makes the user's participation in the design process easier. Figure 7 highlights the steps that incorporate immersive technology (I.T.) in the SBE design framework.

This implementation assists in the SBE design process by leveraging the MR platform for incorporating the immersive simulation with the user's physical surrounding. The user is able to test the smart functionalities and make design choices for preferred configuration of smart environment for different activities.

SBE design process also requires selection of interaction modalities like gesture, voice command, etc. based on user preference. The MR based implementation allows the user to test interaction scenarios like voice commands and hand gestures to control the state of a physical smart object by manipulating its virtual counterpart and decide upon a preferred interaction method. Moreover, the SBE designer can use the MR based implementation for visualizing different architectural and smart functionality design options.

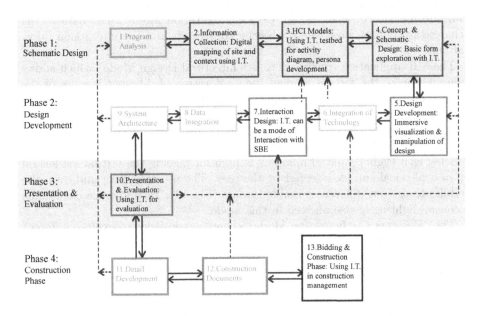

Fig. 7. Steps involved in the MR based reference implementation of the SBE design framework.

The services provided by the implementation include immersive visualization, object manipulation at different scales, multimodal interactions (gesture, gaze, voice command), visual representation of interconnected smart functionality, conflict detection based on the data model, digital representation of users, audio/visual cues, collaboration capabilities, situated interaction, view manipulation, navigation and physics modeling/simulation. Object manipulation also includes controlling physical objects by manipulating their virtual counterparts.

Phase 1 Implementation: A 3D digital model created based on a preliminary conceptual architectural design provides the context for the MR application interface. The first phase requires the designer to collect user's preferences on smart functionality. The "User Configuration Mode" allows the designer to create HCI models (e.g., persona) by directly taking inputs from the users about automated smart-functionality. Figure 8 (Left) shows an example scenario where users explore and choose configurations of smart environment for different activities in an immersive simulation, e.g., recording preferred illumination and volume for activities like watching movies, reading etc. in a game-like application setup. This mode also allows the users to test voice-commands and hand-gesture for controlling physical objects using their virtual counterparts. This functionality helps the user to decide upon a preferred interaction modality. The designer later uses these requirements to program the automation and interaction of SBE.

Phase 2 Implementation: The second phase assists in designing smart functionality and physical environment. A BIM-inspired data model is developed from information collected using "User Configuration Mode". The data model includes the context, user, smart objects, constraints and the interaction information.

The MR application consists of a "Architectural Design Mode" which allows manipulation of the virtual models and exploration of different layouts of the physical design of the house. Designer is able to see the object from different perspectives and in different scales. Modification capabilities like copy, transform, scale, etc. are provided. A small scale holographic representation of the house appears in front of the user along with a library of modules floating over the base model (Fig. 9 Right). Spatial mapping is used for placing the virtual models on top of a physical surface selected by the user. The user can drag and drop the modules to try out different possible layouts (Fig. 10). Testing voice commands to control lighting is also allowed in this mode.

The "Designer Configuration Mode" allows the designer to explore different possible combinations of smart devices in the immersive visualization. The data model is used to validate and notify designers if the collection of smart devices is safe, secure and functional.

Fig. 8. Left: User Configuration Mode—Customize configuration of ambient environment to accommodate user's personal preference. Use of data model for configuration of SBE. Right: Designer Configuration Mode—Explore combinations of smart objects and resolve conflicts.

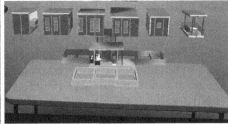

Fig. 9. Left: Preview mode: visualizing design in outdoors. Right: Architectural design mode: visualizing design and module library in MR environment.

It is used to identify conflicts if some event triggers multiple contradictory actions. If any combination of smart functionality violates the safety and security of the environment because of overlapping/conflicting trigger-affect, a warning message is generated for the designer to resolve the conflict by introducing appropriate conditions while programming.

Figure 8 right shows an example scenario where a designer receives warning messages if she attempts to combine conflicting services. Here the smart curtain and the smart bulb are conflicting as both affect lighting.

Another example is that, functionality of a sprinkler system can be hampered by a water leak detection system in case the latter turns off water supply after detecting water pouring into a room with potentially disastrous consequences.

Fig. 10. Architectural design mode: use of MR in the SBE design process.

Phase 3 Implementation: Phase 3 (presentation and evaluation phase) consists of testing the proposed interaction modalities for controlling devices and the overall SBE functionality using the "Preview Mode". In "Preview Mode", the designer/client is able to navigate through the interior of the proposed building in real scale in immersive visualization for understanding the spatial quality. They are also able to visualize the design on actual site (Fig. 9 Left). This helps in smart facade design based on sun path and wind flow to utilize natural light and wind for making it energy efficient.

Phase 4 Implementation: Phase 4 leverages the "Preview Mode" for immersive visualization for assistance in construction management.

MR Application: System Architecture

Figure 11 shows an example of the MR application architecture using light control as the use case.

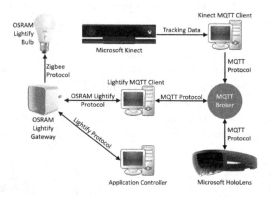

Fig. 11. MR application architecture.

The work-flow for developing a similar MR application consists of three steps:

STEP 1—Preparing the Virtual Components:

The built environment is designed and modeled using digital drafting tools (AutoCAD) and 3D-modeling tools (SketchUp). The models need to be generated in the origin so that transformation in game engine is easier.

STEP 2—Designing the behavior of application:

Application Design: Capabilities like manipulating basic shapes (e.g., change dimensions, add, move), changing color, texture, etc are useful design tools. The virtual model includes BIM information, energy performance, smart functionality and interdependency information with other smart objects. After designing the behavior and capabilities of the application, hand gesture, gaze and voice command are used as interaction modalities. The application provides audio/visual cues in the UI to assist in the design process, e.g., selection menus, shape and color palettes, etc.

System Overview: The interaction model is informed by user data (data from client/designer), smart object data, physical environment data and context data (Fig. 12 Left). The proposed framework creates a virtual twin of SBE using a data model for immersive visualization (Fig. 12 Right). To verify service conflicts, each service registers triggering/affecting factors and the information processor performs reasoning based on space and context.

STEP 3—Developing the application:

Programming the behavior of the application includes developing embodied interaction and testing them using a game engine. For collecting environmental and smart object data, the application needs to connect to the archive and overlay on the virtual model. Building and testing the application for immersive technology platform (VR, MR) requires use of game engines (e.g., Unity, Unreal Engine).

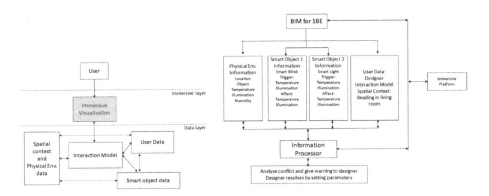

Fig. 12. Left: System overview of MR based SBE design process. Right: Integration of data model with immersive technology.

6   Use Cases and Evaluation

This section discusses the reference implementation of the proposed approaches. An SBE was designed based on the approach described in [7]. The computational and physical infrastructure were perceived as interdependent from the beginning of the design process.

Schematic Design: First, the program analysis step is followed to identify the aim, which is to develop a responsive and energy efficient home with concepts of aging in place and flexible space. Then information collection and HCI modeling is followed to get an overall idea about the conceptual clients, site, context, user's preferences. In a traditional architecture process each basic activity needs a dedicated physical space for supporting functionality. Here we conceptualize an automated, transformable space with multi-functional use. Based on the user's activity, the room would change configuration. For example, the occupants can turn the bedroom into a home office using voice command. Dining space can be turned into family living and formal living into Home Theater.

Design Development: Two major design proposals were developed according to the schemes from phase 1.

1. **Modular, off-site construction using integrated technology:** The proposed design consists of a prefabricated modular design approach combined with site-built components (Fig. 9 Right). The core functional spaces of a house, like kitchen, bathroom, etc., are designed as modules and constructed remotely in a factory. They are constructed fully equipped with the embedded technology like sensors, actuators. Then they are brought to site and anchored to the site built foundation system.

   The proposed system architecture focuses on connecting smart objects, collecting usage data, storage and exploring usage pattern (Fig. 5). Interaction modalities include hand gesture, touch screen, switches and immersive technology based interaction. Touch screen displays are embedded with walls, tables, etc. physical components of the house.

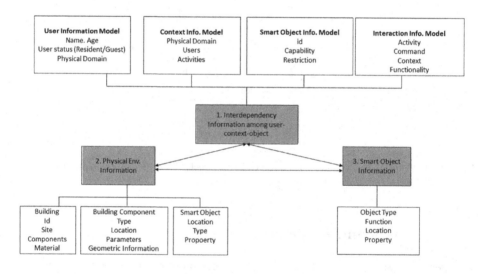

Fig. 13. Proposed user centered data model.

2. **Data model:** The proposed data model consists of semantic information depicting spatial relationships among users, objects and context in addition to geometry information (Fig. 13). User's contextual preferences for different events, smart device information and physical information are modeled here.

7   Conclusion and Future Work

In SBEs, 'things' can autonomously interact with each other and change the state of the physical world. SBEs provide a transformed task-space mapping with changed use-pattern. So during the design of SBE, simply incorporating smart devices into a space without focusing on the holistic design process leads to a rigid and reduced spatial and experiential quality. But current SBE design practices focus primarily on computational capabilities with less importance on holistic approach, resulting in a rigid and sometimes impractical setting. We describe a user centered SBE design approach modified from the traditional architectural process to achieve the desired spatial quality. The proposed framework addresses the issues of situated interaction and underlying technology along with the physical environment design process. A novel data model emphasizing human-space interaction is introduced in the layered framework focusing on increasing user participation in SBE design.

We also describe an immersive technology based reference implementation of the proposed framework using participatory design principles. This implementation allows visualization of invisible services and real-time configuration based on individual preferences before deploying them. Smart home clients can experience the immersive visualization and interact with the designed environment using a game-like application. Data input by actual users is integrated in the data-model assigning an active role to users in the design process. The framework helps testing novel interaction scenarios and complex affordances whereas testing situated interaction is challenging and expensive by following traditional prototyping methods. Moreover, immersive visualization of data generated by smart objects enables more efficient usage of the data in the design process.

Overall, the contributions of our work are as follows:

- A framework for assisting in SBE design process developed by modifying the traditional architectural design process and incorporating user-centred BIM.
- An immersive technology based reference implementation of the framework.

We are working on employing the framework as an education tool for next generation SBE designers. An ongoing user study tests the usability of the application for both the designers and users of SBEs. The study is conducted on two groups—architecture students and people from general population. Architecture students are considered as subject matter experts within the context of SBE design. General people are considered as users of SBE. Participants complete three tasks using traditional methods and mixed reality based implementation of the framework. The first task for the study participants is to configure the ambient environment setting (e.g., illumination, temperature, volume) in a living room context for watching movies. The second task is to use different interaction modalities (e.g., voice command, hand gesture, automatic) for selecting and controlling a device (e.g, lights). The third and final task is to choose smart objects from a menu and place them within the living room context. The participants are provided a feedback in case of a conflict. Finally, the participant completes a survey about their preferences and opinions for the study.

Overall, ours is a novel and comprehensive approach addressing the major aspects associated with SBE design from an interdisciplinary point of view. We hope that the proposed framework would help reduce design failures in SBEs during occupancy period.

References

1. Anderson, L., Esser, J., Interrante, V.: A virtual environment for conceptual design in architecture. In: Proceedings of the Workshop on Virtual Environments, pp. 57–63. ACM (2003)
2. Pandit, A.S.: How virtual environments could help architects? (2018). https://www.arch2o.com/how-virtual-environments-could-help-architects/. Accessed 2 May 2018
3. Atzori, L., Iera, A., Morabito, G.: The internet of things: a survey. Comput. Netw. **54**(15), 2787–2805 (2010)
4. Bridges, A., Charitos, D.: On architectural design in virtual environments. Des. Stud. **18**(2), 143–154 (1997)
5. Campbell, D.A., Wells, M.: A critique of virtual reality in the architectural design process. University of Washington HITL, Technical report R-94 3 (1994)
6. Dasgupta, A.: Towards a unified framework for smart built environment design: an architectural perspective. Master's thesis, Virginia Polytechnic Institute and State University, Blacksburg, VA (2018)
7. Dasgupta, A.: Transience and permanence: an architectural dialogue. Master's thesis, Virginia Polytechnic Institute and State University, Blacksburg, VA (2018)
8. Dasgupta, A., Buckingham, N., Gračanin, D., Handosa, M., Tasooji, R.: A mixed reality based social interactions testbed: a game theory approach. In: Chen, J.Y.C., Fragomeni, G. (eds.) VAMR 2018. LNCS, vol. 10910, pp. 40–56. Springer, Cham (2018). https://doi.org/10.1007/978-3-319-91584-5_4
9. De Biasse and Seminara Architects: The 5 phases of the architectural design process (2018). http://dbsem.com/the-five-phases-of-the-architectural-design-process/. Accessed 21 Sept 2018
10. DiscoverDesign: What is the design process? why is it helpful? (2018). https://www.discoverdesign.org/handbook. Accessed 21 Sept 2018
11. Dourish, P.: Seeking a foundation for context-aware computing. Hum.-Comput. Interact. **16**(2–4), 229–241 (2001)
12. Gračanin, D., D'Amico, A., Manuel, M., Carson, W., Eltoweisy, M., Cheng, L.: Biologically inspired safety and security for smart built environments: position paper. In: Proceedings of the 3rd Workshop on Bio-inspired Security, Trust, Assurance and Resilience (BioSTAR 2018), 2018 IEEE Security and Privacy Workshop (SPW), pp. 293–298, 24 May 2018
13. Gračanin, D., Matković, K., Wheeler, J.: An approach to modeling internet of things based smart built environments. In: Proceedings of the 2015 Winter Simulation Conference, pp. 3208–3209. IEEE Press (2015)
14. Guinard, A., McGibney, A., Pesch, D.: A wireless sensor network design tool to support building energy management. In: Proceedings of the First ACM Workshop on Embedded Sensing Systems for Energy-Efficiency in Buildings, pp. 25–30. ACM (2009)
15. Inada, T., Igaki, H., Ikegami, K., Matsumoto, S., Nakamura, M., Kusumoto, S.: Detecting service chains and feature interactions in sensor-driven home network services. Sensors **12**(7), 8447–8464 (2012)
16. Jeng, T.: Advanced ubiquitous media for interactive space. In: Martens, B., Brown, A. (eds.) Computer Aided Architectural Design Futures, pp. 341–350. Springer, Heidelberg (2005). https://doi.org/10.1007/1-4020-3698-1_32
17. Jeng, T.: Toward a ubiquitous smart space design framework. J. Inf. Sci. Eng. **25**(3), 675–686 (2009)

18. KGA Studio Architects, PC: How does the architectural design process work? (2015). http://kgarch.com/how-does-the-architectural-design-process-work/. Accessed 21 Sept 2018
19. Lertlakkhanakul, J., Choi, J.W., Kim, M.Y.: Building data model and simulation platform for spatial interaction management in smart home. Autom. Constr. **17**(8), 948–957 (2008)
20. Lynch, K.: The Image of the City, vol. 11. MIT Press, Cambridge (1960)
21. Makonin, S., Bartram, L., Popowich, F.: A smarter smart home: case studies of ambient intelligence. IEEE Perv. Comput. **12**(1), 58–66 (2013)
22. McGinty, T.: Design and the design process. In: Introduction to Architecture, pp. 152–190 (1979)
23. Mitropoulos, E.G.: Space networks: toward hodological space design for urban man. Ekistics **39**(232), 199–207 (1975)
24. Nguyen, T.A., Aiello, M.: Energy intelligent buildings based on user activity: a survey. Energy Build. **56**, 244–257 (2013)
25. Norberg-Schulz, C.: Existence, Space and Architecture, 3rd edn. Prager Publishers, Santa Barbara (1974)
26. Rowland, C., Goodman, E., Charlier, M., Light, A., Lui, A.: Designing Connected Products: UX for the Consumer Internet of Things. O'Reilly Media Inc, Sebastopol (2015)
27. Schnabel, M.A., Kvan, T.: Spatial understanding in immersive virtual environments. Int. J. Archit. Comput. **1**(4), 435–448 (2003)
28. Thiel, P.: A sequence-experience notation. Town Plan. Rev. **32**(1), 33 (1961)
29. Weiser, M.: The computer for the 21st century. SIGMOBILE Mob. Comput. Commun. Rev. **3**(3), 3–11 (1999)
30. Wiberg, M.: Interaction design meets architectural thinking. Interactions **22**(2), 60–63 (2015)
31. Zhang, J., Seet, B.C., Lie, T.T.: Building information modelling for smart built environments. Buildings **5**(1), 100–115 (2015)
32. Zhang, L., et al.: Spatial cognition and architectural design in 4D immersive virtual reality: testing cognition with a novel audiovisual CAVE-CAD tool. In: Proceedings of the Spatial Cognition for Architectural Design Conference (2011)

Optimization of a WiFi Wireless Network that Maximizes the Level of Satisfaction of Users and Allows the Use of New Technological Trends in Higher Education Institutions

Leonel Hernandez[1(✉)], Nidia Balmaceda[2], Hugo Hernandez[3],
Carlos Vargas[4], Emiro De La Hoz[5], Nataly Orellano[6],
Emilse Vasquez[7], and Carlos Eduardo Uc-Rios[8]

[1] Department of Telematic Engineering, Faculty of Engineering,
Institución Universitaria ITSA, Barranquilla, Colombia
lhernandezc@itsa.edu.co
[2] Faculty of Basic Sciences, Institución Universitaria ITSA,
Barranquilla, Colombia
nebalmaceda@itsa.edu.co
[3] Faculty of Economic Sciences, Corporación Universitaria Reformada CUR,
Barranquilla, Colombia
Hugo.hp83@yahoo.com
[4] Faculty of Economic Sciences, Corporación Universitaria Latinoamericana
CUL, Barranquilla, Colombia
cvargas@ul.edu.co
[5] Department of Electronic and Computer Science, Universidad de La Costa
CUC, Barranquilla, Colombia
edelahoz@cuc.edu.co
[6] Faculty of Education, Corporación Universitaria Minuto de Dios
UNIMINUTO, Barranquilla, Colombia
nataly.orellano@gmail.com
[7] Department of Accreditation, Universidad Libre, Barranquilla, Colombia
evasquez@unilibrebaq.edu.co
[8] Department of Engineering, Universidad Internacional Iberoamericana,
Campeche, Mexico
carlos.uc@unini.edu.mx

Abstract. The campus wireless networks have many users, who have different roles and network requirements, ranging from the use of educational platforms, informative consultations, emails, among others. Currently due to the inefficient use of network resources and little wireless planning, caused by the growth of the technological infrastructure (which is often due to daily worries, rather than to a lack of preparation by those in charge of managing the network), There are two essential factors that truncate the requirement of having a stable and robust network platform. First, the degradation of the quality of services perceived by users, and second, the congestion caused by the high demand for convergent traffic (video, voice, and data). Both factors imply great challenges on the part of

© Springer Nature Switzerland AG 2019
N. Streitz and S. Konomi (Eds.): HCII 2019, LNCS 11587, pp. 144–160, 2019.
https://doi.org/10.1007/978-3-030-21935-2_12

the administrators of the network, which in many occasions are overwhelmed by permanent incidences of instability, coverage, and congestion, as well as the difficulty of maintaining it economically. The present investigation seeks to propose a process of optimization of the infrastructure and parameters of the configuration of a wireless network, that allows maximizing the level of satisfaction of the users in Higher Education Institutions. In the first place, it is expected to determine an adequate methodology to estimate the level of satisfaction of the users (defining a mathematical criterion or algorithm based on the study variables [1], characterize the environment in which the project will be developed, making a complete study of the wireless conditions and implement optimization strategies with software-defined networks (SDN). SDN is a concept in computer networks that allows network management to be carried out efficiently and flexibly, separating the control plane from the data plane into network devices. SDN architecture consists of an infrastructure layer which is a collection of network devices connected to the SDN Controller using protocol (OpenFlow) as a protocol [2]. Also, SDN will study traffic patterns on the network as a basis for optimizing network device usage [3]. The phases of the research will be carried out following the life cycle defined by the Cisco PPDIOO methodology (Prepare, Plan, Design, Implement, Operate, Optimize) [4].

Keywords: Software-Defined Networks SDN · Wireless Networks · Optimization · PPDIOO · Higher Education Institutions

1 Introduction

Currently, many institutions of higher education have a technological platform that offers a large number of services to students and teachers, which facilitates the teaching and learning process. Within the services provided by students and teachers, there is total access to the Internet, access to virtuals queries in databases and specialized bibliographic resources, access to software and applications on the web, online consultations of notes and activities to develop, etc. These services place educational entities at an advantage since tools and technological means are currently used and are involved in all aspects of daily life. In some institutions of higher education, it is possible to identify the shortcomings in terms of services at a technological level that offers students, professors and members of the institutional community, due to several factors such as the lack of resources to improve the infrastructure of the Reduce, there are planned, connectivity problems, day, day, misuse, resources, media, etc. protocols.

The fact of not having connectivity and total access hinders communication and the development of any activity or work that you want to do with the use of technological tools such as smartphones, tablets, and laptops at any time when the student or teacher is inside of the campus. Given this problem, disinterest in the use of virtual resources offered by the institution is encouraged. The purpose of technological tools in learning environments has become indispensable since they allow interaction in real time. Hernandez et al. [5] in their research on the use of the Internet of Things in the Higher Education Institutions of the city of Barranquilla, made a preliminary diagnosis of the state of the network infrastructure, both wired and wireless, of the leading universities of the city. Only some institutions have adequate technological platform and of which their users have a high level of satisfaction. The vast majority, according to the study, have the flaws already mentioned. On those campus sites where connectivity is inefficient, slow and intermittent according to what is expressed by members of the educational community, it is essential to take some action to improve wireless access.

With the purpose of promoting technological growth in Higher Education Institutions, it is necessary to optimize the wireless network platform or infrastructure, which is capable of efficiently managing the network services offered by the institution and which maximizes the level of user satisfaction. The optimization (and probable implementation in some parts of the campus) of this platform will allow the connectivity and total access to the internet and to the different applications of any person that is inside the institution and that is involved in some process of this. The paper is structured in the following way, first the introduction that has just been specified. The second section shows previous research and the state of the art of the project. The third section emphasizes the research methodology used. The fourth section shows preliminary progress and discussion about the results. It culminates with the conclusions and future work to develop from this work.

2 SDN and WLAN Optimization. A Literature Review

In this section we analyze the existing context in the scientific community and related projects about optimization processes of wireless network infrastructure, using a new trend as SDN. With regards to wireless network optimization, several studies have been carried out [6, 7]. Cisco in its material of the Networking Academy [8] highlights the following essential points about the data network: among all vital elements for human existence, the need to interact is just after the need to sustain life. Communication is almost as important to us as air, water, food and a place to live. The methods we use to share ideas and information are continually changing and evolving. The immediate nature of Internet communications encourages the formation of global communities. These communities motivate the social interaction that depends on the location or the time zone. Being able to communicate reliably with everyone everywhere is vital for our personal and business life. To support the immediate delivery of the millions of messages exchanged between people around the world, we rely on a web of interconnected networks.

A novel and innovative way to optimize the wireless network infrastructure is through the implementation of a solution based on SDN, or networks defined by software. SDN enables organizations to accelerate the deployment and deployment of applications by dramatically reducing IT costs through the automation of policy-based workflow. SDNs converge the administration of network services and applications into centralized and scalable coordination platforms that can automate the provisioning and configuration of the entire infrastructure. In our academic environment, there has been no research related to this issue, let alone a solution for network optimization, whether wireless or wired, based on this new approach. About SDN several essential investigations have been carried out. Sezer et al. [9] in their research explain the fundamentals of SDN and the impact it will have as a future paradigm for the implementation of networks. Jammal et al. [10] present a series of references and important works about SDN and its application for the optimization of connectivity infrastructures. The ONF (Open Networking Foundation) [2] defines SDN as "an emerging architecture that is dynamic, manageable, cost-effective and adaptable, making it ideal for the high bandwidth required by the dynamic nature of today's applications." Figure 1 shows the SDN Architecture:

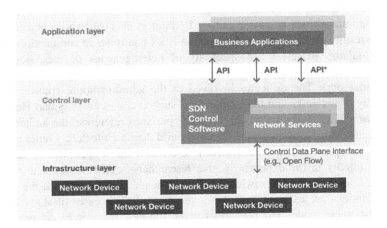

Fig. 1. SDN architecture

Entering SDN, we analyzed the theories related to the topic. Beginning with Bakshi [11], explains that SDN is a new approach to the design of the network, based on the ability to programmatically modify the behavior of network devices. Poses that SDN will provide many benefits to the organizations that implement it since it will allow networks to be more flexible, dynamic and cost-efficient.

Internet of Things (IoT) is a new trend that raises the total connectivity of all devices that can be imagined, using sensor networks, fixed wireless, and mobile solutions, among others. Wifi solutions based on the new IoT trend, in conjunction with SDN, are also susceptible to optimization. Baird et al. [12] in its research, aims to use an approach based on SDN with captive portals and the use of the 802.1X security standard to control access to the network by intermediary or final devices, in such a way that the congestion that may arise in the network does not affect the performance of the same. However, there are also some studies that consider it not so convenient to make a complete migration, but gradual, from the traditional scheme of supervision, monitoring, control and optimization of conventional networks to SDN. Studies such as the one conducted by Sandhya et al. [13], raises some reasons for a gradual transition to SDN. Among these reasons, because the hybrid environment allows SDN and legacy equipment or nodes to coexist, which facilitates the development of an incremental implementation strategy. The hybrid solution provides adaptability to the budgetary conditions of an organization, the programmability of the network, the recovery of mechanisms inherited over time, among others.

Continuing with the line of hybrid SDN solutions, Amin et al. [14], in its research, aims to show different updated studies related to research and development of hybrid SDN networks. Haruyama [15] gave one of the first definitions of SDR to implement SDN oriented wireless networks, he explains "Thanks to the recent advancement of semiconductor technology, it is now possible to process high-speed communication signals in wireless telecommunication systems using as much digital technology as possible.

Other research related to the integration and interaction between IoT, SDN and wireless communications is carried out by Bedhief et al. [16], whose objective is to present the results of the implementation of an SDN controller in conjunction with the MiniNet emulator, to test the connectivity of heterogeneous devices, beyond the heterogeneous wireless networks in which these devices can operate (Ethernet, WiFi, ZigBee, Bluetooth). The difficulty involved in the administration, control and programmability of networks and IoT applications such as Smart cities, Smart Healthcare, Smart Industry, etc., based the research. In the previous reference, the authors use an emulator called MiniNet to make the tests and build their architecture. Fontes et al. [17] in their work, explain in that the objective is to emulate SDN/OpenFlow scenarios that allow high fidelity in the experiments that researchers need to execute to test SDN architectures, to recreate real networking environments. The strengths of the emulator and its limitations are exposed, and they even present three cases of study in which different tests were made. MiniNet arises given the new features of current wireless networks, in which the density of users, the number of base stations and customers, and high traffic rates require the design of cost-effective wireless networks, which have efficient use of resources and ease of administration, due to the challenge involved in managing this complex type of solutions, including IoT applications.

In addition to the emulator mentioned above, other technologies work hand in hand with SDN to manage mobility in IEEE 802.11 WLAN networks. Gilani et al. [18], present the benefits of joint work between SDN and NFV (Network Function Virtualization), for the optimization of traditional wireless infrastructure, the primary objective of its research. A study focused on the control plane of the infrastructure equipment that facilitates virtualization and network administration was carried out by Blenk et al. [19] in their research. The authors explain that hypervisors are logically located between the multiple virtual SDN networks (vSDN), which reside in the SDN physical network infrastructure, and the corresponding tenant controllers (vSDN).

3 Methodology

The following types of research are defined, based on what was pointed out by Hernandez Sampieri et al. [20]:

- According to the object of study: For the execution of this project and according to the problem, it is necessary to use two types of research. First, exploratory research, because innovation is an essential support for the project; therefore, some critical aspects of its development are unknown. As the second type of research, we have applied research, because it is proposed to solve a practical problem of the environment, in this organizational case (maximizing the level of satisfaction of the users of the wireless network, defining an optimization process of the Wireless infrastructure).

- According to the level of measurement, scientific knowledge, and information analysis:
  - Quali-quantitative: because it is based on a working hypothesis, defined in how to maximize the level of satisfaction of the users of the wireless network, optimizing the configuration parameters and the infrastructure of the Wireless network through SDN, to which by means of a proposed process and with a series of procedures, it is intended to provide a solution, evolving with the course of the study.
  - Descriptive: since all the documentation related to optimization and designs of wireless networks will be reviewed, SDN implementation, solutions that have already been provided with advanced wireless equipment and contribute to the scientific literature on the subject based on what was compiled.
  - Correlational: It is intended to visualize how a variable can behave knowing the behavior of another related variable and evaluate the degree of relationship between them, that is, cause-effect analysis between independent and dependent variables will be performed.
- Research design. The present project is part of the experimental design type, considering the collection of the necessary information to answer the research questions, since a series of experiments will be carried out, testing each one of them, and verifying the respective results of each.
- Phases of the project. For this research, the life cycle defined by the Cisco network design methodology, PPDIOO, will be adopted, explained by Oppenheimer [4]. As shown in Fig. 2, PPDIOO consists of five stages:

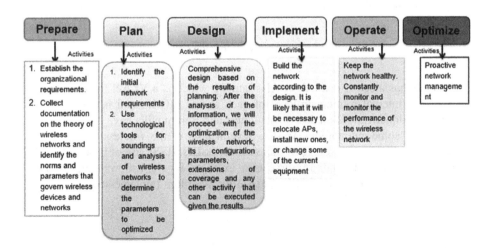

Fig. 2. PPDIOO life cycle

4   Results and Discussion

The project is in the design phase of a network topology that allows optimizing the performance of the wireless infrastructure. The results to present will be those collected by a survey to measure the level of satisfaction of users for identified service variables. Likewise, the results of the site survey and response times of the current network will be exposed, as well as the design of the simulated topology in the Mininet tool, on which tests like those performed in the existing network will be executed. The next phase of the project is to establish the gap between both measures to conclude which solution is more favorable and, in this way, provide the recommendations of the case to the directors of the University for the acquisition of network infrastructure equipment that enhance the performance of the same. The current infrastructure does not support SDN, so it cannot be implemented, and no more real measures can be taken. However, Mininet is a test very close to the actual implementation and can serve as a support to justify the investment.

A. *Network Topology. Current Network Vs. SDN Simulation*

Figure 3 shows the current network topology of the University:

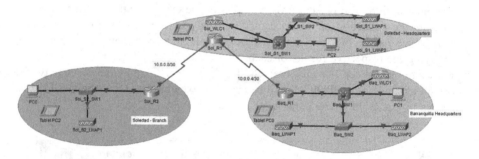

Fig. 3. ITSA current network topology – all venues

Each site has a set of defined VLANs, among which is a VLAN for the wireless network. The internal routing protocol of each site is EIGRP, and between sites is BGP. The headquarters of Soledad Headquarters and Barranquilla have each a wireless controller and some autonomous WAPs. Several tests of the wireless network were taken, among which are: coverage, response time, SSIDs, RSSI, use of bandwidth. The measurements made in the Library serve as an example. Figure 4 shows a high number of SSIDs in the area, channel, RSSI and security algorithm implemented:

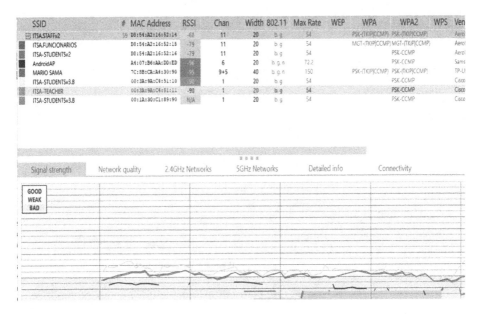

Fig. 4. Site survey – library

As you can see, there is a high RSSI in each SSID, which means that the wireless network in this area is presenting high congestion and intermittency. Figure 5 shows that the overall network quality is poor:

Figure 6 shows that there are SSIDs that overlap each other, which affects the performance of the wireless network in general:

Figure 7 shows a graphical ping to the gateway. It is possible to see the intermittence and instability of the ping, from a wireless client:

On average, the approximate round trip taken with the ping is 130 ms, which is too high for a traditional wireless connection. This same behavior is reflected in the vast majority of the campus (in each location), for which it is essential to make an optimization. The project proposes to measure the performance that an SDN solution can give in a simulated environment, which will give a good measure of the possibility of migration of the current infrastructure.

Figure 8 shows the topology of the network designed with SDN:

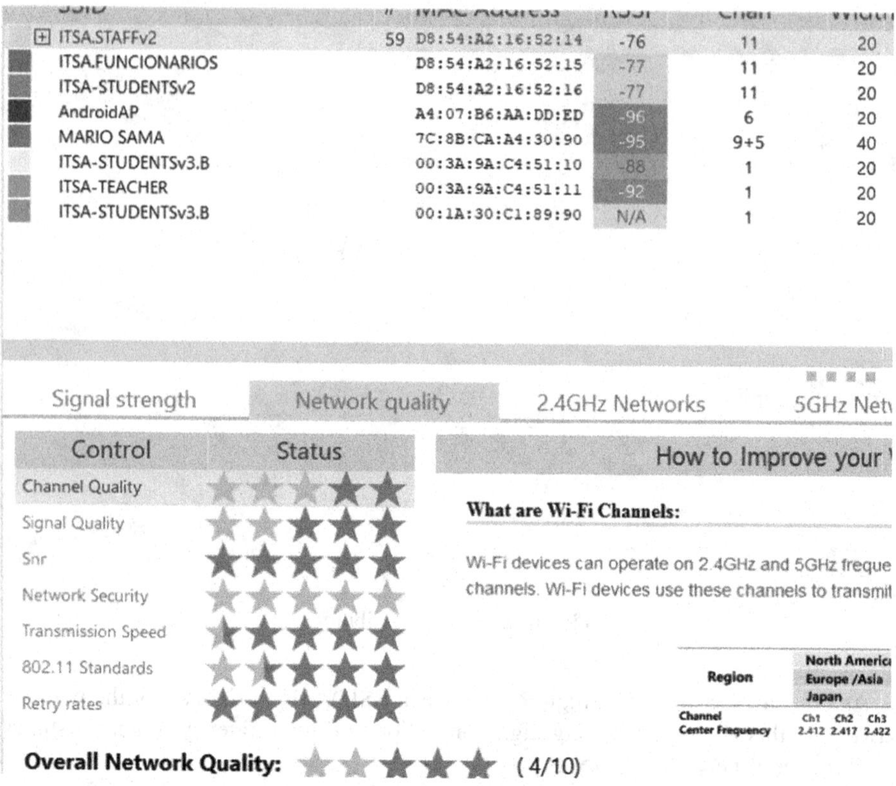

Fig. 5. Total network quality

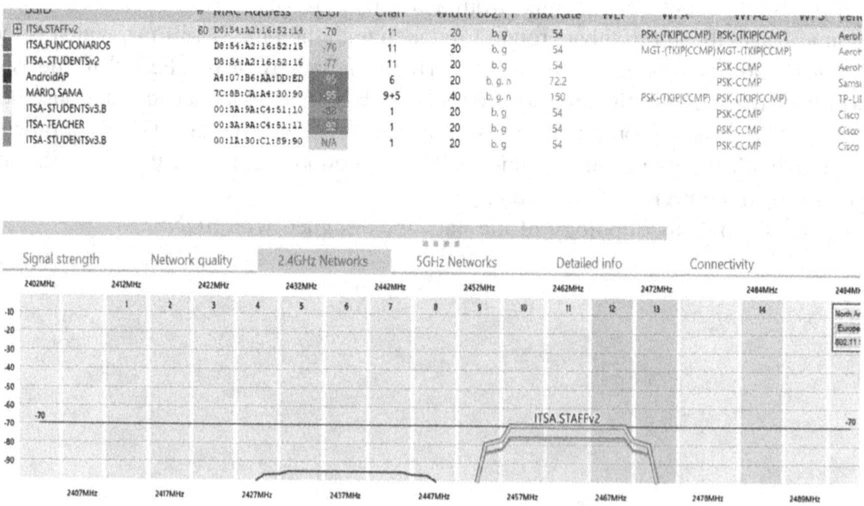

Fig. 6. Overlapping between SSIDs.

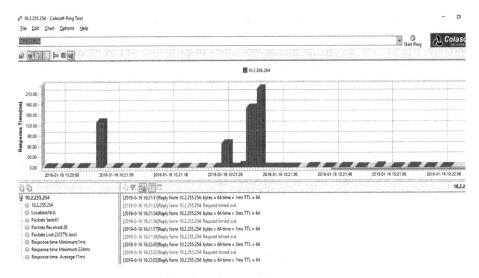

Fig. 7. Intermittence of a ping

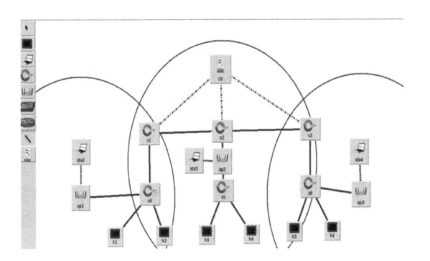

Fig. 8. Network topology – SDN design

The following solution is proposed: there is a single controller that will monitor the behavior of the three sites and all connected devices, including wireless equipment. The traffic behavior between each site is configured through the controller, thus optimizing network response times and overall performance. It is advisable to have an additional backup controller, but it is not included in the design due to its high cost. In this topology, S1, S2, and S3 are the primary switches in each site. At this moment we are testing this topology, there are still not enough results to establish a comparative analysis of the performance of the SDN network concerning the traditional network topology, which is expected to have a short term.

B. *Results and Analysis of Statistical Measurement Instrument.*

A survey was conducted to measure the level of satisfaction of the users of the institution's wireless network, to determine the factors that most affect, and review the parameters that most affect the behavior and expectations of the users of the network. Each question is a variable, which will be shown coded later.

As an initial result of the factorial analysis of multiple correspondences, using software R version 3.5.0, a two-dimensional graph was obtained, which shows the relative positions of the variables that allow measuring the satisfaction of the users for the internet service, as shown in Fig. 9, with which the classification of the observations or individuals was made, through the Factors Map provided by the software R, considering how the individuals responded to the questionnaire. The two dimensions of the survey, collect 21.21% of the variability in the answers obtained.

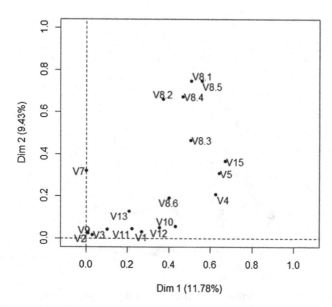

Fig. 9. Two dimensions. relative position of variables

Figure 10 shows three groups of observations or cluster can be identified, from which different groups were obtained taking into account the correspondences in the answers provided when applying the survey:

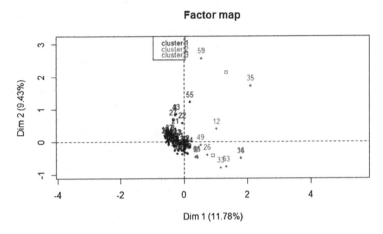

Fig. 10. Factors map

The first Cluster (C1) is made up of 50 individuals, corresponding to 79.37% of the total sample, of which 11 students from Telematics Engineering, 7 from Industrial Engineering and 32 from Technique in Industrial Electronic Maintenance are part. In this group, students are relatively satisfied with the Internet service of the university campus, which are characterized in general terms, for their reasonable satisfaction concerning the technical characteristics and services associated with the provision of Internet service on the university campus. They are mostly students of the Electronic Maintenance Technique program, but it is also made up of people from the Engineering programs, especially Computer Engineering, who know about the technical specifications of the service, 72% of the participants use the WiFi network Frequently.

Among the standard variables of the reasonably satisfied cluster are the regular ratings on the technical characteristics of the internet service, such as speed, availability, signal coverage, response times, real-time connection, stability and network security, as well as other variables evaluated in the survey, which were common, as shown in detail in Table 1. For this group, the current technological infrastructure that supports the Internet service is subject to improvement, given the regular qualifications of both the technical characteristics and the attention provided by the Technology staff, which is reflected in the regular levels of satisfaction in the service. So, it is necessary to focus action plans towards the optimization of infrastructure and quality in the service for the internet service. It is also vital that the processes carried out by the university for the improvement of its technological infrastructure be disseminated since 60% of the participating students do not know about these processes, activities, and progress in this regard.

Table 1. Common variables cluster 1

Technical variables	• 58% of the students in this cluster believe that the speed of connection to the wireless network is regular • 94% of individuals consider that the current technological infrastructure is susceptible to improvement • 42% of the students rated the availability of the Wi-Fi network as consistent, and 52% of the students rated it as regular to poor • 32% of the students consider how to regulate the coverage of the signal; that is, they can not connect from all points of the university campus. • 40% rated the response time of the network as regular, that is, presented delays • 42% of the students rated as regular the connection in a real-time of several users • 38% of the students rated the stability of the wireless network as regular, that is, that it shows drops in the signal or intermittence • 50% of students rate how to regulate network security
Service variables	• 60% of the students in this cluster do not know the processes that the university is carrying out to improve the technological infrastructure • 62% stated how to regulate their general assessment of the access service to the wireless network of the university campus • 56% of students qualify as regulating the level of satisfaction of WiFi network services. • 56% of the student rated the support services and correction of failures of the management unit and campus systems as regular • Despite the regular qualifications, 96% of the participating students consider that the wireless network service facilitates the execution of activities and academic consultations
Connection times/file download times	• 70% of the students said that, on average, they wait between 0–2 min to connect to the wireless network and access the internet and 20% wait between 3 to 5 min • 52% of the students said that, on average, they must wait between 3–5 min to download a file; of course, this depends on the size of the file
The frequency of use of the University's internet/personal mobile networks	• 72% of students have a high frequency of internet use • 59% of the participants said that they use their mobile phone to access Wi-Fi, due to faults in the campus network

Cluster 2 (C2) is composed of 11 individuals, representing 17.46% of the sample. In this group, students are satisfied with the Internet service of the university campus, which are characterized in general terms, for their satisfaction with some of the aspects evaluated in the survey, specifically in the technical characteristics of the Internet service. They are mostly students of the Industrial Engineering program, who do not have as much level of knowledge as students of related programs with the area of ICTs, 63% of participants use the WiFi network frequently.

As common variables of this cluster, there is the excellent perception that students have about the technical characteristics of the service, such as availability, signal coverage, response times, real-time connection, stability and network security. These services were rated in the excellent range by more than 80%, although they did not think the same regarding speed, in which 54% of the participants rated as slow. Another of the key variables of correspondence in this cluster is related to the ease of the wireless network for the development of its activities and consultations, to which 72% of respondents coincided positively. On the other hand, we identified as grouping variables, the time of connection to the network and time of downloading files from the WiFi network, to which the students responded that the waiting time is high, on average, between 6 and 10 min. Although the general results for this group show a general pattern of satisfaction, it is necessary to bear in mind that the favorable perception may be due to the lack of technical expertise or affinity with the area of knowledge of the ICTs. For this reason, their opinion may be less demanding than that of Cluster 1, where students from the computer and electronic areas are grouped. It is also necessary to generate the work plans and projects needed to improve the speed of the network and the times of connection and download of contents.

On the other hand, the third Cluster (C3) is made up of 2 individuals, corresponding to 3.17% of the sample. In this group, students dissatisfied with the wireless internet service provided by the university are located, who are characterized in general terms, by their total dissatisfaction, specifically in the technical aspects of the WiFi internet service. In this cluster, the academic program does not affect general dissatisfaction, since this group is made up of a student of Industrial Engineering and a student of Technical Professional in Industrial Electronic Maintenance, so it is not conclusive to state that the type of program it is associated with the level of satisfaction in this group. As common variables of this cluster, are the technical characteristics of the service, such as availability, signal coverage, response times, real-time connection, stability and network security, which were rated in the lousiest range in most 80% This raises the need to establish action plans that allow improving the technical aspects in the provision of the internet service. Finally, the independence of the variables within the cluster was analyzed, using the Chi-square test. The dependent or significant variables were those that obtained a p-value lower than the level of significance (p-value < 0.05), as shown in Table 2:

Table 2. Determination of significant or dependent variables, according to chi-square test, software R3.5.0

Code	Description of the variable	P-value	Df
V8.5	How it qualifies the stability of the wireless network (little or no intermittency or signal drop)?	1.394047e−12	8
V8.1	How do you rate availability of the wireless network (WiFi network always available or not available)?	6.256282e−12	8
V8.4	Rate the connection in a real time of several users	9.971297e−12	8
V8.3	How do you rate the response time of the network?	3.012736e−09	8
V5	How do you rate the speed of access or connection to the wireless network?	7.436413e−09	8
V15	What is the general assessment of the wireless network access service of the institution?	2.426083e−07	8
V8.2	How do you rate the coverage of the signal? Is it possible to connect from anywhere on the campus?	2.301501e−06	8
V4	The current level of satisfaction of connection to the network services offered through the Wi-Fi network	5.504881e−05	8
V8.6	How it qualifies the security of the network (it has too many filters, it allows to navigate without so many restrictions)?	8.176920e−05	8
V10	How much time do you expect to connect to the wireless network and access the internet?	3.326749e−03	4
V7	Considers that the current technological infrastructure is capable of: being improved, remaining the same	2.780727e−02	2
V9	Do you consider that the wireless network service facilitates the execution of your activities and educational consultations?	3.235995e−02	2
V12	How often do you have to enable the sharing of your mobile to access the internet because the Wi-Fi network of the institution did not allow it?	3.303245e−02	6
V1	Academic program	4.267513e−02	6

In this sense, 14 of the 18 variables in this study were significant or dependent; that is, they are variables with influence on the formation of the clusters or grouping of individuals. Among the significant variables, variables related both to the technical characteristics of the wireless internet connection and attributes of the service and the attention of personnel in the area of systems and technology were found. The academic program was also perceived as a significant variable, which affects not only the level of satisfaction of the users but also the quality of the answers provided by the students, taking into account their affinity or expertise in information technologies and communications. These results allow us to conclude that the variables identified are relevant in the evaluation of Internet service satisfaction by university users and that, through these variables, groups of variables and observations can be identified and characterized and focused. Jointly or multivariate, strategies to improve user satisfaction within the university campus.

5 Conclusions and Future Works

A wireless network optimization process starts from the fact of having a design and implementation of a wireless network infrastructure under international standards. It is necessary to perform an analysis of the state of the wireless network, verify if the design is following the regulations if its implementation has taken into consideration a series of requirements and protocols necessary for its operation. In the present research work, variables such as bandwidth use, network availability, throughput, latency, among others, were analyzed to verify the current status of the institution's wireless network. This analysis applies to any entity.

SDN is an innovative approach in the local environment for the optimization of both wired and wireless networks. Although in the world there are several studies and implementations regarding the subject, in Colombia and especially in our city Barranquilla, little has been investigated and executed. SDN allows organizations to grow in their technological infrastructure, optimizing the behavior of the internal network, in a centralized, scalable and reliable way. Due to costs, it is not possible to acquire equipment that supports SDN, however, a tool such as Mininet is used to simulate the performance of a wireless network configured with SDN, very adjusted to the reality of educational institutions, in order to take the measurements of the variables, and support a change in the infrastructure. The versatility of Mininet allows it to be used in a multi-brand environment such as the one we have in the Institution (and in large part of these in the city), where we have equipment from different manufacturers. The SDN optimization approach that is to be studied and proposed for the optimization of the wireless infrastructure allows new means for network virtualization and programmability, which facilitate how networks can be designed and operated, including the defined characteristics by the user and the personalized behavior, even at runtime.

The present project has two important statistical instruments, from which the results of the second instrument have been shown. The first will be to define a mathematical criterion or algorithm that allows maximizing the level of satisfaction of the users of the network, which helps to validate that the process of optimization of the wireless infrastructure is of impact for the academic community. The second statistical component of the research is a survey, a fundamental tool to measure the success of the project, whose results were shown and discussed previously.

Future works based on the project include completing the mathematical criterion or algorithm to maximize the level of user satisfaction, simulating a functional topology of the SDN wireless network infrastructure with Mininet and presenting the results before the institutional directives, for motivating them to change the current network infrastructure. These results can be replicated in other institutions, considering the factors of each entity.

References

1. Uc-Rios, C.E., Lara-Rodriguez, D.: An efficient scheduler for real and non-real time services maximizing satisfied users in wireless networks. In: Proceeding of the International Conference on Computer Communication Networks, ICCCN (2011)

2. ONF: Software-Defined Networking (SDN) Definition - Open Networking Foundation ONF (2018)
3. Rangisetti, A.K., Tamma, B.R.: Software defined wireless networks: a survey of issues and solutions. Wirel. Pers. Commun. **97**, 6019–6053 (2017)
4. Oppenheimer, P.: Top-Down Network Design, 3rd edn. Cisco Press, Indianapolis (2011)
5. Hernandez, L., Jimenez, G., Baloco, C.: Characterization of the use of the internet of things in the institutions of higher education of the city of Barranquilla and its metropolitan area. In: HCI International 2018 – Posters' Extended Abstracts, vol. 852, pp. 17–24 (2018)
6. Zhao, Y., Li, W., Wu, J., Lu, S.: Quantized conflict graphs for wireless network optimization. In: Proceedings - IEEE INFOCOM, vol. 26, pp. 2218–2226 (2015)
7. Yao, T., Guo, X., Qiu, Y, Ge, L.: An integral optimization framework for WLAN design. In: International Conference on Communication Technology Proceedings ICCT (2013)
8. Cisco Networking Academy, Cisco Networking Academy (2015). http://www.cisco.com/web/learning/netacad/index.html
9. Sezer, S., et al.: Introduction: what is software-defined networking? Future carrier networks are we ready for SDN? Implementation challenges for software-defined networks background: why SDN? Futur. Carr. Netw. **51**, 36–43 (2013)
10. Jammal, M., Singh, T., Shami, A., Asal, R., Li, Y.: Software defined networking: state of the art and research challenges. Comput. Netw. **72**, 74–98 (2014)
11. Bakshi, K.: Considerations for software defined networking (SDN): approaches and use cases. In: Conference Proceedings of IEEE Aerospace, pp. 1–9 (2013)
12. Baird, M., Ng, B., Seah, V: Wifi network access control for IoT connectivity with software defined networking. In: Proceedings of the 8th ACM on Multimedia Systems Conference – MMSys 2017 (2017)
13. Sandhya, Sinha, Y., Haribabu, K.: A survey: hybrid SDN. J. Netw. Comput. Appl. **100**, 35–55 (2017)
14. Amin, R., Reisslein, M., Shah, N.: Hybrid SDN networks: a survey of existing approaches. IEEE Commun. Surv. Tutorials **20**, 1–34 (2018)
15. Haruyama, S.: Software-Defined Radio Technologies. Technol. New Multimed. Syst. (2002)
16. Bedhief, I., Kassar, M., Aguili, T.: SDN-based architecture challenging the IoT heterogeneity. In: 2016 3rd Smart Cloud Networks and Systems, SCNS 2016 (2017)
17. Fontes, R.D.R., Mahfoudi, M., Dabbous, W., Turletti, T., Rothenberg, C.: How far can we go? Towards realistic software-defined wireless networking experiments. Comput. J. **60**, 1458–1471 (2017)
18. Gilani, S.M.M., Hong, T., Jin, W., Zhao, G., Heang, Xu, C.: Mobility management in IEEE 802.11 WLAN using SDN/NFV technologies. Eurasip J. Wirel. Commun. Netw. **2017**, 1–14 (2017)
19. Blenk, A., Basta, A., Zerwas, J., Reisslein, M., Kellerer, W.: Control plane latency with SDN network hypervisors: the cost of virtualization. IEEE Trans. Netw. Serv. Manag. **13**, 366–380 (2016)
20. Hernandez Sampieri, R., Fernandez Collado, C., del Pilar Baptista Lucio, M.: Metodología de la investigación (2010)

From Smart City to Smart Society: China's Journey Towards Essential Urban-Rural Transformation

Tian Liang[(⊠)], Guochao Peng, Fei Xing, Sirong Lin, and Yichen Jia

Sun Yat-sen University, Panyu District, Guangzhou 510000, China
liangt36@mail2.sysu.edu.cn

Abstract. As an economic superpower in the world, China has always been seeking new ways to enhance living environment and improve life equality of its residents. China has thus made substantial progress in the development of smart city with over 700 pilot projects launched over the last decade. However, these smart city pilot projects mainly cover urban areas in China, excluding nearly 600 million Chinese residents living in rural areas. Consequently, the Chinese government proposed the new concept of smart society in 2017 as the next generation of smart city initiative, with the aim of enhancing living standard of residents in not just urban but also rural areas. In this paper, we elaborate the concept and vision of smart society, and present and discuss a variety of issues concerning the transformation from smart city to smart society in China, including cross-departmental coordination, public awareness and participation, and information security and privacy. We conclude the paper by recommended that China's strategy of smart society development can be considered and potentially adopted by other developing countries with similar contexts and urban-rural issues.

Keywords: Smart city · Smart society · China · Transformation · Urban and rural areas

1 Introduction

When decision makers of a country develop strategies, they must contemplate the state's economic development status, percentage of urban population, ecological environment, culture, historical background, and requirements of residents. For instance, Singapore has a population of 5.54 million and a small land area of 277.6 square miles. Driven by the rapid economic growth and a set of urban issues, Singapore launched its smart nation policy agenda in 2014 which was closely connect to its long-lasting strategic development direction [1, 2]. Moreover, facing an aging society ahead of other countries, Japan put forward the concept of "Society 5.0" to solve the plight of aging society and related social problems [3]. There is another case that the Europe 2020 strategy was proposed, which aims to overcome the structural weaknesses in European economy, decrease unemployment rate, and improve overall competitiveness and productivity [4].

© Springer Nature Switzerland AG 2019
N. Streitz and S. Konomi (Eds.): HCII 2019, LNCS 11587, pp. 161–171, 2019.
https://doi.org/10.1007/978-3-030-21935-2_13

In contrast to these nations, however, China, as a developing country, has very different economic conditions, spatial distribution of population and urbanization. In recent years, China has had a good performance in economic development but still has an enormous population pressure and a huge gap between rural and urban areas. In China, the urbanization process picked up in the 1980s, compared to that of Europe and America, is far from maturity. Figure 1 shows pattern of China's urban and rural populations, i.e. statistics provided by the United Nations shows that the urbanization of China is probably only about 60%, and the other part is rural population [5]. Besides, according to the National Bureau of Statistics of China, by the end of 2017, there were still about 567 million people living in rural areas [6].

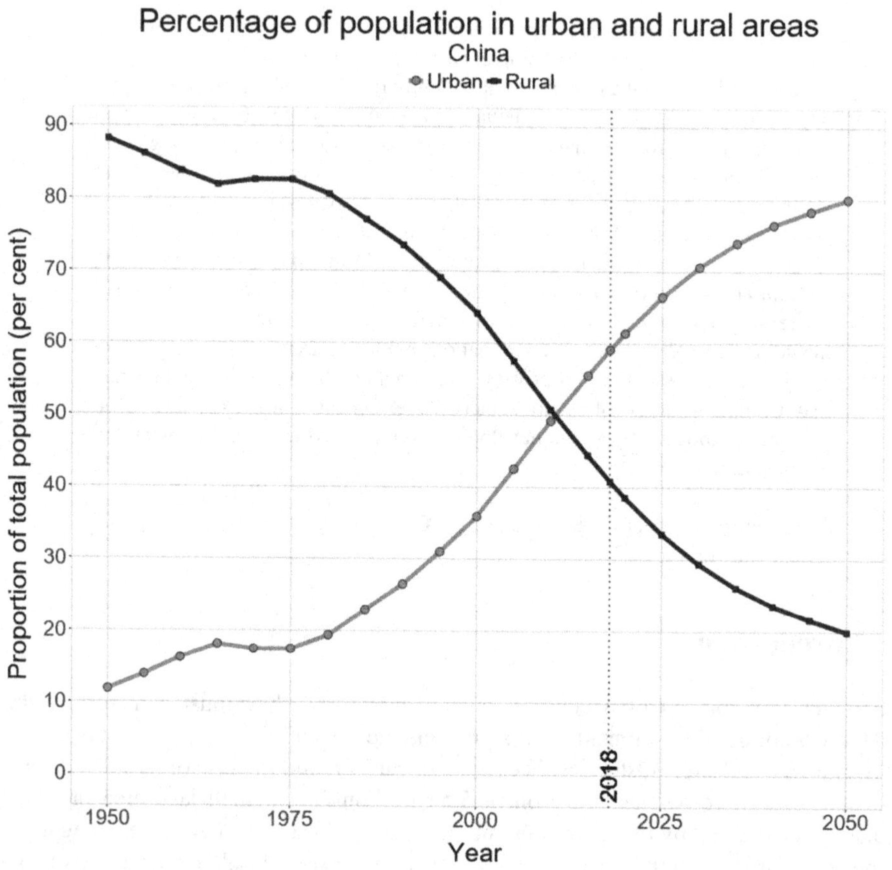

Fig. 1. Urban and rural populations of China Source: United Nations DESA/Population Division

In order to cope with the big gap between rural and urban areas, especially with metropolises, make people's life more conformable and sustainable with special surroundings, China ought to explore its own path of transformation through the development of smart city and smart society.

The paper is structured as follows. First, the main dimensions of smart city are reviewed, followed by a discussion of current smart city achievements made by China. The most important part specifically introduces the local reason why China proposes the smart society strategy, explains the links between smart city and smart society, discusses associated challenges and anticipates the future of smart society development, with conclusions drawn.

2 Smart City

It is generally considered that cities play a significant role in human social and economic development [7]. The term of smart city was originated from IBM's "smart planet" plan which aimed to cope with the enterprise economy recession in 2008 [8]. As it evolved into the concept of smart city, the smart planet vision is not only emphasized by IBM or the industry, but has also successfully attracted attention from policy makers, scientist and citizens. The strategy of smart city emphasizes the important role of information and communication technologies (such as IoT, sensor network and big data) in developing the urban system [9–11]. Although there is no precise definition of smart city, the notion has become widespread in recent years. It can be accepted that smart city means taking advantage of high technology, especially information and communication technology (ICT) in urban subsystems in order to improve the quality of life as well as to create a sustainable, greener city and competitive commerce [12, 13].

However, the model of smart city is more likely to apt to big cities. When it comes to small- and medium-sized cities, which are likely to lose importance and attention against big metropolitan, they are unable to compete in terms of economic foundation and therefore unable to receive or afford the necessary funds for smart city mission [14, 15]. Moreover, most smart city strategies fail to adapt to the local needs of their residents [16].

3 Smart City in China

Over the last decade, China has launched its smart city initiative as a national strategy and has involved large investments in improving city infrastructure. On one hand, as a developing country, China has learned experience from Singapore, Amsterdam and other countries and cities in the beginning, and has got a good performance. On the other hand, the China Smart City Development and Research Center was established in 2012, which is a cross-sectoral research center specially established to provide policy research and decision-making consultation for smart city development, and provide overall planning, top-level design and implementation plan for local government to carry out smart city construction by the National Information Center. Besides, from central government to local departments, a large number of related documents have been released.

Due to strong political and financial support from the government, a large number of Chinese cities have made substantial progress toward the development of smart city, particularly in provincial and municipal cities. Local governments have invested a lot in technology and infrastructure. For instance, Guiyang, a provincial capital city in southwestern China, has committed to big data innovation project and built a complete big data industrial chain by means of big data transactions which will play a strong supporting role in the construction and development of smart cities. Cities like Shenzhen, Ningbo, Shanghai, and Beijing are guided to build digital city subsystems including smart transportation, smart governance, smart healthcare, and smart grid, and so on. In terms of the number of smart city projects under construction, more than 500 pilot cities have emerged, which have also formed numerous smart city clusters in the Yangtze River Delta and Pearl River Delta [17].

In China, however, population and urban factors are very complex. There are still a large population in rural areas and even a great number of migrant workers inside the city who have been ignored by original smart city endeavors. Furthermore, vulnerable groups should be more concerned about. The growth of smart city cannot be disjointed with the support of the surrounding villages and towns which have a positive feedback process as a mutual promotion [18]. Rather, carrying forward cultural traditions and combining Chinese characteristics, the higher period of smart city should consider the coordinated sustainable development of both urban and rural areas [18].

4 Smart Society in China

4.1 Why Does China Need Smart Society?

Although great progress has been made in pilot projects, there exists two major issues in the development of smart city in China:

- There is still a large proportion of population living in rural areas in China. Even for cities, the outer areas of many Chinese cities still have a rural nature and are pretty much under developed. These rural areas, either in countryside or in outer areas of cities, were not really covered in previous smart city projects, and so could not enjoy the convenience and benefits from smart city infrastructure construction and smart public service systems.
- Smart city development focus on sensor, network and platform layer, as for application layer, far from to satisfaction of the public needs and expectation.

As a result, in 2017, the strategy of smart society was delivered at the 19th National Congress of the Communist Party of China by Xi Jinping, the President of China. It was a key strategy to improve the quality of residents, balance the technology and social development based on its own technological development, smart city construction practice and social reality.

To find a new approach to deal with the issues that cannot be solved by smart city project only, smart society is the best solution.

From a realistic point of view, first of all, in addition to urban areas, there are still a large number of rural areas and economically underdeveloped areas in China.

The disparity between urban, rural and regional development needs to be solved urgently. Secondly, China has entered the age of aging, and is also facing social problems such as resource shortage and environmental pollution [19, 20], which require a more intelligent solution.

From a practical point of view, the Chinese government has made some achievements in promoting the construction of smart cities in recent years. China has the experience and ability to push it forward on a wider scale. From the perspective of science and technology, technology and innovation is the motivation. China's scientific and technological strength has rapidly increased. The development of science and disruptive technology has a sizeable impact on society and other aspects of life [21]. Social life will gradually enter the era of intelligence.

4.2 Smart City and Smart Society

There is still confusion about what a smart society is, where its future will be, and also how it performs in comparison to smart city. Smart society and smart city, both with supportive technologies, such as information and communication technology, disruptive AI, big data and cloud computing, have similarity but are not the same. Strictly speaking, smart society which will bring all-round and systematic changes to China's social development is very different from the term of smart city which initially came from IBM.

The notion of smart city is more concerned with cities and urban areas, focusing on city management system, citizens and business, but, in terms of rural areas, nothing has been done for it. In contrast, human plays an even more central role in smart society, especially the public service of the community. In smart society, residents in metropolis, small towns as well as in rural areas play an important role, which have the access to service of smart health care, education, transport, and economic etc. With the model of the smart society, China strives to narrow the gap between urban and rural areas and pays more attention to the satisfaction of people's needs in the society as a whole.

In essence, smart society is an extension and next generation of smart city development, but there are still fundamental differences between these two concepts. On one hand, the construction of smart city more focus on the application of information and communication advanced technology such as wireless network, IoT (internet of things), sensors, cameras etc. The purpose of smart society is offering smart application and service to satisfy the needs of people' life based on big data, cloud computing and AI. On the other hand, the expression of smart city identifies an urban area that, through the widespread and pervasive use of advanced technologies, is able to address the social and economic needs of citizens in a new way. The smart society which not just refers to a smart city, but includes huge rural areas and residents in small towns, is a real revolution for China. Smart society refers to the use of smart means and tools to promote individual relations more inclusive and harmonious.

From smart city to smart society, there are three key issues needed to be concerned about.

- Focus on the software application based on early hardware (mainly imply ICT infrastructure) investment for the public service in key domains. Smart software applications such as smart parking application, smart healthcare application, smart governance application are able to connect sensors, user, vehicle, hospital, government agencies and so on at any time and in any place. Briefly, quick information should be available through smart phone apps by each individual [22]. One such key of cultivating smart mobility application is to develop the digital platforms. Through collecting, analyzing, processing data on digital platforms, the former investment will be switched into smart service.
- Persist people orientation, pay close attention to people's needs and investigate what factors hinder the smart application for inhabitants and improve public service delivery. In the concept of smart society, people is recognized as a key role and the quality of human's life is a crucial axis for the project. The fundamental purpose of launching smart society project is to benefit all the people of society with the development of science, technology and economy. For the purpose, Chinese government will make every effort to put all people's interests above all else, pay more attention to people's living conditions in society, ensure and improve people's wellbeing, so that all people are able to see that the gains of reform and development benefit in a fair way.

Narrow regional gap, which means rural areas equal with urban should be considered carefully. City is an important part of society, and the construction of smart city is also an important part of smart society. At the same time, rural area is less developed than but as important as city. The notion of smart society will pay more attention to the people living rural areas and the vulnerable groups. To narrow the gap between urban and rural areas and between regions, one of the key strategy is to build a three-dimensional, omni-directional and wide-ranging social information service system by taking cities and villages as the support of the strong and the weak. Poverty-stricken rural areas can rely on smart city construction, use information technology to narrow the development gap, eliminate the digital divide between urban and rural areas, regional digital divide. An effective way is to develop the central dominant city in the direction of the surrounding small cities and villages, to form a group of cities, the representative city cluster of such as Guangdong-Hong Kong-Macao Greater Bay Area, the Beijing-Tianjin-Tangshan city group and so on. Taking advantage of the predominance of central city, to drive the surrounding rural areas as well as small and medium-sized cities, develop smart application across the city and ultimately constitute the entire smart society (as shown in Fig. 2).

Compared with smart city, smart society has a wider scope and wider connotation, which includes not only transportation, government and medical aspects in smart city. The perception system of smart society is composed of sensors in cities, factories, villages, human bodies, automobiles and nature. Technology and innovation is the motivation of smart society. Artificial intelligence system and perception system make the city's sensory nervous system more intelligent and sensitive. Sensors continuously transmit all kinds of information from human society and nature to network space. Big data and artificial intelligence algorithm intelligently process all parts of information of intelligent city. Google cloud, Ali elastic compute service, Tencent cloud, Amazon

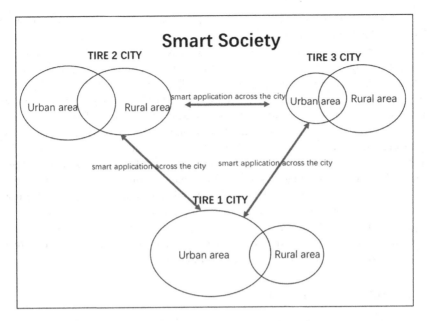

Fig. 2. Concept of smart society

cloud and other companies join in. Big data collected by IoT will be converted into a new type of intelligence by AI and cloud computing and will reach every corner of society. Around people's actual needs of medical treatment, education, social security, employment, pension, transportation and so on, we can make full use of big data and artificial intelligence to realize that everyone can enjoy high-quality services.

4.3 The Challenges of Smart Society

Despite the attractive vision of smart society, China continues to face several significant challenges in the course of smart society. Some challenges exist in the development of smart city, and some appear alongside with the development of smart society. Specifically speaking, the challenges come from administration, social system and ordinary people which should not be ignored.

The most acute challenges lie with cross-departmental and outward partnership and coordination of recourses, closely followed by financial support [23]. The challenge of cross-departmental partnership including the integration of the previous systems is related with interoperability, scalability, infrastructure organization, data privacy and security. Furthermore, the lack of cooperation will impede the construction of unified data platform and also have bad influence on the application of smart service.

The targets of smart society include urban citizens, rural residents, migrant workers in rural areas and so on, which has a certain degree of complexity. Regarding different types of people's social activities, requirements and awareness are different, and they have certain complexity. The awareness and participation of inhabitants is a key factor for the success in smart city [24] as well as smart society and poor participation will hinder the utilization rate of application [25].

There are huge risks behind the widespread interconnection and high perception of society. China's relevant laws, regulations and management mechanism are still subject to improvement, and so there are gaps and weak links currently. The risks of personal privacy, business secrets and national security have been greatly increased. Data and information security issues have attracted the attention of all sectors of the society. In the case of high data sharing, once personal information is leaked or used improperly, it will bring harm to individuals or society [26]. It is necessary to strengthen legislation, reform the judicial system, formulate and implement laws and regulations to ensure information security, which are more suitable for the development of big data in a smart society.

The weaknesses of smart society should be anticipated and planned for. By doing so, China can both avoid the risks of failure and identify and mitigate them as they emerge. In order to address these challenges, the government will need to encourage greater private-sector participation in the initiative and at the same time ensure the robustness and security of its data servers and platforms.

4.4   The Future of Smart Society

The aim of smart society is to safeguard public interest and maximize value for society as a whole, rather than for individuals or companies [26]. Towards essential urban-rural transformation, individuals in urban and rural areas are able to get access to smart public services anytime and anywhere as the journey of smart society gradually turns from information-oriented to people-oriented and services-oriented and offers ubiquitous smart application.

Smart life comes from data. In the course of smart city construction, there is a big data widely collected, including camera data, activity location, action track, behavior data and so on. The original big data acquisition work is basically completed, and data preparation for interconnection and sharing is provided. These data are deeply developed and applied to effectively stimulate the improvement of public services in smart society. In the future, local government will deeply develop and restore the huge data generated by the daily work, study and life of billions of people, to construct a smart public services system and provide information support for people living in society anytime and anywhere, provide necessary services for people living in society, precisely meet he various needs of society beyond the differences of age, gender, region and language, and provide high quality for the whole society. The elderly, disabled and other vulnerable groups in society can also enjoy a comfortable and convenient life.

Smart technology which is the driving force to promote the emergence of smart society and also have a great effect on society. It encourages all sectors of society to participate actively and make effective use of frontier science and technology so as to form an innovative social form driven by production, life and governance cycle based on intelligence and data. Intelligent driving, 3D printing and intelligent manufacturing extend the movement and mechanical operation, and help the residents and producers of the smart society to complete the operation and construction of the smart society. A higher level of automation has made people have more expectations and leisure time in daily routine.

With an aim to establish information platform on smart public services including healthcare, traffic, public security and education, people's lives will be more conformable and sustainable. Smart hospitals, smart learning, smart government and smart home are the cells and foundation of smart society for individuals. Smart hospitals and telemedicine are developing in depth, so that electronic medical records and health records are popularized, big medical data are constantly gathered and used in depth, high-quality medical resources are freely flowing, appointments for diagnosis and treatment are made, electronic payment settlement reduces waiting time for people to register and pay fees, and the difficult problem of seeing a doctor in remote rural areas is effectively solved. Intelligence of social members and intelligence of technology drive people to be intelligent. The application of face recognition, fingerprint recognition and block chain technology is the embodiment of human being's intelligence.

Smart society also breaks the limitations of space and time, integrates the physical world and virtual space, and encourages the search for the joy and significance of individual social life. IoT is the junction between the material world and the virtual world. Machine and material are interlinked and integrated. Cyberspace is not a simple reflection of the physical world, but will become a new development space of human society.

5 Concluding Remarks

Smart society is not a utopia, and it is coming in China. The goal of building a smart society in China lays emphasis on residents both in urban and rural areas in the country by providing people with the integrated smart applications they need with AI, big data, cloud computing and IoT to improve the quality of life. The realization of smart society from central city to the surrounding small cities and villages, forming a group of cities, ultimately constitutes the entire smart society.

The solution of smart society is along with the state and issues of China which can also help solve social problems such as big gap between urban and rural areas, population aging, shortage of medical resources, environmental pollution and so on.

The journey of urban-rural transformation in China means China have developed its own path, theory and system with the complex national conditions and weak infrastructure, blazed a new trail for other developing countries to achieve urban-rural common development. It offers a new option for other countries such as Brazil, India with a large population and a huge gap between urban and rural development. For such countries, China offers a smart approach to solve the problems in human social development.

References

1. The Future of Manufacturing Work in Singapore's Smart Nation Initiative: Imaginations, Realities, and (DIS) Continues Inequalities. https://mmea.hku.hk/wp-content/uploads/2018/09/the-future-of-manufacturing-work-in-singapores-smart-nation-initiative-imaginations-realities-and-dis-continuous-inequalities-by-gayathri-haridas-and-thijs-willems.pdf. Accessed 30 Jan 2019
2. Technology and Governance in Singapore's Smart Nation Initiative. https://ash.harvard.edu/files/ash/files/282181_hvd_ash_paper_jj_woo.pdf. Accessed 30 Jan 2019
3. Society 5.0. https://www8.cao.go.jp/cstp/sogosenryaku/2016.html. Accessed 30 Jan 2019
4. Europe 2020 strategy. https://ec.europa.eu/info/business-economy-euro/economic-and-fiscal-policy-coordination/eu-economic-governance-monitoring-prevention-correction/european-semester/framework/europe-2020-strategy_en. Accessed 14 Feb 2019
5. World Urbanization Prospects 2018. https://population.un.org/wup/Country-Profiles/. Accessed 30 Jan 2019
6. National Bureau of Statistics of China. http://data.stats.gov.cn/easyquery.htm?cn=C01&zb=A0301&sj=2017. Accessed 30 Jan 2019
7. Mori, K., Christodoulou, A.: Review of sustainability indices and indicators: towards a new City Sustainability Index (CSI). Environ. Impact Assess. Rev. **32**(1), 94–106 (2012)
8. Hao, L., Lei, X., Yan, Z., ChunLi, Y.: The application and implementation research of smart city in China. In: Proceeding of the 2012 International Conference on System Science and Engineering (ICSSE), pp. 288–292 (2012)
9. Zanella, A., Bui, N., Castellani, A., Vangelista, L., Zorzi, M.: Internet of things for smart cities. IEEE Internet Things J. **1**(1), 22–32 (2014)
10. Mitton, N., Papavassiliou, S., Puliafito, A., Trivedi, K.S.: Combining cloud and sensors in a smart city environment. EURASIP J. Wirel. Commun. Network. 247–256 (2012)
11. Nuaimi, E.A., Neyadi, H.A., Mohamed, N., Al-Jaroodi, J.: Applications of big data to smart cities. J. Internet Serv. Appl. **6**(1), 25 (2015)
12. Caragliu, A., Del Bo, C., Nijkamp, P.: Smart cities in Europe. J. Urban Technol. **18**(2), 65–82 (2011)
13. Bakıcı, T., Almirall, E., Wareham, J.: A smart city initiative: the case of Barcelona. J. Knowl. Econ. **4**(2), 135–148 (2013)
14. Giffinger, R., Haindlmaier, G., Kramar, H.: The role of rankings in growing city competition. Urban Res. Pract. **3**(3), 299–312 (2010)
15. Angelidou, M.: Smart city policies: a spatial approach. Cities **41**, S3–S11 (2014)
16. Angelidou, M.: The role of smart city characteristics in the plans of fifteen cities. J. Urban Technol. **24**(4), 3–28 (2017)
17. Super Smart City. https://www2.deloitte.com/content/dam/Deloitte/cn/Documents/public-sector/deloitte-cn-ps-super-smart-city-en-180629.pdf. Accessed 30 Jan 2019
18. Opportunities and Challenges for Smart City Development in China. https://www.davidpublisher.org/Public/uploads/Contribute/5b31e7d716e36.pdf. Accessed 30 Jan 2019
19. Vennemo, H., Aunan, K., Lindhjem, H., Seip, H.M.: Environmental pollution in China: status and trends. Rev. Environ. Econ. Policy **3**(2), 209–230 (2009)
20. Li, Y., Lin, Y., Geertman, S.: The development of smart cities in China. In: Proceeding of the 14th International Conference on Computers in Urban Planning and Urban Management, pp. 7–10 (2015)
21. Grübler, A.: Technology and Global Change. Cambridge University Press, Cambridge (2003)

22. Cifaldi, G., Serban, I.: Between a smart city and smart society. In: Karwowski, W., Ahram, T. (eds.) IHSI 2018. AISC, vol. 722, pp. 714–719. Springer, Cham (2018). https://doi.org/10.1007/978-3-319-73888-8_110
23. Angelidou, M.: Shortcomings to smart city planning and development. Exploring patterns and relationships. TeMA-J. Land Use Mobility Environ. **10**(1), 77–93 (2017)
24. Cardone, G., et al.: Fostering participAction in smart cities: a geo-social crowdsensing platform. IEEE Commun. Mag. **51**(6), 112–119 (2013)
25. Peng, G.C.A., Nunes, M.B., Zheng, L.: Impacts of low citizen awareness and usage in smart city services: the case of London's smart parking system. Inf. Syst. e-Bus. Manag. **15**(4), 845–876 (2017)
26. Valkenburg, A.C., den Ouden, P.H., Schreurs, M.A.: Designing a smart society: from smart cities to smart societies. In: Open Innovation 2.0 Yearbook 2016. European Commission (2016)

The Potential of Virtual Real World for Usability Test of Location-Aware Apps

Tomoyo Sasao[1]($\boxtimes$), Ruochen Si[2], Mitsutoshi Shibuya[1], and Min Lu[3]

[1] Tokushima University, Minamijosanjimacho 1-1,
Tokushima City 770-8502, Japan
sasao@tokushima-u.ac.jp
[2] The University of Tokyo, Kashiwanoha 5-1-5, Kashiwa City 277-8568, Japan
[3] Kyushu University, Motooka Nishi-Ku Fukuoka City 819-0395, Japan

Abstract. Recently, many kinds of location-aware applications of smartphone are developed. However, it is difficult to test them for usability in the same way as the non-location-aware ones because of the test environment. For example, in case of supportive applications for emergency situations, the usability test can be carried out only in normal period of outdoor fields. Key competitive technologies beyond the issues will be Augment Reality and Virtual Reality. We focus on advantages of laboratory experiment and present a usability test environment of location-aware apps based on virtual real world using Google Street View. In this paper, we aim at understanding the weaknesses and strengths of this approach. We developed an initial prototype of the usability test environment and a simple map viewer app. The usability test has two conditions from a designated start point: (c1) go to a designated place and (c2) explore the area freely. We observed two participants' behaviors: (b1) movement in the virtual real world, (b2) body motion, and (b3) operation of the map viewer app. From the results, we discuss the better ways to collect these data as well as the weakness and strengths of laboratory-based usability test environment. These outcomes spotlight laboratory survey's strengths of fine grain spatiotemporal data.

Keywords: Smartphone · Usability · Virtual city · Google Street View · Map · Spatial perception

1 Introduction

In recent years, the number of users of location-based applications is increasing with the popularization of mobile devices [1]. The application designers and developers have to consider the ordinary users' ease. User-centered design includes the idea of involving the target users to take part in the design processes to create suitable designs for them. This idea incorporates designs of different aspects and fields, not only application development. To guarantee the diversity of users and the accuracy of the recorded data, user experiments evaluating the applications are often conducted in the laboratories. However, such experiment environments are insufficient for the recent mobile applications, whose operations are responded to the context of ambient environment. It has been proposed that such applications are better to be experimented in

© Springer Nature Switzerland AG 2019
N. Streitz and S. Konomi (Eds.): HCII 2019, LNCS 11587, pp. 172–186, 2019.
https://doi.org/10.1007/978-3-030-21935-2_14

the real-world environment [2, 3]. Operating only in the laboratorial environment is difficult to reveal the problems of interactions and usability issues and their reasons, which are strongly related to the context of ambient environment. With the recent smartphones equipped with Global Positioning System (GPS) and various high-performance sensors, conducting real-world user experiments becomes much easier than before. For example, by overlaying the estimated damage of earthquakes and tsunami to the real world, researches of supporting disaster drills by presenting the emergency situations on smartphones [4] as well as using Augmented Reality (AR) technologies [5, 6] have been conducted.

On the other hand, there are still problems that are difficult to solve in the real-world experiments. One of them is to gather enough target users, whose number can meet the requirements of quantitative evaluations. For example, tests of the applications supporting disaster evacuations often invite local residents near the experimental fields, while usually difficult to gather other target users, such as visitors, strangers, or even foreigners.

The target of this research is to realize the evaluation of the location-based applications by the potential users who are difficult to attend the real-world experiments. For such purpose, we propose a test environment of a Web-based virtual space of the real world to synchronize the location information to the user's smartphone. The users can test the location-based application in the virtual space with their virtual movement reflected on their smartphones in real-time. With this environment, the usability evaluation experiments for certain geographical areas can be conducted anywhere in a laboratory, and can involve more participants with diverse viewpoints to improve the applications. It can contribute to creating easy-to-use location-based applications for everyone, which is also connected to the exploration of better interactions between human and urban environments.

Of course, information and context in the virtual space is not as rich as that of the real world. Understanding how the users will behave in the virtual environment and what kinds of data can be generated is necessary at the first place. Thus, the current stage of this research has developed the prototype of the proposed environment and a map application for tests, and conducted the preliminary experiments with them. In particular, the users' movement in the virtual space, physical information of body motions and operation logs of smartphones are collected, in order to reveal its feasibility of acquiring sufficient data that are helpful to the application evaluation and understanding the ambient context of the smartphone operations, as well as the necessary functions for conducting the usability evaluation.

2   Related Work

2.1   Supportive Environment for Field Tests

The existing supportive environments for user tests of location-based applications emphasize the importance of the real-world context, and developed a lot of supportive systems for field experiments. For example, to record the actual movement, operations and speeches of the participants, they were asked to walk with head cameras and transceivers in addition to the mobile devices with the target application installed, while the experimenters could supervise the processes in the laboratory [7]. Another research comparing the results of user experiments of social applications used in large-scale events between in lab-based and field-based environments has revealed that real-world environment is much better for user evaluations as the quality of context information is dominantly different [8]. On the other hand, it is reported that 71% of the usability tests of the applications were actually conducted in laboratorial environments [9]. In recent years, with the improvement of the sensors' performance in the smartphones and the development of the technologies estimating users' actions from the sensor data, the feasibility of out-door experiments has been dramatically improved. However, the current systems have not been focusing on the issues of participants' diversity. Nakanishi et al. pointed out the difficulty of repeating the field experiments in the case of researching on crowd behaviors in disaster evacuations, and developed a simulator to represent the crowd behaviors in the virtual space from the records of the field experiments [10]. This research intends to take the important context in the experiments into account, which can be missing in the above experiments in virtual spaces, to realize better user test environment.

2.2 "Realness" of Virtual Reality Based on Real World

The "Realness" of virtual space that modeling the real world has been discussed in the fields of architecture and urban design, in which designing with 3D modeling is studied for many years [11]. Accordingly, there are a lot of researches and developments pursuing the "realness", such as the collaborative design environment in virtual space emphasize 3D sound sources, light, shadows, clouds, plants and so on [12, 13], with the revealed importance of the impressions influenced by the context of environment. However, the recent researches also indicate that, "realness" is not necessary in drawing the participants' opinions and creativities. For example, PlacePulse [14] is a Web-based crowdsourcing system to evaluate the impressions to streets. With two images of the streets randomly captured from Google Street View displayed side-by-side, the system collects answers of the questions like "which is safer?" and "which is more beautiful", and then uses the location-based data for quantitative evaluation and mapping the results of safety, beauty and liveliness on maps. Although the context like ambient sounds, crowds, durations and so on, are not included in Google Street View, the reliability of the results could be guaranteed by the conditions in common with certain restrictions. The "Block to Block" project being promoted by United Nations represents the slumified public areas in some developing countries in the virtual space of a popular video game "Minecraft", in which the users can assemble blocks freely to create their unique spaces. Female and young residents around these areas are able to build their ideal space together within the game. Although it may be far from the "realness" when using the highly abstracted blocks, it can be considered as a successful example of involving the participants with the attributes seldomly covered and drawing opinions from them [15].

In a survey of the supportive environments utilizing virtual space for human-centered design in the field of urban design [11], it is proposed that a suitable degree of "realness" is required according to the purpose and context of an experiment. From this discussion, this research is conducted with the viewpoint that, it is possible to construct a user-participating test environment on basis of comprehending the limitation of virtual space and focusing on specific goals.

3 System Design

3.1 Concept

This research proposes a usability test platform for mobile applications, which synchronizes the location information in the virtual real world with real smartphones. From the related works, the importance of represent the context of using the target application in the virtual space is made clear. Thus, this platform is designed to contain the following three processes (as shown in Fig. 1):

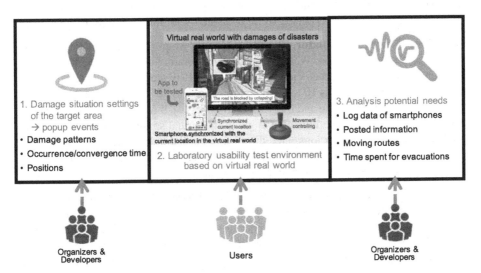

Fig. 1. The user test process of our proposed platform (a case of usability test of a mobile application for disaster)

1. Context Setting: experiment organizers and/or application developers set up the context expected when using the application in real-world environment, and represent it in virtual space. For example, to set up the context of earthquakes, popup events of the damaged places can be set at the blocked roads, which are generated from the past earthquake damage data, to create barriers in the virtual space.
2. Experiment environment: the participants as potential users of the application use a controller to move in the virtual space, which is built based on Google Street View and displayed on the screens. The location of the participant in the virtual space is synchronized to the smartphone with the application to be tested. The organizers

and/or developers inform the scenario, tasks and duration of the experiment. The functions of the location-based application to be tested will work according to the participant's location information in the virtual space. The participant's speech, body motions, movement in the virtual space and smartphone operations are recorded by sensors and cameras.

3. Analysis: the organizers and/or developers analyze the collected data according to the evaluation axis. As the platform focuses on exploring the relations of the spatio-temporal context and the operations of the application, all the data are tagged with time and location, therefore can be visualized on maps or as time-series graphs.

3.2 Prototype Components

This research at first focuses on investigate the effectiveness of the data collected in the preliminary experiments. Therefore, a prototype of the experiment environment with the functions of context setting is developed. At the same time, an experimental location-based application expected to be evaluated with the prototype is developed.

Virtual Real-World Simulator. Based on Google Maps API, a virtual-space environment is implemented on Web browsers for operating and logging in the space represented with Google Street View. JavaScript and PHP are used for the development. As human's viewing angle is 10 to 20 in text reading, 5 to 30° in symbol recognizing, 30 to 60° in color distinguishing and 62° with both eyes [16], three screens are set as shown in Fig. 2. The movement and viewing angle in the virtual space are operated by mouse clicks and drags. Operation logs, including locations (latitude, longitude) and viewing angles (pinch, yaw), are recorded and saved on the server with timestamps and location information at the timing when their values are changed.

Test Sample of Location-Based Application. iPhone A simple map navigation application is developed on iPhone (as shown in Fig. 3). When moving in the virtual space, the update of location recorded in the server will invoke a real-time update of the current location represented in the map application. The viewing range and scale can be operated by pan and pinch gestures. Operation logs in the map application, including map center (x, y), rotation (angle), zoom level (1 to 19) are recorded and saved on the server with timestamps at the timing when their values are changed.

Motion and Eye Sensing. To record the physical information of the participants, JINS MEME ES [17] is applied to measure the head motions (accelerations in XYZ directions, pitch, roll, yow) and eye movements (up, down, left, right, blinking strength). The data are saved on the server with location information.

Voice Sensing. The experiment participants are asked to practice Think Aloud Protocol [18], which need them to speak out all the ideas raised when operating the application. The voices are recorded with videos by the Web camera mounted on top of the screen. The content and timing of the speeches labeled manually for analysis.

Fig. 2. User test environment

Fig. 3. Test sample of location-based application

4 Initial Experiment

4.1 Aims

The initial experiment aims to investigate the advantages and limits of the proposed experiment environment for future improvement through executing the application evaluation processes, which observe how the users are supported by the map application.

4.2 Method

Setup. The prototype shown in Sect. 3 was set up in a laboratory. Except for the log data of the virtual space and smartphone operations, video records of the screens were also taken for confirmation.

Experimental Scenarios. The experiment area was set at Komatsushima City, Tokushima Prefecture in Japan, the start point was Minami-Komatsushima Station. The following two scenarios were prepared:

1. Support of moving to a destination: walk towards Komatsushima Minato Communication Center, and say "arrived" when arriving the destination.
2. Support of strolling: walk freely and say "finished" when the participant likes.

Participants. One participant (P1) often visited the experiment area and one participant (P2) visited the area for the first time (1 female and 1 male, 25–35 years old) attended the experiment. It was still difficult to make quantitative evaluation from the results of the experiment. In this time, the feasibility of observing the interactions with real world through smartphones was focused through analysis of individual cases.

User Experience Measurement. The users' speeches, body motions, movement in virtual space, operations of smartphone were measured and recorded with spatio-temporal information labeling.

Procedure. The experiment organizer explained the purpose, tasks and scenarios of the experiment to the participant, and then a practice in a place other than the experiment area was made for about 1 min. The Think Aloud Protocol was also instructed in the practice. After presenting the start point in the virtual space and starting data recording, "start" was called, and then the participant began to operate the application and virtual space. All the data were collected after the experiments were finished.

Analysis of Data. The recorded data were labeled with timestamps and locations (in latitude and longitude). Time-series graphs and mappings on maps were generated to observe the characteristics of first-visit and often-visit participants, as well as movement to a destination and free strolling, to find out the differences between them.

4.3   Results

Walking Speed. The time spent by the participants in the scenarios (a) moving to a destination and (b) strolling is shown as Fig. 4 (left), and the average is 9 min and 35 s. In scenario (a), the actual shortest path from the start point to the destination is 900 meters (about 12 min on foot), but the average time spent for moving in virtual space is 5 min and 30 s, which means 54% time saved in the experiment. However, the possibility of context information loss comparing to field experiments should be considered. Therefore, it is important to investigate the context information that can or cannot be recorded in this experiment environment. The average number of clicks for moving in Google Street View is 53.5 in scenario (a) and 102 in scenario (b), as shown in Fig. 4 (right). The average speed (number of clicks per minute) in (a) is 9.7 as a baseline for comparisons, while in (b), it becomes 6.4 for P1 and 8.97 for P2, which means the participants tended to have more time between moving actions (clicks) to take other actions. However, in the initial experiment, the number of samples was only 2 for comparing the moving speed, which limited the reliability. More samples are needed in the future to get more accurate baseline moving speed.

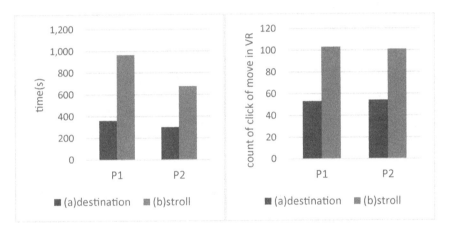

Fig. 4. (left) The time required for the experiments, (right) The number of movements in our VR environment

Operation of the Map Application. Regarding the zooming functions of the map in the smartphone application, the zoom level to view the start point and the destination of (a) on the screen at the same time was 17 (as shown in Fig. 5), but P1, who knew well of the area, kept the zoom level at 19 to display buildings' names and shapes from the start to the end, while never confirmed the overall map. In (b), P1 mainly used zoom level 18 that can show information within about 500 meters when moving. P2, who had never visited the area, tended to use zoom level 15 to 17 more to have an overview in both (a) and (b). P2 also tended to use more different zoom levels in (b) than in (a). The initial experiment revealed that, there was a relation between the experience to the area and the tendencies in operating the map application. Although more samples are needed, the proposed environment can be easier to conduct the experiments investigating behaviors of participants unfamiliar to the place, compared to field experiments.

The sequences of center points of the map displayed in the smartphone application and the moving trajectories in the virtual space were overlaid on maps to find their differences in both scenarios (shown in Figs. 7 and 8). The following three patterns of map operations were found: searching bit by bit along the moving route; moving far away from the route and then return; following the road across the moving route. If adding a visualization of time series variation on a map, it might possible to analyze more deeper relations between the map operations and actual moving routes. In future, we try to figure out the relations between users' mental context and the map operations when users are walking around a real world through virtual testing environment (Fig. 6).

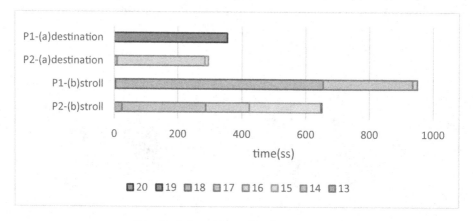

Fig. 5. Sojourn time of each zoom level.

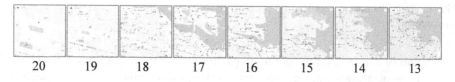

Fig. 6. Map samples of zoom level based on Google Maps API

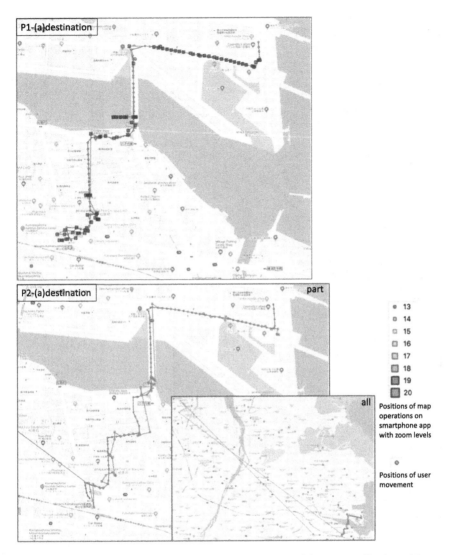

Fig. 7. Mapping movement locus and movement of the center of the map application with zoom levels in (a) destination scenario

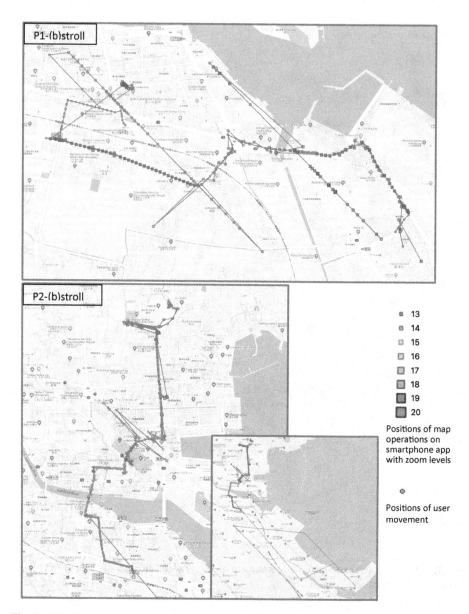

Fig. 8. Mapping movement locus and movement of the center of the map application with zoom levels in (b) stroll scenario

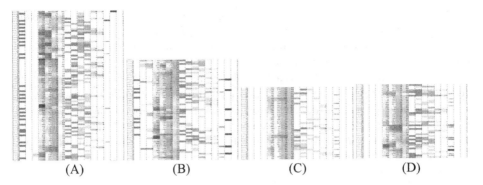

(A)   (B)   (C)   (D)

Fig. 9. Parts of the timeline of P1's (a)destination. From the left row: time(ss), GoogleStreetViewOperation(red rows){movement, heading, pitch}, GlassesOperation1(orange rows){accX, accY, pitch, yaw}, GlassesOperation2(green rows){eyeMoveUp, eyeMoveDown, eyeMoveLeft, eyeMoveRight, blinkSpeed, blinkStrength}, SmartphoneOperation(blue rows) {length of move, map rotation, change of zoom level} (Color figure online)

Eye and Head Movement. The sensors in the glasses recorded the head movement as 6-axis accelerations, eye movement in 4 directions, blinking frequency and strength. The actions of looking at the smartphone were planned to be extracted from these data, but it was not so easy as expected. Fig. 9 shows parts of the log data recorded per 0.1 s for P1 in (a), which include Google Street View operations (red), head accelerations (light blue to orange), eye movement and blinkings (green), smartphone operations (blue). Fig. 9 (A) is in the cases of focusing on moving in the virtual space, and (B) is in the cases of operating the smartphone as well as the virtual space at the same time. In both cases, the eyes were moving frequently in all the directions, therefore it was difficult to distinguish the two cases from only the data recorded this time. Both (C) and (D) were in the cases of focusing on operating the smartphone, however, (C) showed less had movement compared to other cases. To distinguish between (A) and (B), as well as between (C) and (D), analysis using speech and video data with a larger number of samples are required in the future.

5 Discussion

Tang, L. et al. proposed eight open issues that should be covered in supporting rapid design and evaluation of pervasive applications [19]. This research selected five from them, which are effective for evaluations with user experiences of prototypes, to discuss the experiment results in Sect. 4.

5.1 Simulating Pervasive Environment

Tang, L. et al. suggested 3 roles of the simulators for pervasive environment: *"(1) simulating the input space of an application, including the explicit (e.g., mouse or keyboard events) and implicit input (e.g., location sensed input when user moves);*

(2) simulating the logical control flow that jumps between sensors, servers, handhelds (such as PDA) and any other kinds of networking appliances; and (3) simulating the output space of an application, which means to visualize the environment effects caused by the application behaviors."

According to our initial experiment, our prototype seems to cover enough the functions of simulating (1) the input space and (3) the output space because of using real smartphone devices in the simulator. However, especially (2) the network conditions supported by our prototype are not real and it is usually better than outdoor fields. Therefore, it is thought that there is a limitation of the network simulation in our prototype. We might be better to prepare the function creating pseudo network latency in the virtual space.

5.2   Description of Context-Awareness

Tang, L. et al. mentioned *"Integrating the ability of associating digital data with the users' context into a prototype would be a great help to promote easier retrieval."*

From the results of our initial experiment, we could record body motions, speeches and operation logs labeled with spatio-temporal information in the virtual space, though they are still raw data, which are difficult to be analyzed to extract the context. The types of effective context data for retrieval of tested applications depend on the type of them. We will explore the useful context types for the location-based applications having a large number of users, such as applications for navigation, finding restaurants, finding friends nearby, checking public transportation, receiving special deals or offers from retailers [20]. Furthermore, as the reactions to the context in the virtual space can be different from those in the real world, experiments comparing the proposed environment and the real world are necessary.

5.3   Robust Debugging Environment

The debugging environment is important for inspecting the program architecture, data structure and communication flow. However, according to the investigations by Tang, L. et al., debugging of pervasive applications in distributive mode is very difficult. The proposed environment can set the timing of debugging, and is easier to gather necessary data in virtual space for debugging. In the future, the methods and functions of setting debug mode for experiment organizers can be explored.

5.4   Logging Test Data

Tang, L. et al. suggest that, *"When evaluating design, designers have to analyze the test data, especially to collect the feedback from a long-term, in situ test setting."* The proposed environment takes the advantages of virtual space that, all kinds of log data can be automatically recorded with spatio-temporal labeling. The time needed for an experiment is usually short than that in the real world, therefore the burdens of experiment organizers and participants can be reduced. On the other hand, as discussed in Sect. 4, the task of free strolling ended in 15 min averagely, even if there is no time limit, which suggests that long-duration experiments may bring more burdens to participants. For example, it is possible to ask the participants to use certain devices in daily lives for several weeks in the real world, but which is not feasible in the virtual space like the proposed environment.

So far, the methods of extracting context information from the recorded raw data is not established yet, so it is still difficult to arrange and analyze the data efficiently. For example, the body motions and speeches are supposed to be useful to extract the phycological context like confusing in the virtual space. The analysis of eye and head movement in Sect. 4.3 also shows that it can be useful to playback the recorded spatio-temporal data for exploring new findings. Such functions should be implemented in the future.

5.5 Evaluation Criteria

Tang, L. et al. proposed that the evaluation criteria of prototypes should be field specific and distinctive in each phase. The criteria of "easy-to-understand" is suitable for the tests of getting feedbacks, while "latency" is suitable for the tests of the context-aware application's functions. In the former case, if the prototype's functions are easy to understand, the users are expected to have few problems even if the ambient environment is in virtual space. In the latter case, as Google Street View provides limited moving range and fixed context like time and weather, it may not meet the requirements of some evaluations. In the future, context other than location information should be considered, and methods of extending Google Street View to include them need to be investigated.

6 Conclusion

This research developed a prototype of user experiment environment based on the extension of Google Street View for evaluating location-based mobile applications aiming to reduce the costs of user tests compared to field experiments to involve more participants. The initial experiment investigated how the interactions with smartphone application in virtual space could be recorded and represented. The results showed that the proposed experiment environment is useful for user evaluations of location-based applications, and its limits and issues to be improved were also discussed. That means a fieldwork method, which is one of participatory design tools grows up into more collaborative platform and it has potential to influence future urban application design ways.

References

1. Number of location-based service users in the United States from 2013 to 2018 (in millions). Statista (2017). https://www.statista.com/statistics/436071/location-based-service-users-usa/. Accessed 10 Feb 2019
2. Johnson, P.: Usability and mobility; interactions on the move. In: Proceedings of the first workshop on human-computer interaction with mobile devices, GIST Technical report G98–1 (1998)

3. Elzakker, C.P.J.M., Delikostidis, I., van Oosterom, P.J.M.: Field-based usability evaluation methodology for mobile geo-applications. Cartogr. J. **45**(2), 139–149 (2008)

4. Nigetore. https://nigetore.jp/. Accessed 10 Feb 2019

5. Itamiya, T.: The virtual tsunami disaster situation experience system using a head-mounted display, media and communication for disaster risk reduction. In: Showcasing Innovation, An initiative for the Third UN World Conference on Disaster Risk Reduction in Sendai, pp. 2–3 (2015)

6. Kawai, J., Mitsuhara, H., Shishibori, M.: Game-based evacuation drill using augmented reality and head-mounted display. Interact. Technol. Smart Educ. **13**(3), 186–201 (2016)

7. Elzakker, V.C.P., Delikostidis, I., Oosterom, V.P.J.: Field-based usability evaluation methodology for mobile geo-applications. The Cartogr. J. **45**(2), 139–149 (2008)

8. Sun, X., May, A.: A comparison of field-based and lab-based experiments to evaluate user experience of personalised mobile devices. Adv. Hum. Comput. Interact. 2 (2013)

9. Kjeldskov, J., Graham, C.: A Review of mobile HCI research methods. In: Chittaro, Luca (ed.) Mobile HCI 2003. LNCS, vol. 2795, pp. 317–335. Springer, Heidelberg (2003). https://doi.org/10.1007/978-3-540-45233-1_23

10. Nakanishi, H., Yoshida, C., Nishimura, T., Ishida, T.: FreeWalk: A 3D virtual space for casual meetings. IEEE MultiMedia, **6**(2) (1999)

11. Portman, M.E., Natapov, A., Fisher-Gewirtzman, D.: To go where no man has gone before: Virtual reality in architecture, landscape architecture and environmental planning. Comput. Environ. Urban Syst. **54**, 376–384 (2015)

12. Roussou, M., Drettakis, G., Tsingos, N., Reche, A., Gallo, E.: A user-centered approach on combining realism and interactivity in virtual environments. In: IEEE Virtual Reality 2004, pp. 251–252, Chicago, IL, USA (2004)

13. Drettakis, G., Roussou, M., Reche, A., Tsingos, N.: Design and evaluation of a real-world virtual environment for architecture and urban planning. Presence Teleoper. Virtual Environ. **16**(3), 318–332 (2007)

14. PlacePulse. http://pulse.media.mit.edu/. Accessed 10 Feb 2019

15. Block by Block, https://www.blockbyblock.org/. Accessed 7 Feb 2019

16. Royal Naval Personnel Research Committee: Human Factors for Designers of Naval Equipment. Medical Research Council, Swindon (1971)

17. JINS MEME, https://jins-meme.com/en/. Accessed 10 Feb 2019

18. Jaspers, M.W., Steen, T., Van Den Bos, C., Geenen, M.: The think aloud method: a guide to user interface design. Int. J. Med. Inform. **73**(11–12), 781–795 (2004)

19. Tang, L., Yu, Z., Zhou, X., Wang, H., Becker, C.: Supporting rapid design and evaluation of pervasive applications: challenges and solutions. Pers. Ubiquit. Comput. 15(3), pp. 253–269. Springer-Verlag, Heidelberg (2011)

20. Navigation is the most popular type of LBS app, http://www.tnsglobal.com/intelligence-applied/blessing-in-disguise. Accessed 10 Feb 2019

Capturing People Mobility with Mobile Sensing Technology for Disaster Evacuation

Chenwei Song, Masaki Ito, and Kaoru Sezaki[(✉)]

Institute of Industrial Science, The University of Tokyo,
Komaba 4-6-1, Meguro, Tokyo 153-8505, Japan
songchenwei@mcl.iis.u-tokyo.ac.jp,
{mito,sezaki}@iis.u-tokyo.ac.jp

Abstract. In this paper, we propose a client-server-service-based system that provides crowd detection and mobility capture. Crowd detection is to detect and calculate the density of crowds within a specified area. Mobility capture is to track the direction of the people. If a warning mechanism is added, the system can prevent or dissolve the crowd to avoid accidents in public places by sending alerts when the detected number of people exceeds a certain set percentage. The technology also plays a big role after the disaster, by calculating the path with relatively small population density in the disaster area, the high-density crowd can be led to a safe area avoiding secondary injury by crowding. Compared to common methods, such as cameras, our proposed system has the advantages of low cost and location flexibility. The system can detect any area without pre-deployed, as long as there is a sufficient number of users involved. In this article, we conducted several experiments in real environments to determine if the system can accurately capture crowd information and route tracking.

Keywords: Capture mobility · Crowd detection · Bluetooth

1 Introduction

A crowd is a deformable group of people occupying a particular area. We can obtain crowds information by detecting and calculating the density of people within a specified area, such as the number of people, the trend or speed of the crowd. Automatic crowd understanding has a massive impact on several applications including surveillance and security, situation awareness, crowd management, public space design and etc. For example, the government can decide how to widen existing roads to alleviate traffic congestion based on the location information of high-density populations. In addition, merchants can decide place the advertising labels in the place where can attract the most customers according to the walking track of the crowd on the commercial street. In the real-time environment, if an early warning mechanism is added to the crowd detection system, once a large number of people in a certain area are detected, staff can immediately make evacuation work to avoid injury caused by crowding.

In order to achieve the crowd information automatically, specific equipment and techniques are needed to assist in the counting process. The common methods are

© Springer Nature Switzerland AG 2019
N. Streitz and S. Konomi (Eds.): HCII 2019, LNCS 11587, pp. 187–198, 2019.
https://doi.org/10.1007/978-3-030-21935-2_15

cameras, GPS, Wi-Fi and Bluetooth. In general, these methods have the following steps to achieve crowds counting:

1. Obtaining the raw data.
2. Analyzing the relationship between the raw data and the number of people.
3. Displaying the number of people.

Because the equipment and methods used to collect the raw data are different, the above approaches will have different performance in terms of cost, accuracy, and the scope of application. In this paper, we propose a crowd counting and mobility capture system based on Bluetooth. It does not need to deploy devices such as cameras or Radio Frequency Identification (RFID) tag in advance and only needs enough users to carry smartphones with Internet access, which can obtain the crowd information in a certain area. We conducted several experiments in the actual environment to verify the accuracy of the number of people detected by the Bluetooth method, and whether the possibility of walking the trajectory can still be obtained with a small number of users participating.

The rest of the paper is organized as follows. Section 2 describes the related works by other researchers. Section 3 introduces the motivation of developing the system. Section 4 gives details of the system structure and design. Section 5 shows the experiments that we conducted and the evaluation of the results. Section 6 is the conclusions.

2   Related Works

Detecting the crowds to obtain counting number and mobility data is important for today's urban life. The common method of collecting image data by cameras and then analyzing the number of people by image analysis algorithm has already had mature technologies. But the cost of equipment such as cameras has always been a problem for these methods. Recently, the methods of collecting non-image data to obtain crowd information have gradually increased, especially through Bluetooth.

The original purpose of Bluetooth was to meet the need for small-scale data transmission at short range. So, Bluetooth has features like short communication distance, low speed and low cost. This makes Bluetooth very suitable for some special scenes.

In [1, 2], they installed multiple Bluetooth receiving devices in one room. When a person carrying a Bluetooth device enters the room, each receiver can obtain a Received Signal Strength Indicator (RSSI) value to display the distance to the user. Through the trilateration algorithm [2], the user's location in the room can be finally obtained. This method can be used as an alternative to GPS localization indoors. Compared to the Wi-Fi localization method, Bluetooth is cheaper and easier to install.

In [3], they proposed to build a Bluetooth Ad Hoc Network, CrowdBlueNet, to collect data from individual smartphones to support crowd management. The network is completely based on Bluetooth devices, so even if the cellular and wireless networks are not accessible, the network will still work, which means that as long as the user is inside the Bluetooth network zone, the crowd information can be obtained. The users can avoid entering areas with high density of people and causing damage.

In [4], they developed a bus query application based on the crowdsourcing model, using Bluetooth as a crowd counting device and location conversion trigger. Let the users' smartphones provide the number of passengers and traffic conditions instead of the equipment that will be installed on the bus to achieve these proposes. Therefore, reducing the cost of investigating bus operations by using Bluetooth of users' smartphones.

As the researches we have listed above, most of the application scenarios of Bluetooth are to use the low cost and flexibility of Bluetooth to replace the original high cost and non-movable methods.

3   Motivation

In this paper, we propose a client-server-service-based system that provides users with real-time crowd information such as population density and trajectory in a given area.

Our system is designed based on the following three points.

1. No additional devices are other than users' smartphones and the server.
2. Reflect the number of people in the area by counting the number of Bluetooth devices.
3. The users are also sensors that provide information about surrounding Bluetooth devices.

Our goal is to achieve a low-cost crowd detection system that is not limited by the location of the equipment installation, which means that the system can detect crowd information in almost any location without the need to install the detection equipment in advance.

4   System Design

4.1   Data Collection Method

According to existing methods for collecting crowd information, we can divide the methods into two groups by different types of raw data: the image data methods and the non-image data methods. For example, using cameras is a typical method which analyzes image data. The raw data obtained by it is images of the video, then utilize human recognition technology to get the crowd information in the image. About the non-image data methods, the raw data of this kind include the sending time, location coordinates, speed, etc. of a device. How the data of the devices are linked to the information of the crowds becomes the key.

Image data methods, such as using closed-circuit television (CCTV) cameras to capture image data, find the crowd area from the image data and convert it into crowd information. Image recognition technology and equipment that can capture high-resolution images make the method highly accurate [5]. But this method relies on the image collecting equipment, so the method is costly. At the same time, the method will cause problems such as occlusion, insufficient light, inflexibility due to the position where the camera is installed. Therefore, it is more suitable for the government to monitor traffic flow and safety, etc.

In the non-image data methods, the GPS-based method has been published by many map service companies [6]. When using the map service applications, the user can get the crowd information from the server, at the same time, his phone as a participating sensor uploads information. GPS chips integrated into the smartphones are cheap now, and this method does not require complicated image information conversion process. However, the GPS signal cannot reach indoors, therefore, it cannot be applied to every place.

Wi-Fi is a recently popular indoor detection method instead of GPS. By analyzing the change of the Wi-Fi signal between multiple access points (APs) or analyzing the Wi-Fi connection data collected by the AP, we can know the flow of people in that area [7]. This method can be used in any place where an AP is deployed. In other words, it is not restricted by indoor and outdoor. However, due to the need to deploy APs, this method is suitable for indoor detection. In the method of analyzing signals, it is also necessary to do a large number of signal samples in advance for reference, so that the method of analyzing signals is relatively complicated.

A Bluetooth method is similar to a device-based method of Wi-Fi. But because the sender and requester of Bluetooth can be converted to each other. There is no need for additional devices like APs, just make sure that the proportion of people carrying Bluetooth devices in the crowd is enough [8]. Although the effective range of Bluetooth is very short, its low cost and wide usage make this method be applied to almost anywhere (Table 1).

Table 1. Comparison of data collection methods

	Camera	GPS	Wi-Fi	Bluetooth
Money	High	Medium	Medium	Low
Extra equipment	Yes	No	Yes	No
Indoor	Yes	No	Yes	Yes
Precision	High	Medium	Medium	Medium

We make a comparison of the crowd counting approaches mentioned above. This comparison is not to find out which method is the best but to understand the advantages and disadvantages of each method and the scope of application. Meanwhile, find the most suitable method for our system. Finally, we chose Bluetooth as the method to collect data for our system.

4.2 System Overview

After comparing the above methods, we finally use Bluetooth to counting the number of crowds. According to statistics, in 2018, Bluetooth device shipments have reached 3.9 billion, of which smartphones, tablets and other mobile devices have reached

2.05 billion [9]. This proves that Bluetooth is everywhere in people's lives. Bluetooth has two main communication protocol technologies, Basic Rate/Enhanced Data Rate (BR/EDR) and Bluetooth Low Energy (BLE). Due to the low power consumption of BLE and the official announcement that 97% of Bluetooth chips will contain BLE mode in 2022, we decided to use BLE mode to scan.

As shown in Fig. 1, the structure of the system is a client-server model. Each smartphone with our app will become a client. They will scan and upload the surrounding Bluetooth devices information while graphically displaying the crowd data obtained by the server to the user. The server receives and analyzes the information from each client, then it returns the data of the crowd in the area where the client is located in real time.

Fig. 1. Structure of the system

A user can receive the crowd information by carrying a smartphone with our application installed. The application automatically scans Bluetooth devices and logs location data every 10 s. After scanning, the application sends the data to the server through the Hypertext Transfer Protocol (HTTP) method. The server receives the data from smartphones and stores the information in the database. After analysis, the server sends crowd information back to the smartphones. The smartphones display the crowd information to the users through the graphic interface of our application (Fig. 2).

4.3   Data Collection and Analysis Method

We define the following roles to make our system easier to understand.

- The user with a smartphone: After the users installed our application on their smartphones, they can check the crowd information in their area through the application. At the same time, their smartphones become Bluetooth sensors, sending the information of the Bluetooth devices which around them to our server through the network at regular intervals. The rest of this paper will use the smartphone to refer to the user.

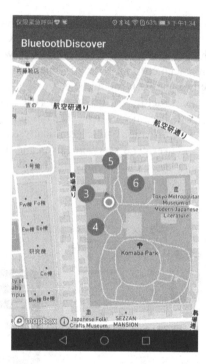

Fig. 2. Screenshot of the smartphone application

- The Bluetooth device: Bluetooth devices are the devices detected by the smartphones through Bluetooth scanning. It may be a mobile phone, a watch, a headset, etc. Through the counting of Bluetooth devices, we can get the number of the crowds.
- The server: The server is the computer we set to provide the crowd information for the smartphones. After processing the information sent by the smartphone, the server sends the result back the smartphone, such as the number of people, the movement and location.

When the application on the smartphone starts working, it will perform a 5 s Bluetooth scan, then upload the device information to the server and stop for 5 s before the next scan. In other words, the smartphone sends a message to the server every 10 s. The message includes the timestamp, the location of the smartphone, and the RSSI value and the Media Access Control (MAC) Address of the scanned Bluetooth.

The RSSI value can be converted into the distance between the Bluetooth device and the mobile phone. The MAC Address is a label for connecting to the network. Like the license plate, it is theoretically unique, so we use it to distinguish different Bluetooth devices. If we detect the same Bluetooth device at multiple points on the timeline, we can track the device. Although the location information belongs to the smartphone since the maximum distance set is 15 m, the route of the device still can be tracked or even pre-judged. Furthermore, if the Bluetooth device is detected by more than three or more smartphones at the same time, we can obtain the actual location of the Bluetooth by using the trilateration method [2]. After the analysis, the server sends the result to the smartphones, and our application display the data to the users with the graphical interface.

5 Experiment and Evaluation

5.1 Effective Distance of the Bluetooth Signal

The Bluetooth signal strength is reflected by the RSSI value, which is a negative number. The closer the value is to zero, the closer the distance to the Bluetooth device.

First, we need to confirm the sending range of BLE devices which often be used in our daily lives. We conducted experiments both indoors and outdoors. We set a smartphone and a Bluetooth headset as the sender separately. Both of them support Bluetooth 5.0, which means they can work in BLE mode. We tested the range at 5-meter intervals starting from 0 m up to 30 m. At each range, we measured the RSSI value. Table 2 shows the average result of this experiment.

Table 2. Result of range test

Distance in meters	RSSI (indoor)	RSSI (outdoor)
0	−40	−40
5	−53	−57
10	−69	−75
15	−75	−80
20	−97	−99
25	−99	−101
30	−101	−103

According to the results of the above table, we can conclude that although the Bluetooth signal can still be detected at around 30 m, from the RSSI value, it is difficult to distinguish the distance of Bluetooth devices when it is more than 20 m. Therefore, in the following experiments, we set the software acceptable threshold to −75 in an indoor environment and −80 in an outdoor environment. In other words, the farthest Bluetooth device that the mobile phone can detect is 15 m.

5.2 Crowd Counting

In order to verify the feasibility of Bluetooth detection, we conducted the experiments in 4 different scenarios and compared them in pairs. They are the classroom where the professor has a lecture, the crowded metro compartment, the street with the low pedestrian flow and the crowded crossroad. To avoid detecting Bluetooth devices outside the test location, we placed the test point in the middle of the 200 m^2 classroom

(20 m × 10 m), and we chose the test point in the middle of the compartment, which is 18 m long, at the tail of the subway hich is 18 m long, at the tail of the subway (Fig. 3).

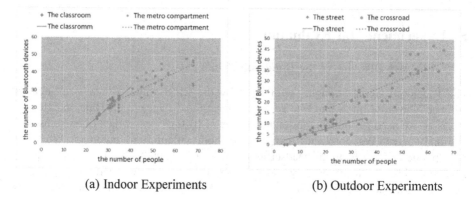

(a) Indoor Experiments   (b) Outdoor Experiments

Fig. 3. Scanning result

Table 3. Correlation between bluetooth devices and people

	Device/per person	Pearson correlation coefficient
The classroom	1.1442	0.9463
The metro	0.6182	0.8047
The street	0.3363	0.7483
The crossroad	0.4867	0.7416

In each experiment, we collected 30 sets of data and took photos at the same time. We manually count the number of people on the photos, then compared with data collected by the smartphone installed our application. About the street and the crossroad, we selected the road of a low-density area and the crossroads with dense crowds in Shimokitazawa. As shown in Table 3, the indoor situation has a higher correlation in the relationship between Bluetooth devices and the number of people. Because almost every student has a notebook or a laptop with a Bluetooth device in that class besides the smartphones. In the other experiments, the relationship between Bluetooth and people is lower, probably because the people being detected is more random. In general, indoor results are more reliable than outdoor results. We consider the reason is that on the one hand, the Bluetooth signal is not easily affected by other factors indoors. On the other hand, indoor flow changes are not as frequent as outdoor.

The results can show that almost one of two people will use a Bluetooth device. This is helpful for the viability and accuracy of our system.

5.3   Mobility Tracking Implementation

After the feasibility test of Bluetooth scanning, we need to further prove the feasibility of tracking and localization.

According to the principle of the trilateration algorithm [2], to obtain location information of the measured point, we need at least three points with known location information and their respective distances to the measured point. In our system, if three or more mobile phones can detect the same Bluetooth device at the same time, by converting the RSSI value into the distance value, we can obtain the specific location information of the Bluetooth device.

If the same Bluetooth device is continuously detected on a continuous time axis, by analyzing the location information at each time point, we can obtain the route information of the Bluetooth device. It should be noted that our system records the location information of users' smartphones, not the location information of the detected Bluetooth device. However, due to the RSSI threshold set by us, the detected Bluetooth device will not exceed 15 m to users' smartphones. If more than three smartphones detect the Bluetooth device at the same time, the actual location of the Bluetooth can also be obtained through trilateration algorithm.

Because the information collected by our system is completed by the participating users' smartphone, in theory, the more users there are in the same area, the more accurate the crowd information will be, the more Bluetooth devices can be tracked and located. We want to further test which factors affect the accuracy of the data when the number of users is fixed. We control the time, the test area, the user's walking route overlap rate, and conducted three sets of comparative experiments.

We selected the test area near the train station in Shimokitazawa. We asked 5 participants to walk around the station, each holding a smartphone installed our application. As shown in Table 4, the first two sets were the comparison of route overlapping under the same experiment time. The latter two sets of experiments were the comparison of time under the same area size. The overlapping in Table 4 refers to the percentage of route repetitions of the 5 people (Fig. 4).

Table 4. Environmental parameters of the experiments

	Time (min)	Area (m^2)	Length (km)	Overlapping
Route 1	15	95048.32	1.78	20%
Route 2	15	37726.35	1.12	54%
Route 3	30	36723.47	1.14	60%

We set the program to record Bluetooth device information every 10 s, which means 6 records per minute. Because there are 5 smartphones, the previous two experiments recorded 450 times respectively, and the third experiment recorded 900 times. Every time a record has information of 0 to multiple Bluetooth devices. We consider Bluetooth devices that have been detected more than 6 times by smartphones as the devices that can be effectively tracked.

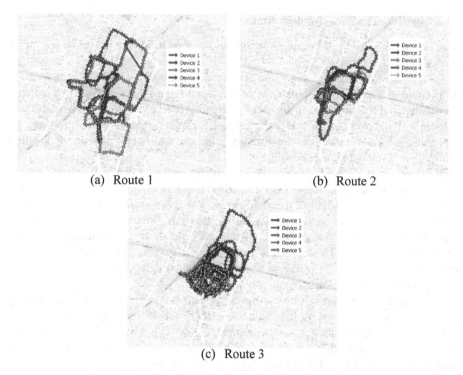

(a) Route 1   (b) Route 2

(c) Route 3

Fig. 4. Walking route

From Table 5 we can see that the route overlapping rate will affect the proportion of effective tracking. A smartphone or several smartphones with a low overlapping rate can obtain device information only within its Bluetooth scan range. A single scan area is very limited. However, if the overlapping rate rises, even if the Bluetooth device is outside the scanning range of one smartphone, it is possible to be captured again by other smartphones in the overlapping range, the tracking continues to be effective. On the other hand, through the comparison of the result of Route 2 and Route 3, we found that the increase in measurement time does not necessarily increase the devices ratio of effective tracking. For the time factor, we consider the reason is the crowd have already gone out of our test range. For this situation, even if the detection time is increased within the same range, it does not work.

Table 5. Effective tracking results

	Detected devices	Detected more than six times	Detected only once
Route 1	726	217 (29.9%)	290 (40.0%)
Route 2	549	357 (65.0%)	126 (23.0%)
Route 3	1122	639 (57.0%)	381 (34.0%)

Tracking not only shows the route of the detected Bluetooth device but also can predict the trend of people flow. With the help of the early warning mechanism, the system can avoid the injury caused by crowds being overcrowded. Tracking also allows us to discover static devices. A static device means the device not carried by a person, such as a desktop computer with Bluetooth. If these devices are counted in the crowd information, the results will be affected. We can remove these static devices by tracking the devices located in a small area for a long time.

The column "Detected only once" in Table 5 is the number of Bluetooth devices that are only detected once by a smartphone. It is difficult to determine if they are mobile devices that can reflect crowd information. Obviously, as the route overlapping rate increases, the number of devices that detected once is reduced.

Table 6. Localization results

	Record times	Times that testers met each other	Record by more than three smartphones at the same time
Route 1	450	26 (5.7%)	59 (13.1%)
Route 2	450	56 (12.4%)	126 (28%)
Route 3	900	64 (7.1%)	167 (18.6%)

We analyzed the feasibility of Bluetooth devices localization. From Table 6 we concluded that in the experimental environment we set, the proportion of device that can be located is not high enough. The device localization in our system is based on the number of smartphones that can detect the same Bluetooth device at the same time, which means that the proportion of participants meeting each other needs to be high. In the three sets of experiments above, the route overlapping rate ensures that multiple smartphones can detect the same device, but this does not mean that these smartphones detected the Bluetooth device at the same time. From the column, 'Times that testers met each other' of Table 6 we conclude that the five participants are mostly distributed in different locations in the test area. In most cases, only two or fewer smartphones in the detected Bluetooth range are the main reasons for the low proportion of devices that can be located. From the above table, we can know that devices localization is not suitable for the area only has a few smartphones.

6 Conclusion

In this paper, we propose a crowd information system based on Bluetooth scanning. It does not require the addition of equipment such as cameras or routers, so it has the advantage of low cost and flexibility. We verified its accuracy and feasibility through the experiments. Meanwhile, we conducted the experiments on the feasibility of device tracking and localization. It is concluded that the tracking of the device is feasible in the experimental environment we set, but the proportion of devices that can be located is too low.

What we can do is to make every effort to make the application more attractive, to encourage people to use our application, therefore improving the accuracy of the Bluetooth detection population.

As future work, we mainly have two tasks, one is to improve the usability and appeal of mobile software to encourage more users to participate in order to improve the accuracy of our system. The other is to use the tracking and localization function to provide users with crowd information forecasting.

References

1. Wang, Y., Yang, X., Zhao, Y., Liu, Y., Cuthbert, L.: Bluetooth positioning using RSSI and triangulation methods. In: 2013 IEEE Consumer Communications and Networking Conference (CCNC), pp 837–842. IEEE (2013)
2. Rida, M.E., Liu, F., Jadi, Y., Algawhari, A.A.A., Askourih, A.: Indoor location position based on bluetooth signal strength. In: 2015 2nd International Conference on Information Science and Control Engineering (ICISCE), pp 769–773. IEEE (2015)
3. Liu, S., Du, J., Yang, X., Li, R., Liu, H., Sha, K.: CrowdBlueNet: maximizing crowd data collection using bluetooth ad hoc networks. In: Yang, Q., Yu, W., Challal, Y. (eds.) WASA 2016. LNCS, vol. 9798, pp. 356–366. Springer, Cham (2016). https://doi.org/10.1007/978-3-319-42836-9_32
4. Cianciulli, D., Canfora, G., Zimeo, E.: Beaconbased context-aware architecture for crowd sensing public transportation scheduling and user habits. Proc. Comput. Sci. **24**, 1110–1115 (2017)
5. Baqui, M., Ohner, R.L.: Real-time crowd safety and comfort management from CCTV images. In: 2017 International Society for Optics and Photonics Real-Time Image And Video Processing, vol. 10223, p 1022304 (2017)
6. Blanke, U., Troster, G., Franke, T., Lukowicz, P.: Capturing crowd dynamics at large scale events using participatory GPS-localization. In: 2014 IEEE Ninth International Conference on Intelligent Sensors, Sensor Networks and Information Processing (ISSNIP), pp 1–7. IEEE (2014)
7. Depatla, S., Mostofi, Y.: Passive crowd speed estimation and head counting using wifi. In: 2018 15th Annual IEEE International Conference on Sensing, Communication, and Networking (SECON), pp 1–9. IEEE (2018)
8. Basalamah, A.: Sensing the crowds using bluetooth low energy tags. IEEE Access **4**, 4225–4233 (2016)
9. Bluetooth Special Interest Group: Bluetooth 5 Core Specification, Version 5, 06 December 2016 (2018)

Multi-modal Sensor Based Localization and Control Method for Human-Following Outdoor Security Mobile Robot

Taeyoung Uhm$^{(\boxtimes)}$, Ji-Hyun Park, Gi-Deok Bae, and Young-Ho Choi

Korean Institute of Robot and Convergence, Pohang, Republic of Korea
{uty,jipark78,bgd9047,rockboy}@kiro.re.kr

Abstract. Recently, mobile robots are attracting attention in various industries. Outdoor unmanned security mobile robot is a key issue for surveillance. The main task of these security robots is to protect people and property. For this purpose, the robot should be able to autonomously navigation and interaction with people is essential. Especially, it is required to perform autonomous driving by avoiding collision with humans and obstacles, tracking a certain human for intruder surveillance or safety of people. For the outdoor security task, we propose the novel localization and control methods that is not only overcome the weather conditions for positioning, but also build a safety route for avoiding and following relative to human position. The robust localization method is based on detecting the salient features by the information filters for multi-layered knowledge (e.g. sensory, episodic, semantic and cloud big data), and then estimate an accurately position of the moved robot. Next, the safety route is defined a rollover model of a security robot on slope and suggests a path generation using DWA (Dynamic Window Approach) method with safety ratio. The method of evaluating rollover is the ZMP (Zero Moment Point) concept. If there is a ZMP between the wheels of the steering mobile robot, it can be safe. The results show that the autonomous navigation is possible with robust localization method, and then it can follow a specific human by the safety path generation. The proposed method is expected to be usable in various applications requiring outdoor surveillance.

Keywords: Multi-layered knowledge · Most weather conditions · Outdoor autonomous navigation · Rollover model · Security robot · Human following robot

1 Introduction

Interaction technology between human and robot has been continuously developed. Among the applications for surveillance, outdoor unmanned security robots have attracted attention in recent years. The robots have to perform autonomous navigation and human interaction in various outdoor environments. First, autonomous driving has been carried out steadily, and many researchers are conducting it. First, autonomous driving has been continuously studied by many researchers. Especially, the navigation techniques for the outdoor environment have been performed mostly for good weather,

© Springer Nature Switzerland AG 2019
N. Streitz and S. Konomi (Eds.): HCII 2019, LNCS 11587, pp. 199–211, 2019.
https://doi.org/10.1007/978-3-030-21935-2_16

and it is difficult to cope with most weather conditions. This is because effective feature extraction is difficult in complex weather environments. In order to overcome this problem, robust features are extracted by utilizing all of the multi-modal sensor data available to the robot. Then, there is a need for a method of locating the most useful features using prior knowledge of the current weather, location, and topography.

On the other hand, the security robot is required to interact with humans to perform missions to track or guide interested humans. For this purpose, it is necessary to consider both the control method of measuring and maintaining the distance from the human, the method of driving safely by recognizing the speed and the humility. Therefore, a safe control method is required for rollover that does not overturn while measuring distance.

In this paper, we propose a robust localization method for outdoor environment and a control method for interaction with human. The proposed method can drive outdoors for most weather conditions, and can track and guide humans on the unpaved road or slope way. Experimental results show that robust position estimation is feasible based on knowledge-based features, and a stability model can be defined to enable safe travel with less risk of rollover.

The remainder of paper is organized as follows. In Sect. 2, some related works are summarized. Section 3 describes localization for outdoor autonomous navigation, including multi-layered knowledge based salient map, information filter, and some results. The safety path generation method with ZMP model is described in Sect. 4. Section 5 presents the human robot interaction by following in surveillance application. Finally, we summarize the proposed method.

2   Related Works

Research on the position estimation of robots has been carried out steadily. The Researches based on various sensors estimate a location with a fixed map using vision data [1] or sensor data [2] in indoor environment. However, in order to carry out unmanned security, localization method should be possible in outdoor environment.

There is a method [3] of recognizing the road environment by mixing LiDAR based on GPS, a method [4, 5] using a laser sensor, a method using a single camera [6] or a stereo vision [7] for outdoor localization. These methods determine the location by mixing the global GPS and the local pose estimation using the sensor data. In the same way, there is also research on location recognition using only global and local vision data [8]. However, for practical security, robust driving methods are needed in most weather conditions, including seasonal changes.

In order to overcome the environmental changes, a method of estimating the location using robust features in the image for seasonal changes [9], a method that is useful not only for seasons but also for night and daytime conditions [10, 11], and techniques have been proposed for rain or snow weather conditions [12]. These methods are solving some of the changes in the outdoor environment depending on the feature quantity using a specific image only. Therefore, in this paper, we propose a localization method considering most of season, night/day and weather conditions.

On the other hand, there were various efforts for stable control of robots. However, it seems that most of them are not suitable for roads that have roughness for active steering [13], steering and braking [14, 15], which are mostly controls for flat roads. Therefore, we propose a stable model-based control algorithm by the centrifugal force generated in the turning process in order to prevent the rollover on the road with the slope.

Most of the interaction methods between human and robot were performed based on sensor data in indoor environments [16, 17]. However, in this paper, we propose a human-following interaction method using the above-mentioned location recognition and control method for outdoor unmanned security robot. It performs interactions that follow specific humans for outdoor security applications. Consequently, the proposed interaction method is expected to improve the service of the outdoor unmanned security robot.

3   Localization for Outdoor Autonomous Navigation

3.1   Multi-layered Knowledge Augmented Based Strategy Map

A multi-layered knowledge augmented map database for extracting valid data from multi-modal sensor is shown in Fig. 1. This map is based on a multi-layer including semantic knowledge (semantic data, episodic data, semantic and cloud big data), climate, time, geographical features and driving strategies. The information is used to enhance a dynamic navigation map. Figure 2 shows an example of fusion of valid salient data based strategy map at the current location by query from the multi-layered knowledge augmented DB map. This is a way to represent the most useful data at the current position using a high-level knowledge database. Moreover, each data has a level of robustness and reliability can be measured using it. Therefore, we can choice the salient data which has strong and weak data in the given knowledge data (weather condition, current time, season, temp, RH, etc.).

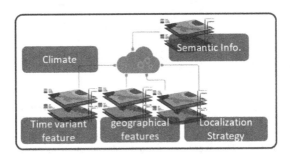

Fig. 1. Multi-layered knowledge augmented map database configuration.

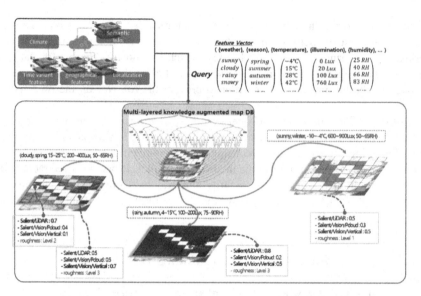

Fig. 2. An example of valid salient data based strategy map.

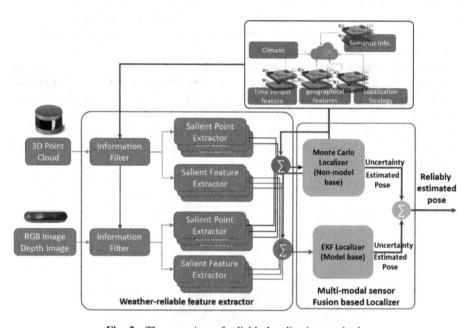

Fig. 3. The overview of reliable localization method.

3.2 Reliable Localization Method

Reliable localization estimation is performed by extracting salient pointers and features with the multi-layer prior knowledge-based information filters. This method is estimated by fusion of non-model based Monte Carlo Localizer [18] and model-based EKF

Localizer [19] in a reliability pose. Each localizer considers the knowledge-based robust level to determine its uncertainty. The final pose estimation using this is a reliable result, as shown in Fig. 3.

The proposed method employs an information filter for multi-modal sensor data, the salient points and features can be extracted as,

$$X_i = I(x_i, k) + V_k \tag{1}$$

where X_i is observed data, and V_k denotes the noise vectors. The $I(\cdot)$ derived from the information state vector Y_k

$$Y_k \triangleq I(\cdot)^{-1}. \tag{2}$$

Therefore, the information filter can be extracted a reliable position from the multi-modal sensor data. Finally, we can estimate the accurate position for security robots.

3.3   Experimental Results for the Proposed Localization Method

In order to show the usefulness of the proposed method, a salient dominant vertical structure was extracted from the heavy rain images. The Fig. 4 shows the results of extracting valid salient features by using information filter. In Fig. 4(a), the image shows a result in the good weather condition. Figure 4(b) is the start image in the heavy rainy day. The third image is a result without filter, as shown in Fig. 4(c). Finally, Fig. 4(d) shows the result image with the proposed information filter (e.g. blurring, lens flare effect repression). Table 1 shows that the salient feature extraction rate improves.

Fig. 4. The results of information filter: (a) sunny day, (b) rainy day, (c) result without filter and (d) result with filter.

Table 1. The comparison of salient feature extraction rate for weather conditions.

Weather condition (without filter or proposed)	Sunny Day (without filter)	Rainy Day (without filter)	Rainy Day (proposed)
Salient feature extraction rate	100%	9%	77%

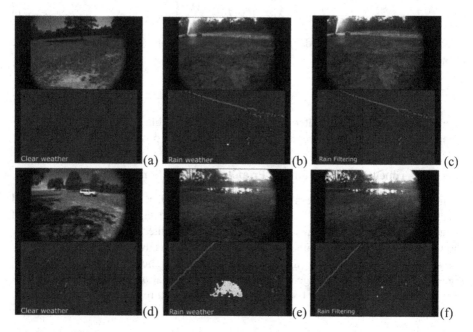

Fig. 5. The result of the proposed method: (a) sunny start location, (b) rainy start location without filter, (c) rainy start location with filter, (d) sunny final location, (e) rainy final location, and (f) rainy final location with filter. (white points are localization error)

Table 2. The comparison of 3D LiDAR feature error rate for weather conditions.

Weather condition (without filter or proposed)	Sunny day (without filter)	Rainy day (without filter)	Rainy day (proposed)
Feature error rate	0%	20%	0.14%

Figure 5 shows the results of applying the proposed method to 3D LiDAR data in a factitious rainy situation. Figure 5(a) and (d) show the start image and final image in a sunny day, and there is no position error. In Fig. 5(b) and (e), the images show that localization error is caused by the raindrops. Finally, the results of our method can reduce the error and obtain a valid location, as shown in Fig. 5(c) and (f). Therefore, the precise location in clear weather loses its accuracy in rainy conditions, but it can be seen that the proposed method is capable of reliable localization by elimination feature error, as shown in Table 2.

4 Safety Path Generation for Human Computer Interaction

4.1 Robot Modeling for Overcoming Rollover

The rollover of the mobile robot is determined by the gravitational force in the ramp and the centrifugal force generated in the turning process of the mobile robot [20]. Figure 1 shows a graphical representation of a turn at a ramp and the resulting force. At this time, the case where the robot is rolled over is expressed by Eq. (3),

$$vw = g\theta + \frac{gd}{2h} \tag{3}$$

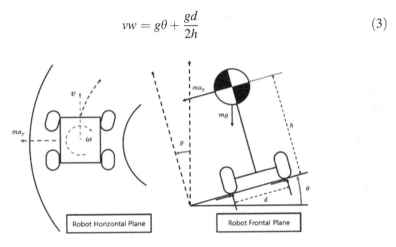

Fig. 6. The robot model on a slope.

where v is velocity of robot, w is angular velocity of robot, θ presents the angle of slope. This equation represents that the rollover is dependent on v, w, and θ. Moreover, in this equation, only the occurrence of rollover is known, and the risk of rollover is unknown. Therefore, it is necessary to quantify the risk of rollover using ZMP (zero moment point). This model is modified to introduce the ZMP concept, as shown in Fig. 7.

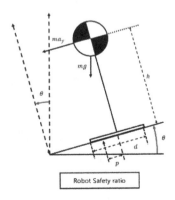

Fig. 7. The robot ZMP model on a slope.

The risk of rollover of a robot can be expressed numerically by the concept of ZMP, and if ZMP model exists between the outer and inner wheels of the robot, it can be said to be stable against rollover. Furthermore, this ZMP model was represented, as Eq. (4),

$$p = h\theta + \frac{vw}{g}h \qquad (4)$$

where p is ZMP, even if it is the same size, which the risk of rollover depends on the robots should be normalized, as Eq. (5),

$$s = \left| \frac{2}{d}\left(h\theta + \frac{vw}{g}h \right) \right| \qquad (5)$$

where stable factor s must be between 0 and 1 to be stable, and if it is negative, it can be determined that rollover has been occurred. If the risk of rollover can be determined numerically, a stable path can be created.

The algorithm used in this paper is DWA (dynamic window approach). DWA calculates the cost according to each cost function in the area consisting of robot velocity and angular velocity set, and determines the most suitable robot velocity and angular velocity. This can be expressed by Eq. (6),

$$G(v, w) = a(\alpha \cdot heading(v, w) + \beta \cdot dist(v, w) + \gamma \cdot vel(v, w) + \delta \cdot rollover(v, w, \theta)). \qquad (6)$$

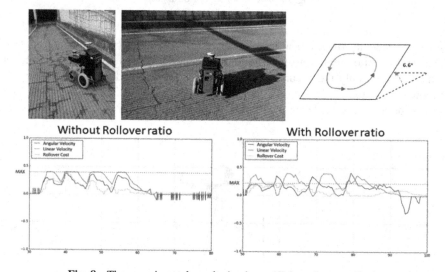

Fig. 8. The experimental results in slope. (Colour figure online)

Figure 8 shows the experimental result through the algorithm applying the rollover model. The robot is turning in a slope, and the result is the same as the graph. In the graph, Rollover cost (sky blue color) indicates the risk of rollover. The results show that the value was 0.4 or higher when the risk of overturning was not taken into consideration, and the risk of overturning was lowered to 0.25 when the risk of overturning was considered.

5 Human-Robot Interaction by Following

In the security mission, the unmanned robot must perform the role of tracking or guiding the human. In particular, a mission to track a specific human is initiated by a tracking command received from an administrator, extracting a human region from an image obtained from a camera mounted on the robot. To do this, we employ a method for extracting human regions from the camera image and an interaction method for performing mission based on tracking method [21].

5.1 Human-Robot Distance Measurement

In order to perform various missions in the outdoor environment, the robot is equipped with a multimodal sensor module. The mission for extracting and tracking human regions in various camera modules conducts by RGBD cameras. When a tracking command is received from the control tower, the robot measures the distance of the tracking area from the depth image. The area from the center (x_i, y_i) of the region to the width and height of the region is divided as shown in Fig. 9(a) (green rectangle), and the depth of the region is accumulated in units of 1 m, and then the final distance D is calculated, as shown in Fig. 9(b) and Eq. (7).

$$D = \frac{1}{N} \sum_{i=1}^{N} d_i \qquad (7)$$

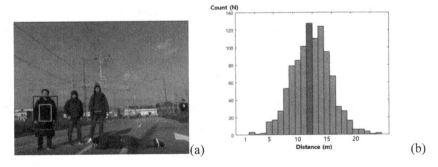

(a)   (b)

Fig. 9. An example of tracking: (a) distance calculation region, (b) histogram by distance. (Colour figure online)

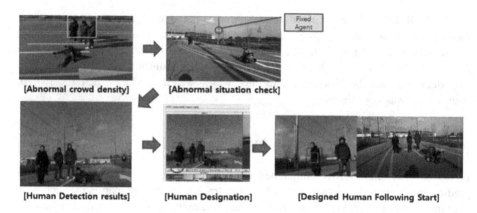

Fig. 10. Human following mission execution flow

5.2   Human-Following Interaction

The interaction of tracking and following the robot human was performed based on the following scenarios. First, when the abnormal situation (extraction of the crowd density based on the threshold) occurs in the fixed agent, the robot receives the abnormality confirmation command from the control tower. Second, the robot moves to the fixed agent where the abnormal situation occurs, identifies the abnormal situation, and transmits the image to the control tower by distinguishing the person who is falling from the person standing. Next, the robot receives the specific human tracking command, and then starts tracking the specified human, as shown in Fig. 10. Finally, the robot carries out the below sequence to perform the human following interactions.

Human Following Interaction Sequence

1. Calculate the straight line distance between the robot and the center coordinates of the human from (x_i, y_i) and D.
2. Calculate the relative angle between the robot and the human.
3. Tracking Flag is executed when straight line distance is over 1.5 m.
4. Left/Right Flag is executed when relative angle is more than 15°.
5. When the Tracking Flag is executed, a linear velocity tv* is generated in proportion to the straight line distance to the object.
   *tv = (tv_gain)*(z_distance) The tv_gain is experimentally determined to be 0.2.
6. When the Left/Right Flag is executed, the rotation speed rv** is generated in proportion to the relative angle with respect to the object.
   **rv = (rv_gain)*(d_angle) The rv_gain is experimentally determined to be 0.35.

Figure 11 shows a result image of human following interaction.

Fig. 11. Human following interaction results: (a) control tower command, (b) drone view, (c) side view, (d) robot view.

6 Conclusion and Future Work

Interactions between robots and humans are very important in outdoor unmanned security missions. Among the interactions, the task of following the human is one of the most active that the robot can perform on the control tower orders. In this paper, we propose a localization method robust to outdoor weather environment and a control method for safe driving in rough load for human following interaction. The results of the localization showed the robustness to the weather, and the control method proved to be safe path generation. Human robot interaction based on these methods showed usefulness to perform a given task, and it was found that robot could actively respond. Therefore, it is expected that the proposed methods can be applied to the security robot more practical.

In the future, we will add a snow removal filter to secure application to most robots by using autonomous navigation based on semantic information and driving techniques for various locomotion. Moreover, we are also developing a human following interaction method for collaborative tracking of multiple robots.

Acknowledgements. This work was supported by the ICT R&D program of IITP, 2017-0-00306. Development of multimodal sensor-based intelligent systems for outdoor surveillance robots.

References

1. Ullah, M.M., Pronobis, A., Caputo, B., Luo, J., Jensfelt, P., Christensen, H.I.: Towards robust place recognition for robot localization, In: International Conference on Robotics and Automation, pp. 530–537. IEEE, USA (2008)
2. Emidio, D., Francesco, M.: Mobile robot localization using the phase of passive UHF RFID signals. IEEE Trans. Ind. Electro. **61**(1), 365–376 (2014)
3. Jesse, L., Michael, M., Sebastian, T.: Robotics: Science and System, 3rd edn. MIT, Cambridge (2008)
4. Jose, G., Eduardo, N., Stephan, B.: Localization and map building using laser range sensors in outdoor applications. J. Robot. Syst. **17**(10), 565–583 (2000)
5. Martin, A., Sen, Z., Lhua, X.: Particle filter based outdoor robot localization using natural features extracted from laser scanners. In: Proceedings of the International Conference on Robotics & Automation, pp. 1493–1498. IEEE (2004)
6. Eric, R., Maxime, L., Michel, D., Jean-Marc, L.: Monocular vision for mobile robot localization and autonomous navigation. Int. J. Comput. Vision **74**(3), 237–260 (2007)
7. Motilal, A., Kurt, K.: Real-time localization in outdoor environments using stereo vision and inexpensive GPS. In: Proceedings of the 18th International Conference on Pattern Recognition (ICPR 2006). IEEE (2006)
8. Christian, W., Hashem, T., Andreas, M., Andreas, Z.: A hybrid approach for vision-based outdoor robot localization using global and local image features. In: Proceedings of the 2007 IEEE/RSJ International Conference on Intelligent Robots and Systems, San Diego, CA, USA, pp. 1047–1052 (2007)
9. Tayyab, N., Luciano, S., Wolfram, B., Cyrill, S.: Robust visual robot localization across seasons using network flows. In: Proceedings of the Twenty-Eighth AAAI Conference on Artificial Intelligence, Canada, pp. 2564–2570 (2014)
10. Christoffer, V., Achim, J.L.: SIFT, SURF & seasons: appearance-based Long-term localization in outdoor environments. Robot. Auton. Syst. **58**(2), 149–156 (2010)
11. Michael, M., Eleonora, V., Walter, S., David, C.: Vision-based simultaneous localization and mapping in changing outdoor environments. J. Field Robot. **31**(5), 780–802 (2014)
12. Naoki, A., Yasunari, K., Shogo, Y., Koichi, O.: Development of autonomous mobile robot that can navigate in rainy situations. J. Robot. Mechatron. **28**(4), 441–450 (2016)
13. Robert, B.: Safety, Comfort and Convenience Systems, 3rd edn. Wiley, Hoboken (2006)
14. Ackermann, J., Odenthal, D.: Advantages of active steering for vehicle dynamics control. In: International Conference on Advances in Vehicle Control and Safety, France (1998)
15. Brad, S., Tore, H., Anders, R.: Vehicle dynamics control and controller allocation for rollover prevention. In: Proceedings of International conference on control applications, Munich, Germany (2006)
16. Donato, D.P., Annalisa, M., Grazia, C., Arcangelo, D.: An autonomous mobile robotic system for surveillance of indoor environments. Int. J. Advan. Robot. Syst. **7**(1), 19–26 (2010)
17. Jiale, G., Hong, W., Zhiguo, L., Naishi, F., Fo, H.: Research on human-robot interaction security strategy of movement authorization for service robot based on people's attention monitoring. In: Proceedings of the International Conference on Intelligence and Safety for Robotics, pp. 521–526. IEEE (2018)
18. Sebastian, T., Dieter, F., Wolfram, B., Frank, D.: Robust Monte Carlo localization for mobile robots. J. Artif. Intell. **128**(1–2), 99–141 (2001)
19. Ling, C., Huosheng, H., Klaus, M.: EKF based mobile robot localization. In: Proceeding of International Conference on Emerging Security Technologies, Italy, pp. 149–154 (2012)

20. Ji-Hyun, P., Tae-Young, U., Gi-Deok, B., Young-Ho, C.: Stability evaluation of outdoor unmanned security robot in terrain information. In: Proceedings of 18th International Conference on Control, Automation and Systems, Korea, pp. 955–957 (2018)
21. Jongwon, C., et al.: Context-aware deep feature compression for high-speed visual tracking. In: Proceedings of Conference on Computer Vision and Pattern Recognition, pp. 478–488. IEEE (2018)

Designing Mobile and IoT Solutions for Sustainable Smart Cities

Studies with Electronic Waste Disposal

Alex Rodrigo Moises Costa Wanderley[1] and Rodrigo Bonacin[1,2(✉)]

[1] UNIFACCAMP, Campo Limpo Paulista, SP, Brazil
alexr.wanderley@gmail.com
[2] Center for Information Technology (CTI), Campinas, SP, Brazil
rodrigo.bonacin@cti.gov.br

Abstract. Sustainable smart cities use technology to improve the quality of life of their citizens and future generations. In this context, electronic waste disposal is still a challenge to be investigated, since electronic devices contain substances that may cause serious damage to the environment. Mobile and IoT technologies may contribute to the design of advanced solutions to this problem. However, it is still necessary to improve design methods so that they consider the citizens' needs, and to integrate mobile technology with Internet of Things technology to promote the development of sustainable smart cities. In this paper, we propose the Participatory Hackathon Method for Sustainable Smart Cities. This method uses Personas and Design Thinking to structure activities during Hackathon sessions with experts and citizens. The Hackathon's results are analyzed, and a final prototype is designed in a participatory way. We carried out a case study with students from technical level courses in Computing, Electronics, Logistics, and Work Safety, as well as developers, and citizens. The participants designed a prototype solution to collect electronic waste using smart recycling bins and mobile technology.

Keywords: Sustainable smart cities · Hackathon · Electronic waste disposal · Personas · Participatory Design

1 Introduction

The development of Smart Cities is based on the intensive use of technology and urban planning. This process allows for the design of new solutions, by promoting the conscious use of resources, and preserving them for future generations.

In this context, electronic waste disposal is a challenge to be investigated. Technological devices are frequently disposed of in common waste bins. These items contain several substances that may cause serious damage to the environment and human health and, at the same time, have economic value.

The Mobile and IoT (Internet of Things) technologies can, for instance, provide alternatives by informing citizens of the importance of electronic waste disposal, the location of collection points, and characteristics and status of recycling bins. In addition, they can support waste disposal management and planning. However, it is still

N. Streitz and S. Konomi (Eds.): HCII 2019, LNCS 11587, pp. 212–226, 2019.
https://doi.org/10.1007/978-3-030-21935-2_17

necessary to improve the design methods and solutions for systems that integrate mobile applications and IoT in the context of sustainable smart cities.

In this paper, we propose a design method focused on the effective participation of citizens and experts during the entire design process of mobile and IoT solutions to electronic waste disposal in sustainable smart cities. This method is based on principles and techniques of Participatory Design (PD) [1], hackathon events for smart cities [2], and Personas [3].

According to Vácha et al. [4], citizens will be more willing to accept a smart city solution if they participate in its design. Participation can also increase citizens' initiative, leading them to carry out activities to support sustainability and improve quality of life in the city. Alba et al. [2] emphasizes that thematic hackathons on the theme of smart cities have increased as governments, universities, and corporations have been engaging in the subject.

Personas are fictional characters, which represent users, and include their characteristics, goals, and behaviors. In our method, Personas are used to stimulate the participatory process, and to express citizens' characteristics and needs in the hackathons' descriptions.

We propose the Participatory Hackathon Method for Sustainable Smart Cities (PHMSSC). This method is composed of five main phases that are executed iteratively, as follows: (1) Problem Definition and Design of Personas, (2) Hackathon Design, (3) Hackathon Application, (4) Design of the Final Candidate Solution, and (5) Prototype Development.

The PHMSSC was evaluated through the design of a mobile application, integrated with IoT devices of smart recycling bins, in the context of Brazilian cities. First, an initial description of the problem was produced to delineate the system's scope.

Subsequently, an expert (first author) designed Personas. He created an initial version of the Personas, based on demographic information from big cities in Brazil. These Personas were complemented by other experts, and validated and improved by students and local citizens using feedback from forms on the Web. The Personas were then revised and included in the Hackathons' descriptions. We created four Personas, two males and two females. All of them have information about the importance of recycling electronic waste, but they have experienced difficulties with the electronic waste disposal of different devices.

Four Hackathon sessions were performed. The participants are technical level (high school) students in Computing, Electronics, Logistics, and Work Safety from Centro Paula Souza, in São Paulo State, in Brazil, as well as invited citizens from the city of São Paulo.

A system prototype was constructed from the results of the Hackathons, and focus group sessions with citizens and experts. Characteristics of this prototype are presented and discussed in this paper. The solution includes a mobile application with georeferenced information to support users in the process of finding the nearest disposal bin, as well as the use of IoT devices that provide information on the status of these bins, as well as management information for the city hall and citizens.

Therefore, the main expected contributions of this paper include: (1) a better understanding of the design process of Sustainable Smart Cities solutions, (2) the proposal of an innovative participatory method based on Hackathons and Personas, and

(3) a prototype and empirical results regarding the execution of this method in an application design scenario.

The remainder of this paper is organized as follows: Sect. 2 presents background information. Section 3 details the PHMSSC method. Section 4 presents the case study and reports on the obtained results. Section 5 concludes the paper and suggests future work.

2 Background

This section presents the definitions of key concepts and background information on related fields, including sustainable smart cities (Subsect. 2.1), IoT (Subsect. 2.2), PD (Subsect. 2.3), Personas (Subsect. 2.4), and Hackathon and Design Thinking (Subsect. 2.5).

2.1 Sustainable Smart Cities

Smart cities can be understood as the use of technology to enable the communication, mediation, and integration of information systems, infrastructure, among others [5]. This results in innovative environments, conducing to the balanced development of technological solutions for cities' problems. The components of a smart city include smarts [6]: transportation, health, security, education, energy, environment, among others smart policy domains.

A sustainable city can be defined as an urban space, which aims to meet the physical, cultural, social, environmental, economic, and political needs and aspirations of the population. Resources should be used in an efficient way in order to achieve this objective.

Sustainable smart cities use information and communication technologies, and other technological resources, to improve quality of life, the efficiency of urban services and operations, as well as increase competitiveness. They arise to meet present and future generation's needs, including social, economic, cultural, and environmental aspects. In a sustainable smart city, citizens' needs are met without compromising the needs of other people and future generations [7]. These objectives must be considered in the design of information technology based solutions for sustainable smart cities.

In the Brazilian context, a law [8] provides for the shared responsibility of waste generators. Manufacturers, distributors, importers, merchants, public services providers, and citizens share the responsibility of addressing the issue of waste from electronic devices.

2.2 IoT and Sustainable Smart Cities

A large increase in the number of IoT connected devices is expected over the next few years [9]. Nowadays, the IoT is developing in various domains, for instance, smart grid and transportation. Novel IoT solutions are also present in the context of sustainable smart cities, particularly in waste management, including solutions such as smart trash bins [10]. For instance, Dublin has smart trash bins using solar energy and wifi connections. A smart trash bin can, for example, inform public services that it needs to be emptied or needs maintenance, as well as automatically compacts waste (improving their capacity).

There are various possibilities for using IoT by integrating it with mobile applications. Smart trash bins can support citizens by informing their characteristics and current status to users nearby, guiding users to go to the correct place and dispose of waste properly.

At the same time that there are innovative IoT solutions, new challenges must be faced. Such challenges are related to the various aspects that must be considered during the design process. These aspects range from technical ones (e.g., calibration of sensors) to the social ones (e.g., usage habits and privacy).

2.3 Participatory Design and Smart Cities

PD [1] has its roots in the democratization of design practices in industry during 60's in Scandinavia. PD can be used to provide a broader and more accurate view of requirements, as well as elicitation of design alternatives, through effective user participation during all phases of the design process.

PD can also boost the innovation process [4] of solutions for smart cities. Such solutions are developed with the participation of the stakeholders, who can, for instance, express and clarify their needs, and propose, improve, and evaluate solutions. Citizen participation during the design process allows for the incorporation of different perspectives in Smart City projects.

One expected benefit of the use of PD in Smart City projects is the improvement of the user acceptance rates. Users tend to be more flexible and open to changes when they participate of the design process [4]. Participation in these projects can increase the citizens' initiative towards sustainability, and quality of life in the city. Users can develop a more systemic view of the projects by sharing their needs and preferences with each other, by creating solutions based on real evidences, and by increasing their sense of responsibility.

In this paper, PD principles and techniques are used in conjunction with Personas to stimulate and facilitate the design-participants' communication. Hackathon and DT activities presuppose the stakeholders' participation, and are complemented by participatory sessions. The next sections present Personas, Hackathon, and DT respectively.

2.4 Personas and Smart Cities

The Personas technique makes use of fictional characters during the design process [3]. These fictional characters are designed by means of analysis and a combination of users' profiles [11]. They reproduce their desires, needs, motivations, and expectations; thus, represent key characteristics of a group.

The design of Personas [3] is based on the analysis of demographics and bibliographic data, as well as creativity, aiming to create a character nearest to the reality of the users at the time that the application is designed.

Empathy maps [12] can support the design of the Personas, since we can consider how the users' think, feel, see, hear, say, and do things. Considering the context of the design of sustainable smart cities, it is necessary to describe how the Personas are committed to environmental aspects and sustainability of the city.

2.5 Hackathon, Design Thinking and Smart Cities

Hackathons are events with participants who have various profiles (e.g., designers, programmers, engineers) working collaboratively on a specific theme/problem over a period of time [2, 13]. Frequently, hackathons have small groups (although there are cases with large groups) working intensively during a short period of time.

Hackathons, in the context of smart cities, are relatively new. In 2008, a pioneer smart city hackathon in Washington DC occurred, named "Apps for Democracy". This event was followed by a series of events to promote innovative solutions for the city, engagement of its citizens, and mapping of the citizen's real needs. In the last decade, organizations, such as the "Code for America" [14], have been promoting smart city hackathons.

According to [2], the number of hackathons linked to smart city themes increased as governments, universities, and corporations became engaged in the issue. Global Urban Datafest [15], CityOS Hackathon [16] and Barcelona Smart City App Hack [17] are examples of events with hackathons focused on themes related to smart cities and innovation.

DT is used to structure the activities and promote good design practices during hackathons. DT aims to solve design problems in a collaborative way, with the stakeholders at the center of the design process. DT can support innovation in information technology, increasing the perceived value of the solution by affecting peoples' lives [18]. DT can benefit the hackathon by structuring insight generation and improving proposals [19] in an interactive way. DT can be used with hackathons [20] to improve public services in an iterative innovation process as well.

3 The Participatory Hackathon Method for Sustainable Smart Cities (PHMSSC)

As shown in Fig. 1, the PHMSSC has 5 phases, detailed in the following paragraphs.

Phase 1: Problem Definition and Design of Personas. This phase contains three steps that aim to describe the problem and to design Personas that represent the citizens' characteristics and needs.

- Step 1.1 – *Problem definition*: Designers and stakeholders work together, aiming to clarify the problem in focus. Well-structured methods or even unstructured meetings can be used according to the complexity of the problem. A well-defined problem description is imperative for the next steps of the design.
- Step 1.2 – *Design of personas*: Starting from the definition of the problem, designers should consider demographic aspects to base their design of an initial version of the *Personas*. Qualitative aspects related to the users' behavior should also be considered.

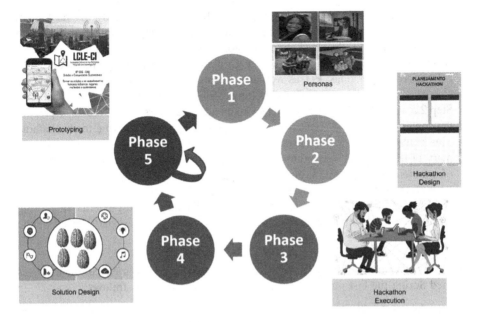

Fig. 1. Overview of the PHMSSC

- Step 1.3 – *Validation of personas*: Quantitative and qualitative analysis is performed using face-to-face workshops and online resources (to achieve a wider audience). Web forms should be carefully designed, and the audience well defined. The audience should include citizens and experts. Meetings with experts and users are necessary to evaluate the collected data and discuss their impacts on the design of the Personas. If necessary, the three steps in this phase can be repeated until a satisfactory evaluation of the Personas is achieved.

Phase 2: Hackathon Design. Experts and citizens work together to design the hackathon events according to the following steps:

- Step 2.1 – *Choose a hackathon platform.* The designers, in the role of hackathon administrators, should select and setup a hackathon platform according to the problem and objectives.
- Step 2.2 – *Create a new hackathon.* The hackathon administrators should create a new hackathon in the platform, give it a name, and define a time period for its completion according to the problem and project' objectives.
- Step 2.3 – *Select the participants.* The hackathon's administrators should select the team members, mentors, and judges. They should invite members with various profiles (e.g., designers, developers, managers), and citizens according to the scope and objectives of the project. It is important that citizens participate in the role of judges as well.

- Step 2.4 – *Create/prepare training resources.* By using online platforms, hackathon administrators should create or prepare necessary training resources to be made available prior to the hackathon sessions. These resources include concepts specifically related to the hackathon (e.g., platform tutorial, tools, methodologies, DT concepts), personas, PD, as well as concepts related to the project domain (e.g., electronic waste disposal, IoT technology, Mobile technology).
- Step 2.5 – *Prepare for execution.* Hackathon administrators should create or prepare the content (text, image, presentations, video) to be presented during the hackathon. This content includes, for instance, a review of the hackathon's concepts, a summary of the problem's definition, a definition of related concepts, and descriptions of previous projects (if any). In this step, the administrators create the teams, attributing responsibilities and roles according to the step 2.3.
- Step 2.6 – *Mentorship requests.* The team members may request external mentoring through the hackathon tool, which can be provided by other participants of the project.

Phase 3 - Hackathon Execution. This phase is the hackathon's execution itself, as planned during the last phase. This phase includes four steps as follows:

- Step 3.1 – *Opening presentations.* Hackathon administrators (and mentors) present the initial content, as produced during the step 2.5.
- Step 3.2 – *Present the Personas to the hackathon teams.* The administrators present the Personas to the teams. The teams will collaboratively propose solutions with the support of these personas.
- Step 3.3 – *Execute the hackathons.* The hackathon team proposes design solutions according to the Personas and problem descriptions.
- Step 3.4 – *Hackathon's evaluation.* Judges evaluate the teams' design proposals. Aspects related to citizens' needs, innovation, environmental requirements, viability of the project, business, and technical aspects should be balanced in the project evaluation. Democratic principles (from PD) should also be observed.

Phase 4 - Design of the Final Candidate Solution. This phase has the objective of answering the following question: "How to consider the results of the hackathon in the design of a final candidate solution?". This phase has two steps:

- Step 4.1 – *Analysis of the projects.* Designers and guest citizens verify the evaluation scores and the judges' comments (step 3.4). A designer makes an initial report based on the judges' comments and score, emphasizing the strengths and drawbacks of each project. This repost is evaluated in a meeting with other designers and citizens. The best design alternatives are selected to be used as input for the next step.
- Step 4.2 – *Adapt solutions.* The designers (with citizen participation) adapt, complement, and merge the best alternatives presented during the hackathon. For instance, a team could propose a good design for a smart recycling bin, but with bad sensors and energy solutions, while another team (with a lower overall score) could propose a good solution for sensors and energy use. Those solutions can be integrated in this step.

Phase 5 – Prototype Development. In this phase, there is the iterative development of functional prototypes.

- Step 5.1 – *Iterative development.* This step is the iterative development of functional prototypes, including redesign, implementation, and testing of solutions. This step must be adapted according to the development process and technologies required by the design solution. For instance, the complexity of the adopted IoT technology must be considered. Citizens should also participate of this step. Usability evaluations can be carried out.
- Step 5.2 – *Field evaluation.* After prototyping cycles, the final version of the solutions should be analyzed in field studies. The empirical feedback can be used in the development of the next versions of the solution.

4   Case Study

This section presents a case study conducted with the objective of evaluating and improving the PHMSSC, and analyzing solutions for collecting electronic waste using smart recycling bins and mobile technology. Subsection 4.1 presents the context, participants, and tools. Subsection 4.2 describes the preliminary results including the design alternatives (from the *hackathon*), and the evaluation of these alternatives to base the construction of a functional prototype.

4.1   Context, Participants and Tools

The case study took place in São Paulo City, Brazil, during October 2018. The hackathon activities occurred during the *"034 Jornada Hacker - Etec Prof. Aprígio Gonzaga"*, Centro Paula Souza, in São Paulo State – Brazil. The other activities in the case study also used Centro Paula Souza's infrastructure.

The participants were invited in person, including professionals, students (classroom invitations), and citizens. Considering the phases, the participants of this case study include:

- *Twenty (20) Students* from Centro Paula Souza, in São Paulo State – Brazil. The students were divided in four groups. Each group is composed of one Informatics/Software Development student, two Electronics students, one Logistics student, and one Work Safety student. The students participated in phases 1 to 3.
- *Three (3) Professional Developers*: two hardware and one software expert. The developers participated in phases 2 to 5.
- *Eight (8) hackathon judges, co-designers, and evaluators*: These participants represent citizens with an interest in the solution. They are teachers and public servants in the role of citizens interested in sustainable smart cities. They participated in phases 3 to 5.
- *A hackathon mentor*, with experience in mentoring innovation oriented hackathons.

The Google Forms[1] platform was used in phase 1 to register both online and face-to-face activities. We used the Shawee[2] platform to manage our hackathon activities. The students participated in an online training (as proposed by PHMSSC) before the hackathon, which included the following topics: active methodologies, DT, empathy maps, and canvas. Four teams were created in the Shawee platform, and internal roles (UX designer, developer, businessman) were attributed according to their profiles and interests.

The description of the hackathon included the Personas, as well as a prototype of the mobile application named LCLE (*Localizador Coletor de Lixo Eletrônico*) [21]. This application was used as a starting point for the activities. The LCLE informs users of the current location of nearby recycling bins.

4.2   Preliminary Results

This subsection presents results of the case study, considering the application of the PHMSSC method in the context presented in the last subsection.

Modeled Personas

As a key result of the first PHMSSC phase, there are four modeled Personas (two male and two female). We considered demographic information, the problem's definition, as well as qualitative aspects discussed in meetings with the participants in the design of the Personas. The focus was to design personas that experienced situations and have concerns regarding electronic waste disposal. Subsequently, the Personas were validated with students and citizens using online forms. Key Personas' characteristics can be briefly summarized as follows:

- *Persona 1 – Vitória*. She is 28 years old; she is single, and is an undergraduate student of Architecture and Urbanism courses. She is doing an internship in an architecture office. As most Brazilians, she has a smartphone with internet access and uses it to access social networks. Recently, the office where she is interning exchanged its computers. She had serious concerns regarding this change, since they had not found an appropriate alternative for disposing of the electronic products. She tried to share her concerns in the office. Vitória believes that it is possible to improve the efficiency of urban operations and services, as well as to improve sustainability by considering architecture and technology together.
- *Persona 2 – Melissa*. She is 34 years old; she is married, and is a project manager at a telecommunication company. As most Brazilians, she has a smartphone with internet access and uses it to access social networks. Melissa has serious concerns about the future of her children. The organization she works in generates huge amounts of electronic waste, such as computer components, telecom devices, smartphones, and batteries. She would like to develop a culture of recycling electronic waste in her department. She believes it is possible to make cities more sustainable by using technology, since this allows for the use of resources in an efficient and balanced way.

---

[1] https://www.google.com/forms/about/.

[2] https://shawee.io/.

- *Persona 3 – Marcos.* He is 29 years old; he is single, and is a trainee in a law office. He has a smartphone with internet access and use it to watch videos, to listen to music, to make banking transactions and, less frequently, to access social networks. Recently, the law office where he is working discarded two computers in a common trash bin. Marcos believes that a better destination could be given to this electronic waste, but advances in the city's administration are needed. He emphasizes that information technology is a key aspect to improve the efficiency of urban operations and services, as well as competitiveness.
- *Persona 4 – Lucas.* He is 30 years old; he is married, and is a military officer. He is patriotic and understands the importance of sustainability for future generations. He is responsible for the informatics office of a military base. There is a storehouse on the base, where electronic waste was stored for years. However, it is almost full, and he understands that this electronic waste can cause damage to nature. He is looking for a sustainable alternative to dispose of part of the electronic waste.

The Personas were analyzed by students from Centro Paula Souza, in São Paulo State – Brazil during October 2018. Twenty-three (23) students answered the evaluation form of the Persona *Vitória*, 32 *Melissa*, 27 *Marcos,* and 13 *Lucas.* Table 1 presents results of this analysis of the problem posed by each Persona described above. The researchers analyzed the qualitative responses, and ranked three questions to represent typical responses. These responses were included in this paper. Table 1 presents results of three of the representative responses for two qualitative questions and two quantitative questions:

- *Question 1*: What are the actions that Persona XX can take to solve his/her problem?
- *Question 2*: Have you faced a situation similar to the described by Persona XX? () Yes or () No.
- *Question 3*: If yes, describe this situation.
- *Question 4*: Do you think Information Technology can be used to solve this problem/situation? () Yes or () No (Table 1).

Hackathon Results

The four groups used different approaches, focusing in one Persona each. They described their prototype and ideas as follows:

- Group 1 – Persona *Vitória.* We prototyped a standard recycling bin with an integrated display. This display shows the items that should be discarded in the respective bin. This recycling bin also helps the users evaluate if the waste should be discarded. The group also proposed that the recycling bin could include sensors to identify electronic object (before opening it). The recycling bins are integrated with a mobile App to inform their locations, characteristics, and status.
- Group 2 – Persona *Melissa* – We will use App Inventor to include the IoT Technology into the LCLE. We projected a prototype using NodeMCU, which integrates weight sensors, gas sensors, ultrasonic sensors, and some motors that will give better function and safety to the project. The ultrasonic sensors are used to automatically open the recycle bins. These sensors will inform a transportation system,

Table 1. Examples of responses and quantitative results of the Personas' evaluation questions

Persona	Question 1	Question 2	Question 3	Question 4
Vitória	Present a project to the company, where the old PCs would be sold or donated	*26.1%* Yes *73.9%* No	Frequently, I see people disposing of things in inappropriate places	*100%* Yes
	Select the valuable pieces from the computer and use them for some kind of handicraft		Recycling of iron, copper, metal cans, and paper	*0%* No
	Invest in an electronic waste company		I have concerns about the electronic devices embedded in cars	
Melissa	Spread information regarding the importance of disposing of these materials in appropriate places	*58%* Yes *42%* No	I also have a propensity to consider ideas and actions to make the world better	*96.9%* Yes *3.1%* No
	Create activities and content with information about electronic waste. . . this is still not very well known by the population		We are organized and we are considerate of others	
	Present a project and try to convince the directors. . .		I also think about reusing computer parts . . .	
Marcos	The devices could be donated to NGOs . . .	*51.9%* Yes *48.1%* No	I, as the majority of the population, do not have access to recycling (electronic waste) bins . . .	*100%* Yes *0%* No
	Create an application to donate the devices to people in need . . .		. . . lack of a proper disposal alternative . . .	
	Sell the devices		When I have to discard batteries	
Lucas	Reuse of various components that may still be working. . .	*61.5%* Yes *38.5%* No	. . . it is difficult to know where we can discard of electronic devices	*100%* Yes *0%* No
	. . . map the stored products, disassemble the equipment, and send it to recycling centers. . .		I have too many computer components . . .	
	Donate the electronic devices to NGOs and schools. . .		I have a notebook (that no longer works) stored for a long period of time. I am looking for sustainable alternatives to discard it	

which will pick up the material to be discarded when it is full, reorganizing the process, and avoiding waste of time. We also propose a safety protocol, where experts evaluate the risks in the transportation and recycling process, according to the sensors' data.

- Group 3 – Persona *Marcos* – To solve this problem, we created an app that informs citizens of where to dispose of electronic waste. This app is integrated with the system in a company that collects, processes, and forwards waste to other companies specialized in electronic waste recycling. This waste should be disposed in waste bins with sensors that will identify when it is full, and automatically inform the company.
- Group 4 – Persona *Lucas* – The organization that produces the electronic waste can use the LCLE application to inform the type/content of the waste. This organization could search a container nearby (using geolocation) and contract another company, which is responsible for recycling electronic waste. There are volume and weight sensors to notify the status of the container for both the organization that produces the electronic waste, and the company responsible for recycling electronic waste.

Table 2. Judge's score and comments for the Hackathon prototypes

Group	Score	Examples of comments
1 Vitória	1.56	The team needs to continue validating the project, aiming to explore other alternatives
		The proposal is innovative. However, the cost of production can be a problem in the future. . .
		Congratulations. In my opinion, the idea is very good; it will effectively assist users in the disposal of electronic waste
2 Melissa	1.44	The group identified a real problem and developed a solution using current technology. They have been able to propose something innovative using single circuit boards, sensors, . . .
		Great idea, but now it needs to be validated, aiming to identify possible improvements
		The idea is interesting, but a lot of work is needed to make it viable. In fact, what the group presented was just a possible solution for the problem
4 Lucas	1.38	The use of microcontrollers and geolocation tools are well projected and documented
		The idea is interesting and has potential; however, it is not clear how it will be feasible from a business viewpoint
		There is no canvas for the project, and it is not possible to verify its technical and economic viability. . .
3 Marcos	1.34	The project was well designed and presented
		It is necessary to model the canvas to verify possibilities from a business viewpoint, as well as to analyze the social value of the project. . .
		The idea is interesting, but the prototype is in a preliminary stage

Judges Scores and Comments

The judges (cf., Subsect. 4.1) attributed scores to each hackathon group according to their proposals and prototypes. In addition, they provided text comments. Table 2 presents the final score for each group as well as three comments selected by the researchers to represent typical responses.

Design and First Prototype

The researchers and judges listed the design alternatives presented by the groups and selected those that were considered the most interesting. For instance, Group 1 uniquely presented a display in front of the recycling bin, Group 2 proposed the use of ultrasonic sensors, Group 3 used sensors to identify when the recycling bin is full, and Group 4 proposed the use of volume and weight sensors. Using this analysis, a design proposal was elaborated with the following characteristics:

- The prototype makes use ultrasonic sensors for the automatic opening of the bin. The user can move their hand near the recycling bin to automatically open it.
- The researchers considered that alternative proposed by group 3 was the best one to identify when the trash is full. This is due to the resources available to implement the prototype. Thus, lasers were inserted internally to identify when the recycling bin is full.
- The prototype also used a display to inform the type of electronic waste disposable in a specific recycling bin.

Fig. 2. Recycling bin prototype

Figure 2 presents a prototype, considered the first prototyping cycle of Step 5.1 of the PHMSSC method. Thus, this case study is comprised of the five phases of the PHMSSC. It is important to note that the execution of the method resulted in a set of valuable design alternatives, which is a result of the interaction between participants of the hackathons, judges (citizens), and designers.

5 Conclusion and Future Work

Electronic waste disposal is one of the key challenges in the development of sustainable smart cities. In this paper, we presented the PHMSSC method, and a case study involving several students, citizens (in the role of hackathon judges and co-designers), and experts. Four groups proposed a set of design alternatives, which make use of mobile applications and IoT technologies to provide solutions for smart recycling bins. The Personas technique acted as an important resource to support a better understanding of the problems and communication with the students (*88.8%* of the students considered that Personas improved their understanding of the problem). In addition, citizens (as judges) had a broader view of all the projects, which made is possible for them to select the best alternatives (from the groups) to implement in a prototype.

As the next steps of this research, we propose the evaluation of a prototype, including field studies in Centro Paula Souza's campus.

References

1. Ehn, P.: Scandinavian design: on participation and skill. In: Schuler, D., Aki, N. (eds.) Participatory Design: Principles and Practices, pp. 41–77. Erlbaum, Hillsdale, NJ (1993)
2. Alba, M., Avalos, M., Guzmán, C., Larios, V.M.: Synergy between smart cities' Hackathons and living labs as a vehicle for accelerating tangible innovations on cities. In: 2016 IEEE International Smart Cities Conference (ISC2), Trento, pp. 1–6 (2016)
3. Cooper, A.: The Inmates are Running the Asylum: Why High-Tech Products Drive Us Crazy and How to Restore the Sanity, 2nd edn. Sams, Indianapolis (2004)
4. Vácha, O., Přibyl, T., Lom, M., Bacúrová, M.: Involving citizens in smart city projects: systems engineering meets participation. In: 2016 Smart Cities Symposium Prague (SCSP), Prague, pp. 1–6 (2016)
5. Komninos, N., Tsarchopoulos, P., Kakderi, C.: New services design for smart cities: a planning roadmap for user-driven innovation. In: Proceedings of the 2014 ACM International Workshop on Wireless and Mobile Technologies for Smart Cities (WiMobCity 2014), pp. 29–38. ACM, New York (2014)
6. Nam, T., Pardo, T.A.: Conceptualizing smart city with dimensions of technology, people, and institutions. In: Proceedings of the 12th Annual International Digital Government Research Conference: Digital Government Innovation in Challenging Times (dg.o 2011), pp. 282–291. ACM, New York (2011)
7. Höjer, M., Wangel, J.: Smart sustainable cities: definition and challenges. In: Hilty, L.M., Aebischer, B. (eds.) ICT Innovations for Sustainability. AISC, vol. 310, pp. 333–349. Springer, Cham (2015). https://doi.org/10.1007/978-3-319-09228-7_20
8. Brazil, National Policy on Solid Waste, law N° 12.305, 2 August 2010. http://www.planalto.gov.br/ccivil_03/_ato2007-2010/2010/lei/l12305.htm. Accessed 14 Jan 2019

9. Press GBW: Internet of things by the numbers: market estimates and forecasts, 22 August 2014. https://www.forbes.com/sites/gilpress/2014/08/22/internet-of-things-by-the-numbers-market-estimates-and-forecasts/#4adcad3fb919. Accessed 14 Jan 2019
10. Lemos, A., Bitencourt, E.: Performative sensibility and the communication of things. MATRIZes 12(3), 165–188 (2018)
11. Vianna, M., Vianna, Y., Adler, I.K., Lucena, B., Russo, B.: Design Thinking: Inovação em negócios. MJV, Rio de Janeiro (2012)
12. Osterwalder, A., Pigneur, Y.: Business Model Generation: A Handbook for Visionaries, Game Changers, and Challengers. Wiley, Hoboken (2010)
13. Tandon, J., Akhavian, R., Gumina, M., Pakpour, N.: CSU east bay hack day: a university hackathon to combat malaria and zika with drones. In: 2017 IEEE Global Engineering Education Conference (EDUCON), Athens, pp. 985–989 (2017)
14. Code for America homepage. https://www.codeforamerica.org/. Accessed 14 Jan 2019
15. Global urban datafest homepage. http://www.global.datafest.net/ Accessed 14 Jan 2019
16. CityOS hackathon homepage. https://cityos.io/ Accessed 14 Jan 2019
17. Barcelona smart city app hack homepage. http://barcelona.smartcityapphack.com/ Accessed 14 Jan 2019
18. Brown, T.: Change by Design: How Design Thinking Transforms Organizations and Inspires Innovation. HarperBusiness, New York (2009)
19. Hecht, B.A., et al.: The KumbhThon technical hackathon for Nashik: a model for STEM education and social entrepreneurship. In: 2014 IEEE Integrated STEM Education Conference, Princeton, NJ, pp. 1–5 (2014)
20. McGowan, B.S.: Hackathon planning and participation strategies for non-techie librarians. Public Serv. Q. 12(3), 271–276 (2016)
21. Wanderley, A., Ratusznei, J., Silva, W.: LCLE-Localizador Coletor de Lixo Eletrônico. In: anais do XXIII Workshop de Informática na Escola (WIE 2017), Recife, pp. 89–97 (2017)

Spatial Perception and Humanistic Innovation in Smart Cities: A Systematic Review

Tongwen Wang[✉] and Wuzhong Zhou[✉]

Design Institute, Shanghai Jiao Tong University, Shanghai, China
{wangtongwen,wzzhou}@sjtu.edu.cn

Abstract. The literature on spatial perception from the context of China and abroad generally presents situation in which the research perspective is rich, and the research methods are diverse. From the research content of the literature, almost all of them cover the objective existence of space and the subjective perception of people. This paper uses the literature review method to analyze and summarize 50 documents in the world which it draws conclusions related to spatial perception. This paper explores the relevant elements of spatial perception in the traditional sense from the microscopic and macroscopic perspectives. At the level of reflection, under the scope of smart city construction, we will explore more on the interactive spatial perception for the future because of the additional technology. This paper is based on the existing literature on how to integrate spatial perception with humanistic innovation in smart cities.

Keywords: Spatial perception · Systematic review · Chinese and foreign · Smart city · Culture

1 Introduction

"Space" are being understood differently in different academic areas: early scientists represented by Newton in physics considered space to be substantial, while in Einstein's theory of relativity, the connection between space and phenomena was emphasized. Roger Jones believes that the concept of modern space is a compound metaphor. Heidegger believes that space needs to be considered relative to people is neither a simple external object nor a pure internal experience. And all the concepts cover the relative relationship between "space" and "people": people walk through space and experience it, which is often associated with time elements. And this relationship stimulates people's multi-level perception of space, including visual, phenomenological and spiritual aspects. Christian Norberg-Schulz calls it "space perception." The concept of "space perception" in this article is also based on this.

The literature on spatial perception in China and abroad generally covers both the objective existence of space and the subjective perception of people. This paper uses the literature review method to analyze, compare and summarize Chinese and foreign literatures. It attempts to draw microscopic and macroscopic conclusions and provide insight for future research on spatial perception as an introspective and reflective work, especially in the context of the rise of smart city planning, where understanding the characteristics of human spatial perception is crucial. At present, the wisdom of urban

© Springer Nature Switzerland AG 2019
N. Streitz and S. Konomi (Eds.): HCII 2019, LNCS 11587, pp. 227–237, 2019.
https://doi.org/10.1007/978-3-030-21935-2_18

discourse is fixated with technical ability and development. From the relevant research results, part of the problem that exists in the construction of smart cities can be summarized to be: the lack of humanistic care in smart city planning; the lack of humanistic considerations in smart applications and the lack of culture in urban public spaces. Taking the current situation in China as an example, technology-based and management-oriented smart cities have been highly valued. A digital government, digital transportation and government platforms have been launched based on digital technology, but due to the construction of smart and managed smart cities, the indispensable coordination and symbiosis between "technology", "society" and "culture" has been neglected to some extent. Technology has not been actively used to establish the unique cultural identity of cities, such as "smart cities" just focusing on the objective existence of development. But subjective perception of the city to the citizens is the key to urban sustainability.

The traditional urban space is dominated by static objective existence, while the smart urban space is an environment with more dynamic changes due to technology and may actively respond to human behavior. Therefore, smart urban spatial planning needs to consider the subjective perception of spatial users. This article reviews previous research on spatial perception based on such a starting point. The literature on spatial perception in China and abroad generally presents a situation in which the research perspective is rich and the research methods are diversified. From the research content of the literature, almost all of them cover the objective existence of space itself and the subjective perception of the people in it. Based on objective existence, the subjective perception of spatial users will be influenced by aesthetics, values, knowledge base, personal interests and living conditions, allowing space to produce another dimension related to time outside the physical existence dimension. In this sense, in addition to objectively defined physical facts, there are also the historical events and memories. The subjective perception of literature research in China and abroad can be roughly divided into the architectural narrative perception, perception of cultural symbols, local memory or collective memory. This article uses systematic literature research methods such as text analysis and comparative analysis to study the domestic and foreign literatures and summarizes the current conclusions from micro to macro in the direction of spatial perception. This work also summarizes the characteristics of human spatial perception at the level of reflection, thus provides insights for future research on spatial perception.

2   Rich Research Perspective

With the development of humanities and social sciences, spatial design has become an interdisciplinary multi-dimensional comprehensive discipline. As emphasized at the National Environmental Protection Act (NEPA) conference, culture and natural resources will generate new land uses and landscapes, and knowledge needs of different disciplines will be incorporated into larger planning areas [1].

From the results of foreign search engines, many foreign related articles related to the "landscape" and "space" topics cover psychology, human geography, sociology, communication, landscape semiotics, etc. Rouhvand started with immigration stories and found geography landscape symbols in the text [2]. Simpson et al. used historical evidence behind the human landscape to infer the social norms of early local fuel use from the perspective of historical archaeology [3]. Peter's article emphasizes the operational concepts and inferences of anthropology and archaeology in space. He believes that space is a social bond that is generated through dynamics in the historical process [4]. From the perspective of sociology and communication, Javier investigates the narratives of local feelings, studies the emotional impact of local spatial changes on tourists, and provides relevant insights into the driving forces of spatial change in tourism [5]. Thomas studies the influence of landscape space on people in space from the perspective of psychology. He feels that the environment has a potential effect on the restoration of human internal state, and it can bring more psychological benefits to humans through landscape space [6].

3 Diverse Research Methods

The research methods used by Chinese scholars are often combined with field surveys, questionnaires, etc. based on qualitative descriptions. Most of the foreign literatures on the space use empirical methods, combined with field trips in geography, while also integrate other humanities and social science research methods: such as historical documentary methods in history, image and photographic methods in art history and quantitative analysis in archaeology, etc. In terms of research methods, more advanced science and technology have been gradually used globally [7]. For example, using GIS techniques is to explore the cultural significance attached to the space from the perspective of cultural geography [8]. These research methods are improving the study of paradigms, theoretical methods, etc. to promote future theory and practice [9].

4 Objective Existence in Research Content

"Spatial perception" can be divided into "space" and "perception". Predecessors' research is based on the existence of objective space, and then to study the subjective perception that objective existence inspires [10].

Gabriel Zuolun believes that the discussion of space issues should be based on the fictional world of texts. He creatively proposes three levels of narrative space reproduction: geography space, time space and text space. These three levels interact and complement each other on the basis of objective existence [11]. Peter Eisenman emphasized that "the objective existence should be seen through the form" [12].

Alison Blunt has proposed two basic characteristics of a historical city: one is the environmental capital it represents (including architecture and urban infrastructure), and the other is the social and cultural values it expresses. In his theory, physical attributes and social attributes are inseparable, that is, the existence of objective space is inseparable from subjective perception [13].

Li-Shin Chang uses the example of the Wiltshire Landscape Park in the United Kingdom: the objective design of the Temple of Florence, the Grotto, the Pantheon, the Rock Arch, the Temple of Apollo, etc., is to reveal the journey of Aeneas and the story of Rome [14]. Tanga begins with the public art of modern urban spaces, taking Boston's bronze food memorial sculpture as an example. The designer redefines the "monument" in the urban environment using an objective existence like "monument" but not "monument". It evokes the public's subjective memory of people and events [15]. Ebru studied the objective existence of a specific type of urban space such as a commemorative public space. It is believed that a single or closed memorial site is not as good as a commemorative venue integrated into the urban public space, which can arouse the public's subjective memory and recognition of urban history [16].

In Hamzah Muzaini's article, attention is paid to the general problem in the existence of commemorative spaces, the neglect of gender issues. In the subject of the study, the Singapore's Changi Church Museum, the objective space for women's commemoration has somehow re-emphasized the gender issues in the commemorative landscape. Such design not only affects the individual subjectivity of the viewer but also affects the collective-subjective view at the national level [17]. Maria surveyed the cities of Lviv and Wroclaw, and the "place attachments" (i.e. apartments, streets, houses, urban areas, cities) in this article are an objective existence, and the "place memory" (including local identity, local attachment, and even racial prejudice in collective memory) is part of subjective perception [18]. Mahbub Rashid believes that "space" is an objective entity defined by coordinates and scales, while "place" is more like an emotional entity and has undergone subjective definitions emotionally [19].

5 Subjective Perception in Research Content

Centered on the objective existence, as an actor in space, every move affects the change of "subjective space", that is, another dimension related to time outside the physical existence dimension. In this dimension, in addition to objectively defined physical facts, more are historically related events and memories.

When people evaluate landscapes, their subjective perceptions are influenced by aesthetics, values, knowledge base, personal interests, and living conditions [20].

In Desiree Geib's book, "place" is defined by emotional experiences and subjective feelings. The "space" media is very different in terms of narrative potential and nature [21, 22]. With the change of human material concept, when the basic material needs to be satisfied, it is more important to have more stories than to have more items [23], that is, having better subjective perception is more important than objective existence itself.

In the predecessors' literature, subjective perception can be roughly divided into architectural narrative perception, cultural symbol perception, local or collective memory, and other memory perceptions.

5.1 Architectural Narrative Perception

Most of China's papers on spatial perception focus on architectural narrative. Ma Jie's article is based on architectural narrative to study commercial space design. The article is based on the subjective perspective of the "recipient" (space user). It analyzes the subjective intention that the "sender" (space designer) wants to express using information conveyed by "media" such as architectural forms [24]. Chen Tianyu studied urban furniture in urban space. He believes that urban furniture is involved in urban "story" for people in the city [11].

Foreign scholars mostly use empirical research methods for architectural narrative research to explore the relationship between form and perception of famous architectural spaces.

After studying the interaction between the intrinsic and external meanings of buildings, Mahbub's article found that the geometry and configuration of buildings impose varying degrees of visual constraints on visitors in space. The article argues that subjective perceptions brought about by objective existence make buildings understood as different visual and spatial complexes. For example, when the Chiswick villa moves along the main pedestrian flow line, there is a lack of change in vision, so subjectively feel a strong sense of symmetry [19].

As Penz believes, from the architectural narrative, all movements of people in the building play a key role in constituting a storyline [25].

5.2   Cultural Symbol Perception

In the field of architectural design, in addition to architectural narrative perception, there is also cultural symbol perception.

In Spain, modern architecture such as the Bank of Bilbao has become a cultural symbol to some extent, representing the political change and modernization movement in Spain at the time. As Catherine Schonfeld said, when people see the role of architecture and its role in urbanization, it begins to consider the city's technology [26].

Architecture as a public object in the process of urban culture, like urban cultural symbols can arouse people's perception of the city's capital flow and modern identity.

In addition to modern cultural symbols such as architectural space, natural landscapes can also serve as cultural symbols. The Mongolian prairie and its nomadic people, horses, herds and small figures form a cultural landscape, which is the landmark of the region and the core image of Mongolian marketing. In other Mongolian and adjacent grasslands, natural and cultural heritage is considered an independent attraction. The concept of cultural landscape is widely used in the context of world heritage. The elements of the cultural landscape have become cultural symbols that can attract tourists. Visitors choose to travel to the local area because of the perception of these cultural symbols. Therefore, cultural symbolic perception plays an important role in tourism [27].

5.3   Memory Perception

Memory is an important concept in the current Western humanities and social sciences. The study of memory has increasingly becoming an area of concern for Western human geographers [28]. While "memory" is associated with "spirituality" and "spirit" in the West, western scholars believe that the physical environment can improve the level of individual sense of consciousness [29]. Urban memories use urban space as a backdrop, and they stimulate the local spirit of historical cities [29]. Mariam et al. also pointed out that collective memory is a "database" that encompasses the tangible and intangible social and cultural values of cities, thus plays an important role in promoting the sustainable protection of historical cities [30]. Joaquim Sabaté Bel's article describes Barcelona's old industrial area, Poblenou, which was transformed into a creative district due to large-scale urban intervention. Urban memory based on elements such as community organization and collective life has been strengthened by the transformation of urban space [31].

In the commemorative landscape, collective memory is spatialized through objective material and symbolic commemorative landscapes [32, 33], and related memories include not only collective, political memory or memory of a generation, but also viewers' own experiences and pains.

In addition to cultural memories such as local memory, collective memory, and urban memory, western scholars have also studied the concept of practical memory in space. Lofland pointed out in the book: "Citizens' perceptions of the community are called 'community identity' and are reflected in the interaction between individual residents and the community" [34].

When studying the "spiritual" dimension of tourism, Gregory explores how people seek subjective meaning after experiencing various objective things on the way to viewing the landscape [35].

The "embedded activism" in Susan Haedicke's article is an appeal to the practice of embedding public affairs in space. It is believed that the practical story connects the narrative with the space and achieves a "reflexive narrative" [36].

Daugstad also believes that the experience space is beginning to turn to deeper perceptions, such as through personal experience to perceive local lifestyles [37].

In the memory landscape, practical perception is more compatible with cultural symbolic perception. Wasserman believes that "a truly good memorial will allow visitors to experience space, watch and touch artifacts, participate in ceremonies or community events, and the audience becomes a participant in the memory experience" [38].

6 Conclusion

6.1 Micro Level

From the related literatures such as "landscape", "space" and "perception", we can summarize the relevant enlightenment on the micro level, macro level and even reflection level of landscape space perception.

The landscape space is not only the story background, but also the narrative process that produces the story [39].

From the micro level, the various elements of landscape space affect the perception of landscape space. As Potteiger said, "landscape narrative" refers to the interaction and relationship between landscape elements and narratives. In the garden of Shinagawa, the narratives brought by landscape elements such as water, wood and stone give memory and respect to the history and customs of this area, express their attachment to natural things, dependence and rational thinking on human living environment [40].

In the landscape space, the relevant architectural form is also part of the narrative. It is interwoven with local and social practice and is the social capital of the narrative structure [41].

Franken believes that contemporary architecture not only satisfies the function of space. In the design of the Frankfurt Motor Show, he uses material integration narratives to view architecture as part of the BMW belief system [42].

However, spatial elements do not exist in isolation. In practice, there are often situations of contradiction, and reasonable choices should be made according to actual conditions [43].

6.2   Macro Level

From the macro level, thinking about "landscape space perception", more scholars have already fostered it to the research category of urban planning development. It is known in previous studies that it is important for cities to achieve future sustainability, recognizing and protecting all tangible and intangible socio-cultural values, since the nature of sustainability includes socio-cultural and economic aspects. This shows a strong interdependence between the environment and people [30]. ESRA Yaldız examined the relationship between Konya's urban architecture and urban ownership, emphasizing the role of buildings in forming unique urban brands [44].

When urban culture is homogenized, a space with nostalgic emotions like the market can stimulate tourists to be more emotionally concerned [45]. In the study of tourism narrative, there is also an inspirational article on the development of urban space: when urban culture is homogenized, spaces with nostalgic emotions, such as the market, can stimulate tourists to be more emotional.

In the design of museums that play a key role in urban cultural communication, local narratives also form part of the national narrative to a certain extent, which can shape local and local identity, realize local and national interactions and regulate community members [46].

There is great potential with external society and other aspects [47]. Urban memories evoked by space have been shown to influence urban competition rankings in urban renewal [31].

6.3   Reflection Level

At present, the contemporary landscape space lacks cultural connotation, and some landscapes are one-sided pursuit of visual impact [48]. Narrative has almost become a marketing tool. Most designers are indifferent to whether the story is clearly stated and whether the information is effectively conveyed [49].

It can be seen from the research literature that the research on spatial perception in China is significantly less than that in foreign countries, where most of the articles are examples of famous foreign architecture.

It can also be seen that for the domestic space design field, there are not many excellent cases that can truly apply the spatial perception to the design and correctly produce the perceived effect. From the perspective of academic research, most of China's articles on spatial perception design stay in the case of empirical analysis and qualitative description, while foreign journal papers are combined with data model analysis methods commonly used in humanities and social sciences.

Therefore, it can be concluded that the lack of scientific exploration with data analysis in Chinese spatial perception research makes it difficult to draw more specific and objective conclusions. However in today's big data context, the study of objective and subjective relationships in the topic of "space perception" can be analyzed using software such as SPSS [50].

Urban landscape space already covers modern landscape spaces such as public art, while the existing literature rarely focuses on the study of modern landscape space perceptions such as public art. In the wave of building a "smart city" around the world, spatial perception is more related to human innovation. Urban space has gradually transitioned from the traditional static, passive experience space to a dynamic, interactive space. In this process, taking the situation in China as an example, many places have launched digital cities, digital government, digital transportation and other platforms based on digital technology. However, these are only functionally satisfying the requirements of efficiency and convenience, while ignoring the spiritual needs of most users in the city.

Furthermore, spatial perception, if combined with the concept of a smart city, can make the experience break the limits of time and space. As an example, we can combine the new generation of information technology with modern garden space and community space by designing smart gardens and smart communities. This makes people connect with space in a smart way, and based on previous spatial perception, it can increase interaction. In the space of cultural communication education, the development of smart apps such as digital museums can make local identity more interesting using microscopic elements such as symbols.

Inheritance of cultural heritage, intangible cultural heritage can be digitally stored in the cloud or online. Is it better if the material heritage also able to build a platform through smart cities, allowing citizens to participate in future related designs while being aware of space entities. Such an intelligent technology system will help to develop better contexts and strengthen building consensus and local sense.

For the humanistic innovation of smart cities, designers can combine the characteristics of human spatial perception and think from the macroscopic and microscopic perspectives, such as considering the aesthetic differences, cognitive differences, personal interests of different users and other factors related to subjective perception. In-depth integration of culture and technology. It is also possible to use the platform system of the smart city to collect, organize and analyze relevant data for analysis. Based on the characteristics of urban space, the cultural symbols of the city can be extracted and internalized into various media of the smart city, and the identity of the culture as one of the core factors together with the scientific and technological factors can promote the sustainable development of the city.

References

1. Rodiek, J.E.: Landscape planning: its contributions to the evolution of the profession of landscape architecture. Landscape Urban Plan. **76**(1–4), 291–297 (2006). https://doi.org/10.1016/j.landurbplan.2004.09.037
2. Rouhvand, H.: Human geography: semiotics of landscape in Jhumpa Lahiri's narratives. Proc. Soc. Behav. Sci. **158**, 132–139 (2014). https://doi.org/10.1016/j.sbspro.2014.12.057
3. Simpson, I.A., Vésteinsson, O., Adderley, W.P., McGovern, T.H.: Fuel resource utilisation in landscapes of settlement. J. Archaeol. Sci. **30**(11), 1401–1420 (2003). https://doi.org/10.1016/S0305-4403(03)00035-9
4. Johansen, P.G.: Site maintenance practices and settlement social organization in iron age Karnataka, India: inferring settlement places and landscape from surface distributions of ceramic assemblage attributes. J. Anthropol. Archaeol. **29**(4), 432–454 (2010). https://doi.org/10.1016/j.jaa.2010.06.002
5. Caletrío, J.: Tourism, landscape change and critical thresholds. Ann. Tourism Res. **38**(1), 309–313 (2011). https://doi.org/10.1016/j.annals.2010.06.003
6. Morton, T.A., van der Bles, A.M., Haslam, S.A.: Seeing our self reflected in the world around us: the role of identity in making (natural) environments restorative. J. Environ. Psychol. **49**, 65–77 (2017). https://doi.org/10.1016/j.jenvp.2016.11.002
7. 侍非, 高才驰, 孟璐, 蒋志杰: 空间叙事方法缘起及在城市研究中的应用. 国际城市规划 (06), 99–103 (2014)
8. Bagheri, N.: What qualitative GIS maps tell and don't tell: insights from mapping women in Tehran's public spaces. J. Cult. Geogr. **31**(2), 166–178 (2014). https://doi.org/10.1080/08873631.2014.906848
9. 审美体验下的当代西方景观叙事研究_邱天怡: 审美体验下的当代西方景观叙事研究_邱天怡
10. 刘欣: 叙事景观与景观心理. 旅游纵览(下半月)(09), 236 (2017)
11. 陈天宇: 叙事空间视角下城市家具设计研究. 工业设计(05), 62–66 (2016)
12. 纪铮: 彼得·埃森曼访谈——欧洲犹太死难者纪念碑设计. 世界建筑(10), 110–112 (2005)
13. Blunt, A.: Collective memory and productive nostalgia: Anglo-Indian homemaking at McCluskieganj. Environ. Plan. D: Soc. Space **21**(6), 717–738 (2016). https://doi.org/10.1068/d327
14. Chang, L., Bisgrove, R.J., Liao, M.: Improving educational functions in botanic gardens by employing landscape narratives. Landscape Urban Plan. **86**(3–4), 233–247 (2008). https://doi.org/10.1016/j.landurbplan.2008.03.003
15. Tanga, M.: Burnishing history: Mags Harries' 1976 Asaroton. Public Art Dialogue **8**(1), 50–71 (2018). https://doi.org/10.1080/21502552.2018.1430293
16. Gurler, E.E., Ozer, B.: The effects of public memorials on social memory and urban identity. Proc. Soc. Behav. Sci. **82**, 858–863 (2013). https://doi.org/10.1016/j.sbspro.2013.06.361
17. Muzaini, H., Yeoh, B.S.A.: Reading representations of women's war experiences in the Changi Chapel and Museum, Singapore. Geoforum **36**(4), 465–476 (2005). https://doi.org/10.1016/j.geoforum.2004.07.011
18. Lewicka, M.: Place attachment, place identity, and place memory: restoring the forgotten city past. J. Environ. Psychol. **28**(3), 209–231 (2008). https://doi.org/10.1016/j.jenvp.2008.02.001
19. Rashid, M.: Architecture and narrative: the formation of space and cultural meaning. J. Archit. **15**(4), 543–549 (2010). https://doi.org/10.1080/13602365.2010.486570

20. Soliva, R., Hunziker, M.: Beyond the visual dimension: using ideal type narratives to analyse people's assessments of landscape scenarios. Land Use Policy 26(2), 284–294 (2009). https://doi.org/10.1016/j.landusepol.2008.03.007

21. Geib, D.: Mapping the city: narratives of memory and place. UWSpace (2017)

22. Azaryahu, M., Foote, K.E.: Historical space as narrative medium: on the configuration of spatial narratives of time at historical sites. GeoJournal 73(3), 179–194 (2008). https://doi.org/10.1007/s10708-008-9202-4

23. 张学东: 设计叙事:从自发、自觉到自主. 江西社会科学(02), 232–235 (2013)

24. 马捷, 华峰: 起·承·转·合——基于建筑叙事学角度研究商业步行交通空间设计. 华中建筑(03), 18–21 (2012)

25. Penz, F.: The architectural promenade as narrative device: practice based research in architecture and the moving image. Digit. Creativity 15(1), 39–51 (2010). https://doi.org/10.1076/digc.15.1.39.28152

26. Larson, S.: Shifting modern identities in Madrid's recent urban planning, architecture and narrative. Cities 20(6), 395–402 (2003). https://doi.org/10.1016/j.cities.2003.08.005

27. Buckley, R., Ollenburg, C., Zhong, L.: Cultural landscape in Mongolian tourism. Ann. Tourism Res. 35(1), 47–61 (2008). https://doi.org/10.1016/j.annals.2007.06.007

28. 李彦辉, 朱竑: 国外人文地理学关于记忆研究的进展与启示. 人文地理(01), 11–15 (2012)

29. Sharpley, R., Jepson, D.: Rural tourism. Ann. Tourism Res. 38(1), 52–71 (2011). https://doi.org/10.1016/j.annals.2010.05.002

30. Ardakani, M.K., Oloonabadi, S.S.A.: Collective memory as an efficient agent in sustainable urban conservation. Proc. Eng. 21, 985–988 (2011). https://doi.org/10.1016/j.proeng.2011.11.2103

31. Bel, J.S.: Rankings, creatividad y urbanismo

32. Muzaini, H., Yeoh, B.S.A.: War landscapes as battlefields of collective memories: reading the reflections at Bukit Chandu, Singapore. Cult. Geogr. 12(3), 345–365 (2016). https://doi.org/10.1191/1474474005eu335oa

33. National Identity and Commemorative Space Connections to the Nation through Time and Site: National Identity and Commemorative Space Connections to the Nation through Time and Site

34. Stewart, W.P., Liebert, D., Larkin, K.W.: Community identities as visions for landscape change. Landscape Urban Plan. 69(2–3), 315–334 (2004). https://doi.org/10.1016/j.landurbplan.2003.07.005

35. Willson, G.B., McIntosh, A.J., Zahra, A.L.: Tourism and spirituality: a phenomenological analysis. Ann. Tourism Res. 42, 150–168 (2013). https://doi.org/10.1016/j.annals.2013.01.016

36. Haedicke, S.: The aroma-home community garden project's democratic narratives: embodied memory-stories of planting and cooking, 8(1), 114–130 (2018). https://doi.org/10.1080/21502552.2018.1430290

37. Daugstad, K.: Negotiating landscape in rural tourism. Ann. Tourism Res. 35(2), 402–426 (2008). https://doi.org/10.1016/j.annals.2007.10.001

38. Sumartojo, S.: Commemorative atmospheres: memorial sites, collective events and the experience of national identity. Trans. Inst. Br. Geogr. 41(4), 541–553 (2016). https://doi.org/10.1111/tran.12144

39. Scheltema, A.: the power of the narrative (2018)

40. 吴庆书, 三谷徹, 曲赛赛: 现代景观设计中叙事手法的应用——以日本东京都品川中心花园设计为例. 中国园林(04), 48–51 (2011)

41. Childs, M.C.: Storytelling and urban design. J. Urbanism: Int. Res. Placemaking Urban Sustain. 1(2), 173–186 (2008). https://doi.org/10.1080/17549170802221526

42. Jo, S., Lee, K.: Architecture as narrative: on Bernard Franken's ruminations on characterization, integration, and imagination. J. Asian Archit. Build. **6**(2), 213–220 (2007). https://doi.org/10.3130/jaabe.6.213
43. 王佐, 沈敏: 叙事学视角下的工业遗产保护与再利用交通空间规划设计研究. 遗产与保护研究(05), 49–51 (2018)
44. Yaldız, E., Aydın, D., Sıramkaya, S.B.: Loss of city identities in the process of change: the city of Konya-Turkey. Proc. Soc. Behav. Sci. **140**, 221–233 (2014). https://doi.org/10.1016/j.sbspro.2014.04.413
45. Aiello, G., Gendelman, I.: Seattle's Pike Place Market (de)constructed: an analysis of tourist narratives about a public space. J. Tourism Cult. Change **5**(3), 158–185 (2008). https://doi.org/10.2167/jtcc093.0
46. 杜辉: 在国家叙事与地方叙事之间_英国北约克郡乡村博物馆实践. 博物馆新论
47. Gillette, M.B., Hurley, A.: Vision, voice, and the community landscape: the Missouri Place Stories pilot project. Landscape Urban Plan. **173**, 1–8 (2018). https://doi.org/10.1016/j.landurbplan.2018.01.005
48. 邱天怡, 常兵, 杨艳茹: 当代景观空间叙事新模式探析. 华中建筑(03), 1–3 (2018)
49. 孙元熙: 当代叙事性景观体验的认同感研究. 中外建筑(05), 46–48 (2018)
50. Sevenant, M., Antrop, M.: Cognitive attributes and aesthetic preferences in assessment and differentiation of landscapes. J. Environ. Manag. **90**(9), 2889–2899 (2009). https://doi.org/10.1016/j.jenvman.2007.10.016

Perception and Emotion in DAPI

Engaging with Sense of Smell Through Textile Interactions

Jyoti Kapur[✉]

The Swedish School of Textiles, University of Borås, Borås, Sweden
jyoti.kapur@hb.se

Abstract. This research paper discusses dimension of smell for designing spatial interactions through textiles. The focus in these design examples is combining the sense of touch to actuate the smells. Sense of touch is explored in terms of different tactile sensations that include pressing, rubbing and movement of the body. Through these tactile interactions smells embedded in the textile objects are released. The temporal textile expressions of smells open up for further investigations for designing spaces, as these design examples bring forward the olfactory expressions and proposes frameworks for future research in potential human-computer interactions through our everyday objects and surroundings. The proposal of textile interactions that engage sense of smell and create slow interactions with objects and situations from our daily lives opens up the opportunity to encourage more social interactions within the physical world. These interactions will include computational things, however, in a discreet manner, helping build deep bonds between human to human and human to environment.

Keywords: Sense of smell · Textile interactions · Movement ·
Texture and haptics

1 Introduction

1.1 Sense of Smell

An introduction to our environment is through our senses. There is a deep and extensive discourse by many philosophers on the senses and their classification. Differentiating perception from sensation, Gibson emphasizes that a sense as a verb, has two meanings, firstly it is "to detect something" and secondly "to have a sensation" [1]. He explains, that the senses as perceptual systems, imply that senses detect something. Whereas Rodaway´s definition of perception is two-fold. One, perception as sensation where stimuli from environment gets mediated through senses and helps form a relationship between human and the environment. Secondly, perception as cognition where in it is culturally mediated in thinking processes, making associations and memories [2].

Smell molecules are usually invisible and are airborne. They come in contact with the olfactory receptors (organ for smelling) in the nasal cavity. When we inhale the air, we are able to detect smell. Olfaction is a chemoreception, that means the chemosignals are sent

© Springer Nature Switzerland AG 2019
N. Streitz and S. Konomi (Eds.): HCII 2019, LNCS 11587, pp. 241–257, 2019.
https://doi.org/10.1007/978-3-030-21935-2_19

to the brain and in this process, the chemical composition is detected. On an average human beings can differentiate between ten thousand different smells, according to the pioneering works of Buck And Axel[1] [3]. Each receptor has a specialized function and detects some limited number of smells. According to Buck and Axel, the chemosignals or the information is passed through the neurons to the receptors and the olfactory bulb that is located in the limbic system which is known as the emotional center of the brain. The information is passed to other parts of the brain to form a pattern and these patterns are recognized from previous memories of encounters with that particular smell.

On a broadly classified way there are five senses, where in sight, hearing, taste and touch comprised the four basic senses and the sense of smell according to Aristotle took a middle place connecting sight and hearing with taste and touch [4]. Sense of smell has taken a back seat in many areas and until today in the field of design there is a lack in understanding, vocabulary, methods and tools to work with smells. Stating the decline in importance of the sense of smell in the western culture since the start of the modern period, Classen quotes the arguments of few of the scholars who emphasize on the olfactory poverty and decline in the private and public spaces. Classen argues that it is not only the olfactory sense but also all the non-visual senses have declined when compared to sense of vision. She emphasizes the major difference in the sense of smell that was once a higher sense of spirituality and medicine in the pre-modern Europe is now being a "non-sense" in the modern western culture [3] and western culture is often reluctant to consider other dimensions that are, nevertheless, fundamental to the experience of architecture, design and habitation.

1.2 Smell and Space

Designing through the sense of smell means designing an experience. At this point, the question we ask is, how far have we in the western society developed our understanding for olfactory experience and encounter with the smells itself ? What differentiates us today in olfactory acceptance to the ancient societies in the premodern west? Designing with the non-visual sensory sensitivity and experience is not a commonly seen practice within the design studies and research that includes user experience especially in the fields of architecture and spatial designing in public and private spaces. However, Lally is convinced of the future areas of research that would incorporate the increased human body sensory sensitivity and the material energy for architectural applications [5]. Such as using artificial intelligence for augmenting the human senses to be able to understand our surroundings near and far better than, we are able to do so now. For example, to be able to hear certain frequencies that are below or higher than normal human audible frequencies.

Designing spatial qualities through the tangible and intangible materials essentially focuses on the human interactions in a space. Although the conventional choice of materials are their physical and visual attributes like color, pattern and textures, where invisible materiality like smell is seldom a design choice. What if we can add olfactory

[1] Buck and Axel won a Nobel Prize in 2004 for the research investigating the olfactory system, written in a paper in 1991.

attributes by using smell as a material in spatial designing? What kind of interactions with smell will emerge in spaces? "Olfaction would seem to be largely extraneous to the formulation of spaces, and yet a careful reading of cognitive, perceptive, cultural, social, planning and anthropological phenomena would suggest that odors are not only profoundly inherent components of places, but at times actually essential to defining them" [6]. Smells can be a social tool for communication among human beings and also to interact with our immediate environment, like navigating through a space. Classen, suggests that in the ancient times, the senses were taken as a media for communication as opposed to the present day thinking of senses as passive recipients of the data. Especially the sense of smell in an Amazonian tribal culture by defining the tribes based on their odours, since each tribe smelled differently based on their customary eating habits and their hunting professions; such as one tribe did fishing and another hunted animals for the meat and a third tribe looked for the roots and plants [4], these social orders were communicated through the olfactory.

If the spaces could be designed using the sense of smell; boundaries, openings and closings of a space defined by smells could be a navigation tool. As an example, without having rigid hard walls, sometimes smells act like a wall, when it is foul smelling and one can hardly enter in that zone. However, the same quality of the smells could be used to create spatial cues for a visually impaired person and offer not just a guiding tool but also help navigating in a directional way, since smells gives a sense of position in relation to its source. Quoting Hall, Rodaway writes that different cultures define their olfactory experience differently in the context of geographical experiences [2]. The spatial concepts of depth, distance, openings and closing help to create a composition of a space in a metaphorical sense, according to Tufnell et al. [7], but also do so through subliminal and past experiences, wherein smells in a space may create boundaries or open up a space, setting a stage for making relationships within that contained space for example in a given space a particular smell reminds a person of an associated event with particular person/s back in time may open or close up a space for present and future encounters for the person.

Pallasmaa suggests that modern architectural theory and criticism has a strong tendency to regard space as an immaterial object that is delineated by material surfaces, instead of understanding space in terms of its dynamic interactions and interrelations. Japanese thinking, by contrast, is founded on a relational understanding of the concept of space [8].

Olfaction and its characteristics become a part of a smellscape, that in turn helps make a space - a place through olfactory memory, as smells are associative of materials, people and events in a particular time. Adaptive sensitivity of smells make sense of smell an important communication tool to respond to the changes in the near environment [2]. Also, through the smells of our own bodies and the spaces around us, we interact subliminally and communicate within our environment [9]. Smells make one linger on longer in a space, rather than making hurried steps and moving from point A to B in order to complete a business, spaces could provide an element of freedom of movement and composure [10] and an opportunity to discover a space which appears to be familiar due to its smells.

Using practice-based design research tools and methods, this paper explores olfactive interaction at an intersection of textiles, spatial and interaction design. In this paper, taking smell as a design material, methods of designing interactions through textiles in a spatial context are explored. The olfactive interactions are initiated by activating smells through the touch or the body movement. Surface textile processes like impregnation, coating and printing, are applied when investigating the applications of smell on the textiles. By using these methods, different textile expressions of smell for spatial interactions are proposed which can activate and release smells.

2 Design Examples

The following two interactive installations, *Sight of Smell* and *Touch of Smell* explore olfactive interactions through the touch of textiles. These textiles are treated with micro-encapsulated smells that gets released only upon physical interaction that break-opens the smell molecules. In the design example of *Temporal textile interactions through dynamic forms*, the final iteration combined smell induced yarns and the spacer knitting technique, creating a temporal form of origami folded knitted textile that is imbued with natural smells and embodies the concept of playing with and intensifying smells through haptic interactions. And the performance - *Smell, space and Body Movement* was carried out with a textile object that is designed by soaking the material in the synthetic smell molecules and is interacted-with through improvised dance movements.

2.1 Sight of Smell

This lighted installation evokes a visual interest from a distance. Only once approached inside in this created space, one realizes another spatial quality to it. The strings of balloons become the object of curiosity and with an intuitive reflex one tries to hold the strings (coated with microencapsulated smells) in the hand. Only with this physical interaction and touch, that the smells get activated. Since the micro-encapsulations are so designed that get broken with a physical abrasion, touch or rubbing, it then releases the smells in the space (Figs. 1 and 2).

Fig. 1. Sight of smell installation at the exhibition speculate, collaborate, define – textile thinking for future ways of living, the Textile Museum Borås, Sweden, 23 March–15 May 2017

Fig. 2. Expression of smell through haptic interactions

This expression of smell intrigues the senses and opens up the space for not only the soft transitions of movements through it but also for the interactions in the space through the tangible expression of smells.

2.2 Touch of Smell

How does it feel to touch a smell?

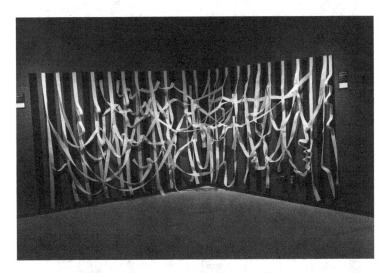

Fig. 3. Touch of smell installation at the exhibition speculate, collaborate, define – textile thinking for future ways of living, the Textile Museum Borås, Sweden, 23 March–15 May 2017

This installation is designed for a playful interaction through velcro tapes. Visitors interacted with this installation by touching, rubbing, sticking together, and peeling the loose ends of the velcro tapes across the corner of the walls, and thereby releasing the smells. The intensities of the smell could be experimented and played with, by varying the length of the tape and the speed at which they were peeled apart. Eucalyptus smell was used in this installation which was quite pleasant and almost all the visitors had some associations with the smell, this however was not planned in the designing nor it was important that the visitor is able to correctly determine what smell it is. However, it was playful for some visitors to be able to determine the smell and in doing so, the action of peeling and sticking across the tapes was multiplied (Fig. 3).

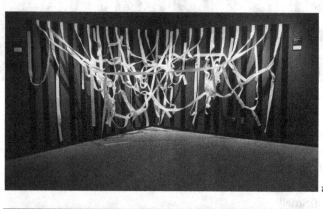

a

b

c

Fig. 4. (a–c) changes in installation over days "touch of smell"

The soft side of the velcro tapes were coated with the micro-encapsulated smells. The placement of these tapes alternated with the uncoated loop side of the velcro tapes. This logic was followed also in the colors across the whole corner installation. As a result, upon their placement from one wall of the corner to the other, the velcro tapes physically created a space that was on one hand difficult to de-entangle but on the other hand, quite inviting for further interaction (Fig. 5).

Fig. 5. Expression of smell through haptic interactions

Combining conventional textile materials and smart paints with micro-encapsulated smell molecules, these textile objects are designed to carry the smells in a discreet way. As a result, only through bodily interactions of touch and movement, embedded and enclosed smells on the textile objects are opened, released and transported in the space. By changing the scale, the purpose and the context of a two-dimensional material (velcro tapes) created an unexpected three-dimensionality; a space through the smells.

2.3   Temporal Textile Interactions Through Dynamic Forms

The aim in this project with the origami folded textiles was to translate the action of releasing smells through haptic interactions with the dynamic and playful origami folded textile structures. The design sample was developed using flatbed industrial knitting machine. The challenge was to design knitted textiles with integrated fold lines so that when the fabric is laid flat, it automatically takes on a three-dimensional, folded form, suggesting an interaction based around unfolding that releases the smells (Fig. 6).

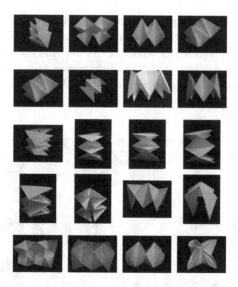

Fig. 6. Temporal textile interactions through dynamic forms, origami paper fold sketches

This investigation followed on from an experimental workshop that explored various hand gestures and actions performed on natural materials like whole spices; cardamom, clove, cinnamon or fruits like oranges etc. to actuate smells. The action of unfolding and folding a textile was initially explored on paper in the form of three-dimensional sketches. Some of these were translated on the knitting software, wherein the lines of folds were crucial to investigating the automatic folding action. The fabrics were knitted using industrial knitting machines, with various stitch patterns and yarn materials explored in relation to enhancing the folding action. Through various iterations, it was then possible to define the folding pattern and combination of yarns that induced the optimal folding of the fabric (Fig. 7).

Fig. 7. Process of treating yarns with natural moss for impregnating the smells

In the final sample yarns were beforehand treated with natural moss and lichens as a natural dyeing process for textile materials. These yarn was provided by textile designer, Worbin [11]. The moss had been collected from the forest and therefore it did have some soil attached to the roots. The smell of this bath is a combination of moss greens, soil and some mushroom smells. The microorganisms present in soil could be a reason for the mushroom like smell [12], however, it is a pleasant smell and transports one back to the nature, in the forest. Provided one has experienced some walks in the forest in the past and is familiar with the natural smells of the moss and mushroom.

The final iteration combined smell induced yarns and the spacer knitting technique as shown in Figs. 8 and 9. Spacer technique involves knitting with yarn A on the two outer sides of the fabric and using yarn B to fill-in between two sides. This construction makes the fabric sturdy and gives it a structural character.

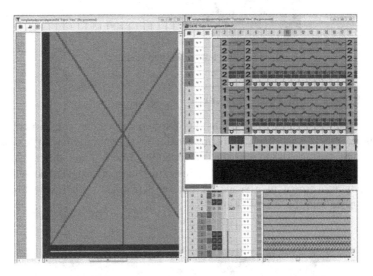

Fig. 8. Computer program for spacer construction of knitted textile

Fig. 9. Cross sectional view of the spacer knitted textile

This technique helped create a temporal form that is able to stand on its own as shown in Fig. 10, imbued with smells that embodied the concept of playing with and intensifying smells through haptic interaction.

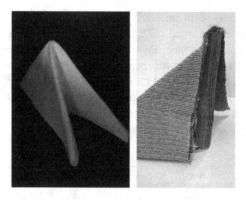

Fig. 10. Folded knitted textile

2.4   Smell, Space and Body Movement

Yet another method of activating smells; i.e. through movement, is explored through a performance; Smell, space and body movement in collaboration with a dancer. As ephemeral are the smells so are the movements. Smells trace the movements or movement makes the smells perceivable. This exploration investigated actuating smells through body movement in a space. A dancer performed with textile objects as a medium to distribute the smells (Fig. 11).

Fig. 11. Performance smell space and body movement in collaboration with dancer, Giedre Kirkilyte - Jankauskiene, at Vilnius Academy of Arts and presented at an exhibition at the VAA Gallery, Vilnius, Lithuania November 28–December 2, 2016.

The textile object functioned as a free standing object in a space, and was not fixed at any point. The dancer interacted with this object, creating an artistic performance by exploring the object with regards to volume, shape, surface, size, and smell. She played with them, slipping, sliding, cuddling, curling, twisting, wrapping, fanning, pinching, pressing, releasing, rotating, and twirling, improvising her movements [9]. The movements of the dancer were based on the interaction with the textile object, as the object was bouncy in nature due to the materials used. Handling of the textile object and more importantly the smells emanating from the sponge directed the moves of the dancer.

The textile object was designed and knitted on an industrial flatbed machine for this exploration, and several two meter by two centimeter sponge strips were prepared in a bath of tatami (rice straw) smell, dried at room temperature, and inserted into tubular structures. The textile piece is a knitted tube and four meters long by twenty centimeters wide. Polyamide monofilament yarn was used to knit the textile structure and the textile object was made to be interactive. The tubular knitted panel was filled with two bunches of sponge strips, each of which was tied together at one end. The tied ends of the two bunches were then attached together head-on, and drawn through the tubular structure, such that the sponge strips protruded from both ends. The textile object has a spongy and resilient character to invite different ways of interactions with it.

The textile object allowed an interaction on a near-to-body scale, with the dancer improvising movements with the textile object as guided by smells. Through her movement in relation to the textile object the air in the space was moved and so the smells were too. The frequency – as to how often, with what intervals and with what intensity- these smells were spread in the space with the dancer's movements seemed like an olfactory orchestra in a space. As the dancer moved with the object in the space, her steps back and forth and the textile object was swirled in the air, the smells get dispersed in the room at the intervals - somehow if one were to close the eyes and concentrate on the time difference between the whiffs of smell, one could relate that to the time that the dancer swirled the textile object in the air. The movement of the dancer were in harmony with the smells at times, where she walked in slow steps and at times she moved the textile object in a rather persistently fast and rhythmic movements. These changes in her movements had an immediate effect on the smells being dispersed in the room and therefore it reminded one of a symphony orchestra. From the dancers perspective, it was an intense interaction, as she could weave her way through the smells in the space and make smells follow her movements. In this way, her ephemeral movements transited to be perceived from being visual to olfactory sense.

3 Discussions

The above design examples are investigating tactile stimulations through textile textures, haptic gestures and movements of body to connect to the smells by actuating them with physical interaction. These examples actuate the smells through the touch. Different tactile sensations involved as muscle movements of skin, or the action of rubbing, pressing etc. are akin to Montagu's explanation of the term haptic, which is a mentally extended sense of touch that comes to being through the experience of living in a space. Montagu argues that haptic is an acquired sense, in terms of the objects already been seen, touched and acted upon [13]. Through the interactions in these individual installations and design objects, although sensory stimuli are focused on touch and smells, we assimilate and understand our environment not exclusively through one sense, rather in a multi-sensorial way.

The sense of touch, is reaching out (extending oneself) with the body. According to Rodaway, there is a reciprocity of the haptic system that is three-fold; simple contact, exploratory activity and communication [2]. Through touch, one feels connected to the surroundings, people and community. This relationship gets manifested through the senses to (re)locate oneself geographically. In the above examples, touch is explored as a simple contact which is just one directional and as exploratory activity, where the visitor tries to find out how to explore with the textile installations. When the touch and reciprocal activity of opening and disseminating of smells is present, it is a two way process or communication in the interaction through touch.

Gibson argues that the senses should be conceived as active rather than passive. These should be interrelated and not exclusive and be taken as systems rather than channels for information of the environment [1]. Exemplifying the intimate relationship between the sense of taste and smell or tactile consciousness of vibrations and auditory experience, Rodaway writes that "sensuous experience is, in any case, often a complex of sense working together offering a range of clues about the environment through which the body is passing" [2]. Olfactory and haptic sensations are at an intimate distance to the body, and these two senses are essential to locate oneself in a space, distinguish danger in food or other beings (ibid). Also in certain ways there is an interaction with smells and sense of touch [14] where the smell stimuli may be experienced with facial nerves.

In the installation *sight of smell*, the visitors are moving through the space while being constantly "in touch" with the ribbons induced with the smell. At times the sense of touch is active and at times passive and so is the sense of smell. Very likely, both the sense of touch and smell are involuntary and cannot be shut off as we can do when closing our eyes or ears [14]. The interaction designed within this installation is an analogue and slow interaction that induces fluid movements through the space. The interaction can also be seen as time based, since the smell molecules upon being released are dynamic and random in their movement also in relation to the movement of the body (visitor) in the space. These smell molecules are perceived instantly and with high intensity just as they get released and slowly the perception is reduced as the molecules move away, and then randomly they appear again. Although, it is not just the movement of the smell molecules but also the nature of sense of smell that is adaptively sensitive due to familiarity [2]. These interactions are designed, to induce the movement and explore the space around the installation, perhaps trace the smells outside the installation space in relation to the thresholds and perception of smells.

Smell being an intimate sense, generates a local geography and also emotionally creates a bond between the person and the environment, and quite similar to the sense of touch there is a direct bonding between the body (chemical contact) and the space [2]. Through the olfactory experience, there is a bond and olfactory memory that is created and that is a relationship between the person to environment or person to person or another being as in case of an animal pet. The olfactory notes taking subliminal cues in the near environment of what is in the way and navigate the way through these cues would be of significance to the temporal spatial designing tools and methods. Designing with olfactive dimension in urban setting, would add to the wayfinding toolset for the people with visual disabilities where smells would help one navigate the space. Although above design examples are designed specifically for interactions in the interior spaces, the textural element that could be reached through the body (not just the hands) to actuate the smells could offer potentials of creating patterns for walking in a public space, where the smells get released by walking over the path in a similar intensity and pressure, as an example; walking twice in this pattern in a difference of a minute. This will not only create playful interactions in space, rather it would also lend time for the passersby to enjoy few moments of walking and creating a "signature smellscape".

The design examples of tactile interactions in the installation *touch of smell*, and textile interactions through *dynamic forms* exemplify experience of space through olfactory embodied interactions. The *Touch of Smell* installation demanded from the visitors to apply some force while detangling or peeling off the velcro surfaces. Figure 4(a–c) shows difference in the installation as it had been interacted with over the time. Although the aim of the installation was not to collect data from the visitors, yet the installation was photographed randomly over days to watch if there are differences to note if it has been interacted with. In the last picture (c) it is evident that the force applied for pulling was sometimes even stronger than expected as some of the velcro strips came out of the wall leaving a mark behind. Here the tactile sensations on the soft side of the velcro (containing smells) are different than on the loop side of the velcro (help peeling off micro-encapsulations). Active touching and peeling of the velcro tapes leads to the dissemination of the smells in the space. Textile interactions through *dynamic forms*, enables one to engage in the act of folding and unfolding through hands and by that experience the smells that get disseminated from the textile object. The perception of smells at this closer scale to the body would be varied depending on many factors. Firstly, the act of folding and unfolding is each time different, and therefore the dissemination differs. Secondly, the ambient conditions of flow of air, moisture levels and room temperature would make a difference in the perception of smells. Thirdly, the familiarity of smell would bring in the habitation and thereby reduce the perception of smell. Unlike the embodied interactions as we know in ubiquitous way with the computer systems, these are physical, analogue and embodied interactions with the materials and backwards. It is to explore how to design responsive materials and design systems in our living environment. Here both the sense of touch and smell are active during the interaction with the textile and are equally motivating the visitor to engage themselves interacting with the textile objects.

Through the active physical interaction with the textile objects combined with ambient conditions where the sensory inputs of touch (texture, air flow, temperature change and humidity) and smell create embodied interactions and spatial experiences. This interaction is not a typical computer-human interaction, rather the information of the environmental changes like in air-flow or temperature is delivered through visual and non-visual cues [15] is interesting to design new digital experiences. Since the sense of smell is passive and working in the background, this sensory stimuli can be used to design subtle cues to help us navigate in our environment. As a future research, this could be explored by developing 'tactile smell maps' layered on digital street maps. Adding the dimension of smells to the maps, for browsing the cities would make it more interactive and attractive especially for pedestrians and cyclists, and add quality to ways of living within Urbanscapes [9]. Such as creating real-time geo-mapping in the pedestrian and biker lanes in an urban setting. The computational technology informs of the olfactive walking or biking trail using augmented reality as an example and where the biking tracks and walking paths are designed with embedded smells, so that walking or riding on these paths would actuate the smells. In addition, natural smells could be added by planting trees and floral beds around the pedestrian and biking paths in the city. Taking inspiration from the fragrance gardens or the designed gardens for the blind where certain herbs were planted that would release the odor only upon touching specifically actions like either rubbing or crushing [16]. In this way, the urban landscape or the real physical environment would be a collaborator with the digital tools and computing systems to have an impact in experiencing the environment in a multisensorial way. Playful interactions in the physical world would take precedence over the digital interfaces, the computational tools are important guiding tools to such experiences, however, by remaining in the background.

Also, through the body movements and the air that shifts around the dancer interacts in the space with the smell as she follows the smells. This dual tracing of smell movement is creating a relationship of the body and material in the space and also opens the space for encounters. As Rodaway emphasizes on the role of smells in geographical experience - which is the organization of space and spatial relationships, orientation in the space and relationship to a place with its smell characterization. This collaborative work with dancer, helps put the movement of smells in relation to the body in perspective and this interactive relationship in a space is an interesting element to designing spaces.

Smellscapes as designed by the urban planner Henshaw [17] and artist Mclean [18] define and articulate the experiences of being in these particular cities through the joint narratives and memories of the people, events and places. Although the combined memories of a place or the way one feels of being in a certain space and time are solely not very idiosyncratic, rather these can also be a shared memory and space through the chemosignals. Chemosignals through which animals and also humans communicate [19] are present in our daily living environment and situations. Due to the perceptible connection of chemosignals between the humans, when these chemosignals are left in the space by one person and get picked up by another person even after a long difference of time, therefore sometimes it can make a person embody a certain emotion left in the space by someone else. Utilizing sensory sensitive information [5] of near environments such as living and working spaces and perceived through our bodies and skins is the next step in designing spaces that extend beyond the physical boundaries of architecture as we know it today.

4   Potentials of Designing Interactions Through Smells

Physical spaces today, are becoming more of a misfit in the light of changing human behavior induced by new technology that keeps our sense of vision and hearing overly stimulated and occupied, architectural elements or vegetation (bushes, trees etc.) in the public spaces become more like a hindrance when one walks while looking only downwards to the digital device. The connections and bonding between the person and the environment are not yet possible in human-computer interactions, since sight and hearing are termed as abstract senses and miss the direct contact. As smell and touch are intimate senses, as these are in reach of the body, whereas sight and hearing are distant senses, where the perception of the environment happens beyond the reach of the body [2]. In the definition of embodied interaction as defined by Dourish, an interaction with the computer systems that occupy our world of physical and social reality [15], the dimensions of smell and touch are a missing piece to make these human-computer interactions as rich as our real physical world. As smell and touch are intimate senses, they not only create a sense of position (geography) but also an emotional bond between the person and the environment [2].

Human-computer interactions that only incorporate the visual and auditory stimulants engaging the attention of the people through the smart devices, dis-engages people from the real physical environment at the same time. Therefore designing interactions for daily living situations, where the focus of the interaction design is on the connectedness to the real physical environment, would be beneficial if the computational technology is in the background rather than being in the forefront [20].

Akin to the above, Dourish uses tangible computing as an overarching term for the computation that is embedded in everyday objects and experiences of the real physical and social world. Among approaches in his suggested investigations, interacting directly through the physical artefacts to inform the computational activities [15] is of a great value for designing multi-sensory experiences that are tangible and also intangible by the way of sensory stimuli.

With a perspective to design experiences in the physical public spaces made for today's scenarios where HCI, AI and AR/VR is a big part of our lives, these spaces would be very different than the status quo. Here, the temporality of a space becomes an interesting concept, as it can help engage the attention of the people with multi-sensorial inputs in that little time and space (Fig. 12).

Fig. 12. Proposed expression of a smell scape in a space

Spaces could have a deeper connection to the inhabitants and a perceptual depth [21] when designing through sensory-sensitive thinking, where smell is an invisible matter to the eyes, but not for the olfactory sense. It is highly intriguing to aesthetically design with smells, with their movements and flow be orchestrated in the space in relation to the body and spatial interactions. Understanding the dynamic characteristic of smells, from their existence in nature, for example in trees, plants, flowers, fruits etc., smells are never obtrusive on the dimension of time, by being equally perceptible all at the same time, rather, these get released as part of a natural process. It unfurls slowly and gets carried away with the flow of air and the intensity of the smell varies when the temperature and humidity level changes.

This paper proposes a potential framework for future research for new ways of designing spaces where it is about slow technology. As an agenda for an interdisciplinary design research based on the design example of Smell, Space and Body movement, can be tracing the patterns of flow of smell molecules in a given space with the help of computational fluid dynamics. This research would be essential to design smellscapes based on the presence of people and their movement in the space (interior or outside). Also, by varying the design drivers such as airflow, temperature and humidity these digital tools could add to the quality of life in terms of facilitating social interactions in public spaces. Hallnäs suggests focus on presence of time to be essential in designing of the computational things, where design is for reflective use rather than for the efficiency which relates to disappearance of time [20] and where the human-computer interactions could connect the physical spaces with the digital spaces, in bringing about everyday life experiences through our senses mediated with the objects and materials in our environment, tangible interactions based on familiarity similar to the social interaction in the real physical world [15]. Through the textile interactions in the discussed design examples, it is the expression of interaction [22] that brings forward the olfactory expressions and potential interactions through our everyday objects and surroundings.

References

1. Gibson, J.J.: The Senses Considered as Perceptual Systems. Houghton Mifflin, Boston (1966)
2. Rodaway, P.: Sensous Geographies: Body, Sense and Place. Routledge, London (1994)
3. Buck, L., Axel, R.: A novel multigene family may encode odorant receptors: a molecular basis for odor recognition. Cell **65**, 175–187 (1991)
4. Classen, C.: Worlds of Sense: Exploring the Senses in History and Across Cultures. Routledge, London and New York (1993)
5. Lally, S.: The Air from Other Planets : A Brief History of Architecture to Come. Lars Müller, Zurich (2013)
6. Barbara, A., Perliss, A.: Invisible Architecture: Experiencing Places Through the Sense of Smell. Ringgold Inc., Portland (2006)
7. Tufnell, M., Crickmay, C.: Body, Space, Image: Notes Towards Improvisation and Performance. Dance Books (1993)
8. Pallasmaa, J.: The Eyes of the Skin: Architecture and the Senses. ed. L. Academy. Wiley, London (2012)

9. Kapur, J.: Smells: olfactive dimension in designing textile architecture (2017)
10. Zumthor, P.: Atmospheres: Architectural Environments: Surrounding Objects. Birkhäuser, Basel (2006)
11. Worbin, L.: Irreversible Colour Expressions. Hogskolan I Borås, Borås (2013)
12. Kaiser, R.: Headspace. In: Future Anterior: Journal of Historic Preservation, History, Theory, and Criticism, pp. 1–9 (2016)
13. Montagu, A.: Touching: The Human Significance of the Skin, 3rd edn. Harper & Row, New York (1986)
14. Erwine, B. (ed.): Creating Sensory Spaces - The Architecture of the Invisible. Taylor & Francis Ltd., Abingdon (2016)
15. Dourish, P.: Where the Action Is: The Foundations of Embodied Interaction. MIT Press, Cambridge (2004)
16. Diaconu, M.: Olfactory design: strategies and applications. In: International Congress of Aesthetics "Aesthetics Bridging Cultures", Turkey (2007)
17. Henshaw, V.: Urban Smellscapes: Understanding and Designing City Smell Environments. Routledge, New York and London (2014)
18. McLean, K.: Smell map narratives of place - Paris. NANO (6) (2014). https://nanocrit.com/issues/issue6/smell-map-narratives-place-paris
19. Semin, G.R.: Mysterious communication: the secret language of chemosignals. In: van Brakel, M., Duerinck, F., Eikelboom, W. (eds.) Sense of Smell, pp. 156–161. Eriskay Connection, Breda (2014)
20. Hallnäs, L., Redström, J.: Interaction Design: Foundations, Experiments. The Interactive Institute. The Textile Research Centre, The Swedish School of Textiles, University College of Borås, Borås (2006)
21. Mori, T.: Immaterial/Ultramaterial: Architecture, Design, and Material. Harvard Design School in Association with George Braziller, Cop., Cambridge (2002)
22. Hallnäs, L.: Textile interaction design. Nord. Text. J., Special Edition Smart Textiles, 104–115 (2008)

Emotion-Aware Ambient Intelligence: Changing Smart Environment Interaction Paradigms Through Affective Computing

Alex Altieri$^{(\boxtimes)}$, Silvia Ceccacci, and Maura Mengoni

Department of Industrial Engineering and Mathematical Sciences,
Università Politecnica delle Marche, Ancona, Italy
a.altieri@pm.univpm.it,
{s.ceccacci,m.mengoni}@univpm.it

Abstract. This paper describes the conceptual model and the implementation of an emotion aware system able to manage multimedia contents (i.e., music tracks) and lightning scenarios, based on the user's emotion, detected from facial expressions. The system captures the emotions from the user's face expressions, mapping them into a 2D valence-arousal space where the multimedia content is mapped and matches them with lighting color. A preliminary experimentation involved a total of 26 subjects has been carried out with the purpose of assess the system emotion recognition effectiveness and its ability to manage the environment appropriately. Results evidenced several limits of emotion recognition through face expressions detection and opens to several research challenges.

Keywords: Emotion-aware system · Ambient intelligence ·
Emotion recognition · Smart environment · Face expression recognition ·
Affective computing · Emotion detection

1 Introduction

Ambient intelligence (AmI) refers to the concept of a smart environment sensitive to its inhabitants, able to support them in an unobtrusive, interconnected, adaptable, dynamic, embedded, and intelligent way, and even capable of anticipating their needs and behaviors [1].

To be reliable and robust, such systems should have the ability to recognize the affective state of the person communicating with, so as to manage their behavior according to this information. Consequently, AmI systems should be equipped with emotional skills and must be able to adapt their users' emotional mood expressing feelings [2].

The recent increase in interest, concerning embedding emotion recognition to HCI systems, gave birth to a newly introduced facet of human intelligence, named as "emotional intelligence" within the more general field of ambient intelligence (AmI) [3]. However, despite for several years, affective computing and emotion analysis have been the focus of researchers in the field of Human-Computer Interaction,

© Springer Nature Switzerland AG 2019
N. Streitz and S. Konomi (Eds.): HCII 2019, LNCS 11587, pp. 258–270, 2019.
https://doi.org/10.1007/978-3-030-21935-2_20

the development of effective AmI systems applications still represents a great challenge today.

A lot of basic research has been carried out in the last years, which has determined some important advances regarding emotion recognition systems. However, despite several studies proposed framework that embedded emotion recognition systems with the purpose to enable AmI systems with emotion regulation capabilities, the majority of them are described only at a conceptual level. By our knowledge, no studies reported experimental results with the aim to assess the effectiveness of the proposed systems. Only [4] reported the results of an experimentation involved users, with the aim to assess user's satisfaction about the emotion regulation capability of the proposed system.

In this context, this paper describes the design of an emotion aware system able to manage multimedia contents (i.e., music tracks) and lightning scenarios, based on the user's emotion, detected from facial expressions. The system conceptual modelling and its implementation and validation in a real scenario are the main contribution of this research work.

2 Related Works

Affective computing, emotion analysis and study of human behaviors have been the focus of researchers in the field of Human-Computer Interaction over a long time [5].

Today several methods and technologies allow the recognition of human emotions, which differ in level of intrusiveness. The majority of such techniques, methods and tools refer to three research areas: facial emotion analysis, speech recognition analysis and biofeedback emotion analysis. Obviously, the use of invasive instruments (e.g., ECG or EEG, biometric sensors) can affect the subjects' behavior and, in particular, it may adulterate his/her spontaneity and accordingly the emotions experienced by them.

In the last years several effort have been made to develop reliable non-intrusive emotion recognition systems, in particular based on facial expression recognition. Facial emotion analysis aims to recognize patterns from facial expressions and to connect them to emotions, based on a certain theoretical model.

Nowadays, the majority of facial expression recognition system implements Deep Learning algorithms, in particular based on Convolutional Neural Networks (CNN), a Deep Learning mathematic model that takes in input different kind of pictures and make predictions on the trained model basis. There have been several models that have been proposed for analyzing emotions from facial expressions. However, the majority of facial expression databases currently available are based on the Ekman and Fresner's primary emotions (i.e., anger, fear, disgust, surprise, joy and sadness) [6]. Consequently, it is not surprising that most of the algorithms developed until now allow to recognize only these emotions. Among the main commercial tools currently available for visual emotional analysis, there is Affdex by Affectiva [7] and the Microsoft Cognitive Services based on the Azure platform [8].

Several studies have been conducted with the aim to develop emotion-aware systems, which embed cognitive agents, to regulate human emotions, for example by managing music and lighting color [2, 9–12].

The proposed framework implements the results of a lot of basic research regarding for example the link between human emotion and color association [13, 14] and the associations between music and colors [15]. Moreover, several methods have been proposed in literature with the aim to classify music tracks according to human emotions [16, 17].

Nowadays, all this knowledge together with the technology available may lead to the effective implementation of new human-computer interaction paradigm, e.g. symbiotic interaction [18]. However, by our knowledge, most of the proposed system are only at a conceptual level. No studies report experimental results able to evidence in a clear manner the real effectiveness of the proposed emotion-aware systems.

3   The Proposed System

A schematic layout of the proposed system architecture is reported in Fig. 1. Five processing nodes characterize it: the face detection, the facial expression recognition, the mood identification, the emotion/music track matching and the emotion/lighting color matching.

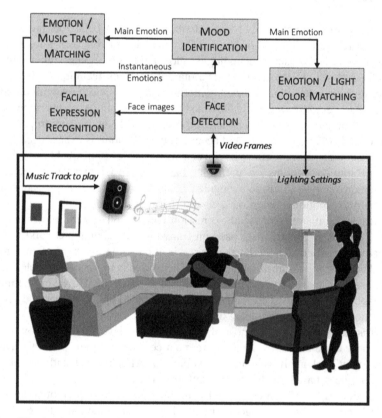

Fig. 1. General architecture of the proposed emotion-aware environment

The face detection node processes the video streams captured by a video camera (e.g., an IP camera). It detects, crops and aligns, frame by frame, the user's face by the original image. The resulted image is resized to 64 × 64 and converted in grayscale.

The facial expression recognition node (FERN) implements a CNN, based on a revised version of the VGG13 [19], which consists of 10 convolution layers spaced with max pooling and dropout layers. It was trained from scratch on the FER+ dataset [20], so that it is able to recognize the six basic Ekman's emotions (i.e., joy, surprise, sadness, anger, disgust and fear), plus the neutral emotion condition. The CNN takes in input the aligned 64 × 64 grayscale images provided by the face detection node and gives in output an array of seven values (Eq. 1), each representing the respective emotion probability.

$$Emotion(t) = (a_t, b_t, c_t, d_t, e_t, f_t, g_t), \quad a_t + b_t + c_t + d_t + e_t + f_t + g_t = 100 \quad (1)$$

The FERN was already tested in a real environment to determine its emotion detection effectiveness compared to a traditional video analysis. Results of experimentation are reported in [21].

Each face image with the associate related emotion data are saved time by time in the background. The mood identification node allows evaluating the main emotion experienced by the user in a certain period. To this end, second by second, it gets and aggregates emotion data related to the video frames collected during a certain acquisition window (e.g., 30 s) and it processes them through an algorithm, in order to determine the resulting "average" emotion.

Emotion data, related to the considered acquisition window, are aggregated within 7 arrays (one per each emotion). To eliminate non-significant emotion data, values lower than 1 are discarded. Then, for each acquisition window, the emotion resultant, representing the user's mood, is determined as the maximum values of the sums of each emotional array elements (Eq. 2).

$$EmotionResultant = \text{MAX}(Joy, Surprise, Fear, Sadness, Anger) \quad (2)$$

Where:

$Joy = \sum_{i=1}^{n} a_i, \quad a_i > 1$
$Suprise = \sum_{i=1}^{n} b_i, \quad b_i > 1$
$Fear = \sum_{i=1}^{n} c_i, \quad c_i > 1$
$Sadness = \sum_{i=1}^{n} d_i, \quad d_i > 1$
$Anger = \sum_{i=1}^{n} e_i, \quad e_i > 1$
$Disgust = \sum_{i=1}^{n} f_i, \quad f_i > 1$
$Neutral = \sum_{i=1}^{n} g_i, \quad g_i > 1$

In order to manage ambient lighting and music playlist according to the user's emotion feelings, it is then necessary to match the detected user's mood with the music tracks and the lighting color that best suit it. To this end, proper algorithms have been defined, which are described in the following paragraphs, with the aim to match lighting color and music with five basic emotions: Joy, Surprise, Fear, Sadness and Anger.

Emotion feelings related to the Neutral mood, have not be considered to actuate ambient modification: the system does not perform any action when it detects a "Neutral" mood. Otherwise, because it is not considered useful to create experiences that arouse disgust, the system immediately stops any music stimulus and provides white lighting when it detects "Disgust".

3.1   Managing Lights Based on Emotions

In order to manage ambient lighting according to users' emotion feelings, by projecting the most appropriate chromatic light through a RGB led lighting system, it has been necessary to define a total of 5 color transitions. To this purpose, a survey was carried out involving about 300 people (58.4% females and 41.6% males), to determine the most suitable color-emotion associations. The questionnaire was managed through Google Surveys and anonymously administered. The user, at first must indicate his generalities (e.g., sex and age). Then he is asked to associate a color with each of the considered basic emotions (i.e., Joy, Surprise, Fear, Anger, Sadness). For each emotion the user is asked to answer to the question: "According to the following color palette, which color would you associate with the emotion X?"

The user must choice a color among a color palette made up of 8 colors (Fig. 2), which can be easy reproduced through an RGB led lighting system.

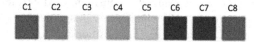

Fig. 2. The color palette

Table 1. Predominant emotions-color associations

Emotion	Color	Result (%)
Joy	C3 (yellow)	46,6
Surprise	C2 (orange)	41,1
Fear	C7 (purple)	42,7
Anger	C1 (red)	71,5
Sadness	C6 (blue)	62,2

Table 1 shows the colors that users have predominantly associated with the five considered emotions. Results revealed in almost all cases a prevalence of a color among the 8 available. At this point, it was possible to associate a color with each emotion and reproduce them through a RGB lighting system.

3.2   Managing Playlist Based on Emotions

In order to classify music tracks according to the emotion feelings they arouse, it is possible to map them on the bi-dimensional valence-energy space, according to the model proposed by Russell in [22]. In fact, based on the results discussed in [23], music characterized by "high-valence/high-arousal" seems to be more related with exciting sensations, while music with "low-valence/low-arousal" is more sad, melancholic and boring and music with "low-valence/high-arousal" are generally associated with tension. Accordingly, we identify on the space valence-arousal a total of 5 areas, which can be respectively associate with five Ekman's basic emotions: surprise, joy, fear, anger and sadness (see the image on the top left corner of Fig. 3). The barycenters of these areas have been considered as starting centroids in a k-means clustering process, which has been applied to subdivide a generic music playlist in a total 5 cluster, respectively related with the five considered emotions.

4   System Implementation and Experimental Test

A system prototype has been deployed in order to support experimentation. A preliminary test has been carried out to assess the system effectiveness. The experiment involved 26 participants: 13 males, 13 females, aged between 23 and 47.

4.1   The Experimental Set-Up

The experimental set-up consists of the following hardware systems:

- A 49" Samsung 4K TV;
- A webcam Logitech Brio 4K;
- Two stereo speakers Logitech Z130;
- An iPad 2018, 9.7", wi-fi;
- A Brightsign Media Player XD233;
- An Intel NUC mini-PC;
- A Crestron DIN-DALI-2 controller;
- Two LINEARdrive 720D eldoLED;
- Two strip led RGBW;
- A router NETGEAR Nighthawk XR500.

The system is based on an architecture of clients/servers positioned within a local network to guarantee the security of the system and not have problems of interference and loss of data between the client and the server and between the various modules and physical peripherals that they are activated by the server (Fig. 4).

A Netgear Nighthawk XR500 router is used for communication within the network and routing packets.

The ipad is connected to the local wifi network and represents the Client of the architecture: the user sends the selection of his favorite kind of music through a web page developed and realized in.Net language.

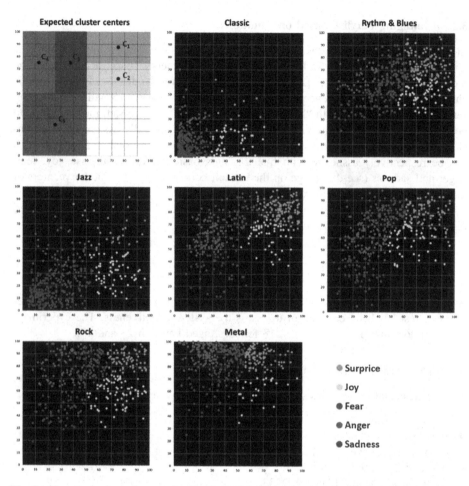

Fig. 3. Hypothetical areas most related with the five basic emotions in the valence-arousal space (on the top left) and results of the k-means process applied to various music playlists

The Samsung TV is positioned on a table 90 cm high and 150 cm distant from the user. The NUC acts as a central server and it is connected via USB to the Logitech webcam, positioned in front of the user on the top of the Samsung TV, which captures 8 frames per second (equal to a frame-rate of 0.125 f/s) and streams the video that will be processed frame by the FERN. The NUC embeds software and REST services that allows to receive the client requests. Such software consists of various modules:

- The FERN CNN developed in Python, which allows to detect and evaluate the facial expressions of the subject and convert them into emotions;
- The data storage in a MySql database;
- The management of data logic developed in C # code.

In particular, the NUC central unit processes the client requests and creates an information package containing:

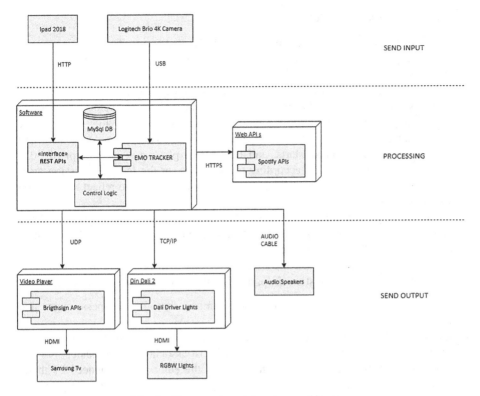

Fig. 4. The experimental system architecture

- The favorite music genre, selected by the user, which is stored in the database;
- The video selected by the user, among a pre-loaded video playlist, which is inserted into an Udp packet and routed through the network to reach a Brightsign xd233 Video player device connected to the LAN.

While the user watching the video on the TV, the system acquires and processes the video streamed by the USB camera, detect the user's face, and recognizes the user's emotions. At the end of the video the decision-making process is activated, and the system provides two outputs, based on the result of the mood identification algorithm, to proper manage respectively the music playlist and lighting.

In particular, the NUC, through an http call to the Spotify web APIs [24], select music tracks belonging to the music genre selected by the user and according on the results of the music management algorithm, it selects the song most related to the detected user's mood.

At the same time, the NUC, based on the result of the color management algorithm builds a DALI package and sends it to the DIN-DALI 2 device via TCP/IP in order to properly manage the two RGBW strips-led through the Eldoled drivers.

4.2   Experimental Procedure

The experimental tests took place in a dimly illuminated room. The experience proposed to the participant was characterized by two phases: a "stimulus phase" and a "reaction phase".

During the "stimulus phase", the subject underwent the viewing of a 30-s video clip (stimulus) selected from the FilmStim database validated by Schaefer's studio and collaborators [25], in order to arouse a particular emotional state. While watching the videos, the subject's facial expressions were analyzed by the system. Once the video has ended, the reaction phase starts, and the system plays a song excerpt of 30 s, through the Spotify Web APIs, according to the results of the facial expression analysis. Moreover, the light system will adapt its color and intensity to reflect the emotion felt by the user during the video.

Before starting the experience, the subjects was asked to select, through the tablet, a music genre between Classic, Rock, R and B, Jazz, Pop, Latin and Metal. Then they were asked to start the video-player.

At the end of the experience, the subject was asked to fill out a questionnaire to assess the reliability of the system. In particular, the subjects were asked to report:

- The main emotion aroused by the video (among fear, joy, sadness, anger and surprise);
- Whereas the proposed music was coherent with the emotion experienced by them. Otherwise, they had to indicate the emotion most associated with music;
- Whereas the proposed light was coherent with the emotion experienced by them. Otherwise, they had to indicate the emotion most associated with the proposed lighting.

Overall, the experience lasts 1 min plus the time needed to fill the questionnaire. The subject were asked to repeat the experience four time: four videos has been proposed to each subject, in order to arouse them: fear, anger, sadness and joy (i.e., amusement). The order of the video clips was previously defined in order to ensure counterbalance across subjects.

In order to avoid any distraction from the tasks, the room has been organized with as fewer objects as possible. To limit the researcher intervention, the experiment was supervised from a different room.

4.3   Results

Experimental results evidenced several issues and limitations that should be addressed to ensure system effectiveness.

In particular, by comparing the system outputs in term of detected mood and emotions the users reported they had experienced (Fig. 5), it is possible to infer that the system is slightly able to effective detect the main emotion the user experiences in a certain time period (i.e., within 30 s).

Despite the CNN, used to detect the facial expressions, as demonstrated by the experimental results reported in [21], is characterized by a good level of reliability, the percentage of mood recognition resulted by the experiment is very low. This may be

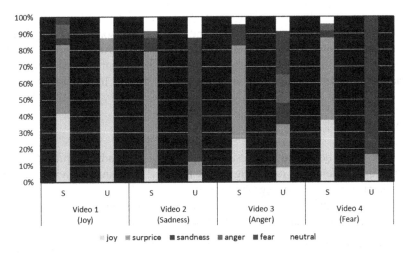

Fig. 5. System effectiveness in terms of mood detection: comparison between mood percentages detected by the system (S) during each video playing and the percentages of emotions the users reported they had experienced.

due to the limits of the algorithms used to determine the prevailing emotion in a time window.

However, although the scarce effectiveness of the system in mood recognition has proved to be poor, it is surprising most of the subjects anyhow have positively evaluated the experience.

In particular, the 73% of the subjects found the color of the proposed lighting coherent with the emotional state they experienced.

This is probably because the majority of users' moods detected by the system are related to the surprise, which has been associate with orange lighting, and a wide variability in user's judgement regarding the emotions associated to the orange color has been observed (Fig. 6).

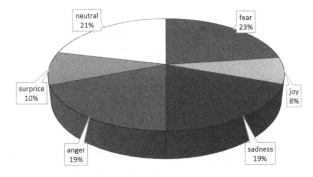

Fig. 6. Emotions aroused to users by orange color. (Color figure online)

Furthermore the 54% of the subjects found a correct association between the emotional experience aroused by the video and the proposed song. However, the small sample of users involved in the experimentation does not allow to deep analyze these results, given the variability of proposed music. Probably, also this result may be due to the variability of user's opinions about the emotions aroused by a song.

5 Conclusion

The present paper described the design, the deployment and experimentation of a emotion-aware system for managing some features of a smart environment (i.e., lighting characteristics and background music).

Experimental results evidenced that the proposed system is still far away from being effective. In particular, several issues have emerged:

- The system resulted slightly able to correctly identify the main emotion perceived by the users during the viewing of the videos, although the FERN can be considered reliable, given the results of previous experimentation [21].

This can be due to the limits of the implemented mood identification algorithm. Several studies have to be carried out to improve the algorithm. For example, several experiments should be carried out to test its effectiveness by varying the threshold value (currently set to 1) defined to limit the effect of ambiguous facial expressions on the user's mood evaluation. However, the conceptual hypothesis on which the algorithm is based (i.e., "The total emotions experienced in a certain period of time is equal to the sum of all the emotions experience in that period") probable is too simplistic and must be revised. As the emotions are time-related, because they occur in response to certain events [26], the algorithm should consider also the temporal relationships between the various facial expressions. Moreover, it is also possible that facial expressions are not sufficient to determine the actual emotional state of the person, so that the collection of other contextual information are needed. In fact, Russell and Fehr [27] argued that context is the principal determinant in interpreting person' s emotion from facial expressions, despite Ekman and O'Sullivan [28] stated that contextual information is only useful to interpret neutral or ambiguous face expressions.

- Even if the system has not been able to detect users' emotions correctly, most of the people involved in the test were satisfied with the music and lighting offered by the system.

In our opinion this result is surprising and can be motivated only if it is admitted that the personal preferences play a role so considerable in the emotion-color association and in the music-color association that it is not possible to hope that an environment management system, according on univocal rules, even if based on statistical findings, can satisfy all users. In this context, the system customization capability seems to be crucial and must be improved. In particular, the possibility to enhance the system adaptability by introducing self-learning functions should be considered.

Acknowledgements. This research has been co-funded by Videoworks spa and Marche Region within the POR Marche FSE 2014/2020 - Asse 1- P.I. 8.1- R.A. 8.5.

References

1. Chen, T.C.T., Chaovalitwongse, W.A., Hong, I.H.: Optimization of ambient intelligence systems. Oper. Res. Int J. **18**, 575 (2018)
2. Acampora, G., Vitiello, A.: Interoperable neuro-fuzzy services for emotion-aware ambient intelligence. Neurocomputing **122**, 3–12 (2013)
3. Frantzidis, C.A., Bratsas, C., Papadelis, C.L., Konstantinidis, E., Pappas, C., Bamidis, P.D.: Toward emotion aware computing: an integrated approach using multichannel neurophysiological recordings and affective visual stimuli. IEEE Trans. Inf. Technol. Biomed. **14**(3), 589–597 (2010)
4. Muñoz, S., Araque, O., Sánchez-Rada, J.F., Iglesias, C.A.: An emotion aware task automation architecture based on semantic technologies for smart offices. Sensors **18**(5), 1499 (2018)
5. Mengoni, M., Peruzzini, M., Mandorli, F., Bordegoni, M., Caruso, G.: Performing ergonomic analysis in virtual environments: a structured protocol to assess humans interaction. In: ASME International Design Engineering Technical Conferences and Computers and Information in Engineering Conference, pp. 1461–1472 (2008)
6. Ekman, P., Friesen, W.V.: Facial Action Coding System: Investigator's Guide. Consulting Psychologists Press, Palo Alto (1978)
7. Affdex. https://www.affectiva.com/product/affdex-for-market-research/. Accessed 7 Feb 2019
8. Microsoft Azure: Cognitive Services. https://azure.microsoft.com/en-us/services/cognitive-services/emotion/. Accessed 7 Feb 2019
9. Fernandez-Caballero, A., et al.: Smart environment architecture for emotion detection and regulation. J. Biomed. Inform. **64**, 55–73 (2016)
10. Acampora, G., Loia, V., Vitiello, A.: A cognitive multi-agent system for emotion-aware ambient intelligence. In: 2011 IEEE Symposium on Intelligent Agent (IA), pp. 1–8 (2011)
11. Acampora, G., Loia, V., Vitiello, A.: Distributing emotional services in ambient intelligence through cognitive agents. Serv. Oriented Comput. Appl. **5**(1), 17–35 (2011)
12. Hsiao, S.W., Chen, S.K., Lee, C.H.: Methodology for stage lighting control based on music emotions. Inf. Sci. **412**, 14–35 (2017)
13. Hemphill, M.: A note on adults' color–emotion associations. J. Genet. Psychol. **157**(3), 275–280 (1996)
14. Naz, K., Epps, H.: Relationship between color and emotion: a study of college students. Coll. Student J. **38**(3), 396 (2004)
15. Palmer, S.E., Schloss, K.B., Xu, Z., Prado-León, L.R.: Music – color associations are mediated by emotion. Proc. Natl. Acad. Sci. **110**(22), 8836–8841 (2013)
16. Kim, Y.E., et al.: Music emotion recognition: a state of the art review. In: Proceedings ISMIR, pp. 255–266. Citeseer (2010)
17. Chang, C.Y., Lo, C.Y., Wang, C.J., Chung, P.C.: A music recommendation system with consideration of personal emotion. In: 2010 International Computer Symposium (ICS), pp. 18–23. IEEE (2010)

18. Jacucci, G., Spagnolli, A., Freeman, J., Gamberini, L.: Symbiotic interaction: a critical definition and comparison to other human-computer paradigms. In: Jacucci, G., Gamberini, L., Freeman, J., Spagnolli, A. (eds.) Symbiotic 2014. LNCS, vol. 8820, pp. 3–20. Springer, Cham (2014). https://doi.org/10.1007/978-3-319-13500-7_1
19. Simonyan, K., Zisserman, A.: Very deep convolutional networks for large-scale image recognition. arXiv preprint arXiv:1409.1556 (2014)
20. Barsoum, E., Zhang, C., Ferrer, C.C., Zhang, Z.: Training deep networks for facial expression recognition with crowd-sourced label distribution. In: Proceedings of the 18th ACM International Conference on Multimodal Interaction, pp. 279–283 (2016)
21. Generosi, A., Ceccacci, S., Mengoni, M.: A deep learning-based system to track and analyze customer behavior in retail store. In: 2018 IEEE 8th International Conference on Consumer Electronics-Berlin (ICCE-Berlin), pp. 1–6. IEEE (2018)
22. Russell, J.A.: A circumflex model of affect. J. Pers. Soc. Psychol. **37**(3), 1161 (1980)
23. Kim, J., Lee, S., Kim, S., Yoo, W.Y.: Music mood classification model based on arousal-valence values. In: 13th International Conference on Advanced Communication Technology (ICACT), pp. 292–295 (2011)
24. Spotify web APIs. https://developer.spotify.com/documentation/web-api/. Accessed 7 Feb 2019
25. Schaefer, A., Nils, F., Sanchez, X., Philippot, P.: Assessing the effectiveness of a large database of emotion-eliciting films: a new tool for emotion researchers. Cogn. Emot. **24**(7), 1153–1172 (2010)
26. Ekman, P.: Facial expression and emotion. Am. Psychol. **48**(4), 384 (1993)
27. Russell, J.A., Fehr, B.: Relativity in the perception of emotion in facial expressions. J. Exp. Psychol. Gen. **116**(3), 223 (1987)
28. Ekman, P., O'Sullivan, M.: The role of context in interpreting facial expression: comment on Russell and Fehr (1987). J. Exp. Psychol. Gen. **117**(1), 86–88 (1988)

Emotion Detection Affected Soothing Device

Shijian Luo[1,2(✉)], Ping Shan[1], Chengyi Shen[1], Yuke Song[3],
Yufei Zhang[1], Ze Bian[1], and Zhitong Cui[1]

[1] Department of Industrial Design, Zhejiang University,
Hangzhou 310027, China
sjluo@126.com, 403191990@qq.com, 634906847@qq.com,
359243864@qq.com, {shenchengyi,21721008}@zju.edu.cn
[2] Design Industrial Innovation Center, China Academy of Art,
Hangzhou 310024, China
[3] Faculty of Industrial Design Engineering, Delft University of Technology,
2600 AA Delft, The Netherlands
yuke_song@sina.com

Abstract. The fast-paced life of modern metropolises often makes people busy with their lives, working hard for their ideals and accumulating tremendous psychological pressure. The thirst for success has led people to gradually ignore their mental health problems, and people's emotional communication is also decreasing.

Although Emotional comfort products on the market fill the gaps in such products in the market to a certain extent, and plays a certain role in promoting emotional stability in the short term, it cannot attract users to use it for a long time. They are often not smart enough, so they require high learning costs; the interaction is relatively simple, so the utilization rate is usually not high. There is a lack of such mental health products in the market that are closely related to the emotional life of the metropolis.

We find a method appease emotions by obtain emotional data and interact with the acousto-optic device based on physiological detection, to explore the possibility of effectively and empirically managing emotions. The main functions realized are: monitoring emotions, giving interactive feedback on the sound, and giving interactive feedback on the light.

The research was carried out in three stages, using desktop research, key user interviews and other methods to collect analysis and design requirements, using the arduino suite to build prototypes, using questionnaire interviews, scenario reconstruction and other methods to collect improvement suggestions.

Keywords: Interactive design · Smart devices · Emotional appeasement · Urban youth's pressure

1 Introduction

Health is the eternal pursuit of mankind. People not only pursue physical health, but also mental health. Emotional life is closely related to people's mental health. However, with the fast-paced life of contemporary people, the contradiction of material richness and lack of emotions has gradually entered people's sight. Busy urban life

© Springer Nature Switzerland AG 2019
N. Streitz and S. Konomi (Eds.): HCII 2019, LNCS 11587, pp. 271–285, 2019.
https://doi.org/10.1007/978-3-030-21935-2_21

often puts people's emotions in a state of high tension and exhaustion. Once a fuse event occurs, it is easy to get out of control. If such a stressful group lacks basic emotional comfort for a long time, it will aggravate their emotional instability, causing excessive emotional excitement and causing unnecessary troubles for daily work.

Young people in urban areas tend to be more impulsive. They often want to live a happy life and are full of fighting spirit for their careers. However, the reality may not be satisfactory in the short term, and the huge pressure is easy to make them into an impatient state of mind, leading to problems such as excessive emotions. In the long run, it will affect mental health, even from mental health to physical health. For example, their bad mentality makes them fall into the infinite loop of working overtime and night, thus affecting their health.

Nowadays, daily necessities are gradually becoming wearable and intelligent. The mainstream intelligent wearable devices on the market are more targeted at the field of physiological health management. Most of them are monitoring the heart rate, pulse, and number of steps in various scenarios. The homogenization is very serious. Emotional awareness products focusing on the field of mental health management are few, and often stop at the collection and presentation of front-end data, and rarely interact with the user substantially. Even though there are some interactive smart product exploration studies that can provide people with a healthy and safe lifestyle [1], their target population is rarely urban youth.

Therefore, we study a kind of intelligent emotional comfort products that focus on the mental health of urban youth. Products are divided into monitoring modules and feedback modules. The monitoring module is based on an emotional signal acquisition method. The MIT Media Lab's Emotional Computing Research Group was the first to systematically study the emotion recognition based on physiological signals, and proved that it is feasible to extract feature patterns from physiological signals for emotion recognition. A large number of studies have shown that people's information measured by physiological indicators has a strong correlation with emotions and music [2]. Among dozens of physiological indicators, we selected the Galvanic skin response (GSR), which is commonly used in physiological signals for sentiment analysis research, to design the monitoring module [3].

The feedback module explores the channels of product interaction that are appropriate for emotional comfort. We are inspired by the interaction of several sets of innovative attempts [4, 5]. These studies focus on the emotional changes of the user, classify the GSR signals and control the module to provide feedback on different modes. In this way create a subtle sense of communication, generate appease impact on user emotion, even if it comes from their own exchanges. Under the trend of intelligence, attempts to emotionally appease have also been tried in wearable smart products [6, 7]. We also try to make product prototypes more wearable and naturally integrate into people's daily lives.

2   Method

2.1   User Interviews with Target Groups

In order to better understand the user's understanding of emotional comfort products and user demand functions, we used a single interview with the target users to gain a deeper understanding of the target population. The target population is mainly young people aged 20 to 35 who are prone to temperament. In this interview, a total of 4 young people with temperament tendencies were invited. The basic information is shown in Table 1. These four people already have some emotional comfort products. We arranged four in-depth interviews for them. Each interview lasts approximately 40 min and is recorded in a comfortable environment with notes and recordings. The content and purpose of the interview outline are shown in Table 2.

Table 1. Basic information maps of the interviewed participants

Code	Identity	Gender	Age	Background description
A	Single	Male	24	Designer, bachelor's degree No emotional management knowledge background
B	Single	Female	26	Ph.D., bachelor degree Have emotional management knowledge
C	Married	Male	28	Programmer, master's degree No emotional management knowledge background
D	Married and have child	Female	35	Clerk, college degree No emotional management knowledge background

Through interviews, we learned that although the subjects had ordinary emotional comfort products at home, the utilization rate was not high. Mainly because these types of emotional comfort products interact in a single way, or require a lot of extra efforts from users. People would lose novelty after a period of time, and instead bored. Users are often attracted to the efficacy of such products, but they do not use these products for a long time, and soon lose interest. Even if the user does not give up using it, it is usually unsatisfactory due to the lack of background in their emotional management knowledge. Such products are also often complained of being idle, easy to accumulate, and occupying living space.

Through interviews, we learned a few key points:

1. Enhancing the interaction of such emotional comfort products is conducive to attracting users to use the product for a long time.
2. Users want to improve the utilization of emotional comfort products.
3. Most emotional comfort products are not smart enough, requiring users to have a certain emotional management knowledge background, in order to make reasonable use of them, the learning cost is high.

Table 2. Contents and purposes of the interview outline

Interview stage	Time	Content	Purpose
First stage	5 min	Self introduction; the rules described; warm field	Allow participants to relax and gain trust, paving the way for the smooth progress of the following interviews
Second stage	10 min	The situation of the participants; the traditional emotional comfort products and the Intelligent emotional comfort products that participants usually contact	Get the basic personal information of the participants, and explore their interests in the product, the motivation to purchase and the high frequency factors considered
Third phase	15 min	The situation of ordinary emotional comfort products and intelligent emotional comfort products in the home of the participants	Learn about the current use of emotional comfort products and find our design opportunities
Fourth stage	10 min	Understand the relevant content of the emotional management knowledge background of the participants; the daily activities of the participants at home and their future emotional management plans	Get the emotional management skills of the participants and their interest in the way of appeasement; get their views on emotional management

4. Users hope that these products are small in size and easy to store and clean.
5. The factors that users often consider: price, utilization, use effect, aesthetics and land occupation factors.

2.2 Design Testing and Verification Based on Emotional Signal Acquisition and Analysis

Test Purposes. According to the personality scale filled out by the subjects, the emotionally unstable persons are selected. We mimicked the preference of tempers in a home environment for specific sensory stimuli to determine the main function of our product prototype. And test the manifestations of specific sensory stimuli suitable for emotional comfort. For example, light, music, family voice, smell, etc.

Subject Selection. Based on the grasp and understanding of the characteristics of the tempers, a questionnaire was prepared, supplemented by the Eysenck Personality Questionnaire, and 20 subjects were selected. 10 of them were normal, as a control group; the other 10 were emotionally unstable, as an experimental group.

Test Environment. The laboratory is arranged in an environment similar to the living room, with dim light and room temperature controlled at a suitable temperature of 26 ° C. During the experiment, the experimenter and the participant use the voice plug-in to communicate with each other, and use the front camera of the computer to record the test video (Fig. 1).

Fig. 1. Lab environments

Test Content. Based on previous research, we decided to use the GSR data as the main measurement data. Specific music and breathing lights are used as the main emotional inducing material, supplemented by olfactory stimuli (such as sandalwood scent) to induce the subject's emotions. After the experiment, the self-reported report method and the questionnaire survey method are used to evaluate the feedback effect.

Test Results. The participants were better emotionally evoked with music and lights. Musical changes have a greater impact on emotions. Users are generally able to accept music, lighting stimuli, and show emotional consistency with certain music. However, in the sense of smell, individual differences are large, and it is difficult to find a certain law. So we choose music, lights to interact with users.

2.3   User Requirements Summary

Target users: emotional Irritable urban youths in Asia, with $15,000 to $25,000 pear year incomes.

1. User Insight
    i. Users expect a calm mood, but often lack knowledge of emotional regulation.
   ii. The lack of energy distribution and lack of learning ability caused by fast-paced modern life.
  iii. The pursuit of the principle of convenience and efficiency, the consumer psychology brought about by public opinions.
2. Benefit commitment
    i. Reducing the ineffective emotional regulation of emotionally unstable urban youth, due to lack of experience.
   ii. Reduce the time allocation of emotionally unstable urban youth who want to relieve symptoms but are busy with work.

iii. Reducing the physical and mental exhaustion and health hazards caused by repeated emotional outbursts among emotionally unstable urban youth.
3. Support points
    i. The GSR monitoring module.
    ii. The music selective playing module and the light-prompting module.
4. Summary

Save time and effectively alleviate emotional instability in urban youth. "Easy, experienced" regulates emotions.

3   The Experimental Description

3.1   Hardware System Concept Design

The design of this equipment is mainly divided into four parts, product modeling and structural design, intelligent hardware and circuit design, monitoring unit and hardware communication implementation, experimental design and evaluation.

Realize the functions of 3 products:

1. Monitor GSR data in real time, judge and send instructions. The feedback mode is adjusted according to the intensity change of the excessive emotion. Through the preliminary research and experimental verification, the most intuitive and convenient GSR monitoring method was selected.
    i. Real-time monitoring of the user's GSR value and quick response to read data;
    ii. Based on the results of previous studies, make reasonable judgments on physiological monitoring data and grade excessive emotions;
    iii. Send the corresponding instruction according to the level of emotion;
    iv. Read and record in a natural way. Comply with the humanized improvement trend of monitoring methods, optimize the monitoring experience, and simplify the operation procedures. Users do not need to take the initiative to operate, only need to touch the sensor, and then the monitoring module can monitor and record.
2. Adjust the excessive emotions by performing different audible feedback according to the received instructions. The instructions are passed through the processor, and the commands are communicated to the feedback device to enable a targeted response mode, provide a follow-up processing solution for monitoring and judgment, and perform acoustic stimulation. After receiving the GSR grading instruction, the music of the appropriate emotion is selected according to the emotion level for playing.
    i. After receiving the excessive emotion leveling instruction, the corresponding sounds (music, voice, etc.) can be played according to the type preset by the user to stimulate their emotional relief response.
    ii. The SIM card stores the sound library, and when the instruction is received, the corresponding track can be adjusted.
    iii. Tap to turn off the sound feedback.

3. According to the received instructions, the light feedback of different blinking frequencies is adjusted to relieve the excessive emotion. The instructions pass through the processor, the commands are communicated to the feedback device, the targeted response mode is turned on, the subsequent processing scheme for monitoring and judgment is provided, and visual stimulation is performed. Using the principles of phototherapy, combined with music therapy, it is suitable for the home environment, providing a calming training in daily life.

    i. After receiving the over-excited emotion grading instruction, the corresponding light flashing frequency can be controlled according to the type preset by the user, the mood fluctuation is visually displayed, the user is prompted to control the emotion, and the user can enter the state of peace of mind with a slight delay.

    ii. Set the phototherapy flicker frequency and time period for different modes.

    iii. Tap to turn off the light feedback.

Implementation of communication between the monitoring unit and other hardware:

The main method to realize the communication between the monitoring device and other hardware is to connect the single-chip microcomputer through the Bluetooth module, and connect the monitoring device and other hardware devices to the same Bluetooth communication environment, so that the two can communicate.

The wireless module of the monitoring device mainly sends the judged information to the hardware device, such as whether the emotion is excessive, the degree of excessive stimulation, and the like. The Bluetooth module of other hardware devices receives, and after processing, the corresponding feedback command is sent to the feedback device, thereby changing the feedback mode of the feedback device, such as performing a voice interaction mode or a visual interaction mode.

The information transmitted by the monitoring device to the hardware device is mainly the human physiological signal data collected by the components in the detecting device. Maintain a real-time feedback and prepare for the next calculation. With the development of open source hardware platforms such as Arduino, the project can transmit the information of user emotional judgment and user status information to the user's mobile phone application in real time through the Bluetooth module through the combination of various monitors and single-chip microcomputers. The monitor includes sensitive electronic components such as SRG electrodes, and one of the best experimental results is suitable for the product.

Hardware Prototype System Principle. Both the monitoring device and the intelligent hardware portion of the main body will be designed in one piece to simplify the cumbersome operation. In the structure of the device, the monitoring device and the feedback device are separated, and Bluetooth communication is used for data transmission. The main body of the monitoring device is a ring-shaped object that can be worn on the end of the user's limb, such as an arm, thereby reducing the impact on the user's activity experience. Considering that the monitor has a certain degree of vulnerability, it is designed as an independent, integrally detachable part. This layout also facilitates the replacement of physiological indicators monitors of different characteristics according to the user's monitoring preferences, and the overall design has certain environmental adaptability. The sound and light equipment is hidden in the main device box, and the position of the voice device will be slightly higher, thereby increasing the sound quality and convenience of voice input and output. The position of the sensor is arranged in the monitor section, and the information collected for different human parameters should be adaptive.

From the outside to the inside, the main body of the device can be divided into three parts: the inner layer is the intelligent hardware board, which stores the single-chip microcomputer and the power amplifier board; the external unit of the inner layer is equipped with the Bluetooth module and the power supply part such as the battery; The outer layer is a monitoring or feedback mechanism, since all sensors, voice equipment, and bulb parts need to be exposed for good results, so all relevant parts are placed separately.

Through previous research, we began to develop prototypes with original features based on our design concepts for product testing in the later evaluation phase. The basic working principle of the hardware system is:

1. Bluetooth connects the prototype of the monitoring device and feedback device.
2. According to the results of the previous experiments, music tracks with good emotional comfort are selected and stored in the TF card in advance. The sensor of the GSR module detects the change of the physiological reading, and when the value of the single chip determines that the value is greater than the reference value, the voice module plays the corresponding music, and the sound is emitted through the power amplifier board and the speaker.
3. At the same time, the sensor of the GSR module detects the change of the physiological reading, and when the value of the single chip determines that the value is greater than the reference value, the bulb flashes at different frequencies.

Motherboard and Sensor Selection. Under the trend of open source, DIY intelligent hardware has become a lot of fun. We can buy various types of hardware accessories through many ways such as online shopping, and assemble monitoring, processing and feedback devices that can complete this design function.

1. Motherboard

The core of the functions in this system is the open source motherboard microcontroller. The Arduino Yun from Arduino comes with WIFI module, Ethernet function and Bluetooth function, which is very suitable for the development of this project. Motherboard's size, only 53 × 19 × 12 mm, comes with integrated Bluetooth 4.0 module, which can achieve the interconnection between the two controllers, and has a strong Bluetooth communication capabilities, ideal for the current prototype development needs. However, during the actual construction of the prototype, we used the more easily understood Arduino Yun R3 board and HC05 Bluetooth module to achieve the function.

2. Bionic sensor

We chose the Grove - GSR module to collect the user's physiological data. This module measures GSR to measure skin conductivity. Strong emotions can stimulate the sympathetic nervous system, causing sweat glands to secrete more sweat, which affects skin conductivity. Simply connecting the two electrodes to the appropriate skin surface reveals strong mood swings. This fun piece of equipment is great for creating emotionally relevant projects that are great for our projects.

3. Broadcast module

We chose Waveshare's Music Shield module as an audio player to provide music interaction. It is based on the Arduino standard interface design and is compatible with UNO and Leonardo development boards. The board has a 74VHC125 level conversion chip that is compatible with 3.3 V and 5 V microcontroller interfaces. The module has a TF card slot, and can access the TF card to play audio files therein. The module is based on the VS1053B audio decoder chip and supports common audio file formats such as MP3/AAC/WMA/WAV/MIDI. Moreover, there is a MIC recording function on the board, and 2S and MIDI interfaces are introduced in this area, which is advantageous for function expansion (Fig. 2).

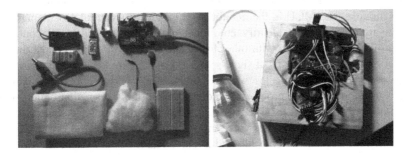

Fig. 2. Monitoring module materials, feedback module materials

In order to implement the product module function, the following materials are required (Tables 3 and 4):

Table 3. Monitoring module materials

Name	Model	Number
Arduino Uno board	R3	1
GSR module	Grove - GSR	1
GSR electrode	/	2
Bluetooth module	HC05	1
Battery	/	1
Battery holder	/	1
DuPont line	/	Several

Table 4. Feedback module materials

Name	Model	Number
Arduino uno board	R3	1
Arduino data transmission line	/	1
Music shield module	VS1053	1
Speaker	/	2
Light bulb	220 V	1
Electromagnetic Relay	TM58H	1
Touch switch	TTP223B	1
Amplifier board	PAM8403	1
Bluetooth module	HC05	1
DuPont line	/	Several

Hardware Prototype Design and Implementation. The entire product intelligent hardware prototype is divided into two modules: the monitoring module and the feedback module. The MCU in the mainboard area acts as a central processing unit to coordinate user commands, identify emotional grading commands, and control the operation of the entire system with other hardware devices; the sensing area monitors the user's emotional physiological signals and transmits them back to the main board; the Bluetooth area communicates with the monitoring device. Obtaining hardware control instructions from the processing end or transmitting information obtained from the monitoring system such as GSR signal or temperature, heart rate, etc. to the processing end; the sounding area has voice input and output devices related to the voice service; the light area has a light bulb and a relay. The modular system uses a lithium battery to power the entire system and can also be powered by USB (Fig. 3).

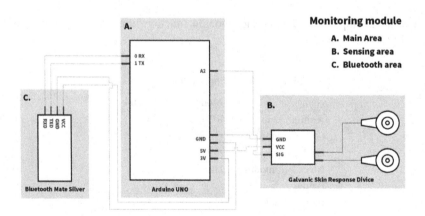

Fig. 3. Circuit design of the monitoring module

1. **Monitoring module**

The monitoring module realizes its function of detecting, transmitting and receiving commands through the GSR electrode, the single chip microcomputer and the Bluetooth module. It can monitor the user's GSR value in real time, quickly respond to the read data and analyze it to grade the emotional value, and finally output the control command. The instructions are simple and the operation is easy to control. The entire hardware prototype is divided into three areas: the main board area, the sensing area and the Bluetooth area (see Fig. 4).

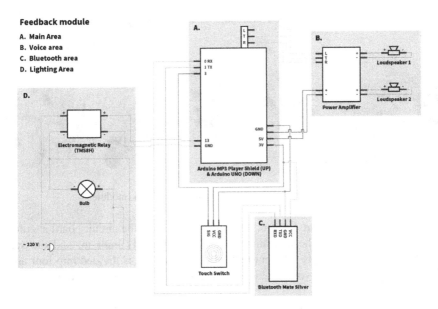

Fig. 4. Circuit design of the feedback module

Motherboard area: This area is the Aduino Yun controller that records the program. It mainly includes two functions: Accepting the GSR signal; transmitting the signal to the Bluetooth module.

Sensing area: This area integrates 2 GSR electrodes and Grove - GSR module board. Logic flow: The GSR electrode detects the GSR analog signal and transmits it to the Grove - GSR module board for processing and conversion to become a digital signal. Thereby measuring the skin conductivity and collecting the physiological data of the user.

Bluetooth area: Sends the monitored physiological signal (Fig. 5).

2. **Feedback module**

The information is collected through the Bluetooth module, and the data is processed by the single-chip microcomputer carried by the feedback module to drive the external music module and the light bulb module to realize sound interaction and light interaction. Due to indoor environment restrictions, the size of the monitoring module

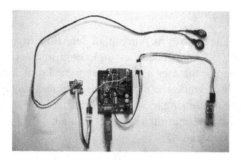

Fig. 5. Prototype construction of the monitoring module

Fig. 6. Prototype construction of the feedback module

and the feedback module are limited. Therefore, the size of the circuit board should be reduced reasonably, and the appearance should be properly built in, and the space should be arranged carefully. The entire hardware prototype is divided into four areas: the main board area, the voice area, the lighting area, and the Bluetooth area (see Fig. 6).

Motherboard area: This area is the Aduino Uno controller that has programmed the program. It mainly includes four functions: Identifies and grades the received GSR signals; Control the flashing of the light according to the level mode; Control the playback of music tracks according to the level mode.

Light area: The main board control light flashes at different frequencies to guide the user to calm down. This area consists mainly of a light bulb and a relay.

Sounding area: The Music Shield module accepts the grading signal from the output of the motherboard, plays the corresponding music track in the TF card, and sounds through the speaker enhanced by the power amplifier.

Bluetooth area: Receives monitored physiological signals.

3.2 Product Design System Testing

Test Purposes. A total of two experiments were performed, once when the functional unit was basically implemented, once when the initial model was established. This facilitates immediate adjustment of the product's function and verification of the product's user experience.

The first experiment tested the main function of the product: user preferences in auditory stimulation. Create an audio library with the best effect audio type.

The second experiment tested the user experience of the product: to correct the poor user experience details found, and to improve the product's unreasonable settings.

Subject Selection and Environment. Based on the grasp and understanding of the characteristics of the violent people, a questionnaire was prepared, supplemented by the Eysenck Personality Questionnaire, and 5 typical subjects were selected.

The laboratory is arranged in an environment similar to the living room, with dim light and room temperature controlled at a suitable temperature of 26 °C.

Test Content. In order to optimize the experimental results, we hid the prototype of the previously built circuit into the appearance of the product, and made a product prototype for test evaluation. Use the observation method, oral report method, and questionnaire survey method to carry out evaluation tests.

1. Learning Adaptation: Use observation method combined with video observation and record the duration, fluency and difficulties encountered by users in learning products.
2. The dictation report intuitively describes the experience: using the method of think aloud to visually describe the user's experience of the product.
3. Suggestions for improvement: Use the model of questionnaire survey to obtain suggestions for improvement of users (Fig. 7).

Fig. 7. Product prototypes for testing

Test Results. Participants were curious about the way and principle of prototype interaction, so prototype stimulated their interest in operation to some extent. Most of the time, they showed positive emotional feedback and a good emotional calming effect. Few participants experienced obstructive pauses in operation, and only one was dissatisfied because he could not change his mood in a short time to achieve the effect of switching mode. Most participants can quickly learn how to use the prototype, but some think that the monitoring module is too large and affects the activity experience.

Others have suggested improving the color and shape of the light module, hiding more exposed wires in the prototype, and associating them with the mobile app to make it easier to operate.

4 Discussions

Paper introduces an emotional comfort device based on physiological detection. We analyze and locate the product functions according to the user's wishes and usage scenarios. Then we conducted a design study on the prototype of the product system, and summarized the comprehensive influencing factors and potential contradictions and divergence points that the target users usually have in the process of using the product. Finally, we constructed an intelligent prototype based on the conclusions obtained, and realized the code writing and hardware construction of each module. In the process, we also conducted two evaluation tests on the prototype, providing directional suggestions for improving the prototype.

Combining the analysis of users and products, refining the principles of user expectations and functional design features of products; summarizing the design methods guiding product design, providing new ideas for the design of emotional comfort products. The purpose of designing and developing intelligent emotional comfort products in this paper is to design a smart wearable product that can naturally integrate into the living habits of target users; increase the interest of users to interact with products, and attract users to maintain emotional management for a long time. This allows users to maintain emotional stability and promote their mental health for a long time.

In our research, the stability of the sensor components and the spatial layout of the circuit have much room for improvement and can be further studied. Nor do we have a quantitative and qualitative study of the relationship between the level of understanding of emotional management knowledge and the appropriate way of interacting. This kind of analysis needs to study the correlation between the emotional management background of a large number of target users and their operational data and error rate, thus providing guidance for emotional management behavior.

Acknowledgement. This research was supported by the National Natural Science Foundation of China (No. 51675476).

References

1. Capodieci, A., Budner, P., Eirich, J., Gloor, P., Mainetti, L.: Dynamically adapting the environment for elderly people through smartwatch-based mood detection. In: Grippa, F., Leitão, J., Gluesing, J., Riopelle, K., Gloor, P. (eds.) Collaborative Innovation Networks. SESCID, pp. 65–73. Springer, Cham (2018). https://doi.org/10.1007/978-3-319-74295-3_6
2. Huang, W., Bortz, B., Knapp, R.B.: Exploring the causal relationships between musical features and physiological indicators of emotion. In: International Conference on Affective Computing and Intelligent Interaction, vol. 6, pp. 560–566. IEEE (2015)

3. Healey, J.: Sensing affective experience. In: Westerink, J.H.D.M., Ouwerkerk, M., Overbeek, T.J.M., Pasveer, W.F., de Ruyter, B. (eds.) Probing Experience. PRBS, vol. 8, pp. 91–100. Springer, Dordrecht (2008)
4. Müller, L., Keune, S., Bernin, A., Vogt, F.: Emotional interaction with surfaces - works of design and computing. In: Herrlich, M., Malaka, R., Masuch, M. (eds.) ICEC 2012. LNCS, vol. 7522, pp. 457–460. Springer, Heidelberg (2012). https://doi.org/10.1007/978-3-642-33542-6_52
5. You, Y., Tang, T., Wang, Y.: When arduino meets kinect: an intelligent ambient home entertainment environment. In: International Conference on Intelligent Human-Machine Systems and Cybernetics, vol. 2, pp. 150–153. IEEE (2014)
6. Williams, M.A., Roseway, A., O'Dowd, C., Czerwinski, M., Morris, M.R.: SWARM: an actuated wearable for mediating affect. In: International Conference on Tangible, Embedded, and Embodied Interaction, pp. 293–300. ACM (2015)
7. Luo, S., Wang, Y., Xiong, N., Shan, P., Zhou, Y.: An interactive smart music toy design for children. In: Streitz, N., Konomi, S. (eds.) DAPI 2018. LNCS, vol. 10921, pp. 372–390. Springer, Cham (2018). https://doi.org/10.1007/978-3-319-91125-0_31

Sensing Creatures: Tools for Augmenting Our Sensory Awareness of Space

Athina Papadopoulou[✉]

Massachusetts Institute of Technology, Cambridge, MA 02139, USA
athpap@mit.edu

Abstract. Architecture education has prioritized vision over the other senses and has been detached from the direct experience of space. To extend our sensory understanding of space, this paper proposes the use of computational tools for body-centered situated learning of space, and discusses precedents in sensory pedagogies and embodied learning. The paper demonstrates the pedagogical implications of the use of such tools by describing the method, procedure, and results of a narrative-based study that utilizes wearable devices in the role of "sensing creatures" limited to a particular sense. In the study, participants were asked to explore a physical space while being the host of a sensing creature. It was hypothesized that the sensing creatures can act as perceptual filters, allowing us to focus on each of our senses individually in order to expand our understanding of space. It was demonstrated that the sensing creatures augmented participants' sensory awareness of space by engaging them in a sensory exploration, which, while stemming from the specific sense under study extended to the rest of the senses. The study suggests a new direction towards a sensory pedagogy of space based on the perceptual and psychological impact of wearable computational tools when used in the exploration of physical spaces.

Keywords: Sensory experience · Wearable tools · Architecture education

1 Introduction

Although we experience space through all of our senses [1], architecture education tends to focus on the formal visual qualities of space at the expense of the rest of the senses. Moreover, common teaching approaches tend to detach design from the direct experience of space, limiting the creative process within the design studio. Architecture, through the sensory qualities of its material and environmental properties, has a direct impact on our psychology and wellbeing. The impact of the built environment on our sensory experience, health, and psychology has been the subject of research in environmental psychology for decades [2]. Unfortunately, relevant studies have so far had only tangential influence on the formal education of architects. Architectural discourse and studio culture continue to prioritize vision over the other senses and abstract, formal knowledge over in-situ, experiential spatial exploration.

© Springer Nature Switzerland AG 2019
N. Streitz and S. Konomi (Eds.): HCII 2019, LNCS 11587, pp. 286–303, 2019.
https://doi.org/10.1007/978-3-030-21935-2_22

Fig. 1. A participant in the study exploring the MIT Chapel, designed by Eero Saarinen, using the "sensing creature" as an Object-to-sense-with.

In order to incorporate a greater sensory awareness of space into the design process, we need to develop tools for situated learning strategies focused on the interaction between our bodies and the built environment. This paper presents the procedure and results of a study on a sensory spatial learning method that utilizes wearable sensing tools in the exploration of physical spaces (Fig. 1). The suggested method aims to expand our sensory understanding of space by focusing on each of the senses individually, an idea inspired by Maria Montessori's sensory training exercises [3], which were later integrated in design teaching at the Bauhaus school [4]. In previous work, the author discussed the use of sensing tools in spatial learning and coined the term "objects-to-sense-with" [5] alluding to Seymour Papert's term "objects-to-think-with," a term Papert used to signify the role of technological tools as vehicles for situated and self-directed learning [6]. The study presented here demonstrates how tools can become extensions of our bodies and minds, an idea supported by theories and research on distributed cognition [7] and extended cognition [8].

2   Framework

2.1   Education of the Senses

To suggest a methodology that addresses matters of sensory perception in situated learning of space, this study draws upon the sensory pedagogies of Maria Montessori and László Moholy-Nagy. Maria Montessori, a radical educator of her time, was inspired by the sensory training methods used by physicians of special education in the middle of the 19th and the beginning of the 20th centuries, including Jean-Marc Gaspar Itart and Edouard Seguin [9]. The goal of the education of the senses as formulated by Montessori in the Montessori Method was "the refinement of the differential perception of stimuli by means of repeated exercises" [3]. In the Montessori Method, Montessori describes techniques for the training of each of the senses individually through the use of special sets of didactic material, from wooden blocks and textured tactile samples to train the sense of touch, to sets of bells to train the sense of sound.

Focusing on each of the senses individually was an important aspect of Montessori's sensory education, because isolating the sensory modality of the particular qualities under study allowed students to gain greater insights. For example, to train their sense of touch, children had to be blindfolded in order to focus on the differences between a variety of textures, undistracted by the primacy of the eye (Fig. 2). To train the sense of sound, children would be asked to discriminate between the different played sounds while seated in a dark room. Montessori motivated students to develop their own tools for acquiring knowledge and evaluating the world around them. Part of what made Montessori's methods so progressive was that they were to a great extent focused on self-discovery and self-instruction [3].

Montessori's radical pedagogical approaches were introduced into architecture education at the Bauhaus school, in László Moholy-Nagy's design studio. His studio focused on sensory training exercises and the development of tools to enhance the appreciation of the sensory qualities of the material environment. The studio's agenda, addressed to first-year students of the Bauhaus school, aimed at broadening the students' sensory experiences and allowing them to gain a more refined appreciation of textures and tectonics based on direct sensory knowledge of material objects rather than on descriptions. Through the sensory training exercises introduced in the studio, students were able to build a sensory repertoire by distinguishing between subtle sensory differences. To study tactile qualities, they designed tactile charts like the "Luna park for the fingers"; to study the senses of smell, they designed special instruments like the "smell-o-meter." The developed projects allowed students to both study the subtleties of particular modalities and document them diagrammatically by visualizing them [4].

2.2   Objects-to-sense-with

Montessori and Moholy-Nagy's experiments were limited to classroom exercises and engagement with material objects. Such exercises, although important in familiarizing students with the different sensory qualities of objects, do not engage students in the actual physical exploration of spaces. Today's sensing technologies can help us invent new didactic tools towards a body-centered, sensory-based education of space, reframing the education of the senses of the early 20th century within today's technological and cultural context.

Fig. 2. Training the sense of touch. *The Montessori Method* (Montessori, 1912, p. 283)

Sensing technologies are often used today to track changes in our body and mood and to help us organize our work life, regulate our emotional health, and manage our physical health. The action of tracking oneself is viewed by some, and particularly by the proponents of the "Quantified Self" movement, as a means to increase self-awareness and to allow greater access to information regarding one's body. Self-Tracking, according to Gary Woolf, co-founder of the movement, is a way to take control of one's own data and turn digital technologies into tools of self-evaluation and discovery [10]. Such proclamations sound similar to those made by the proponents of the biofeedback methods in the 1960's and 70's, who argued that wearable medical devices giving direct information about one's own emotional and physical health could empower individuals [11].

Just as sensing technologies and wearable tracking tools are used to empower individuals by providing access to bodily data, these same technologies could be used to provide us with a body-centered awareness of space. One of the first examples in this area was Christian Nold's 'Bio-Mapping' project, for which he used a biometric sensor and a GPS device to capture people's emotional response to the environment, allowing him to develop body-centered, emotion-based maps of urban spaces [12]. At about the same time came the "Running Stich" art project by Jen Southern and Jen Hamilton. Running Stich was a 5 m × 5 m projection of a map of the trajectories of participants as captured by a GPS device. The participants were asked first to explore the city and then to observe their route in the exhibition [13].

If tracking devices can offer an alternative mode of spatial exploration focused on the body and the self, why can't we use such devices to help us explore architecture from a body-centered point of view? Reflecting on that concept, in previous work the author discussed the development of a wearable sensing and tracking tool that could help individuals track their sensory interactions in space and allow them to develop map and notation systems to evaluate architecture based on experiential aspects. The tool was provided as an example of an "object-to-sense-with," which, as mentioned earlier, alludes to the notion of an "object to think with."

Seymour Papert used the notion "objects to think with" in Mindstorms to refer to technological tools that can act as vehicles for situated and self-directed learning. He introduced the LOGO programming language as an "object-to-think-with," helping children to learn abstract computing concepts in a concrete manner [6]. In the LOGO language, abstract computing concepts become concrete with the aid of a little turtle which generates lines as it moves, allowing for a body-centered knowledge of computing and shapes. As Ackermann notes, one of Papert's greatest insights was "to tap children's knowledge about their own movement in space" [14]. Drawing a circle using the Logo turtle is, according to Papert, "body syntonic," because the manner it is created directly relates to children's sense of and knowledge about their own bodies [6].

A great deal of literature is dedicated to the importance of body-centered knowledge, including embodied cognition [15], extended cognition [8], and enactive cognition [16]. The term "objects-to-sense-with" emphasizes the embodied aspect of Papert's educational approach reinforcing the connection between technological tools and sensory-based knowledge. Empowering self-directed education through computers was an important aspect of Papert's vision, similar to Montessori's aspiration for self-directed knowledge.

The term "objects-to-sense-with" refers to "the use of objects that promote sensory-based learning by allowing knowledge to emerge through our bodily actions in the physical environment in a self-directed manner" [5]. In previous work, the author explained how objects-to-sense-with can be used as tools for registering our sensory spatial interactions, allowing us to go beyond traditional architectural modes of representation to arrive at sensory based drawings of environments and buildings centered on the body [5].

2.3   Reflections on a Design Workshop with Sensing Creatures

The focus of this paper is not placed on the actual function of the objects-to-sense-with as sensing devices, but rather on the psychological impact they can have on the wearer by becoming an extension of the wearer' s body and mind. The idea of studying the impact of such tools on our experience emerged from a design workshop developed and taught by the author, Cagri Zaman, and Terry Knight in January 2014. The workshop was titled "Perception Creatures: Ways of sensing and making space" and was conceptualized as a creative and playful way to motivate students to approach the design of space from a body-centered perspective. Students had to invent their own "creature," which could be a wearable or autonomous device, and then use it to explore different spaces on MIT campus. They were asked to imagine a particular perceptual mechanism for their creature, embed sensors within its structure, and define the rules of its behavior in space. Then they had to visualize the data recorded from the creature's spatial explorations and reflect on its sensory experiences.

One of the students designed a color-dancing creature that made sense of its environment by sensing its color and then dictated the wearer's body directions based on the sensed color. The student developed particular rules for body movements resulting in a semi-improvised choreography in space guided by the colors of the environment. Two other students designed a timid sound creature that would move autonomously in space but move away from loud noise or sound. They placed the creature in different campus locations and compared the data related to the auditory qualities of the spaces. Finally, another student designed a hybrid of a plant and an animal that was shaped like a flower and would turn its head towards light.

Because students had to reflect on different perceptual mechanisms and implement them within the creature, the creatures became objects-to-sense-with both in the research, design, and analysis processes of the workshop. It appears that the creatures began to influence the students' own perceptions, channeling their spatial awareness in the direction of the particular modality their creature was designed to be sensitive to: the student working on the color-creature began to comment on the differences in the color qualities of spaces; the students working on the sound creature started noticing the subtle differences in environmental noise and sounds in spaces, and so on. Thus, whether wearable devices, or objects designed to autonomously perceive the environment, sensing creatures became extensions of the students' bodies and minds, increasing their curiosity about sensory spatial exploration and focusing their attention on specific spatial sensory qualities.

2.4   Sensing Creatures as Objects-to-sense-with

As was observed in our workshop, sensing devices, when functioning as objects-to-sense-with, can have an impact on our psychology: they seem to channel the user's attention to the specific sensory qualities under study. The fact that the objects designed by the students took on the role of creatures mimicking the behavior of sentient beings, seems to have reinforced this psychological impact. This is not surprising if one considers that we tend to become more attached to objects with anthropomorphic characteristics, and that children from early infancy attribute anthropomorphic characteristics to objects and engage in imaginary relationships with objects. The things we play with become the "transitional objects" from the egocentric world to a decentralized reality constructed through the perspectives of 'others' [17–19].

Designing a sensing device as an animate creature can be particularly useful as a tool for sensory education because it allows the users to step in and out of their own viewpoint, taking on the perspective of the creature. As Ackermann points out, stepping in and out of our own viewpoint is crucial in order to bring multiple fragmented experiences into a whole [14]. "Only when a learner actually travels in a world by adopting different perspectives, or putting on different 'glasses,' can a dialogue begin between local and initially incompatible experiences" [14]. Sharing our spatial experiences with the sensing creatures is like empathizing with another being. In "Anthropomorphic Epistemology" Sayeki argues that it is by extending our empathy into objects that we experience our surroundings. He argues that we dispatch "Kobitos," which are analogous to imaginary selves, into people and things. Through this distributed self we identify with objects, mimic imaginary behaviors, and feel through others [20].

The argument that the objects we interact with shape our experience by allowing us to "think with them" (and by extending this argument here, by allowing us to "sense with them") is also supported by other theorists in anthropology and science and technologist studies. Turkle uses the term "evocative objects" to refer to technological objects that shape our culture and personal experiences – from personal diaries, to toys, to digital tools, symbolic objects and personal devices [21]. Drawing upon anthropological, archeological and cognitive science studies, Malafouris, in his Theory of Material Engagement, places material objects in the center of our cognitive processes and cognitive development, arguing that "things shape the mind" [22].

3   A Spatial Study with Sensing Creatures

3.1   Scope, Method and Hypothesis

Considering the ideas discussed so far and building upon the outcomes of the design workshop, we can argue that objects-to-sense-with, as technological tools that sense our spatial environment in a body-centered manner, seem to offer opportunities for alternative modes of experiencing space, channeling our attention to the properties sensed by the objects. A series of questions emerged through outcomes of the design workshop: How can we evaluate the use of objects-to-sense-with as perceptual filters? Does the narrative of the sensing creature actually help us focus on spatial qualities revealed by projecting ourselves into the creature? Could we indeed claim that by using sensing tools to explore space we can channel our senses in ways that extend our spatial understanding, uncovering sensory dimensions neglected in the common ways of perceiving space?

A controlled study was designed and conducted by the author in order to provide answers to the these questions. As in the workshop, participants used sensing creatures equipped with sensors to explore physical spaces on the MIT campus. The prototype-creature was given to the participants along with a particular narrative and a specified space to explore. Participants were tested in different groups, each given a different narrative regarding the creature that would allow them to focus on the study of specific sensory qualities. The first group was told that the creature could only see (Vision group), the second group that the creature could only hear (Sound group), the third group that creature could only touch (Touch group), and the fourth group -which functioned as a control group- was told that the creature could see, hear, and touch (All-senses group).

Montessori's sensory training exercises were designed to make students focus on the study of the qualities of a particular sense through the isolation of the senses under study. Similarly, the hypothesis for the conducted study was that by focusing on each of our senses individually through the sensing creature, we can augment our understanding of space by uncovering qualities associated with that sense that would otherwise remained unnoticed. Based on the assumption that we are accustomed to perceiving spaces primarily through vision, it was also hypothesized that the Vision group would yield similar results to those of the All-senses group.

3.2   Procedure

Twenty-four graduate students from the MIT Department of Architecture participated in the study. The participants were divided into two groups. The first group was asked to explore the interior of the MIT Chapel and the second group was asked to explore the interior space of MIT's Morss Hall. The MIT Chapel was designed by Eero Saarineen and built in 1955. Morss Hall is a multipurpose room on the ground floor of the Walker Memorial Building at MIT, designed by Welles Bosworth and built in 1916. These two spaces were chosen for the study because they have significant differences that allow them to be used as different cases but significant similarities that allow a comparison of the results (Fig. 3).

In terms of its architectural language, the Chapel has a modern architectural vocabulary, evident in the pure geometry, simple layout, and materials used. The architecture language of Morss Hall, on the other hand, has classical references and was designed after the gentlemen's clubs of the 19th century. Whereas the Chapel functions as a church, Morss Hall is used as a multipurpose room with no specific function. The spaces are of similar size, are symmetrical in terms of a central axis that leads to a significant visual element, and have walking areas along the perimeters of the space. In the case of the Chapel, the significant visual element is the altar along with the roof lighting and a hanging metal sculpture designed by Harry Bertoia. In the case of Morss Hall, the significant element is a mural painted by Edwin Howard Blashfield.

In the study, each of the two groups of participants was subdivided into four groups, each comprised of three participants to be tested individually (the Vision group, the Sound group, the Touch group, and the All-Senses group). Participants were provided with the following narrative: "A creature of another kind is visiting MIT. It experiences the world only through the sense of [specific sense named here] and can also sense your movement. You have volunteered to act as a host for the creature and provide him/her the experience of this space." Depending on the group they belonged to, participants were told that the creature could only see (Vision group), could only hear (Sound group), could only touch (Touch group) or could see, hear, and touch (All-Senses group). Participants were then instructed to explore the space for ten minutes.

Each of the participants was given the same prototype that would function as the sensing creature. The prototype was a 3d printed wearable device that participants were asked to wear on their wrists. The prototype had embedded sensors (a microphone, proximity sensor, real-time clock and camera). Additional sensors were attached to a chest-strap (compass, accelerometer, magnetometer) and a hat (camera) that participants had to wear in addition to the prototype (Fig. 4). Participants wore the wearable device "creature," chest-trap, and hat during the entire 10-min spatial exploration.

Each wearable device-creature was equipped with the same sensors, but depending on the group, participants were told that the sensors were able to capture only their movement path in space and information regarding one other sense: auditory information (Sound group), tactile information (Touch group), visual information (Vision group), or all of the above (All-senses group). The author collected data regarding the participants' movement path, sound interactions, tactile interactions, and data captured by the two cameras, one placed inside the creature and the other on the participant's

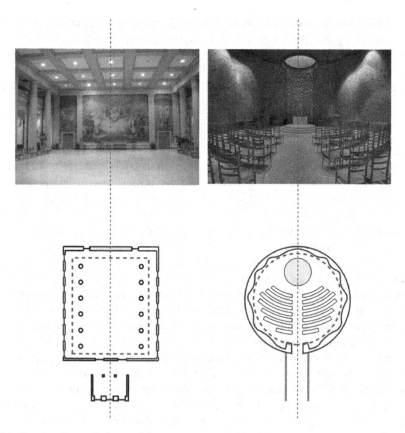

Fig. 3. Plan drawing and views of the two spaces used in the study. Left, the MIT Morss Hall. Right, the MIT Chapel.

hat. The goal was to use these data to analyze and compare the participants' routes and experiences in the spaces. However, beyond the camera recordings, not all of the rest of the data were used in the study analysis, as the movement tracking tool needed further development to accurately capture data for comparisons.

After experiencing the space, the participants were given two templates to fill out, specifically designed for this study. The templates were provided in printed format along with a set of colored markers. The first was the Action template, which depicted the plan of the space under exploration and prompted the users to mark on the template

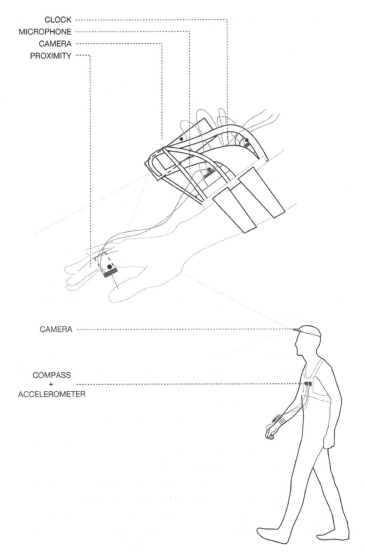

Fig. 4. Diagram depicting the sensors incorporated in the wearable device – creature (top), and the additional equipment the participants had to wear in the study (bottom).

their path in space as well as the salient points of sensory interaction. A basic notation system was provided for that purpose: a red continuous line signified fast movement whereas a red dashed line signified slow movement. A circle filled with black along this line signified points of rest or stops along the route. A circle with a varying radius was used to denote different volumes of sound in particular source locations. An array of black lines denoted points of spatial interaction and a triangle denoted points of visual focus (Fig. 5). The participants were asked to draw their path from memory and recall their basic points of interaction in the space. The purpose of this template was to study what parts of the participants' experience were highlighted after their exploration.

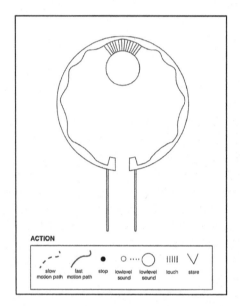 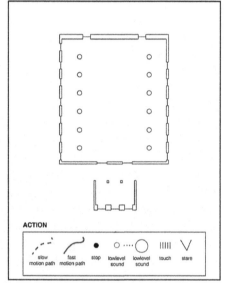

Fig. 5. The Action templates given to the participants in the study.

The second template the participants were given to fill out was the *Mood template* which consisted of two parts, one addressing the experience of the participant and the other the experience of the creature (as imagined by the participant). The template especially designed for the study included a plan drawing of the space and an index of colors, each corresponding to a specific mood. The participants were prompted to fill in the space with colors according to how they felt in particular areas of the space while exploring it. They were also prompted to do the same on behalf of the creature in another plan drawing included in the template (Fig. 6).

After filling out both parts of the mood template, the participants were asked to elaborate on their choices, describe their experience in the space and explain the differences or similarities between their own experience and the creature's experience. The purpose of the mood template was to study the participants' subjective evaluation of their spatial experience and also to test whether having participants think on behalf of the creature's experience would allow them to gain greater awareness of the contribution of the different senses to spatial understanding.

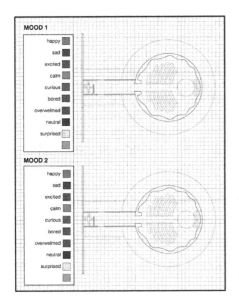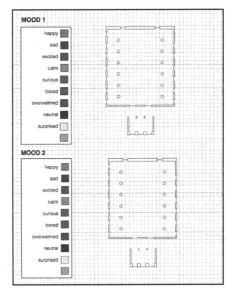

Fig. 6. The Mood template given to the participants in the study. The upper part of the template corresponds to the participant's experience; the bottom part corresponds to the creature's experience as imagined by the participant.

3.3 Results

The Planned and the Unplanned Approach Based on the Action Templates.
Comparing the Action templates, we observe two main approaches regarding participants' movement and action in space (Fig. 7). The first seems "unplanned," as the participants seem to move in an unorganized manner. In the oral interviews, participants who took the unplanned approach said that they moved according to what attracted their attention, which could be an object of interest such as the sculpture or piano in the Chapel or the centrally placed painting in Morss Hall. This approach produced a complexity and multiplicity of movements with no identifiable pattern.

The other main approach was the one seeming strategically "planned." The participants started their exploration by walking along the perimeter of the space and then gradually moved toward the center, discovering the space in sequential layers. For example, participants in the Sound or Touch groups who followed this approach in the Chapel, first walked along the undulating outer wall while interacting with it, touching it, and knocking on it to produce sounds. They then gradually moved towards the altar and finally towards the center of the space, where they rested on a chair. A similar movement strategy was adopted by the participants who explored Morss Hall, with the difference that what functioned as the outer layer was the colonnades rather than the outer wall.

Four of the six participants in the Sound group and four of the six participants in the Touch group followed the planned approach, whereas only two of the six participants in the All-senses group and only one of the six participants in the Vision group followed the planned approach. This difference is possibly due to the different ways our spatial perception unfolds through different modalities: Spatial perception through touch develops though continuous bodily contact with materials. On the other hand, with vision one can gain an understanding of large areas of space with one look. In order to 'scan' the space, the participants in the Vision and the All-senses groups (who apparently relied mostly on vision), moved from one location to another in an unorganized manner in order to obtain complementary views of the space, whereas participants in the Touch and Sound groups (which also relied a lot on sounds generated through tactile interaction) had to walk around the entire perimeter in order to obtain meaningful information.

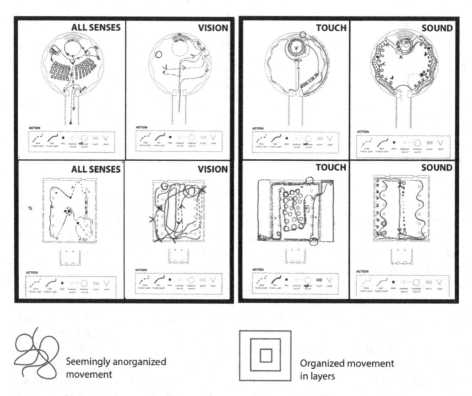

Fig. 7. Examples of templates filled-out by participants demonstrating the Unplanned approach (left) and the Planned approach (right).

The participants in the Sound group used the sense of touch many times in order to communicate auditory information, and participants in the Touch group often produced sound while conveying tactile spatial information. This fact resulted in a similar approach in these two groups regarding the participants' movement in space. Most of the participants in the Sound group adopted an active approach, generating sounds with their own bodies by running inside the space with heavy footsteps, producing sounds with their voices, or tapping the materials to convey spatial information.

The Participants' Experience Based on the Mood Templates. Regarding participants' own experience, the prevalent mood was "calm" in the Vision and the All-senses groups (seven out of twelve participants) (Fig. 8). In the Chapel, most participants marked the center area and pathway leading to the altar with colors denoting "calmness." They also marked the outer area of the space including the wall with colors denoting general "curiosity." Finally, they marked specific areas in this perimeter with colors denoting "happiness" and "excitement," usually associated with particular objects of attraction such as the altar, the podium, and specific spots explored in the wall. In Morss Hall, most participants in the Vision and All-senses group used colors in the template denoting "curiosity" in areas around the main attraction points which were the murals and the windows. Many participants in these groups marked the area from the entrance to the mural in colors denoting "calmness."

Regarding the participants' own experience, in the Sound and the Touch groups the prevalent mood was "excited" (seven out of twelve participants) (Fig. 8). In the Chapel, the colors marked by the participants in the templates revealed an emerging pattern of "excited" mood in the path leading to the altar and in the area around it. There was also an emerging pattern of "bored" and "neutral" mood in the seating areas, and feelings of "happiness," "curiosity" and "excitement" along the external wall. Regarding Morss Hall, feelings of "excitement," "curiosity," and "happiness" were marked around the columns of the colonnade, the windows, and the murals. Finally, comparing the Touch and Sound groups in the two spaces, we can observe that the mood results in Morss Hall and the Chapel are equally rich and diverse, whereas in the Touch group, the mood results recorded in the Chapel are richer and more diverse than those recorded in Morss Hall. This difference is possibly due to the fact that the Chapel has a richer variety in materials than does Morss Hall.

The fact that the prevalent mood – calm – was the same in the All-senses and Vision groups is possibly due to the fact that the participants in the All-senses group mostly relied on their sense of vision. The fact that the prevalent mood – excited – was the same in the Touch and Sound groups was possibly due to the fact that participants were motivated to explore the space in an unusual manner, uncovering qualities that might otherwise remain unobserved. As noted by one of the participants in the Touch group, the Chapel offered "so much potential for touch." Tactile interaction also led to the discovery of visual and auditory qualities. As noted by a participant in the Touch group exploring Morss Hall, "Beginning the path, I felt mostly curious because of the different surfaces, the curvilinear ones and the paintings. Then I saw the hangers where I felt really happy because it was not only the touch but also the sound that I heard."

Participants in the Touch group often discovered auditory qualities of the space through their explorations and participants in the Sound group often discovered tactile qualities by engaging in an active exploration involving the production of sounds. In the case of the Chapel, two significant auditory elements in participants' experience were the sound produced by the metal sculpture above the altar and the sounds of the piano. Interestingly, in the case of Morss Hall, a significant auditory element was produced by a simple set of metal hangers accidentally found there. The participants of the Sound and Touch groups referred to interactions with these objects as "exciting" or "happy" experiences.

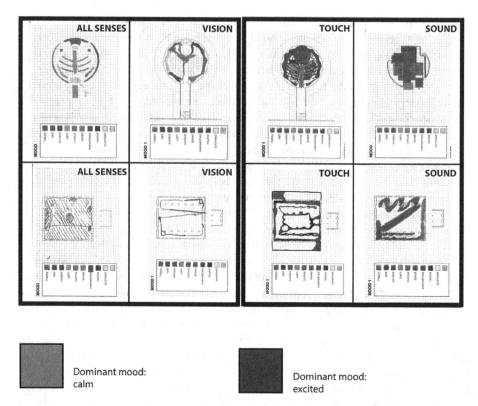

Fig. 8. Examples of Mood templates filled-out by participants having "calm" as the dominant mood (left) and having "excited" as the dominant mood (right).

Overall, participants in the Touch and Sound groups often felt "excited" because they engaged in a playful exploration. As noted in the interview by one of the participants in the Chapel "the space felt like an instrument." On the other hand, participants in the Vision and All-senses groups often felt calm. As no activity was taking place in the spaces at the time they were visited, participants in these groups seemed focused on the visual elements.

The Creature's Experience Based on the Mood Templates. Most of the participants (twenty-three out of twenty-four) reported that their experiences were different from those of the creatures. The exception was a participant in the Vision group. In the Sound and Touch groups, both in the Chapel and in Morss Hall, participants attributed this difference to the creature's limited sensory abilities. While explaining this difference, participants tried to imagine themselves being limited to the only sense their creature had available, whether this was sound or touch. This brought to participants' awareness the difference between spatial understanding when developed through one sensory modality or the other, or all of them together.

An example that illustrates the awareness of the difference between the senses regarding spatial understanding can be provided by the case of one of the participants in the Touch group. In the mood template, in both the part of the template that addressed her own mood and the part of the template that addressed the creature's mood, the participant used red and blue colors, red signifying an 'excited' mood and blue signifying a 'neutral' mood. However, in the case of the creature's mood, the amount of the red color exceeded the amount of the blue color whereas in the case of the participant's mood the amount of the blue color exceeded that of the red color. When asked to elaborate on the choice of colors, the participant replied that because the creature lacked the sense of vision, its excitement lasted longer:

"I think the difference (between mine and the creature's experience) is that I can see that there is repetition ahead so I am not as excited about it, I am kind of more just neutral, whereas the excitement and happiness lasts longer for the creature because the repetition is unexpected. Because it just touches... the pattern becomes known through the experience and then eventually more towards the middle it becomes monotonous and then it is less exciting...but in the beginning when it recognizes the pattern is exciting. So that's the case for the windows and the columns as well."

The participant's description regarding the creature's experience made apparent that projecting oneself into another "being's" sensory mechanism helps one become aware of the differences between sensory modalities and highlights the way they contribute to understanding space. Unlike the participants in the Sound and the Touch groups, the participants in the Vision and All-senses groups did not explain the difference regarding their own and the creature's experience on the basis of the creature's limited senses, a fact that confirms the hypothesis that we are preconditioned to perceive space mainly through vision.

Interestingly, as mentioned, with the exception of one participant, most participants did not identify with their creature's experience, attributing the differences mostly to its scale – the scale of the creature being very small when compared to the scale of the human body – and the fact that it was supposed to be a creature "from another kind," thus perhaps being alien to this culture and its architecture. Because the creature was worn on the participants' hands and had an embedded camera, it functioned as a "third eye"; participants used it to focus on details of the space, exploring elements that might otherwise have remained unnoticed, such as small objects left in small openings of the undulating wall in the Chapel. The fact that the creature was presented as being "of another kind" allowed participants to "reset" their spatial experiences, allowing them to explore the space through the imagined creature's senses.

Summary of the Results. Comparing the actions and experiences of the participants in the Vision and All-senses groups, we can conclude that these two groups relied primarily on vision. As was revealed in the Action templates, both groups adopted the same strategy of movement in exploring space. Also, as revealed in the Mood templates, participants in those two groups had similar patterns of mood regarding their own experience in space. Moreover, when asked to elaborate on the differences between their own and the creature's experience, participants in the Vision and All-senses groups did not attribute the differences to the lack of other senses. These results support the study hypothesis that we are conditioned to perceive space mainly through vision.

It was hypothesized that focusing on each of the senses individually through the sensing creature would render participants more focused on the sense under study: that the prototype would act as perceptual filter isolating one sense from the others. This turned out to be partially true: the sensing creatures did indeed have an impact on participants' behavior and experience, but instead of making participants perceive the space only through the specific sense designated to the creature, they produced multisensory experiences. The task of communicating auditory information motivated participants to explore the space through touch, and the task of communicating tactile information motivated participants to explore the space through sound.

Although it was expected that focusing only on vision would not result in altering common modes of spatial exploration, the study showed that even in the Vision group the wearable device-creature expanded the participants' perception by offering them a "third eye." Finally, the act of reflecting on the creature's experience turned out to be an additional filter in one's spatial experience and perception as it forced the participants to project themselves into the perceptual mechanism of another being and to feel the space through it.

4 Conclusions

To explore a multisensory approach in architecture education, this paper discussed sensory pedagogies of the twentieth century to arrive at a new proposal for sensory education that takes advantage of current technologies. Objects-to-sense-with were proposed as vehicles for body-centered sensory spatial learning, building upon ideas articulated by Seymour Papert, Maria Montessori, and Lazlo Moholy-Nagy. The paper focused on the psychological impact of Objects-to-sense with on the user, hypothesizing that such objects, by becoming extensions of our bodies and minds can help us augment our sensory awareness of space.

The study conducted utilized Objects-to-sense-with taking on the role of "sensing creatures" to test whether focusing on each of our senses individually through the creatures would allow us to expand our sensory perception of space. The study demonstrated that the use of sensing and tracking devices in the exploration of physical spaces can have an impact on our spatial understanding. Overall, the study showed that we are conditioned to perceive space mainly through vision, and that engaging participants in a sensory exploration focused on a sensory modality other than vision expands their sensory knowledge regarding the space. Participants engaged in creative and multisensory modes of exploration which allowed them to observe material and spatial qualities that might otherwise have remained unperceived.

Results of this study in combination with the observations of the design workshop described in this paper reveal a promising path for the development of sensory pedagogies based on the use of objects-to-sense-with. Incorporating the making and use of such tools in architecture education could allow students to expand their understanding of space by engaging in in-situ exploration and sensory embodied spatial interactions.

Acknowledgments. I am grateful to Professors Terry Knight, Edith Ackermann and Takehiko Nagakura for their advice and comments on this study.

References

1. Millar, S.: Space and Sense. Psychology Press/Taylor and Francis, Hove/New York (2008)
2. Gifford, R.: Environmental Psychology: Principles and Practice, 3rd edn. Optimal Books, Colville (2002)
3. Montessori, M.: The Montessori Method: The Origins of an Educational Innovation: Including an Abridged and Annotated Edition of Maria Montessori's The Montessori Method. Frederick A Stokes Company, New York (1919)
4. Moholy-Nagy, L.: The New Vision: Fundamentals of Bauhaus Design, Painting, Sculpture, and Architecture. Dover Publications, New York (2005)
5. Papadopoulou, A.: Objects-to-sense-with: computational tools for embodied spatial learning. In: Herneoja, A., Österlund, T., Markkanen, P. (eds.) Complexity and Simplicity - Proceedings of the 34th Education and Research in Computer Aided Design in Europe (eCAADe) Conference, Oulu, Finland, 22–26 August, vol. 1, pp. 367–376 (2016)
6. Papert, S.: Mindstorms: Children, Computers, and Powerful Ideas. Basic Books, Inc., New York (1980)
7. Hutchins, E.: Cognition in the Wild. A Bradford Book, Cambridge (1996)
8. Clark, A.: Supersizing the Mind: Embodiment, Action, and Cognitive Extension. Oxford University Press, Oxford, New York (2008)
9. Winzer, M.: The History of Special Education: From Isolation to Integration. Gallaudet University Press, Washington, D.C. (1993)
10. Woolf, G.: The Data Driven Life. The New York Times (2008). http://www.nytimes.com/2010/05/02/magazine/02self-measurement-t.html?pagewanted=all&_r=0. Accessed 12 Dec 2018
11. Brown, B.B.: New Mind, New Body: Bio-Feedback, New Directions for the Mind. Bantam Books, New York (1975)
12. Nold, C.: Technologies of the self (2009). http://emotionalcartography.net. Accessed 12 Dec 2018
13. Sotelo-Castro, L.C.: Participation Cartography: The Presentation of Self in Spatio-Temporal Terms (2009). http://journal.media-culture.org.au/index.php/mcjournal/article/viewArticle/192. Accessed 15 Jan 2019
14. Ackermann, E.: Constructing knowledge and transforming the world, Chap. 2. In: Tokoro, M., Steels, L. (eds.) A Learning Zone of One's Own: Sharing Representations and Flow in Collaborative Learning Environments, DC, Part 1, pp. 15–37. IOS Press, Amsterdam, Berlin, Oxford, Tokyo, Washington (2004)
15. Johnson, M.: The Body in the Mind: The Bodily Basis of Meaning, Imagination, and Reason. University of Chicago Press, Chicago (1990)
16. Noe, A.: Action in Perception. A Bradford Book, Cambridge (2006)
17. Winnicott, D.W.: Playing and Reality. Routledge, London, New York (2005)
18. Ackermann, E.: Perspective-taking and object-construction. In: Kafai, Y., Resnick, M. (eds.) Constructionism in Practice: Designing, Thinking, and Learning in a Digital World. Lawrence Erlbaum, Northdale (1996)
19. Ackermann, E.: Playthings that do things: a young kid's "Incredibles"! In: Proceedings IDC 2005, Interaction design and children, Boulder, Colorado, 8–10 June (2005)
20. Sayeki, Y.: Anthropomorphic Epistemology: when a dialogue with objects starts. In: Keynote Lecture. ISCAR International Congress, Rome, Italy, September 2011
21. Turkle, S.: Evocative Objects: Things We Think With. The MIT Press, Cambridge (2011)
22. Malafouris, L.: How Things Shape the Mind: A Theory of Material Engagement. MIT Press, Cambridge (2013)

Affective Sleeve: Wearable Materials with Haptic Action for Promoting Calmness

Athina Papadopoulou[(⊠)], Jaclyn Berry, Terry Knight,
and Rosalind Picard

Massachusetts Institute of Technology, Cambridge, MA 02139, USA
{athpap, jberry, tknight}@mit.edu, picard@media.mit.edu

Abstract. Although affective computing is most often associated with software intelligence, physical materials can also be programmed to promote wellbeing. Based on recent findings regarding the impact on health of interoceptive awareness and the sensation of touch, we develop the programmable Affective Sleeve, a wearable device that produces rhythmic haptic action (warmth and slight pressure along the arm) to promote calmness and reduce anxiety. Through a controlled pilot study, we demonstrate that the pace of haptic action of the sleeve can influence the participants' breathing rate and perception of calmness. Quantitative findings indicate that faster haptic action is associated with a faster breathing rate, while qualitative self-report findings affirm a positive correlation between perceived calmness and slow pace of haptic action (equal to relaxed breathing rate), and a negative correlation between perceived calmness and fast pace of haptic action (25% faster than relaxed breathing rate).

Keywords: Affective Sleeve · Programmable materials · Intervention · Breathing · EDA

1 Introduction

Although most research on affective computing focuses on software applications [27], there is an emerging interest in extending affective computing to applications utilizing physical materials [1, 33, 36]. In the past few decades we have seen the development of smart and programmable materials that grow, adapt and transform to respond to environmental conditions and accommodate functional needs [25, 35]. We have also seen a significant shift in response to human-computer interaction, through the development of tangible, embodied, and other novel interfaces that allow the coupling of physical and digital information through the direct manipulation of materials [17, 37]. In addition, we have seen programmable materials offering novel solutions in biomedical applications through their use as artificial muscles [3, 4, 29], and augmented physical and sensory experiences when incorporated in body suits [11, 24]. It is becoming more and more apparent that materials have qualities that can help us respond better not only to functional needs, but also to our health and emotional needs, enhancing our wellbeing.

Recent applications in affective computing have demonstrated that technological interventions utilizing rhythmic sensory stimuli, such as sound, vibration and light can

© Springer Nature Switzerland AG 2019
N. Streitz and S. Konomi (Eds.): HCII 2019, LNCS 11587, pp. 304–319, 2019.
https://doi.org/10.1007/978-3-030-21935-2_23

aid in emotion regulation by affecting our physiological functions and interoceptive awareness [9, 14]. Interoceptive awareness, the awareness of the physiological state of our own bodies, is highly interrelated to our emotional awareness - our ability to process and express our emotions [10, 19]. Disruption in emotion processing and expression has been associated with various serious mental health and developmental disorders [19, 20]. The fact that sensory stimuli can have an impact on emotion regulation has been associated with the phenomena of physiological synchrony and emotional contagion [14, 15, 22] and demonstrates a promising path for non-invasive interventions for emotion regulation.

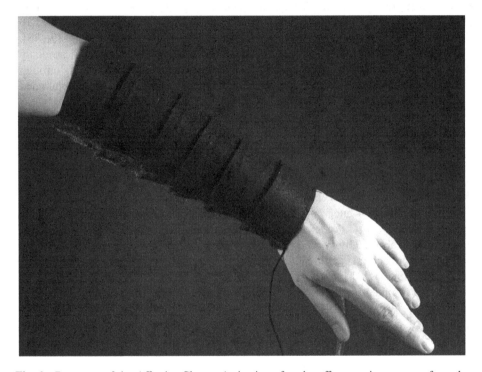

Fig. 1. Prototype of the Affective Sleeve. Activation of each cuff occurs in sequence from the palm towards the elbow.

In this study we take advantage of the affective impact of material sensory properties to explore the effect of programmable materials as emotion regulation systems. We designed a controlled study to test how different paces of rhythmic haptic action (slight pressure and warmth), induced through a programmable Affective Sleeve that we developed, can affect a subject's psychophysiological signals. In particular, we test whether the haptic sensations induced by the sleeve may influence breathing rates and changes in calmness.

2   Related Work

2.1   Breathing Regulation and Interoceptive Awareness

As indicated by meditation practices, cultivating awareness of one's bodily signals is important for reducing anxiety and promoting calmness. Sensory stimuli can help promote and guide such awareness. For example, Canales-Johnson et al. show that auditory heartbeat feedback plays a significant role in maintaining homeostasis and regulating our behavior [8]. The benefits of controlled slow breathing can also be achieved through the aid of technological interventions. As demonstrated by Elliot et al., device-guided breathing has positive effects on graded blood pressure reduction [13]. Based on such findings, several mobile applications have been developed to provide guided breathing by providing visual, auditory or tactile stimuli [7, 30]. Material-based mindfulness interventions have also been proposed though specially designed furniture, that can focus one's attention on different parts of the body through incorporated heating mechanisms, or guide one's breathing through programmed lighting patterns [33].

Although cognitive access to our interoceptive processes has been associated with healthy emotion regulation mechanisms, interestingly, high levels of interoceptive awareness have been positively correlated with anxiety symptoms [12, 28]. Research shows that higher than necessary levels of interoceptive awareness can be a symptom of emotion dysregulation [19]. Aligned with such findings, studies have demonstrated that providing false interoceptive awareness (false heart or breathing rate feedback) through technological intervention can regulate the heart or breathing rate to reduce anxiety levels [9, 14]. For example, Ghandeharioun and Picard demonstrated that barely perceivable auditory and visual interventions on a computer, rhythmically oscillating to match relaxed breathing rates, can increase both focus on a work-related task and calmness [14].

The development of the Affective Sleeve takes into account research findings on interoceptive awareness and the regulation of physiological signals though technological intervention. We suggest that the Affective Sleeve can regulate breathing through rhythmic sensations of warmth and slight pressure to reduce stress levels.

2.2   Benefits of Touch in Emotion Regulation

Through studies on married couples, Holt-Lunstad et al. provided evidence of the positive effects of human touch on health, particularly for lowering anxiety levels [16]. The effects of human touch on health have also been achieved through technological interventions. For example, Sumioka et al. demonstrated that the stress-reducing effect of interpersonal touch can also be achieved through huggable devices that provide tactile sensations [34]. In the HCI field, Bonanni et al., discussed the design and therapeutic effects of wearable haptic systems that have the ability to record and play back human touch [6]. Other studies, like the one by Boer et al. have explored the aesthetic potentials of haptic wearable interfaces and their impact on sensory experience [5].

Related to the aforementioned studies, our goal is to utilize the Affective Sleeve to achieve therapeutic effects similar to those of human touch. In the case of the Affective

Sleeve, the sensation of touch is defined by both the stimulus of warmth and the stimulus of pressure. Warmth alone has significant benefits for health. Lowry et al. provide evidence on how warmth may alter neural connections regulating mood and cognitive processes, including serotonergic circuits that affect stress-related disorders [23]. Pressure stimulus of the touch sensation also has significant benefits in health. Research demonstrates that pressure stimulus in massage therapy significantly decreases the perception of pain, improves mood and lowers anxiety levels [18, 21].

Finally, recent contributions to the HCI and affective computing communities have focused on valence and arousal measures of temperature changes and vibrotactile stimuli, demonstrating that such stimuli can have a distinct impact on psychophysiology [31, 32, 38].

Through the intervention of the Affective Sleeve, we plan to examine the impact of pressure and warmth stimuli on human psychophysiology. We aim to provide the beneficial effects of human touch in cultivating calmness and lowering anxiety levels. In particular, we plan to examine the impact of different paces of rhythmic pressure and warmth stimuli on psychophysiology.

3   Method

3.1   The Affective Sleeve

We designed the Affective Sleeve as a series of autonomous cuffs to explore the impact of different types and paces of haptic action on wearers' psychophysiology (Fig. 1). Each cuff can be actuated independently and controlled for various durations of time to provide flexibility for setting haptic rhythms. The final prototype consists of six cuffs of adjustable circumference that cover an adult's forearm.

The rhythmic haptic action of the Affective Sleeve was made possible by sandwiching 0.5 mm Nitinol wire (a shape memory alloy) between two insulating layers of thick felt in each cuff (Fig. 2). Although the wires took on an arc shape when sewn into the Affective Sleeve, they were "programmed" to return to a flat, linear shape when heated to temperatures above 45 °C. Based on this property, we were able to pass current through the wires to transform the geometry of each cuff and cause a slight sensation of pressure and warmth on the forearm. When the electrical current is disconnected and the wires cool, they are forced back into an arc due to the geometry of the sleeve and stiffness of the fabric.

We chose to use a shape memory alloy because it allowed us to simultaneously induce pressure and warmth by actuating a single material. However, the limitation of the shape memory alloy used is that it allows only for a one-way transformation. Thus, a mechanical solution was necessary to create a repetitive actuation with the wire. After testing various solutions with plastics, elastics and springs, we decided that designing the sleeve using cuffs made of a stiff felt fabric created the best actuation and reversible behavior, as well as the most comfortable wearable experience.

For this study, we programmed each cuff of the Affective Sleeve to be activated periodically from the palm toward the elbow. The time of the activation for each cuff was set in response to the duration of the wearer's breathing cycle (inhale and exhale)

Fig. 2. The Affective Sleeve consists of a sequence of independent cuffs containing nitinol wire, a shape memory alloy, sewn between two layers of thick felt. Current passed through the nitinol wire activates the cuffs, creating pressure and warmth.

after which it returned to the cool state. The pace of the rhythmic haptic action varied according to three test groups, as will be explained in the experiment procedure. The periodic activation of each cuff creates the sensation of warmth and pressure along the forearm. The temperature of the fabric in contact with the human skin ranges from 26 °C (off) to 38 °C (on) (Fig. 3).

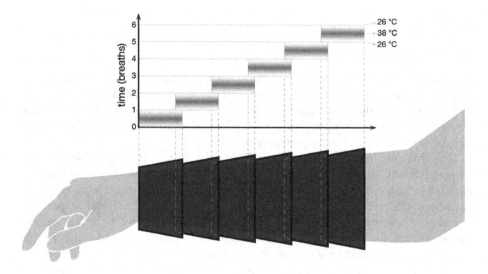

Fig. 3. Diagram depicting the periodic change of temperature over time for each cuff.

We intended the Affective Sleeve to be an example of emotion-regulating clothing, stimulating different locations on the body. Unlike other wearable solutions for emotion regulation, such as the EmotionCheck application by Costa et al., which provides steady vibration stimuli in one specific location on the wrist, the Affective Sleeve induces sequential tactile stimuli at six distinct locations along the forearm, creating a flow of warmth and slight pressure [9]. The idea of the flow of induced rhythmic haptic sensations along the forearm was inspired by the body scan technique in breathing meditation that transfers the focus of attention along the body while synchronizing with rhythmic breathing, as well as by techniques of deep pressure stimulation along the body in massage therapy [2, 18, 26]. These connections, while not deeply explored in this study, are important aspects of the sleeve's design that could be further explored in the future.

3.2   Experiment Method and Hypothesis

To evaluate whether the haptic action of the sleeve has a positive effect on lowering anxiety levels, we designed a randomized controlled experiment to measure the difference between stressed-state and relaxed-state physiological signals. Given prior research findings on false interoceptive awareness and sensory stimulation we hypothesized that the pace of the sleeve would have a positive correlation with breathing rate. Our hypothesis was that slow and fast rhythmic haptic action of the Affective Sleeve would decrease and increase, respectively, participants' psychophysiological symptoms of stress.

We recruited 18 healthy adult college students to participate in a study that would require them to wear the sleeve while taking a spatial cognition quiz in order to induce high stress levels. The participants were told that the quiz would measure the effect of the sleeve on their cognitive performance. We chose to use the quiz as a stressor because simulating an exam setup was relevant to students and could be easily controlled and reproduced for further studies.

To ensure that the measured effects were a result of the haptic action of the sleeve and not a result of the texture of the fabric or other factors, we randomized participants into three test groups: the Control Group (inactive sleeve, but participants were told it was active and barely perceptible), the Fast Group (fast rhythmic haptic action of the sleeve) and a Slow Group (slow rhythmic haptic action of the sleeve). All participants wore the Affective Sleeve for the habituation and performance tasks of the experiment. Based on our hypothesis, we expected that participants in the Slow Group would exhibit lower electrodermal activity (EDA), a noninvasive measure of the sympathetic nervous system's "fight or flight" response, and lower breathing rates than those in the Control and Fast Groups. Also, we expected that participants in the Fast Group would exhibit higher increases in EDA and breathing rates than those in the Slow and Control groups. Such results would provide evidence that the haptic action of the sleeve has an impact on participants' stress levels and associated physiological processes.

3.3   Experimental Procedure

The participants were told in advance that they would be compensated with a $10 gift card, and given an additional $50 gift card if they achieved one of the two highest scores on the spatial cognition quiz. We gave the opportunity for this additional compensation in order to make the task competitive, eliciting more stress and aspiration for good performance.

We decided to withhold the true aim of the study at the onset of the experiment to ensure that participants would not consciously manipulate their physiology or behavior in a way that would affect their breathing rate and skin conductance levels. Instead, the participants were told that they would participate in a study measuring the effect of the sleeve on cognitive performance.

In addition to the Affective Sleeve, participants were asked to wear an Empatica E4 wristband sensor to record EDA levels, as well as a Zephyr BioPatch chest sensor to record respiration rate and its variability (Fig. 4). Because participants would need to use their dominant hand for the performance task, the programmable sleeve was worn on the non-dominant hand and the E4 wristband was worn on the dominant hand.

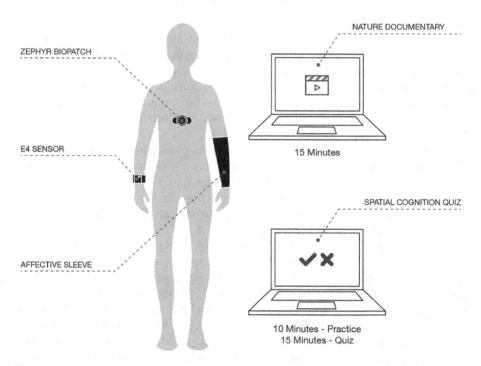

Fig. 4. Experiment setup and procedure. Participants wore the Zephyr Biopatch on their chest, the E4 sensor on their wrist and the Affective Sleeve on their forearm.

The experiment consisted of four phases: (1) establishing baseline conditions, (2) habituation task, (3) performance task and, (4) qualitative surveys (Fig. 5). In the first phase of the experiment, participants wore the E4 wristband and Biopatch sensor while watching a relaxing nature documentary for 15 min. to collect relaxed-state baseline conditions for breathing rate and EDA. Participants were not wearing the sleeve during this task. The baseline measurements allowed us to account for variations in skin conductance and respiration rates among individuals at rest.

The sleeve's action was programmed to be different for each test group. For the Control Group, the haptic action was inactive. For the Slow Group, the haptic action was programmed to match the average relaxed-state breathing rate of individual participants. For the Fast Group, the haptic action was programmed to be 25% faster than the average relaxed-state breathing rate of individual participants. The pace of haptic action for the Fast Group was chosen based on the material properties of the sleeve (how fast the material could actuate) and initial experiments exploring the perceivable difference in actuation rates.

Fig. 5. Participants watched a nature documentary to collect baseline metrics for breathing rate and EDA (left). They then completed the habituation and performance tasks while wearing the Affective Sleeve (middle). Finally, participants filled out qualitative surveys describing their experience (right).

In the habituation and performance tasks, participants wore the Affective Sleeve, the E4 sensor and the Zephyr Biopatch sensor. The habituation and performance task required taking a spatial reasoning quiz of multiple-choice format. The duration of the habituation task was 10 min. but participants were allowed to finish earlier if they completed all the questions in less than the allocated time. The participants were told that results of the practice quiz would not count towards the final score. The habituation task was necessary so that participants' psychophysiological response would not be influenced by the novelty of the intervention.

In the performance task, we designed the quiz to be impossible to complete within the given 15-min. timespan. The average score among all participants was 36%, the median 33%, the highest 57%, and the lowest 18%. The quiz consisted of multiple-choice spatial reasoning questions. We chose a spatial reasoning test as a method for eliciting stress to make sure that all participants (coming from different departments) would be able to respond to the questions. We wanted the stress to be elicited not because of a lack of knowledge of a particular subject but because of cognitive demands and time pressure.

After the performance task, the participants were asked to remove the Affective Sleeve and sensors and proceed to the qualitative survey task and oral interviews. The participants first filled out a multiple-choice questionnaire about their experience of wearing the sleeve during the study. Second, the participants filled out the Perceived Stress Scale (PSS) questionnaire, which has been scientifically verified and widely used. The PSS was used as a post-study screening method that would allow us to evaluate whether very high stress responses and/or poor performance during the study were due to other circumstances in the participant's life. While the mean for our participants (16.27) was much higher than the mean provided in the PSS (12.1 for males, 13.7 for females), the association of PSS results to quiz performance and physiological data for each individual in the study did not show any significant correlation, which supports that there was no prior stress bias or cognitive ability bias among the random group assignments. Finally, the study ended with a brief oral interview regarding the experience of the study.

The setup of the experiment remained the same throughout the study: each participant sat at a desk with a computer and remained seated until the end of the study. Participants were tested one at a time. The experimenters interacted with the participants between the phases of the study to adjust or remove the sensors if required. Otherwise, participants did not interact with anyone during the tasks of the experiment. The room was isolated from other distractions to the best extent possible in a common academic environment.

4 Results

4.1 Physiological Data Analysis

The 18 participants (aged 19–34) were all students at Massachusetts Institute of Technology (MIT); 16 were graduate and two were undergraduate students. Of the participants nine were female and nine were male. Out of the 18 participants, 15 were students in the School of Architecture and Planning, one was a student in the Mathematics department, one in Bio-electrical Engineering, and one in Materials Science.

For every participant, we computed the mean and standard deviation for the first three phases of the experiment (baseline, habituation, performance), excluding any data outside two standards of deviation from the mean. Data from the first three phases were scaled horizontally to fit within a 15-min., 10-min., and 15-min. window respectively. After removing noise, we normalized the data per participant (maximum over the whole session = 1, minimum over the whole session = 0) to eliminate any difference in individual ranges. We calculated the difference between the mean value of the performance phase and mean value of the baseline phase for each participant. We then calculated the average difference between the performance phase and baseline phase for each test group as a whole. Given that this pilot study had a small n and we did not have a normal distribution of data, we used the Kruskall-Wallis test to evaluate our results.

Results from the EDA data (Fig. 6) show that the mean change in EDA in the Slow Group was 0.095 μS less than the Fast Group and 0.078 μS less than the Control Group. However, with such a small n, we cannot reject the null hypothesis. Additional studies must be conducted to determine how the haptic action of the Affective Sleeve affects EDA.

The results from the breathing rate data are more promising (Fig. 7). A comparison of the mean change in breathing rates from relaxed to stressed conditions show that subjects in the Slow Group breathed 0.021 bpm faster than the Control Group and 0.142 bpm slower than the Fast Group. Given our small study, we cannot reject the null hypothesis for these results. However, when comparing the Fast and Control Groups, the data show that the Fast Group breathed 0.164 bpm faster than the Control Group, ($p = 0.0105$). This result suggests that the rate of haptic action of the sleeve correlates positively to breathing rate; that is, a faster haptic action is associated with a higher breathing rate.

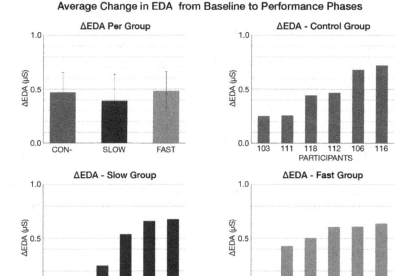

Fig. 6. The average difference in EDA from baseline to performance tasks.

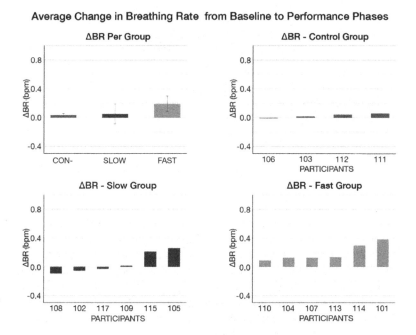

Fig. 7. The average difference in breathing rate from baseline to performance tasks.

4.2 Self-reported Data Analysis

Participants were given qualitative surveys designed to evaluate their experience of wearing the sleeve. Out of the 13 questions, 11 had a multiple-choice format providing a scale of 0 to 4—0 indicating negative, 2 neutral, and 4 positive. Specific responses associated with the scale were provided for each question. Two out of the 13 questions prompted written feedback. We compared the results of the three groups to gain insight into the experience of wearing the sleeve and its effectiveness for regulating anxiety.

When asked about the comfort of the sleeve, 50% of the Control Group reported that they were either neutral or uncomfortable, and only 16.7% reported they were very comfortable. In the Slow Group, 50% of participants reported that they felt a bit comfortable and 50% reported that they felt very comfortable. In the Fast Group, 66.7% of the participants reported that they felt a neutral level of comfort. These responses suggest that the pace of haptic action is negatively correlated with perception of comfort: the faster the pace of haptic action, the less comfortable it is. Additionally, the absence of haptic action is perceived as more uncomfortable than either slow or fast haptic action (Fig. 8).

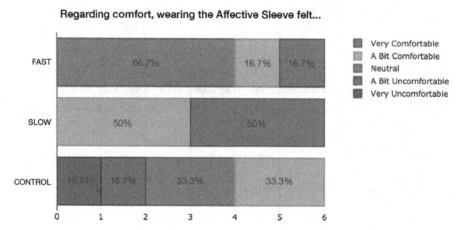

Fig. 8. Participants' responses to the question "Regarding comfort, wearing the sleeve felt…"

To inquire whether the sleeve affected participants' performance, we asked participants whether they felt that the sleeve was distracting or helped them focus. Of all participants, 66.7% reported that it neither helped them focus nor felt distracting, 16.7% of participants reported that it helped them focus a bit, 16.7% of participants felt that it was a bit distracting, and none felt it distracted them significantly. In addition to the self-reported data, the mean scores from the performance task for each test group were very similar: the Control Group averaged 32%, the Slow Group averaged 34% and the Fast Group averaged 34%. These results suggest that the participants' performance was not greatly affected by the sleeve.

Regarding the warmth produced by the sleeve, 66.7% of the Control Group reported the warmth was neutral and only 33.3% felt it was a bit calming. In the Slow

Group, 16.7% reported the warmth was neutral and 83.3% reported it was either a bit calming or very calming. From the Fast Group, 50% reported that the warmth was neutral and 50% reported it was either a bit calming or very calming (Fig. 9). Overall, participants in the Slow Group perceived the warmth of the sleeve as more calming than the Fast or Control Groups.

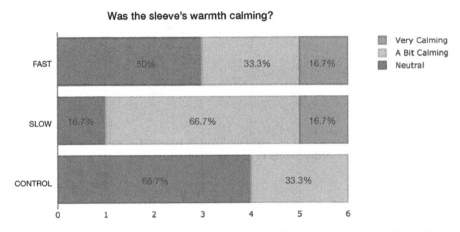

Fig. 9. Participants' responses to the question "Was the sleeve's warmth calming?"

When asked to describe the sensation of wearing the sleeve, all participants in the Slow Group described the experience as positive. Responses ranged from simply "Pleasant," "Warm and comforting," to more imaginative such as "Felt like a cat was lying on my arm." In the Fast Group only half of the participants found the experience positive; the other half described it as slightly discomforting, mostly due to the sensation of movement or pressure. In the Control Group, 83.3% of participants described the experience as neutral, reporting that they did not notice any warmth or movement. Only one participant in the Control group reported the perception of change of temperature of the sleeve, which may have been the result of placebo effect. Participants' feedback regarding their experience of wearing the sleeve suggests an association between slow pace of haptic action (matching their resting respiration rate) and participants' positive experience, and an association between fast pace of haptic action and participants' slightly negative experience.

Finally, participants were asked if they would wear the Affective Sleeve in their everyday lives if it was proven to decrease stress levels (Fig. 10). Of the Control Group 66.7% were neutral and 33.3% responded "most likely." In the Slow Group 33.3% responded neutrally or "probably not" while 66.6% responded either "most likely" or "definitely." In the Fast Group, 50% of participants responded neutrally and the remaining 50% responded "most likely" or "definitely." This and other survey responses suggest that participants in the Slow Group had a more calming and positive experience than the Fast and Control Groups and that the valence of participants' experience while wearing the sleeve possibly biased their opinion of its application in everyday life, as the Slow Group was the most receptive to the idea of wearing the sleeve.

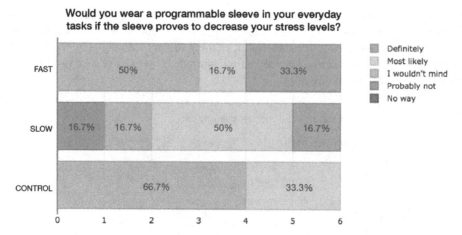

Fig. 10. Participants' responses to the question "Would you wear a programmable sleeve in your everyday tasks if the sleeve proves to decrease your stress levels?"

5 Conclusion

The results from the analysis of the breathing rate data demonstrate a positive correlation between the pace of the haptic action and the change in measured signals, indicating that the rate of activation in the Affective Sleeve may have a subtle impact on breathing regulation. These results suggest that a faster pace of haptic action along the sleeve may increase the rate of respiration. However, our quantitative analysis does not yet demonstrate that a lower pace of haptic action can lower breathing rates. Further quantitative analysis with a greater number of participants and a slightly different experiment design are necessary to prove or disprove this statement of causality.

As our current hypothesis assumes that lowering breathing rate reduces anxiety levels, additional studies will be necessary to associate the change in breathing rates with the change in anxiety levels. Also, based on the comparison of the mean change in EDA per group, we believe that with a larger group of participants we may begin to see statistically significant results in the EDA results. Future studies with a greater number of participants and possibly with different methods for inducing different kinds of stress (e.g. in a social context) need to be conducted for further conclusions.

The results from the self-reported data show a positive correlation between calmness and slow pace of haptic action, and a negative correlation between calmness and fast pace of the haptic action. The experience of wearing a sleeve producing slow periodic haptic action, at a rate matched to resting respiration rate, was perceived as more comforting and positive than the experience of wearing a sleeve with no haptic action or 25% faster-than-resting-respiration haptic action. The experience of wearing a sleeve producing fast haptic action was perceived as more discomforting than wearing a sleeve with no haptic action. The results from the self-reported data suggest that the slower pace of the sleeve's haptic action may help promote calmness.

As the haptic action in this study combines the stimulus of warmth, the stimulus of pressure, and movement along the arm, future studies on the impact of each of these sensations on calmness independently would be useful. Because shape memory alloys require heat activation for their actuation, perhaps an alternative future sleeve design could include inflatable materials as one component and heating wires as another component, each controlled independently, to allow for individual testing of the warmth and pressure stimuli.

Finally, it is important to note that the results of the performance task indicate no correlation between overall performance and pace of haptic action, indicating that the haptic interventions did not distract participants from their ability to perform. Taking into account the results of both the physiological and self-reported data analysis, we can conclude that the effect of Affective Sleeve on emotion regulation seems promising, although more studies need to be conducted to explore the range of emotional influence that is possible.

References

1. Alonso, M.B., Keyson, D.V., Hummels, C.C.M.: Squeeze, rock, and roll; can tangible interaction with affective products support stress reduction? In: Proceedings of the 2nd International Conference on Tangible and Embedded Interaction (TEI 2008), pp. 105–108. ACM, New York (2008). http://dx.doi.org/10.1145/1347390.1347413
2. Arch, J.J., Graske, M.G.: Mechanisms of mindfulness: emotion regulation following a focused breathing induction. Behav. Res. Ther. **44**, 1849–1858 (2006)
3. Belforte, G., Eula, G., Ivanov, A., Sirolli, S.: Soft pneumatic actuators for rehabilitation. Actuators 3(2), 84–106 (2014). https://doi.org/10.3390/act3020084
4. Bar-Cohen, Y.: Electroactive polymers as artificial muscles: a review. J. Spacecr. Rockets **39**(6), 822–827 (2002)
5. Boer, L., Cahill, B., Vallgårda, A.: The hedonic haptics player: a wearable device to experience vibrotactile compositions. In: Proceedings of the 2017 ACM Conference Companion Publication on Designing Interactive Systems (DIS 2017 Companion), pp. 297–300. ACM, New York (2017). https://doi.org/10.1145/3064857.3079178
6. Bonanni, L., Vaucelle, C., Lieberman, J., Zuckerman, O.: TapTap: a haptic wearable for asynchronous distributed touch therapy. In: CHI 2006 Extended Abstracts on Human Factors in Computing Systems (CHI EA 2006), pp. 580–585 (2006). http://dx.doi.org/10.1145/1125451.1125573
7. Bumatay, A., Seo, J.H.: Investigating the role of biofeedback and haptic stimulation in mobile paced breathing tools. In: Schmorrow, D.D., Fidopiastis, C.M. (eds.) AC 2017. LNCS, vol. 10284, pp. 287–303. Springer, Cham (2017). https://doi.org/10.1007/978-3-319-58628-1_23
8. Canales-Johnson, A., et al.: Auditory feedback differentially modulates behavioral and neural markers of objective and subjective performance when tapping to your heartbeat. Cereb. Cortex **25**(11), 4490–4503 (2015)
9. Costa, J., Adams, A.T., Jung, M.F., Guimbretière, F., Choudhury, T.: EmotionCheck: leveraging bodily signals and false feedback to regulate our emotions. In: Proceedings of the 2016 ACM International Joint Conference on Pervasive and Ubiquitous Computing (UbiComp 2016), pp. 758–769 (2016). https://doi.org/10.1145/2971648.2971752

10. Craig, A.D.: How do you feel? Interoception: the sense of the physiological condition of the body. Nat. Rev. Neurosci. **3**(8), 655–666 (2002). https://doi.org/10.1038/nrn894
11. Delazio, A., Nakagaki, K., Klatzky, R.L., Hudson, S.E., Lehman, J.F., Sample, A.P.: Force jacket: pneumatically-actuated jacket for embodied haptic experiences. In: Proceedings of the 2018 CHI Conference on Human Factors in Computing Systems (CHI 2018), Paper 320, 12 p. ACM, New York (2018). https://doi.org/10.1145/3173574.3173894
12. Dunn, B.D., Stefanovitch, I., Evans, D., Oliver, C., Hawkins, A., Dalgleish, T.: Can you feel the beat? Interoceptive awareness is an interactive function of anxiety- and depression-specific symptom dimensions. Behav. Res. Ther. **48**(11), 1133–1138 (2010)
13. Elliot, W.J., et al.: Graded blood pressure in hypertensive outpatients associated with the use of a device to assist with slow breathing. J. Clin. Hypertens. **6**(10), 553–559 (2004). https://doi.org/10.1111/j.1524-6175.2004.03553.x
14. Ghandeharioun, A., Picard, R.: BrightBeat: effortlessly influencing breathing for cultivating calmness and focus. In: Proceedings of the 2017 CHI Conference Extended Abstracts on Human Factors in Computing Systems (CHI EA 2017), pp. 1624–1631 (2017). https://doi.org/10.1145/3027063.3053164
15. Hatfield, E., Cacioppo, J.T., Rapson, R.L.: Emotional Contagion. Cambridge University Press, Cambridge (1993)
16. Holt-Lunstad, J., Birmingham, W.A., Light, K.C.: Influence of a "warm touch" support enhancement intervention among married couples on ambulatory blood pressure, oxytocin, alpha amylase, and cortisol. Psychosom. Med. **70**(9), 976–985 (2008). https://doi.org/10.1097/psy.0b013e318187aef7
17. Ishii, H., Lakatos, D., Bonanni, L., Labrune, J.B.: Radical atoms: beyond tangible bits, toward transformable materials. Interact. **19**(1), 38–51 (2012). https://doi.org/10.1145/2065327.2065337
18. Jane, S.W., Wilkie, D.J., Gallucci, B.B., Beaton, R.D., Huang, H.Y.: Effects of full body massage on pain intensity, anxiety, and physiological relaxation in Taiwanese patients with metastatic bone pain: a pilot study. J. Pain Symptom Manag. **37**(4), 754–763 (2009). https://doi.org/10.1016/j.jpainsymman.2008.04.021
19. Kanbara, K., Fukunaga, M.: Links among emotional awareness, somatic awareness and autonomic homeostatic processing. BioPsychoSocial Med. **10**(1), 16 (2016). https://doi.org/10.1186/s13030-016-0059-3
20. Khalsa, S., et al.: Interoception and mental health: a roadmap. Biol. Psychiatry: Cogn. Neurosci. Neuroimag. **3**(6), 501–513 (2018)
21. Kutner, J.S., et al.: Massage therapy versus simple touch to improve pain and mood in patients with advanced cancer: a randomized trial. Ann. Intern. Med. **149**(6), 369–379 (2008). https://doi.org/10.7326/0003-4819-149-6-200809160-00003
22. Levenson, R.W., Ruef, A.M.: Physiological aspects of emotional knowledge and rapport. In: Ickes, W. (ed.) Empathetic Accuracy, pp. 45–72. Guilford Press, New York (1997)
23. Lowry, C.A., Lightman, S.L., Nutt, D.J.: That warm fuzzy feeling: brain serotonergic neurons and the regulation of emotion. J. Psychopharmacol. **23**(4), 392–400 (2008). https://doi.org/10.1177/0269881108099956
24. Maimani, A.A., Roudaut, A.: Frozen suit: designing a changeable stiffness suit and its application to haptic games. In: Proceedings of the 2017 CHI Conference on Human Factors in Computing Systems (CHI 2017), pp. 2440–2448. ACM, New York (2017). https://doi.org/10.1145/3025453.3025655
25. Menges, A.: Material Computation: Higher Integration in Morphogenetic Design. Wiley, London (2012)

26. Mirams, L., Poliakoff, E., Brown, R.J., Lloyd, D.M.: Brief body scan meditation practice improves somatosensory perceptual decision making. Conscious. Cogn. **22**, 348–359 (2013)
27. Picard, R.: Affective Computing. MIT Press, Cambridge (2000)
28. Pollatos, O., Traut-Mattausch, E., Schroeder, H., Schandry, R.: Interoceptive awareness mediates the relationship between anxiety and the intensity of unpleasant feelings. J. Anxiety Disord. **21**(7), 931–943 (2007). https://doi.org/10.1016/j.janxdis.2006.12.004
29. Ramasamy, R., Juhari, M.R., Sugisaka, M., Osman, N.A.: Pneumatic artificial muscle in biomedical applications. In: Ibrahim, F., Osman, N.A.A., Usman, J., Kadri, N.A. (eds.) 3rd Kuala Lumpur International Conference on Biomedical Engineering 2006. IP, vol. 15, pp. 219–221. Springer, Heidelberg (2007). https://doi.org/10.1007/978-3-540-68017-8_57
30. Roquet, C.D., Sas, C.: Evaluating mindfulness meditation apps. In: Extended Abstracts of the 2018 CHI Conference on Human Factors in Computing Systems (CHI EA 2018), Paper LBW575, 6 p. ACM, New York (2018). https://doi.org/10.1145/3170427.3188616
31. Salminen, K., et al.: Emotional responses to thermal stimuli. In: Proceedings of the 13th international conference on multimodal interfaces (ICMI 2011), pp. 193–196. ACM, New York (2011). http://dx.doi.org/10.1145/2070481.2070513
32. Salminen, K., et al.: Cold or hot? How thermal stimuli are related to human emotional system? In: Oakley, I., Brewster, S. (eds.) HAID 2013. LNCS, vol. 7989, pp. 20–29. Springer, Heidelberg (2013). https://doi.org/10.1007/978-3-642-41068-0_3
33. Ståhl, A., Jonsson, M., Mercurio, J., Karlsson, A., Höök, K., Banka Johnson, E.C.: The soma mat and breathing light. In: Proceedings of the 2016 CHI Conference Extended Abstracts on Human Factors in Computing Systems (CHI EA 2016), pp. 305–308. ACM, New York (2016). https://doi.org/10.1145/2851581.2889464
34. Sumioka, H., Nakae, A., Kanai, R., Ishiguro, H.: Huggable communication medium decreases cortisol levels. Sci. Rep. **3**, 1 (2013). https://doi.org/10.1038/srep03034
35. Tibbits, S. (ed.): Active Matter. The MIT Press, Cambridge (2017)
36. Vaucelle, C., Bonanni, L., Ishii, H.: Design of haptic interfaces for therapy. In: Proceedings of the 27th International Conference on Human Factors in Computing Systems (CHI 2009), pp. 467–470. ACM, New York (2009)
37. Wiberg, M.: The Materiality of Interaction: Notes on the Materials of Interaction Design. The MIT Press, Cambridge (2018)
38. Yoo, Y., Lee, H., Choi, H., Choi, S.: Emotional responses of vibrotactile-thermal stimuli: effects of constant-temperature thermal stimuli. In: Proceedings of the 2017 Seventh International Conference on Affective Computing and Intelligent Interaction (ACII), San Antonio, TX, pp. 273–278 (2017). https://doi.org/10.1109/acii.2017.8273612

DAPI for Health and Learning

A Framework of Longitudinal Study to Understand Determinants of Actual Use of the Portable Health Clinic System

Masuda Begum Sampa[1]([✉]), Md. Nazmul Hossain[2], Rakibul Hoque[2],
Rafiqul Islam[3], Fumihiko Yokota[4], Mariko Nishikitani[4],
Akira Fukuda[1], and Ashir Ahmed[1]

[1] Graduate School of Information Science and Electrical Engineering,
Kyushu University, 744, Moto'oka, Nishi-ku, Fukuoka 819-0395, Japan
sampa@f.ait.kyushu-u.ac.jp
[2] Faculty of Business Studies, University of Dhaka, 1000 Dhaka, Bangladesh
[3] Medical Information Center, Kyushu University, 744, Moto'oka, Nishi-ku,
Fukuoka 819-0395, Japan
[4] Institute of Decision Science for Sustainable Society, Kyushu University,
744, Moto'oka, Nishi-ku, Fukuoka 819-0395, Japan

Abstract. Due to the scarcity of medical infrastructure including doctors and hospitals, ICT based healthcare services is getting popular around the world including low facilities rural areas of Bangladesh. Portable Health Clinic (PHC) system is one of the ICT based healthcare systems. Speciality of this system is that the clinic box is carried and operated by a pre-trained healthcare worker. However, longitudinal study in this context wasn't undertaken before. In order to draw strong inferences about new technology use we need to do longitudinal study. Therefore, the aim is to identify key determinants of *actual use* of the PHC system and to understand how their influence changes over time with increasing experience to explain detailed action sequences that might unfold over time. Face to face survey will be conducted to collect data. Structural Equation Modeling will be used to analyze data. By analyzing data using AMOS 25.0 this study will identify most important time that are key to increase *actual use* of the PHC system. The proposed model can make it possible to offer important practical guidelines to service providers in enhancing *actual use* of the PHC system. The study can suggest way of increasing health awareness to policy makers and way to build awareness to use the system. The study can also contribute to make policy to improve health care situation i.e., reduce morbidity rate in the country.

Keywords: Structural equation modeling · Technology acceptance model · Longitudinal study

© Springer Nature Switzerland AG 2019
N. Streitz and S. Konomi (Eds.): HCII 2019, LNCS 11587, pp. 323–332, 2019.
https://doi.org/10.1007/978-3-030-21935-2_24

1 Introduction

Though dramatic advances in hardware and software capabilities, low usage of already developed information systems continue and low return from organizational investment has been identified. Therefore, understanding and creating the conditions under which the information system will be accepted by human remains a high priority research issue of information systems research and practice. Better understanding of the determinants of *use* behavior would increase user acceptance and usage of new system [1]. Significant changes have been made in the most of the countries in the world over the last decades in explaining and determining user acceptance of information technology at health care sectors [2]. In addition, due to the scarcity of medical infrastructure including doctors and hospitals, and to expensive access to quality health care services remote healthcare services by using advanced Information and Communication Technology (ICT) is getting popular around the world including Bangladesh.

Currently Grameen, Bangladesh and Kyushu University, Japan have developed one of remote healthcare systems called portable health clinic (PHC) system which is carried and operated by one pre-trained health care lady to deliver health care services to the unreached people in Bangladesh who are deprived of quality health care services where doctors from urban area can consultant with patients.

Due to potential benefits and various eHealth initiatives in place, many recent studies have been done to enhance the acceptance of eHealth services by all citizens. Therefore, through proper study of growing popularity of ICT based health care services, it is possible to enhance the actual use of the PHC system. There are four broad categories of factors that can influence consumers' usage of any new product or service - (i) demographic factors (ii) socio-economic factors (iii) cultural factors, and (iv) psychological factors [3]. Understanding factors that influence technology acceptance is essential for its successful adoption [4]. However, there are only few studies conducted in regards to consumer acceptance [5]. A study among 600 families in one particular area in Bangladesh to determine the demographical and socio-economic factors found – consumers' age, occupation and purchasing power have significant influence on their acceptance of eHealth services from PHC system. But this study identified temporary and contemporary solutions or dynamics of determinants of acceptance of the PHC system [6].

Moreover, longitudinal study of a cohort of consumers in the context of Portable Health Clinic (PHC) system wasn't undertaken before to understand the consistent causal relationship among factors of PHC and how their influence changes over time. In order to draw strong inferences about acceptance of new technology we need to do longitudinal study.

Therefore, the main aim of this study is to identify key determinants of actual use of the PHC system and to understand how their influence changes over time with increasing user experience by using the PHC system to explain detailed action sequences that might unfold over time. More detailed objectives are following:

- To develop a general decision making model across time and geographic area for the actual use of PHC system in Bangladesh.
- To identify consistently cited most significant factors in predicting actual use.

- To identify cause and effect relationships among factors over time.
- To explore changing factors of use the system over a 1 year period.
- Testing significant differences among 3 times survey per year: survey 1, survey 2, and survey 3 data, to examine whether the respondents' use of PHC service changed over the period.

A sample of 300 people from both areas (urban and rural) of Bangladesh have been collected by face to face questionnaire survey.

2 Theoretical Basis for Building the Proposed Model

There have been many previous studies targeted to explore the factors influencing the use behavior of a new technology. The present study reviewed previous literature and develops the proposed model. Theory of Reasoned Action (TRA) is the major theory to explain people's behavior [7].

Based on the reasoned action theory, theory of planned behavior was developed which is an extension of TRA [8]. Based on the above models Technology Acceptance Model (TAM) was developed [9]. TAM is the major theory to understand how users come to accept and use a new technology/system. By 10 years, TAM has become a well-established, robust, powerful, and parsimonious model for predicting user acceptance but this model did not include some important external variables. TAM2 model supported well basic TAM relationships and extended TAM model by adding additional determinants of the basic TAM model (TAM1)'s perceived usefulness and usage intention constructs. Later Unified Theory of Acceptance and Use of Technology (UTAUT) model was developed by adding four constructs in the basic technology acceptance model: facilitating conditions, social influence, performance expectancy, and effort expectancy [10].

Based on TAM1, TAM2, UTAUT and other existing user acceptance model we would like to propose a generalized theoretical model that can investigate factors behind actual use of PHC system in Bangladesh. In our proposed model, we incorporated TAM1 [9], TAM2 [1], and UTAUT [10] model moreover; we are arguing that illness, health awareness, and self-efficacy directly affect actual use of Portable Health Clinic (PHC) system (Figs. 1 and 2).

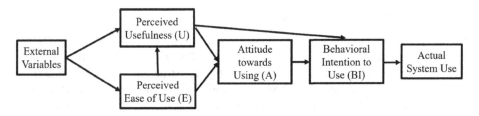

Fig. 1. TAM1 - First version of TAM [9]

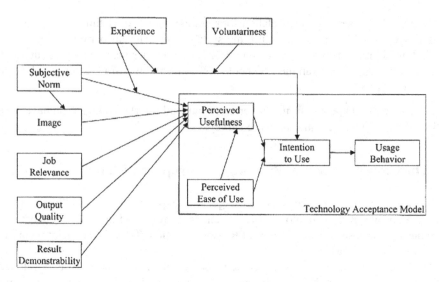

Fig. 2. TAM2 - a theoretical extension of TAM1 [1]

3   Methodology

3.1   Study Place

We have selected two areas of Bangladesh to collect our data. One is the urban area and another one is the rural area. (i) Urban area: Grameen Bank Complex, Mirpur, Dhaka, and (ii) Rural area: Ekhlaspur village, Matlab, Chandpur.

3.2   Study Population

The target population is those who have used the PHC system at least once. The target population size is: 300 from both areas. And participants must be: (1) Adult aged older than or equal to 35 years, (2) Residents who live at the targeted survey areas, (3) Those who provides informed written consent, and (7) Those who are healthy enough to be able to participate in this research.

3.3   Statistical Basis of the Sample Size and Sampling Procedures

There is considerable variation in the opinions observed in the literature in regard to the selection/calculation of optimum sample size in different types of statistical analysis [11]. For example, statistical analysis including structural equation modeling (SEM) recommends sampling of 200 as fair and 300 as good [12]. Hair et al. also recommended a sample size of 200 to test a model using SEM. A 'critical sample size' that can be used in any common estimation procedure for valid results [13]. As per previous studies, a sample size of 300 was selected in this study for data analysis using SEM [14].

The sample was drawn by a simple random sampling procedure. In this study, we informed people first about our PHC system. After initial introduction about PHC system, survey1 will be conducted among those who come to the service point and have received the PHC service at least once. The same respondent will be interviewed in the post-survey.

3.4   Data Collection Methods

Longitudinal field survey through structured questionnaire will be conducted to measure factors/variables. Data will be collected in 3 different points in time per year: First survey (survey 1) - after initial introduction of the PHC system (T1), Second survey (survey 2) - 4 months after the first survey (T2), Third survey (survey 3) - 4 months after the second survey (T3). The same respondent will be interviewed in the post-survey.

3.5   Pretesting

Pilot survey was conducted in both areas. 35 respondents were interviewed after receiving the PHC healthcare service. Furthermore, we have analyzed their responses. Based on feedback from the pilot survey, we have finalized our questionnaire.

3.6   Questionnaire Design

The questionnaire contains the following two parts: (1) Part A (Socio-demographic information)-Name, age, education level, gender, having phone, having access to internet, past experience, and, having any kind of illness etc. and (2) Part-B (Cognitive or Perceptional questions)-13 Psychological factors which are used in the initial hypothetical model (Fig. 3). Every factor will be measured by 3 questionnaire items. Respondent will read each statement and rate each statement on 5-point Likert scales by putting $\sqrt{}$ (tick) in the number that best describes she/he. All statements will be measured on a 5-point Likert scale, where 1 = Strongly disagree, 2 = Disagree, 3 = Neither Disagree nor agree, 4 = Agree, and 5 = Strongly agree.

3.7   Outcome Variables

Our outcome variable is the *actual use* of the Portable Health Clinic (PHC) system. We have asked three questionnaire items to measure the dependent variable.

3.8   Hypotheses of the Study

Based on previous related researches we propose following hypotheses:

H1. Perceived usefulness will have a positive and direct effect on actual use of the Portable Health Clinic (PHC) system.

Perceived usefulness is defined as the extent to which a person believes that using the PHC system will improve his or her health [1].

H2. Social influence will have a positive and direct effect on actual use of the Portable Health Clinic (PHC) system.

Social influence is defined as the degree to which an individual perceives that important others believe he or she should use the system. Social influence is similar to subjective norm and social norm [10]. Social norm or subjective norm is defined as an individual's perception most people who are important to him think that he should or should not perform the specific behavior [7]. In other words, social influence means reference from friends or family members or loved one. Social norm consists of two influences: 1. Informational norm to enhance knowledge and 2. normative to conforms expectations of others [15]. Subjective norms concern the perceived social pressures to undertake or not undertake a behavior [8, 16]. And moral norms are personal feelings of moral responsibility or obligation to perform a certain behavior which may have a significant contribution to explain the variance of the behavior [8, 17]. Social reference was a direct determinant of acceptance of eHealth technology [18]. Study analyzed energy saving behavior among University students in Vietnam and identified Social norm was the most important determinants for energy saving behavior such as avoiding AC use [19]. Social norm had also direct positive influence on waste reduction behavior [20].

H3. Illness will have a positive and direct effect on actual use of the PHC system.

H4. Health awareness will have a positive and direct effect on actual use of the PHC system.

Health awareness is measured to assess the degree of readiness to undertake health actions [21]. This construct reflects a persons' readiness to do something for his or her own health [22].

H5. Privacy will have a positive and direct effect on actual use of the PHC system.

Privacy is defined as the extent to which a respondent believes that PHC system will not compromise his or her privacy [23].

H6. User self-efficacy will have a positive and direct effect on actual use of the PHC system.

Perceived self-efficacy is defined as the judgement of one's ability to use a technology [10, 24]. That is belief that using the PHC system can improve or benefit his or her health condition.

H7. Past experience of using any eHealth system other than PHC system will have a positive and direct effect on actual use of the PHC system.

H8. Internet access will have a positive and direct effect on actual use of the PHC system.

H9. Having mobile will have a positive and direct effect on actual use of the PHC system.

H10. Intention to actual use will have a positive and direct effect on actual use of the PHC system.

The theory of reasoned action (TRA) by Ajzen et al. [25] has identified that intention to perform behavior as the immediate determinants of behavior.

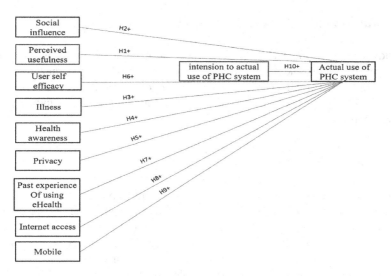

Fig. 3. Initial hypothetical model. Note: H indicates hypothesis, + indicates positive effect between two variables.

3.9 Statistical Methods of Data Analysis

We will apply two well established statistical methods to analyze our data, which are: Exploratory Factor Analysis (by using Statistical Package for Social Sciences (SPSS) 25.0): We will use factor analysis to measure factors that were used in our proposed research model. Structural Equation Modeling (by using Analysis of a Moment Structures (AMOS) 25.0 software tool): We will use Structural Equation Modeling statistical technique to identify cause and effect relationship among factors.

4   Expected Results

The result can identify the degree (value) of relationship between statistically significant variables. We will examine the direct and indirect roles of *social norm, perceived usefulness, user self-efficacy, health awareness, privacy, illness, past experience of using eHealth,* and *access to internet connection* on actual use of the eHealth system in Bangladesh. The study can also offer important practical guidelines to the PHC service providers in enhancing *actual use* of the PHC system. Results can suggest way of increasing health awareness and to build awareness to use PHC system to policy makers. The results of this study can also contribute to make policy to reduce morbidity rate in the country.

5   Limitations and Future Directions

The study will be conducted to only two specific geographic areas due to time and budget constrain. Thus the results may raise concern about the generalizability of the findings. Due to the small sample size our model could able to explain less % of the variance. In future, we could include more geographic areas. Future study could also increase sample size.

6   Conclusion

This study will theoretically develop a modified and improved eHealth acceptance model. The study will be the first longitudinal study to identify the key psychological factors and socio-demographic characteristics behind *actual use* of the PHC system by potential users. It can offer important practical guidelines to service providers and policy makers in promoting *actual use* of the PHC system.

We will examine the direct and indirect roles of *social norm, perceived usefulness, user self- efficacy, health awareness, privacy, illness, past experience of using eHealth,* and *access to internet connection on actual use* of the eHealth system in Bangladesh. Structural equation modeling statistical technique will be used to test the hypotheses of the study. Some factors those who have direct and positive effects on *actual use* of the PHC system will be also identified.

The proposed model through this study will make it possible to offer important practical guidelines to service providers and policymakers in promoting *actual use* of the eHealth system in Bangladesh.

For policy recommendation, we should take into account more the most important predictor of *actual use* of the PHC system. And for this identified predictor we can inform policy maker the way of increasing this predictor. We should also focus on followed by predictors of the actual use of the PHC system. In addition, our result can also suggest the way of increasing significant predictors based on indirect effects.

Therefore, the result of this study can offer important practical guidelines to the PHC service providers in enhancing actual use of the PHC system. Results can also suggest way of increasing health awareness and to build awareness to use PHC system to policy makers. The results of this study can also contribute to make policy to improve the healthcare system in the country i.e., to reduce morbidity rate in the country.

Acknowledgement. This research work has been supported by multiple organizations. JSPS KAKENHI, Grant Number 18K11529 and the Future Earth Research Fund, Grant Number 18-161009264 jointly financed the core research. Institute of Decision Science for a Sustainable Society (IDS3), Kyushu University, Japan provided travel expenses for data collection, and Grameen Communications, Bangladesh provided technical assistance.

References

1. Venkatesh, V., Davis, F.D.: A theoretical extension of the technology acceptance model: four longitudinal Studies. Manag. Sci. **46**(2), 186–205 (2000)
2. Hoque, R., Sorwar, G.: Understanding factors influencing the adoption of mHealth by the elderly: an extension of the UTAUT model. Int. J. Med. Inform. **101**, 75–84 (2017)
3. Armstrong, G., Adam, S., Denize, S., Kotlar, P.: Principles of Marketing. 14th edn. Pearson
4. Randike, G., Renato, I., Tony, S.: Consumer acceptance of accountable eHealth systems, eHealth Contin. Care **205**, 980–984 (2014)
5. Petkovic, M., Ibraimi, L.: Privacy and security in e-health applications, e-health, Assist. Technol. Appl. Assist. Living Chall. Solut., 23–48 (2011)
6. Hossain, M.N., Okajima, H., Kitaoka, H., Ahmed, A.: Consumer acceptance of eHealth among rural inhabitants in consumer acceptance of eHealth among rural inhabitants in developing countries developing countries (a study on portable health clinic in Bangladesh). Procedia Comput. Sci. **111**, 471–478 (2017)
7. Fishbein, M., Ajzen, I.: Belief, Attitude, Intention and Behavior: an Introduction to Theory and Research. Penn State University Press, University Park (1975)
8. Icek, A.: The theory of planned behavior organizational behavior and human decision processes. Organ. Behav. Hum. Decis. Process. **50**(2), 179–211 (1991)
9. Davis, F.D.: Perceived usefulness, perceived ease of use, and user acceptance of information technology. MIS Q. **13**(3), 319–340 (1989)
10. Venkatesh, V., Morris, M.G., Davis, G.B., Davis, F.D.: User acceptance of information technology: toward a unified view. MIS Q. **27**(3), 425–478 (2003)
11. Hair, J.F., Anderson, R.E., Tatham, R.L., Black, W.C.: Multivariate Data Analysis, 5th edn. Bowling Green (1998)
12. Kline, R.: Principles and Practice of Structural Equation Modeling. Guilford Publications, New York (2015)
13. Hoelter, J.W.: The analysis of covariance structures. Sociol. Methods Res. **11**(3), 325–344 (1983)
14. Roscoe, J.T.: Fundamental Research Statistics for the Behavioral Sciences. Holt, Rinehart and Winston (1975)
15. Hsu, C.-L., Lin, J.C.-C.: Acceptance of blog usage: the roles of technology acceptance, social influence and knowledge sharing motivation. Inf. Manag. **45**(1), 65–74 (2008)
16. Neal, P.W.O.: Motivation of Health Behavior. Nova Science Publishers Inc., New York (2007)
17. Botetzagias, I., Dima, A.-F., Malesios, C.: Extending the theory of planned behavior in the context of recycling: the role of moral norms and of demographic predictors. Resour. Conserv. Recycl. **95**, 58–67 (2015)
18. Hossain, N., Yokota, F., Sultana, N., Ahmed, A.: Factors influencing rural end-users' acceptance of e-health in developing countries: a study on portable health clinic in Bangladesh. Telemed. e-Health **25**(3), 221–229 (2019)
19. Goto, N., Tokunaga, S., Nga, D.T., Ho, V., Thanh, T.: Analysis of energy-saving behavior among university students in Vietnam. J. Environ. Sci. Eng. B **5**, 355–362 (2016)
20. Hirose, Y.: Two-phase decision making model of environmental conscious behavior and its application for the waste reduction behavior. Soc. Secur. Bull. **5**, 81–91 (2014)
21. Ophuis, P.A.M.O.: Measuring health orientation and health consciousness as determinants of food choice behavior: development and implementation of various attitudinal scales, EMAC XVIII. Athens School of Economics and Business, Athens, Greece (1989)

22. Schifferstein, H.N.J., Ophuist, P.A.M.O.: Health-related determinants of organic food consumptions in the Netherlands. Food Qual. Prefer. **9**(3), 119–133 (1998)
23. Vijayasarathy, L.R.: Predicting consumer intentions to use on-line shopping: the case for an augmented technology acceptance model. Inf. Manag. **41**, 747–762 (2004)
24. Rockmann, R., Gewald, H.: Elderly people in eHealth: Who are they? Procedia Comput. Sci. **63**, 505–510 (2015)
25. Ajzen, I., Fishbein, M.: Understanding Attitudes and Predicting Social Behavior. Prentice-Hall, Upper Saddle River (1980)

Feasibility of Digital Health Services for Educating the Community People Regarding Lifestyle Modification Combating Noncommunicable Diseases

Mithila Faruque[1], Mohammad Badruddozza Mia[2],
Moinul H. Chowdhury[3], Farhana Sarker[3,4],
and Khondaker A. Mamun[3,5(✉)]

[1] Department of NCD, Bangladesh University of Health Sciences (BUHS),
Dhaka, Bangladesh
mithilafaruque@gmail.com
[2] School of Business and Economics, United International University (UIU),
Dhaka, Bangladesh
badruddozza@bus.uiu.ac.bd
[3] CMED Health Limited (A Research Commercialization of AIMS Lab, UIU),
Dhaka, Bangladesh
moin@cmedhealth.com
[4] Department of CSE, University of Liberal Arts Bangladesh (ULAB),
Dhaka, Bangladesh
farhana.sarker@ulab.edu.bd
[5] AIMS Lab, Department of CSE, United International University (UIU),
Dhaka, Bangladesh
mamun@cse.uiu.ac.bd

Abstract. Mobile health (mHealth), or the use of mobile technology to improve health, is a rapidly expanding field. There have been a number of intervention studies based on mobile apps and most of these focused on specific medical issues. A majority of the available health apps are for health and wellness promotion and disease prevention for the general public. But the pace of traditional academic research is slow and less nimble relative to commercial app development resulting in huge lags in dissemination into commercial settings for public health. This paper assessed the content, usability and efficacy of the commercially launched digital healthcare platform developed by CMED Health for the purpose of preventing major noncommunicable diseases in the rural communities of Bangladesh. A combining approach of quantitative, qualitative and participant observation were used in this study following the principles and process of Action Research methodology. The study evaluated the CMED health app by content analysis, usability testing, health observational study, and efficacy testing. The view of the service receivers, service providers and health managers of the concerned organization was evaluated to test the feasibility. The quantitative data was collected using a semi-structured questionnaire from 393 service receivers and qualitative data was collected through Key Informant Interview (KII) of key-informants of service providing team, senior staff members and village opinion leaders and Focus Group Discussions (FGDs) with the direct service providers and service receivers. The study

© Springer Nature Switzerland AG 2019
N. Streitz and S. Konomi (Eds.): HCII 2019, LNCS 11587, pp. 333–345, 2019.
https://doi.org/10.1007/978-3-030-21935-2_25

analyzed quantitative health data generated from the service delivery during 6-month piloting with the members of more than 7,000 households in 21 villages. The main reasons for accepting the CMED health app was showing the results instantly on the screen, instant advices and getting health services in a smart system within a short period of time. This also increased their trust on the health care providers and they were benefitted by the health records stored in the cloud of the user for their next visit to physicians and getting medicines. The people also mentioned about the suitability of the digital healthcare services for preventing diabetes and hypertension in the community.

Keywords: Mobile health app · Usability · Noncommunicable diseases · Prevention · Health records · Smart device

1 Introduction

Mobile health (mHealth), or the use of mobile technology to improve health, is a rapidly expanding field [1]. As of 2015, more than 165,000 mHealth apps were available on the Apple iTunes and Android app in play stores, and 34% of mobile phone owners had at least one health app on their mobile device [2–4]. Commercial mobile apps for health behaviour change are flourishing in the marketplace. Although health apps have drawn great public interest and use, little evidence exists about the usability and efficacy of the majority of commercially available apps [5, 6]. Producing an app for public use requires content, programming, design expertise, the ability to continually host and update the app, and the resources to provide both customer service and technical support [7–9].

CMED Health is an Internet of Things (IoT) enabled Artificial Intelligence (AI) driven cloud based preventive and primary health care service provider [10]. CMED uses portable smart medical sensors and devices connected to a smart phone application for the measurement of vital signs or health parameters and store data to its secured cloud server. Based on acquired data, CMED clinical decision support systems (CDSS) perform health risks assessment and provide instant feedback to the user about their health status, and moreover, it connects to a doctor if he/she has risks. CMED digital healthcare platform also generates sharable health reports from stored health data which helps doctors to minimize diagnostic time and to provide better treatment. The architecture of CMED digital healthcare platform for providing preventive and primary healthcare services is shown in Fig. 1.

Unlike the existing systems used usually, CMED system keep records of the user's data automatically. It also give suggestions to the users to consult with the physician when their health condition is at risk. At this current stage, CMED system can monitor the vital parameters of human health like blood pressure, blood glucose, pulse, blood oxygen saturation (SpO2), body temperature, weight, height and body mass index (BMI) [10]. The pictorial representation of CMED Smart devices, health kit, and App showing color coded measurement records as well as example of measuring blood glucose using smart devices, App and CDSS feedback is shown in Fig. 2.

Over the last two decades, Bangladesh, a lower middle-income country, has experienced a rapid demographic and epidemiological transition [11]. The population is

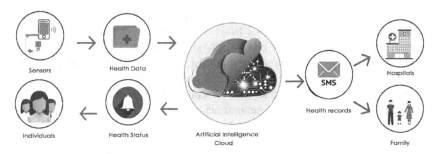

Fig. 1. Architecture of CMED IoT enabled Artificial Intelligence driven Cloud based Preventive and Primary Healthcare Platform, which includes CMED smart devices, mobile App, CDSS, and Cloud platform.

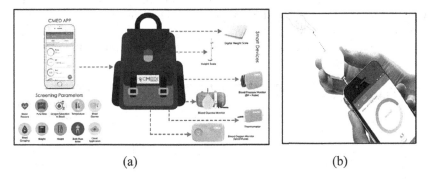

(a)   (b)

Fig. 2. (a) Smart devices for screening health parameters (blood pressure, blood glucose, pulse, blood oxygen saturation (SpO2), body temperature, weight, height and body mass index) equipping in CMED health kit, and CMED App showing color coded measurement records; and (b) example of measuring blood glucose using smart devices, App and CDSS feedback based on the blood glucose value in the CMED Digital preventive and primary healthcare platform.

projected to increase substantially from 147 million in 2007 to 218 million in 2050 [12]. In 1986, the total deaths due to chronic diseases was 8% which increased to 68% by 2006 in rural Bangladesh [13]. At least in part, this can be explained by changes in nutritional status. People in Bangladesh are not conscious about their health. Bangladesh is actually facing a major crisis in this sector. Being one of the highly populated country, a number of people are suffering due to obesity, cardiovascular diseases, diabetes and many other non-communicable diseases. In a nationally representative study among adults (>35 years) 18.9% were overweight and 4.6% were obese [14] whereas about 17.9% school children were obese [15], around 21% people are suffering from hypertension [16], and more than 10% are diabetic [17]. On the other hand, due to the unhealthy dietary habit, physical inactivity and other behavioural factors health risks are increasing simultaneously. According to World Health Organization, 67% of the deaths occurs in low-and middle-income countries due to non-communicable diseases with 31% of these deaths is due to cardiovascular diseases and 3% is due to diabetes [18]. Best way to deal with non-communicable disease is preventive healthcare. Research has claimed that preventive healthcare can reduce the risk of NCDs – upto 90% strokes, 80% heart attack and 73% diabetes can be prevented by changing lifestyle with healthy diet and physical exercise [19–21]. Thus preventive healthcare with regular health monitoring and lifestyle modification can minimize the healthcare risk, cost and time of an individual and of the nation as a whole [22].

CMED Health Platform is designed to reduce the risk of life threatening non-communicable diseases like stroke, heart attack, diabetes, obesity, etc. With the regular health monitoring systems, users would be able to reduce diagnostic time, follow up cost, cost of hospitalization and hospital days significantly. Community Health Workers (CHW) can also play a vital role in the rural areas by using CMED systems. This paper assessed the content, usability and efficacy of the commercially launched digital healthcare platform developed by CMED Health for the purpose of preventing major noncommunicable diseases (cardiovascular diseases, hypertension and diabetes) and improving primary health care in the rural communities of Bangladesh. Figure 3 showing CMED App user registration process with demographics and household information collection, health parameters screening using App and smart devices and measurement records of the user (a); and CMED Digital Healthcare Platform Dashboard

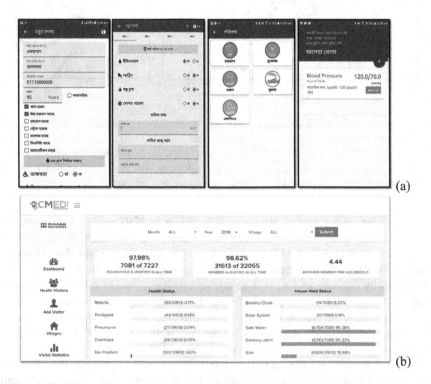

Fig. 3. (a) CMED App showing user registration process with demographics and household information collection, health parameters screening using App and smart devices as well as showing color coded measurement records of the user. (b) CMED Digital Healthcare Platform Dashboard showing aggregated information and statistics on household visits, health conditions, household and demographic status, health workers work performance and so on.

with aggregated information and statistics on household visits, papulation health conditions, household and demographic status, health workers work performance and so.

2 Methods

A triangulation of research methods combining quantitative, qualitative and participant observation were used in this study following the principles and process of Action Research Methodology. The study was conducted through a pilot project on digital health services implemented with more than 32,000 people in about 7,000 households of 21 villages in Dhamrai upazila (sub-district) of greater Dhaka district in Bangladesh. The study was conducted during the period of July to December of 2019 with joint initiative of CMED Health; AIMS Lab, Department of CSE, United International University; Department of NCD, Bangladesh University of Health Sciences; Palli Karma Sahayak Foundation (PKSF) and local Non-Government Organization (NGO), SOJAG. Demonstration of digital healthcare services in rural areas of Bangladesh using CMED preventive and primary healthcare platform is shown in Fig. 4. The study evaluated the digital healthcare services model implemented through mobile health apps developed by CMED Health. It includes content analysis, usability testing, health observational study, and efficacy testing as discussed below.

Fig. 4. Demonstration of digital healthcare services delivery using CMED preventive and primary healthcare platform in Dhamrai upazila, a rural areas of Bangladesh.

(a) The contents were evaluated by comparing the cut off values and interpretation with the National Protocol on Diabetes and Hypertension. The contents of the CDSS were evaluated by the stakeholders such as medical professionals, health service providers, health service receivers, service supervisors and management staff members of the NGO. As a guiding standard, the content evaluation study followed the national protocol in the rural setting for pilot implementation.

(b) The health information and advices incorporated in the digital healthcare services model were validated by expert consultation through arranging a workshop at the policy level.

(c) During piloting, the usability testing of the services model has been conducted. Through a testing-and-fixing process the interfaces of the mobile health service app were established. The field health service providers and the management staff members were used for this usability testing in the working environment. It has been assessed how well the app functions and serves its intended purpose for a target population which was explored through a piloting or field testing.

(d) The efficacy of the digital health app was evaluated through comparing the measurement values with the manual and traditional methods. Through 6-month piloting the efficacy of the app and underlying systems has been evaluated in the socio-cultural setting of rural Bangladesh.

The rural health service providers provided health services to the every household members of 21 villages using the CMED digital healthcare platform for 6 months. The study team observed the participants, the process of providing health services, and the use of smart devices and mobile app on a continuous manner, and went through a process of evaluation. The study team collected quantitative and qualitative data from (1) Rural Health Service Providers, (2) Senior Management Staff Members, (3) Selected Village Opinion Leaders, and (4) Service Receivers. And the feasibility of the digital health services was evaluated by taking the view from the service receivers, providers and health managers of the concerned organization.

The study analyzed quantitative health data generated from the service delivery during 6-month piloting with the members of more than 7,000 households in 21 villages. The quantitative data was collected using separate semi-structured questionnaire from 393 service receivers of the piloting area. Qualitative data has also been collected through Key Informant Interview (KII) of key-informants of service providing team, senior staff members and village opinion leaders and conducting four Focus Group Discussions (FGDs) with the key participant groups of the pilot project. Two FGDs were conducted with the service providers who used both the CMED smart devices and app, and another one was conducted with the group who used manual devices and app for providing digital services. Two more FGDs were conducted among the service receivers in two different villages. Prefixed separate FGD guidelines were used for conducting FGDs among the service providers and receivers. The discussion was recorded in a tape recorder and also noted in pen and paper. The transcription of the discussion findings has been done and presented as speech mark in the result. Figure 5 showing Focused Grouped Discussion on digital health service with the rural people (service receivers) and the health workers (service providers).

Fig. 5. Focused Grouped Discussion on digital health service with the rural people (service receivers) and the health workers (service providers).

3   Results

During the CMED digital health services pilot project, 17,907 adult population out of 32,122 have received the primary health screening services through the use of CMED digital platform and smart medical devices. The services include regular blood pressure monitoring, glucose monitoring, BMI, SPO2 and MUAC for child nutrition measurement of aged under 5 years.

Table 1 shows the number of services provided in different measurements during pilot study. Of the 17907 people, blood pressure, BMI and SPO2 have been measured for the highest number of times among all other health screening.

Table 1. Number of measurements taken in each category during pilot study.

Measurement type	BP	Glucose	BMI	SPO2	MUAC
Number of measurements	36326	1348	34721	38400	1229

3.1   Quantitative Findings

Gender of the Respondents from Service Receivers. The responses were taken at the day time when most of the men remain busy with their works outside. As a result, most of the respondents were female, which consists of 92.10% female and 7.90% male.

Types of Services Received. Figure 6 shows the primary health screening services taken using CMED digital healthcare system as percentage of survey population. On average, more than 90% of the adult population have taken the primary health screening services. On the other hand, 21% children of the total population have received MUAC test to measure malnutrition.

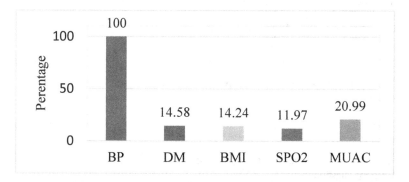

Fig. 6. Type of services and its percentage received by the community people using Digital Healthcare Platform.

Acceptance and Preference. About 99.5% of the respondents exhibited satisfaction when asked about the acceptance of CMED digital health services. The respondents also expect continuation of the CMED digital health services in future. Almost all respondents could mention about the services they received from the local NGO (SOJAG) health workers including blood pressure, blood glucose, SPO2, MUAC, height, weight and BMI measurements. Most of the respondents told that the new digital method (CMED health app with smart devices) is better than the old manual method. The study found that majority of the service receivers accepted the service delivery model using smart devices and app. However, a very few service receivers recommended for the old manual machines as they are used to it and thought those are more reliable. When we explored the reasons of liking the new digital system, it was observed that more than quarter (27.3%) of the respondents mentioned new method is digital and smart looking, 14.7% of the respondents mentioned the results can be seen instantly on the screen, and can be compared with previous record (14.4%), about 13% respondents liked it as they can get the advices instantly through the app as shown in Fig. 7. Rest of the participants/population had different views like they are getting the accurate health results in a short time at their doorsteps. All the respondents told that the digital method using smart device and app is suitable for providing health services at the community level. A minor proportion of the respondents (1.6%) mentioned about the reasons of their dissatisfaction as they do not get the services and instant medicine completely free which is out of scope of the study and completely depends on the providers service model.

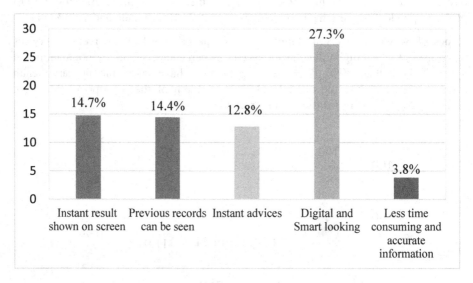

Fig. 7. Reasons for acceptance of the CMED digital healthcare platform and its percentage based on survey questionnaires.

We found that the majority of the sample liked CMED system in their regular health monitoring services for many reasons. Previously, they could not see the results with their own eyes. All they had to do is to rely on what the health workers say to them. As a result there was a certain level of understanding gap. On top of that, they could not remember the records provided by the health workers or lost the written reports. Now they can see the reports on the screen with their eyes instantly which they can believe. They now do not have to worry about maintaining their previous records as well. In addition, they find the system is very efficient and effective with the advices provided by the CMED CDSS. Based on the advices provided by the app, they are acting upon it by doing lifestyle modification with various exercises such as started walking or walking more than before.

Usability of the App. All the respondents responded positively when asked about the usablity of CMED health services in the community level. They were satisfied with the interfaces and output formats of the app. Also regarding detection of the heath conditions, the smart app and device was more effective as it identified more diabetic and hypertensive patients in the community. For example, only 2.7% of the population knew that they have diabetes whereas 15.8% were found with diabetes after blood glucose measurement. After this finding, people have been found to be more concerned about the NCDs and they are acting upon to prevent it. For example, some of them started to exert physical efforts to stay healthy and fit. This has been possible due to the visibility of results on the phone's screen in native language, which they can understand easily. On the other hand, only 6.5% of the population knew that they have hypertension while after screening, 11.5% people were identified as hypertensive. Accordingly, more adult population who came to know their health condition through primary health screening services using CMED digital system can now reduce the risk of stroke, cardiovascular diseases and other related NCDs through life style modifications.

3.2 Qualitative Findings

FGD Findings from the Health Visitors. The health workers of the local NGO are working in this field for around six years and provide primary health services to the community people. These primary health services includes blood pressure monitoring, blood glucose monitoring, height measurement, weight measurement, SPO2 monitoring and MUAC measurement for the children who are aged under 5 years. Besides, they arrange two days of satellite clinic service in every week and help the rural people consult with the doctors in real time. Also they set various health camps for the villagers such as eye health camp, heart camp, ENT camp etc. Each health visitor covers at least 25 households every day. The FGD findings of the different health workers are presented as below-

"Previously we didn't measure the height and weight of all people. We didn't monitor BMI of the people as manual BMI calculation is very complicated and time consuming, which was very hard to do at the field level. However, now we can monitor BMI through the CMED system very easily."

"Now I can give proper advice to the villagers using CMED app and smart devices for which they respect us more than before."

"Now the villagers can see their blood pressure status directly on the screen through CMED health app, which helped them to trust the health workers more than before. Also they want to know the previous record of blood pressure, weight etc. and compare with the current measurements. With all these facilities, the villagers are satisfied and excited."

When they were asked about the usability of the app in measuring blood pressure and glucose at the field level they told that smart device and app is very suitable to use in the field. It will be helpful for the villagers. Now the villagers are more aware of their health condition. They are now satisfied as the health workers provide services using digital technique. More comments from health workers on digital services are presented below.

"The messages are very useful to the villagers and they try to obey their advices."

"The machine can say whether one is diabetic or not, hypertensive or not, overweight or not. As a result, the villagers are now more eager to test their primary health vitals. Also the result accuracy of the devices is more than 90 percent."

The health workers also mentioned that relatives of the piloting villages regretfully say that,

"You have so many advantages in your village. You get the health services in modern technique, but we don't have that service in our village. We didn't see it before. We also want this service in our village".

One of the villagers told to a health visitor,

"After measuring my weight, when I saw it was more than normal, I started walking. Now I walk regularly and feel better than before".

FGD Findings from the Service Receivers. The people in the village, who received digital healthcare service and participated in the FGD mentioned that,

"Previously when the health workers measured the blood pressure or other parameters, only we could not see it, but now in digital system we can see it directly on the screen and we get the suggestions at the same time. As we couldn't see the results before, we hardly trusted them thinking that could be wrong."

"We can take our previous records from the app and use it when we go to the doctors for consultation."

About the feasibility of the CMED app the villagers mentioned that,

"We think this health services provided by the smart device and app would be feasible to implement at the field level for detection of hypertension and diabetes among the community."

4 Discussion

In our country, 67% deaths occur due to noncommunicable disease like, heart attack, stroke, diabetes, cancer and chronic obstructive pulmonary disease and our health system is not ready to handle this soaring burden [23]. Cardiovascular (CVD) mortality raised from 17% in 2014 to 30% in 2018 and 85% of these deaths are due to heart attack and stroke [24]. Still the people do not know their health status and there are about 36 lacs undiagnosed cases of diabetes in Bangladesh [22]. So people come to the physicians for solution with complications leading to increased morbidity, mortality and health expenditure. According to Bangladesh National Health Accounts, our out-of-pocket health expenditure is one of the highest (67% of the country's total health costs) in South-East Asian Region. Seventy percent of the health expenditure is spent on drugs, health care services, and curative health care while just 10% accounts to preventive care [25]. Still more than 70% people in our country live in rural area where health service delivery is not within the reach of the general people [26]. In these circumstances, we need a cost-effective health intervention which is acceptable and available at the community level. To make the health services accessible to the people CMED Health launched a digital healthcare services which can identify the health conditions at an early stage with low cost. Thus CMED Health is bringing upon change and creating impact in the health sector by saving lives. However, the actual behaviour change in the community couldn't be measured due to short duration of the study.

Regarding feasibility we have identified the following advantages of CMED digital healthcare platform-

1. Through this smart app health managers can constantly supervise the health workers and easily identify the gap in the system.
2. Due to the collection and storage of information in the digital system the usability of the app has been increased and now it is possible to do the research in various directions like socio-economic, gender based, environmental, disease risk factors identification and association with different factors.
3. Health administrators and policy makers can visualize the overall information of a population in a defined geographical area sitting in one place through the dashboard of the platform, like the total birth, death, marriage, pregnancy, disease prevalence, sufferings, medical expenses etc.
4. Collecting and recording the information at the same time has reduced the additional hassle for further data collection.
5. As the digital system works in offline, so the health workers could work uninterruptedly and finish their work in time even though the areas doesn't have good internet coverage.
6. Using this app, the workload of the health workers has been reduced a lot and their interest in work has been increased. As a result, the efficiency of the organization is also increasing.
7. The knowledge of the community people regarding their health risks and its prevention has been increased as instant advices are provided through the CDSS of the app during health monitoring.

CMED health created a cloud based digital healthcare platform through which specific health interventions can be designed against a particular health condition among a group of population (gender, age based). Also the app can be used to design a health insurance policy for the people based on their socio-economic characteristics.

5 Conclusion

As per opinion of the service providers and service receivers the CMED digital preventive and primary healthcare system is suitable and feasible to use at the rural and urban community level throughout the country. It was noticeable that awareness has been developed among the villagers after getting the health services through smart device and app with CDSS. So this digital method can be used as the primary prevention intervention model to prevent the exposure to risk factors of NCDs and reduce the burden of chronic diseases in a low resource setting like Bangladesh where there is a dearth of healthcare services in remote areas.

Acknowledgement. We would like to thank Palli Karma Sahayak Foundation (PKSF); Enhancing Resources and Increasing Capacities of Poor Households Towards Elimination of their Poverty (ENRICH) program of PKSF; Partner Organization SOJAG (a local NGO); and United International University, Bangladesh as well as the team for their support and cooperation to implement the pilot program.

References

1. Istepanian, R., Laxminarayan, S., Pattichis, C.: M-Health: Emerging Mobile Health Systems. Springer, New York (2006). https://doi.org/10.1007/b137697
2. Fox, S., Duggan, M.: Mobile Health 2012: Half of smartphone owners use their devices to get health information and one-fifth of smartphone owners have health apps. Pew Res. Cent. Internet Technol. (2012). http://www.pewinternet.org/2012/11/08/mobile-health-2012/
3. Terry, K.: Medscape: number of health apps soars, but use does not always follow (2015). http://www.medscape.com/viewarticle/851226
4. Smith, A.: U.S. Smartphone Use in 2015. Pew Res. Cent. Internet Technol. (2015). http://www.pewinternet.org/2015/04/01/us-smartphone-use-in-2015/
5. Boulos, M.N.K., Brewer, A.C., Karimkhani, C., Buller, D.B., Dellavalle, R.P.: Mobile medical and health apps: state of the art, concerns, regulatory control and certification. Online J. Public Health Inform. 5(3), 229 (2014). https://doi.org/10.5210/ojphi.v5i3.4814
6. Chan, S., Torous, J., Hinton, L., Yellowlees, P.: Towards a framework for evaluating mobile mental health apps. Telemed. J. E Health 21(12), 1038–1041 (2015). https://doi.org/10.1089/tmj.2015.0002
7. Riley, W.T., Glasgow, R.E., Etheredge, L., Abernethy, A.P.: Rapid, responsive, relevant (R3) research: a call for a rapid learning health research enterprise. Clin. Transl. Med. 2(1), 10 (2013). https://doi.org/10.1186/2001-1326-2-10. http://www.clintransmed.com/content/2/1/10
8. Joorabchi, M.E., Mesbah, A., Kruchten, P.: Real challenges in mobile app development. In: International Symposium on IEEE Empirical Software Engineering and Measurement. ACM/IEEE, Baltimore (2013)
9. Turner-McGrievy, G.M., et al.: Choosing between responsive-design websites versus mobile apps for your mobile behavioral intervention: presenting four case studies. Transl. Behav. Med. 7(2), 224–232 (2016). https://doi.org/10.1007/s13142-016-0448-y
10. Sailunazn, K., Al-Hussein, M., Shahiduzzaman, M., Anowar, F., Mamun, K.A.: CMED: cloud based medical system for rural health monitoring in developing countries. J. Comput. Electr. Eng. 53, 469–481 (2016). https://doi.org/10.1016/j.compeleceng.2016.02.005

11. Karar, Z.A., Alam, N., Streatfield, P.K.: Epidemiological transition in rural Bangladesh 1986–2006. Glob. Health Act. **2**(Suppl.), 1–9 (2009)
12. Islam, A., Biswas, T.: Chronic non-communicable diseases and the healthcare system in Bangladesh: current status and way forward. Chronic Dis. Int. **1**(2), 6 (2014)
13. Macro, O.: National Institute of Population Research and Training (NIPORT), Dhaka, Bangladesh (2005)
14. Streatfield, P.K., Karar, Z.A.: Population challenges for Bangladesh in the coming decades. J. Health Popul. Nutr. **26**(3), 261 (2008)
15. Saquib, N., Saquib, J., Ahmed, T., Khanam, M.A., Cullen, M.R.: Cardiovascular diseases and type 2 diabetes in Bangladesh: a systematic review and meta-analysis of studies between 1995 and 2010. BMC Public Health **12**(1), 434 (2012)
16. Biswas, T., Garnett, S.P., Pervin, S., Rawal, L.B.: The prevalence of underweight, overweight and obesity in Bangladeshi adults: data from a national survey. PLoS ONE **12** (5), e0177395 (2017). https://doi.org/10.1371/journal.pone.0177395
17. Mohsin, F., Tayyeb, S., Baki, A., Sarker, S., Zabeen, B., Begum, T., et al.: Prevalence of obesity among affluent school children in Dhaka. Mymensingh Med. J. **19**, 549–554 (2010)
18. Akter, S., Rahman, M.M., Abe, S.K., Sultana, P.: Prevalence of diabetes and prediabetes and their risk factors among Bangladeshi adults: a nationwide survey. Bull. World Health Organ. **92**, 204–213A (2014). https://doi.org/10.2471/BLT.13.128371
19. O'Donnell, M.J., Xavier, D., Liu, L., Zhang, H., Chin, S.L., Rao-Melacini, P., et al.: INTERSTROKE Investigators. Risk factors for ischaemic and intracerebral haemorrhagic stroke in 22 countries (the INTERSTROKE study): a case-control study. Lancet **376**, 112–123 (2010). https://doi.org/10.1016/s0140-6736(10)60834-3
20. Johnson, S.R.: CDC: majority of heart-related deaths in 2016 were preventable. https://www.modernhealthcare.com/article/20180906/NEWS/180909953/cdc-majority-of-heart-related-deaths-in-2016-were-preventable
21. O'Donnell, M.J., Chin, S.L., Rangarajan, S., Xavier, D., Liu, L., Zhang, H., et al.: INTERSTROKE Investigators. Global and regional effects of potentially modifiable risk factors associated with acute stroke in 32 countries (INTERSTROKE): a case-control study. Lancet **388**(10046), 761–775 (2016). https://doi.org/10.1016/s0140-6736(16)30506-2
22. Zaman, M.M., Rahman, M., Rahman, M., Bhuiyan, M.R., Karim, M., Chowdhury, M.J.: Prevalence of risk factors for non-communicable diseases in Bangladesh: Results from STEPS survey 2010. Indian J. Public Health **60**, 17–25 (2016)
23. Noncommunicable Diseases Country Profiles. World Health Organization (2018). ISBN 978-92-4-151462-0
24. WHO Factsheet on Cardiovascular Diseases. World Health organization (2017) https://www.who.int/news-room/fact-sheets/detail/cardiovascular-diseases-(cvds). Accessed 17 May 2017
25. International Diabetes Federation. IDF Diabetes Atlas, 8th edn. (2017)
26. Al-Masum Molla, Md.: People fork out most: govt report shows healthcare costliest in South Asia, 21 September 2017. https://www.thedailystar.net/backpage/people-fork-out-most-1465246

Vocabulary Learning Support System Based on Automatic Image Captioning Technology

Mohammad Nehal Hasnine[1]([⊠]), Brendan Flanagan[1],
Gokhan Akcapinar[4], Hiroaki Ogata[1], Kousuke Mouri[2],
and Noriko Uosaki[3]

[1] Kyoto University, Kyoto 606-8501, Japan
nehalhasnine@gmail.com
[2] Tokyo University of Agriculture and Technology, Tokyo 184-8588, Japan
[3] Osaka University, Osaka 565-0871, Japan
[4] Hacettepe University, 06800 Ankara, Turkey

Abstract. Learning context has evident to be an essential part in vocabulary development, however describing learning context for each vocabulary is considered to be difficult. In the human brain, it is relatively easy to describe learning contexts using pictures because pictures describe an immense amount of details at a quick glance that text annotations cannot do. Therefore, in an informal language learning system, pictures can be used to overcome the problems that language learners face in describing learning contexts. The present study aimed to develop a support system that generates and represents learning contexts automatically by analyzing the visual contents of the pictures captured by language learners. Automatic image captioning, a technology of artificial intelligence that connects computer vision and natural language processing is used for analyzing the visual contents of the learners' captured images. A neural image caption generator model called Show and Tell is trained for image-to-word generation and to describe the context of an image. The threefold objectives of this research are: First, an intelligent technology that can understand the contents of the picture and capable to generate learning contexts automatically; Second, a leaner can learn multiple vocabularies by using one picture without relying on a representative picture for each vocabulary, and Third, a learner's prior vocabulary knowledge can be mapped with new learning vocabulary so that previously acquired vocabulary be reviewed and recalled while learning new vocabulary.

Keywords: Artificial intelligence in education · Automatic image captioning ·
Learning context representation · Ubiquitous learning ·
Visual contents analysis · Vocabulary learning

© Springer Nature Switzerland AG 2019
N. Streitz and S. Konomi (Eds.): HCII 2019, LNCS 11587, pp. 346–358, 2019.
https://doi.org/10.1007/978-3-030-21935-2_26

1 Introduction

1.1 The Advancement and Challenges of Vocabulary Learning Using Various Technologies

In recent years, computer-assisted technologies have received considerable attention for language learning particularly to support foreign vocabulary learning. One of the many reasons for that is, unlike available traditional teaching methods, technology-mediated learning environments offers the flexibility to learn at at-time and anyplace. With regard to the adaptation of technologies to support learning systems, Stockwell stated that the range of technologies is broad and includes courseware (commercial and self-developed), online activities, dictionaries, corpora and concordance, and computer-mediated communication (CMC) technologies [1]. It has already been observed that vocabulary with various annotation styles linking for textual meaning, audio, graphics etc. [2], intelligent language tutoring systems that included sophisticated feedback systems [3], hypermedia-enhanced learning systems [4] etc. been developed. While various technologies provide various advantages but questions remain regarding how these technologies have been used in achieving learning objectives. For example, ubiquitous learning technologies, a renowned technology to support vocabulary learning often provide the facility to learn anytime and anywhere. Also, in this kind of learning environments, previous learning experiences are used to measure one learner's current knowledge level, which can be used to learn new knowledge. However, there are certain limitations namely, the scope of learning new vocabulary is limited, students often cannot determine on which words to be learned next, a learner's engagement with the system is low, and describing each learning context for each word may be difficult etc. are often discussed.

1.2 The Roles of Learning Context in Vocabulary Learning

Generally learning context refers to the learning environment including socio-cultural-political environment where learning takes place [5]. According to Gu [5], the learning context may include educators, classmates, classroom atmosphere, family support, social and cultural tradition of learning, academic curriculum etc. Learning contexts constrains the ways learners' approach to different learning tasks. Research also evident how meaningful context can help learners in acquiring foreign languages. To describe the importance of meaningful context, Firth, in the late 1950s, said that the complete meaning of a word is always contextual and no study of meaning independent of complete context can be taken seriously [6]. Firth also articulated that each word, when used in a new context, becomes a new word that assists us in making statements of meaning [6]. Robert Sternberg stated that most vocabulary is acquired from contexts [7]. Nagy said that, apart from explicit instruction, what a word means often depends on the context in which it is used, and people pick up much of their vocabulary knowledge from context [8]. Concluding therefrom, in the context of informal learning of foreign vocabulary, the role of learning contexts evident as important in enhancing vocabulary development.

1.3   The Aim of the Research

Earlier, we have discussed how important learning contexts are in enhancing vocabulary development but describing each learning context for each word is considered to be difficult. Therefore, this research investigates how technology can be applied to generate special learning contexts. To generate learning contexts, we used pictures that are captured by the learners of foreign languages. We analyzed the visual contents of images in order to produce learning contexts which we refer to as special learning contexts for vocabulary learning. The assumption was that those special learning contexts will help learners in enhancing their vocabulary.

This research also attempts to find answers to the following research questions:

1. Can we build technology that provides multiple visual learning contexts for learning multiple words from one picture?
2. Can we develop a support system that will provide visual cues to highlight the word to be learned which can be related to visual mnemonics?
3. Can we apply learning analytics to learning vocabulary with the context-vs- without learning context?
4. Can we use one picture to learn multiple vocabularies?
5. Can we use learning analytics and knowledge graph to map a learner's prior vocabulary knowledge in order to recommend new vocabulary to be learned?

2   Literature Review

In recent years, the successful application of deep neural networks to computer vision and natural language processing tasks have inspired many AI researchers to explore new research opportunities at the intersection of these previously separate domains [9]. Caption generation models have to balance an understanding of both visual cues and natural language. In this present work, we used automatic image captioning technology to generate learning contexts from images.

2.1   Google's Image2Text

Google's Image2Text system is a real-time captioning system that generates human-level natural language description for any input image. In this model, a sequence-to-sequence recurrent neural networks (RNN) model for image caption generation. This system also enables users to detect salient objects in an image, and retrieve similar images and corresponding descriptions from a database [10].

2.2   O'Reilly-Show and Tell

O'Reilly-Show and Tell Model is an image caption generation models combine advances in computer vision and machine translation to produce realistic image captions using neural networks. These models are trained to maximize the likelihood of producing a caption given an input image and can be used to generate novel image descriptions [9].

2.3 Deep Visual

Deep visual is a model that generates natural language descriptions of images and their regions. The deep model leverages datasets of images and their sentence descriptions for learning the intermodal correspondences between language and visual data [11]. This caption descriptor model is capable of producing state of the art results on Flickr8K [12], Flickr30K [13] and MSCOCO [14] datasets.

2.4 Microsoft Cognitive API

Microsoft Cognitive API for images' visual content analysis is an API (Application Program Interface) that returns features about visual contents found in a natural image. This API, in order to identify contents and label uses tagging, domain-specific models and descriptors [15].

We have found several recognized models and APIs that generates texts and sentences from images. Most of the studies using this technology are carried out for NLP applications, explaining frame-by-frame video clips, social media such as Facebook where faces are inferred directly from images, computer vision, robotics, machine learning etc. We have not found many recognized studies on building educational technology using this promising technology. Therefore, we aimed to use this technology to solute a recognized problem in language learning namely learning contexts generation in informal learning.

3 Overview of the Research

3.1 Background and Motivation

While previous research indicates that most of the vocabulary is learned from context [7] particularly for recalling learned vocabulary but describing learning context for each word is difficult. To begin with, we analyzed a dataset that contains ubiquitous learning logs. The aim of the analysis was to observe whether or not leaners of foreign language have difficulties in describing learning contexts while learning via ubiquitous learning tool. Therefore, we analyzed SCROLL (System for Capturing and Reminding of Learning Logs) dataset [16]. a dataset that consists of foreign language learners lifelong learning experiences (i.e. lifelogs). Logs are chronologically collected from a context-aware ubiquitous language learning system called SCROLL [16].

To elaborate more, in this system, a foreign language learner can create his/her own vocabulary learning materials using this system [17]. A learning material consists of a contextual image, the translation data, and the pronunciation. Moreover, the system is capable of recording a learner's vocabulary learning experience (such as the geolocation information, vocabulary knowledge, quiz, learning context, contextual image information etc.) into its server. The interface of the system is displayed in Fig. 1.

Fig. 1. Interface of the SCROLL system

We analyzed 31258 ubiquitous learning logs. The analysis indicates that 82% (13931 out of 16844), 62% (6224 out of 10034), and 94% (6648 out of 7044) learning logs that are created by English-native, Japanese-native and Chinese-native are created without learning contexts, respectively. Note that, we use the term -*native* because learners registered themselves as either of these languages as the default language. Figure 2 shows the result of the log analysis. This analysis indicated that describing learning context is an area that most of the learners skipped while learning context is an essential component in vocabulary development. Hence, we aimed to develop this support system that will support learners by providing special learning contexts.

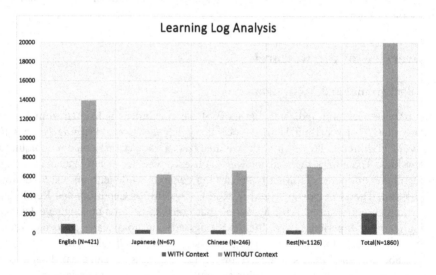

Fig. 2. Result of the learning log analysis

3.2 How Does Image Captioning Technology Fit into Educational Research?

Imagine a situation where a learner has previously learned words such as *sun, mountain, river,* and *sunrise.* In a new learning situation, the same learner captures a picture and uploads it into our server. The system will analyze the visual contents of the image and generate multiple special learning contexts (for instance, 1. *sunrise in the mountains,* 2. *sunrise paints the sky with pink,* 3. *sunrise offers beautiful view in mountain*) by which –the learner's prior vocabulary knowledge will be mapped with the special learning contexts. It is possible when you develop an intelligent technology that can understand the context of the picture and capable to generate the learning context automatically. We aimed to develop a system that will take pictures that are uploaded by learners as input. Then, the system will analyze the visual contents of those pictures. And based on those visual contents, the system will produce special learning contexts.

By doing this, this study aimed to assist foreign language learners in several ways, as follows:

- Map a learner's previous knowledge with new so that he/she can review and recall the previously acquired vocabulary
- To memorize new vocabulary in context
- To acquire multiple vocabulary from the same picture
- Provide visual mnemonics that will work as visual cues to highlight that particular word

In Fig. 3, mapping between a learner's prior knowledge with a new knowledge using special visual context is shown.

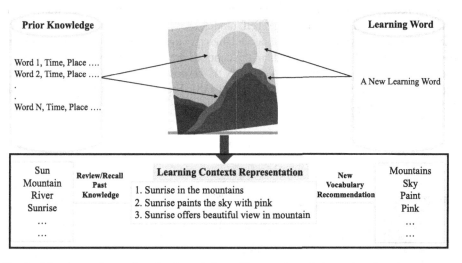

Fig. 3. Mapping a learner's prior knowledge with new knowledge using learning contexts representation

However, producing learning contexts is not an easy task. Now-a-days, artificial intelligent is gaining much popularity to build various system. Image captioning, a technology that connected computer vision and artificial intelligence is capable of generating captions from a picture. However, connecting learning analytics with computer vision and natural language processing is a quite challenging task. In this study, we hypothesized that by developing a computer program to automatically generate language description from an image may be helpful for learners to new words. Therefore, by using image captioning technology, we aimed to build an environment where learning context, multiple vocabulary acquisition and reflection of prior knowledge to learn new knowledge are supported. At this point, it can be mentioned that the adaptation of various technologies to support vocabulary learning is not new. New technology opens scopes to new research.

4   System Implementation

In this study, the Show and Tell model [18], a state-of-the-art model is trained for the image-to-word generation and special context generation tasks. In this section, we discuss about the architecture of the model along with its implementation in our server.

4.1   Architecture

The diagram below illustrates the architecture of the model. In this model, the image encoder is a deep convolutional neural network (CNN). Recently, deep CNN is widely adopted for object recognition and detection tasks. We used Inception v3 image recognition model [19] that was pretrained on the ILSVRC-2012-CLS image classification dataset [20]. In recent days, this type of neural and probabilistic framework is used for sequence modeling tasks such as language modeling and machine translation. The architecture of the Show and Tell model uses the Long Short-Term Memory (LSTM) network which is trained as a language model conditioned on the image encoding. In LSTM network, words in the captions are represented with an embedding model where each word in the vocabulary is associated with a fixed-length vector representation that is learned during training [18]. Figure 4 shows the general architecture of the model.

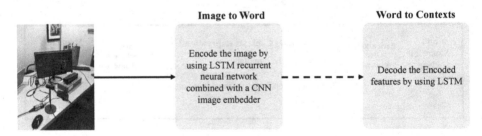

Fig. 4. General architecture of the LSTM-based show and tell model

4.2   Dataset

There are several popular datasets available in computer vision such as ImageNet, PASCAL VOC and SUN etc. Each of these datasets contains different types of images that can perform well for designated tasks. For example, ImageNet was created to capture a large number of object categories, many of which are fine-grained; while PASCAL VOC's primary application is object detection in natural images; and SUN focuses on labeling scene types and the objects that commonly occur in them [14]. In this study, we trained the Show and Tell model on MSCOCO image dataset [14]. The images were in native TFRecord format. The dataset contains a total of 2.5 million labeled instances in 328k images that performs well precisely for category detection, instance spotting and instance segmentation [14]. The dataset contains images of complex everyday scenes containing common objects in their natural context, hence it performs well on pictures that are captured in daily-life. This is why we used this dataset for training our model.

4.3   Details on Hardware and Training Time

In Table 1, we summarize the hardware details and the training time require to train the model.

Table 1. Hardware and software configuration of the model

Heading level	Example
GPU	ZOTAC GAMING GeForce RTX 2080 Ti AMP ZT-T20810D-10P
Time	10 to 14 days
Libraries/Packages	Bazel, Python, Numpy, punkt
Natural Language Toolkit	NLTK
Dataset	MSCOCO

4.4   Advantages of the Model

In this present study, we used this model because: Firstly, this neural network-based model is capable of viewing a natural image and generating reasonable contexts in plain English. Hence, it is readable without further interpretation. Secondly, the model encodes an image into a compact representation, followed by a recurrent neural network that generates a corresponding sentence. Thirdly, the deep recurrent architecture of the model preforms well in limited computation power. Finally, the performance of the model improves as the amount of data increases.

5   Result

We tested the performance of our system on the natural pictures that are uploaded by foreign language learners while using SCROLL system. To demonstrate the result, we choose three random pictures associated with three learning logs from SCROLL dataset. Each of the three logs contained a picture and the context described by the log creator. We used the pictures to generate learning contexts using our system.

First (refer to Fig. 5), for the word *lunch box* created by a Japanese-native, the learner described the learning context as 食べる *(ate,* in English*)*. While our system generated top-three learning contexts are: (1) a lunch box with a variety of food items (p = 0.000009), (2) a lunch box with a variety of food and a drink (p = 0.000001), and (3) a lunch box with a variety of vegetables and a sandwich (p = 0.000000).

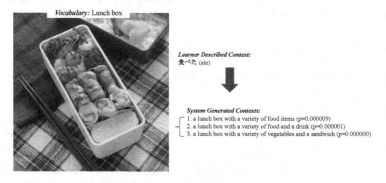

Fig. 5. Sample result (1)

Second (refer to Fig. 6), for the word *computer*, the learner described the learning context as: *this is a computer running Oculus Rift for language research.* In contrary, our system represented the learning contexts as: (1) a laptop computer sitting on top of a desk (p = 0.008150), (2) a laptop computer sitting on top of a wooden desk (p = 0.007242), and (3) a laptop computer sitting on top of a table (p = 0.001166). We noticed that the Oculus device was not detected but the objects like desk and table were identified.

Third (refer to Fig. 7), in learning the word *carpet*, the learner described its context as: 買った (which mean *bought* in English). After analyzing the visual contents, our system represented its contexts as: (1) a living room filled with furniture and a window (p = 0.001004), (2) a living room filled with furniture and a fire place. (p = 0.000599), and (3) a living room filled with furniture and a window (p = 0.000045).

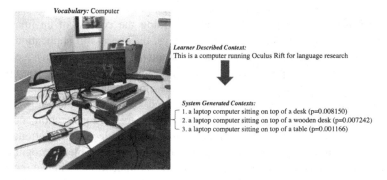

Fig. 6. Sample result (2)

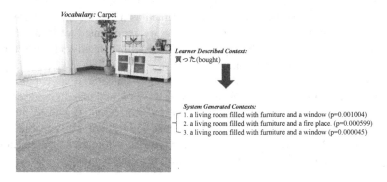

Fig. 7. Sample result (3)

6   Discussion

Ubiquitous learning technologies provide the facility to learn anytime and anywhere. These technologies help to capture ones learning experiences. Also, in this kind of learning environments previous learning experiences are used to measure one learner's current knowledge level, which can be used to learn new knowledge. Hence, there are certain limitations, namely the scope of learning new vocabulary is limited, students often cannot determine on which words to be learned next, a learner's engagement with the system is low, and describing each learning context for each word may be difficult etc. are often reported by many researchers. From that standpoint, this paper describes an approach to represent learning contexts by analyzing the visual contents of an image that is captured by a leaner of a foreign language. The three-fold advantages of this technology are: First, to develop an intelligent technology that can understand the context of the picture and capable to represent learning contexts automatically, Second, to develop a technology in which a leaner can learn multiple vocabulary using one picture, and Third, relating with their prior knowledge, new vocabulary can be learned.

Automatic image captioning, a technology of artificial intelligence that connects computer vision and natural language processing is used for analyzing the visual contents of an image. A neural image caption generator model called Show and Tell is trained for image-to-word generation and describing the context of an image automatically. It can be mentioned that, in recent days, the successful application of deep neural networks to computer vision and natural language processing tasks have inspired many AI researchers to explore new research opportunities at the intersection of these previously separate domains. Caption generation models have to balance an understanding of both visual cues and natural language. We trained the Show and Tell model, a state-of-the-art model is trained for the image-to-word generation and context generation tasks. In this model, the image encoder is a deep convolutional neural network (CNN). Recently, deep CNN is widely adopted for object recognition and detection tasks. Our particular choice of network is the Inception v3 image recognition model pretrained on the ILSVRC-2012-CLS image classification dataset. The decoder is a long short-term memory (LSTM) network. This type of network is commonly used for sequence modeling tasks such as language modeling and machine translation. In the Show and Tell model, the LSTM network is trained as a language model conditioned on the image encoding. Words in the captions are represented with an embedding model. Each word in the vocabulary is associated with a fixed-length vector representation that is learned during training.

We tested the performance of the system on the pictures that are captured by the learners of foreign languages while using SCROLL. We found that, in representation of learning contexts, some objects are not detected correctly. However, many new vocabularies are generated by the system because the system was capable to detect many important objects. We believe this system will assist foreign language learners in learning new vocabulary along with representing learning contexts.

7 Limitations and Directions to Future Works

The goal of image captioning is to produce sentences that are linguistically plausible and semantically truthful to the contents embedded in it [21]. Also, the original reason behind this technology is to generate simple descriptions for images taken under extremely constrained conditions [21]. However, in this study, we used this sophisticated technology to generate the learning contexts, which may be questionable to some extent. In other word, we used an image-to-word often address as automatic word captioning model to produce visual learning contexts assuming that those learning contexts will be helpful in learning foreign vocabulary. We aim to carry out an evaluation experiment in the near future to assess the learning effect of this system. In future, this model is planned integrated with a ubiquitous language learning system called SCROLL (System for Capturing and Recording of Learning Logs).

Acknowledgement. This work was partly supported by JSPS Grant-in-Aid for Scientific Research (S)16H06304 and 17K12947; NEDO Special Innovation Program on AI and Big Data 18102059-0; and JSPS Start-up Grant-in-Aid Number 18H05745.

References

1. Stockwell, G.: A review of technology choice for teaching language skills and areas in the CALL literature. ReCALL **19**(2), 105–120 (2007)
2. Yeh, Y., Wang, C.: Effects of multimedia vocabulary annotations and learning styles on vocabulary learning. Calico J. **21**(1), 131–144 (2003)
3. Heift, T.: Error-specific and individualised feedback in a Web-based language tutoring system: do they read it? ReCALL **13**(1), 99–109 (2001)
4. Coll, J.F.: Richness of semantic encoding in a hypermedia-assisted instructional environment for ESP: effects on incidental vocabulary retention among learners with low ability in the target language. ReCALL **14**(2), 263–284 (2002)
5. Gu, P.Y.: Vocabulary learning in a second language: person, task, context and strategies. TESL-EJ **7**(2), 1–25 (2003)
6. Ibrahim, W.J.: The importance of contextual situation in language teaching. Adab AL Rafidayn **51**, 630–655 (2008)
7. Sternberg, R.J.: Most vocabulary is learned from context. Nat. Vocab. Acquis. **89**, 105 (1987)
8. Nagy, W.E.: On the role of context in first- and second-language vocabulary learning. University of Illinois at Urbana-Champaign, Center for the Study of Reading, Champaign (1995)
9. Daniel, R.P.R.: Caption this, with TensorFlow. O'Reilly Media, 28 March 2017. https://www.oreilly.com/learning/caption-this-with-tensorflow
10. Liu, C., Wang, C., Sun, F., Rui, Y.: Image2Text: a multimodal caption generator. In: ACM Multimedia, pp. 746–748 (2016)
11. Karpathy, A., Fei-Fei, L.: Deep visual-semantic alignments for generating image descriptions. In: Proceedings of the IEEE Conference on Computer Vision and Pattern Recognition, pp. 312–83137 (2015)
12. Hodosh, M., Young, P., Hockenmaier, J.: Framing image description as a ranking task: data, models and evaluation metrics. J. Artif. Intell. Res. **47**, 853–899 (2013)
13. Plummer, B.A., Wang, L., Cervantes, C.M., Caicedo, J.C., Hockenmaier, J., Lazebnik, S.: Flickr30k entities: Collecting region-to-phrase correspondences for richer image-to-sentence models. In: Proceedings of the IEEE International Conference on Computer Vision, pp. 2641–2649 (2015)
14. Lin, T.-Y., et al.: Microsoft COCO: common objects in context. In: Fleet, D., Pajdla, T., Schiele, B., Tuytelaars, T. (eds.) ECCV 2014. LNCS, vol. 8693, pp. 740–755. Springer, Cham (2014). https://doi.org/10.1007/978-3-319-10602-1_48
15. Image Processing with the Computer Vision API—Microsoft Azure. https://azure.microsoft.com/en-us/services/cognitive-services/computer-vision/
16. Ogata, H., Uosaki, N., Mouri, K., Hasnine, M.N., Abou-Khalil, V., Flanagan, B.: SCROLL Dataset in the context of ubiquitous language learning. In: Workshop Proceedings of the 26th International Conference on Computer in Education, Manila, Philippines, pp. 418–423 (2018)
17. Hasnine, M.N., Mouri, K., Flanagan, B., Akcapinar, G., Uosaki, N., Ogata, H.: Image recommendation for informal vocabulary learning in a context-aware learning environment. In: Proceedings of the 26th International Conference on Computer in Education, Manila, Philippines, pp. 669–674 (2018)
18. Vinyals, O., Toshev, A., Bengio, S., Erhan, D.: Show and tell: lessons learned from the 2015 mscoco image captioning challenge. IEEE Trans. Pattern Anal. Mach. Intell. **39**(4), 652–663 (2017)

358 M. N. Hasnine et al.

19. Szegedy, C., Vanhoucke, V., Ioffe, S., Shlens, J., Wojna, Z.: Rethinking the inception architecture for computer vision. In: Proceedings of the IEEE Conference on Computer Vision and Pattern Recognition, pp. 2818–2826 (2016)
20. Russakovsky, O., et al.: Imagenet large scale visual recognition challenge. Int. J. Comput. Vis. **115**(3), 211–252 (2015)
21. Bai, S., An, S.: A survey on automatic image caption generation. Neurocomputing **311**, 291–304 (2018)

Development of Mobile Based In-Home Patient Monitoring System for the Management of Chronic Disease of Indigenous Communities in a Developing Country

Rakibul Hoque[1](✉), Golam Sorwar[2], Ashir Ahmed[3], and Rafiqul Islam[3]

[1] University of Dhaka, Dhaka, Bangladesh
rakibul@du.ac.bd
[2] Southern Cross University, Gold Coast, Australia
Golam.Sorwar@scu.edu.au
[3] Kyushu University, Fukuoka, Japan
ashir@ait.kyushu-u.ac.jp,
rimaruf@mic.med.kyushu-u.ac.jp

Abstract. Indigenous people of developing countries have serious shortage of health support including lack of health professionals and technology. It is often difficult for the indigenous people to receive consultation in the hospitals when they face any chronic disease. In Bangladesh, there are 54 groups of indigenous communities with a base of estimated 3 million in number. There are 300 government registered doctors and nurses, and 800 community health workers to provide health services to approximately 3 million people. By the invention of Information Technology, health care services have been modernized and more accessible in recent times. Information Technology has made the health services available at the door of general people. In recent years, there is large number of people in the indigenous community uses internet in their smart phones. As, there is not enough health care organizations and professional doctors in the indigenous community, for this reason, it will be useful and compatible to provide mobile phone-based services to the people. Mobile phone-based health services have great potentiality in reducing 'digital divide', and acts as a crucial tool for supporting indigenous community especially chronic disease affected people staying at home. This paper aims to develop, implement and evaluate a mobile based integrated framework for in-home or community care and rural health centers' patient monitoring and health management.

Keywords: Indigenous communities · In-Home monitoring · Chronic disease

1 Introduction and Problem Identification

The diseases (i.e. diabetes, asthma, hypertension, cardiac diseases, paralysis, cancers of different types and depression) that undergo more than three months or more are called chronic disease (Bodenheimer et al. 2002). These are the common and direst diseases causing large number of deaths every year in the whole world. Poor eating habits,

N. Streitz and S. Konomi (Eds.): HCII 2019, LNCS 11587, pp. 359–367, 2019.
https://doi.org/10.1007/978-3-030-21935-2_27

tobacco use, lack of physical activity, unhealthy lifestyle are the major causes of such diseases. Every year, a vast majority of people worldwide are affected by chronic diseases, and this fact causes burden of the disease is alarming. Since 2001, chronic disease results in almost 60% of all deaths and the rate is predictable to climb to 73% by 2020. The chronic disease cannot be cured fully, not even it disappears. As a result, chronic disease causes long term health and economic sufferings for both individual and families. As of now, the countries of both low and middle incomes are in a probable state of approximate loss of $7.3 trillion due to chronic diseases by 2025, which is an annual loss of about 4% for those countries (Kelland 2011).

In 2005, a longitudinal study in 23 fast-growing countries revealed that the chronic diseases were accountable for 50% of deaths and illness (Abegunde et al. 2007). With regard to this serious issue, the World Health Organization (WHO) anticipated that the deaths occurred from chronic diseases to increase by 15% within the period of 2010 to 2020, with a higher increase of over 20% in African and South-East Asian counties (Garenne et al. 2014). Although a limited number of studies exists in Bangladesh context, which is a low-ranked middle-income country, the evidence shows that chronic diseases are accountable for more than half of mortality (51%) every year, and possesses almost half of the burden of expenditure caused by diseases (41%).

Indigenous people of developing countries have serious shortage of health support including lack of health professionals and technology. Hence, every year the countries have to take disproportionate burden for patient with chronic disease. Mainly indigenous people are the underserved people of a country who are mostly detached from direct development activities. Moreover, extreme poverty and improper health facilities made the people of the indigenous communities vulnerable to several health problems. Normally, in comparison to other population, a higher number of diabetes, heart disease, tuberculosis, HIV/AIDS and many other disease patients are observed among the indigenous communities (Marrone 2007). In Bangladesh, there are 54 groups of indigenous communities with a base of estimated 3 million in number. The characteristics and the way of life of the indigenous community are remarkably different from other citizens in Bangladesh (Islam and Odland 2011). Their unconscious foods habit and unhealthy daily lifestyle cause them chronic diseases such as diabetics, heart disease, and cancer. For the treatment of the chronic diseases, patients have to face difficulty for consultation in every period of time (Whiting et al. 2011).

There exists a considerable and widespread health service inequality between indigenous and non-indigenous communities in Bangladesh. This inequality deprives the indigenous community from the common fundamental rights in the society, including health facilities (Rahmatullah et al. 2012). The ratio of the number professionally qualified Health Care Providers (HCP) is very poor in compared to the number of patients in indigenous communities. In Bangladesh, there are 300 government registered doctors and nurses, and 800 community health workers to provide health services to approximately 3 million people (El Arifeen et al. 2013). Thus, it is often difficult for the people to receive consultation in the hospitals when they face any chronic disease. Most of the time, it is seen that indigenous people take health services from village doctors, who do not have any formal medical training but provide medical treatment in the indigenous community for the common illness. For their healthcare they also rely on Baddya or Homeopathic practitioners, pharmacists and drug-sellers who lack formal medical training. Often, based on faith, they also seek treatment from the spiritual teachers, who obtained expertise from their ancestors (Rahman et al. 2012). Under such circumstance, scope and experience of getting common and conventional healthcare supports for chronic diseases for the indigenous people in Bangladesh still remains very unsatisfactory.

By the invention of Information Technology, health care services have been modernized and more accessible in recent times. Information Technology has made the health services available at the door of general people. In this regard, E-Health technology provides many benefits such as assisting in self-management, reducing the need for frequent physical visits and treatment spending. However, the indigenous communities, especially in developing countries such as Bangladesh, suffer from 'digital divide' in case of receiving E-Health care due to lack of accessibility to digital devices like smart-phones and computer with internet services. Furthermore, in developing countries, many difficulties, such as lack of infrastructure, health professionals, social resistance, and lack of readiness to accept technology among the indigenous people, make it difficult to receive the benefits of E-health like IT-based hearth services (Hoque et al. 2014).

In recent years, there is large number of people in the indigenous community uses internet in their smart phones. As, there is not enough health care organizations and professional doctors in the indigenous community, for this reason, it will be useful and compatible to provide mobile phone-based services to the people. Mobile phone-based health services have great potentiality in reducing 'digital divide', and acts as a crucial tool for supporting indigenous community especially chronic disease affected people staying at home. As chronic disease needs constant monitoring it can provide proactive and preventive solutions by ensuring availability of doctors who will give instructions and emergency treatment for chronic diseases.

As healthcare specialists and policy makers are looking for newer ways to reduce healthcare expense through improving healthcare system and service delivery, smart phone-based health services can regularly impart significant roles to facilitate in active prevention and proactive chronic diseases management by decreasing related medical expenses and increasing patient outcomes.

This project aims to develop, implement and evaluate a mobile based integrated framework for in-home or community care and rural health centers' patient monitoring and health management. In most of the cases, the existing systems mainly emphasis on monitoring the vital signs in human body. Yet, in the low-resource setting, it is impractical to provide adequate number of specialized monitoring to monitor the vital signs. This project takes into account the limitations and issues of existing in-home health monitoring facilities from the perspectives of both health professionals and chronic patients, and aims for designing and development of a framework that would enable a remote point-of-care (POC) of various health monitoring capabilities, and minimize the complexity of health monitoring for the end users.

Indeed, most of the systems proposed in the literature are specially designed for a specific application scenario. Hence, implementation of a specific system requires an ad hoc information and communication infrastructure. Without an integrating framework, it is technically and economically infeasible for the caregivers to maintain a collection of heterogeneous special purpose monitoring systems. Besides, each of the systems comes with its own user interface. This hinders the acceptance of monitoring systems to healthcare professionals as it is extremely difficult for a person to be familiar with a diverse collection of interfaces.

2 Literature Review

With the rapid change in digital health technology, the practical utility of smart phones in providing healthcare services are becoming ubiquitous (Rise et al. 2016). As the penetration of smart-phone has been increasing for last two decades, the pervasiveness of the scope of using biosensor enabled smart-phone platform has increased accordingly. Today, the benefits of smart phone in home healthcare are better realized (Munos et al. 2016). For example, the use of various types of biosensors such as optical, accelerometer, electrochemical, surface plasmon resonance (SPR) and near field communication (NFC) biosensors in smart phones for remote POC monitoring (Zhang and Liu 2016). The remote POC can simplify three important tasks in which the smart phones based POC can assist remotely in managing chronic disease. These are: (1) providing reminders to the patients to follow guidelines, (2) to provide feedback on the performance or health track records, and (3) register and interact with the service providers. In this regard, WHO has recommended to distribute of IT-based remote POC services across the service providers (Bauer et al. 2014).

In today's time, people do not like to visit doctors as it needs more time and money, especially for the inhabitants in the remote areas (Ajami and Teimouri 2015). In such reality, the biosensors in the smart phone can enable remote services like remote POC diagnostics, which is useful for the reduction of frequent doctor visits and expensive diagnosis, and enhancing the health performance and health deterioration tracking (Sun et al. 2016). The application of biosensors in the smart phones can be as cheap as less than $20, making it cost-effective and more practical to serve the purpose of serving the underprivileged population, especially in the context where the 'digital divide' prevails severely. Furthermore, in many instances, biosensors in the smart phones can assist in remote POC services, which ultimately can replace the cumbersome and expensive medical tests that require frequent visiting laboratories.

The biosensors integrated in the peripheral modules (e.g. camera, Bluetooth, audio receivers and UBS ports) in the smart phones can detect sensitive electrochemical signals, which make it possible to discontinue many bulky equipment typically used for detecting same sensitive signals (Sun et al. 2016). Such multi-purpose use of biosensors in the smart phones makes it convenient to adopt and adhere to IT-based health services, especially in the long-run treatment for chronic diseases (Sun et al. 2016). Besides, the lack of time of the doc tors distributed for the more patients make it harder to health service providers to identify some symptoms.

With the considerable development in micro/nanotechnology in the lase 10 to 15 years, such scope is highly potential because of the availability of a wide range of biosensors that are compatible with biomedical science. A successful case of application of such technology is the use of telemedicine for the prisoners which prevented the incontinence of moving the inmates to central hospital, unless it is emergency (Ajami and Arzani-Birgani 2013). Another notable usefulness of biosensors in the smart phones is the real-time detection of illicit drug use by tracking electrodermal activity, body temperature, and acceleration (Carreiro et al. 2015). For the elderly patients with chronic diseases who are incapable to moving and visiting doctors can be better served with remote POC by using smart phones with integrated biosensors (Ajami and Teimouri 2015). Beside the benefits of being cheap, convenient and portable, the other benefits of smart phone based remote POC include enhanced scalability real-time health status analysis, environment monitoring and food evaluation, which is significant in taking proactive and quick actions to manage chronic diseases (Zhang and Liu 2016).

The continuous follow-up and periodic checkup are essential for the chronic disease management. In such scenario, the wide-spread adoption of POC can eliminate the government's burden of the reducible expense incurred in the healthcare system (Sun et al. 2016). According to Benharref and Serhani (2014), by promoting the service-oriented architecture (SOA) based framework to facilitate remote POC, the governmental and private healthcare systems can minimize various chronic disease driven burdens faced by them. Another economic benefit of using remote POC is that it would save the enormous cost of biomedical information for future clinical research (Munos et al. 2016). Moreover, with the increasing use of Internet of things (IoT), a new and powerful smart health industry is also increasing the opportunity of using biosensor based remote POC.

3   The Framework

The overall framework is depicted in Fig. 1. The system consists of 3 nodes: data acquisition node, Transmission node, and Base Station node (sub-center).

3.1   Acquisition of Bio-signals

The first step in the monitoring system is the acquisition of physiological signals from a patient's body using portable/wearable bio-sensors. Patient may locate in home or rural health care centers in remote areas or any other outdoor environment implemented on mobile phone. Clearly, the biosensors should be low-cost and comfortable to use to be acceptable to the patients. In Bangladesh, various low cost locally produced wearable sensors exist to measure various physical parameters, such as, blood pressure, oxygen level, ECG signal, heart rate, blood sugar, body temperature, respiration rate, skin hydration, body motion, and brain activity.

3.2   Wireless Transmission of Bio-signals

After acquisition of the bio-signal, the measured data will be transmitted to a central database, located in a neatest hospital that can be accessed by healthcare professionals. Portable/wearable bio-sensors usually come with Bluetooth wireless connectivity to provide access to the acquired signals from a short distance. The ubiquitous phones are used to receive and pre-process the data and then transfer them to a central database via GPRS/4G mobile network technology. Patients may have a constant connection or an

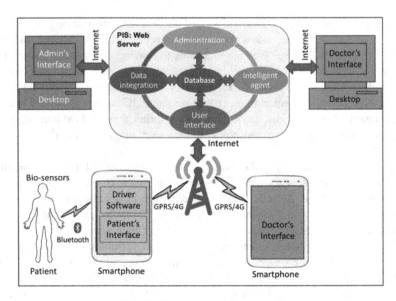

Fig. 1. The proposed framework

intermittent connection based on their needs. A bio-sensing system is thus completely defined by the physical sensing system along with the software running on the phone that coordinates the transmission of the measurements from the sensors to the base station node.

3.3   Patient Information System

Central to the proposed system is a Patient Information System (PIS) running on a base station node. In the future multiple "Base Station" nodes can be interconnected to create a distributed network using a peer-to-peer relationship. Each base station node may represent anything from a small node in a rural area health center to a large node in a local hospital. It defines an abstract interface to receive the measurements about the patients from varying sources. The interface specifies only the format of information exchange leaving the implementation details to the monitoring systems. A bio-sensing system is compatible with PIS if its driver software, running on the phone, transmits the data according to this interface. It is this abstract interface that enables the PIS to receive data from heterogeneous systems. The PIS is driven by the database storing all the patient information. The database stores patients' information coming from all possible sources such as laboratory test, imaging test, and those acquired by the remote bio-sensors. Finally, the PIS provides consistent and coherent web-based Interfaces to healthcare professionals as well as to the patients. If necessary, for example in the case of emergency, the base station node can directly communicate with a specialist consultation. If any clinical test is required, the rural center/hospital will complete those tests and directly send the report to the specialist doctor through Internet for their further diagnosis.

3.4   Intelligent Agent

One of the major issues to be addressed for successful adaptation of an in-home monitoring system is scalability. As the system grows in terms of number of patients and systems, automation of patients' risk assessment, prioritization, and recommendation becomes essential. Therefore, advanced artificial intelligence techniques should be employed to prioritize the patients based on the expert knowledge in the relevant domain. Since most artificial intelligent algorithms are computationally intensive, they are expected to run on the base station node server system. However, the smartphones are general purpose computing devices with processors, memory, and wireless connectivity managed by an operating system. Their main limitation is that they are low-powered devices. Therefore, low-complexity intelligent algorithms can also run on the smartphones that can detect critical conditions and alert relevant personnel using text messages.

One of the salient features of this framework is that it is scalable and it supports heterogeneous bio-sensors. The smart phone is a general-purpose computing device that can support various software and connectivity. Similarly, the PIS is also a general-purpose system defined by its abstract interface and driven by the underlying database. This general-purpose setting enables easy integration of a new monitoring device. The new monitoring systems only need to provide 'driver software' that will run on the smartphones. The drivers will access the signals from the bio-sensors and transmit them to the database hosted in the web-server.

4   Initial Prototype

As a proof-of-concept (Jahan and Chowdhury 2014), we implemented an initial prototype of the framework, presented in the previous section, using off-the-shelf bio-sensors and open source technologies. Initial implementation of the prototype focuses on heart related problems and fall detection because of their prevalence as a chronic disease. For continuous acquisition of ECG signal from a patient, we used the commercially available Heart & Activity Monitor. This single channel bio-sensor uses wireless Bluetooth technology for real-time transmission of ECG and accelerometer data. The driver software for receiving the data from the sensors and transmitting to the base station was implemented in a Samsung Galaxy mobile phone running on Android platform. The driver software also provides interfaces to doctors and patients for visualization of ECG signal (Fig. 2(a)). The driver software at the mobile phone implements an algorithm to detect falls from the accelerometer data. Since a fall is a critical condition, it needs to be detected at the mobile phone. This will enable alerting the relevant personnel directly without relying on the Internet connectivity to reduce the communication latency and uncertainty. Thus, we implemented the threshold-based fall detection algorithm. The essential idea of scheme stems from the observation that the magnitude of acceleration during fall is greater than those during normal activities. Therefore, the algorithm continuously computes the magnitude of acceleration in three-dimensional space from the acceleration values along three axes. If at any point the magnitude of acceleration exceeds a threshold (imperially defined) then it assumes that a fall has been occurred. Figure 2(b) shows that at the time of the fall, the magnitude of acceleration exceeds this threshold.

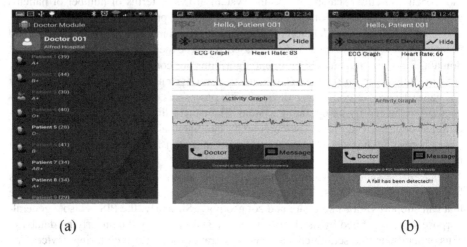

(a)   (b)

Fig. 2. (a) Doctor's portal showing a list of patients; and (b) Patient's portal showing the ECG graph and the magnitude of three-dimensional acceleration. It follows from the graph that the magnitude of acceleration crosses the threshold τ during the fall.

5 Implication and Conclusion

No previous study in Bangladesh has explored the scopes and possible resultant benefits of using remote POC for chronic disease using smart phones integrated with biosensors and software driver, let alone for the indigenous communities. After observing the benefits of remote biosensor based POC in the developed countries, and developing our own prototype, we are optimistic about reducing the existing 'Digital Divide' and inconvenience of the people in the indigenous communities, and as well as contributing in the better management of their chronic disease and achieving wellness. Once proven cost effective and useful, our proposed system (app) would be commercially available for the smartphones.

References

Bodenheimer, T., Lorig, K., Holman, H., Grumbach, K.: Patient self-management of chronic disease in primary care. JAMA **288**(19), 2469–2475 (2002)
Rahman, S.A., Kielmann, T., McPake, B., Normand, C.: Healthcare-seeking behaviour among the tribal people of Bangladesh: can the current health system really meet their needs? J. Health Popul. Nutr. **30**(3), 353 (2012)
Kelland, K.: Chronic Disease to Cost $47 Trillion by 2030: WEF (2011)

Abegunde, D.O., Mathers, C.D., Adam, T., Ortegon, M., Strong, K.: The burden and costs of chronic diseases in low-income and middle-income countries. The Lancet **370**(9603), 1929–1938 (2007)

Garenne, M., Masquelier, B., Pelletier, F.: Future mortality in high mortality countries. World Population and Human Capital in the Twenty-First Century, p. 273 (2014)

Marrone, S.: Understanding barriers to health care: a review of disparities in health care services among indigenous populations. Int. J. Circumpolar Health **66**(3), 188–198 (2007)

Whiting, D.R., Guariguata, L., Weil, C., Shaw, J.: IDF diabetes atlas: global estimates of the prevalence of diabetes for 2011 and 2030. Diab. Res. Clin. Pract. **94**(3), 311–321 (2011)

Islam, M.R., Odland, J.O.: Determinants of antenatal and postnatal care visits among Indigenous people in Bangladesh: a study of the Mru Community. Rural Remote Health **11**(2), 1672 (2011)

Rahmatullah, M., et al.: Survey and scientific evaluation of medicinal plants used by the Pahan and Teli tribal communities of Natore district, Bangladesh. Afr. J. Tradit. Complement. Altern. Med. **9**(3), 366–373 (2012)

El Arifeen, S., et al.: Community-based approaches and partnerships: innovations in health-service delivery in Bangladesh. The Lancet **382**(9909), 2012–2026 (2013)

Hoque, M.R., Mazmum, M., Bao, Y.: e-Health in Bangladesh: current status, challenges, and future direction. Int. Tech. Manag. Rev. **4**(2), 87–96 (2014)

Jahan, S., Chowdhury, M.M.H.: mHealth: a sustainable healthcare model for developing world. Am. J. Model. Optim. **2**(3), 73–76 (2014)

Bauer, A.M., Thielke, S.M., Katon, W., Unützer, J., Areán, P.: Aligning health information technologies with effective service delivery models to improve chronic disease care. Prev. Med. **66**, 167–172 (2014)

Rice, E.S., Haynes, E., Royce, P., Thompson, S.C.: Social media and digital technology use among Indigenous young people in Australia: a literature review. Int. J. Equity Health **15**(1), 81 (2016)

Munos, B., et al.: Mobile health: the power of wearables, sensors, and apps to transform clinical trials. Ann. N. Y. Acad. Sci. **1375**(1), 3–18 (2016)

Zhang, D., Liu, Q.: Biosensors and bioelectronics on smartphone for portable biochemical detection. Biosens. Bioelectron. **75**, 273–284 (2016)

Ajami, S., Teimouri, F.: Features and application of wearable biosensors in medical care. J. Res. Med. Sci.: Official J. Isfahan Univ. Med. Sci. **20**(12), 1208 (2015)

Sun, A.C., Yao, C., Venkatesh, A.G., Hall, D.A.: An efficient power harvesting mobile phone-based electrochemical biosensor for point-of-care health monitoring. Sens. Actuators B: Chem. **235**, 126–135 (2016)

Benharref, A., Serhani, M.A.: Novel cloud and SOA-based framework for E-Health monitoring using wireless biosensors. IEEE J. Biomed. Health Inform. **18**(1), 46–55 (2014)

Ajami, S., Arzani-Birgani, A.: The use of telemedicine to treat prisoners. J. Inf. Technol. Softw. Eng. **S7**, e002 (2013)

Carreiro, S., et al.: Real-time mobile detection of drug use with wearable biosensors: a pilot study. J. Med. Toxicol. **11**(1), 73–79 (2015)

Supporting Human Relationship-Building in a Daily Life Community

Koya Iwase[✉], Kota Gushima, and Tatsuo Nakajima

Department of Computer Science and Engineering, Waseda University,
Tokyo, Japan
{chocochan_i, gushi, tatsuo}@dcl.cs.waseda.ac.jp

Abstract. A wide friendship network helps us in our daily lives, and there are merits to expanding personal connections. Newly developed communication services have been developed as a means to expand the network of connections, and they enable the building of new relationships on the Internet without meeting people directly. While these tools are spreading, currently in Japan, various warnings and instructions are communicated regarding Internet encounters, and due to interactions of young people via the Internet, many people recognize that it is dangerous to have relationships with unknown partners. We want to alleviate the distrust users have for unknown partners and contribute to relationship-building on the Internet. This paper proposes ComFriends, a communication tool that reduces the resistance of an initial conversation and helps expand friendships more easily and safely. ComFriends provides users with conversations between people who belong to the same community and are in a state of mutual interest, and it supports relationship-building. We first present a ComFriends design approach and then describe its evaluation via a user study.

Keywords: Civic computing · Personal informatics · SNS

1 Introduction

A wide friendship network helps us in our daily lives, and there are merits to expanding personal connections [1, 2]. Newly developed communication services can expand the network of people, and we can build new relationships on the Internet without meeting directly. Therefore, expanding personal connections has become much easier. While these tools are spreading, communication among young people on the Internet in Japan is facing various warnings and education about Internet communication concerns; many people recognize that it is dangerous to have relationships with unknown partners on the Internet [3]. However, in the current information society, SNS interaction is convenient and frequently used and also will be a major way to build relationships in the future [4]. We want to alleviate distrust of unknown partners and contribute to relationship-building on the net.

This paper proposes ComFriends, a communication tool that reduces the resistance of an initial conversation and helps us expand our friendships more easily and safely. ComFriends provides conversations between mutually interested people in the same

N. Streitz and S. Konomi (Eds.): HCII 2019, LNCS 11587, pp. 368–380, 2019.
https://doi.org/10.1007/978-3-030-21935-2_28

community and supports relationship-building. We thought that if the users and partners belong to the same community, distrust of the unknown would be slightly relieved, and we could focus on applications that expand relationships within the community. In this research, we want to confirm how sharing communities influences the affinity and usefulness of relation building. In addition, we would like to investigate other obstacles in SNS exchanges in order to promote smooth relationship building.

We first introduce the current approach to assisting initial relationship building and then our ComFriends approach. This research provides clues for better SNS development and contributes to its future development.

2   Related Work

Various systems have been developed to assist relationship building or utilize relationships according to purpose. We will introduce some of them and consider which elements are necessary for relation building.

2.1   Support for Directly Facing Communication

Several approaches for people directly face each other when communicating for the first time. For example, conversation contents (what you talk about when you first meet someone) are important [5]. To eliminate this obstacle, various content conversation systems were developed to help users talk more easily. However, the problem was that these systems proposed topics that speakers did not want to discuss with a first-time partner. It also seems that many people were resistant to directly face a first-time partner, except when they had to face each other directly and talk.

2.2   Virtual Relationship Expansion

There are also studies on virtually broad connection via other means [6]. In this system, an individual's personal network can be shared via a database, allowing each individual to connect to another. If you face a problem at work and you need human resource support, you can find suitable people through your acquaintances.

2.3   People Proposal Based on Common Elements

We are unconsciously looking for commonality with our partner when interacting with them for the first time, and it is said that this sense of familiarity will remove psychological barriers [7]. Researchers grasp elements such as hobbies where people need help and support for artificially matching similar people in order to make the sharing process smoother. In fact, results show that pairs with many commonalities have many conversation topics and tend to get along. In particular, hobby commonalities seem to have a large positive impact on familiarity. However, since a third party's evaluation carried out the artificial matching, it is an uncertain means for relation building, and the administrator presents a significant burden. We believe that it is good to find common points with the partner depending on the user's will.

3   Design Implementation

To explore the problems of existing relationship building and chat applications, before creating ComFriends we created a concise, similar design, and asked for user evaluation. The first design implementation procedures are shown below.

3.1   Questionnaire

To produce the initial ComFriends design, we surveyed eighteen people ages 20 to 57, and addressed five issues: (1) Do you feel resistance to conversation in the first meeting? (2) Do you feel resistance to talking on the SNS with someone you have never met before? (3) Have you experienced easy conversation with the person you were within the first meeting? (4) Do you think that interaction within the community is necessary? (5) Do you want to expand the network of people in the community?

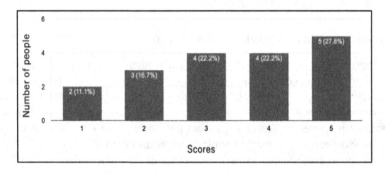

Fig. 1. Result of the first question - Do you feel resistance in the first meeting? (The higher the score, the stronger the sense of resistance.)

Figure 1 shows the result of the first question. More participants felt resistance in the first-time conversation and their main reasons were *"I don't know what to talk about."*, *"I don't know what kind of person this is."*, *"I don't know the speed of partner's reply."*, etc.

Figure 2 has results of the next question and, contrary to the previous question, the number of people who feel resistance is very low in an SNS conversation. Reasons for decreasing resistance were *"I can't see the other's expression, so I don't have to worry about it."*, *"I can get the information necessary for conversation through the users' profile."*, etc. In addition, participants felt it was easy to talk with each other for the first time under the following situations: when the content is decided, when they have a common hobby, and when they can clearly see a reaction.

Next, are the results of an exchange within the community. As shown in Fig. 3, half of the participants felt that an exchange within the community was necessary, and half did not. While the former argued that it is necessary in the event of emergency, the latter argued that it would be difficult to complain about group living there when they know each other. We believe that these merits and demerits apply to "residential

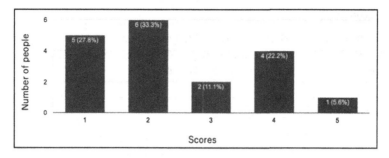

Fig. 2. Result of the second question - Do you feel resistance to talking on the SNS with someone you have never met? (The higher the score, the stronger the sense of resistance.)

communities" such as residential areas and apartment houses, not "affiliation communities" such as schools and workplaces. As shown in Fig. 4, fewer people want to expand the network within the community, and some mentioned that this is mainly due to the difficulty of building a new relationship regardless of whether it is a community interaction or not.

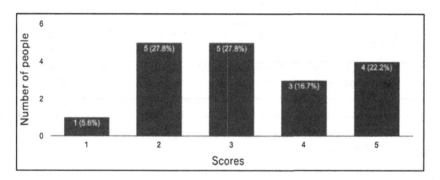

Fig. 3. Result of the fourth question - Do you think that interaction within the community is necessary? (The higher the score, the more they feel it is necessary.)

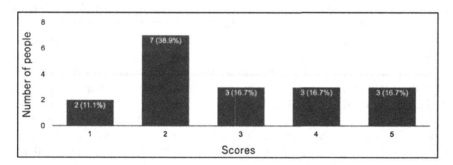

Fig. 4. Result of the fifth question – Do you want to expand the network of people in the community? (The higher the score, the more they have motivation to build new relationships.)

3.2   Approach

Given the questionnaire results, we decided to create an application with the following approach: (1) Provide a concise profile required for conversation, (2) Prepare on the premise that there is mutually favorable reaction (Fig. 5).

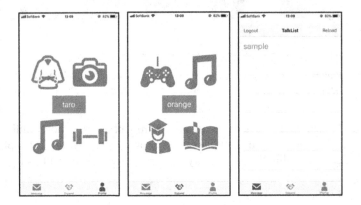

Fig. 5. Initial design - Profile Scene, Expand Scene, Message Scene

This design has three main scenes. The first is "Profile Scene" where you can check your brief profile. Next is "Expand Scene" which proposes users in the same community, one after the other. The application users will indicate whether or not they are interested in the proposed profile by dragging the image. If they are not interested in the opponent, they move the image up, and if they are interested, they pull it in front to accept. The last is "Message Scene", which uses the "Expand Scene" to create a talk room between users who are mutually interested. The talk room allows them to talk like an existing chat and check the partner's profile.

3.3   User Study

We conducted a user study for five participants ages 20 to 25 using the initial Com-Friends design. In a prior questionnaire, we asked if they would like to expand their network in the community, their hobbies, and what kind of partner information they need when building an SNS relationship. We thought that it was necessary to treat the "school and workplace" and "region and apartment house" communities separately, so we checked each one's motivation for personal network expansion. All the participants are students and results show that they do not want to expand the network in the region and apartment house, but many strongly desire it in schools and workplaces; therefore, we decided to conduct experiments only with their university community. Next, regarding the hobby from the preliminary questionnaire and the information participants needed to build relationships, we prepared several profiles and asked for their reaction. We then asked participants to talk to a fictitious user whom he/she was interested in via chats, and the conversation was simulated. Conversely, another user whom participants were interested in, talked to them via chat and simulated the conversation.

3.4   Interview

After the study, we asked participants to evaluate the design and we interviewed them.

Theme 1: Usability
Figure 6 shows the initial design evaluation in term of usability. Results show that several functions had to be extended and some participants did not give the initial design a high score. We will explain these issues in other themes in detail.

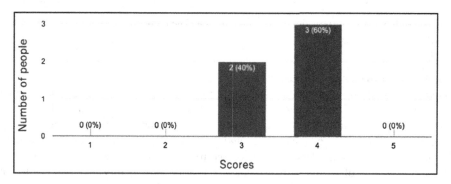

Fig. 6.   Usability of the initial design. (The higher the scores, the higher the usability.)

Theme 2: Ease of Talking
Regarding ease of talking, evaluation scores were divided as shown in Fig. 7. People who often talk with someone they have never met on SNS and who are motivated to expand relationships said that they were able to talk easily based on the displayed partner's characteristics. Others who are not good at conversation and have low motivation for relationship building said that it was difficult to speak because they didn't know the conversation tempo with a new person or how to write the opponent's chat. To solve the problem of not knowing the conversation tempo, they suggested displaying whether or not each other is entering the sentence.

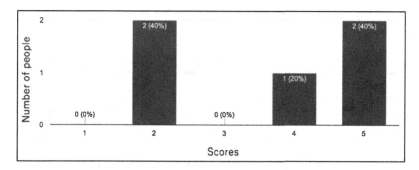

Fig. 7.   Ease of Talking in the initial design. (The higher the scores, the easier it was to talk.)

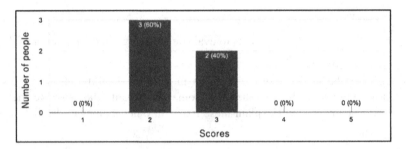

Fig. 8. Sufficiency of Information in the initial design (The higher the scores, the more they feel the information is sufficient.)

Theme 3: Sufficiency of Information

As shown in Fig. 8, information provided in the initial design is inadequate. The first common result was that gender information is necessary, but in this design, the only way to get gender information was to guess from the partner's name, which was an uncertain method. Participants mentioned that building relationships or changing behavior in conversation depended on the partner's gender. In addition, related to the above theme, one of the participants stated that brief introductory text was needed in order to write the other party's chat. She stated that she would estimate the other's writing style and the sense of distance, even if she could not get detailed characteristics from the sentence. Finally, the strongest opinion was that the profile characteristics were too brief. For example, even if the user and opponent have music and reading in common, because these comprise several genres and pieces of work, they insisted that they do not necessarily get along well with each other. We used a brief profile, even with the chance that users will be selective and not interested in anyone, because it allows for the possibility of a wide community. But, this actually may not be a problem even if detailed information is used. They also wanted to change how much detailed information can be disclosed depending on the partner; some participants did not want to show their detailed information if they could not get along with the other person.

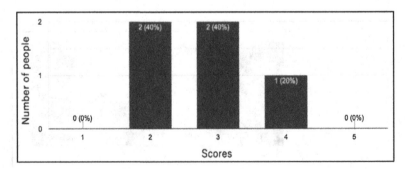

Fig. 9. Whether they feel that they could build a relationship with the opponent. (The higher the scores, the more they feel they build new relationships.)

Theme 4: Relationships Building

Figure 9 shows the results of investigating whether this design could help participants build relationships with the conversation partner. Participants' awareness towards friendships from usual means was a significant influence. Participants with some SNS relationships recognized the other person as an acquaintance only by this chat conversation, but those who did not, said that if they do not meet directly, they could not recognize them as an acquaintance. Since we think this application is the first step to building relationships, it is good if a relationship can be made with only chat, otherwise, this is a good path to direct exchange. Additionally, current information is insufficient to recognize the other as an acquaintance. This experiment showed that a conversation about the community greatly changed the participants' impression. If they cannot recognize that the partners are close to them, they will become unrelated, so we felt that we should present more information related to the community.

3.5 Results

As a result of the initial study, the following main elements are necessary for ComFriends.

1. Enhancement of chat
2. Refinement of proposed profile
3. Addition of community elements

The next chapter has details for each element. We also could roughly identify three participant patterns:

1. People with a wide range to recognize partners as acquaintances in short SNS conversations and who have high relationship building motivation.
2. People who have high relationship building motivation but do not recognize opponents as acquaintances in short SNS conversations.
3. People with low motivation for relationship building.

Since we want to utilize the premise of community chat to assist relationship-building, we narrowed down the target to the second group of people after that.

4 Improvement

4.1 Enhancement of Chat

The first improvement is the expansion of the chat function. One of the initial design evaluations was the lack of clarity around the partner's conversation speed. This is considered a major obstacle in the first meeting, so to eliminate this, we fixed the chat design so the user can get visual information about whether or not the other party is entering text. If the conversation partner inputs text, the displayed partner name in the talk room changes to yellow as shown on the right in Fig. 10; otherwise, it turns white as shown on the left.

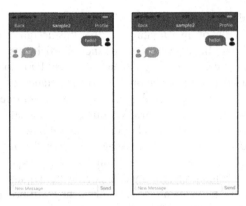

Fig. 10. Improved talking scene.

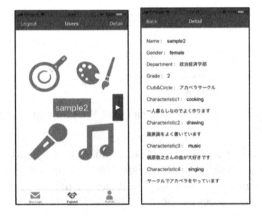

Fig. 11. Improved expand scene and detail.

4.2 Refinement of Proposed Profile

The next improvement is refinement of the proposed profile. In the initial design, due to the many genres of displayed characteristics, the user would not necessarily know if the conversation would be successful with a simple characteristic. Therefore, in order for the user to know the partner's characteristics in more detail, we added a one-word comment field for each characteristic to be displayed as shown in Fig. 11. Users can check this information by pressing the "detail" button on the upper right of the screen. This also gives users a clue about how to write their partner's chat. Based on findings that gender information is important for selecting partners, we modified the proposed profile to grasp partner gender by color difference. A male partner profile is displayed in gray and a female partner profile is displayed in light orange. Finally, in the initial design, we learned that participants remember their partner by associating with their icon in conventional SNS, so we made it possible to display the user's icon in the talk room.

4.3   Addition of Community Elements

The last improvement is the addition of community elements. The initial design does not contain community information in the proposed profile and the user had to propose that topic in the conversation. We thought that users felt close to each other when the partner belonged to the same community, so we added profile information on the grade, department, and club activities of the participants' university. In addition, because some participants did not want to disclose community information to people they did not know, we allow users to arbitrarily set the community information disclosure range to three types: (1) Public to all, (2) Public only to partners who are interested in each other, and (3) Not public to anyone.

5   User Study and Evaluation

We conducted a user study on six college students ages 21 to 25, who were highly motivated to build new relationships with an improved ComFriends. Half of the participants used the first design and the other half used ComFriends for the first time. We first asked participants to set up their profile and prepare five fictitious profiles that they would be interested in getting referred to them. Profiles include name, gender, characteristics that indicate hobbies, community information such as grade and department, and icons used for talking. They reacted to whether or not they were interested in the proposed fictitious users and, similar to the initial user study, they simulated conversation for approximately 10 min in one of the talk rooms generated by mutual interest. Then, we asked them to evaluate the app and we briefly interviewed them.

The application evaluation criteria are as follows: (1) Usability, (2) Ease of Talking, (3) Affinity for conversation partner, and (4) Motivation to build relationships with this application. Figure 12 shows a comparison of the initial design and improved design evaluation results. The score is the average of all participants between 1 to 5 points, with higher scores representing higher ease of use, less resistance to conversation, greater affinity, and higher motivation for the app.

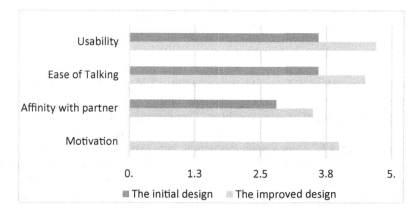

Fig. 12. The evaluation of the initial design and the improved design

As shown in Fig. 12, the improved design got a better evaluation than did the initial design. From the usability point of view, the initial design gained 3.6 points and the improved design gained 4.7 points, which was a significant improvement. Participants seemed to be able to use the app naturally, like a conventional talk application. Next, for ease of talking, the initial design gained 3.6 points and the improved design gained 4.5 points. Participants seemed to have a good impression of the new design because they were able to grasp the speed of the partner's conversation and avoid conflict by checking the partner's display name color. Regarding partner affinity, the initial design gained 2.8 points and the improved design gained 3.5 points. Many participants could recognize that their partners are located in familiar places because they got partner information about community. In particular, participants with community related topics in the conversation simulation give high points to the improved design. Participants who did not give high points said the reasons were insufficiency of conversation time and lack of community-related topics. In terms of motivation to use this app, the improved design got 4 points. We did not compare this result to the initial design since we did not get this evaluation then. Participants said they would like to actively use this app when enter a new community.

6   Discussion

6.1   Obstacle in the First Meeting

In this section, we will discuss whether ComFriends could assist first-time conversations. According to the survey of 18 users, we found that the obstacles in the first meeting were the unclear conversation content and the ambiguity of the partner's conversation speed.

To solve the problem of conversation content, ComFriends gave the user information on the characteristics of their partner's hobby and their status in the community, and at the time of profile selection, made it possible for users to freely choose people they wanted to talk to. If a talk room is created, there is a presumption that they want to talk with each other, so users can be highly motivated for conversation. In the user study, participants seemed to have a smooth conversation proposal with reference to characteristics. Participants said that due to the four simple profiles, they could easily sort out those who are not interested at all versus interested parties, which avoided the need to confirm details; we thought that this visually easy-to-understand design was useful in selecting multiple partners. We added these details in the new design, which reduced the mismatch of hobbies. As shown in Fig. 12, this made it easier for users to select the partner and propose the conversation topic.

To solve the conversation speed problem, ComFriends made it possible for the user to check whether the conversation partner is entering a chat. This function reduced conversation conflict so it got a good evaluation, but users found it difficult to see the design. Several participants said that since a chat is added at the bottom of the conversation, the design should confirm whether or not the conversation partner has entered the chat in at the lower side of the screen (from the user's perspective).

Throughout the experiment, some participants were less familiar with their opponents due to lack of conversation time, but all participants said they were not resistant to conversation with the other party.

6.2 Usefulness of Community Sharing

This section discusses the usefulness of personal expansion within the community. Our first hypothesis was that expanding the community network would increase the user's sense of security and affinity compared to using SNS. In the interview, participants mentioned that they were able to recognize the partner as a familiar presence through topics and information related to their community, which were displayed in detail.

As shown in Fig. 12, partner affinity was greatly enhanced by adding community information. They also felt that they could provide more information to people in the same community than to other partners on the Internet who they do not know at all. We believe that sharing a lot of information brings partners closer and it seems that maintaining the community helped relieve user anxiety about unknown parties and helped build relationships. Participants' interest in expanding relations within the community via this application was also high.

7 Conclusion and Future Work

In this work, we investigated obstacles to interacting in a first meeting, proposed an application design for expanding the community network, and got evaluation results. The main design concepts are the display of the characteristic as conversation seed, the conversation by mutual interest, and preparing the assumption that users belong to the same community. A study of six users showed that a concise design with characteristics that promote conversation and belonging to a community, gave users a sense of intimacy.

In the future, it is necessary to confirm actual interaction among users in the community. Since this was a simulation experiment using fictional users, results from a more natural environment will be required. For the community, we need to try this concept at different scales. This time it was a big community, such as a university, but we have to confirm how this application works in a smaller community or a resident community such as an apartment house.

References

1. Rath, T.: Vital friends: The People You Can't Afford to Live Without. The Gallup Press, Washington (2006)
2. Ellison, N.B., Steinfield, C., Lampe, C.: The benefits of Facebook "Friends:" social capital and college student's use of online social network sites. J. Comput.-Mediat. Commun. 12(4), 1143–1168 (2007)

3. Murata, I., Suzuki, N.: A newspaper-based analysis of minors' legal responsibility for mobile phone-induced crimes: with special reference to articles of online dating sites related crimes. Japan J. Educ. Technol. **32**(4), 435–442 (2009)
4. Ishii, Y., Aburai, T., Takeyasu, K.: An analysis of user attitudes to SNS. OIU J. Int. Stud. **26**(2), 1–21 (2013)
5. Nguyen, T.T., Nguyen, D.T., Iqbal, S.T., Ofek, E. : The known stranger: supporting conversations between strangers with personalized topic suggestions. In: Proceedings. of CHI, pp. 555–564 (2015)
6. Ogata, H., Yano, Y., Furugori, N., Jin, Q.: PeCo-mediator: development and modelling of a supporting system for sharing and handling personal connections. Trans. Inf. Process. Soc. Japan **36**(6), 1299–1309 (1995)
7. Iwasaki, H., Yano, E., Sinohara, I., Kato, T.: Modeling of personal sense of intimacy using common points of contents. Kansei Eng. Int. **8**(3) (2009)
8. Matsuo, Y., Yasuda, Y.: How relations are built within a SNS world-social network analysis on mixi-. Trans. Jpn. Soc. Artif. Intell. AI **22**(5), 531–541 (2007)
9. Hamasaki, M., Takeda, H., Ohmukai, I., Ichise, R.: Proposal and analysis of a community system using personal networks. Trans. Jpn. Soc. Artif. Intell. AI **19**(5), 389–398 (2004)
10. Uehigashi, N., Sakabe, S., Yamazaki, H.: Relationship between communication on social network service and empathy. Papers Environ. Inf. Sci. **30**, 273–278 (2016)

Comparison of User Listening Attitude for Birdsongs Recorded in Fukushima Restricted Area to Prepare Training Data for AI

Hill Hiroki Kobayashi[✉] and Daisuke Shimotoku

Center of Spatial Information Science, The University of Tokyo, Kashiwa,
Chiba 277-8568, Japan
kobayashi@csis.u-tokyo.ac.jp

Abstract. This article reports experiments conducted using non-experts to create a training dataset for detecting birdsong using AI. Herein, the authors focused on the number of enthusiasts instead of the number of bird experts, and conducted birdsong voice detection experiments on 21 non-expert participants, i.e., the participants were neither bird experts nor hobbyists. The experiment did not focus on the accuracy of the listening rate; rather, it aimed to evaluate the difference between the numbers reported to have been heard per subject. The authors conducted an experiment to detect two distinct bush warbler songs from randomly selected natural environmental sounds over 4 h. Among the obtained results, the largest number of reports was 196, whereas the smallest number of reports was two. These results demonstrate the expected user behavior when creating a participatory survey system of remote birds using the Internet or SNS. These results would help us create a training data set for AI that leverages the boundary of the real and virtual worlds by engaging ecological cognition to perform soundscape interaction with a wild animal through HCI.

Keywords: Participatory sensing · Acoustic ecology · Radioecology

1 Introduction

Human beings can imagine the bush warbler (*Horornis diphone*) in a nature environment because our brain has the ability to record and store the creature as an ecological context of a textbook. Since each person's history and experiences differ, the imagined presence of an ecological creature differs relative to the size, shape, and type of country. A contemporary approach to observing the presence of the songbird is to listen to "*ho ho ke kyo, chi chi chi*" in the national park. By listening to bird sounds, we can observe and share the presence of songbirds in natural environments. According to Ishida [1], the singing voice of the bush warbler is being investigated to understand the impact on the ecosystem caused by the Fukushima nuclear power plant accident.

This study attempted to understand the processes of soundscape interaction between users and remote uninhabited environments using information technologies to reveal new knowledge by examining the counting calls of animals. This study hopes to

© Springer Nature Switzerland AG 2019
N. Streitz and S. Konomi (Eds.): HCII 2019, LNCS 11587, pp. 381–389, 2019.
https://doi.org/10.1007/978-3-030-21935-2_29

discover the differences in individual listening skills, which is expected to help us design a training dataset for AI (Fig. 1, right) that leverages the boundary of the real and virtual worlds by engaging ecological cognition to perform Human-based computation with a wild animal through HCI.

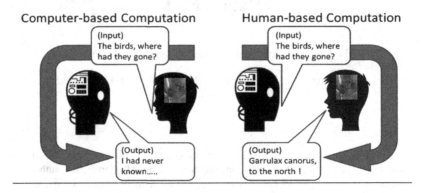

Fig. 1. Proposed method (right).

This paper discusses the progress of this study, as well as the design, development, and evaluation of a system used to examine the counting calls of animals in a contemporary real-world setting. First, based on related studies, we have designed an experimental system based on related observation methodologies. In addition, the processes of soundscape interaction (Human-based computation) of users are evaluated by quantitative content analysis. Finally, based on the experimental results, overall findings are discussed, including potential applications of the system. The remainder of this paper is organized as follows. Section 2 provides background information, and Sect. 3 presents the proposed method. Section 4 describes results and discussions, Sect. 5 summarizes future work, and Sect. 6 concludes the paper.

2 Background

To monitor such species, counting recorded calls is an effective method because by various animals, including mammals, birds, amphibians, fish, and insects, use acoustic communication [2, 3]. In addition to using visual counts, this method is commonly used to investigate the habitats of birds and amphibians [4], where an observer manually listens to calls and identifies species in the field. Therefore, it has a disadvantage. i.e., results are affected by the observer's ability to identify each species by calls. Therefore, it is necessary to develop a monitoring system with AI that can operate over multiple years to ensure long-term stability under unmanned operating conditions. Thus, we decided to create training data for an AI system that counts these calls. If such a system can be achieved using the Internet or SNS, safe surveys and a communication mechanism will be realized for both experts and enthusiasts.

In ecological studies, it is desirable to develop a technology that effectively supports study while consuming minimal resources. Specifically, we aim to establish a long-term, continuously operating, ubiquitous system that delivers environmental information, such as sound, in real time. Researchers worldwide are conducting ecological studies by recording and analyzing the spatial information of wild animal vocalizations [5]. Furthermore, ecological studies of the environment near urban areas are being conducted using smartphones [5]; however, it is difficult to confirm the behavior of wild animals using cell phones. To record the vocalizations of wild animals whose behaviors are difficult to predict, it is necessary to employ a monitoring system that operates continuously. It is difficult to conduct system maintenance due to the environmental conditions of wild animal habitats (e.g., out of infrastructure service areas and high temperature and high humidity environments); thus, system redundancy is crucial.

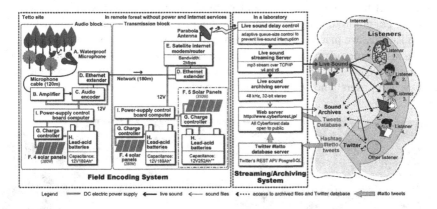

Fig. 2. Cyberforest project system diagram.

Our previous system was continuously operational on Iriomote Island (Okinawa, Japan) from 1996 to 2010. To date, the fundamental research performed at Iriomote Island was expanded into the Cyberforest (Fig. 2) project we are conducting at the University of Tokyo [6]. We have also observed user behavior via our developed system through a project website [6]. We have a record of casual comments and analyses from more than 2000 users who wrote during experiments we conducted from 1996 to 2010 [6]. The phrase that appeared most frequently was "animal voices." No specific names of animals plants or words associated with the sound of falling trees or of wind or ocean tides appeared [6]. This implies that if we continue to stream real-time environmental sounds to users who are interested in environmental issues, such users will share the names of animals with others. Moreover, despite being in situations where users do not know when an animal will make a noise, a user can continue to listen carefully until an animal does make a sound. Then, this can be reported. Note that in most cases, we do not ask users to do anything specific, i.e., the users act on their own accord. Given these behaviors, we decided to examine how the numbers reported to have been heard per subject differs. Based on the results obtained to date, our research questions are as follows.

How much input can be expected per unit time to have Internet users participate and make a training dataset for AI using real-time comment information? Note that we do not consider the birdsong identification accuracy. The sounds heard by the user are presented randomly. For a future AI system, it will be used as knowledge for participatory type sensing to prepare the training data required to realizing it.

3 Proposed Method

Based on the discussed background, this study attempted to understand the soundscape interaction processes between users and remote uninhabited environments using information technologies to reveal new knowledge to perform Human-based computation by examining the counting calls of animals (Fig. 1, right). We hope to discover the differences in individual listening skills, which would help us design a training dataset for AI that leverages the boundary of the real and virtual worlds by engaging ecological cognition to perform soundscape interaction with an ecological creature. To accomplish this, we placed an Internet-connected microphone in places where easy-to-understand environmental problems occurred. We then recorded environmental audio over the 20 years and processed it as experimental data. Finally, we conducted an interview with users who are neither bird experts nor amateur enthusiasts.

Fig. 3. Location of project site in exclusion zone (37° 28′ 04.3″ N, 140° 55′ 27.5″ E), which is 10 km from the Fukushima Daiichi Nuclear Power Plant. (right) Remote microphone system installed in exclusion zone.

This project installed a bioacoustic transmitter station [7] in the exclusion zone area (10 km from the Fukushima Daiichi Nuclear Power Plant; Fig. 3). A map of the exclusion zone is shown in Fig. 2. The transmitter station is located in the Oamaru district in Namie, Fukushima (37° 28′ 04.3″ N, 140° 55′ 27.5″ E). We developed a "Live Sound System" and a "Streaming/Archiving System (Fig. 2)," which enables us to (1) distribute sound data in the exclusion zone to the public via the Internet in real time and (2) distribute the sound data to the public over the Internet. The Live Sound System (Fig. 4) comprises two separate subsystems, i.e., a "Field Encoding System"

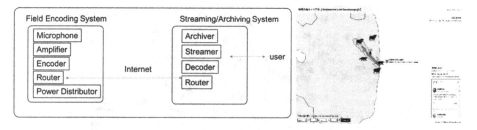

Fig. 4. (left) System diagram of Live Sound System (Field Encoding and Streaming/Archiving Systems) and (right) web interface (http://radioactivelivesoundscape.net/).

(to digitize the live sounds) and a "Streaming/Archiving System" (to delivery live sound via the Internet and archive the sound data). The technical operational testing notes for the Live Sound System can be found in the literature [8].

The recording was conducted from June 2016 to June 2017 in Japan Standard Time in the Fukushima exclusion zone. The summer and winter seasons in this zone last from June to September and December to March, respectively. The average monthly temperature is highest in August (23.0 °C) and lowest in January (2.0 °C). The average annual rainfall is 1511 mm (Namie Meteorological Station; JMA 2017) [9]. The acoustic activity of birds is highest near sunrise; thus, the acoustic survey analyzed live streaming audio data from 10 min before sunrise and 60 min after sunrise [10]. Primarily following the procedures in the literature [10] and [11], we also studied sunset sounds. The recordings began six minutes after the hour and lasted for one hour (i.e., streaming events were recorded at 00:06–01:05, 01:06–02:05, and so on). Denoting the sunrise or sunset time by n:m, if $6 \leq m < 36$, we take the first 30 min of the sound file containing the sunrise or sunset time. Otherwise (i.e., if $0 \leq m < 6$ or $36 \leq m < 60$), we take the last 30 min of the file. To alleviate listener workload, these 30-min audio files were separated into two parts. The audio files were processed by peak normalization high-pass filtering with a 500-Hz cutoff and 20 dB/decade attenuation. These calculations were made using the sox software (version 14.4.2).

The participants acquired two sounds made by nightingales, which is a very common species in Japan. Japanese nightingales vocalize in two way, i.e., using a "song" to attract females and a "call" to present himself or warn others of the presence of predator. The participants demonstrated typical calls and songs using a public addressing speaker and were asked to use headphones. Using the Audacity software, which can show the Fourier frequency-time transformation spectrogram of a sound file, the participants were instructed to describe each song or call in terms of the following information: time the sound started, (ii) time the sound ended, (iii) type of sound (song or call) or environmental noise (rain or wind), which were expected to be recognized automatically, and (iv) sound quality or signal level. Here Audacity provides the time information (in milliseconds), which was then recorded by the participants, and the sound type and quality were identified subjectively.

Fig. 5. Experiment conducted on June 24, 2017 (Komaba, Tokyo).

4 Results and Discussions

A human listening experiment was conducted on June 24, 2017 in Komaba, Tokyo (Fig. 5). Here, 48 audio files were allocated to 21 listeners. This experiment accumulated 2225 events, including 711 calls, 572 songs, 628 winds, and 314 rains. In this task, the listeners were asked to evaluate as many files as possible in four hours. To minimize human error, each audio file was scanned at least three times by different listeners. Note that the participants were paid 10,000 Japanese yen.

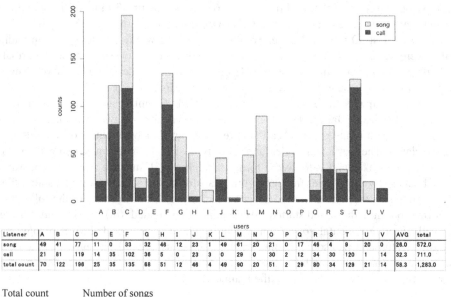

Listener	A	B	C	D	E	F	G	H	I	J	K	L	M	N	O	P	Q	R	S	T	U	V	AVG	total
song	49	41	77	11	0	33	32	46	12	23	1	49	61	20	21	0	17	46	4	9	20	0	26.0	572.0
call	21	81	119	14	35	102	36	5	0	23	3	0	29	0	30	2	12	34	30	120	1	14	32.3	711.0
total count	70	122	196	25	35	135	68	51	12	46	4	49	90	20	51	2	29	80	34	129	21	14	58.3	1,283.0

Total count	Number of songs
Time cost	Number of calls
Total count	Total number of songs and calls

Fig. 6. Number of songs and calls per user.

Table 1. Hourly and economic costs per report.

Listener	A	B	C	D	E	F	G	H	I	J	K	L
total count	70	122	196	25	35	135	68	51	12	46	4	49
time cost	205.71	118.03	73.47	576.00	411.43	106.67	211.76	282.35	1200.00	313.04	3600.00	293.88
economic cost	142.86	81.97	51.02	400.00	285.71	74.07	147.06	196.08	833.33	217.39	2,500.00	204.08

Listener	L	M	N	O	P	Q	R	S	T	U	V	Average
total count	49	90	20	51	2	29	80	34	129	21	14	58.32
time cost	293.88	160.00	720.00	282.35	7200.00	496.55	180.00	423.53	111.63	685.71	1028.57	849.12
economic cost	204.08	111.11	500.00	196.08	5,000.00	344.83	125.00	294.12	77.52	476.19	714.29	589.67

Total count	Total number of songs and calls
Time cost (sec)	Time required for one report (obtained by dividing working time of 14400 seconds (four hours) by total number of reports of songs and calls)
Economic cost (yen)	Amount of remuneration obtained from a single report (obtained by dividing 10000 yen by the total number of reports of songs and calls.

An annotation experiment was conducted on June 24, 2018. Here, 21 undergraduate students were recruited to count 711 calls and 572 songs. The participant who detected the most events counted 196 events (119 calls and 77 songs), and the user who detected the fewest events worked with only two calls (Fig. 6). The user who detected the most counted spent 73.5 s to detect one event (either a call or song), meanwhile the user with the minimum count spent 7200 s to detect a single voice (Table 1). The user who detected the most counted earned 51 yen to detect one voice (either a call or song), and the user with the minimum count earned 2 yen to detect a single voice. Those events (call and song) do not distribute uniformly; thus, these differences cannot attribute to user performance. However, it shows the time and economic cost for non-experts to annotate two Japanese nightingales sounds.

This experiment described the preparations and problems required to investigate birdsongs using the Internet. When delivering birdsong in real time using the Internet, the time to reach the user depends on the network environment. In other words, even if different participants hear the same environmental sound, there may be a time difference for each user, i.e., better communication quality results in better real-time performance.

As mentioned previously, those events (call and song) events do not distribute uniformly; thus, these differences cannot attribute to user performance. However, there is great variation relative to how each user can detect. There are various reasons for this. For those who think the natural environment sounds comfortable, continuing to listen with headphones can cause drowsiness. Meanwhile, despite significant effort, some users were unable to distinguish between call and song events. In addition, some people became sleepy and other perceived the experiment as a game.

For this experiment, we paid all participants 10,000 yen after four hours. Therefore, the resulting earnings were equal. If this was calculated by unit price per detection, a difference of 51 to 5000 yen would occur. In other words, if we calculate according the amount paid for detection efficiency, it would be approximately 100 times greater for people with better skills than that of people with less skills. Experts must be compensated appropriately; thus, this method allows non-experts to perform work for considerably less. As a result, this method is an effective way to increase the amount of training data at low cost.

We presented natural environmental sound randomly using 21 participants and conducted bush warbler song in two kinds of listening tests over four hours. In some reports, up to 1283 call or song detections were generated, and the number of reports varied from two to 196 depending on the participant.

There were three types reactions during the evaluation experiment, i.e., some people became sleepy because they were comfortable listening to the natural environment, some people detected a lot because they perceived the experiment as a game, and some people found it difficult to detect when many sounds were present in the natural environment.

When participatory sensing is used to create training data for AI, a single report from one person can be generated every 849 s. Recall that we did not consider accuracy. In other words, if we seek detection of approximately once per minute to identify these sounds over the Internet in real time, only approximately 14–15 non-experts are required to work at all times. However, this is only true relative to creating training data for dawn sounds, which is when animals' sounds are heard most frequently.

5   Future Work

As mentioned, we did not evaluate accuracy. In future, it will be necessary to evaluate the correct answer rate it consideration of both economic and temporal costs. For that purpose, it will be necessary to analyze the recorded data to extract the birdsong data and compare it to our experimental results. However, even if this is realized, the birdsong detection accuracy will not be understood. Ultimately, groups of results with similar trends must be grouped, and expert confirmation will be required.

6   Conclusion

A training dataset for detecting birdsong using AI has played an important role in the development of bioacoustic monitoring in uninhabited environments. It could play a key role in understanding the impact on the ecosystem caused by the Fukushima nuclear power plant accident. To increase the amount of training data set, the authors focused on the number of enthusiasts instead of the number of bird experts to increase the amount at low cost. We propose that our Human-based computation approach to count calls of animals using information technologies.

Acknowledgments. This study was supported by JST Presto 11012.

References

1. Ishida, K.: Agricultural Implications of the Fukushima Nuclear Accident. Springer, Minato (2013). https://doi.org/10.1007/978-4-431-54328-2
2. Krebs, J.R., Davies, N.B.: An Introduction to Behavioural Ecology, 3rd edn. Blackwell Scientific Publications, Hoboken (1993)
3. Searcy, W.A., Nowicki, S.: The Evolution of Animal Communication: Reliability and Deception in Signaling Systems, 3rd edn. Princeton University Press, Princeton (2005)
4. Heyer, W.R.: Measuring and Monitoring Biological Diversity: Standard Methods for Amphibians, 1st edn. Smithsonian Institution Press, New York (1994)
5. Hans, S., Peet, M.: Ecology: birds sing at a higher pitch in urban noise. Nature **424**(6946), 267 (2003)
6. Kobayashi, H.: Basic research in human-computer-biosphere interaction. Ph.D. thesis. The University of Tokyo (2010)
7. Kobayashi, H., Kudo, H.: Acoustic ecology data transmitter in exclusion zone, 10 km from Fukushima Daiichi nuclear power plant. Leonardo **50**(2), 188–189 (2017)
8. Saito, K., et al.: Utilizing the cyberforest live sound system with social media to remotely conduct woodland bird censuses in Central Japan. Ambio **44**, 572–583 (2015)
9. Agency JM Namie Meteorological Station (2013). http://www.jma.go.jp
10. Ueta, M., Hirano, T., Kurosawa, R.: Optimal time of the day to record bird songs for detecting changes of their breeding periods. Bird Res. **8**, T1–T6 (2012)
11. Ishida, K., Tanoi, K., Nakanishi, T.M.: Monitoring free-living Japanese bush warblers (Cettia diphone) in a most highly radiocontaminated area of Fukushima Prefecture, Japan. J. Radiat. Res. **56**(Suppl. 1), i24–i28 (2015)

Take a Photo for My Story: Social Connectedness for the Elderly

Xu Lin[(✉)], Xuechen Liu, Matthias Rauterberg, and Jun Hu

Eindhoven University of Technology, 5612AZ Eindhoven, The Netherlands
X.Lin@tue.nl

Abstract. Along with the declining physical and mental condition, the living range and the social circle of elderly people shrink gradually, which indicates a relatively negative effect on the social connectedness of the elderly. The rapid development of the Internet and related technologies, however, bring new opportunities for researchers and designers to help improve elderly people's feeling of being connected and reduce their risks of becoming socially isolated. This paper presents the case study of MemoriesSharing Project, a participatory platform designed for senior residents in care homes to connect with other people and local communities through location-based story sharing. This design consists of an interactive installation and an online platform. Through 2 iterations, we introduce the design and implementation of the system, share the insights for design in care home contexts, and discuss the potentials of interaction design in semi-public spaces for improving elderly peoples' feeling of connectedness.

Keywords: Elderly people · Social connectedness · Care home · Story sharing · Interactive installation

1 Introduction

Since 1980, the number of people who is 60 or over has been doubled, and the number of people aged 65 or over will be more than the population of the children under age of 14 before 2050 [1, 2]. Ageing has become a serious topic for modern society and brings critical challenges not only in safety, mobility and physical health, but also in mental health and social well-being [3, 4].

In recent years, with the maturing of Internet and the rapid development of ICT and IoT technology, people are becoming much more connected with each other through different kinds of smart devices, services and networked environment. The merging of our cyber and physical life also brings new potentials to involve the ageing group, who are relatively away from the digital life, back into the public and mainstream networks through tangible solutions and embedded technologies in real-life context [5, 6].

In this paper, we take the local care homes in Eindhoven as examples to share our understanding about senior residents' social life in long-term care environment. Based on our investigation and design practice, we present the case study of Project MemoriesSharing and discuss the possibilities of embedding the interactive products

N. Streitz and S. Konomi (Eds.): HCII 2019, LNCS 11587, pp. 390–407, 2019.
https://doi.org/10.1007/978-3-030-21935-2_30

and systems into the daily environment of semi-public spaces inside local care homes to support senior residents' social well-being.

The following sessions of the paper include the preliminary studies and investigation with the care givers and residents in local care homes, as well as the design process of two main design iterations and the initial user test in real-life environment.

2 Background and Related Works

2.1 Social Connectedness for Elderly People

Along with the decline of physical and mental health and the shrinking social circles, elderly people usually suffer from the gradually limited mobility and less engagement in social activities. Meanwhile, many of the elderly people also face with the growing threshold in technology caused by the high learning load and the high-speed changes of modern technology. The gap between the ageing group and the mainstream media with new communication tools also increases the difficulty for elderly people to be active and engaged with others. These changes may lead to the increasing risks of being socially isolated, which is claimed to be highly related with the poor physical and mental health in many research studies [7, 8].

In the study of Giummarra et al. [9] on the relationship between ageing and social isolation, the interviewed older people considered social connectedness and social activities to be strongly associated with their overall health. They described social and mental health as being even more important than their physical health. The health professionals interviewed in the study also reported mental and physical health deteriorating when older people were socially isolated. They claimed social health to be at least as important as mental and physical health. Maintaining a good level of social connectedness and preventing social isolation are considered to be important for keeping elderly people's life quality.

However, social connectedness is a complicated concept which can be hardly explained with a universal definition or measurement. A lot of factors can influence how people experience social connectedness, such as age, context, gender, personality, culture, individual preferences, previous social relationship and so on [10, 11]. According to the review of different research studies and investigation tools [12–14], we consider social connectedness as a concept with three main aspects: (1) the quality of social relationship (including factors like the range and scale of the social circle, the frequency and quality of contact etc.); (2) the engagement in social interactions and activities (including general social interactions in daily living environment, the involvement in public social activities, voluntary work etc.); (3) the subjective feeling of being connected and perceived quality of social contact.

2.2 Related Design Works

There have been many solutions and explorations in the direction of improving or maintaining elderly people's social connection with other people. So far, more studies are focused on the bonding between elderly people and their families. For instance, the multi-player games, smart home products [15], photo sharing system, story sharing devices [16] and so on.

Although the social tie with family members is one of the most important parts in most elderly people's life, it should not be the only support for a good social life. In the context like a care home, the interaction between residents, and the connection between people living inside the care home and the local society also have essential influences on elderly's social connectedness. Both intimate and peripheral relationships in elderly people's social circles can provide a sense of connectedness and contribute to their social wellbeing [17–19].

There are also research studies and design explorations aiming to improve elderly people's social connection in care home contexts. So far, the main solutions to provide social support is to provide activities and services to encourage senior residents to share experiences and meet people, like the social groups, recreational activities, workshops, and home visiting [12, 20]. These solutions have strong influences in improving the social interaction between elderly people and others, but meanwhile they also need relatively heavy investments in organizing, managing and maintaining for keeping the activities and services sustainable. Besides, the support from the programed activities is lack of continuous influence on elderly people's feeling and behaviour. When there are no activities, residents have to entertain themselves, while most of the people turn back to the mode of doing nothing at home.

To have sustainable influence as well as to support the social activities ambiently, another direction of designing interactive products or smart environment derives in recent years. At the beginning, many of the explorations still looked into solving mobility and safety problems, but currently there are more and more studies turning to the direction of supporting and improving elderly people's social life experience and other emotional needs. Uitkijkpost [21, 22] is an interactive installation employing the real-time photo sharing experience as a way to build up the connection between people inside and outside the care homes, taking advantages of the strong emotional connection between elderly people and places. The Photostroller [23] is a device presenting the photos retrieved from Flickr website to engage senior residents in the living room and trigger conversation between them. Closer-to-Nature [24] is an interactive installation using the pumping metaphor to trigger elderly people's memory of farm life and facilitating the feeling of being connected to the outdoor nature space.

In most of the projects, elderly people are playing a role as the receiver of the information and services, while there may be possibilities for them to be involved as the generator of the content as well. In MemoriesSharing project, we are not only interested in the exploration to design interactive products and systems in the daily environment to support elderly residents' social needs, but also expect to see whether senior people can be involved into the system as a role to provide meaningful contribution to other stakeholders.

3 Context of Local Care Institution

In order to get a better understanding of senior residents' daily life in local care homes, the researchers in MemoriesSharing team did preliminary studies in three care institutions (Home G, Home B and Home K). The user studies mainly included the ethnographic observation and semi-structured interviews. The observation was conducted to understand elderly people's daily routine and social activities. The interviews were focused on basic information and more detailed questions on social interaction with different groups in elderly people's social circles. Considering the private issues, video recording was not employed. Instead, the observers took notes for the key variables with a semi-structured form manually. In total, we interviewed 24 residents and 2 care givers in this step.

In this paper, we take Home B as an example to present the basic lifestyle in a local care home in Eindhoven. Home B is a senior apartment with more than 200 apartments, providing care services not only for its residents but also for some people living around in the neighbourhood. Half of the residents (around 100–120 apartments) live in the apartment for the care service, and the others rent rooms but live more independently. On the ground floor, there is a small library next to the entrance of the building, a coffee area along the hallway, a big canteen as the activity center and a small rest space next to it. There are daily services (e.g. the coffee hours and regular meals), weekly activities (e.g. Bingo) and monthly activities (e.g. Chorus and Historical Day) organized for the residents by the care providers. There are also activities open to both residents and people outside the care home.

According to the interviews with the care givers in Home B, many of the residents taken care by them are from different areas of the city, while now they spend most of the time inside the care home due to the mobility and safety concerns of going out. Happiness and excitement can be easily found when families and familiar friends or volunteers come to visit, and the mood depression can also be noticed after the visits. These contacts are important but also limited in elderly people's daily life. More social activities that can keep the seniors cheered up and connected with other people are needed. This is also one of the reasons why they hold many events to involve both residents and the people from the neighbourhood around.

Meanwhile, many residents in the care home stick to their daily routine and resist to have changes. During the observation, noted by the researchers, it was always the similar group of people doing the similar things at the same place. Even in different kinds of activities, the people who would like to join were very likely to be the similar group of residents. Small social groups also gradually formed within these people, and the new comers sometimes reported difficulty of joining the social circle inside the care home. In the coffee area on the hallway, the situation was quite similar, and there was another phenomenon that many residents spent hours sitting and looking outside through the big windows, doing nothing.

Most of the residents in the care home are not familiar with new technologies like computers and smart phones, except some individuals who are able to contact families and friends with emails, Facebook and WhatsApp. The major of the residents still stay with the traditional media like TV, telephone and newspapers. Photos play an important role in their social life, not only providing the way for them to recall the old memories, but also trigger new conversations with other peers or visitors. Some of the residents even bring their important albums together with them every day, in order to show other people with the photos of their old experiences or families.

During the interviews, many people showed a great passion in talking about their stories and experiences in the old days. If there was a suitable trigger like the photos, a map or a news, they would like to talk for a very long time, with personal opinions and some experiences from the old days which younger generations can hardly know. Usually, it is the family members like the children and grandchildren who listen to them talking about the stories. The residents who joined our interviews admitted that they would like to share those stories with more people, but normally they would not take the first step to actively post or share the experience, since they did not have a way to share and also were not sure whether other people, especially the younger generations, would be interested in those talks or not. When there were organized activities specially for memory sharing, like the Historical Day or workshops for storytelling (Fig. 1), they were willing to join and open to talk. The residents told us if there were people listening to them carefully, it could give them a feeling of being concerned and respected.

Fig. 1. Photo wall from story sharing workshop in care home

4   Design of MemoriesSharing System

Inspired by the related works and the preliminary studies in local care homes, we choose memories sharing as a trigger to build the connection between elderly people and others, taking advantages of elderly people's passion of storytelling and their strong emotional connections with the places and things related to the past. Besides, the rich experience and memories of elderly people can also be considered as a part of the local history, which is meaningful for the younger generations to know. This is also a reason for a lot of social communities and care institutions to organize workshops and activities for intergenerational communication on local history.

Design Process and Methods
Following the process of research through design, the whole study included 3 design cycles, in which the approaches like brainstorming, interaction prototyping, constructive storytelling, Wizard of Oz, semi-structured interview, and observation were employed to help designers conduct analysis, synthesis, simulation, evaluation and decision [25].

In this project, the first design cycle included the preliminary study and concept generation. Ideas were generated through brainstorming, based on the information we collected from the ethnographic observation and interviews. The design concepts were described in storyboards, concept videos and paper prototypes. 4 potential target users were invited to use and evaluate the concept in the early stage.

The second cycle was the first iteration of the design concept, the implementation of the mid-fi prototype on tablet and the user test. In this cycle, another 4 residents were invited to try the prototype with the Wizard of Oz method, in order to simulation the real experience of sharing stories and receiving photo feedbacks.

The third cycle was the second iteration based on the knowledge from cycle 2. In this phase, the concept was refined into a combination of an indoor interactive installation and an online platform. A 3-week initial field trial was conducted in one of the local care homes and 19 people joined for the initial qualitative study.

4.1 Concept Generation and Evaluation

In the first version of the concept, the target users were the senior residents who have unforgettable memories somewhere and would like to visit or have a look at the places again. They were invited to share the memories and express their wishes at the end of the stories. They could share the stories through different ways, including handwriting, audio recording, video recording and face-to-face storytelling to a volunteer. For each story, the key information like time and location would be highlighted by the volunteers and readers online, so that the stories could be recommended to more suitable people. The people outside the care homes could use a map application to receive the stories when they appeared at the location near the stories. They could leave comments or took photos to realize the wishes for the elderly if they liked the stories. If a story received a lot of feedbacks, the story and the replies would be re-organized into a small brochure or a nice poster that could be presented inside the care home.

Fig. 2. (A), (B) Props for interview; (C) Screenshot of video sketch; (D) Interviews with residents.

Paper Prototypes and Concept Evaluation

Taking a memory of a trip to Paris and England as an example, the initial concept was made into a simple scenario with a short video sketch and a paper prototype for a quick evaluation (Fig. 2). The physical evidence in the concept (the brochure and the poster) were made for elderly users to understand the concept more easily. During the evaluation, the research assistant (native Dutch speaker with good English level) explain the background and goal of the concept, played the video sketch and explained the scenario with the video to the interviewees. Then the props in the set of the paper prototype were showed to help them experience the concept. After introducing the concept, prepared questions were asked to make sure the interviewees understand the concept and see how they liked or disliked the design. Feedbacks were collected in notes and audio recordings for analysis.

4 residents (1F, 3 M) were randomly chosen and interviewed in Home B. In general, all the 4 interviewees liked the concept and gave their opinions. The first interviewee (S1) started the discussion particularly on the concrete example in the scenario. He hated the places in the story for personal reasons but would like to see similar stories happened in the country he liked. He also emphasized that he would like to know the local life from real people instead of the introduction written in books. Two interviewees (S2 F, S3 M) used to travel a lot around the world, thus they liked the concept very much and would like to see the photos of current days in those places. The female interviewee reached this goal mainly with the help from her daughter since she hurt her hips seriously and had limited mobility from then on. The man didn't mention any related experience with family's help and was looking forward to the product. Besides, he also expressed curiosity to the countries and places where he didn't have chances to go. One of the interviewees (S1, M) mentioned one common reaction that he thought he didn't have stories (worth) to share with others. Many elderly people held similar opinions that they assumed younger generations might not be interested in listening to or reading an old person's old story. This can be solved with two ways: (1) recommend and push the information to the suitable potential users who are interested in historical stories or the topics mentioned in the story (e.g. the certain location, events, hobbies etc.), and the feedbacks with interest may encourage the senior people to share; (2) encourage the residents to explore other people's stories and get inspired from the shared topics. The feedbacks from the 4 interviewees also indicated that the residents were to some extent interested in personal and real-life experiences shared from other peers.

4.2   First Design Iteration: Touch Screen Application & Website

Design Concept Iteration

The first design iteration was mainly a website with mobile application and webpage versions (Fig. 3A). The basic functions of sharing and exploring stories were implemented. A special interface for public interaction on touch screen were also designed, which was expected to be used by the residents in the semi-public space to share memories and explore other people's stories.

The preliminary study showed that most of the residents were not familiar with computer and Internet, while the care givers mentioned that it would be possible for the residents to try if the interface and the operation were simple and clear enough for them to understand. Most of the people who came downstairs to meet people in the canteen every day were relatively open to the new things, especially when the products meet their interests. Besides, there were also residents who could use smart phones and computers, and were very familiar with touch screens. For this group, either the touch screen in the canteen or the website would work.

Considering the major group of the users often sit and chat with each other during the coffee time, a desktop size was suggested for the prototype, so that the users would stay at the table and use the system together. In this way, the prototype could not only combine the groups inside and outside the care home, but also became a trigger for residents to start more various topics in their daily conversations, instead of repeating the superficial conversations like "good weather".

The basic idea of the design concept was similar to the initial one, but the details were revised. The way of sharing stories was clearly described as posting stories on the website or using the touch screen in the canteen. The concept of promoting the stories was also described in details as recommending the stories to the people who were near the location where the story happened before or the ones who were interested in certain topics.

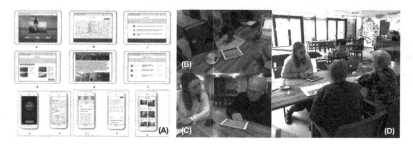

Fig. 3. (A) Interface of the touch screen version; (B), (C), (D) Interviews with residents.

Mid-Fi Prototype Implementation

Due to the time limitation and the needs of fast prototyping for evaluation, the system was built with the prototyping tool called Mockingbot. The basic interaction of the system was implemented in the mid-fi prototype, and the system of posting stories and receiving feedbacks were simulated with the method Wizard of OZ.

The interfaces on the tablet was kept simple. Most pages are fixed without sliding bar, and the interactions with double tap or holding operation were reduced, so that all the information could be directly seen when the elderly users took the screen, and the system can be easily explored though several buttons.

The start page was a slideshow to introduce the whole project with a sample story. At the bottom, there was one big button with small ones on each side. The big button was the visual center to draw people's attention. It was the starting point of story sharing on this platform. The small buttons were linked to the detailed introduction of the whole project (left) and the showcase of the shared stories (right). Clicking on the start button, users would go to the page of the story map centered by the current location of the device. After choosing the place where the story happened through touching the map or typing the location in the search bar, the users went to the second step of choosing how to tell the stories. At the moment of the first iteration, there were three possible ways: typing, handwriting for photo taking or scanning, and audio recording. After sending out the stories, users would receive messages when the story receives feedbacks. They could also check the stories in the showcase or through the account information at the top-right corner. Besides reading the replies and checking the photos, the elderly storytellers would also react and edit the content together with the photo, or even add the photo into their original story. The system would automatically generate a layout for either a poster or a brochure style with both the stories and the replied comments and photos, which could be printed out as a physical evidence and a small reward.

Prototype Evaluation
4 people (3 Female, 1 Male) were invited for the user test in this step to see elderly people's acceptance of the version on touch screen and collect the feedbacks on usability (Fig. 3). The interviewees were chosen randomly from the canteen of the care home. 2 of them were not familiar with computer and Internet, the other 2 said they used computer and Internet before.

Similar with the first concept evaluation, the user test started with the introduction of the background and the goal of the project. Then, a sample story of using the product was introduced through research assistant's storytelling and the video sketch. After the introduction, interviewees were invited to recall their own experiences that might be similar with the story as a warm-up, and were triggered to imagine if they were the person mentioned in the story, what they would like to share and what they wished to receive as the reply. Based on the conversation, interviewees were invited to try the system. At the beginning, they were asked to explore and try finishing the tasks of sharing stories and checking replies by themselves. If they met problems and could not reach the goal on their own, the research assistant would give hints and help them to finish the steps. All the conversations were audio recorded for qualitative analysis.

Although showing a lot of interest in the project, the 2 interviewees who did not ever use computer expressed high threshold in adopting technologies in different perspectives. One of the ladies (S1) refused to use the tablet on her own since she did not know how to deal with the device and it was still difficult for her to understand the logic in the interface, even though there were only 3 buttons. The other lady (S2), however, felt it difficult because of her poor eyesight. She spent most of her life in Eindhoven and did not really have a chance going out to other places. Before this concept, she did not think about that she can share the memories with others. Instead of the places and events, she was more interested in animals like horses and dogs, and would like to see more content related to her interests.

For the 2 interviewees who could use computer, the touch screen was much more easily accepted, while the man (S3) preferred the traditional keyboards rather than the soft keyboard on the screen. Both of the interviewees understood the concept and talked about their own experiences. They both chose to type the stories, but none of them finish a detailed and complete story in a short term (10–15 min). The typed content was short with some simple content mentioned in their stories. As mentioned by S3, they needed to think of the wording for written version of the stories, and this would take time and need concentration, which was difficult in a semi-public environment.

According to the user test, it was still difficult for senior residents with little experience of using computer or related technologies to understand and accept the unfamiliar interaction on smart products, although the care givers were optimistic with their openness towards new things. A tangible solution with intuitional interaction or suitable metaphor of traditional lifestyle was needed to involve the users in this generation.

4.3   Second Design Interaction: Interactive Installation and Online Platform

Design Concept Iteration
According to the feedback from the evaluation of the first iteration, an interactive installation with tangible interactions was considered to be employed for reducing residents' difficulty in using technology.

A metaphor of "writing a letter" was introduced for the elderly people to share their stories and memories. In this version, we designed an interactive mailbox to collect stories in semi-public space, and provided participants with the special letter cards to write stories. On the letter cards, simple questions like when and where the story happened were asked as a hint for participants to highlight the key information, so that the story could be marked on the story map easily and sent to more suitable target readers.

Although most of the residents were not familiar with smart products, the public screen and television were not strange to them at all. To achieve a better effect on presenting the stories and drawing people's attention for participating, a big screen was installed together with the mailbox. The nice sentences and interesting paragraphs of the stories as well as the photos and replies would be presented for more people to see.

Meanwhile, the interaction on the webpage were kept and revised for the users who did not go to the shared spaces regularly but were able to use computers at home.

Ideally, the written stories should be recognized automatically by the system. Due to the technology limitation, in current version, we used the crowdsourcing way to transcribe the documents. There were two solutions: one was to hide the personal information and use the existing online crowdsourcing platform like Mechanical Turk, which would make some cost but the service was relative stable; the other one was to take advantages of the power of social media, while the quality and efficiency needed to be estimated.

Prototype Implementation
The final iteration of MemoriesSharing (Fig. 4A) consisted of the interactive installation in the care home (a special mailbox and a big screen), a website with both gallery and map version for presenting stories, and the social media accounts for promotion.

In details, elderly people who wanted to tell their stories could share the contents via the special mailbox by "writing a letter". The stories would be presented and promoted on a collective "story map" online based on the location data of the stories. On the big screen with the mailbox, the senior storytellers could check the feedbacks to their stories and read other people's stories as well. On the other side, people who were interested in the stories, could receive the stories via social media, or search the stories near them or at particular locations through the "story map". If they liked the stories, they could leave comments or help enrich the stories by taking new photos of the places, or spreading the stories to more people. Through the interaction between readers and story-tellers, the stories were expected to be continuously updating on the platform, connecting the past and the current local life. The growing stories with new photos and comments, in turn, would also be sent back to the elderly people in a nice visual and physical style as a reward.

Fig. 4. (A) Set-up of MS project; (B), (C) Photos of people using the prototype in care home.

Interactive Installation to Collect Stories (Mailbox)

In the prototyping phase, with the consideration of lower the cost and being flexible to change, the mailbox (Fig. 5A) was made of Mdf and the inside structure for embedding cameras and sensors was created by laser-cutting. The box was in a size around $30 \times 40 \times 68$ cm, covered with the good-quality wallpaper with wood patterns to form a natural and vintage style, which was suitable for the indoor environment in the care home.

Fig. 5. (A) Mailbox; (B) Set-up of MS installation; (C) Screen layout.

Inside the mailbox, a photoelectric sensor (TCRT5000), a camera and a LED ring (WS2812B) were installed and controlled via an Arduino Nano, connected to a laptop. Arduino, processing and python 2.7 were used to build up the system of letter sensing, data collecting and uploading. The work process of the mailbox was: (1) when the user put the letter card into the box, the photoelectric sensor installed near the entrance sensed the paper and sent out the signal; (2) the laptop hidden in the mailbox received the signal and turned on the LED ring and the camera on the inner top of the box; (3) After 8500 ms (the duration for elderly user to fully put the letter into the box), the processing program took a photo of the letter card automatically and saved it into a particular folder; (4) 2000 ms later, the camera and LED ring would be turned off again; (5) the photo would be sent to the work email address via Wi-Fi and counted in a backup txt document.

Showcase of Stories (Big Screen)

Stories and feedbacks would be presented on the big screen (Fig. 5C) in the semi-public area like a canteen via the showcase of the system. The stories would be showed on the right side, automatically scrolling-up to show the full content. On the left side, the replied comments and photos through the social media would be captured and presented. If the story was too long, a group of selected paragraphs would be showed instead of the full story. The interface showed on the screen was built with html5 and JavaScript, and a python program was employed to provide content resources for the showcase by monitoring and capturing the data from the Twitter account of the project.

In this version, Twitter, as a mature social media. was one of the main ways to collect feedback. A Twitter account named MemoriesSharing was created to post new tweets when new stories were collected. The readers could leave comments and photo reactions under the story tweets. The python program used the Tweepy API to monitor the twitter account and captured the data from it. For each tweet, a folder was built by the python program. The tweet content (description of the story, and image version of story content), the replied contents (comments, photos, account information) would be captured and saved into different folders under the tweet folder. The data would be read by the JavaScript program and used as the content resource for the html5 interface on the public screen.

Website and the Story Map

Based on html5, the online website was built to show the stories in gallery style as well as the map style. People who were interested in the project can explore the stories on the website, and even joined to help as a volunteer for promoting the stories or transcribing and translating the stories for more potential users.

The story map was an important part of the website. It was a search page built with Google Maps JavaScript API. According to the geographic information (latitude and longitude) of the location where the story happened, the icons representing the stories were created and marked at the certain locations on the map. When the mouse hovering on the icon, visitors could see a short introduction of the story. Double-clicking the icon, visitors can go to the particular story page directly. Through the map, people could explore stories according to the location information, which might also remind the visitors of their own experience in a place and facilitate some emotional connection between the readers and the storyteller.

Initial Field Test and Result

For the second iteration of the project, an initial field test was conducted for about 3 weeks. Several weeks before the field trial formally starting, we set up a pilot experiment at the corner of the canteen of Home K. This corner was a part of the big canteen, where a lot of residents visited every day in the morning and afternoon for the free coffee. There was a TV on the wall which was convenient for us to connect the mailbox and the MS system without building up new constructions to interrupt elderly residents' daily activities.

The pilot experiment was conducted every morning from 10:00 to 12:00, and 4 residents joined short interviews to give feedbacks for the improvement in details of the design and the preparation of the formal field trial. Based on their comments, several changes were made: (1) the fonts and layouts were slightly adjusted to become easier for the residents to read at the tables (1.2–1.8 m away from the screen), and the details like the speed of scrolling were also adjusted for better reading experience; (2) the sample stories were changed into the ones more related to the local life and typical memories of the generation (e.g. the old life after WWII); (3) cooperation with the local college on historical storytelling was employed and promotion materials like the flyers and posters were created to attract more residents.

After the pilot study, we revised the design, took a warming-up step with the introduction day and then formally started the field trial. In this paper, we reported the initial qualitative feedbacks in the first phase of the field trial.

Introduction Day

To prepare for the field trial, we organized a 1.5-h workshop in Home K (Fig. 6). A presentation was made by a research assistant (speak both Dutch and English) to introduce the background and the goal of the project, as well as to show the residents how to use the system with a prepared example. Questions from residents were answered after the presentation, and the promotion materials including the introduction of the project and a schedule of the whole field trial were given to the participants, working as a reminder of the project and also a potential promotion to the elderly people's family members.

Field Trial and Initial Feedbacks

Fig. 6. Photo of the introduction day.

The field trial took place at the same location with the pilot study, from 9:30 am to 4:30 pm every weekday. One table in front of the screen was regularly assigned to our project. The other one next to our table was occupied by a group of ladies every afternoon. They did not mind us doing experiment next to them, but insisted very much to sit at that corner and refused to move to the bigger table 3 m away, due to the noise of the radio above that table. Thus, the final set-up of the project included the special mailbox, the big screen of the canteen and one set of the table and chairs. At the beginning, there were 7 sample stories presented on the screen: 3 samples were collected from the residents before the formal field trial, and 4 samples were prepared by MS team.

19 residents were invited for interviews. Most of them were already invited to the introduction day, while some of them noticed the project later by themselves. In order to guarantee that the participants understand the concept clearly, the research assistant shortly repeated the concept and the goal of whole project again. Then the semi-structured interviews started with the basic information and their recent use of the system.

Due the preferences of the elderly people, 11 interviewees were interviewed individually and 8 interviewees were interviewed in pairs and groups (1 couple, 2 ladies together, and 4 ladies insisted to join as a group together). Some of the interviewees did not finish the whole question list. The interviews looked into the following aspects: whether and how much the residents liked the concept; which aspects contributed to their motivation of using the system; how they actually interacted with the installation; whether there were any social interactions with others triggered by the project; personal preferences and expectations in the content on the platform; feedbacks and suggestions on interaction, as well as the input and output way (e.g. handwriting, audio recording, or video recording for input); and their expectations on the quality and frequency of the feedbacks.

In general, most of the interviewees liked the project and the concept, but some of the participants were questioning about the feasibility in technology and the applied context of the system as it looked into a quite new field in their mind. "I am not sure if the installation would actually work" said by one of the interviewees. "It's funny, but you have to have something to talk about to start it" another interviewee mentioned since she was wondering whether it would be difficult for people without interesting memories to join the project. One of the interviewees who was active and sometimes worked as a volunteer in the care home suggested the project could be connected to other on-going projects, like the project they had for different people to meet and talk on specific topics every month. When discussing that some of the residents might be afraid of using the installation, one interviewee said "It is easy to use", "just create some groups at the beginning and let them use the concept together with a care giver to get familiar with it". These comments might indicate a further development direction to combine with the social activities in the care home and to involve the care givers more into the system.

About the feedbacks on input and output methods, most of the residents still chose handwriting as the first priority of sharing the stories, while one man expressed his worries about the feasibility of handwriting for some of the residents, not only because some of the elderly people were too old to write, there were also worries that some of the residents were not able to write properly and were even bullied because of their poor grammar. Some people preferred voice recording because of the "efficiency", and "easier and faster than writing". Face-to-face was chosen by 1 interviewee because she could "do it during the coffee time".

For the story content and the expectation on the feedbacks, some interviewees mentioned that some stories were "too far away" and "hard to connect with", since they prefer to read the stories of the local neighbourhood around them or shared by the people similar with them in age or experiences. When asked about what kind of feedbacks they would like to see and how often they would like to receive the feedbacks, most of the residents were interested either in the comments talking about similar experiences or reactions from different generations which would be new and fresh for them. They did not hold any expectations on the frequency as many of them were not confident enough about their stories to get replies. "I appreciate all the feedbacks. Any time will be good if there are replies" said one interviewee who was quite active in participating the project.

In the beginning, due to the lack of promotion online and outside the care home, the feedbacks were not enough, thus some of the comments during the first weeks were given by the MS team members. Later, other designers and friends were invited to read the stories and help commenting and promoting the project to more people.

In the first 5 days, many letter cards on the table were taken away and 6 stories were collected through the mailbox, 2 stories were sent directly to designer's email address. The 6 hand-writing story providers chose to take the postcards away and wrote their stories in other places, few people really sat at the table in the canteen and wrote their stories, according to our observations. One of the participants explained in the interview that he preferred to recall the memory and write in a quiet and private place. One storyteller sent a very long story through email and he said that typing was faster for him for such a long story. The other storyteller who used email had Parkinson Disease and said he could type but not write.

5   Discussion and Future Work

Based on the lessons and insights from the iterations in this case study, we discuss the possible directions for design interventions in care home contexts to improve and to better support elderly people' s social life.

Tangible and Intuitive Interaction with Suitable Metaphor

In all of the iterations in this design case, we noticed that the preference of elderly people on tangible interaction and metaphor of traditional behaviour was still very strong. Although in recent years, more and more elderly people are becoming familiar with the new technologies, there are still a large group of senior users who have difficulties in adopting new technologies. Furthermore, some of the senior people in the care homes are with relatively high age and have to face with the decline in physical and mental health, which is also one of the reasons for people to be afraid of using technologies and smart products. For most of the senior residents, an interaction that can be understood intuitively or associated with traditional life styles can always be more friendly and easier to try.

However, there are special situations as well. Taking the examples of our storytellers, there are also people with problems of using the traditional way, like the writer who has stories far too long for handwriting and editing, and the participant with PD who can think and type clearly while writing is a big challenge. Thus, even though the tangible solution is widely recommended, the best choice is still based on the specific context of the design.

Multiple access for Information Input and Output

In the design practice, we started to notice that within the ageing group, individuals were very different from each other, not only because the varieties in aspects like characteristics and personal preferences, but also because their mood, thought and decisions were highly influenced by the health condition, sometimes as well as the changes in social relationships.

Thus, for different residents, the feasible methods are often different, and it is difficult to find a universal solution that can satisfy all the participants in the project. There is a need for the design in a care institution to leave space for openness in content and interaction, which means providing multiple accesses for people to join in their preferred ways.

Sustainable System and Long-Term Evaluation

MemoriesSharing Project is a platform combined the installation and the online service. In the whole project, elderly people are not the only user group. The ideal context of memory sharing experience should be a sustainable and long-term experience, so that the casual interaction and communication between storytellers and the readers can actually bring influences on elderly people's social behaviour and subjective feeling of social connectedness.

One of the possible directions for MS project is to cooperate with the existing social activities, like the activity mentioned by one of the interviewees that people meet and talk on certain topics every month. Compared with the traditional solutions, the advantages of system like MS is the low cost of human resource in maintaining and organizing activities, as well as the continuous effects embedded in the daily environment, so that the residents can join the interaction in a more flexible and casual way.

However, no matter it is the current version of the MS or the future direction, MS project requires the service system that involves different kinds of stakeholders in elderly people's social circle, like the care givers, family members, other residents etc. A suitable service system is needed for further iteration, especially the design to involve care givers and the public readers. Care givers as stakeholders are important since they sometimes have strong influences on elderly people's decisions and behaviours, but at the same time, they are always too busy to join any extra activities. Thus, how to properly involve the care givers without bringing extra burden for them is a critical challenge in the following iteration. In MS project, the participation of the public readers is also very important. However, although the life stories from the ageing group are expected to be a motivation for people to join the project, it cannot be the only motivation and reason. More reasonable triggers are needed to attract the public, especially the younger generation to join the system.

With the consideration of the service system and the sustainable influences on elderly people's social connectedness, project like MemoriesSharing should be evaluated in a longer time period in the real-life environment. This need also raises up the design needs for better details and a more stable system for long-term run.

6 Conclusion

MemoriesSharing Project was a participatory platform designed to enrich elderly people's social interaction by encouraging them to share memories and co-create stories with other people in a crowdsourcing way. The whole design process of the project includes 3 design cycles with 2 main design iterations. According to the insights from the preliminary study, the possible design intervention in this case aims to provide new activities or services for the senior residents in local care homes to enrich the social interaction in their daily environment, especially help improving the connection between residents inside the care home and the people outside.

Through the presenting of the design and evaluation process of the, we share the findings and lessons from our practice, and introduce the typical lifestyle in local care institutions in Eindhoven, the Netherlands. Based on our users' feedbacks, MemoriesSharing project needs to consider the improvement in: (1) tangible solutions with intuitive interaction; (2) multiple accesses for input and output to better meet users' different preference; (3) exploration and design of sustainable system that can cooperate with different stakeholders; (4) longer field evaluation for more reliable feedbacks.

Acknowledgement. We thank all the participants of the experiment, and the cooperation from Vitalis Berckelhof, De Horst/Kronehoef, Genderstate and Summa College. We also thank China Scholarship Council for support with the research.

References

1. World Health Organization: World Health Day 2012 - ageing and health - toolkit for event organizers
2. Tinker, A.: The social implications of an ageing population. Mech. Ageing Dev. **123**(7), 729–735 (2002)
3. Hilt, M., Lipschultz, J.: Elderly Americans and the Internet: E-mail, TV news, information and entertainment websites. Educ. Gerontol. **30**(1), 57–72 (2004)
4. Namazi, K., McClintic, M.: Computer use among elderly persons in long-term care facilities. Educ. Gerontol. **29**(6), 535–550 (2003)
5. Townsend, A.M.: Smart Cities: Big Data, Civic Hackers, and the Quest for a New Utopia. W. W. Norton & Company, New York (2013)
6. Alves Lino, J., Salem, B., Rauterberg, M.: Responsive environments: user experiences for ambient intelligence. Ambient Intell. Smart Environ. **2**(4), 347–367 (2010)
7. Findlay, R.: Interventions to reduce social isolation amongst older people: where is the evidence? Ageing Soc. **23**(5), 647–658 (2003)
8. Pettigrew, S.: Reducing the experience of loneliness among older consumers. J. Res. Consum. **12**, 1–14 (2007)
9. Giummarra, M.J., Haralambous, B., Moore, K., Nankervis, J.: The concept of health in older age: views of older people and health professionals. Aust. Health Rev. **31**, 642–650 (2007)
10. Global Council on Brain Health: The brain and social connectedness: GCBH recommendations on social engagement and brain health. Technical report, AARP Policy, Research and International Affairs; AARP Integrated Communications and Marketing; and Age UK (2017). www.GlobalCouncilOnBrainHealth.org

11. Davis-Owusu, K., Owusu, E., Marcenaro, L., Regazzoni, C., Feijs, L., Hu, J.: Towards a deeper understanding of the behavioural implications of bidirectional activity-based ambient displays in ambient assisted living environments. In: Ganchev, I., Garcia, N.M., Dobre, C., Mavromoustakis, C.X., Goleva, R. (eds.) Enhanced Living Environments. LNCS, vol. 11369, pp. 108–151. Springer, Cham (2019). https://doi.org/10.1007/978-3-030-10752-9_6
12. Nicholson, N.R.: A review of social isolation: an important but underassessed condition in older adults. J. Primary Prevent. **33**(2), 137–152 (2012)
13. Cordier, R., Milbourn, B., Martin, R., et al.: A systematic review evaluating the psychometric properties of measures of social inclusion. PLoS One **12**(6), 0179109 (2017)
14. Zavaleta, D., Samuel, K.: Social isolation: a conceptual and measurement proposal. In: Oxford Poverty & Human Development Initiative (OPHI) (2014)
15. Schell, R., Hausknecht, S., Kaufman, D.: Barriers and adaptations of a digital game for older adults. In: Proceedings of ICT4AgeingWell2015, Portugal, pp. 269–275 (2015)
16. Biemans, M., van Dijk, B., Dadlani, P., van Halteren, A.: Let's stay in touch: sharing photos for restoring social connectedness between rehabilitants, friends and family. In: 11th International ACM SIGACCESS Conference on Computers and Accessibility, Pittsburgh, PA, USA, pp. 179–186 (2009)
17. Ten Bruggencate, T., Luijkx, K.G., Sturm, J.: Social needs of older people: a systematic literature review. Ageing Soc. **38**(9), 1745–1770 (2018)
18. Steverink, N., Lindenberg, S.: Which social needs are important for subjective well-being? What happens to them with aging? Psychol. Aging **21**(2), 281–290 (2006)
19. Register, M.E., Scharer, K.M.: Connectedness in community-dwelling older adults. West. J. Nurs. Res. **32**(4), 462–479 (2010)
20. Dickens, A.P., Richards, S.H., Greaves, C.J., Campbell, J.L.: Interventions targeting social isolation in older people: a systematic review. BMC Public Health **11**(1), 1–22 (2011)
21. Lin, X., Kang, K., Li, C., et al.: ViewBricks: a participatory system to increase social connectedness for the elderly in care homes. In: Intelligent Environments (Workshops), pp. 376–385 (2016)
22. Kang, K., et al.: Designing interactive public displays in caring environments: a case study of OutLook. J. Ambient Intell. Smart Environ. **10**(6), 427–443 (2018)
23. Gaver, W., Boucher, A., Bowers, J., et al.: The photostroller: supporting diverse care home residents in engaging with the world. In: Proceedings of the SIGCHI Conference on Human Factors in Computing Systems, pp. 1757–1766. ACM (2011)
24. Valk, C., Lin, X., Feijs, L., Rauterberg, M., Hu, J.: Closer to nature interactive installation design for elderly with dementia. In: 3rd International Conference on Information and Communication Technologies for Ageing Well and e-Health, ICT4AWE 2017, pp. 228–235. SciTePress (2017)
25. Roozenburg, N.F.M., Eekels, J.: Product Design: Fundamentals and Method. Wiley, New York (1995)

The Information Infrastructure for Analyzing and Visualizing Learning Logs in Ubiquitous Learning Environments

Songran Liu[1]([⊠]), Kousuke Mouri[2], and Hiroaki Ogata[3]

[1] BiiiiiT, Inc., Tokyo, Japan
liu.songran@biiiiit.com
[2] Institute of Engineering, Tokyo University of Agriculture and Technology,
Fuchu, Japan
mourikousuke@gmail.com
[3] Kyoto University, Kyoto, Japan
hiroaki.ogata@gmail.com

Abstract. In this paper, we describe about an information infrastructure and data flow in SCROLL Data Tracking Module for analyzing and visualizing students' learning logs in ubiquitous learning environments. There are lots of behaviors log in SCROLL, which not be used to analyzed and visualized yet. To build the information infrastructure in SCROLL, we send learning behaviors data to xAPI (Experience API) for analyzing and visualizing and share students' learning logs with LTI (Learning Tools Interoperability).

Keywords: Ubiquitous learning · xAPI · LTI · SCROLL

1 Introduction

Recently, researchers in the educational engineering area have been studying based on ubiquitous theme. For example, context aware ubiquitous learning (u-Learning), PDA Education Support Assistance (PESA), or Computer Supported Ubiquitous Learning (CSUL). Lots of education researching have constructed using mobile computing technologies such as mobile devices, QR-code, RFID tag and wireless sensor networks (Hwang et al. 2008; Ogata and Yano 2004). These learning takes place in a variety of learning space such as classroom, home and museum. Also, it provides the right information using the contextual data like location, surrounding objects and temperature (Liu et al. 2014).

Furthermore, many researchers have been focusing on effective learning using ubiquitous technologies. We have developed ubiquitous learning system called SCROLL (System for Capturing and Reminding of Learning Log) as well (Ogata et al. 2011). The system will support students to do their language learning. For example, international students take a photo, record some videos even upload a pdf file what they have learned in their daily lives. However, how to analyzing and visualizing is still a problem. This paper describes the information infrastructure for analyzing and

© Springer Nature Switzerland AG 2019
N. Streitz and S. Konomi (Eds.): HCII 2019, LNCS 11587, pp. 408–418, 2019.
https://doi.org/10.1007/978-3-030-21935-2_31

visualizing learning logs in SCROLL with xAPI (Experience API) and LTI (Learning Tools Interoperability).

With xAPI, learning logs in SCROLL will be send to xAPI server, and available to check by students. Furthermore, students and researchers can analyze students' learning behavior. With LTI, students and researchers can share their learning logs to other educational system or application. After learning logs have been send to xAPI and LTI, the logs will also be saved in LRS for more researching.

2 Related Works

2.1 SCROLL

With the evolution of the mobile device, People prefer to record learning contents using mobile devices instead of taking memos on paper. Most of the language learners have their own learning note. In this paper, learning log is defined as a recorded form of knowledge or learning experiences acquired in our daily lives.

SCROLL has been developed for supporting international students in Japan to learn Japanese language from what they have learned in formal and informal setting. It adopt an approach of sharing user created contents among users and is constructed based on a LORE (Log-Organize-Recall-Evaluate) model which is shown in Fig. 1 (Ogata et al. 2011).

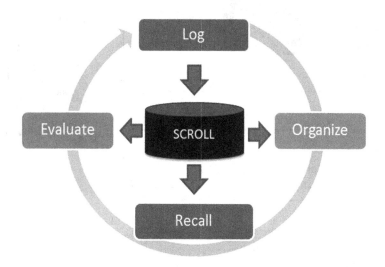

Fig. 1. LORE model in SCROLL

SCROLL is a client-server web-application, which runs on different platforms including PC browser, SP browser and general mobile phones shown in Fig. 2. The server side runs on CentOS 7. It is developed by Java, Spring Boot 2 and Mybatis in server side. In frontend, it is developed by Javascript with Vue.js framework.

Moreover, all application resources is containerized by docker. So every framework and technology idea is up to date. Therefore SCROLL is a high availability and high reliability system.

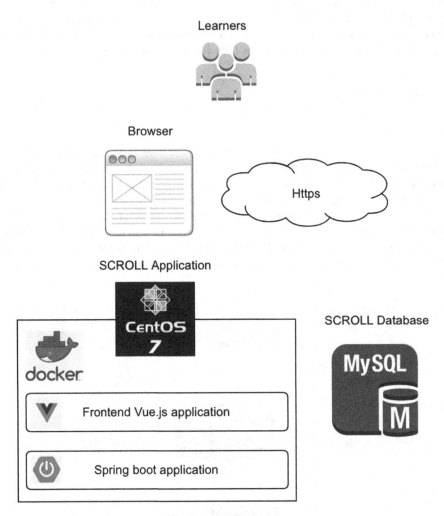

Fig. 2. The architecture of SCROLL

2.2   xAPI and LRS

xAPI is a simple, lightweight way to retrieve action records about learners into system and make the records as data for analyzing or to share these data across platforms. These records can be captured in a consistent format from any number of sources and they are aggregated in a learning record store (LRS).

The x in xAPI is short for "experience", and implies that these activity providers are not just limited to traditional AICC- and SCORM-based e-learning. With xAPI we can track learners' learning activities, usage of performance support tools, participation in online communities, mentoring discussions, performance assessment, and actual business results. The goal is to create a full picture of an individual's learning experience and how that relates to her performance.

2.3   LMS and LTI

IMS Global Learning Consortium published the Learning Tools Interoperability (LTI) standard for defining the process of connecting two systems (Fig. 3), and how users will transition across these systems without having to authenticate once again with the destination system. During the LTI transition process, information about the user and the context in which the external tool was launched can be transferred from the source system to the target system.

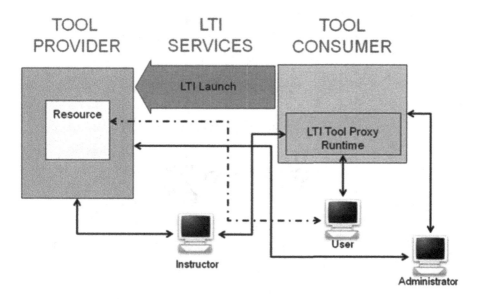

Fig. 3. Learning tools with LTI

3   Implementation

3.1   Architecture of Data Tracking Module in SCROLL

Figure 4 shows the architecture of Data Tracking Module in SCROLL to build information infrastructure. After students log in SCROLL with LTI, SCROLL will save their user data that is managed by LTI. Therefore their learning logs will ready to share with other educational system, such as, LRS, moodle etc. After learners have logged in SCROLL, Learner Action Tracking Library will track grasped all learners' action in SCROLL, such as "Write log", "see all logs" and so on. Then, Learner Action Tracking

Library will send learners' action data to server side, which is a spring boot data streaming application, with JSON format.

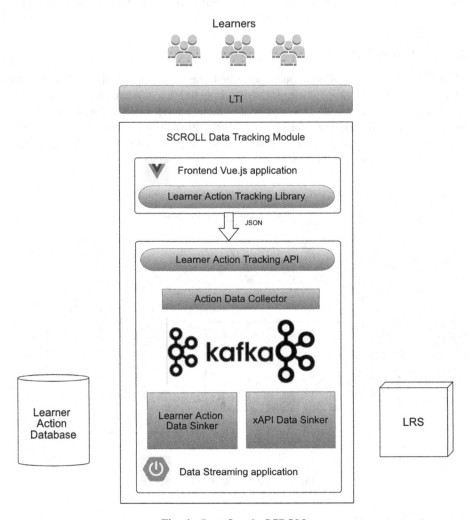

Fig. 4. Data flow in SCROLL

Data Streaming application will get learners' action data with web API, and produce to kafka topic as data streaming. Action Data Collector is a data streaming sourcing component to receive streaming data in kafka's topic at real time. Action Data Collector will also aggregate and transform data into a appropriate format to next topic in kafka.

Learner Action Data Sinker is a data sinking component in SCROLL data tracking module. Learner Action Data Sinker is a data consumer to kafka topic. When there are new data produced by topic, Learner Action Data Sinker will get the data and save the data into database, without any transformation process.

xAPI Data Sinker is also a data sinking component in SCROLL data tracking module. xAPI Data Sinker can receive streaming data from kafka topic and send data to LRS with appropriate formatting.

3.2   LTI with SCROLL

Figure 5 shows the login flow chart in SCROLL with LTI.

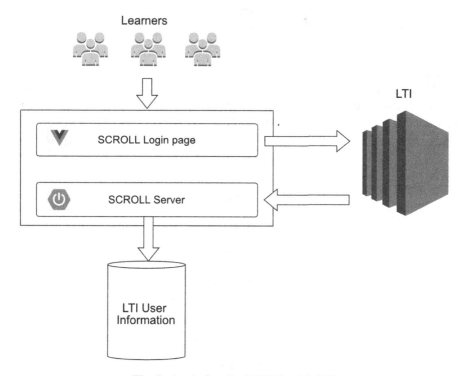

Fig. 5. Login flow in SCROLL with LTI

1. Learners access to SCROLL login page, and login.
2. SCROLL login module begins authentication flow and calls LTI user API and Person API to get learners' LTI data.
3. LTI system does a callback to SCROLL authentication API to send learners' data to SCROLL.
4. SCROLL server saves learners user data and person data to database.
5. SCROLL server redirect to SCROLL index page, and finish authentication and LTI login flow.

There are lots kinds of learners learning data in LTI user API and person API, shows in Table 1.

Table 1. LTI user API and person API variables

Message variable name	Description
$User.id	LTI user id
$Person.sourcedId	source id
$Person.name.full	full name
$Person.address.locality	address
$Person.address.country	country
$Person.address.postcode	postcode
$Person.address.timezone	timezone
$Person.email.primary	email address
$Person.webaddress	website address

With LTI user API and person API, SCROLL will get learners' learning data in LTI. Besides a lot of learning situation data, such as current learning course and so on shown in Table 2. With these data, SCROLL can also analyze learners learning situation in other LMS and even provide SCROLL learning data for other LMS.

Table 2. LTI APIs for LMS

APIs
LIS Course Template
LIS Course Offering
LIS Course Section
LIS Group
LIS Membership
LIS LineItem
LIS Result

3.3   xAPI with SCROLL

When learners use SCROLL to learn, Learner Action Tracking Library will grasped almost all of learners' action.

Figure 6 shows the data flow and data format transformation in server side data streaming application.

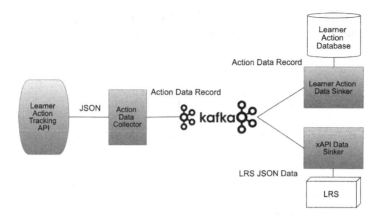

Fig. 6. Data format transformation in Data streaming application

6. Learner Action Tracking API receive JSON data from Learner Action Tracking Library.
7. Then transform JSON data into binary data stream and produce the data stream to kafka topic. Data in kafka topic is always ready to be consumed. We call this data streaming as Action Data Record.
8. Learner Action Data Sinker and xAPI Data Sinker are always listen to kafka topic. When new Action Data Record is produced, Learner Action Data Sinker and xAPI Data Sinker will receive new data record.
9. Learner Action Data Sinker will transform Action Data Record into a database data format and sink to Learner Action Database.
10. Besides, xAPI Data Sinker will transform Action Data Record into JSON format to post to xAPI.

For example, when learner open all logs function in SCROLL, Learner Action Tracking Library will grasped three kind of data, including who, what, where and when. With this three kind of data. SCROLL can analyze learners' learning habit. as we all know, SCROLL can analyze learners' learning habit and recommend more appropriate learning content. SCROLL is very helpful for the learners and they benefit from the context-based recommendation and learning-style based prompting well. the parameters is shown in Table 3 below.

Table 3. Tracking data type

Type	Parameters
who	user_id, user_name, first_name, middle_name, last_name, nationality, native_language, target_language, known_country
what	log_id, l1_word, tl_translation, picture, video, note
where and when	latitude, longitude, study_place, item_zoom

Figure 7 shows a example of xAPI JSON format. Like this, SCROLL Data Tracking Module will track learners behaviors in SCROLL and send data to xAPI.

```
{
      "id":"7ccd3322-e1a5-411a-a67d-6a735c76f119",
      "timestamp": "2015-12-18T12:17:00+00:00",
      "actor":{
      "objectType": "Agent",
            "name":"Example Learner",
            "mbox":"mailto:example.learner@adlnet.gov"
      },
      "verb":{
            "id":"http://adlnet.gov/expapi/verbs/attempted",
            "display":{
                  "en-US":"attempted"
            }
      },
      "object":{
            "id":"http://example.adlnet.gov/xapi/example/simpleCBT",
            "definition":{
                  "name":{
                        "en-US":"simple CBT course"
                  },
                  "description":{
                        "en-US":"A fictitious example CBT course."
                  }
            }
      },
      "result":{
            "score":{
                  "scaled":0.95
            },
            "success":true,
            "completion":true,
            "duration": "PT1234S"
      }
}
```

Fig. 7. xAPI request JSON example

3.4   SCROLL with LRS

With xAPI, SCROLL Data Tracking Module can send learners' data to LRS. Figure 8 shows how learners using SCROLL to store there learning experience into LRS. Learners use SCROLL to learn, SCROLL send their learning data to LRS. LRS not only show what learners' learning in SCROLL, but also can allow learners to analyze their learning situation.

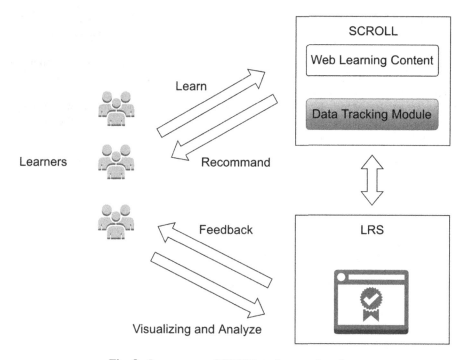

Fig. 8. Learners use SCROLL to learn and analyze

4   Conclusion

This paper described the how SCROLL grasp students' learning behavior learning logs and the information infrastructure to combine with LTI and xAPI, witch for analyzing and visualizing in LRS.

In the future, we will consider that recommend educational content with analytics result and feedback content with visualizing.

Acknowledgements. The part of this research work was supported by the Grant in-Aid for Scientific Research No. 17K12947 from the Ministry of Education, Culture, Sports, Science and Technology (MEXT) in Japan.

References

BookLooper. https://www.kccs.co.jp/ict/service/booklooper/

Li, M., Ogata, H., Hou, B., Uosaki, N., Mouri, K.: Context-aware and personalization method in ubiquitous learning log system. J. Educ. Technol. Soc. **16**(3), 362–373 (2013)

Hwang, G.J., Tsai, C.C., Yang, S.J.H.: Criteria, strategies and research issues of context-aware ubiquitous Learning. Educ. Technol. Soc. **11**(2), 81–91 (2008)

Ogata, H., Yano, Y.: Context-aware support for computer-supported ubiquitous learning. In: IEEE International Workshop on Wireless and Mobile Technologies in Education, pp. 27–34 (2004)

Ogata, H., Li, M., Bin, H., Uosaki, N., El-Bishoutly, M., Yano, Y.: SCROLL: Supporting to share and reuse ubiquitous learning logs in the context of language learning. Res. Pract. Technol. Enhanced Learn. 6(3), 69–82 (2011)

Liu, S., Ogata, H., Mouri, K.: Location based context-aware support for second language learning using ubiquitous learning lots. In: Proceedings of the 22nd International Conference on Computers in Education, ICCE 2014, pp. 13–16 (2014)

Advanced Tools for Digital Learning Management Systems in University Education

Atsushi Shimada[1]([✉]), Tsubasa Minematsu[1], and Masanori Yamada[2]

[1] Faculty of Information Science and Electrical Engineering,
Kyushu University, Fukuoka, Japan
`atsushi@ait.kyushu-u.ac.jp`
[2] Faculty of Arts and Science, Kyushu University, Fukuoka, Japan

Abstract. This paper introduces advanced tools in the digital learning management system M2B. The M2B system is used in Kyushu University, Japan, and contains three sub-systems: the e-learning system Moodle, the e-portfolio system Mahara, and the e-book system BookRoll. We developed useful tools to help improve both teaching and learning.

Keywords: Digital learning environment · E-learning system ·
E-book system · Learning management system · E-portfolio system ·
M2B · Moodle · Mahara · BookRoll

1 Introduction

Digital learning environments enable teachers to conduct lectures online. Several effective tools are available to support these environments, including learning management systems to track students' activities, e-portfolio systems to encourage student self-reflection, and e-book systems to provide textbooks in digital form. Thanks to learning management systems, collecting large-scale data about education practices has become easier in recent years. For example, learning management systems such as Blackboard and Moodle record clickstream data when users submit reports, access materials, and complete quizzes. This data plays a crucial role in learning analytics and educational data mining.

Learning analytics is a research domain which involves collecting and analyzing data about learners and their environments in order to understand what contexts best facilitate learning and how those contexts might be created [2]. Various studies thus far have focused on learning analytics, including learning activity analysis [15], identifying at-risk students [10,14], understanding learning paths [4], pattern mining [7], performance prediction [3,5], and learning support [13]. One common characteristic of these studies is that they focus on collected learning logs but do not pay much attention to how these logs might be created. To maximize the effectiveness of learning analytics, a learning management system itself has to be well considered and well designed.

© Springer Nature Switzerland AG 2019
N. Streitz and S. Konomi (Eds.): HCII 2019, LNCS 11587, pp. 419–429, 2019.
https://doi.org/10.1007/978-3-030-21935-2_32

In this paper, we discuss an advanced digital learning environment using examples from Kyushu University, Japan. Kyushu University uses the M2B learning management system, which contains three sub-systems: the e-learning system Moodle, the e-portfolio system Mahara, and the e-book system BookRoll. All students use their own laptops so they can access these systems from anywhere, either on or off campus. Students submit reports, take quizzes, access materials, and reflect on their learning activities using Moodle and Mahara. BookRoll creates reading logs by tracking activities such as when a student opens a material or turns a page. In Kyushu University, additional self-developed plugins are installed in these systems, which enabled us, among other things, to collect real-time responses from students, analyze more precise learning and teaching activities, and give quick feedback to students and teachers. The following sections of this paper present the details of the M2B system and its additional plugins.

2   Advanced Functions in M2B

2.1   M2B

In Kyushu University, the learning management system M2B was introduced in 2014. M2B's three subsystems are Moodle, Mahara, and BookRoll. BookRoll is a self-developed e-book system used for providing digital lecture materials and collecting browsing logs.

Various kinds of educational logs are collected by the M2B system. Basic logs of when students submit reports and complete quizzes, for example, are collected in Moodle and Mahara. BookRoll creates more precise learning logs about when a student opens a material or turns a page, for example.

The collected learning logs are converted into active learner points (ALPs), which are barometers of learning activities. In this study, we utilized three activities in Moodle (quizzes, reports, and logins), four activities in Mahara (highlights, memos, actions, and browsing), and one activity in BookRoll (diary length). Each activity was measured for all students and converted into one of five scores. Please refer to literature [8] for a more detailed explanation of ALPs.

2.2   Clicker Plugin for Collecting Student Responses

A clicker is a well-known device for collecting answers on quizzes and questionnaires from students in real time. We developed a clicker system plugin for Moodle (see the right-hand side of Fig. 1). In our study, we utilized the clicker plugin to collect data on seating location in the classroom in order to perform relationship analytics between learning activities and where students sat. The classroom, which contains about 240 seats, is divided into 12 subareas, and the M2B system keeps track of which students are seated in which area so that we may analyze the correspondence between seating areas and clicker responses.

Figure 2 is the visualized result of seating changes over 14 weeks. The horizontal axis represents the i-th week, and the vertical axis represents the individual

Seating capacity: 240

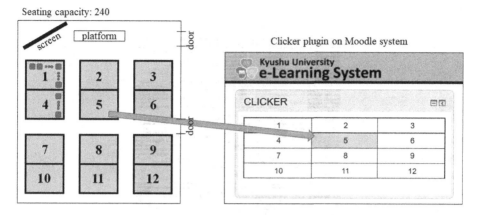

Fig. 1. Left: top view of the classroom. About 240 seats are available in the classroom. The classroom is divided into 12 areas to collect the seat area of students. Right: clicker plugin on Moodle system. Students answer their seat area by clicking the corresponding area number.

student. Therefore, a single row shows the seating changes of a single student. The color of each cell corresponds to the color map on the bottom part of the figure. The gradient from darker to brighter colors represents seating areas #1 through #12. Figure 2 shows that most students did not change seats very much; they sat in the same or nearby seats over several weeks. On the other hand, some students frequently changed seats week by week. Such students were more likely to be absent from class.

We analyzed the relationship between seating areas and ALPs. Through experiments with about 200 students over 14 weeks, we found that seat location has a strong correlation to learning activities. Overall, we can see that the scores of students seated in the front areas (from #1 to #3) are higher than those of students in the back areas (from #10 to #12). This result suggests that students seated in the front of the classroom had higher activity levels than those in the back. For more details on seating area analytics, refer to literature [12].

2.3 Recommending Related Content in Lecture Materials

Recommending related content when presenting lecture materials is effective for promoting deeper understanding in students. We developed a plugin for BookRoll which provides web links to related websites on each page of lecture materials. Figure 3 shows the overview of the recommendation system. The system consists of the e-book system, three databases, and a program which recommends related content. Each database stores the e-textbooks used in lectures, their recommended supplementary teaching materials (STMs), and e-book activity logs. The system flow is as follows: First, teachers register e-textbooks in the database via BookRoll. Next, the recommendation system analyzes the e-textbooks and identifies STMs corresponding to each page. That related

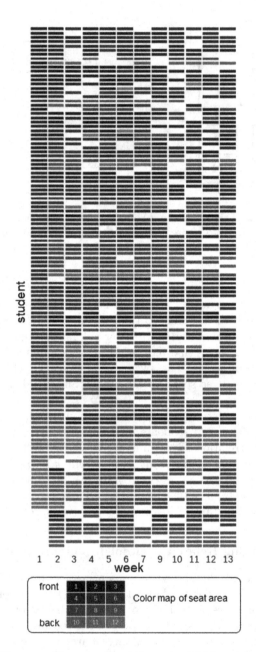

Fig. 2. Area transition over 12 weeks. The 8th week and 14 week are removed because of examination weeks. The row corresponds to each student. From top to down, and from 1st week to 13 week, the seat area is sorted by the area number.

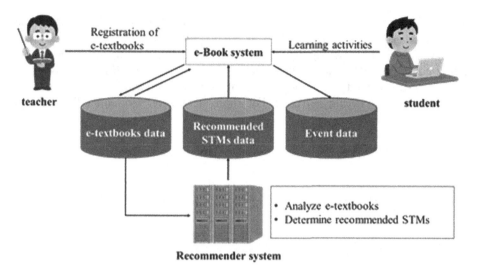

Fig. 3. Overview of recommendation system

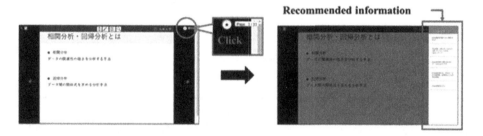

Fig. 4. Overview of recommendation system

content is then stored in the database. When a teacher conducts a lecture using BookRoll and students open the e-textbook during the lecture, the students can access the STMs as necessary (Fig. 4).

The web links are automatically generated by analyzing the contents of the lecture materials. A text mining approach discovers important keywords throughout the lecture as well as page-specific keywords. In each page of lecture material, the most important keywords are used for web searching, matching keywords to the titles of retrieved websites. Good matches are automatically registered as web links directly on the corresponding pages of lecture material. We conducted preliminary experiments using the recommendation plugin and got positive responses from students.

Figure 5 shows the number of clicks on the recommended STM links for each page of the e-textbook. It is apparent that there were numerous clicks on and around page 32 of the e-textbook. During the lecture, the contents of page 32 and its surrounding pages were not explained. Instead, students were given time to browse the pages themselves. It can be assumed that the reason the number of clicks increased here is that students learned by exploring the recommended STMs rather than the lecture itself. In addition, since there were many clicks on pages that contain exercises or pages with difficult contents, it can be assumed that recommending supplementary information on each page is useful for supporting learning. For more details on recommending related content, refer to literature [6].

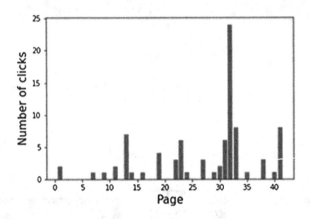

Fig. 5. Number of clicks on recommended information about each page

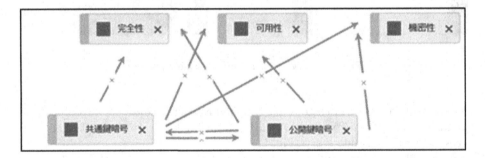

Fig. 6. Example of BR-Map

2.4   Concept Maps for Learning Reflection

Tools which assist cognitive learning? in particular, concept maps and knowledge maps? enhance awareness and comprehension of important concepts, ideas, and relationships. Integrating a concept map creation tool driven by student input can promote learning and support learning analytics in investigating the process of comprehension. Our study aims to develop a visualization tool which aggregates input logs and constructs concept maps in order to make teachers and students aware of potential areas for improvement. We developed a concept map

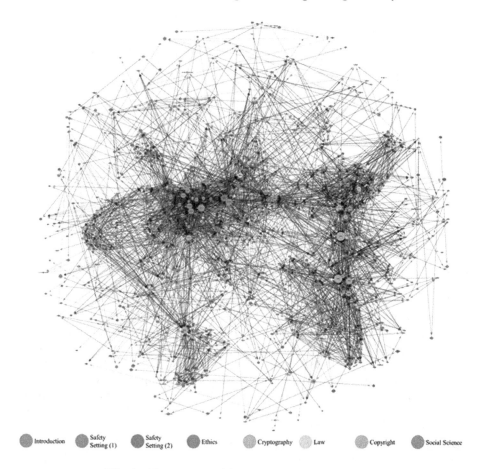

Introduction   Safety Setting (1)   Safety Setting (2)   Ethics   Cryptography   Law   Copyright   Social Science

Fig. 7. The integrated knowledge map of all nodes

tool called BR-Map which integrates with BookRoll to support the generation of concept maps.

In our study, BR-Map [16] used logs from BookRoll to create concept maps in this way: First, a learner reads an e-book and highlights words or sentences which he or she finds interesting, important, or difficult. The highlighted words and sentences become candidates for nodes in the BR-Map. Finally, the learner creates their own concept map by arranging the nodes on a canvas and drawing links between nodes as shown in Fig. 6.

The words in the nodes of the BR-Map are automatically extracted from the e-book by referring to the words the learner highlighted. Ideally, each node should have one keyword representing a single knowledge point. However, some nodes have a sentence (or a set of words) because the learner highlighted a complete phrase. For example, one learner highlighted the sentence "Cybersecurity is the protection of computer systems," and another highlighted the keyword "Cyber-

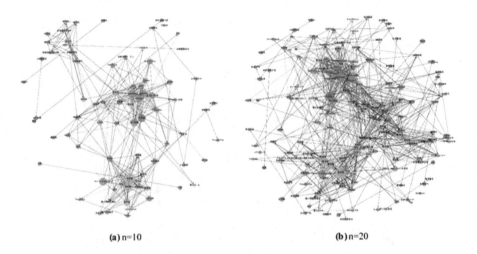

(a) n=10   (b) n=20

Fig. 8. The integrated knowledge maps of the top n important nodes at each lecture

security." These highlights are differentiated as separate nodes on the concept map. Therefore, we have to perform a text mining process to identify shared keywords in sentences. There are two steps to determining nodes in the concept map. For a detailed methodology of concept map analysis, refer to literature [9].

In our experiments, students drew their concept maps after eight weeks of lectures. We performed an integrated analysis of the concept maps to explore which keywords (nodes) many students had interest in. The concept map (see Fig. 7) shows the relationships between the contents of each lecture. There is a trade-off between readability of the content and the number of nodes. In order to evaluate the level of readability, we presented five kinds of concept maps, which are visualized as different numbers of important nodes (Figs. 7 and 8). The size of the node is proportionate to its level of importance. A larger-sized node represents an important node, which means that many learners drew links to or from the node. Additionally, the node's color corresponds to the lecture in which that word was frequently used. Furthermore, the thickness of the lines connecting the nodes represents the number of links that the learners drew. The thicker the line, the more times learners drew it. We found that important keywords are bridged not only within a lecture but also across lectures.

2.5 Real-Time Visualization of E-Book Reading Logs

Real-time feedback helps teachers know where student's attention is during lectures. We utilized Moodle and BookRoll to collect real-time data regarding learning activities during lectures. We developed a real-time analytics graph using student's BookRoll activity logs which performed analytics in real time and displayed how many students were following the teacher's explanation, which helped the teacher control his or her lecture speed.

During the lecture, as the teacher explained the content of the materials, students browsed the materials on their laptops. In our university, students are asked to open and browse the same page as the teacher and to highlight or add notes on the important points. During the lecture, learning logs were sequentially collected and stored. The analyzed results were immediately displayed on the web interface, as shown in Fig. 6, and updated every minute. Therefore, the teacher was able to monitor the latest student activity. The visualization included real-time information regarding how many students were following the lecture, how many students were browsing previous pages, and so on. The teacher adaptively controlled the speed of the lecture according to what he or she saw on the graph. For example, if many students were not following the lecture and were still on the previous page, the teacher slowed down the lecture. For detailed information about this graph's implementation, refer to literature [11] (Fig. 9).

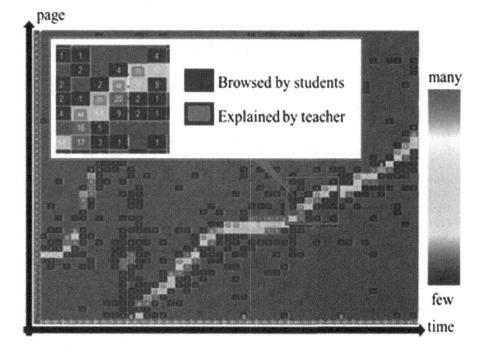

Fig. 9. Real-time heat map of browsed pages. The horizontal axis is the time of day and the vertical axis is the page number. A column corresponds to the distribution of the number of students browsing each page. The page explained by the teacher is highlighted by a red colored rectangle. The heat map is automatically updated minute-by-minute.

3   Conclusion

In this paper, we described the advanced digital learning environment M2B as used in Kyushu University, Japan. We developed and implemented four useful tools in this system: a clicker plugin to monitor how student seating areas affect learning, a recommendation tool for integrating supplementary content into e-books, a concept map tool to visualize each student's chosen focus areas, and a real-time graph of student's browsing activities. We will continue to develop new tools for the purpose of improving education in digital learning environments. The latest information on our research is available on our website [1].

Acknowledgements. This work was partially supported by JST PRESTO Grant Number JPMJPR1505, JSPS KAKENHI Grand Number JP18H04125, Qdai-jump Research Program of Kyushu University, Japan.

References

1. Learning and educational data science research unit. https://www.leds.ait.kyushu-u.ac.jp/
2. (SoLAR). https://solaresearch.org/
3. Brinton, C.G., Chiang, M.: MOOC performance prediction via clickstream data and social learning networks. In: 2015 IEEE Conference on Computer Communications (INFOCOM), pp. 2299–2307, April 2015
4. Davis, D., Chen, G., Hauff, C., Houben, G.: Gauging MOOC learners' adherence to the designed learning path. In: Proceedings of the 9th International Conference on Educational Data Mining, EDM 2016, pp. 54–61 (2016)
5. Mouri, K., Okubo, F., Shimada, A., Ogata, H.: Bayesian network for predicting students final grade using e-book logs in university education. In: IEEE International Conference on Advanced Learning Technologies (ICALT 2016), pp. 85–89 (2016)
6. Nakayama, K., Yamada, M., Shimada, A., Minematsu, T., Taniguchi, R.: Learning support system for providing page-wise recommendation in e-textbooks. In: Society for Information Technology and Teacher Education (SITE 2019) (2019, Under review)
7. Oi, M., Okubo, F., Shimada, A., Yin, C., Ogata, H.: Analysis of preview and review patterns in undergraduates e-book logs. In: The 23rd International Conference on Computers in Education (ICCE 2015), pp. 166–171 (2015)
8. Okubo, F., Yamashita, T., Shimada, A., Konomi, S.: Students performance prediction using data of multiple courses by recurrent neural network. In: 25th International Conference on Computers in Education (ICCE 2017), pp. 439–444 (2017)
9. Onoue, A., Yamada, M., Shimada, A., Taniguchi, R.: The integrated knowledge map for surveying students learning. In: Society for Information Technology and Teacher Education (SITE 2019) (2019, Under review)
10. Park, J., Denaro, K., Rodriguez, F., Smyth, P., Warschauer, M.: Detecting changes in student behavior from clickstream data. In: Proceedings of the Seventh International Learning Analytics & Knowledge Conference, pp. 21–30 (2017)
11. Shimada, A., Konomi, S., Ogata, H.: Real-time learning analytics system for improvement of on-site lectures. Interact. Technol. Smart Educ. 15(4), 314–331 (2018)

12. Shimada, A., Okubo, F., Taniguchi, Y., Ogata, H., Taniguchi, R., Konomi, S.: Relation analysis between learning activities on digital learning system and seating area in classrooms. In: 11th International Conference on Educational Data Mining (2018)
13. Shimada, A., Okubo, F., Yin, C., Ogata, H.: Automatic summarization of lecture slides for enhanced student preview-technical report and user study. IEEE Trans. Learn. Technol. **11**(2), 165–178 (2018)
14. Shimada, A., Taniguchi, Y., Okubo, F., Konomi, S., Ogata, H.: Online change detection for monitoring individual student behavior via clickstream data on e-book system. In: 8th International Conference on Learning Analytics & Knowledge, pp. 446–450, March 2018
15. Wang, G., Zhang, X., Tang, S., Zheng, H., Zhao, B.Y.: Unsupervised clickstream clustering for user behavior analysis. In: Proceedings of the 2016 CHI Conference on Human Factors in Computing Systems, CHI 2016, pp. 225–236 (2016)
16. Yamada, M., Shimada, A., Oi, M., Taniguchi, Y., Konomi, S.: Br-MAP: concept map system using e-book logs. In: 15th International Conference on Cognition and Exploratory Learning in Digital Age 2018 (2018)

Elicitation of Appropriate Scratching Zones Based on Lecture Slide Layouts

Fumiya Suzuki[1]([envelope]), Kousuke Mouri[1], Noriko Uosaki[2],
Atsushi Shimada[3], Chengjiu Yin[4], and Keiichi Kaneko[1]

[1] Tokyo University of Agriculture and Technology, Tokyo, Japan
s152995t@st.go.tuat.ac.jp
[2] Osaka University, Osaka, Japan
[3] Kyushu University, Fukuoka, Japan
[4] Kobe University, Kobe, Hyogo, Japan

Abstract. In recent times, researchers in pedagogy have focused on digital learning logs collected by learning tools such as Learning Management Systems and digital textbook systems. By analyzing and visualizing these, they aim to improve learning and/or teaching methodologies in the future. Using a digital textbook system, it is possible to collect information on which textbook pages were browsed by learners. However, these tools cannot decipher which zones of the textbook were browsed. In order to collect this information, eye-tracker technology would be necessary, but providing each learner with an eye-tracker would be too expensive. To solve this problem, a previous work proposed a method that used masks to detect and conceal each section of the slides in a digital textbook. The learner then clicked the masks one by one to delete them while browsing the contents of the digital textbook. By recording the learner's clicking operations, the method collected information about the zones browsed by the learner. However, this method was found to cause a decline in learning achievement and system usability as a large number of zones were hidden. Therefore, we propose a grouping method, based on the layout information of the slides, in order to identify the appropriate zones to hide with masks.

Keywords: Digital textbooks

1 Introduction

The Japanese government announced that digital textbooks will be introduced in K12 schools by 2020 [1]. The policy regarding the digital textbooks focuses on introducing the digital textbook technologies. Here are reasons why digital textbooks are going to be introduced:

(1) Interactive multimedia: The digital textbooks can respond to learners' actions by presenting contents such as texts, images, animations, videos, audios and video games in themselves.

N. Streitz and S. Konomi (Eds.): HCII 2019, LNCS 11587, pp. 430–441, 2019.
https://doi.org/10.1007/978-3-030-21935-2_33

(2) Portability: Paper-based textbooks can be bulky and heavy. On the other hand, the digital textbooks can be read on a mobile device, enabling learners to access more than a hundred textbooks.

(3) Functionality: Learners can use functions such as highlight, bookmarks, zoom-in, zoom-out, and copy and paste.

For the reasons stated above, the majority of educational institutions have introduced digital textbook systems in schools and universities, but little attention has been paid to analyzing and visualizing the collected logs to improve learning and teaching.

To tackle the issue, Ogata et al. [2] introduced a digital textbook system in universities and analyzed the logs collected by the system. By analyzing the logs, it is possible to collect information on which textbook pages were browsed by learners. However, it is difficult to collect the more specific information of which zones of the textbook were browsed. Mouri et al. [3, 4] proposed a scratching method to collect information regarding the zones browsed. The method detects and hides with masks each section of the slide in a digital textbook. Thereafter, the learner clicks the masks one by one to delete them while browsing the textbook contents. By recording the learner's clicking operations, the method can collect information regarding the zones browsed by the learner. However, this method was found to cause a decline in learning achievement and system usability as a large number of zones were hidden.

Therefore, we propose a grouping method based on the layout information of the slides in order to identify the appropriate zones to hide with masks. The rest of this paper is structured as follows. Section 2 describes previous work regarding digital textbook systems. Section 3 describes the system we propose. Finally, Sect. 4 describes our conclusions followed by future works.

2 Digital Textbook Systems

In many countries, their policies regarding the digital textbooks focus only on introducing the technology of the digital textbooks to K12 schools [5–7]. For example, the digital textbook system called BookLooper was developed by Kyocera Maruzen Systems Integration Co., Ltd [8]. The system provides a cloud service and the digital textbooks are managed in the cloud based on digital right management. Learners can download the digital textbooks using BookLooper. However, if a certain analyst wants to analyze the log data of the digital textbooks, s/he needs to download them because the company manages the collected logs. Therefore, it is difficult for the analyst to analyze them in real time. If the analyst could analyze the logs in real time, it would be possible to support each learner in accordance with his/her browsing status.

To solve the problem, Mouri et al. [3, 4] developed a digital textbook system called SEA (Smart E-textbook Application) to collect the digital textbook logs. Figure 1 shows the interface of SEA.

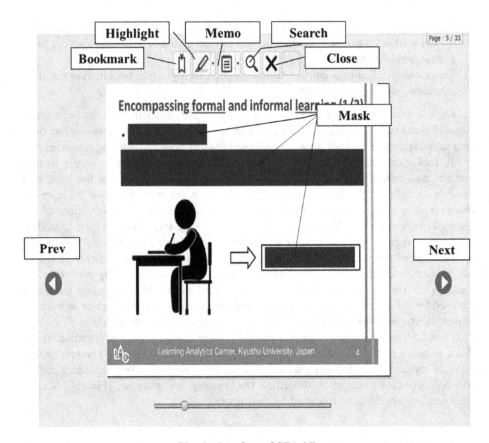

Fig. 1. Interface of SEA [4]

A learner can read the digital textbooks on a web browser at any time and any place. The system supports six functions: Next, Prev, Bookmark, Highlight, Memo, and Search. By clicking on the Bookmark button, the current page will be saved as a favorite for easier future access. When the learner feels some words, phrases, or sentences important, s/he can Highlight them. When the learner clicks on the Memo button, s/he can post a note about the target words.

Unlike previous digital textbook systems [3, 4, 9–11], the proposed system automatically hides the text in the digital textbooks with mask processing before the learner browses the texts. If the learner clicks on a masked text, the system gets rid of the mask and the text appears. Then, the system can identify the x- and y-coordinates of the position where the learner clicked on the texts. From this, the system can identify which zone of the page the learner was browsing in the digital textbook. Table 1 shows the difference between the previous digital textbook systems and SEA.

Table 1. Difference between previous digital textbook systems and SEA

Data unit	Previous digital textbook systems	SEA
Names of digital textbooks	☑	☑
Pages of digital textbooks	☑	☑
Section of the pages of digital textbooks		☑

3 Proposed System

3.1 Overview

In this section, we propose a system for grouping texts in the slide based on the layout information of the slide in order to improve scratching. Figure 2 shows an overview of our system.

1. **Input.** Teachers prepare lecture slides with PowerPoint. By uploading the slides to the SEA (digital textbook system), SEA can gather information on the character areas and slide images. The details of the input are described in Sect. 3.2.
2. **System.** Our system executes text processing and image classification.
   a. Text processing executes three processes, (1) Single-line processing, (2) Multiple-line processing. The proposed system determines relation among texts through (1) and (2). The detail of these processes is described in 3.3.
   b. To process the image, the system extracts shapes from the slide image and detects the corners of each shape. Based on the positions of the corners, the system detects an arrow and a balloon. The detail of image processing is described in 3.3
3. **Output.** The system groups texts based on the result of 2.a and 2.b. The output is shown to teachers; they confirm the relation between texts in a slide, and can apply scratch to the important areas of a slide.

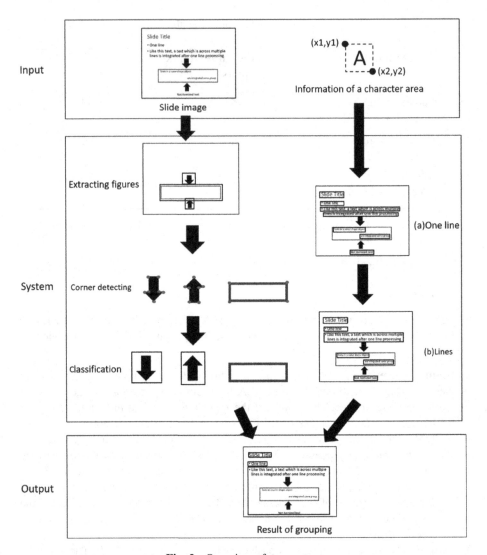

Fig. 2. Overview of our system

3.2 Input

We used two types of input data: slide images and information of the character areas. A slide image includes sentences, images and shape objects. As shown in Fig. 3, the information of the character area consists of a single character and the upper-left and bottom-right coordinates (x1, y1), (x2, y2) of the rectangle surrounding the character in the slide image.

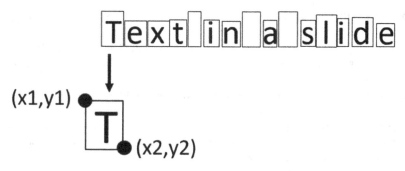

Fig. 3. Information of a character area

3.3   System

Processing the Information of Character Areas
Integration processing carries out (a) Single-line processing, (b) Multiple-line processing.

(a)   Single-line processing

Figure 4 shows the Single-line processing.

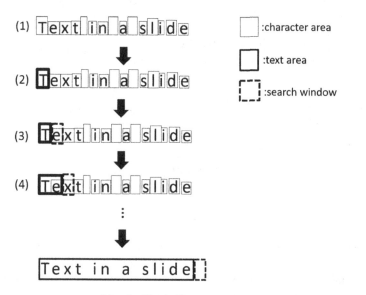

Fig. 4. Single-line processing

(1) In the slide image, search the top-left character area that is not included in any text area.

(2) If a such character area exists, introduce a new text area that consists of the character area and has a search window whose size is identical to the character area.

(3) Locate the top-left point of the search window to the top-right point of the current text area.

(4) If there is the top-left point of another character area inside the search window, extend the text area so that it contains the character area and go back to (3). Otherwise, the Single-line processing terminates.

(b) Multiple-line processing

This process decides whether there is relation between the vertically juxtaposed text areas. Figures 5 and 6 show the multiple-line processing.

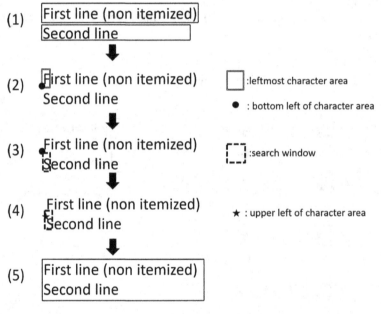

Fig. 5. Multiple-line processing

(1) If there are two text areas that are vertically juxtaposed as shown in Fig. 5(1), select the upper text area.

(2) Locate the search window so that its top-left point overlaps the bottom-left point of the upper text area.

(3) Note that the size of the search window is identical to the size of the character area of the top-left character of the upper text area.

(4) Search the text area below the upper text area. If an item symbol is included in the search window, recognize that the lower text area does not belong to the upper text area. If the text area is not detected, the processing terminates.

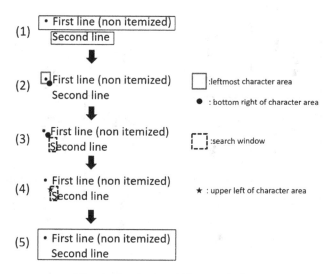

Fig. 6. Itemized multiline processing

(5) Otherwise, that is, if a text area is detected, integrate the upper and lower text areas into a new text area, and go back to (1).

(1) If there are two text areas that are vertically juxtaposed as shown in Fig. 6(1), select the upper area.

(2) Locate the search window so that its top-left point overlaps the bottom-right point of the top-left character of the upper text area.

(3) Note that the size of the search window is identical to the size of the character area of the top-left character of the upper text area.

(4) Search the text area below the upper text area. If an item symbol is included in the search window, recognize that the lower text area does not belong to the upper text area. If the text area is not detected, the processing terminates.

(5) Otherwise, that is, if a text area is detected, integrate the upper and lower text areas into a new text area, and go back to (1).

Shape Object Classification

In the slide, in order to extract shape objects such as circles, squares, triangles, and so on, this study carries out the following image processing.

(1) Generate a binary image by binarizing the slide image. After binarization, label each shape object.

(2) By using a corner detection technology [12], classify shape objects. This paper describes how to classify arrows.

(3) Judge if the shape object is an arrow or not by using the pattern in Fig. 7. That is, judge if the shape object is an arrow or not by overlapping it onto the 3×3 zones shown in Fig. 7 and checking the number of the corners in each zone to be equal to the corresponding integer in Fig. 7.

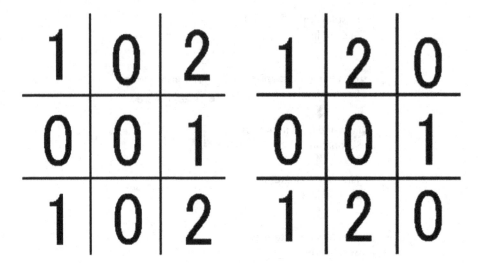

Fig. 7. A 3 × 3 detection pattern for a right arrow using horizontal and vertical lines

(4) If the shape object is not judged to be an arrow in (3), Judge if the shape object is an arrow or not by using the pattern in Fig. 8. For example, as shown in Fig. 9, each red point means each corner. From the results, we can find the arrow and the direction. That is, judge if the shape object is an arrow or not by overlapping it onto the 2 × 2 zones shown in Fig. 8 and checking the number of the corners in each zone to be equal to the corresponding integer in Fig. 8.

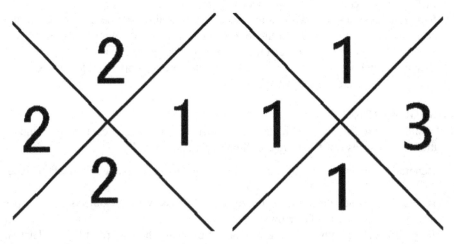

Fig. 8. A 2 × 2 detection pattern for a right arrow using diagonal lines

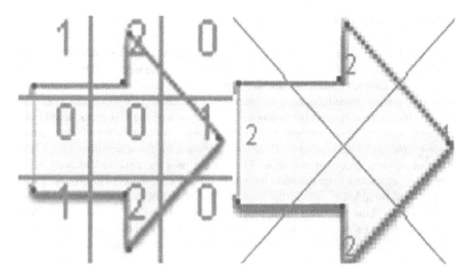

Fig. 9. An example of detection of a right arrow (Color figure online)

Output

Figure 10 shows the output of our system. The slide consists of three groups of texts. The two-line texts were successfully integrated. In addition, there are three nested subgroups of texts, which are related by the up and down arrows. The system also successfully integrated them into one group by detecting the arrows. The system can output the result of grouping as a two-dimensional array. The size of the array is equal to the resolution of the input image. Each element of the array has a natural number, which represents a group number. That is, if a point in the slide belongs to a group whose group number is 2, the corresponding element of the array has the value 2. If the point does not belong to any group, the element has the value 0.

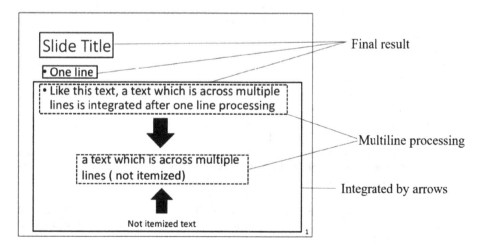

Fig. 10. Example of output of the system

4   Conclusions and Future Works

In this paper, we proposed a system for grouping areas in a slide of a digital textbook. Grouping is based on the layout information of the slide. The input of the system is the information of character areas and the slide images. The system detects the relationship among texts using the information of character areas. Based on the position of each character, the system decides the positions and the sizes of the text areas. In addition, the system extracts shape objects from slide images. Among shape objects, arrows represent context of text groups. Therefore, the system classifies arrows to extract context of the text groups in the slide. The system uses the positions of corners in a shape object extracted from the slide image. In other word, the system groups texts in the slide with the relation among the texts and the shape objects.

The system helps to extract the appropriate zones to hide with masks by grouping texts in a slide. Note that the system doesn't extract the appropriate zones themselves. Grouping the texts prevents hiding too many zones, but it doesn't show the appropriate zones to hide. To solve this problem, it is necessary to define priority of masking.

Acknowledgments. This part of this research was supported by the Grant-in-Aid for Scientific Research No.17K12947 from the Ministry of Education, Culture, Sports, Science and Technology (MEXT) in Japan.

References

1. MEXT, Japanese Ministry of Education, Culture, Sports, Science and Technology. "The Vision for ICT in Education" (2011). http://www.mext.go.jp/b_menu/houdou/23/04/__icsFiles/afieldfile/2012/08/03/1305484_14_1.pdf
2. Ogata, H., Yin, C., Okubo, F., Shimada, A., Kojima, K., Yamada, M.: E-book-based learning analytics in university education. In: Proceedings of the International Conference on Computers in Education, pp. 401–406 (2015)
3. Mouri, K., Shimada, A., Yin, C., Kaneko, K.: Discovering hidden browsing patterns using non-negative matrix factorization. In: Proceedings of the 11th International Conference on Educational Data Mining (2018)
4. Mouri, K., Uosaki, N., Shimada, A., Yin, C., Kaneko, K., Ogata, H.: Redesign of a data collection in digital textbook systems. In: Proceedings of the International Conference on Learning Technologies and Learning Environments (2018)
5. Shin, J.H.: Analysis on the digital textbook's different effectiveness by characteristics of learner. Int. J. Educ. Learn. 1(2), 23–38 (2012)
6. Shepperd, J.A., Grace, J.L., Koch, E.J.: Evaluating the electronic textbook: is it time to dispense with the paper text? Teach. Psychol. 35(1), 2–5 (2008)
7. Fang, H., Liu, P., Huang, R.: The research on e-book-oriented mobile learning system environment application and its tendency. In: Proceedings of the International Conference on Computer Science and Education, pp. 1333–1338 (2011)
8. BookLooper. https://www.kccs.co.jp/ict/service/booklooper/
9. Kiyota, M., Mouri, K., Uosaki, N., Ogata, H.: AETEL: supporting seamless learning and learning log recording with e-book system. In: Proceedings of the 24th International Conference on Computers in Education, pp. 306–314 (2016)

10. Yin, C., Okubo, F., Shimada, A., Kojima, K., Yamada, M., Ogata, H.: Smart-phone based data collecting system for analysing learning behaviors. In: Proceedings of the International Conference on Computers in Education, pp. 575–577 (2014)
11. Shimada, A., Mouri, K., Ogata, H.: Real-time learning analytics of e-book operation logs for on-site lecture support. In: Proceedings of the 17th IEEE International Conference on Advanced Learning Technologies, pp. 274–275 (2017)
12. Harris, C., Stephens, M.: A combined corner and edge detector. In: Proceedings of the 4th Alvey Vision Conference, pp. 147–151 (1988)

Seamless Collaborative Learning Method to Learn Business Japanese with eBook and Chat System

Noriko Uosaki[1(✉)], Kousuke Mouri[2], Fumiya Suzuki[2],
Mohammad Nehal Hasnine[3], Takahiro Yonekawa[4], Chengjiu Yin[5],
and Hiroaki Ogata[3]

[1] Osaka University, Osaka 565-0871, Japan
n.uosaki@gmail.com
[2] Tokyo University of Agriculture and Technology, Tokyo 184-8588, Japan
[3] Kyoto University, Kyoto 606-8501, Japan
[4] Brain Signal, Inc., Tokyo 105-6027, Japan
[5] Kobe University, Kobe 657-8501, Japan

Abstract. The breakthrough of information technology has accelerated the evolutionary change in teaching and learning methodologies. In particular, pervasion of high-efficiency smartphones has raised the potential to generate a new learning environment called seamless learning, which has been drawing much attentions from researchers in pedagogy of any domains.

The Japanese government, in 2016, declared "Japan Revitalization Strategy 2016". It includes the increasing of the number of foreign workers who gain employment in Japan after graduation. They set the goal from 30% to 50% of the international job hunting students find jobs in Japan. Therefore, career education for international students has become an urgent issue to tackle with in Japan. In fact, many universities in Japan have started providing international students with career education such as business Japanese, business communication and career design. Since Japanese job hunting process is very unique, most foreign students have anxieties about it. The objective of this study is to propose an effective business Japanese learning support system. Our ultimate goal is to contribute to the enhancement of their employment rate in Japan.

Keywords: Career support · Digital textbook · Job-hunting ·
International students · Seamless learning · Collaborative learning · Chat tool

1 Introduction

Seamless learning has been recognized as an effective learning approach across various dimensions and domains. Quite a few researchers are exploring to make learning seamless between formal and informal learning, individual and collaborative learning, and physical world and cyberspace [1]. So far, majority of researches in the seamless learning focus on realizing a seamless formal and informal learning [2, 3]. However there is no the researches on challenging to make individual-learning and collaborative learning seamless. Therefore in our study, the focus was on entwining individual and collaborative learning.

According to Japan Student Services Organization (JASSO), 298,980 foreign students are studying in Japan as of May 1st, 2018 [4]. "Japan Revitalization Strategy 2016" declared by the Japanese government includes the increasing of the number of international workers who got jobs after graduation [5]. They set the goal from 30% to 50% of the international job hunting students who actually find jobs in Japan. Therefore, career support for international students is an urgent issue to tackle with. Job-hunting process is complicated in Japan. It imposes a heavy workload on their academic lives. Students start job-hunting more than 1 year before graduation. They start with writing CVs (curriculum vitae) and entry sheets, taking exams, written or web-based, such as general knowledge tests, aptitude tests, and personality tests, participating group discussion observed by recruiters, and receiving group interviews and individual interviews at the final stage until they finally obtain official job offers. According to the survey conducted by [6], the top two anxieties that international students had about job hunting in Japan were (1) language-related anxieties: writing CVs and entry sheets (writing skill) and job interviews (listening and speaking skills) and (2) an anxiety about how to get information to find a job. There are many terms used in job-hunting processes, which are so rarely used in daily conversation that even advanced learners of Japanese are yet to learn. The survey result also showed that more than half of the questiones selected "I don't know how to get information".

The objective in this study is to propose an effective business Japanese learning system to facilitate international students' job hunting in Japan. The system seamlessly supports indivisual learning and collaborative learning with SCROLLeBook and a chat system, InCircle. Our research question is:

(1) whether or not our system contributes to international students' leaning business Japanese.

The rest of this paper is constructed as follows. Section 2 describes related researches to clearly identifying the difference between related works and our research. Section 3 describes the design of SCROLL eBook and InCircle. Section 4 describes evaluation and our conclusions.

2 Related Researches

2.1 Seamless Learning Environments

Seamless learning is used to describe the situations where students can learn whenever they want to in variety of scenarios and that they can switch from one scenario to another easily and quickly using one device or more per student as a mediator. Researchers in the seamless learning used mediating tools such as smart phone and PDA to realize a seamless learning environment. For example, Wong et al. [7] reported a seamless learning system called MYCLOUD (My Chinese UbiquitOUs learning Days), which allow students to learn the Chinese language in both in-school and out-of-school learning spaces using mobile devices. MYCLOUD consists of three components to bridge formal learning and informal learning: mobile dictionary, digital textbook and Social network service. In a formal learning setting, learners use the digital textbooks to highlight unfamiliar vocabularies and the vocabularies will be added to the mobile dictionary. In an informal learning setting, they use the social network service to record the artifacts (photo(s)+sentence(s)) of the experiences in their daily life. The seamless learning environment is realized by linking the vocabularies between the digital textbooks and the social network service.

On the other hand, Uosaki et al. [8] reported a seamless learning system called SMALL (Seamless Mobile-Assisted Language Learning support system) to support students who aimed to learn the English language in a formal and informal setting. SMALL has been developed with newly functions added to SCROLL. In a formal setting, learners use digital textbook to record vocabularies that they want to remember and the vocabularies will be added to the SCROLL database. In an informal setting, learners can record the digital records (a vocabulary with a photo or a video) of their learning experiences in their daily lives. The seamless learning environment is realized by linking the vocabularies between digital textbook and SCROLL. Therefore, in designing seamless learning environments, researchers need to consider how formal and informal learning are linked with use of computer technologies.

However there is no report so far on the researches challenging to make self-learning and collaborative learning seamless. This study, therefore, designed and developed a seamless learning environment by integrating the digital textbook system called SCROLL eBook with a chat system called InCircle. As far, researchers have constructed a seamless learning environment and evaluated whether the seamless learning environment can be enhanced learners' learning efficacy and autonomy learning, while this study considers learning analytics perspective with designing successfully the seamless learning environment because the collected learning logs aren't utilized to support teaching and learning.

2.2 Technology Enhanced Career Education

The emergence of IT technologies such as multimedia technology, Internet technology, ubiquitous and mobile technology provoked new learning concepts such as WBL (web based learning), CSCL (computer supported collaborative learning), and MAL (mobile assisted learning) [9]. Besides, various kinds of learning supports have been made into reality by accessing resources of web sites, or by linking learners and numbers of learning objects [10]. However career education using information technology is still in the stage of emergence. There are some reports on ICT implementation to career education such as portal sites for students' career support [11], the use of ePortfolio in career education [12], e-Learning in career development for university students [13], and e-mentoring for career development [14]. But no such learning system using seamless mobile learning technologies to enhance career education for international students has been developed yet.

2.3   Self-learning vs. Collaborative Learning

There is a trend in a pedagogical field that there goes the shift from teacher-centered to student-centered learning in any level of education [15]. According to [16], student-centered and small-scale course programmes resulted in more academic success than lecture-based course programme. It is also reported that a student-centered collaborative learning is one of the most effective ways of learning in language class [17]. In fact, most studies investigating the link between the extent to which course programmes are student-centered on the one hand and promote academic success on the other hand, find positive relationships between the two [16].

However, according to the result of the questionnaire conducted in [18], 70% of them prefered learning alone to learning in a group. It should be considered that fact that more than two-third of students preferred indivisual learning. How can we design the class which could satisfy both students who prefer study alone and those who prefer study in a group? In this study, we challanged the learning secnario to be combined self-learning with group learning seamlessly.

3   System Designs

3.1   SCROLL eBook

SCROLL [19] stands for System for Capturing and Reusing Of Learning Log, which has been developed since 2010 [20]. SCROLL supports learners to record what they have learned in both informal and formal settings as a log using a web browser and a mobile device and to share them with other learners anytime and anywhere beyond the limits of time and space. This on-going project is still in progress with new functions being added to the system one after the other. SCROLL eBook is one of the functions of SCROLL developed based on EPUB format.

Fig. 1. Login interface of SCROLL (left) and SCROLL top page (right).

Figure 1(Left) shows the login interface of SCROLL. Figure 1(right) shows top page of SCROLL. Book icon is the link to eBook system. Figure 2 shows SCROLL eBook contents. Teachers can create e-book contents using PowerPoint or Keynote prior to the class and use them in their courses. The uploaded e-book contents are converted to EPUB format and it is supported to access the contents by using smart-phones and PCs. Figure 1(Right) shows digital textbooks uploaded by the teachers.

Figure 3 shows the eBook viewer interface and its functions. When a learner clicks the highlight button, he/she can highlight the word. he/she can find the page number corresponding to the target word in the e-book by clicking the search button. When a learner clicks the memo button on the digital textbook viewer system, he/she can write a description concerning the target words. In order to facilitate memorization of the target words, the masking function was implemented. When they read the content for the first time, the target terms were masked and by clicking them, the words appear (Fig. 4).

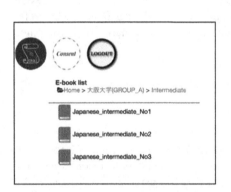

Fig. 2. SCROLL eBook contents

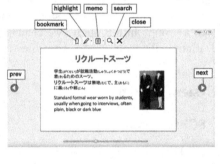

Fig. 3. SCROLL eBook viewer interface

3.2   InCircle

InCircle [21] is a product developed by AOS Mobile Inc., Tokyo, Japan [22] with the fifth author joining this project as a chief software architect. It is a client-server application. The server side runs on Linux OS and Windows Server. The client side is working on iOS, Android, and PC Web browser. Chat messages are transmitted and received through the network (Fig. 5).

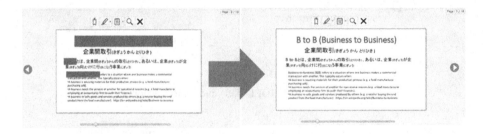

Fig. 4. Masking function of SCROLL eBook

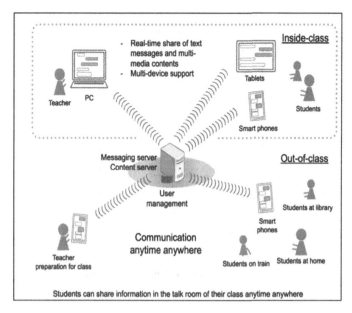

Fig. 5. InCircle system configuration

The system allows users to create groups. Group members are able to send and receive messages and multimedia files in their chat room with an easy operation. Chat messages are synchronized in real-time to realize smooth communication. Figure 6 shows a chat room interface when the instructor posted an interrogative sentence: "Do you have textbook authorization system in your country?" since interrogative sentences trigger active interaction among learners which leads to mutual cross-cultural understanding.

In our system, we have mainly four major advantages:

Teachers can be Administrators of the System
Teachers can be administrators of the system so that they can watch the users/their students' behaviors. Therefore, they can avoid their students' malicious behaviors via InCircle. In case of inappropriate behavior from the part of a student, teachers can delete or close the student's account.

Teachers can Pre-register User Accounts
Unlike other SNS or chat tools, such as Facebook and LINE, user accounts are pre-registered. Teachers create accounts for their students and make a group for the class in advance. There are always some students who do not want to use the existing SNS systems. In fact, in one of the authors' classes, some students rejected to create a Facebook account and some students did not want to use LINE. Unless all the students agree to use it, it is not appropriate to use it as a communication tool in class. Besides, the existing SNS users usually post their private information on their profiles. However, some students may not wish to share private information with some of their classmates. In our system, on the contrary, there is no page in the first place to fill in their private information, such as school career, birth place/date.

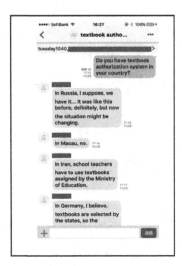

Fig. 6. InCircle chat room interface on mobile

(a) Security is ensured

Every effort was made in order to ensure the security, such as encryption of the cache data in the client terminal, channel coding, encryption of database, the use of different cryptography keys for each company or school in the server side. Therefore, it is highly protected against divulging of information or account hacking.

(b) Users can delete the sent messages.

In our system, we can delete messages after they are sent not only on the sender's side but on the recipient's side. It is likely to happen that we send messages by mistake. Our system can handle such human errors.

3.3 SCROLLeBook and InCircle Combined Learning

In this study, the learning secnario was desgined to combine self-learning with group learning. Figure 7 shows SCROLLeBook & InCircle combined learning. Students learn career-related things with SCROLLeBook alone and interact with other classmates and the teacher at the same time. In order to encourage students to collaborate during the task, the teacher posted a topic which would be helpful to learn career-related things via InCircle. Students were encouraged to interact via InCirle by telling them the number of InCircle posts will affect their grades.

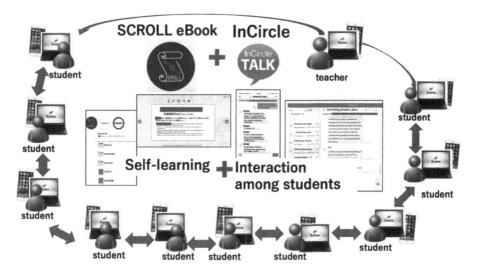

Fig. 7. SCROLLeBook & InCircle combined learning

4   Evaluation

4.1   The Target Class

Twenty-two international students (6 Chinese, 3 Korean, 2 Americans, 2 Filipinos, 1 French, 2 Germans, 1 Canadian, 1 Danish, 1 Dutch, 1 Finnish, 1 Hong Konger, 1 Taiwanese), who are studying at the University in the western part of Japan participated in the evaluation experiments. The target class was held on a once-a-week-basis in a CALL (computer assisted language learning) room during the fall semester, 2018. Each student had a PC in class. The class was one of "international exchange subjects" which was targeted mainly for international exchange students whose length of stay varies from half a year to one year. Some are regular students who aim to graduate from the university in Japan. The objectives of the target class were (1) to improve the skills of their target language, Japanese and (2) to enhance cross-cultural understanding as well as to learn Japanese affairs. The evaluation was conducted during the class held in January 22nd, 2019.

4.2   Procedures

Figure 8 shows the learning scenario.

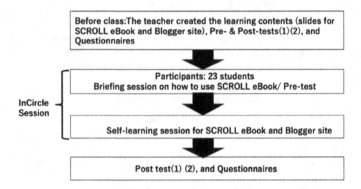

Fig. 8. Evaluation procedures

The teacher created 15 slides (8 for SCROLL eBook contents, 7 for Blogger contents), of career related terms such as "年功序列" (promotion by seniority), "PREP 法" (PREP method). The objective of the contents was to learn business Japanese, especially useful terms in terms of job-hunting. At the beginning of the session, the participants took the pre-test to examine whether they know the meanings of the target terms. The students were given a briefing on how to use SCROLL eBook and given the URL of the Blogger site to be learned. Then they were assigned to learn the target terms on a self-learning basis using SCROLL eBook and Blogger site (Figs. 9 and 10). In order to examine the effectiveness of SCROLL eBook, the comparison was made between SCROLLeBook and Blogger's site. A class blog was created by the teacher using Google Blogger service at the beginning of the semester and used for the whole semester for class communication. Therefore the students were all familiar with handling Blogger site. The teacher created a new Blogger site for learning career-related terms which were given in the pre-test. In order to give an equal opportunity of

Fig. 9. SCROLL eBook content "年功序列" (promotion by seneority)

education using the cutting-edge technology, there was no control group created. Therefore the whole class experienced both medias. During the session, students were free to use InCircle on PC to communicate with other classmates and the teacher. After the evaluation, Post-tests (1) & (2) were taken by the participants and the questionnaire was conducted in the whole class.

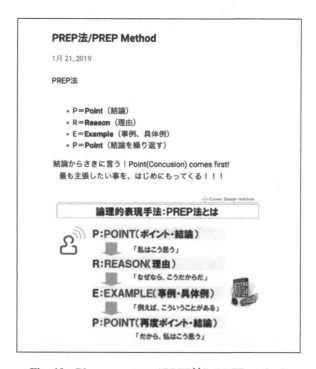

Fig. 10. Blogger content, "PREP法" (PREP method)

4.3   Results

Table 1 shows the result of the Pre- and Post-test (1) and (2). Pre- and Post-test (1) were identical to ask them the meaning of 8 Japanese career-related terms to be taught via eBook. Pre- and Post-test (2) were also identical to ask them the meaning of 7 Japanese career-related terms to be taught via Blogger site. Two points were given for each question, thus the full mark was 16 points for Pre- and Post-test (1) and 14 points for Pre- and Post-test (2). The mean scores of the Pre-test (1) and (2) taken by the Japanese language learners in class were 4.45(27.8%) and 3.57(25.5%) with the standard deviation(SD) of 3.46 and 2.10. After the learning session, the result of Post-test (1) jumped into 11.86(74.1%) with the standard deviation of 4.18(26.1), while that of Post-test (2) was 9.18(65.6%) with the standard deviation of 5.14(36.7). T value, 5.03 shows that there is a statistically significant difference between them. Figure 11 shows that the mean scores increased in both medias but the mean score increased more when they learned with eBook.

Table 1. The result of Pre- and Post-test

	Pre-test(1) (full mark 16)	Post-test(1) after eBook use (full mark 16)	t-value of Pre-test(1)& (2)	t-value ofPost-test(1) & (2)
Mean	4.45 (27.8%)	11.86(74.1%)		
SD	3.46(21.6)	4.18(26.1)		
	Pre-test(2) (full mark 14)	Post-test(2) after Blogger use (full mark 14)	1.78 (p=0.08<0.05)	5.03 (p=0.00000963<0.05)
Mean	3.57(25.5%)	9.18(65.6%)		
SD	2.10(15.0)	5.14(36.7)		

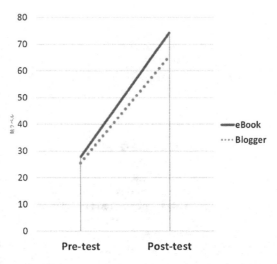

Fig. 11. Comparison between eBook learning and Blog learning in terms of the means of Pre- and Post tests

Table 2 shows the number of InCircle post of the students and the teacher during the evaluation. Since the students were free to communicate via InCircle, the contents are not necessarily related to job-hunting. Totally there were 78 posts by the students and 27 by the teacher. As the number shows, the students were active in posting messages on InCircle. However, even though [18] reported that there was an active interaction among students when they used InCircle, which did not happen in other communication tools, such a phenomenon did not happen in this evaluation. When the teacher posted a message to encourage students' interaction: "Talk about job-hunting system in your home country! When do you usually start job-hunting?", 12 students posted their comments. But unlike the teacher's expectation, one student's post did not lead to another students' reaction. They just answered to the teacher's question (Fig. 12).

Table 2. The number of InCircle post during the evaluation

	The number of InCircle post	Job-hunting related post	Job-hunting unrelated post
Students	**78**	12	66
Teacher	**27**	3	24

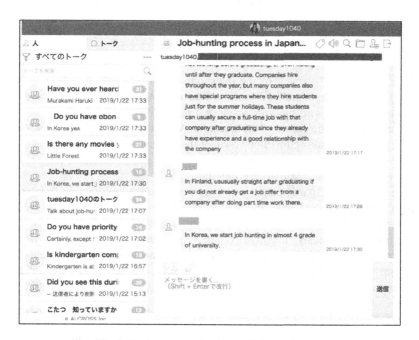

Fig. 12. InCircle communication on job hunting systems

5   Discussion and Conclusion

5.1   Discussion

At the end of the evaluation, they were asked to answer the five-point-scale-questionnaire on the individual- & interactive-learning-combined class as shown in Table 3. Q1 was created to examine the fun factor of our system. Q2 was created based on the technology acceptance model proposed by [23]. Q3 and Q4 were created to examine its effectness of masking function of eBook. Q5 was created to examine the user acceptance of its interface. The highest score, 4.5 was given when they were asked about the usability of the system (Q.2). The lowest score, 3.8 was given when they were asked about the effectness and likability of its masking function (Q.3 and 4).

Table 3. The results of the 5-point-scale questionnaire

	Questions	Mean	SD
Q.1	Was it fun to learn career related terms with SCROLL eBook contents?	4.2	0.60
Q.2	Was it easy for you to handle SCROLL eBook?	4.5	0.66
Q.3	Was the masking function helpful for you to memorise the terms? ✕masking function: by clicking the masks, important terms appear	3.8	0.69
Q.4	Did you like the masking function?	3.8	1.07
Q.5	Please rate its interface of SCROLLeBook	3.9	0.76

Figure 13 shows the result of the question: which one was the easier to handle, SROLLeBook or Blogger site? 62% of the students felt SCROLLeBook was easier to handle. It was in line with the high score of Table 3 Q2.

Figure 14 shows the result of the question: Which do you prefer eBook contents with or without the masking function? 54% of the students preferred "with the masking function" to "without". Even though their evaluation rate was not so high (3.8), the majority preferred "with the masking function".

Table 4 shows the participants' free comments on the individual- & interactive-learning-combined class. Unlike the author's expectation, most comments were concerned with eBook functions and not focued on the hybrid class, but most are positive ones and there is no clearly negative comment. As student #7 pointed out, late introduction of InCircle might have affected the effectiveness of its use. Student #7 also pointed out the diversion of attention, which he himself regards as a personal issue, but it is an important issue to cope with for an implementation of a successful PC-based learning.

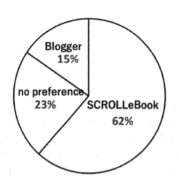

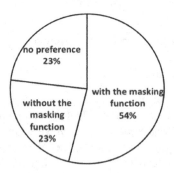

Fig. 13. Which was easier to handle?   **Fig. 14.** Which did you like?

Table 4. The students' impressions of the individual- & interactive-learning-combined class

Student No.	Comments
#1	It's interesting to read about the Japanese career system and its related terms, but it's more beneficial for me to discuss them (such as using InCircle) during class. I can always read on my own time, but discussing in real-time is hard to do outside of class
#2	We can share our opinion with other classmates
#3	Nothing special, I don't figure out what's the point of InCircle when we can also start a line group to communicate in the same way
#4	Convenient to use
#5	It is very convenient to read
#6	It was interesting. But the masking is not for me
#7	The eBooks were quite useful. I don't really see how InCircle contributed to my learning experience, but that might be because it was only introduced towards the end of the class and I didn't really have much time to include it into my learning. Might have been nicer to introduce it earlier (and to provide an app, because for me, messengers need to be in an app - I don't like having to go out of my way and log in online for "just" a messenger. For that matter, I don't like facebook either, if it wasn't for the app. Might also be connected to the fact that I would have to scroll through my bookmarks until I find InCircle - and there are lots of interesting things to find that might divert my attention away from learning. A bit of a personal issue and need for self-discipline, but an app is just nicer)
#8	I didn't really have an opinion
#9	I think it is very helpful and in an easy form for us to learn
#10	eBook was pretty okay. InCircle was convenient as well as a messaging tool
#11	It is complicated, but fun to learn

Table 5. The results of the 5-point-scale questionnaire

	Questions	Mean	SD
Q.1	Was it easy for you to use InCircle?	4.6	0.70
Q.2	Was it fun for you to use the system?	4.1	1.02
Q.3	Was it helpful as a means of communication with your classmates and teacher?	4.2	0.79
Q.4	Was it helpful for understanding Japanese culture and other cultures?	4.1	0.94
Q.5	Was it helpful for your target language learning?	3.5	1.07
Q.6	Please rate its interface	4.0	0.91
Q.7	Please rate the whole system	3.9	0.76

They were also asked to answer the five-point-scale-questionnaire on InCircle function as shown in Table 5. Q1 and Q3 were created based on the technology acceptance model proposed by [18]. Q2 was created to examine the fun factor of our system. Q4 and Q5 were created to examine its contribution to the class objectives. Q6 and Q7 were created for examining the user acceptance of its interface and the whole system.

Table 6 shows the participants' free comments on InCircle. Most comments were positive ones, but there is one clearly negative comment: #12. As mentioned in the Sect. 2.2, the fact that 70% of the students preferred learning alone. There might be a possibility that the negative attitude toward group learning reflected the negative comment on InCircle. This is not directly connected with the effectiveness of the system itself, but we need to consider this fact.

Table 6. The students' impressionos of InCircle

Student No.	Comments
#1	Easy to use and fresh system
#2	It's solid chatting app. But I don't know if people will use it over LINE or Facebook Messenger
#3	simplified LINE
#4	It's not so attractive since we can also have such a talk in Line or some apps
#5	It simple and good to use
#6	Many functions is not available e.g. correcting others' sentences
#7	I thought it was a great way to exchange information with everyone, especially about our culture differences, while listening to the teacher or the presentations
#8	It seems very simple, but not very practical for use outside of class. There are simply more convenient apps to communicate with classmates
#9	First time using these kind of tools, interesting, I felt like I was chatting with friends during class
#10	It makes us talk more and involve more in the class. Convenient and nice
#11	We can talk about Japanese culture
#12	I don't really like group chats, so I found it rather annoying when people sent stuff in the group
#13	User interface was very clean and nice
#14	Simple and useful, especially when you want everyone's opinions. Everyone can answer at the same time
#15	I love it. Students can share their stories through this platform, I found it very helpful

5.2 Conclusions

In this study, we describe facilitating business Japanese learning using SROLLeBook and InCircle. When compared with Blogger site, SCROLLeBook showed its superiority in many aspects as described in Discussion section. The questionnaire results showed that the students were satisfied with its usability. There was a statistically significant difference in the Post-test results between SCROLLeBook learning and Blogger learning. Therefore our hypotheses (our system contributes to international students' leanring business Japaese: Research Question (1)) was proved to be correct. However, it was found out that our system was not supportive for entwining indivisual learning with interactive learning. Since interactive and collaborative learning is essential in language learning, it is necessary to consider how to encourage learners to interact with each other It is among our future works to find out some solutions to implement hybrid learning method via SCROLLeBook and InCircle.

Acknowledgements. Part of this research work was supported by the Grant-in-Aid for Scientific Research No. 18K02820, No. 17K12947, No. 16H06304 and 16H03078 from the Ministry of Education, Culture, Sports, Science and Technology (MEXT) in Japan.

References

1. Wong, L.H., Looi, C.K.: What seams do we remove in mobile-assisted seamless learning? A critical review of the literature. Comput. Educ. **57**, 2364–2381 (2011)
2. Looi, C.K., Sun, D., Xie, W.: Exploring students' progression in an inquiry science curriculum enabled by mobile learning. IEEE Trans. Learn. Technol. **8**(1), 43–54 (2015)
3. Milrad, M., Wong, L.H., Sharple, M., Hwang, G.J., Looi, C.K., Ogata, H.: Seamless learning: an international perspective on next generation technology enhanced learning. In: Berge, Z.L., Muilenburg, L.Y. (eds.) Handbook of Mobile Learning (Chap. 9), pp. 95–108. Routledge, New York (2013)
4. Japan student services organization (JASSO). https://www.jasso.go.jp/sp/about/statistics/intl_student_e/2018/index.html. Accessed 30 Jan 2019
5. Japan revitalization strategy (2016). https://www.kantei.go.jp/jp/singi/keizaisaisei/pdf/hombun1_160602_en.pdf. Accessed 19 Jan 19 2019
6. Uosaki, N., Mouri, K., Yin, C., Ogata, H.: How we can support international students' job hunting in Japan seamlessly. In: Proceedings of International Conference on Computer in Education, 26–30 November, Philippines, pp. 527–529 (2018). http://icce2018.ateneo.edu/wp-content/uploads/2018/12/C4-26.pdf
7. Wong, L.H., Chai, C.S., Aw, C.P., King, R.: Employing the TPACK framework for research-teacher co-design of a mobile-assisted seamless language learning environment. IEEE Trans. Learn. Technol. **8**(1), 31–42 (2014)
8. Uosaki, N., Li, M., Hou, B., Ogata, H., Yano, Y.: Supporting an English course using handhelds in a seamless learning environment. In: Workshop Proceedings of the 18nd International Conference on Computers in Education (ICCE 2010), pp. 185–192 (2010)
9. Ogata, H., Uosaki, N.: A new trend of mobile and ubiquitous learning research: towards enhancing ubiquitous learning experiences. Int. J. Mobile Learn. Organ. **6**(1), 64–78 (2012)
10. Inoue, G., Uosaki, N., Ogata, H., Mouri, K.: Enhancing outside-class learning using online tools: a review work. In: Proceedings of LTLE2014, pp. 332–337 (2014)
11. Calitz, A., Evert, C., Cullen, M.: Promoting ICT careers using a South African ICT career portal. African J. Inf. Syst. **7**(2), 40–61 (2015). Article 1
12. Arame, M., Naganuma, S., Kobayashi, M., Komatsu, M., Tamaki, K.: Consideration about how to use the e Portfolio in career education (Japanese) IPSJ Trans. Comput. Educ. (Kenkyu Houkoku: Computer to Kyouiku) 2013-CE-120(3), 1–8 (2013)

13. Teshima, H., Kawasaki, C., Komatsu, Y.: Integrated program of the academic skills and the career development for university freshers: a report on the course "Skills for Self Establishing" at Osaka Jogakuin College (Japanese). Bulletin of Osaka Jogakuin College 5, 119–144, (2008)
14. Headlam-Wells, J., Gosland, J., Craig, J.: "There's magic in the web": e-mentoring for women's career development. Career Dev. Int. 10(6/7), 444–459 (2005)
15. Morimoto, Y.: E-portfolios: theory and practice. J. JSiSE (教育システム情報学会誌) 25(2), 245–263 (2008). (in Japanese)
16. Severiens, S., Meeuwisse, M., Born, M.: Student experience and academic success: comparing a student-centered and a lecture-based course programme. Higher Educ.: Int. J. Higher Educ. Educ. Plann. 70(1) (2015). https://doi.org/10.1007/s10734-014-9820-3
17. Chen, T.X.: Interactive learning of a foreign language. J. Acoust. Soc. Am. 114(1), 30 (2003). https://doi.org/10.1121/1.1601085
18. Uosaki, N., Yonekawa, T., Yin, C.: Supporting collaborative interaction among learners using collaborative learning system InCircle. In: Proceedings of COLLA 2018, the Eighth International Conference on Advanced Collaborative Networks, Systems and Applications, pp. 1–6 (2018)
19. SCROLL: (2019). https://scroll.let.media.kyoto-u.ac.jp/learninglog/signin(last. Accessed 29 Jan 29
20. Ogata, H., Hou, B., Li, M., Uosaki, N., Mouri, K., Liu, S.: Ubiquitous learning project using life-logging technology in Japan. Educ. Technol. Soc. J. 17(2), 85–100 (2014)
21. InCircle: (2019).)https://www.incircle.jp/. Accessed 29 Jan
22. AOS Mobile Inc., Tokyo, Japan. http://www.aosmobile.com/. Accessed 29 Jan 2019
23. Davis, F.D.: Perceived usefulness, perceived ease of use, and user acceptance of information technology. MIS Q. 13(3), 319–339 (1989)

Supporting Weight Loss Through Digitally-Augmented Social Expression

Nan Yang[1]([⊠]), Gerbrand van Hout[2], Loe Feijs[1], Wei Chen[3], and Jun Hu[1]

[1] Department of Industrial Design, Eindhoven University of Technology,
5612AZ Eindhoven, Netherlands
{n.yang,l.m.g.feijs,j.hu}@tue.nl
[2] Obesity Centre, Catharina Hospital, 5623 EJ Eindhoven, Netherlands
gerbrand.v.hout@catharinaziekenhuis.nl
[3] Department of Electronic Engineering, Fudan University,
Shanghai 200433, China
w_chen@fudan.edu.cn

Abstract. In this paper, we present the design, prototyping and implementation of i-Ribbon—a wearable device designed to support weight loss through digitally-augmented social expression. Starting with an Obesity Awareness Ribbon, we introduced the exploration process and formation of the i-Ribbon concept. Prototypes of different fidelity were built during the design process, including a working system that could extract the user's personal health-related data through a mobile application and sent it to a wearable expression device. Evaluation through interview has been conducted. Base on the reflection on design, prototyping and evaluation process, we summarize the insights and discuss the options for future work.

Keywords: Wearable · Weight loss · Quantified-self · Healthcare · Social interaction · Interaction

1 Introduction

With the development of sensing technology and the popularity of wearable devices, more and more types of health-related data can be monitored. In most existing wearable applications, quantified-self data is visualized and fed back to the end users. Supporting users in their self-management have become an important role in wearable applications. However, the starting point of this research—the Obesity Awareness Ribbon (Fig. 1) [1] inspired us about the social attributes of the wearable device. Instead of staring at the increasing sensing capabilities of wearable devices, we try to discover its potential in social expression.

The original role of wearable devices is to monitor the wearer's health-related information. However, just like the role of conventional apparel is no longer just to shield the wearer's body, wearable devices should also not be restricted to their most primitive roles. If we consider wearable devices as apparel augmented by the integration of digital technology, they could have properties similar to conventional

© Springer Nature Switzerland AG 2019
N. Streitz and S. Konomi (Eds.): HCII 2019, LNCS 11587, pp. 459–470, 2019.
https://doi.org/10.1007/978-3-030-21935-2_35

460   N. Yang et al.

apparel, reflecting wearer's identity, taste, attitude, and values. Additionally, with the help of sensing and display technology, quantified-self data can also become a type of social cue, enrich the social expression through wearable devices.

Different from the existing tracking devices, the wearable devices we present in this paper—i-Ribbon, is designed as a channel for social expression rather than a self-tracking terminal. By introducing the design and research process of i-Ribbon, we discussed the opportunities of wearable devices in promoting social expression in the context of weight loss.

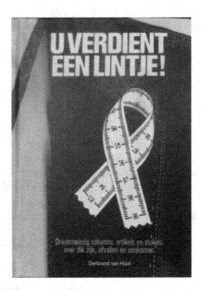

Fig. 1. The book of Gerbrand van Hout, entitled "U Verdient een Lintje!" (in Dutch) which means "You deserve a ribbon!" The cover of the book shows the physical version of the Obesity Awareness Ribbon.

2   Related Work

2.1   Wearables in Social Interaction

A number of prior researches explored the social aspect of wearable device. Fajardo et al. [2] proposed a contextual wearable display model to describe the typical relationships between display devices, wearers, onlookers and the context, the model was subsequently used to evaluate a pilot study that compared the abstract and overt visualization of skin conductivity on a wearable display device. Some other research also considered the relationship between the wearer of a wearable device and people in proximity [3, 4]. Moere and Hoinkis [5] proposed a wearable folding display that is able to convey wears' behavioural typology. The concept was defined as "an electronically enhanced form of self-expression for increased social awareness in physical reality".

2.2   Social Applications of Quantified-Self Data

Some previous efforts integrated quantified-self data into social applications to motivate physical exercise. The most used data type in these applications is heart rate [6–10]. Mueller presented "Jogging over a Distance" to support runners in different cities to jog at the same time, runners' heartbeat audio are shared between each other to facilitate a social experience [11]. In some other research, the user's activity level has also been publicly displayed to motivate physical activity [12, 13].

3   Starting Point and Initial Exploration

The starting point of this research is the Obesity Awareness Ribbon presented by Dr. van Hout (Fig. 1) [1, 14]. Similar to the pink ribbon design for breast cancer awareness [15], this ribbon is designed for everyone "who wants to show awareness for obesity and wants to hearten obese people" [14]. The physical version of the ribbon was given to the patients and staffs in the Obesity Centre of Catharina Hospital in Eindhoven.

Fig. 2. The upper four pictures showing the explorations on ribbon wearing behaviour and the lower pictures showing the potential interaction related to a digitalized Obesity Awareness Ribbon.

Starting with the concept of the original Obesity Awareness Ribbon, an initial exploration has been conducted. We tried to enhance the expressive feature of the ribbon by integrating digital technology. In order to explore the potential values related to this digitalized Obesity Awareness Ribbon, several low fidelity prototypes were built (Figs. 2, 3, 4). Figure 2 shows the explorations on ribbon wearing behaviours and potential interaction related to a digital ribbon. Figures 3 and 4 show the different possibilities for digitalizing the ribbon.

With the help of these prototypes, evaluation through interview was carried out, two persons with weight loss experience participated and provided some inspirational feedback. The most significant finding from the initial exploration was the value of "weight-loss efforts". In the process of weight loss, efforts are usually invisible before the significant changes appear. Therefore, the users would like to show their weight-loss efforts through the digitalized ribbon in more expressive ways.

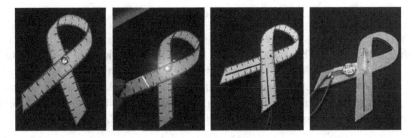

Fig. 3. Two versions of the digitalized Obesity Awareness Ribbon, the first two pictures showing a concept based on visual output, the last two pictures showing the tactile output (vibration).

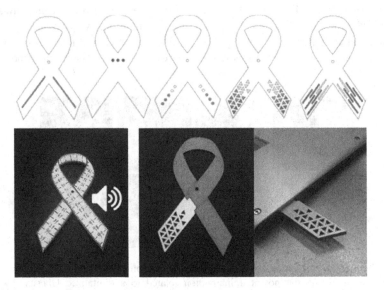

Fig. 4. Additional possibilities for the digitalized Obesity Awareness Ribbon.

4   First Iteration: Visualize Efforts

4.1   Concept of I-Ribbon

Based on the result of initial exploration, we presented the concept of i-Ribbon, a wrist-worn wearable device that expresses the wearer's weight-loss efforts. A dynamic pattern which represents the wearer's physical activity was integrated with the conventional ribbon to enhance its social expressiveness. The pattern on i-Ribbon change according to the wearer's amount of physical activity (reflected by steps, distance and floors), see Figs. 5 and 6. The wearer can also personalize the expression of i-Ribbon through a mobile application (Fig. 5). Therefore, the concept of i-Ribbon consists of two parts:

- A wrist-worn device, which is visible to onlookers and carries symbolic meanings. At the same time, it has a built-in accelerometer to detect movements, similar to other commercial activity trackers.
- A mobile application, providing an additional interface, which would not fit on the limited size of the wrist-worn device.

There are many ways to wear conventional awareness ribbon. The decision to make i-Ribbon a wrist-worn device was motivated by the following factors: first of all, the wrist is a body location that can be seen by both the wearer and onlooker. Therefore, a wrist-worn device offers the opportunity for the wearer to express more actively [2]. Additionally, the wearers can conceal the device worn on their wrist, so they will have more freedom to decide where and when to show i-Ribbon to others. Moreover, as a product designed to support weight loss, a wrist-worn device will not cause inconvenience in most physical activities.

4.2   Prototype and Evaluation

In order to completely present the original concept of i-Ribbon, the first prototype we built is a non-functional simulation of i-Ribbon under the ideal condition. This prototype consisted of two complementary parts, including a set of mock-up of i-Ribbon (Fig. 5), and a screen-based simulation of the dynamic pattern (Fig. 6).

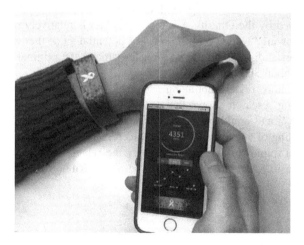

Fig. 5. The prototype of the wrist-worn device and the mobile application of i-Ribbon (non-functional simulation).

Evaluation with early prototypes (Figs. 5, 6) has been conducted through semi-structured interviews, the process and results have been presented in a published paper [16]. Participants showed a positive attitude towards the idea of "showing weight-loss efforts", they described i-Ribbon as a trigger that can start conversations and expect a more obvious way to show their weight-loss efforts. We also found that the symbolic meaning of the original Obesity Awareness Ribbon is obscure for some participants.

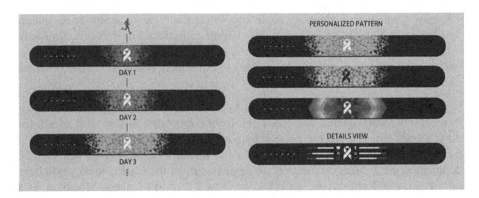

Fig. 6. The prototype of the wrist-worn device of i-Ribbon (screen-based simulation of the surface).

5   Second Iteration: Embody Values

5.1   Symbol, Design and Values

The original Obesity Awareness Ribbon was essentially a symbol [1]. From the initial exploration and first iteration, we realized that due to the short history of the symbol, it has not been widely spread and recognized. Compared to the famous Pink Ribbon [15], the values conveyed by the Obesity Awareness Ribbon is relatively obscure for some of its wearers. Showing "weight-loss efforts" is a potential value that we identified. We need further understanding about the relationship among the original Obesity Awareness Ribbon, i-Ribbon and the values it conveyed.

A further literature review about human values and values elicitation has been conducted. Existing research shows that values could be integrated into technology through design [17] and could be elicited through a variety of ways [18–21]. With a deeper understanding of value theory [22] and its relationship with system and product [23], we present a framework (Fig. 7) to clarify the relationship between the symbol (the original Obesity Awareness Ribbon), design (i-Ribbon), values (weight-loss efforts) and user.

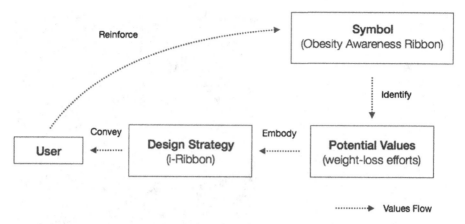

Fig. 7. The relationship between the symbol (the original Obesity Awareness Ribbon), design (i-Ribbon), values (weight-loss efforts) and user.

As shown in Fig. 7, potential values could be identified from the symbol of the Obesity Awareness Ribbon. Design strategy can be used to embody the identified values in a specific product. Through interacting with the product, the user may have a better understanding of the values that symbolized by the Obesity Awareness Ribbon. We have identified the value of "supporting weight-loss efforts" in the previous study, with other values identified in further research, corresponding design strategies can be used to embody these values and convey them to users.

5.2   Working Prototype

The prototype we built at second iteration is not only a technical upgrade of the previous version (Figs. 5, 6), but also a flexible system that has the potential of embodying different values. The working prototype of i-Ribbon includes a wrist-worn device as a medium of social expression (Figs. 8, 9), and a mobile application connected to the Google Fit platform to access user's physical activity data (Fig. 12).

The core function of the wrist-worn device was implemented through LightBlue Bean with an RGB LED matrix. With the built-in Bluetooth LE module on LightBlue Bean, the device can receive wearer's health-related data from the mobile application and represent through the RGB LED matrix (Figs. 8, 9). In addition, a button with the abstract version of the Obesity Awareness Ribbon (Fig. 10) was assembled into the device as a button. The wearer could turn on/off the display by pressing this button. The display will automatically turn off after ten seconds if there is no other operation. Wearer's interaction with the button could strengthen the connection between the symbol of Obesity Awareness Ribbon and the values we expect to elicit through i-Ribbon. Other electronic components such as lithium battery, charging module and main switch were also included in the wrist-worn part of the prototype.

Fig. 8. Two sides of the working prototype of i-Ribbon's wrist-worn part.

Fig. 9. Two examples of the representation of
wearer's health-related data through the RGB LED
matrix on an i-Ribbon.

Fig. 10. The abstract version of the Obesity Awareness Ribbon.

In addition to the hardware of the wearable device, we developed an Android
mobile application to access the user's physical activity data and provide an extended
user interface. With the Google Fit API, the application can extract data from any
device connected to the same Google Fit account and send it to the wrist-worn device
through the smartphone's built-in Bluetooth LE module. This feature technically
separated the expression and sensing function of the prototype and brought the possibility of getting data beyond the wrist-worn sensing device (Fig. 11).

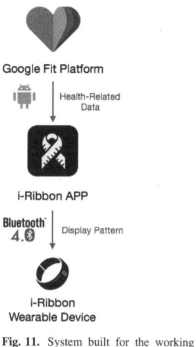

Google Fit Platform

Health-Related
Data

i-Ribbon APP

Bluetooth
4.8

Display Pattern

i-Ribbon
Wearable Device

Fig. 11. System built for the working prototype of i-Ribbon.

Fig. 12. Screenshot of the Android mobile application for i-Ribbon's working prototype.

Although we only used the smartphone's built-in accelerometer and Xiaomi Mi Band as a data source at this stage. Data from any other device that compatible with Google Fit platform could be used in further research. The main interface of the mobile application consists of two parts: (1) a pie chart showing user's calorie consumption of walking, running and biking, and (2) a "WEAR IT" button enabling user to convert the data into the visual pattern and display on the wrist-worn device (Fig. 12) [24].

Evaluation with the working prototype should be conducted in further research, with the flexible system we built for the working prototype, we are also able to embody other values by using different data sources and design strategies.

6   Discussion

6.1   Visualization of Weight-Loss Efforts

"Effort" is a concept that is difficult to quantify, but with the help of existing sensing technologies, many indicators can be used to represent efforts in the context of weight loss. In this study, we used some common data type that can be monitored by most exiting wearable devices, such as step, distance and calorie consumption. However, due to the diversity of the user's physical condition, the same value under the same indicator may not mean the same level of effort for different users. Therefore, choosing appropriate indicator is very important for objectively presenting "weight-loss efforts". The historical data of the same user can be compared, and the degree or speed of change is more appropriate than the absolute value to reflect efforts. Data types like calorie consumption are directly related to the user's age, gender, and weight. These types of data are more suitable for representing efforts than steps, distances or floors.

In addition to the choice of data types, the strategy of visualization is also very important. Due to the limited space on wearable devices, visualization for social expression on wearables differs from statistically oriented visualization. Our purpose is not to show specific data details, but to represent "weight-loss efforts" intuitively and clearly. Therefore, one direction of further research is to identify the appropriate data types and visualization strategies for "weight-loss efforts".

6.2 Wearables and Digitally-Augmented Social Expression

Based on the design and research process of i-Ribbon, we summarize two perspectives of enhancing social expression through wearable devices. Firstly, the wearable devices themselves can incorporate digital technology to enable dynamic information display. In this perspective, wearable device can be seen as apparel that augmented by digital technology, it can be a garment, watch or jewellery and does not necessarily have the sensing ability. Secondly, quantified-self data detected by wearable devices can become a new type of social cue. Some users are already sharing their fitness tracking record on social networks. With appropriate visualization, quantified-self data not only can be displayed in the mobile application but also can be combined with user's cloth, jewellery, vehicles or other daily accessories to enrich user's social expression channels.

These two perspectives also provide two directions for future research: (1) Explore the social potential of a particular type of wearable device. (2) Investigate the social properties of Quantified-self data in specific scenarios.

6.3 The Influence of Context on Social Expression

An important difference between wearable devices and awareness ribbons is that they are worn in the different context. Most people only wear awareness ribbons on specific occasions, such as charity gatherings or events. And in these occasions, there are usually many people wearing the same ribbon for similar reasons. However, wearable devices are usually worn all day by users, like other clothing and accessories, they may be seen by others on a wide variety of occasions. When we add some social expression feature to wearable devices, some autonomy should be given to users, because the user may not want to present this information on all occasions. Autonomy can be given to the user in two ways: (1) Set a switch that lets the user decide whether to present or hide the information in different situations. (2) Present the information in an abstract way, leaving the user with the space to explain to others.

6.4   Symbol and Values

It's difficult for people to realize the values represented by a symbol by simply watching or wearing it. The values behind a symbol could be embodied into a specific application and conveyed to its user. In this research, we identified the value of "supporting weight-loss efforts" in the initial exploration and embodied it into a wearable application to, by using i-Ribbon, the user will have a deeper understanding of the values represented by the symbol. A framework was presented to explain the relationship between symbol, design, and user (Fig. 7). From the perspective of symbol and values, there are two directions for future research, (1) Identify other values related to the Obesity Awareness Ribbon. (2) Embody the value of "supporting weight-loss efforts" into other applications by different design strategies.

7   Conclusion

In this study, we presented the design and research process of i-Ribbon —— a wearable device designed to support weight loss through digitally-augmented social expression. Starting with the Obesity Awareness Ribbon. The value of "weight-loss efforts" was identified through an initial exploration. We designed a wearable device to visualize the user's "weight-loss efforts" in the first iteration. In the second iteration, a working prototype was built and the relationship between symbol, values, design and user was clarified. Serval insights and options for future works were identified.

References

1. Van Hout, G.: U verdient een lintje! - drieëntwintig columns, artikels en stukjes over dik zijn, afvallen en aankomen. Houterig, Middelbeers (2015). (in Dutch)
2. Fajardo, N., Moere, A.V.: ExternalEyes: evaluating the visual abstraction of human emotion on a public wearable display device. In: Proceedings of the 20th Australasian Conference on Computer-Human Interaction: Designing for Habitus and Habitat, pp. 247–250. ACM (2008)
3. Fortmann, J., Müller, H., Heuten, W., Boll, S.: Designing wearable light displays for users and observers. In: CHI 2014, CHI Conference on Human Factors in Computing Systems, Workshop on Peripheral Interaction: Shaping the Research and Design Space, pp. 33–36 (2014)
4. Pearson, J., Robinson, S., Jones, M.: It's about time: Smartwatches as public displays. In: Proceedings of the 33rd Annual ACM Conference on Human Factors in Computing Systems, pp. 1257–1266. ACM (2015)
5. Moere, A.V., Hoinkis, M.A.: Wearable folding display for self-expression. In: Proceedings of the 18th Australia conference on Computer-Human Interaction: Design: Activities, Artefacts and Environments, pp. 301–304. ACM (2006)
6. Curmi, F., Ferrario, M.A., Whittle, J., Mueller, F.F.: Crowdsourcing synchronous spectator support: (go on, go on, you're the best) n-1. In: Proceedings of the 33rd Annual ACM Conference on Human Factors in Computing Systems, pp. 757–766. ACM (2015)
7. Magielse, R., Markopoulos, P.: HeartBeat: an outdoor pervasive game for children. In: Proceedings of the SIGCHI Conference on Human Factors in Computing Systems, pp. 2181–2184. ACM (2009)

8. Mauriello, M., Gubbels, M., Froehlich, J.E.: Social fabric fitness: the design and evaluation of wearable E-textile displays to support group running. In: Proceedings of the SIGCHI Conference on Human Factors in Computing Systems, pp. 2833–2842. ACM (2014)
9. Sonne, T., Jensen, M.M.: Race By hearts. In: Pisan, Y., Sgouros, Nikitas M., Marsh, T. (eds.) ICEC 2014. LNCS, vol. 8770, pp. 125–132. Springer, Heidelberg (2014). https://doi.org/10.1007/978-3-662-45212-7_16
10. Walmink, W., Wilde, D., Mueller, F.F.: Displaying heart rate data on a bicycle helmet to support social exertion experiences. In: Proceedings of the 8th International Conference on Tangible, Embedded and Embodied Interaction, pp. 97–104. ACM (2014)
11. Mueller, F.F., O'Brien, S., Thorogood, A.: Jogging over a distance: supporting a jogging together experience although being apart. In: CHI 2007 Extended Abstracts on Human Factors in Computing Systems, pp. 1989–1994. ACM (2007)
12. Burns, P., Lueg, C., Berkovsky, S.: Activmon: encouraging physical activity through ambient social awareness. In: CHI 2012 Extended Abstracts on Human Factors in Computing Systems, pp. 2363–2368. ACM (2012)
13. Lim, B.Y., Shick, A., Harrison, C., Hudson, S.E.: Pediluma: motivating physical activity through contextual information and social influence. In: Proceedings of the Fifth International Conference on Tangible, Embedded, and Embodied Interaction, pp. 173–180. ACM (2011)
14. Van Hout, G.: You deserve a ribbon. Obes. Surg. 25(7), 1251 (2015)
15. Harvey, J.A., Strahilevitz, M.A.: The power of pink: cause-related marketing and the impact on breast cancer. J. Am. Coll. Radiol. 6(1), 26–32 (2009)
16. Yang, N., van Hout, G., Feijs, L.M., Chen, W., Hu, J.: i-Ribbon: social expression through wearables to support weight-loss efforts. In: Intelligent Environments (Workshops), pp. 524–533 (2016)
17. van de Poel, I., Kroes, P.: Can technology embody values? In: Kroes, P., Verbeek, P.-P. (eds.) The Moral Status of Technical Artefacts. PET, vol. 17, pp. 103–124. Springer, Dordrecht (2014). https://doi.org/10.1007/978-94-007-7914-3_7
18. Halloran, J., Hornecker, E., Stringer, M., Harris, E., Fitzpatrick, G.: The value of values: Resourcing co-design of ubiquitous computing. CoDesign 5(4), 245–273 (2009)
19. Pommeranz, A., Detweiler, C., Wiggers, P., Jonker, C.M.: Self-reflection on personal values to support value-sensitive design. In: Proceedings of the 25th BCS Conference on Human-Computer Interaction, pp. 491–496. British Computer Society (2011)
20. Ross, P.R., Trotto, A., Overbeeke, C.J.: Ethics through aesthetics: a trefoil design research agenda. In: Proceedings of the International Association of Societies of Design Research. pp 1–10, (2009)
21. Woelfer, J.P., Iverson, A., Hendry, D.G., Friedman, B., Gill, B.T.: Improving the safety of homeless young people with mobile phones: values, form and function. In Proceedings of the SIGCHI Conference on Human Factors in Computing Systems, pp. 1707–1716. ACM (2011)
22. Schwartz, S.H.: An overview of the Schwartz theory of basic values. Online Readings Psychol. Cult. 2(1), 11 (2012)
23. Kujala, S., Väänänen-Vainio-Mattila, K.: Value of information systems and products: understanding the users' perspective and values. J. Inf. Technol. Theory Appl. (JITTA) 9(4), 4 (2009)
24. Yang, N., van Hout, G., Feijs, L., Chen, W., Hu, J.: Eliciting values through wearable expression in weight loss. In: Proceedings of the 19th International Conference on Human-Computer Interaction with Mobile Devices and Services, p. 86. ACM (2017)

Learning Behavioral Pattern Analysis Based on Digital Textbook Reading Logs

Chengjiu Yin[1]([⊠]), Zhuo Ren[2], Agoritsa Polyzou[3], and Yong Wang[4]

[1] Kobe University, Kobe, Japan
yin@lion.kobe-u.ac.jp
[2] Jinan University, Guangzhou, China
[3] University of Minnesota, Twin-Cities, USA
[4] Ocean University of China, Qingdao, China

Abstract. Since various features have different degrees of association with learning outcome, it is necessary to evaluate each feature by giving a reasonable weight. In this paper, we propose a different weighting of the features, weighting the features is different from other researches, when we carry out Correlation Analysis between these features and grade achieved (in the end of the semester). By using this weighting of the features and the students' grade achieved, we grouped students into five clusters and analyzed their learning behavioral patterns. We found some interesting patterns, such as the students who always use the MEMO or MAKERS function, always get better grade achieved.

Keywords: Clustering · Weighted variables · Learning analytics · Digital textbook

1 Introduction

Recently, it is easy to collect learning logs to do learning analysis by using data collecting tools. For example, the digital textbook system can be seen as a kind of educational data collecting tool. Both traditional and online platforms are using the digital textbook system. Many countries plan to use digital textbooks replaced the traditional textbooks in schools. Such as Korean, Japan (Yin et al. 2014). The traditional textbook has been replaced gradually (Yin et al. 2018). By using digital textbooks, it is possible to collect a significant amount of logged educational data. These log data are a recording of learning practices such as marking, memo. Recently, researchers have begun to pay attention to the utilization of the learning logs of the digital textbook systems (Yin and Hwang 2018).

On our previous research (Yin et al. 2018), by using digital textbooks reading logs, a k-means clustering is employed to group students into clusters, and analyzed the learning behavioral patterns of each group by using some features, such as number of pages read, reading times, and backtrack reading rates. Students were grouped into four clusters and their learning behavioral patterns were analyzed. We examined whether the learning behavioral patterns are related to the learning outcomes. To be more specific, we considered the students' grade achieved (in the end of the semester) as a way to evaluate their performance.

© Springer Nature Switzerland AG 2019
N. Streitz and S. Konomi (Eds.): HCII 2019, LNCS 11587, pp. 471–480, 2019.
https://doi.org/10.1007/978-3-030-21935-2_36

However, some features stronger association with learning outcomes than others. Therefore it is essential to assign a reasonable weight to each features of clustering (Nie et al. 2017). In this paper, weighting the features is different from other researches, when we carry out Correlation Analysis between features and grade achieved. If the correlation coefficient is bigger, then add a bigger weight to the feature; if the correlation coefficient is smaller, then add a smaller weight to the feature.

After weighting the features, we grouped students into five clusters and analyzed their learning behavioral patterns. We found some interesting patterns, such as the students who always use the MEMO or UNDERLINE function, are the ones who always get better grade achieved.

2   Literature Review

2.1   Learning Analytics (LA)

LA can positively influence on learning effectiveness (Archer et al. 2014; Hrastinski 2009; Yin et al. 2017; Yin and Hwang 2018). LA can be used to optimize learning and teaching processes (Colvin et al. 2015). Yin and Hwang (2018) indicated that LA can benefit different roles:

LA can help students to improve and share their learning experience;
LA can help teachers to get feedback from learners and identify the learning strategies;
LA can help to evaluate the structure of course content, and to evaluate teaching materials;
LA can help to evaluate teachers and students.

Digital textbooks reading log data based LA is an emerging topic. Yin and Hwang (2018) proposed several potential research directions of LA for digital textbooks:

(1) *Prediction.*

  • *By analyzing digital textbooks based learning logs to provide supports and make predictions.*

(2) *Structure Discovery.*

  • *Discovering learning behavioral patterns.*
  • *Identifying the impacts of different learning strategies.*
  • *Investigating the factors affecting students' performances.*

(3) *Relationship Mining.*

  • *Investigating the correlations between students' behaviors and performances.*

A lots of research is focused on using LA for Structure Discovery. Clustering, Factor Analysis, Knowledge Inference and Network Analysis are common analysis methods of structure discovery. This paper is also focused on Structure Discovery, which attempts to find learning patterns by using e-book reading data.

2.2   Clustering

The k-means clustering involves grouping similar records together in a large multidimensional data set (Aggarwal and Yu 1999). The records within a cluster exhibit high similarity to each other; however, they are dissimilar to records in other clusters. Dissimilarity and similarity features are based on the attribute values that describe the records and generally involve distance metrics (Han et al. 2011).

Clustering Analytics are widely used as a tool for analyzing multivariate data. Utilizing k-means clustering, Cheng and Tsai (2014) reported their success in identifying the features of reading behaviors in an augmented reality picture book. Our research purpose is to identify the features of reading behaviors on digital textbooks, in a more educational context. Therefore, k-means clustering analysis is conducted in the current work.

2.3   Previous Work

On my previous research (Yin et al. 2017), we examined whether the learning behavioral patterns exhibited relations with the learning outcomes and identified learning patterns from e-book log data. To achieve these objectives, we used visualization technologies to identify unobserved learning behaviors. We then analyzed their learning behavior patterns by using k-means clustering.

The students were grouped into four clusters of varying learning behavior patterns: the "preview and diligent group," "efficient group," "diligent group," and "poor performance group." The following observations emerged from the analysis results:

(1) Backtrack reading learning behavior has its merit because it can aid students in saving time while studying. The results reveal that the learning behavior of "backtrack" style reading exerts a significant positive influence on learning effectiveness, which can aid students to learn more efficiently.
(2) A reasonable learning behavior complemented by sufficient learning time can yield excellent learning results.

There are three differences with the previous research:

(1) In current research, the e-book reading log data used come from a commercial law course. In the previous research, the e-book reading log data is collected from programming learning courses.
(2) The previous research did not care about weighting the features of clustering.
(3) The number of features used in the previous research is smaller than current research.

3   DITeL

3.1   System

Collecting data is the first step in learning analysis (Yin et al. 2013; Yin et al. 2013b). In order to collect educational data, we build a digital textbook system, which is named as digital textbook for improving teaching and learning (DITeL). Teachers upload all the teaching materials needed to the DITeL. The DITeL system has been developed to collect textbook reading data such as "turning to next/previous page," "memo," "zoom in/out," "adding marker." The aforementioned reading actions are termed as events in this study. The DITeL system can be used not only on a personal computer, but also on mobile devices such as smartphones and tablets, thereby making it usable anywhere and anytime.

The learning logs of the students were collected to analyze their learning behaviors for improving the DITeL system (Yin et al. 2017; Li et al. 2018).

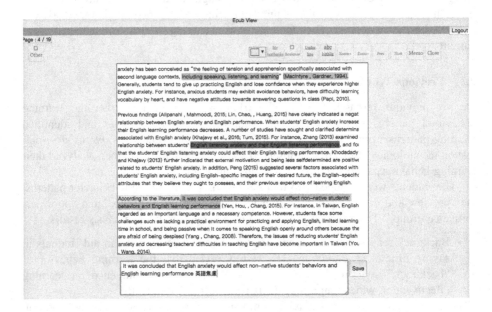

Fig. 1. Interface of DITeL

Figure 1 shows the interface of DITel. The interface has some buttons at the top. The students can interact with the e-book, to navigate through its contents, add notes and highlights. All of these actions are stored in the database. These data were used to analyze learning behaviors of the students. More specifically, the available events are the following:

Turning to next/previous page: Students can read the contents multiple times; they navigate to the next page by clicking the "Next" button, and backtrack to the previous page by clicking the "Prev" button.

Memo: A user can click the "Memo" button to write something in the learning content. After the user finishes writing the memo in the textbox provided, the action name will be saved as "Memo."

Zoom in/out: The zoom in/out function can expand and reduce font size so that it can help students read the contents clearly.

Adding marker: A user can click "Highlight" or the "Under line" button when s/he wants to highlight text in the learning content, and the action name will be saved as "Highlight" or "Underline.

3.2 Participants

The data used in this study were collected during a commercial law course in March 2017- July 2017and March 2018–July 2018 at Jinan University in China. The learning goal of the course was to teach students the basic commercial law.

The students were provided the teaching materials for the subsequent class and were asked to prepare the lesson before the subsequent class. A total of 234 graduate students (aged 18 to 19) attended the course. Nine students were removed from the study sample after data processing, including drop-out students among others. The data from the remaining 225 students were used. Among the participants, 22.4% were female and 77.6% were male. In these students, 6% were from the School of Education, 10% were from the School of Letters, 13% were from the Faculty of Science, three were from the School of Medicine, and 69% were from the Faculty of Engineering.

Prior to entering the class, they had no previous experience of using DITeL, an e-book system that records students' learning behaviors when they read e-books.

The experiments were conducted following the ethics criteria suggested by an authorized ethics committee in Japan in order to protect the participants. Further, the personal information of the participants was hidden.

3.3 Data Collection

Collecting data is the first step in learning behavior analysis (Yin et al. 2013b, 2013; Yin et al. 2018). Table 1 presents a sample of reading action logs. Each data log contains date, time, user ID, Content ID, page number, user action, devices, and other data. A total of 200,000 records were gathered from 2017 to 2018.

The reading action logs for "Action Time" listed the students who engaged in this behavior, and we calculated the number of times this occurred.

The e-book features were used in this research:

- Log in times(LGI): The number of times a student log in to DITeL system.
- Number of "Memo" (NM): The number of times a student writes memo.
- Number of "Underline"(NUL): The number of times a student makes underline.
- Number of "Highlight" (NHL): The number of times a student makes highlight.
- Number of "Next" (NN): The number of times a student turns to subsequent pages.
- Number of "Prev" (NP): The number of times a student returns to previous pages.
- Reading Pages (RP): The total number of pages that a student read. The reading action logs for "Page No." and "Action Time" listed the number of pages the students read. Many of them repeatedly read specific pages.
- Read Time (RT): The total time spent reading the learning contents. The reading action logs "Action Time" listed the lengths of time students spent reading the learning content. RT was calculated on an hourly basis.
- Backtrack reading rate (BRR): BRR is a hidden measure, which is also calculated using NN and NP. This will be described in the following section.

Table 1. Sample of records

User ID	User action	Content ID	Page no.	Time	Devices
S1	NEXT	0NBU1	15	2017/05/22 14:40:55	Mobile
S1	PREV	0NBU1	6	2017/05/22 14:45:55	PC
S2	HIGHLIGHT	0NBU2	6	2017/05/22 14:46:55	Tablet
S3	MEMO	0NBU3	10	2017/05/22 14:47:55	PC

4   Method

4.1   Correlation Analysis

The Grade Achieved (GA) was used to measure the learning outcomes. We analyzed a number of variables that could affect performance, including the behaviors and their related variables (time spent reading pages, etc.). SPSS (IBM SPSS Statistics, New York, USA) was used to determine the partial correlation of GA with these variables.

Table 2. The correlation GA with features

	LGI	NM	NHL	NUL	BTR	RT	RP
GA	0.202	0.445	0.546	0.162	0.615	0.777	0.840

GA = Grade Achieved; LGI = Login Count; Memo = Memo Count; HL = Highlight Count; UL = Underline Count; BTR = Backing Track Rate; RT = Reading Time; RP = Reading Pages

Table 2 lists the results, which indicate that the variable GA exhibits a significant positive correlation with LGI, NM, NHL, NUL, BTR, RP, and RT. In addition, based on the results of partial correlation, a k-means clustering analysis was conducted to cluster students into groups to analyze the features of the learning behaviors in each group.

The partial correlation values are used the weighted the features of k-means clustering.

5   Learning Behavior Patterns

After clustering, we got five clusters: C1, C2, C3, C4 and C5. Compare these 5 groups, C4 and C3 obtained similar learning achievement (there is no difference between the GA of C4 and C3), and C4 and C3 exhibited a higher learning achievement. The performance of C4 and C3 is higher than C2, the performance of C2 is higher than C1, and the learning achievement of C1 is higher than C5 (GA: $3 > 2 > 1 > 5$; $4 > 2 > 1 > 5$) (Table 3).

Table 3. The result of clustering

	C1 (n = 52) (mean/SD)	C2 (n = 53) (mean/SD)	C3 (n = 46) (mean/SD)	C4 (n = 41) (mean/SD)	C5 (n = 33) (mean/SD)
LGI	.0873/.05915	.1392/.05694	.2337/.08084	.3471/.13020	.1136/.10532
NM	.0494/.04889	.3717/.06354	.0437/.03362	.4361/.07064	.0300/.03279
NHL	.0463/.03464	.3002/.06341	.0533/.03120	.3988/.08773	.0242/.02586
NUL	.0071/.00893	.0266/.02738	.0107/.01104	.1927/.27569	.0045/.00754
BTR	.0987/.04247	.1006/.03645	.1693/.04896	.1712/.05120	.1930/.18841
RT	.1285/.07411	.1936/.05962	.2459/.07443	.4305/.10414	.1445/.10168
RP	.1350/.07302	.1972/.06181	.2904/.07659	.4817/.10212	.1591/.11083
GA	.56192/.1062	.65962/.1565	.75739/.1302	.75341/.1531	.19303/.0938

Compare C1 with Other Groups:
C1 (n = 52) (Table 4): C1 students obtained higher learning achievement (GA: mean = 0.56192, SD = 0.1062) than C5. While C5 students exhibited significantly higher tendency to go back the previous pages of the learning content compared with the C1 students (BTR: 1 > 5).

In the previous research, it is found that (Backing Track Rate) BTR is a good learning strategy which can help students to save time; Although students learn with BTR learning strategy, it is still necessary to spend more time reading the learning content in order to ensure higher learning achievement (Yin et al. 2018). Comparing these students in C5 and C1, the BTR learning strategy does not work for the C5, because these students did not spend more time reading the learning contents.

Among all the students, those of C4 exhibited the low learning achievement (GTA: 1 < 2, 1 < 3, 1 < 4) as well as the lowest total count of login count, reading pages and reading time (LGI, RP, RT: 1 < 2, 1 < 3, 1 < 4). Therefore, owing to their behavior of only reading the pages of the learning content in sequence, C4 is identified as the "poor performance group."

Compare C2 with Other Groups:
C2 (n = 53) (Table 5): C2 (n = 29, Table 5: C2): C2 students also exhibited a significantly higher tendency to write memo and make highlight compared with C5 and C1 students (NM, HL: 2 > 5; 2 > 1). C2 students reported significantly higher learning achievement than C5 and C1 students (GTA: 2 > 5; 2 > 1). While the BTR of C5 shows a significantly higher tendency compared with C2 students (BTR: 5 > 2), and compare to the BTR, there is no difference with C1 and C1. Therefore, Memo and Highlight exert a significant positive influence on learning effectiveness, Memo and Highlight are "good" reading strategies, and BTR could not influence the learning effectiveness, if the Memo and Highlight have significantly difference.

Compare C3 with Other Groups:
Compare these 5 groups (Table 6), C4 and C3 obtained similar learning achievement (there is no difference between the GA of C4 and C3), and C4 and C3 exhibited a

higher learning achievement. The learning achievement of C4 and C3 is higher than C2, the learning achievement of C2 is higher than C1, and the learning achievement of C1 is higher than C5 (GA: 3 > 2 > 1 > 5; 4 > 2 > 1 > 5).

Table 4. Compare C1 with other groups

		C2	C3	C4	C5
C1	LGI	<	<	<	
	MEMO	<		<	
	HL	<		<	
	UL			<	
	BTR		<	<	<
	RT	<	<	<	
	RP	<	<	<	
	GA	<	<	<	>

Table 5. Compare C2 with other groups

		C1	C3	C4	C5
C2	LGI	>	<	<	
	MEMO	>	>	<	>
	HL	>	>	<	>
	UL			<	
	BTR		<	<	<
	RT	>	<	<	
	RP	>	<	<	
	GA	>	<	<	>

Table 6. Compare C3 with other groups

		C1	C2	C4	C5
C3	LGI	>	>	<	>
	MEMO		<	<	
	HL		<	<	
	UL			<	
	BTR	>	>		
	RT	>	>	<	>
	RP	>	>	<	>
	GA	>	>		>

6 Discussion and Conclusion

Yin and Hwang (2018) indicated that several potential research issues of LA for e-books: such as Identifying students' behavioral patterns from e-book-based learning logs, investigating the impacts of different learning strategies on students' behavioral patterns, using LA approaches to investigate the factors affecting students' learning performances.

This paper focused on using LA to investigate the factors affecting students' learning performances by using clustering method. To further understand students' possible behavior patterns, cluster analysis was employed. Students were clustered into groups according to the similarity in their learning behaviors. We then analyzed the learning behavior features in each group.

In this research, the k-means clustering method is improved by weighting the features of clustering, and the number of features is also increased, such as the number of MEMO, the count of UNDERLINE and the count HIGHLIGHT. According to the analysis result, we found some interesting patterns, such as the students who always use the MEMO or MAKERS function, who always get better GA.

Acknowledgements. A part of this research work was supported by the Grant-in-Aid for Scientific Research No. 16H03078 and No. 16H06304 from the Ministry of Education, Culture, Sports, Science and Technology (MEXT) in Japan.

References

Aggarwal, C.C., Yu, Philip S.: Data mining techniques for associations, clustering and classification. In: Zhong, N., Zhou, L. (eds.) PAKDD 1999. LNCS (LNAI), vol. 1574, pp. 13–23. Springer, Heidelberg (1999). https://doi.org/10.1007/3-540-48912-6_4

Archer, E., Chetty, Y.B., Prinsloo, P.: Benchmarking the habits and behaviours of successful students: a case study of academic-business collaboration. Int. Rev. Res. Open Distance Learn. **15**(1), 62–83 (2014)

Cheng, K.H., Tsai, C.C.: Children and parents' reading of an augmented reality picture book: analyses of behavioral patterns and cognitive attainment. Comput. Educ. **72**, 302–312 (2014). https://doi.org/10.1016/j.compedu.2013.12.003

Colvin, C., et al.: Student Retention and Learning Analytics: A Snapshot of Australian Practices and a Framework for Advancement. Australian Government for Office of Learning and Teaching, Canberra (2015)

Han, J., Kamber, M., Pei, J.: Data Mining Concepts and Techniques, 3rd edn. Elsevier Inc., Amsterdam (2011)

Hrastinski, S.: A theory of online learning as online participation. Comput. Educ. **52**(1), 78–82 (2009)

Li, L., Uosaki, N., Ogata, H., Mouri, K., Yin, C.: Analysis of behavior sequences of students by using learning logs of digital books. In: Proceedings of 26th International Conference on Computers in Education, Manila, Philippines, 26–30 November, pp. 367–376 (2018)

Nie, F., Li, J., Li, X.: Self-weighted multiview clustering with multiple graphs. In: Proceedings of the Twenty-Sixth International Joint Conference on Artificial Intelligence, pp. 2564–2570 (2017)

Yin, C., Hwang, G.J.: Roles and strategies of learning analytics in the e-publication era. Knowl. Manage. E-Learn. **10**(4), 455–468 (2018)

Yin, C., Uosaki, N., Chu, H., Hwang, G., Hwang, J., Hatono, I., et al.: Learning behavioral pattern analysis based on students' logs in reading digital books. In: Proceedings of 25th International Conference on Computers in Education, Christchurch, New Zealand, 4–8 December, pp 549–557 (2017)

Yin, C., Hirokawa, S., Yau, J., Nakatoh, T., Hashimoto, K., Tabata, Y.: Analyzing research trends with cross tabulation search engine. Int. J. of Distance Educ. Technol. **11**(1), 31–44 (2013). https://doi.org/10.4018/jdet.2013010103

Yin, C., et al.: Learning by searching: a learning approach that provides searching and analysis facilities to support research trend surveys. J. Educ. Technol. Soc. **16**(3), 286–300 (2013b)

Yin, C., et al.: Exploring the relationships between reading behavior patterns and learning outcomes based on log data from E-books: a human factor approach. Int. J. Hum.–Comput. Interact. (2018). https://doi.org/10.1080/10447318.2018.1543077

Yin, C., Okubo, F., Shimada, K., Yamada, M., Fujimura, N., Ogata, H.: Mobile devices based data collecting system for analyzing learning behaviors. In: Liu, C.-C., et al. (eds.) Proceedings of International Conference of Computers on Education, pp. 575–577 (2014)

Author Index

Printed in the United States
By Bookmasters